Gerry Frank's

Where to
Find It
Buy It
Eat It
in
New York

MANHATTAN

INWOOD

FORT GEORGE

181st

WASHINGTON HEIGHTS

151st

125th

HARLEM

MORNINGSIDE HEIGHTS

110th

HARLEM RIVER

HUDSON RIVER

96th

ST. NICHOLAS

CENTRAL PARK WEST

CENTRAL PARK

FIFTH

PARK

YORKVILLE

79th

WEST SIDE

EAST SIDE

59th

THEATER DISTRICT

47th

MIDTOWN

SUTTON

42nd

TUDOR

34th

38th

GARMENT DISTRICT

MURRAY HILL

28th

GRAMERCY

FIRST

STUYVESANT

CHELSEA

14th

14th

GREENWICH VILLAGE

B'WAY

EAST VILLAGE

LOWER EAST SIDE

HOUSTON

SOHO

LITTLE ITALY

BOWERY

LOWER BROADWAY

CHINATOWN

FULTON

CIVIC CENTER

WALL STREET

BATTERY

EAST RIVER

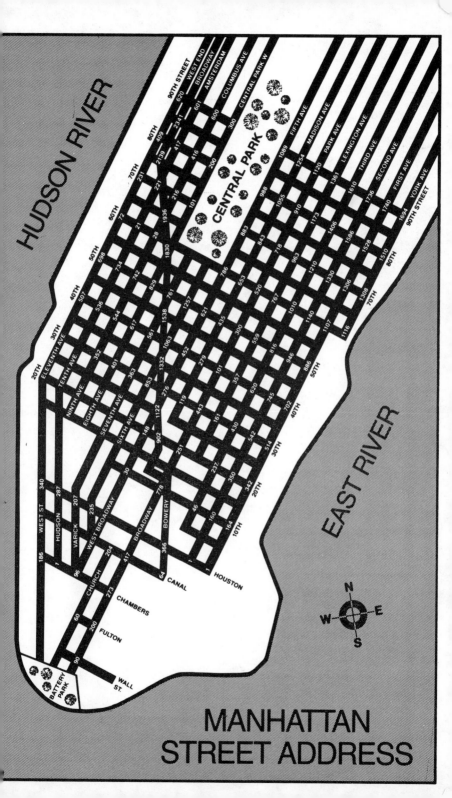

MANHATTAN
STREET ADDRESS

Gerry Frank's
Where to
Find It
Buy It
Eat It
in
New York

For additional copies (special quantity prices available),
write or call:

Gerry's Frankly Speaking

P.O. Box 2225
Salem, Oregon 97308
(503) 585-8411

Preface

It hardly seems possible this is the seventh edition of *Where to Find It, Buy It, Eat It in New York*. What started as a hobby in 1980 has developed into considerably more than that, with nearly half a million copies now in print. It is the best-selling and most complete guidebook to the city of New York. Of course, this could not have been possible without the loyalty and interest of my readers. Thanks!

The question I am asked most often is, "How could someone who lives in Oregon and works in Washington, D.C., write a guide to New York?" My answer makes sense, I think. I was born into an Oregon department-store family and spent 17 years in the retail business. I often traveled to New York with our store buyers, spending time in the various markets of the city. During that period I fell in love with New York. Today I find myself more fascinated than ever with the energy and excitement of the Big Apple.

After the family business was sold, I joined forces with United States Senator Mark Hatfield of Oregon. I have served as his Chief of Staff for over a quarter of a century. During that period I have visited New York on an average of twice a month, spending time walking the streets, visiting the stores, eating in the restaurants, sampling the food shops, trying out the services, exploring the different districts. What I have found is contained in this volume.

As a former retailer I have an eye for the values and service that are the keystone of a successful store. As a world traveler who has visited over 130 countries, I know what good food and accommodations should be like. As the proprietor of a restaurant and specialty food operation in Oregon, I have developed an eye for what customers are looking for in the taste category. Over the years I have eaten at more than 1,600 restaurants in Manhattan. Thank goodness all the walking around has enabled me to wear the same belt I had when the first edition was published!

You're probably wondering what makes this book different from the dozens of other guides to the city. First and foremost, this one is complete. There are excellent books available on various aspects of life in Manhattan, but this one alone combines all the ingredients most folks are interested in—residents and visitors alike. Whereas many books of this nature are the combined product of a number of people who handle different sections, this book is *my* evaluation only (except for beauty shops), so there is consistency throughout. You may not always agree with my comments, but I have tried to make them as interesting, relevant, and personal as I can.

A city as dynamic as New York changes rapidly. This is especially true of eating establishments. It is impossible, of course, to be absolutely up-to-date, but because I self-publish, my deadlines are much closer to printing time than most books. Therefore, my information is as current as possible. Every entry is checked and updated with each new edition.

The story of this book has become somewhat of a legend in the book business. I had no idea, at the start, that I would write a book. My only previous adventure in journalism had been the publishing of a newspaper when I was a youngster. Because people know I spend a lot of time in New York, I've always been asked questions about where to buy this or that, where to eat, where to stay, and so on. I collected and assembled a great deal of data—after 25 years of exploration in every corner of the city—and took it to the New York publishers.

To say the big publishing houses were aghast that "some hick from Oregon" was writing a book about their city was an understatement. They wouldn't give me the time of day. I am not the sort of individual who likes to be told no, so I decided to publish and distribute it myself. It was a lot of work, and sometimes I got discouraged, but the end result was worth the effort. Not only are we number one in the marketplace, but some of the same publishers who turned me down now want to handle the book! (Thanks, but no thanks.)

Where to Find It, Buy It, Eat It in New York is also available in an abridged pocket-sized edition ($5.95), which contains the introductory sections of the book, the restaurants, and highlights of tours and shopping. It is used a great deal by groups visiting Manhattan. Special prices on quantity lots of either volume are available. Please feel free to call me at (503) 585-8411 or write me at P.O. Box 2225, Salem, OR 97308.

The success of the book would not have been possible without the support of my readers. You have been wonderful in commenting about what is included and what is not. Your suggestions and criticisms are taken very seriously, and each edition is more useful because of the ideas gleaned from readers of previous volumes. Because of your comments, several new sections have been added in this edition, while others have been expanded. You expressed interest in more inexpensive places to eat, shop, and stay, so I've added them. I encourage you to pass along your comments. Whenever a particular establishment in the book does not live up to readers' expectations, I contact that firm personally. No one pays to be included.

A number of people have helped with the logistics of putting out a volume as complex as this one. Esther Benovitz, who knows the city so well, has been of particular assistance. Her knowledge of New York has been sharpened as a student, mother, and housewife. Cheryl Johnson has handled the administrative details. Parke Puterbaugh has served in the important position of my editor. Jeryme English and LaVelle Blum have each helped with their particular expertise. Tim Prock, a talented young artist, designed the cover.

This volume was not meant to be a set of Yellow Pages. It is, however, a compilation of the best and the most interesting establishments in the city—in most every category and in every price range. I (or Esther, in some cases) have visited every place included. I hope the book will enhance your enjoyment of this fascinating metropolis, whether you call it home or just come to visit once in awhile.

Contents

V. WHERE TO FIND IT: NEW YORK'S BEST SERVICES

VI. WHERE TO BUY IT: NEW YORK'S BEST STORES

VII. WHERE TO "EXTRAS"

I. The World's Greatest City

Where to and Where Not To!

Like any great city, New York not only has a host of wonderful things to do and see, but it has its share of unpleasant things. The following list is certainly not complete, but it will give you an idea of what to expect.

On the plus side, try:

Visiting the Statue of Liberty.

Browsing through the 2.5 million volumes in the New York Public Library (Fifth Ave at 42nd St).

Viewing one of the more than 50 parades that excite the city each year.

Touring the Museum of Immigration at the newly reopened Ellis Island.

Taking a ride on one of the 388 (!) elevators in Rockefeller Center (preferably to the top).

Sitting on one of the 7,674 benches in Central Park on a glorious, warm spring day.

Looking down one of the open grates that expose 238 miles of subway tracks below the city streets.

Visiting the Romanesque/Byzantine-style St. Bartholomew's Church (built in 1919) on Park Avenue between 50th and 51st Sts.

Ogling the authentic American Indian crafts at Saity Jewelry (Trump Tower, 5th level, 725 Fifth Ave, at 57th St).

Letting your hair down as you eat Americana-style at Ed Debevic's (661 Broadway, at Bond St).

Enjoying a musical performance at Lincoln Center for the Performing Arts (Broadway at 64th St).

Spending a day at the Metropolitan Museum of Art (Fifth Ave at 82nd St).

Browsing through the new C.P. Company in the historic Flatiron Building (23rd St at Fifth Ave and Broadway).

Taking in the farmer's market on Wednesdays, Fridays, and Saturdays at Union Square (14th St and Broadway).

Visiting 75^1/$_2$ Bedford St (in Greenwich Village), site of the city's narrowest house.

Having a romantic dinner at "One if By Land, Two if By Sea," Aaron Burr's former carriage house (17 Barrow St).

Getting up as early as four a.m. to witness the activity at the Fulton Fish Market (South Street Seaport).

Visiting the Federal Hall National Memorial (26 Wall St), where George Washington took oath as the first U.S. President.

Touring the most important collection of decorative arts in the country at the Cooper-Hewitt Museum (Fifth Ave at 91st St).

Taking the kids to see the medieval collection at the Cloisters (Fort Tryon Park, 193rd St and Fort Washington Ave).

Having a special birthday party at Trumpet's Bar & Grill in the Grand Hyatt Hotel (at Grand Central Station).

Taking a Circle Line cruise around Manhattan's 31 miles of shoreline (call 269-5755).

Answering the question "Who is buried in Grant's Tomb?" (Riverside Drive at 122nd St).

Visiting the priceless collection at Aunt Len's Doll and Toy Museum in Harlem (6 Hamilton Terrace).

Taking a boat trip in Central Park on a summer day (Loeb Boathouse).

Ice skating at the renovated Wollman Rink in Central Park.

Taking a ride on the Staten Island Ferry for just 50¢.

Shopping Orchard Street on Sunday.

Visiting the United Nations.

Touring St. John the Divine, the world's largest Gothic cathedral (Amsterdam Ave at 112th St).

Feasting your eyes on the marble and glitter of Trump Tower (Fifth Ave at 56th St).

Having an evening meal in the Crystal Room at Tavern on the Green in Central Park.

Taking a ride through Central Park in a hansom cab.

Buying a hot bagel from H&H Bagels (80th St and Broadway or 1551 Second Ave).

Having drinks and conversation in the Rainbow Room atop Rockefeller Center.

Attending the flea market and antiques sale on Sunday at Sixth Avenue and 26th Street.

Having tea or Sunday brunch in the Palm Court at the Plaza Hotel (Fifth Ave and Central Park S).

Enjoying the awe-inspiring view from atop the World Trade Center.

Touring backstage at the Metropolitan Opera.

Sampling dim sum in Chinatown.

Having a cup of espresso or cappuccino in Little Italy.

Watching the lights on the Statue of Liberty while walking along the promenade at Battery Park.

Viewing the model furniture rooms at Bloomingdale's (Third Ave and 59th St).

Enjoying the New York skyline from the River Cafe in Brooklyn (1 Water St).

Buying fresh coffee at Zabar's (80th St and Broadway).

Catching the Knicks and the Rangers at Madison Square Garden (Seventh Ave and W 33rd St).

Getting lost in the downstairs stacks at the Strand Book Store (12th St and Broadway).

Enjoying the open-air entertainment at the South Street Seaport.

Getting stuffed at the Carnegie Deli (Seventh Ave and 55th St).

Enjoying the Easter flower show at Macy's (Herald Square).

Gawking at the dinosaurs in the American Museum of Natural History (79th St and Central Park W).

Watching the Christmas show at Radio City Music Hall (50th St and Sixth Ave).

Getting the early edition of the Sunday *New York Times* to read in bed on Saturday night.

Running in Central Park before heading to the office.

Taking the kids for an after-dinner treat at Peppermint Park (1225 First Ave).

Browsing through the "New York Is Book Country" book fair on Fifth Avenue in September.

Taking advantage of the weekend package at the Vista International.

Spending an afternoon at the Museum of Modern Art (11 W 53rd St).

Getting a loaf of Eli's bread at almost any gourmet shop.

Spending the day getting pampered at Elizabeth Ardens (691 Fifth Ave).

Having one of the finest French dinners anywhere at La Reserve (4 W 49th St).

Visiting Theodore Roosevelt's birthplace (28 E 20th St) and George Washington's headquarters (1785 Jumal Terrace).

Securing a bargain ticket for a Broadway matinee at the TKTS booth in Times Square.

Getting into a political discussion with a cab driver.

Going dancing at the Palladium (126 E 14th St).

Having a mountainous burger at Jackson Hole Wyoming Burgers (232 E 64th St).

Taking home fresh fruit and vegetables from Balducci's (426 Sixth Ave).

Getting a glass of fresh-squeezed orange juice at 1428 Sixth Avenue (just off 58th St).

Buying a new outfit for a discount price at Ben Farber (462 Seventh Ave).

Visiting the Winter Garden shopping area at the World Financial Center.

Strolling through the "Place des Antiquaires" (Lexington Ave and 57th St).

Eating until you burst at the Polish Veselka Coffee Shop (Second Ave and Ninth St).

Enjoying happy hour at Molly Bloom's (150 W 47th St).

Finally, taking advantage of any rest room you come across, especially those in hotels. Others may not be so handy or clean.

Then there are the negatives:

Walking around alphabet land (Avenues A, B, C, D).

Knockoff Hard Rock Cafe sweat shirts from street vendors.

Restaurant maitre d's who seat you in the bar when the dining room is not filled.

Cab drivers who take you on the Triboro Bridge rather than the 59th Street Bridge to La Guardia Airport.

Upper East Side singles bars.

New York in August.

Buying drinks at the Palladium.

Buying an overpriced pretzel on Fifth Avenue near Central Park.

Trying to find a bargain apartment in the Real Estate section of the Sunday *Times*.

Street phones that don't work.

Street addresses, especially on Fifth Ave and Park Ave, that don't really exist because entrances are on side streets.

Cabs that take short corner turns, moving the puddle from the gutter to your new suit.

Restaurants that include tax in the check total so the tip will be larger.

The person who knows so much about New York that no one can tell him or her anything ("I've lived here all my life").

Department store clerks who remind the customer, "That isn't my section."

People who need to draw attention to themselves by having the largest and loudest portable radio on the street.

The VIP (in his or her mind only) who instructs the secretary not only to ask who is calling, but also to inquire about the subject matter.

Garbage bags rotting in the hot summer sun.

Dogs whose manners are unacceptable to everyone but their owner.

Trying to get a cab at five p.m. on a wet Friday afternoon.

Watching an unsuspecting person buy a fake Rolex watch from a street vendor.

Getting ripped off by an electronics store on Fifth Ave.

Restaurants that automatically add a 15 to 20 percent service charge to the check.

"Happy Birthday" being sung off-key by waiters at quality restaurants.

Wearing a gold necklace! You're bound to attract ripoff artists.

Getting Around the City

It helps to know a little history and geography to get around New York. Here are some basics to keep in mind.

New York City comprises five boroughs: Manhattan, Staten Island, the Bronx, Queens and Brooklyn. All of the boroughs except the Bronx are located on islands. (A bit of trivia: The Bronx is the only portion of New York City attached to the U.S. mainland.)

Historically speaking, New York started on the southern tip of Manhattan and worked its way north and east. For both geographical and historical reasons, New York City is limited in the directions that it can physically grow. The last growth spurt occurred when the city of Brooklyn was annexed into the city of New York in the 1890s.

As a result, most streets in Manhattan are carefully thought out and resemble a grid pattern of north-south avenues and east-west streets. Fifth Avenue is the dividing line between east and west addresses, with 1 West 59th Street being the first building west of Fifth Avenue and 1 East 59th street being the first building east of Fifth Avenue. (Of course, to have the coveted ''1'' address implies that a building is actually *on* Fifth Avenue.)

In recent times the city has seen a spate of buildings erected whose locations, in relationship to their prestigious addresses, are imaginative at best. The only exceptions to the above rules are streets that predate the grid plan (such as Broadway, the longest continuous street in the world, extending all the way to Albany) and all of lower Manhattan below 4th Street. Streets there have names rather than numbers, often following Dutch farm trails as opposed to logical routes. Wall Street takes its name from the outer wall erected there to protect the city. It is not even as wide as a suburban driveway, and the actual Stock Exchange entrance is on Broad Street. Fourth Street isn't always clear, either, since it runs through Greenwich Village. (To New Yorkers, it is simply ''the Village.'') In addition to curving and changing names, streets there actually meet themselves. But the gridlike arrangement of streets and avenues is the basic pattern. Incidentally, 20 city blocks equal one mile.

Downtown is where the city started. Over time, the lines have been blurred by both erosion and landfill. Battery Park City is built upon the earth displaced by the World Trade Center excavations, sitting in what once was the Hudson River. But basically, downtown runs from the tip of Manhattan through the Financial District to 14th Street. This includes the Battery, Wall Street, the World Trade and World Financial Centers, Battery Park City, City Hall, Chinatown, the South Street Seaport, the Lower East Side, Little Italy, the East Village, Greenwich Village, SoHo (meaning ''south of Houston''—pronounced *how-stun*), TriBeCa (Triangle Below Canal Street), Washington Square, and Union Square.

All of this occupies less than two square miles, so it is quite possible to cross neighborhood lines on the same block. I don't think anyone can tell you where Chinatown ends and the Lower East Side begins. The same can be said for where the "Wall Street" district ends and municipal offices begin.

Downtown streets are confusing. Most have names, and even when they do have letters or numbers they can't be counted on. Here are some examples to confuse you: 12th Street (not "Little West 12th Street") runs into West 4th Street at the intersection of Greenwich and Seventh Avenues. All the numbered avenues end on Houston street, but not before Fourth Avenue joins Third Avenue and becomes Bowery. Broadway starts in Battery Park and runs parallel to Fourth (which is called Park Avenue South from 14th to 34th Streets) until it reaches 14th Street. On its trek uptown it crosses Fifth, Sixth, Seventh, and Eighth Avenues before running into Columbus Circle (which is at 59th Street). At the point where downtown Manhattan is wider than uptown, between Houston and 14th Streets on the East Side, Avenues A, B, C, and D can be found. Locally this is known as alphabet land, and you have very little business—legal or otherwise—being there.

Midtown begins at 34th Street. What, you might ask, happened between 14th and 34th Streets? Well, nothing much. This, too, is largely residential. With the exception of the nineteenth-century "Ladies Mile" along Broadway, this was never the chic part of town.

Getting around midtown is easy. Numbered streets run in order. From east to west, you'll encounter First, Second, and Third Avenues. There is also a Sutton Place, as well as York and East End Avenues. (Park Avenue South lies below 34th Street. It was changed from Fourth Avenue because residents liked "Park Avenue" better than "Fourth Avenue.") After Third comes Lexington, Park, Madison, Fifth, and Sixth, with Broadway occasionally crossing the avenues at a diagonal.

In the 1950s Sixth Avenue became Avenue of the Americas, although no one except landlords called it that. Lately, it has become acceptable for a "real" New Yorker to use "Avenue of the Americas." This is a really revolutionary statement, appearing for the first time in any New York guidebook. It certainly is the first time that I've allowed it! (However, if you want to show off, stick to Sixth Avenue.) After Sixth comes Seventh, Eighth, Ninth, Tenth, Eleventh, and Twelfth Avenues.

At 59th Street, Central Park divides the city into "the East Side" and "the West Side." It is more than a geographical division, since the two sides are both uptown. With the physical division at 59th Street there is a philosophical division as well. Both sides at this point are mainly residential.

The East Side consists of Park Avenue, Madison Avenue, and Fifth Avenue, with "Museum Row" occupying the major portion of Fifth Avenue in the 70s, 80s, and 90s. Yorktown (in the 80s) used to be very middle-European. It still has remnants of Hungarian pork stores and German bakeries, but many of the old buildings and tenants have been replaced by yuppies and singles.

The West Side has Central Park West, Columbus (which is, in fact,

Ninth Avenue), Broadway, Amsterdam (Tenth), and West End Avenues (Eleventh). All of these have reputations as shopping streets that are just a little more funky, bookish, and theatrical than the staid East Side. Jackie O. lives on Fifth. Yoko Ono lives in the Dakota, on Central Park West and 72nd Street.

Above the West Side is Columbia University and Morningside Heights, where work on St. John the Divine is proceeding into its second hundred years. Local artisans are being trained for the project, and there's no end in sight. Above that lies Harlem, Washington Heights, Inwood, Fort Tryon Park, and the Cloisters. Atop the East Side is Gracie Mansion (the mayor's home), then El Barrio (also known as Spanish Harlem or East Harlem) before Manhattan Island narrows in the vicinity of Harlem. That is Manhattan Island.

Key to Manhattan Addresses

To determine the approximate cross street for addresses located on the avenues, try the following formula. Cancel the last figure of the house number. Divide the remainder by two, and add the key number below. The result is approximately the nearest cross street.

Ave A, B, C, D	Add 3
First and Second Ave	Add 3
Third Ave	Add 9 or 10
Fourth Ave (Park Ave South)	Add 8
Fifth Ave	
Up to 200	Add 13
Up to 400	Add 16
Up to 600	Add 18
Up to 775	Add 20
From 775-1286	
Cancel last figure and subtract 18	
Up to 1500	Add 45
Above 2000	Add 24
Ave of the Americas (or 6th Ave)	Subt 12 or 13
Seventh Ave	Add 12
Above 110th St	Add 20
Eighth Ave	Add 9 or 10
Nineth Ave	Add 13
Tenth Ave	Add 14
Eleventhth Ave	Add 15
Amsterdam Ave	Add 59 or 60
Audubon Ave	Add 165
Broadway ....Up to 750 is below 8th St	
756 to 846	Subt 29
847 to 953	Subt 25
Above 953	Subt 31
Columbus Ave	Add 59 or 60

Convent Ave .... Add 127
Ft. Washington Ave .... Add 158
Lenox Ave .... Add 110
Lexington Ave .... Add 22
Madison Ave .... Add 26
Manhattan Ave .... Add 100
Park Ave .... Add 34 or 35
St. Nicholas Ave .... Add 110
West End Ave .... Add 59 or 60
Central Park West
   Divide house number by 10 and add 60
Riverside Drive
   Divide house number by 10 and add 72

To determine which avenue is nearest to a street address, use the following chart. Example: 356 West 34th Street is located between Eighth and Ninth Avenues.

East Side
1 at Fifth Ave
101 at Park or Fourth Ave
201 at Third Ave
301 at Second Ave
401 at First Ave
501 at York Ave or Ave A
601 at Ave B

West Side
1 at Fifth Ave
101 at Sixth Ave (Lenox Ave
   north of 110th St)
201 at Seventh Ave
301 at Eighth Ave
401 at Ninth Ave (Columbus
   Ave north of 59th St)
501 at Tenth Ave (Amsterdam
   Ave north of 59th St)
601 at Eleventh Ave (West Ave
   north of 59th St)

Given a midtown street address, you can tell between which avenues it is located from this chart.

East Side
1-49/Fifth and Madison
50-99/Madison and Park
100-149/Park and Lexington
150-199/Lexington and Third
200-299/Third and Second
300-399/Second and First
400-499/First and York

West Side
1-99/Fifth and Sixth
100-199/Sixth and Seventh
200-299/Seventh and Eighth
300-399/Eighth and Ninth
400-499/Ninth and Tenth
500-599/Tenth and Eleventh
600-up/Eleventh and Twelfth

Even-numbered addresses are located on the downtown (south) side of the street. Odd-numbered addresses are located on the uptown (north) side of the street.

If the above formula is too confusing, try this chart guide, which roughly covers the area between Union Square and Times Square.

CROSSTOWN GUIDE

Fifth Avenue	
Sixth Avenue	100W
Seventh Avenue	200W
Eighth Avenue	300W

STREET GUIDE

Street	Madison Avenue	Fifth Avenue	Sixth Avenue	Seventh Avenue	Broadway
18		130	615	135	875
20		150	655	170	900
22		170	695	210	935
24	20		730	245	1100
26	45	210	770	285	1135
28	80	250	810	320	1180
30	120	275	855	365	1215
32	155	320	885	405	1255
34	185	350		440	1315
36	215	390	980	480	1350
38	250	420	1020	525	1400
40	280	450	1065	560	1430
42	300	500	1100	600	1470

Transportation

There are the usual ways to get around the city. But in New York, very little goes by "the usual way." Here's why:

Walking: Shank's mare is always the optimal choice in New York. The city is really very compact, and unless you are going from Columbia University (116th Street) to New York University (West 4th Street), there's no reason why you shouldn't walk. In all likelihood, the weather won't deter you. If it rains or snows, much of your traveling can be done indoors or along the sides of buildings. In addition, you are less likely to make wrong turns, and you won't get stuck in traffic. Traffic is the bane of every other mode of transportation except the subway. It doesn't take long to pick up the pace of New York walking. There's no stopping at corners, lights, or one-way streets. If you've got any daredevil in you, walking can be lots of fun.

Driving: Don't. It never ever pays. Getting into Manhattan costs exorbitant tolls (there are free bridges from Brooklyn and Queens, but you'd better be a very good driver), the traffic is murder, and parking the car is either expensive (in a garage) or impossible (in midtown). One garage across from Radio City charged me $18 per *half*-hour, and then cheated on the clock! There are municipal garages around town, as well as some reasonable private ones (a mere $10 an hour is as good as you're going to get), but is it worth the headache of driving in gridlocked city traffic and locking horns with the hothead behind you? I think not. You also have to worry about the day before Thanksgiving and Christmas, opening day at Yankee Stadium and the UN, and anytime the president is in town. Movie stars, film shoots, parades, Woody Allen, pickets, and political riots are routine on the streets of New York.

Cabs: Taxis in New York are very carefully regulated. There are a finite number of yellow "medallion" cabs and they are subject to many constraints. They are not allowed to refuse fares. Neither are they allowed to refuse a reasonable amount of passengers (usually not more than four), even though the fare is computed per trip and not per person. In addition, a passenger has the legal right to select the music, smoking or nonsmoking conditions, and the route, which may include stops at no additional charge. It's the law!

Now, let's talk reality. All the jokes you've heard about not getting a cab in the rain or not getting one to travel outside Manhattan are based on truth. It's almost impossible. You may even have a problem getting one to go to the airport. As for telling the cabbie that rap music is not your favorite—well, just try it. Many of the cabbies are newcomers to the city (and the country), so their knowledge of the streets is not always the best. It never hurts to have a route and directions mapped out before you hail the cab. Avoid asking the cabbie's advice on how to go—that can hurt! Every yellow cab has a light and a number atop the roof. If the number is lit, the cab is available and is required to stop for anyone who hails it. The same number is displayed inside the cab, alongside the cabbie's name and license number. If you have a problem, do *not* bring it to the driver's attention. Instead, contact the Taxi and Limousine Commission (221 W 41st St, New York, NY 10036; 212/869-4513 or 382-9301), making note of the number.

To hail a cab put your arm straight out and step slightly into the street. Do not wave. Someone may wave back at you, but a cab won't stop. To better the odds, face uptown in the morning rush hour, downtown at night. You can always reverse the cab's direction on the next block. Other good spots are in front of hotels and expensive restaurants, or the cabbie diners on 10th and 11th Avenues. There are cab lines at the airports. They are legitimate and there's no reason to jump the line.

Buses: Most buses run along north-south or east-west routes, and despite the existence of special bus lanes, most of the time they are navigating the same vehicular traffic as cars and pedestrians. The M101 has a route of several miles that ends in the Bronx while the 42nd Street crosstown bus goes less than a mile. Usually the only reason to take a bus is if you have a lot of time and are afraid of the alternatives. The exception is the Jacob Javits Convention Center, which has no parking facilities or convenient subway stops. There, the bus is your best option.

The bus requires exact change or tokens. Stops are usually every two or three blocks, and you are supposed to exit via the rear door. Hold onto your wallet at all times, but especially when getting off a bus. Theoretically, every stop is marked with the route number and a map. Before you board check out the stop and the route number. Several buses use the same stop, and it's a matter of lore as to where each one stops.

Subways: Some tourists can't wait to ride the subways; some won't come to New York because it *has* subways. The truth lies somewhere in between. Millions of people ride the subways every day. It is the cheapest and quickest way around town. Statistically, it is no more dangerous than any other means of travel. But there are stations that are decidedly hazardous. Use common sense. Don't aimlessly wander the subway system. Don't ride during off hours or enter deserted stations. Stay in the middle of the platform, and find another forum to impress the locals with your wealth and jewels.

The subway system is derived from the merger of several different private systems that sprang up to serve the population at the turn of the century. Old-timers still refer to the lines as the BMT, IRT, and IND. All but a few lines go north-south or out to Queens and Brooklyn. You can, however, cross town via the 14th Street and 42nd Street shuttles. Along 42nd Street you also have the option of taking the Flushing train as it heads to or from Queens. It makes an extra stop, but you avoid having to trek to the tracks of the shuttle. For the most part, the subway is concentrated downtown and sparsely spaced out above 59th Street. In Queens and Brooklyn, there are miles between stations, and even in Manhattan there are key areas that have no local stations. Museum Row, large sections of Harlem, and the Bronx are just some of the places that have no subway access.

Entering the subway requires tokens. These are available at token booths within the station. These booths also supply subway maps, or you can call 718/330-1234. A light system at the entrance to the station alerts passengers to the hours of the booth. Red globes means that no tokens are ever sold at that entrance. (Many stations have more than one entrance.) Green lights mean the token booth is open and manned. No lights means that someone broke them.

Neighborhoods

One of the most unique features of Manhattan is the diversity of the various neighborhoods. It is almost like a collection of smaller communities, each with its own special flavor and excitement. To really get the most out of the city, one should try to spend time in each of the following areas:

Upper West Side. For many years this was a pleasant, relatively less expensive, and convenient place to live and shop. All of a sudden folks discovered the advantages of the Upper West Side, and things changed dramatically. Most of the change was in the rents charged for apartments and retail outlets. The boom is over now, however, and there are plenty of available spaces in what was a hot Columbus Avenue and Amsterdam Avenue district. Best bets are some of the smaller restaurants, the famous Zabar's gourmet and housewares emporium, Fairway Market, and dozens of pleasant side streets where comfortable, old-fashioned living quarters are still possible to find.

Upper East Side. This is still the classiest neighborhood in which to live and shop. Madison Avenue is the home of many famous names in clothing, accessories, household furnishings, and antiques. Scattered along the street are some great specialty shops, but high rents are taking a toll on many of the smaller, owner-operated establishments. Ralph Lauren's Polo mansion is a must-see. Park Avenue and Fifth Avenue addresses are preferred by those who want the best in the "price doesn't matter" world. Upper Fifth Avenue contains some of the finest museums in the city, and a stroll on the avenue provides great views of Central Park. As you move east, Bloomingdale's dominates the retail world, but literally hundreds of specialty stores are worth a visit. Although many of New York's pricier restaurants are located on the Upper East Side, you can still find excellent specialty houses in my Restaurant section. Grace's Marketplace is the best quality food emporium.

Midtown. The name is a catchall for the central part of the city. In the northern reaches of the area are a number of the better hotels in Manhattan. The closer to the park, the pricier. Fifth Avenue is the major shopping street of New York, with the better quality stores starting at 58th Street. Prices decline the further south you go. Famous names like Tiffany, F.A.O. Schwarz, Lord & Taylor, Bergdorf-Goodman, Henri Bendel, and Saks all have Fifth Avenue addresses. Trump Tower is a singular statement about what makes New York different . . . and exciting. Most of the major theaters are crowded around Broadway as it runs diagonally through midtown. Macy's and the new A&S Plaza occupy two of the busiest shopping blocks in town. Don't miss famous buildings like Grand Central Station, Madison Square Garden, and the Empire State Building. Numerous old-time places to have a quick, decent meal abound. Times Square, of course, is world famous—and is *not* recommended for leisurely inspection! The Chelsea area, home of the famous Barney's clothing store, abounds with good, moderately priced eateries.

The Villages. Once the heart of Bohemian life, the East and West Villages now are a mixture of what is great and not so great about New York. There are still wonderful old buildings and small parks, interesting specialty stores, excellent restaurants and enough local color to put a Crayola box to shame. Balducci's and Dean and Deluca are the premier food stores, with top quality items (and prices to match). Interwound with all of this is an unsettling crime and drug situation, and an unattractive collection of filth on some of the streets. If meeting a few of New York's more interesting characters is part of your scene, this is certainly the place to start. Unique emporiums on Lower Broadway sell every type of contemporary merchandise you might be looking for.

SoHo. Translated, this means south of Houston Street! SoHo is the home of some of the best galleries and specialty stores in New York. Once just a warehouse area, enterprising real-estate folks converted lofts into attractive, moderately priced places to live, and the young and the adventurous moved in. The turnover in restaurants is high, but there are many excellent places to eat inexpensively and without the hassle of getting dressed up. The area comes alive late in the day and on weekends, so plan accordingly.

Flatiron District. The Flatiron Building is enjoying a wave of popularity it didn't have when it was erected in 1902 as headquarters for the Fuller Company. Its shape was dictated by the crossing of Broadway and Fifth Avenue at Madison Square. The city noticed the triangular building's resemblance to an iron, and even the Fuller Company recognized that name eventually. The current company headquarters at 41 E 57th St has a flatiron embedded in the mosaic lobby floor. The Flatiron district extends from the south side of 23rd Street (where Broadway and Fifth Avenue meet) to 14th Street. The building itself houses an exciting new sportswear store, C.P. Company, featuring Italian unisex clothing. Gathered around are a number of new retail outlets and eating spots. Some of the better shops include Emporio Armani (110 Fifth Ave, clothing), Kenneth Cole (95 Fifth Ave, shoes), Paul Smith (108 Fifth Ave, clothing), Saint Laurie (897 Broadway, clothing), Fishs Eddy (889 Broadway, vintage dinnerware), and Chevignon (79 Fifth Ave, clothing). Restaurants worthy of mention are: America (9 E 18th St, a big place with a big menu and small prices), Book Friends Cafe (16 W 18th St, intimate and unique, just as it sounds), Coffee Shop (29 Union Square West, zero ambiance but good food at reasonable prices), Mesa Grill (102 Fifth Ave, very noisy and very "in"), Union Square Cafe (21 E 16th St, classy food), and Caffe Bondi (7 W 20th St, an Italian neighborhood favorite).

Lower East Side, Bowery, Chinatown, Little Italy. Color these areas brightly. The Lower East Side represents one of the last chances to catch a glimpse of how New York was in the early days. There are bargains to be found among the clutter and the smells, particularly along Orchard Street on Sundays. Places like Fine and Klein, Ezra Cohen, Russ and Daughters, and Katz's Deli are world famous. The Bowery is not as romantic as books claim it is; today, it is mainly the home of electrical equipment houses. Chinatown and Little Italy have a few good eating places, but be very selective. Shopping is not quite like it is in Florence or Hong Kong. Street fairs present a good opportunity to see and taste the uniqueness of these areas.

Lower Manhattan. Here, we've put together diverse districts such as the South Street Seaport, Wall Street, and Battery Park City. The Seaport has faded a bit, but it is still a fun place to visit, particularly in nice weather. The canyons of the financial district hide some of the more interesting old-time restaurants and stores in the city. A view from the top of the World Trade Center is not to be missed, especially as evening comes to the Big Apple.

Battery Park City. Over 30,000 people work in the World Financial Center, where four huge towers house the businesses. Next door two dozen apartment buildings have become chic places to live. The centerpiece of the development is the stunning Winter Garden, a magnificent setting for parties or just plain ogling. The vaulted roof soars 120 feet into the sky. Surrounding this grand space are dozens of interesting stores and restaurants. There are no bargains and no great gourmet meals, but the entire development is an opulent must-see for residents and visitors alike.

Shopping Districts

In most cities, each neighborhood is a self-contained entity. You might find a butcher, a grocer, and a hardware store, with the same types of businesses present in a shopping center several miles away. Almost never will a series of specialty stores group together to sell the same exact merchandise. New York is different. New Yorkers do not just *thrive* on competition, they consider it a way of life. In any event there are two givens to shopping in New York: (1) You can get anything below retail, and (2) if you want to pay the least possible amount, then shop "the districts."

There is a district for everything from beef to shoes. This is not to say that New Yorkers buy milk and eggs from wholesalers, although it is possible. If they are in the market for something very special, or simply the best, the first choice is always the districts. In one afternoon they can see an entire line and every aspect of it. Following are locations for some of the districts. Keep in mind that places move and that, like everything in Manhattan, boundaries are not exact.

Antiques: In antiquarian times the antique district was quite clearly Madison Avenue in the 70s. That was before Madison Avenue became boutique country and Ralph Lauren's "back in time" country store displaced shops that sold the real thing. The thrift shops (many of whom lived off the castoffs of the Madison Avenue boutiques) inhabited Lexington and Third Avenues in the same area. Most have now been forced to move further north or east or into collective quarters, such as the Antiquarium Market or Manhattan Art and Antiques (at 1050 Second Avenue).

Many dealers moved downtown, taking space abandoned by used-book dealers. Check out the area below Union Square, particularly 10th, 11th, and 12th Streets, near University Square and Fourth Avenue. That's for the fine quality merchandise. The "near antique" dealers are in the early 20s, the East Village, and the Village proper. Greenwich Avenue, however, is home to the real—i.e., expensive—items. (Refer to the Antique section under "Stores.")

Appliances and Electronics: Originally, the *only* place to go was the Lower East Side. A dozen or so places there made department-store sale prices seem sky high. But then the entire electronics scene changed, and with it the merchandising scene as well. Whereas "electronics" once meant washing machines and other appliances, these days we are talking computers, teletronics, and compact-disc players. These items are now sold via huge ads in the Sunday *Times* at specialty stores, many of which are located off Sixth Avenue in the 40s. The pioneer was 47th Street Photo, which as the name implies, was originally a camera store. Nowadays there are "800" numbers, specialized locations, and dozens of stores that will match or beat prices. Shopping can be done from your room. Just read the ads very carefully. One ripoff is to require cash or to stock a very limited supply. The buys are there, but stay away from the Fifth Avenue electronics stores.

Art: The formal, traditional galleries are usually located near the large art museums. Look near the Whitney, for example, and the Madison and Park Avenue areas in the 60s. These are prime areas with primo prices. The art market has been among the first to feel the repercussions of the financial downturn, as many galleries are barely hanging on, if they haven't already let go! Smaller fringe galleries with lesser known names (and lesser price tags) can be found in the Village. The pioneer Village galleries, such as Leo Castelli and Mary Boone, have moved to SoHo, where they offer uptown deals in a downtown setting.

Books: In the old days, the Union Square/Cooper Square area was book country. The only remaining vestiges are Barnes and Noble and the Strand. But even they have become big business. Barnes and Noble operates two stores at Fifth Avenue and 17th Street, and the Strand is a destination in itself. Today the antiquarian dealers have moved uptown, and virtually every new-book dealer discounts.

Carpets: Tread lightly here. If you don't know what you're doing, you can get badly burned. First, there's a world of difference between "floor coverings" and carpets or Oriental rugs. There's even a big difference between Oriental carpets and Oriental rugs. And we haven't begun to discuss hand-woven, hand-knotted, all wool, Persian wool, etc. The designer carpets are still in the designer's haunts: the Decorative Arts Building or the formidable Decoration and Design Building. These days you can get into the latter, but that doesn't mean you'll have any better knowledge of what you're viewing. You'll still need someone to explain what the salesman is saying.

Traditionally, dealers in area and Oriental rugs of less than museum quality clustered downtown, around 27th and 28th Streets between Madison and Park Avenues. That neighborhood is undergoing a trendy resurgence, and high rents have driven carpet dealers to an area near West 12th Street and the Hudson River. The warehouses there were originally built for distributors and wholesalers.

Diamonds: The epitome of New York district shopping, the Diamond District has been on 47th Street between Fifth and Sixth Avenues for eons. There is no one in New York who doesn't "know someone in the business." New York must have the lowest percentage of engagement rings sold at retail in the world!

Periphery businesses deal in castings, fittings, pearls, and other precious stones, but diamonds are the business's best friend on 47th Street. If you *don't* "know someone," do not take the advice of any new-found friend, and definitely don't take a stone you are considering to the appraiser that the dealer recommends. For the most part, the street is honest (business in the millions of dollars is conducted with a handshake), but that's not to say honesty will necessarily be extended to you.

We recommend several places. Stick to them. Take any gem you are considering to a certified gemologist. You also have the right to see the Gemological Institute of America's (GIA) report on the stone. Every stone has one; don't think of buying one without seeing the report.

Feathers, Beads, and Trimmings: An auxiliary to the Garment District, the area off Sixth Avenue in the upper 30s offers flowers, bows, and buckles. There are probably more beads and bangles on 38th Street than in all of Ohio. Every season, enterprising, fashion-conscious people uncover the latest accessory fad for pennies.

Fish: The Fulton Fish Market, across from the South Street Seaport, is the source of nearly every fish or seafood item in the metropolitan area, if not the Eastern Seaboard. If you want it fresh, six a.m. is considered a late time to get there. But the price is right, and the attitude is getting to be almost friendly. They do sell to the general public, and a series of lectures and tours is offered that imply they are interested in attracting you. And the smell isn't *that* bad!

Flowers: The Flower District, which runs from 26th through 30th Streets between Sixth and Seventh Avenues, is another longstanding area that has felt the economic pinch and become more receptive to retail customers. Time was when the Public Flower Mart (which is a flowery nomenclature, not a description) was the only retail business in the area, and it wasn't truly in the district at that! But recently business has been blooming, albeit only during the traditional early-morning shopping hours. This is definitely the place to go to save bouquets of money on flowers for parties or formal affairs. The stores adjacent to the area offer support and plant accessories such as baskets, pots, planters, and artificial flowers.

A final note: A few years ago enterprising Mexican immigrants began selling roses, first from buckets on the street and then from stores such as Rosa Rosa. The quality is top-notch and there are frequent price wars between the street merchants and the legitimate florists, as well as the "roses only" stores and their neighbors. It's all good news to New Yorkers because quality is unusually high and a dozen long-stemmed roses can be had for $15. Many old-time florists don't even bother with roses anymore, because they can't match the rose shops.

Fur: I wonder what is going to happen here. The wholesale fur district resides between 27th and 30th Streets along Seventh Avenue. But the animal rights activists ("It takes 30 dumb animals to make a fur coat, but only one to wear it") have made great inroads into the business. Companies are dropping like flies, and every day we read of another "final liquidation" sale. You can get great buys, particularly in the showrooms on 28th Street. But don't wear it out of the showroom!

Furniture: The fraternal headquarters of the furniture industry (not the manufacturing plants, which are in the Carolinas) are on Lexington Avenue between 29th and 33rd Streets. Usually the public can't get into those buildings, but several auxiliary places are open to lone customers. They include upholsterers, cooperative showrooms, and clearance centers. Some of the best furniture buys in town can be had when the showrooms change their decor.

Handbags: The 30s off of Fifth Avenue. No one knows why they're there, but keep your eyes peeled. Most of them are on upper floors.

Hats and Fabrics: Part of the spillover from the Garment Center, these stores can be found in the upper 30s and lower 40s between Sixth and Seventh Avenue. The bargain prices will knock your socks off.

Junk: This is not Junque, this is the real thing—whatever it is. Walk along Canal Street between the Financial District and SoHo and you'll find everything from rusty motor parts to used raincoats. Take it for granted that *nothing* good is in the bins outside, but hardware enthusiasts can spend hours inside the stores. You just never know when you might find the air-conditioner manifest you were looking for. The scene makes last year's rummage sale look tame.

Kitchenware, Lighting and Restaurant Supplies: The neighborhood down around Bowery and Houston is as sleazy as can be, but most of the locals are sleeping it off at any given moment, so it's probably quite safe. Still I would take a partner and either have a cab wait or ask the store where to park. Is it worth it? Definitely! Starting at Bowery and Houston and going north to Cooper Square is "restaurant row," *the* source for professional kitchen equipment and lighting. When you're buying appliances in the thousands of dollars, you can put up with the neighborhood to get wholesale prices and a selection that the local guy never carries. Everything from Garland stoves to specialized light bulbs can be had at wholesale, and the dealer is not only knowledgeable, he can service it, too!

If you don't want to try the neighborhood, lighting can also be found along Second Avenue in the 60s and 70s. Even the hardware stores there are primarily lighting specialists.

Men's Clothing (Discount): Walk along Fifth Avenue between 18th, 19th, and 20th Streets. This is another place to keep your eyes turned up because virtually all of these places are lofts on the higher floors. (The exception is Saint Laurie, on street level.) We list many of them, but also look for hand-lettered notices on signposts. The usual comment is, "I got two suits for what I paid for my last *one.*"

Musical Equipment: Classical sheet music and piano stores are located near Carnegie Hall (57th Street and Seventh Avenue). After all these years, they still haven't recognized Lincoln Center or spread throughout the city! Other instruments, acoustic and electronic, are found in shops clustered on the block between Sixth and Seventh Avenue on West 48th Street.

Photographic Supplies: This is a changing scene. It depends in part on what you mean by "photographic supplies" and in part on a rapidly changing industry, which has now subdivided.

Historically, the photo industry was located directly adjacent to the garment center, whose showrooms needed their expertise for models and fashion layouts. So the area in the lower 30s and 40s between Seventh Avenue and Broadway was home to many a photographer's studio. At the same time, the photo *developing* industry was further downtown, around Union Square or what is now known as the Flatiron District.

The area was always industrial, but it is now undergoing a revival with law and advertising firms taking over manufacturing space. Advertising agencies rely heavily on the artistic and photo processing in the area below 14th Street, and lawyers have great fun shopping for used cameras or "gray market" accessories. There's yet a third area of the city for photo equipment: the electronics houses. With 47th Street Photo the granddaddy of that genus, look for new discounted camera equipment in the 40s off Broadway. There's another big outlet near the World Trade Center, and as we said with appliances, check out the Sunday *Times.*

Theater: Okay, even folks in Anchorage know the words to "Give My Regards to Broadway" and "42nd Street," and consequently think that they can locate New York's Theater District. They'd be wrong. The *real* Broadway is *west* of Broadway and uptown from 42nd Street. (42nd Street and Broadway form the end of Times Square, which is not a square but a double *X.*) The only theaters there are locally called the "Bimbos" for reasons best left unexplained. They should remain unvisited as well. Forty-fourth Street to 51st Street is the *real* Theater District, unless you're talking *off*-Broadway. In theater, off-Broadway refers to any production that is quasi-legitimate but not produced in the Theater District. The Manhattan Light Opera company, on the Upper East Side, is off-

Broadway. So is Circle in the Square, in the Village. And then there's off-off-Broadway. That is experimental, workshop, or non-equity playhousing. It can be weird, too. There are a lot of theater companies on the extreme west of 42nd Street (subsidized artists' housing is across the street) and in the East Village, particularly along First, Second, and Third Avenues, where a lot of stages are left over from either vaudeville or Yiddish theater use.

Thrift Shops: First, Second, and Third Avenues in the upper east 70s, 80s, and lower 90s is resale country. Note the neighborhood. Goodwill and the Salvation Army are elsewhere. "Antique" or funky clothing stores are not what they once were, but the people in the East Village, especially along Avenue A and 7th Street, don't know that the rest of the world has moved on. Most of the other stores that sold "antique" clothing have branched out.

Women's Clothing: The Garment Center, Seventh Avenue, Fashion Avenue—each term describes the same place, and each one says it all. From 35th to 39th Streets, from Broadway to Seventh Avenue, there is only one industry: the wholesale dressing of America's women. There's nothing like it anywhere in the world.

Manhattan at Night

If you've ever ambled down Fifth Avenue on a Sunday morning, or been in any New York office at 8:30 on a Monday morning in August, you'd swear you were hallucinating. The quiet and lack of bustle is eerie. Most people think of New York at night as a cross between that pastoral image and the chase scene in *The French Connection,* throwing in a little reality from the last time you walked around the city for theater and dinner. The true situation is nothing like that. A sizable number of city residents are *exclusively* night people, and an entire economy revolves around them.

Here's a list of things to do and places to go at night. Most of them are open all night. The exceptions are noted.

AMBULANCE—The citywide emergency number is 911.

ANIMAL SERVICE—The Animal Medical Center (510 E 62nd St, 838-8100) is the first choice for animal care, day or night. (Avoid the A.S.P.C.A.) They are open 24 hours a day.

AUTO SERVICE AND REPAIR—It seems like cars need servicing only in the dead of night in New York. If you're in that position, you have enough trouble without getting involved with ripoff artists. Take some basic measures of protection: If you can drive your car to a well-lit, active street, do so. One mechanic's wife hit a pothole that blew her tire. Her husband told her, "Drive home anyway. I can always replace a wheel. I can't replace you!" If the car cannot be moved, turn on the flashers and get to the nearest phone. Call the AAA, if you're a member, or one of the following, if you're not. Above all do *not* let your car be towed by anyone who lacks written credentials or by a 24-hour towing company. They will tow your car but do nothing else. In the morning, your car will be untouched but held hostage for major bucks for "towing and storage" and unneeded repairs.

AAA Road Service (757-3356)

A Manhattan Towing (466 Tenth Ave, 239-4953) Mechanics are available around the clock, and their road service will provide minor repairs on the spot. They will tow from any of the five boroughs. Disadvantage: they don't take credit cards.

Express Towing (276 Seventh Ave, 242-5811) Towing and service are available 24 hours a day.

Gaseteria (2 West End Ave, at 59th St and Eleventh Ave, 307-1099) The repair franchise is Sammi Transmission, and they have a mechanic on duty 24 hours a day. They also tow.

Golden European Towing Corp. (539 W 47th St, 307-0945) They have flat-bed road service and mechanics on duty around the clock.

Jake's Auto Repair (236 W 60th St, 800/343-8785, 315-3094) Mechanics are on duty all the time, and they do both flat-bed and wheel-lift towing.

Jimmy's Towing Service (35 West End Ave, 489-6718) This is the affiliate of the Amoco and Allstate motor clubs. (800/782-7887) The towing alone is available 24 hours.

JRS Towing (323 W 96th St, 800/334-3300) This is an Amoco Club affiliate. The towing and emergency road service is 24 hours.

BANKS—The automatic cash machine has changed the face of banking. It is possible never to have to enter your bank, and you can even do your banking via home computer. In the city, a series of networks can get you instant money. If you use a cash machine, never give your card to the previous customer to "test" the machine because his card didn't work. It's a common scam. In fact, don't even enter an area where another customer is waiting. If someone comes while you're operating the machine, shield your transaction and get out fast.

For locations of the nearest ATMs call:

CIRRUS	800/4-CIRRUS
CITIBANK	868-1100
NYCE	914/899-6777
PLUS	800/843-7587

American Express traveler's checks information is 800/CASH NOW. Emergency cash can be received from a machine at the Western Union office (1440 Broadway, 354-9750). It gets charged to your credit card.

BILLIARDS
Tekk Billiards (75 Christopher St, bet Seventh Ave S and Bleecker St, 463-9282)

BOOKSTORES
Doubleday Book Shop (724 Fifth Ave, at 57th St, 397-0550) When I started out, the Doubleday chain gave me encouragement. Even before that, I had hours of reading enjoying from late-night purchases here. They are open Mon-Sat: 9 a.m.-midnight; Sun: noon-5.

Gryphon (2246 Broadway at W 80th St, 362-0706) Gryphon takes its name from its collection of rock and roll records, but it has branched out into all sorts of books. It's a great place for fiction, particularly Oz and Baumiana as well as first editions and out-of-print books. Hours are Sun-Thurs: 10 a.m.-midnight; Fri, Sat: 10 a.m.-1 a.m.

St. Mark's Place Bookshop (12 St Mark's Pl, bet Bowery and Second Ave, 260-7853) A strange place, befitting the Village, this store specializes in underground literature, radical politics, and alternative lifestyles. As best we could ascertain, their hours are 11 a.m.-11:30 p.m., every day. When we expressed surprise because that didn't jibe with our information or experience, the retort was, "Okay, so maybe they're not." A strange place, St. Mark's.

Shakespeare & Company (2259 Broadway at 81st St, 580-7800; 716 Broadway, 529-1330) They are open seven days a week, from 10 a.m.-midnight.

CLEANERS
Midnight Express Cleaners (25-15 41st Ave, Long Island City, 921-0111) Mon-Fri: 9 a.m.-11 p.m.; Sat: 9 a.m.-3 p.m. Relax. You don't have to go to Long Island City (which is in Queens) to have your clothing cleaned. The hours are the hours of service, and they can have your order back the next day. Prices are competitive with regular cleaners and a fraction of those at the hotel valet. They will pick up and deliver.

COMPUTER RENTAL
PC Express Rentals (26 W 23rd St, bet 43rd and 44th St, 807-8234)

DELIVERY AND MESSENGER SERVICES
AAAAAAAA James Bonded Courier Service (42-19 192nd St, Queens, 752-1007) 24 hours a day, seven days a week.

Able Motorized Deliveries (41-41 38th St, L.I.C., 800/225-2253, 687-5515) Always open, but they restrict delivery to the tri-state area. Midtown delivery is guaranteed within a half-hour, within the city in an hour, and 90 minutes anywhere else in their delivery area. There is no weight restriction up to an entire truckload.

Metro Express (606 W 47th St, 765-2729) 24 hours, every day, trucking and messenger.

Quality Messengers Inc. (2 Lincoln Sq, 877-5608) They offer 24-hour, seven-day-a-week service for up to a truckload, mostly within the city.

Whooshhhh (100 Sixth Ave, 966-7747, 800/942-7747) Ditto.

ELECTRICIANS

Marty Allen Electrical Services (200 Park Ave S, 254-9600) Twenty-four-hour service, seven days a week.

Michael Altman (80 Fifth Ave, 681-2900) Twenty-four-hour service, every day.

A. C. Green Electrical Contractors (412 W 48th St and 134 W 70th St, 541-4100)

Joseph Weinstein (94-24 88th St, Queens, 877-4600) Two-hour service anytime, any day.

EMERGENCIES–the city-wide emergency number is 911. To report a fire or look for a fire-call box, call 628-2900. Fire-call boxes are found on streetposts and have an orange light. See the "Emergency Numbers" section of this book.

FLORISTS–To amend that late-night quarrel, here are a few suggestions:

Piccadilly Florist (110 E 59th St, bet Park and Lexington Aves, 421-5176) They offer same day delivery, seven days a week, and are open nights, Sundays, and holidays. Hours vary.

Rialto (707 Lexington Ave, bet 57th and 58th St, 688-3234) The granddaddy of them all, the Rialto is open 24 hours, seven days a week. Legends are built upon their services.

FOOD

Eat In. (See also "Manhattan à la Carte")

Time was that cabbies alone could support half a dozen all-night diners. A few dozen more were chichi down-home places frequented by the "in" crowd. Nowadays, the cabbie haunts are all but gone and the smart set sticks to nightspots and goes home. (Even Ratner's burned down!) So don't expect great food or a gourmet chef at three in the morning. Basically, these places are open:

Around the Clock Cafe and Gallery (8 Stuyvesant St, bet Second and Third Ave, 598-0402) Call for directions. Stuyvesant Street is *not* in Stuyvesant Town, and few people have ever heard of it. (It's actually the continuation of Astor Place in the East Village). It's really *breakfast* that's served around the clock here, but the food and prices are good.

Big City (572 Eleventh Ave, at 43rd St, 244-6033) Originally the Market Diner, this was a cabbie and truck driver's hangout until it was discovered by the uptown crowd. Nowadays, it's a private club Thursday through Saturday night, but there is a restaurant that takes reservations and is still open 24 hours.

Brasserie (110 E 53rd St, 751-4840)

Chelsea Square Restaurant (368 W 23rd St, 691-5400)

Cooper Square Restaurant (87 Second Ave, 420-8050)

Empire Diner (210 Tenth Ave, 243-2736) Twenty-four hours a day. American diner menu.

Joyce's Steak House (948 Second Ave, at 50th St, 759-6780, 800/42STEAK) Hours are noon-3 a.m. for steaks, chops, and seafood.

Kiev (117 Second Ave at E 64th St, 674-4040) Kiev is open 24 hours a day. The menu is heavy on Ukrainian-style breakfast, but there are also soups, blini, pierogi, sausages, and stuffed cabbage.

Le Farfalle (209 W 48th St, at Broadway, 582-0352) Located off Broadway and Times Square, Le Farfalle is more of a disco than a restaurant—and more than just a little theatrical. Its hours are Wed-Sun: 10 p.m.-4 a.m.

Midnite Express Restaurant (1712 Second Ave, 860-2320)

Morning Star Restaurant (401 W 57th St, 246-1593)

Munson Diner (600 W 49th St, 246-0964)

Panchito's (105 MacDougal, nr Bleecker St, 473-5239) Panchito's isn't open *late* so much as it's open Village time. From noon-4 a.m., you can get anything from a drink to the full menu, and no one will think it's odd. Mexican food is the specialty of the house.

Sarge's (548 Third Ave at E 36th St, 679-0442) Open 24 hours a day, seven days a week. Sarge's could feed an army; they would be well fed.

Second Ave Deli (156 Second Ave at E 10th St, 677-0606) Sun-Thurs: 7 a.m.-midnight; Fri-Sat: 7 a.m.-2 a.m. A great deli. The pastrami is world famous.

Takeout

Many of the small mom-and-pop outfits are open 24 hours a day. This is especially true of the industrious Korean greengrocers who see no reason to close their stores when they have to get up at 4 a.m. anyway.

Bagels on the Square (7 Carmine St, 691-3041)

Food Emporium (316 1/2 Greenwich St, 215 Park Ave S, 228 West End Ave, 1498 York Ave, 1052 First Ave, 1331 First Ave, 969 Second Ave, 1172 Third Ave, 1450 Third Ave, 452 W 43rd St)

Grand Union (350 E 86th St, 535-2205)

H & H Bagels East (1551 Second Ave, 734-7441) They are rumored to close around two. No one has ever caught them closed, though.

Jumbo Bagels and Bialys (1070 Second Ave, bet E 56th and 57th St, 355-6185)

Pathmark (227 Cherry St, at Pike Slip, 227-8988, and 410 W 207th St, 569-0600)

Shim Si Grocery (524 Columbus Ave, 787-7025)
West Side Supermarket (2171 Broadway, 595-2536)

GAS
Amoco (Broadway and Houston S, Eighth Ave and W 110th St)
Citgo (Bowery and E Third St)
Gaseteria (Houston and Lafayette St, West End Ave and W 59th St)
Gulf (Tenth Ave and W 23rd St)
Mobil (Sixth Ave and Spring St, Eleventh Ave and W 57th St)

HAIR—It used to be that you could get your hair done 24 hours a day.
Here are some *almost* all night hair ports!
   Astor Place Hair Designers (2 Astor Pl, bet Broadway and 8th St,
      475-9854, 475-9790) They are open 8-8 everyday but Sunday (8-6),
      so they really don't qualify. But you have until 8 p.m. to look in
      on the action here. Don't miss it!
   George Michael of Madison Ave/Madora, Inc. (420 Madison Ave
      bet 48th and 49th St, 752-1177) This expert in *looong* hair is open
      until 10 Thursday night and by appointment Sunday and other times.
      They also make house calls.
   Heads & Tails Haircutting (22 St Mark's Pl, 677-9125) Tues-Fri:
      11:30 a.m.-midnight; Sun: 11:30 a.m.-9 p.m. No appointment
      needed.
   Larry Mathews Twenty-four Hour Beauty Salon (536 Madison Ave,
      bet 54th and 55th St, 246-6100) This salon has repeatedly changed
      its hours while retaining the name. They are once again open 24
      hours every day, but if you're going at 5 a.m., I would call first.

LOCKSMITHS
Locksmiths are one of those professions that this section was written
for. It seems they all work nights! The other thing they have in common
is that even Mr. Zibrinski jockeys for position in the phone book by
listing his business under "A." One other thing—these guys know you're
desperate. Always ask for an estimate when you call, and insist on a
written estimate before work begins. If you think a locksmith can be
trusted, you think wrong.
   AAAA Manhattan Locksmiths (2449 A Broadway, bet 90th and 91st
      St, 877-7787) Anytime.
   AAA 1 24 Hour Locksmith (1592 Third Ave, 360-6000)
   AAA Ace Locksmith (1529 Third Ave, 727-2222) One phone
      number, five other locations on the East and West sides. 24-hour
      service, every day.
   A Award NY Locksmith (115 E 96th St, 215 E 79th St, 806-2400)
   Abrruzzi (324 E 48th St, 30 E 53rd St, 509 Madison Ave, 751-1380)
      Ditto.
   All County Locksmith (701 Seventh Ave, 1053 First Ave, 798 Ninth
      Ave, 944-0246)

Delta Locksmiths (1268 Madison Ave, bet 90th and 91st St, 534-1300)

MESSENGERS
Goodwill Messenger Service (1017 Sixth Ave, at W 38th St, 298-5034)

NEWSSTANDS
First Ave at 63rd, 65th, 79th, and 86th St
Second Ave at St. Mark's Pl, 50th, and 53rd St
Third Ave at St. Mark's Pl, 23rd, 35th, and 54th St
Lexington Ave at 64th and 89th St
Park Ave Grand Hyatt at 42nd and 45th St (Pan Am Building)
Sixth Ave at 8th and 48th St
Broadway at 40th, 42nd (first spot for dropoff of the *New York Times*), 72nd, 79th, 94th, 96th, and 104th St
Seventh Ave S at Sheridan Sq
Eighth Ave at 23rd, 41st, 42nd (Port Authority Bus Terminal), and 46th St
Amsterdam Ave at 79th St
Columbus Ave at 81st St
162 E 23rd St (bet Madison and Park Ave)

PHARMACIES
Kaufman Pharmacy (557 Lexington Ave in the Beverly Hotel, at 50th St, 755-2266) Open 24 hours a day.
Plaza Pharmacy (1657 Second Ave, at 86th St, 879-3878) Open 10 a.m.-midnight every day.

PHOTOCOPYING
Acro Duplicating Services (122 Fulton St, 5th floor, 732-5111)

PHOTO DEVELOPING
K&L Custom PhotoGraphics (222 E 44th St, bet Second and Third Ave, 661-5600)

PLUMBERS–The story here is similar to electricians. Many simply take a message in the middle of the night. Make sure they intend to show up and that you get a written estimate. Plumbers must be licensed. For complaints, call 312-8217.
ABAC Contracting Co. (139 W 28th St, 208 E 21st St, 473-2024) They never close.
Brennan Plumbing and Heating (123 W 79th St, 873-8626)
Boro Wide Piping & Heating (315 W 53rd St, 944-7225)
Effective Plumbing Corp (147 E 24th St, 299-0700)
Metro Plumbing (196 Highlawn Ave, Brooklyn, 385-2233)
Roto-Rooter (687-1661)

POST OFFICE–The main post office (James A. Farley Postal Station, 33rd St and Eighth Ave) is open 24 hours. Services are limited sometimes, but on April 15 and the first day for applications for the New York Marathon, or for mail-order rock concert tickets, full service is offered until midnight. The Church Street Station (90 Church St) and Grand Central Station (Lexington Ave at 45th St) have vending machines stocked with stamps at all times.

SECRETARIAL AND OFFICE SERVICES

AB Graphics (106 W 43rd St, bet Sixth and Seventh Ave, 869-7474)

All Language Services (545 Fifth Ave, 986-1688) Typing service open 24 hours.

Around the Clock Staffing (235 W 56th St, bet Seventh and Eighth Ave, 245-1750)

Dial-a-Secretary (521 Fifth Ave, 348-9575, and 126 E 83rd St, 348-8982) All types of secretarial work, at any time.

HQ Services & Offices (237 Park Ave, 949-0722; 666 Fifth Ave, 765-7111; 730 Fifth Ave, 333-8700; and 53 Wall St, 558-6400) A full range of services is available here, and they will process phoned-in dictation 24 hours.

Kinko's—the Copy Center (24 E 12th St, 924-0802) Open 24 hours.

Village Copier (20 E 13th St, 924-3456) They are open 24 hours, and do all kinds of copying work.

Manhattan on Sunday

Sunday in New York is a different world. Most visitors and business people come to the city Monday through Friday. Even residents escape on weekends. With the advent of "supersaver" fares that require a Saturday night stay, weekend packages, and the age of the "couch potato," more and more people are visiting or remaining in the city on weekends. If you want to explore the Big Apple at a more leisurely pace, weekends are your best bet.

Bear in mind the city does not "work" on Sunday. Yes, the department stores are open, and so are most attractions. However, few office buildings and fewer businesses are open before noon. That means the auxiliary functions (newsstands, cabbies, public transportation, and even many restaurants) are also out of commission or operating at a greatly reduced pace. For private car owners, this is a bonanza. You can park with ease for free virtually anywhere. For those taking public transportation, it's a pain in the neck—just the opposite of the rest of the week.

Some attractions are *more* in demand on weekends (i.e., the Statue of Liberty and Saturday night movies). On the other hand, museums are practically empty, particularly in the morning. The Metropolitan and the Cloisters open at 9:30, the American Craft Museum at 10, the

Museum of American Folk Art at 10, and most of the others between 11 and 1. Try to structure your time so that you are doing those things that can only be done on the weekend.

HOTEL PACKAGES: There are some super deals here. Most require a Friday and/or Saturday night stay, but you can check in as early as Thursday night and leave as late as Monday night. Many have elaborate weekend packages revolving around Broadway, shopping, or the sights. Always ask for special rates. Please note that some hotels quote per room rates while others are per person. It can make a substantial difference. One further point: the hotels we might recommend as first choices during the week are not necessarily the best for weekends, and vice versa. The *Salisbury* is a first choice during the week. It's neat, centrally located (close to Carnegie Hall), and reasonable. On the weekend, 57th Street is deserted. The same is true of the *Vista International*. Why would anyone want to be down there on a Sunday morning? Savvy locals who enjoy all the amenities, such as the health club, know the answer: it's a great, cheap getaway. The very best deal might just be the *United Nations Plaza,* with its sky-high swimming pool. That's a place you might never stay at during the week! Most of the following hotels have "800" numbers. You'll be pleasantly surprised at the special package rates.

Algonquin (59 W 44th St, 800/548-0345)

Bedford (118 E 40th St, 800/221-6881)

Beekman Tower (3 Mitchell Pl, across from the UN, 800/ME-SUITE)

Beverly (125 E 50th St, 753-2700)

Doral Inn (541 Lexington Ave, 800/223-5823)

Doral Park Avenue (70 Park Ave, 800/847-4135) Both Dorals have health clubs.

Dorset (30 W 54th St, 800/227-2358)

Drake Swissotel (440 Park Ave, 800/DRAKE NY)

Essex House (160 Central Park S, 800/NIKKO US)

Grand Hyatt (Park Ave at 42nd St, 800/228-9000)

Helmsley Middletowne (148 E 48th St, 800/221-4982)

Helmsley Park Lane (36 Central Park S, 800/221-4982)

Helmsley Windsor (100 W 58th St, 800/221-4982)

Intercontinental New York (111 E 48th St, 800/327-0200) Health club on premises.

Marriott Marquis (1535 Broadway, 800/228-9290) Health club.

Mayfair Regent (610 Park Ave, 800/223-0542 [New York State], 800/545-4000 [U.S.]) Health club.

New York Helmsley (212 E 42nd St, 800/221-4982)

Omni Berkshire Place (21 E 52nd St, 800/THE OMNI)

Parker Meridien (119 W 56th st, 800/543-4300) Health club and swimming pool.

Plaza (Fifth Ave at 59th St, 800/228-3000)

Rihga Royal (151 W 54th St, 800/937-5454)

Salisbury (123 W 57th St, 800/223-0680 [U.S.], 800/228-0822 [Canada])
Sheraton Park Ave (45 Park Ave, 800/325-3535)
United Nations Plaza Hotel (44th St at First Ave, 800/223-1234) Health club and swimming pool.
Vista International (3 World Trade Center, 800/258-0505)
Waldorf Astoria Hotel (301 Park Ave, 800/HILTONS)

SUNDAY BRUNCH: Sunday brunch is a custom unique to New York. Since everyone goes out on Saturday night, there is virtually no Sunday morning in New York. European travelers who arrive in the city Sunday morning are so stunned by the stillness they often think they are in the wrong city. In the old days, the only reason for stirring on Sunday was to get first crack at the Sunday *Times*. However, New Yorkers quickly discovered which newsstands were first to get the Sunday *Times* on Saturday night. Eventually, enterprising dealers began selling crucial sections, such as real estate (which is preprinted), earlier and earlier in the week. Nowadays, subscribers receive half of Sunday's paper as a matter of course on Saturday, and there is absolutely no reason to stir before 11 Sunday morning. Brunch is served from 11-2 (or maybe even 3). It is usually offered in hotel restaurants or formal dining spots, so you can sample some of the best places in town for a fraction of their dinnertime cost. The Plaza Hotel has New York's classiest Sunday brunch. (Please see "Manhattan à la Carte" for brunch listings.)

WHAT TO DO: Check at museums and sights for Sunday hours. Especially on Sunday morning, you can have the city's highlights to yourself! Almost everything is open on the weekend, and some offerings, like walking tours and children's theater, are open only weekends. The same can be true of sporting events and concerts. During the week, there is seldom an afternoon event (baseball is an exception), but on the weekends double bills are not uncommon.

One of the year-round pleasures of Sunday in the city is a simple stroll. Depending on the season, you can chance upon one of dozens of street fairs, indoor exhibits, or shows. Here's what you can expect throughout the year:

January: Winter brings the *Winter Festival* and skating in Central Park (the Louise Lasker and Wollman Memorial Rinks), as well as at *Rockefeller Center*. There are also private rinks around town. If a heavy snow falls, you might see commuters cross-country skiing to work! The *National Boat Show* sails into the Javits Center, and in the midst of winter gales, New York goes nautical. In the middle of the month, the *Winter Antiques Show* is held at the Seventh Regiment Armory (655-5250).

February: *Chinese New Year* falls anywhere from the end of January to late February. No matter when it is, Chinatown is the place to be. If it's the Year of the Dog, it's a double celebration, because the

Westminster Kennel Club Dog Show is held at Madison Square Garden (563-8300). President's Day is celebrated with *big sales* in the department stores. It's not just end-of-the-season merchandise, either. Check out electronics and clothes. This is the big one!

March: The *Cat Show* gets equal time at Madison Square Garden, and the *circus* comes to town in mid-March. The real show is the trek the animals make down 34th Street to the Garden via the Lincoln and/or Midtown Tunnels from their train on the outskirts of town. The street is closed after midnight as the cast parades past you. Lions, tigers, elephants—it's really something! Call the Garden for an exact date (563-8300). Sometimes they try to keep it a secret, but it's a little hard to move a herd of elephants quietly down 34th Street.

March 17th is *St. Patrick's Day,* and the entire town paints itself green. The parade is a citywide celebration so famous that the Lord Mayor of Dublin has, on occasion, forsaken the Emerald Isle to serve as Grand Marshall in New York. Every year the parade gets longer as more groups demand entry. If you're not marching, you're watching. Just don't attempt to cross Fifth Avenue or use a rest room.

Depending upon when *Easter* falls, winter in New York ends with a burst of flowers. Macy's annual display on the ground floor rivals that of the Botanical Gardens, next to the Bronx Zoo. The tulips on Fifth Avenue peek up through the snow, and flowers and pastels suddenly appear all over town. An *Easter Parade* goes past St. Patrick's Cathedral on Fifth Avenue on Easter Sunday.

April: This is *Passover season.* Go down to the Streits Matza Factory (150 Rivington St, 475-7000) on the Lower East Side to watch matza being made. They will break off a strip so you can sample it hot from the oven. Any Sunday you can take the Shapiro's Wine tour (126 Rivington St, 475-7383) which tunnels under the streets of the East Side. It is the city's only wine cellar and active winery. Kedem (107 Norfolk St, 673-2780) is another kosher winery open on Sunday, but they don't give tours, and the actual winery is located upstate. While you're there, tour the East Side for an unrivaled international bazaar and gastronomic feast.

May: The *Ninth Avenue International Food Festival* (581-7217), south of 57th Street along Ninth Avenue, becomes an outdoor fair that anyone can attend. The star of the fair is *food*—ethnic, fast, and finger—and never has so much been hawked, consumed, and appreciated in such crowded conditions. But it's all wonderful, and everyone turns out. It's New York at its very best. And is it delicious!

Spring comes to the Village with the formal *Washington Square Art Show.* The informal exhibition takes place year-round, except in rain or snow, but the officially sanctioned event is held in late May or early June.

June: The month of weddings, graduations, and outdoor fun, June *is* summer in New York. (Real New Yorkers leave the city on weekends in the summer. If you think it's desolate on a Sunday in March, try one in mid-August.) June is when Central Park becomes the site of *Shakespeare in the Park,* the nature programs at Belvedere Castle and the Conservatory, and the playoffs for the city's intramural corporate sports programs. The star-struck will want to catch the Broadway Show League or the Soap Opera League. All of these people (and a whole lot more) play at the Hecksher, 62nd Street, and Sheep Meadow diamonds throughout the week. In the summer, the city streets host fairs and block parties, and the young and able take to skateboards and bikes. Walking tours and private explorations of the city's architecture are at their height. The weather is perfect, and everyone is out enjoying it. Hop aboard the *Circle Line* (Pier 83, 563-3200) or go to the *South Street Seaport* for a day on the water.

June is also when the museums along Museum Mile (Fifth Ave from 82nd to 105th St) offer a free Tuesday evening of viewing. It's not really such a big deal, because most Tuesday nights are free anyway, but for some reason everyone turns out for this particular bargain.

July: June activities continue, but at a slower pace. Lincoln Center holds court to the *American Crafts Festival* (877-2011), which features handmade crafts and accessories, as well as entertainment from passing musicians, jugglers, and puppeteers.

Independence Day celebrations are sponsored by Macy's and consist of fireworks along the East River in the evening. F.D.R. Drive (the East Side Drive to locals) is closed from 14th to 51st Streets, so you can view the fireworks, which emanate from a barge in the river.

August: If a local team is in a pennant race, all eyes are on Shea or Yankee Stadium. (The two teams play each other only once a year for the Mayor's Cup, unless they happen to meet in the World Series.) In August, the *U.S. Open* is played at the Tennis Center, in Flushing Meadow Park (in Queens). You'll understand why everyone leaves town if you get caught in traffic for the U.S. Open on a day when the Mets are playing in town.

Macy's strikes again as the founder of Tap-O-Mania, a one-day assembly of the largest group of tapping feet in history. The sole purpose for this gathering is to make *The Guinness Book of World Records.*

September: Our personal favorite is the *New York Is Book Country* fiesta held on a Sunday in mid-September. I haven't missed one yet, and traditionally each new edition of this book is released at the fair. From 57th Street to 45th Street, Fifth Avenue is turned into a literary wonderland. Authors gather for lunch at the Plaza Hotel or man booths to greet their fans. Roving minstrels offer giant birthday cards to sign or the *Times'* crossword puzzle on sandwich boards to fill out. The *Third Avenue Street Fair* is often held the same day between 68th and 90th Streets. It makes a very pleasant day to stroll between the two fairs.

Mid-September is also the Italian's turn to celebrate downtown. The *Feast of San Gennaro* fills Little Italy for ten days every fall (226-9546).

People whose families moved away 50 years ago "come home" for the festival, and Little Italy literally shines with lights and Old Country specialties. For the more intellectual, the *New York Film Festival* moves into Alice Tully Hall at Lincoln Center every September. This is the local equivalent of Cannes. The awards given here are often followed elsewhere later in the year.

October: Left-over revelry from the San Gennaro Festival is used on Columbus Day. As we approach the 500th anniversary of Columbus' voyage, watch everyone jockey to claim him for their nationality! In the meantime, the parade is still strictly an Italian affair. The Polish get their day with the *Pulaski Day Parade* down Fifth Avenue from 52nd to 26th Streets.

Halloween is not a big time in New York, except in the Village. Elsewhere, the old-time customs have largely been abandoned due to fear of street crime and crowds. Many of the stores and the vertical malls have trick-or-treating for kids. It's all over before dark, except in the Village, where the action begins at 7 p.m. with a parade that starts at Sixth Avenue and Houston Street, and goes to roughly Union Square. People in the neighborhood spend a year preparing (the practice of "voguing" was born here), and it is outrageous. There also isn't much competition elsewhere in town.

The *New York City Marathon* is run in late October or early November. The idea is to pick a time that will have optimal running conditions for record-breaking. It hasn't happened yet, because it has been too warm in November or too cold in October or it has rained. The point is, you'll know when it is, because the city goes marathon-mad. Thousands of people run, the event is televised, and thousands of onlookers turn out to cheer the runners. Every year after the marathon, the papers are full of love letters between runners and fans. It really is a giant lovefest!

November: Although it is *not* on a Sunday, the *Macy's Thanksgiving Day Parade* is the high point of the month. The parade wends down Broadway to Herald Square, and the entertainment industry is represented by floats, balloons, and marching bands. Parade's end heralds the holiday season with Santa Claus's arrival on a toy-loaded sleigh.

December: Don't miss the Rockefeller Center Christmas tree or the store windows on Fifth Avenue. There are always myriad performances of *The Nutcracker* and Handel's *Messiah* in the city.

Manhattan for Kids

Let me level with you. I've been assembling and updating this book for over ten years now. When I started, it was from the vantage point of a businessman who came to the city sans kids. I learned quickly, however, that many people do bring their kids to New York both for business and for pleasure trips, and that exploring the city with kids can heighten the experience. There's something to be said for the sense of wonder children display at the city's treasures.

I've learned to explore and include spots in the city that are most appealing to children. But it's never been easy. For many years the only museums designed exclusively for children were MUSE in Brooklyn and the Staten Island Children's Museum. Initially, the Children's Museum of Manhattan operated out of a storefront as an auxiliary to neighborhood classrooms. Despite several moves and a custom-made home of its own, they still haven't worked the bugs out, and New York remains the only city I know of with no specific museum for youngsters.

Over the years, we have found some pretty exciting places for kids of all ages. But in researching this edition we found that for budgetary or security reasons a great many are no longer in operation. The following are open as of this writing or are temporarily closed. I strongly urge you to call *before* going.

AT&T INFOQUEST
Madison Ave (bet 55th and 56th St)   605-5555
Wed-Sun: 10-6; Tues: 10-9

Infoquest should be first on your list—and not just alphabetically! The free program spans three floors of exciting, interactive electronic displays and games on communications. From the start, when a glass-walled elevator carries you through the AT&T atrium, you know you're in for a treat. Children of all ages love it. Allow about an hour and a half. Incidentally, you are next to IBM and Trump Tower and not far from the Museum of Broadcasting and the Museum of Modern Art.

CENTRAL PARK
The park has numerous activities for children. The newly renovated Central Park Zoo, Fifth Ave at 64th St (439-6500), charges a nominal admission fee. It is now run by the same folks who run the Bronx Zoo, which translates into a professional, state-of-the-art zoo with much to do. Would that the Children's Zoo, at E 65th St (408-1271), were as nice. Every year the Park Department threatens to close it due to budget considerations. Every year it is "saved." I think they were right the first time!

Elsewhere the park offers dozens of playgrounds. Each has its own local traditions—i.e., one is a "nanny" spot, another a sand lot, etc. Central Park also has two skating rinks. Wollman, located midpark at 62nd Street (517-4800), turns into a miniature golf and roller-skating rink in spring. Louise Lasker, located midpark at 106th Street (996-1184), is where the professional hockey players practice. The Dairy (397-3156) has many programs, including free weekend walking tours with the Urban Park Rangers (397-3080). Belvedere Castle, 79th Street south of the Great Lawn (772-0210) has family workshops for ages 5-11. It overlooks the Delacorte Theater, where free Shakespeare in the Park is held every summer. There are two rowing lakes. Boats may be rented at the Loeb Boathouse, midpark at 75th Street (517-2233), as well as facilities for model-boat sailing in the Conservatory Water. Bethesda Fountain, near the latter, is for local color. Sheep Meadow must hold the record for the most concurrent softball games played on one field. Of course, you can also bike, walk, run, or picnic virtually anywhere in Central Park.

CHILDREN'S MUSEUM OF MANHATTAN
212 W 83rd St (bet Broadway and Amsterdam Ave)
721-1234

This was supposed to be a state-of-the-art, ultramodern, high-tech resource for children, but it hasn't worked out that way. First of all, a nine-year-old would be an old child here. Then there is the fact that at any given time some part of the exhibit is not functioning. Finally, I detect a prejudice against one-time visitors, as opposed to members and communal residents. After-school programs, workshops, art classes, and private birthday parties exclude tourists and casual visitors, and the museum often seems to be run like a private club.

ELLIS ISLAND
Ferries leave from Castle Clinton in Battery Park on the southern tip of Manhattan (264-8711, 269-5755). This is one of the hottest tickets in town—and for good reason. The newly renovated Ellis Island is a monument to the immigrants who made America. You can trace a typical arrival into the country, as well as your own ethnic background. It's a fascinating place, and the short ferry ride takes the kids into New York harbor. That ferry ride is also a bone of contention. The bridge from New Jersey used by workmen during the reconstruction was left standing, but it is off limits for "safety reasons." As a result, visitors are required to pay what some regard as an outrageous fee to get to the island. The matter is being discussed in Congress.

EMPIRE STATE BUILDING
Fifth Ave (at 34th St)   736-3100
Daily: 9:30 a.m.-midnight

The World Trade Center may be taller and the Sears Tower in Chicago taller still. It makes no difference. Children want to see the Empire State Building, and New Yorkers still think of it as the world's tallest building. A series of three elevators takes you from the lobby to the 80th floor, then to the 86th floor outdoor overlook and, finally, to the 102nd-floor tower. The line is long, but it moves fast. Don't go if visibility is poor. Instead, you can visit the Guinness Book of World Records exhibit hall (947-2335) next to the ticket counter. Most kids enjoy it as much, if not more!

IBM BUILDING
590 Madison Ave (bet 56th and 57th St)
407-3500, 800/426-3333
Tues-Fri: 11-6; Sat: 10-5

The IBM Gallery of Science and Art features changing exhibits. Virtually all of them involve hands-on activities—and it's free! The problem is that there are periods of down time when exhibits are being prepared and nothing is open, so call ahead. You enter the exhibit through the Bamboo Court, which itself has interactive monitors, the world's largest indoor bamboo stalks, and fascinating shops. Ample seating makes it a first-choice spot for brown-baggers and resters, and IBM thoughtfully provides entertainment throughout the day.

INTREPID SEA-AIR-SPACE MUSEUM
Pier 86 (bet Twelfth Ave and 46th St)   245-0072
Wed-Sun: 10-5

This aircraft carrier, permanently moored in the Hudson River, offers several decks of exhibits on the history of sea, air, and space craft. Two submarines are also part of the museum. The flight deck features models of virtually every type of aircraft flown in air history, including examples from the Persian Gulf War.

NBC STUDIO TOUR
30 Rockefeller Center   664-7174
(see ''Tours'')

NEW YORK STOCK EXCHANGE
20 Broad St   656-5168

We've debated this entry since the first edition. The stock exchange guides have always been charming and helpful to me when I identified myself. However, staffers who have taken kids have found that exhibits were out-of-order, the tour was perfunctory, and the guides downright rude.

Across the street (note that the Stock Exchange is *not* on Wall Street) the Federal Hall National Memorial at 26 Wall Street (344-3830) is one of the few National Parks sites in Manhattan proper. (Theodore Roosevelt's birthplace is another.) Park rangers dressed as they are in Yosemite rule over the site of Washington's inauguration, the first treasury, and the first capitol. (Did you know that New York was the first seat of government in the United States?) The building has huge vaults left from the treasury days, as well as a new Museum of American Constitutional Government. On the second floor is an exhibit on John Peter Zenger, whose trial (which established freedom of the press in the colonies) took place on this site. There are also thematic exhibits, lectures and concerts throughout the year.

POLICE MUSEUM
235 E 20th St (bet Second and Third Ave, 2nd floor)
477-9753

This museum is manned by officers from the police academy who are proud of their history and eager to share it with young citizens. They are in the process of organizing and displaying artifacts acquired during 300 years of city law enforcement. Check on hours.

RADIO CITY MUSIC HALL
Sixth Ave at 50th St
247-4777 (information), 632-4041 (tours)

At holiday time, there is nothing like the Rockettes and the holiday shows, which sell out months in advance. Almost as much fun is the one-hour backstage tour that meets in the lobby seven days a week. The fee is a bit hefty, but wouldn't you love to see the world's largest organ and the elevators that raise and lower the orchestra?

SOUTH STREET SEAPORT
669-9424 (recording), 669-9400 (offices)

This is a living period piece—and much more! Wall Street types come here for lunch and after work to browse, wine, and dine. A heavy-duty singles and retreat scene! Weekends they're gone, and the seaport becomes a street fair, some of which takes place aboard ships or at sea. For kids, the seaport is a wonderland. For adults, it's a place to sample some of the best little shops in the city.

The Seaport Museum requires a ticket and allows boarding of whatever ships currently make up the fleet. Permanent ones include the *Wavertree,* an 1885 three-masted tall ship undergoing restoration; the *Ambrose,* a former lighthouse ship; the *W.O. Decker,* a wooden tugboat; the *Peking* and the *Pioneer,* which sail on charters and at lunchtime; the *Maj. Gen. Wm. H. Hart,* a 1925 steam ferry; and the *Lettie G. Howard,* the last fishing schooner of its kind. A ticket also gains admission to the Museum Gallery, the Children's Center and its hands-on programs and workshops, and the Norway Galleries (in the A.A. Low Building). Free for the walking are dozens of shops in the Fulton Market, Pier 17 Pavilion, and on the Seaport streets. Many of those along Schermerhorn Row, Front Street, and Cannon's Walk are period revivals featuring the crafts and culture of the eighteenth and nineteenth centuries. Also on the Cannon's Walk is the Seaport Experience Theater (210 Front St, 608-7888), featuring a realistic movie, accompanied by sound and light effects, on the seaport's (and New York's) history.

STATUE OF LIBERTY
Liberty Island ferries leave from Castle Clinton in Battery Park. (For information, call 363-3227 [statue], 269-5755 [ferry], 363-8832

[museum].) After the "Miss Liberty" celebrations, this suddenly became the longest line in the city. (One time-saving alternative is to leave from Liberty State Park in New Jersey). Lines are endless for the ferry and at the Statue, where there are, in fact, two lines. One is for the elevator to the top of the pedestal, the other is for the climb (12 stories, 171 steps) to the Statue's crown. Unless you are among the morning's first arrivals, you won't be able to do both. Opt for the pedestal.

UNITED NATIONS
First Ave from 43rd to 49th St   754-7713

Children are fascinated by the United Nations partly for idealistic reasons and partly because entering the UN takes one out of the United States and onto international territory. Eat lunch in the cafeteria or delegates' lounge. Mail a letter from the UN post office after buying UN stamps. The gardens (a gift, as is all the land, from the Rockefellers) are perfect for contemplating the world (or merely the traffic along the East River). Notice I haven't said anything about the tours. Children under five are not admitted. Most of the tour is geared over the heads of kids. There are no facilities for strollers or carriages, and children who can't behave are asked to leave. In time of crisis, tours are canceled and at all times security is a world-class pain.

WORLD FINANCIAL CENTER
Battery Park City

You can get to the World Financial Center from the World Trade Center via enclosed viaducts above West Street, and that alone is reason enough to take the kids here. But there's more. The area was built on landfill (displaced by the World Trade Center) in the Hudson River, and the view is charming. In addition, there's much to see: yacht and boat basins (in the North and South Coves); a sweeping esplanade with views of New York Harbor, the Statue of Liberty, and New Jersey; and the Crystal Palace Winter Garden, which soars high enough to house 16 live palm trees and an outdoor plaza. Throughout the year programs are offered here that rival Broadway productions.

WORLD TRADE CENTER
Observation Deck, 2 World Trade Center   466-7377
Daily: 9:30-9:30

Superlatives don't really do the World Trade Center justice. Nor do statistics. From the 107th-floor observation deck, you can see 55 miles. From the rooftop promenade on the 110th floor, the world's highest outdoor observation point, the view is even better! Fifty thousand people work at the World Trade Center, while another 80,000 visit on any given day. There are 99 elevators in each tower and over 600,000 square feet of glass windows. For kids, in addition to the observation deck, there's the Commodities Exchange Center (4 World Trade Center) and all sorts of shows and programs in the lobbies. Holiday time here is magical.

Rest Rooms

When you gotta go . . . well, no one can say that nearly every possible need isn't addressed in this volume. We hope, for this reason, you always keep it handy.

New York is not the easiest place to find clean, safe rest rooms. By law, public buildings must have public facilities. However, getting in them and finding them in good shape is an entirely different situation. Do *not* place anything on the floor in public rest rooms, as purses, packages, and luggage have a habit of disappearing. A general rule for finding decent, convenient facilities is to try major hotels, busy restaurants (act as if you are a patron), large stores, shopping malls, schools, theaters, libraries, and hospitals.

Specific suggestions:

A&S Plaza (Herald Square)
Citicorp Center (153 Lexington Ave, at 53rd St)
Forbes Building (Fifth Ave at Twelfth St)
Grand Hyatt Hotel (Lexington Ave and 42nd St)
New York Public Library (Fifth Ave and 42nd St)
Olympic Tower (Fifth Ave at 51st St)
Park Ave Plaza (55 E 52nd St)
South Street Seaport
30 Rockefeller Center (concourse level)
Trump Plaza (Fifth Ave and 56th St)
Waldorf-Astoria Hotel (Park Ave and 50th St)
World Trade Center and World Financial Center

Safety in the City

Safety is a consideration in every city in our land today, and New York is no exception. Naturally, one hears more about crime in Manhattan, because there are so many people living and working in a confined area. The percentages are with you. New York is big. Very big. But despite the density of population, it doesn't even make the top ten in the nation's crime statistics. Common sense, as always, is the best advice.

Safety considerations should certainly not deter you from visiting and enjoying the many sights and pleasures of the city. Be prudent. You are your own best security. Don't leave tempting things on the seat of your car. Lock all valuables in the trunk, whether you're parked on the street or in a garage. Don't wear good jewelry in public places, especially on the streets. A favorite trick in New York is ripping gold chains off the necks of unsuspecting women and men. Leave your flashy rings at home. Lock your valuables in hotel safes.

Sticking to so-called "good" neighborhoods is no guarantee of safety. The only time I was mugged was in the "silk stocking" district at Park Avenue and 63rd St. Don't ask for trouble. Stay away from Avenues A, B, C, and D on the Lower East Side. This is drug land. Also stay out of Central Park at night. Never leave bags or belongings unattended. Report any strange package that looks out of place.

Be alert to distractions, as pickpockets work in a hurry. They are watching for persons making phone calls, greeting friends, hailing a taxi, picking up something off the sidewalk. Be alert to people who are persistently asking directions or are too eager to be helpful. Use pocketbooks that have a secure closing, keep wallets in an inside pocket, and don't carry handbags that can be easily grabbed.

CAN PEOPLE STILL MEET UNDER THE BILTMORE CLOCK IN NEW YORK CITY?

Yes, but the clock that once hung over the entrance to the lavish Palm Court salon in the famed Biltmore Hotel — between Madison and Vanderbilt Avenues and Forty-third and Forty-fourth Streets — is now part of the 78 story atrium of the Bank of America Plaza at 335 Madison Avenue. The bronze clock is the only visible remnant of the Palm Court, which was demolished in August 1981 when the hotel was converted into a bank building.

II. Where to Eat It! Manhattan à la Carte

No part of this book receives as much attention as the restaurant section. This is because we all have to eat several times a day and because eating out has become an important part of daily life in Manhattan. With most adult members of a household working, time to prepare meals at home is strictly limited these days. Many residents have found it is less expensive to eat out or pick up a meal from the growing number of stores that sell gourmet dishes for takeout.

To visit all the restaurants in the city would be impossible. The latest count I heard was approximately 25,000. They can be found in every part of the city, with every kind of ethnic orientation, and in every price range. No city in the world has the diversity or the quality that this city's restaurants have. The problem is that with so much available, it can be intimidating and bewildering.

I have tried to uncomplicate the restaurant scene and provide as much information as I can so you can enjoy your meals and get the most for your dollar. At the same time, you benefit from the experience of one who has eaten in over 1600 establishments of every kind and description in Manhattan!

Let me set the record straight. I make no pretense of being an expert food critic, like my good friend Bryan Miller, the talented restaurant writer for the *New York Times*. I am presenting information from my perspective—that of an average patron who has spent over 20 years in the field, who operates his own eating place in Oregon (a Konditorei), who has had the opportunity to make judgments based on travels to every major city in the world. So much for my credentials.

The restaurant scene has changed a great deal in recent years. No longer is it hip to run up huge checks in plushy establishments. Expense accounts, in most cases, are being closely watched. Extravagance in all fields is out of style these days. No one knows this better than the owners and operators of the bistros and dining rooms of this city. A few of the top establishments still draw a small, select clientele who don't look at the prices. But in most cases, they have become more reasonable, just as the food offered has become simpler and healthier.

I want to emphasize that this is not a Yellow Pages of restaurants in New York. It is a carefully culled selection of the best (which does not mean expensive) the area has to offer, whether it is hamburgers and pizza or gourmet French and Italian fare.

New trends abound. Simpler, healthier dishes. "No smoking" rooms. Casual clothes. Marvelously rich desserts. Owner-chef operations. A revival of excellent dining in Manhattan hotels. Interesting new places in unlikely areas, next to warehouses and unsightly storefronts. Places that are more fun. And, best of all, a price structure that tends to be more realistic.

Most restaurant guides give stars or ratings to the places listed in their pages. I've chosen not to go that route. Only those establishments that I feel are worth visiting are included. Every one is recommended because of some unique quality (or qualities) that sets it apart from the rest.

What do I look for? Good food, of course. But the place must also be clean and inviting. The personnel must be informed, polite, and helpful. The value received for your dollar must be there. The presentation must be attractive. Kitchens and rest rooms must be spotless. The noise level should be tolerable. Reservations should be efficiently honored. Tables should be placed so that conversations can take place. To sum up, an establishment should be the best in whatever category (type of food, price, ambiance, etc.) it specializes in.

Certain things I don't like have been taken into account in my evaluations. Imperious maitre d's. Waiters who try to become your friends, not your servers. Restaurants that try unusual ethnic mixes: like Japanese-Italian. Places that try to derail you to the bar (so the tab can be run up), even when you have reservations. Cold bread. Crowded plates. Tepid soups. Overseasoned entrées. Day-old desserts. Greasy menus. Uninformed personnel. Unpleasant odors. Being seated by the kitchen or the rest rooms. Haughty attitudes. You get the picture.

In the sections that follow, I have tried to include everything readers have asked for. The first part of the "Manhattan à la Carte" section features listings for different kinds of meals and occasions (tea, brunch, etc.), Sunday dining, outdoor cafes, places for kids, hamburger spots, cheap eats, listings by ethnic type and by neighborhood, and much more.

Next comes an exclusive listing of major food items or dishes that seem to be the most popular. I have tried to list those places where the best (tastiest, priced right, adequate selection) is available, either to eat in or take out. Of course, each item is not available all the time at all of the places mentioned.

Next comes a listing of several hundred places that are worthy of expanded description. These reviews include the salient features of the establishment (including pricing) and a general feel for the kind of ambiance you will encounter. I have purposely tried not to be too specific on menu descriptions, as these change overnight and can rapidly be out-of-date. However, the general character of these places usually does not change. I have tried to eliminate trendy spots that, in my opinion, will not last in the ultracompetitive restaurant world.

A few housekeeping comments. Inexpensive, to me, means under $15 for a meal, per person, without drinks. Moderate is $16-$35; moderately expensive, $36-$45; expensive $46 and up. Most establishments take the major credit cards (American Express, Visa, Mastercard). Diner's Club cards are also honored in many establishments. Where only certain cards are honored, or where they take cash only, this has been noted in the restaurant description. I take no pretense of being a wine expert, so descriptions of wines are not included. Except for the more expensive places, casual dress is perfectly acceptable. If in doubt, call the establishment. (Most have spare jackets or ties on hand for men who are not appropriately dressed.) In most cases, reservations are preferred. Many establishments will ask for a telephone contact or a reconfirmation. (I object to the latter.) If you arrive on time, you have every reason to ask to be seated at the agreed time. Do not let them put you in the bar to cool your heels. If there is a problem with a particular dish or a complaint about service, you have every right to pass it along to the individual in charge. Check your bill carefully. Figure your tip on the total for food and drink, excluding tax. Remember, you are the guest; how you react to your dining experience is what word-of-mouth is all about. And positive word-of-mouth is the most valuable advertisement a restaurant can have.

A bit of advice about ordering specials that do not appear on the regular menu. Many restaurants use this devise to sell higher-priced meals. If the items announced by your waiter sound appealing, and if price is important to you, don't hesitate to ask the price of the dish described. You will save yourself some real "check shock"!

Be warned of one important factor. The turnover in eating establishments is enormous. Frighteningly so. I can recall one establishment that had a well-known name and menu at noon. By that same evening, the place had reopened under new name, new management, new menu, and a completely different direction. There is also great mobility among the chefs of the city, who hop from one place to another. Naturally, the style and quality of the food can change as fast as the personnel.

If you disagree with some of my evaluations, remember this is an informed but *personal* opinion. If some changes and closings have occurred after publication, I am sorry. All I can say is that my information was current right up until printing time, which, unlike most major publishing houses, is a matter of several weeks after the manuscript is completed. (This is one of the advantages of self-publishing.)

Bon Appetit!

Quick Reference Guide

Here is a quick way to decide where you might like to eat! In one easy listing it tells you the location, type of food, and whether it is open on Sunday. The page reference will direct you to a complete write-up!

Best Taste Treats (Eat In and Takeout): An Exclusive List

Antipasti, hot: Pasta Roma (315 W 57th St)

Appetizers, gourmet: Russ & Daughters (179 E Houston St)

Apple pandowdy: An American Place (2 Park Ave)

Babka: Gertel's (53 Hester St)

Bagels: H&H Bagels East (1551 Second Ave)

Baked Alaska: Rainbow Room (30 Rockefeller Plaza)

Baked Alaska (by order): G&M Pastries (1006 Madison Ave)

Baklava: Alleva Dairy (188 Grand St) and Anatolia (1422 Third Ave)

Barbecue items, Chinese: Quon Jan Meat Products (79 Christie St)

Baskets, corporate: Manhattan Fruitier (210 E 6th St)

Baskets, picnic: In a Basket (226 E 83rd St)

Bass, striped: Scarlatti (34 E 52nd St)

Bean curd, stuffed: Golden Unicorn (18 E Broadway)

Beef, boiled: North Garden Restaurant (24 Pell St)

Beef Bourguignonne: Philippe (1202 Lexington Ave)

Beef, roast: Adams Rib (1340 First Ave)

Beef stroganoff: Pie Restaurant (340 E 86th St)

Beef Wellington: One if By Land, Two if By Sea (17 Barrow St)

Beer, imported (greatest selection): De Roma's (323 Broadway)

Bialys: Kossar's Bialys (367 Grand Ave)

Bigoli (Venetian pasta): Remi (145 W 53rd St)

Biscuits, pepper: Vesuvio Bakery (160 Prince St)

Blini: The Pie (340 E 86th St)

Blintzes, homemade: Mama Leah's (429 Amsterdam Ave) and Kiev Restaurant (117 Second Ave)

Bouillabaisse: La Bonne Soupe (48 W 55th St)

Bratwurst: Schaller & Weber (1654 Second Ave)

Bread, Afghan: 764 Ninth Ave

Bread, basil with mozzarella: Patisserie Encore (141 Second Ave)

Bread, chocolate: Ecce Panis (1120 Third Ave)

Bread, corn: Moishe's Bakery (181 E Houston St, 115 Second Ave)

Bread, Eli's: E.A.T. (1064 Madison Ave) and other gourmet shops

Bread, Indian: Akbar (475 Park Ave) and Dawat (210 E 58th St)

Bread, Italian whole wheat: D&G Bakery (45 Spring St)

Bread pudding: Mark's (25 E 77th St)

Bread, raisin-nut: E.A.T. (1064 Madison Ave)

Bread, Swiss health: Thorough Bread (450 Park Ave)

Bread, whole wheat French: Dean & Deluca (560 Broadway)

Brioche: Cafe Europa (347 E 54th St)

Brownies: Karen's (187 Columbus Ave)

Buns, sticky: William Greenberg (1377 Third Ave)

Burritos (to go): Benny's Burritos (113 Greenwich Ave)

Cake, apple: The Cream Puff (1388 Second Ave)

Cake, Black Forest: Eclair (141 W 72nd St)

Cake, blackout: Gertel's (53 Hester St) and Serendipity 3 (225 E 60th St)

Cake, butter cream and chocolate: Moishe's Bakery (181 E Houston St)

Cake, carrot: Carrot Top Pastries (5025 Broadway, at 220th St)

Cake, chocolate: Hard Rock Cafe (221 W 57th St)

Cake, chocolate meringue with chocolate mousse: Bakery Soutine (106 W 70th St)

Cake, chocolate mousse, individual: City Bakery (22 E 17th St)

Cake, coconut brandy: Metropolis Cafe (31 Union Sq)

Cake, fudge layer: Caffé Bianco (1486 Second Ave)

Cake, fruit, Milanese Italian: Bleecker Street Pastry (245 Bleecker St)

Cake, gourmet: Les Delices Guy Pascal (1231 Madison Ave, 2241 Broadway, and 939 First Ave)

Calamari: Extra! Extra! (767 Second Ave)

Calzone: Little Italy Gourmet Pizza (65 Vanderbilt Ave and other locations) and Piatti Pronti (34 W 56th St)

Cannelloni: Piemonte Ravioli Company (190 Grand St) and Giambelli (46 E 50th St)

Cannoli: Caffe Vivaldi (32 Jones St) and De Roberti's Pastry Shop (176 First Ave)

Caramel, crème: Man Ray (169 Eighth Ave)

Cassoulet: La Côte Basque (5 E 55th St) and La Colombe d'Or (134 E 26th St)

Caviar: Petrossian (182 W 58th St)

Caviar, Beggar's Purses: Quilted Giraffe (550 Madison Ave)

Caviar, Beluga: Iron Gate (424 W 54th St)

Ceviche (marinated seafood): Albuquerque Eats (First Ave bet 76th and 77th St)

Champagne: Garnet Wines and Liquor (929 Lexington Ave) and Gotham Liquors (1543 Third Ave)

Cheese selection: Grace's Market Place (1237 Third Ave)

Cheesecake, combination fruit: Eileen's Cheese Cake (17 Cleveland Pl)

Cheesecake, pineapple: Jimmy Red's (171 Mulberry St)

Cheese plate: Quilted Giraffe (550 Madison Ave)

Cheese sticks and cheese rolls, gourmet: Cheesestick Factory (410 E 13th St)

Chicken, baked: Harper (1303 Third Ave, at 74th St)

Chicken, beggar's: Sun Lee Palace (155 E 55th St)

Chicken, Cajun: Susan Simon (32 E Second Ave)

Chicken, Dijon: Zabar's (2245 Broadway)

Chicken, free-range: Amazing Foods (807 Washington St)

Chicken, fried: Yellow Rose Cafe (450 Amsterdam Ave)

Chicken, grilled: Rainbow Chicken (2801 Broadway, at 108th St) and Les Poulets (27 E 21st St)

Chicken-in-the-pot: Fine & Schapiro (138 W 72nd St) and Golden's Restaurant Deli (148 W 51st St)

Chicken liver with truffle mousse paté: Main Course (1608 Third Ave)

Chicken pot pie: Cafe at Between the Bread (141 E 56th St) and Jim McMullen's (1341 Third Ave)

Chicken salad: China Grill (60 W 53rd St)

Chicken salad, coriander: Petak's (1244 Madison Ave)

Chicken salad, curried: Les Poulets (27 E 21st St)

Chicken salad, sesame: Indiana (80 Second Ave)

Chicken salad, smoked: Madelines (177 Prince St)

Chicken, skinless and marinated: Koo Koo Roo (792 Lexington Ave, at 61st St)

Chicken soup: Second Avenue Kosher Delicatessan and Restaurant (156 Second Ave)

Chili: Manhattan Chili Company (302 Bleecker St)

Chili, Texas: As You Like It (120 Hudson St)

Chinese vegetables: Kam Man (200 Canal St)

Cholent: Second Avenue Kosher Delicatessen and Restaurant (156 Second Ave)

Chorizo (Spanish sausage): La Ideal (166 Eighth Ave)

Cioppino: Coastal (300 Amsterdam Ave)

Clams, tender baked: Frank's Trattoria (371 First Ave)

Coffee, fresh: Porto Rico Importing Company (201 Bleecker St) and Zabar's (80th St and Broadway)

Coffee, morning: Caffe Dante (81 MacDougal St)

Cookie, chocolate chubbie: Sarabeth's Kitchen (423 Amsterdam Ave, at 80th St)

Cookies, almond: Fung Wong Bakery (30 Mott St)

Cookies, fortune (wholesale prices): Key Lee Fortune Cookies (178 Lafayette St)

Corned beef hash: Broadway Diner (1726 Broadway) and Carnegie Deli (854 Seventh Ave)

Cornish hens: Lorenzo and Maria's Kitchen (1418 Third Ave)

Couscous: Provence (38 MacDougal St, on Sunday)

Crab: Pisacane Midtown Corp. (940 First Ave, bet 51st and 52nd St)

Crab cakes: Acme Bar and Grill (9 Great Jones St) and the Coach House (110 Waverly Pl)

Crab-meat salad in dill sauce: Fledermaus (1 Seaport Pl)

Crabs, Maryland spiced: Sidewalkers (12 W 72nd St)

Crème brûlée: Le Cirque (58 E 65th St)

Crème caramel: Barbetta (321 W 46th St)

Crepes: Crepes & Co (30 Carmine St)

Croissants: Paris Croissant (609 Madison Ave, 1776 Broadway, and other locations)

Cucumber salad: Neuman and Bogdonoff (1385 Third Ave)

Danish, cheese: Budapest Pastries (207 E 84th St)

Deli items, Italian: Lisa's (901 Park Ave)

Delicatessen assortment: Dean & Deluca (560 Broadway)

Dessert plate, chocolate: Quilted Giraffe (550 Madison Ave)

Doughnuts, jelly: Gertel's Bake Shop (53 Hester St)

Duck, Peking: Peking Duck House Restaurant (22 Mott St)

Duck, roasted: La Bohème (24 Minetta Lane)

Dumplings: Dumpling House (111 Lafayette St)

Dumplings, Chinese: Pig Heaven (1540 Second Ave) and Great Shanghai (27 Division St)

Egg cream: Carnegie Deli (854 Seventh Ave), Mill Luncheonette (2895 Broadway, at 112th St), and Moisha's Luncheonette (239 Grand St)

Eggplant salad: Juliana (891 Eighth Ave)

Eggs, fresh Jersey (72 E 7th St, only Thurs: 7-5:30)

Eggs, Scotch: Myers of Keswick (634 Hudson St)

Empanadas: Ruben's (64 Fulton St)

Enchiladas: Lucy's Restaurant (503 Columbus Ave)

Espresso: Caffe Dante (79-81 MacDougal St)

Fajitas: Zarela (953 Second Ave)

Falafel: Lox Around the Clock (676 Sixth Ave) and Pita Cuisine of SoHo (65 Spring St)

Fettuccine Alfredo: Parioli Romanissimo (24 E 81st St)

Fish, fresh: Citarella (2135 Broadway) and Central Fish Company (527 Ninth Ave)

Fish, smoked: Russ & Daughters (179 E Houston St), Barney Greengrass (541 Amsterdam Ave), and M. Schacht Company (99 Second Ave)

Fish, smoked, with toasted French bread: Delices de France (289 Madison Ave)

Flapjacks, walnut apple: West Side Storey (700 Columbus Ave)

Food and kitchen extravaganza "best all-around in the world": Zabar's (2245 Broadway)

Frankfurters: Leo's Famous (861 Sixth Ave)

French fries: Tout Va Bien (311 W 51st St)

French toast: Lox Around the Clock (676 Sixth Ave, 1700 Second Ave)

Frog's legs: Le Cygne (55 E 54th St)

Frozen dessert, low calorie: Tasti D-Lite (86th St and Lexington Ave)

Fruit tarts: Bett's Best (203 Eighth Ave) and Laurent (111 E 56th St)

Fruits and vegetables, fresh: Fairway (2127 Broadway, at 74th St) and Balducci's (424 Sixth Ave)

Fruit dessert plate, fresh: Primavera (1578 First Ave)

Galettes: Cafe Galette (23 E 22nd St)

Game, fresh: Ottomanelli's Meat Market (285 Bleecker St)

Gâteau Charlene Blanche: Lanciani (275 W 4th St)

Gelati: Caffe Dante (81 MacDougal St) and Gelateria Siracusa (65 Fourth Ave)

Grill, mixed: Delmonico's (56 Beaver St)

Guacamole: Manhattan Chili Company (302 Bleecker St)

Gumbo: Century Cafe (132 W 43rd St)

Ham, apricot glazed: Word of Mouth (1012 Lexington Ave)

Ham, Westphalian and brie: Food Store (58 Greenwich Ave)

Herbs, Chinese: Hang Fung Tai (78 Mulberry St)

Hamburgers: Jackson Hole Wyoming Burgers (232 E 64th and other locations), Corner Bistro (331 W 4th St), Hamburger Harry's (157 Chambers and 145 W 45th St), and Taste of the Apple (1000 Second Ave)

Heros: Italian Food Center (186 Grand St) and Hero Boy (492 Ninth Ave)

Hot cakes: Royal Canadian Pancake House (145 Hudson St)

Hot Dogs: Hotdiggity (140 Eighth Ave) and Gray's Papaya (8th St and Sixth Ave)

Hotpot, Japanese: Seryna (11 E 53rd St)

Jambalaya: 107 West (2787 Broadway, at 107th St)

Jambon: Raoul's Boucherie (180 Prince St)

Jerk, pork: Vernon's Jerk Paradise (252 W 29th St)

Kale, deep-fried: New Haven Pizza Co. (140 W 13th St)

Kielbasa: First Avenue Meat Products (140 First Ave)

Kosher corned beef: Bernstein-on-Essex (135 Essex St)

Kosher meat, grilled: Cafe Masada (1239 First Ave, at 67th St)

Lamb, rack of: Coach House (110 Waverly Pl)

Lamb stew: Pamir (1437 Second Ave)

Lamb sandwich, baked: Arizona 206 (206 E 60th St)

Lasagna: Green Noodle (313 Columbus Ave)

Linzer Torte: T.A.S.T.E. Sensations (412 E Ninth St)

Liver, chopped: Mama Leah's to Go (429 Amsterdam Ave)

Lobster: Shell Lobster & Seafood (412 W 13th St)

Lobster Bisque: Neuman and Bogdonoff (1385 Third Ave)

Lobster, poached: La Petite Ferme (973 Lexington Ave)

Marzipan: Cream Puff (1388 Second Ave) and Elk Candy Company (240 E 86th St)

Meat loaf: Cafe Mortimer (155 E 75th St)

Meat, wholesale prices: Old Bohemian Meat (452 W 13th St)

Meats and poultry, quality (reasonably priced): Empire Purveyors (901 First Ave)

Meats, prime: Jefferson Market (455 Sixth Ave) and City Wholesale Meats (305 E 85th St)

Meringue, chocolate hazelnut: De Roberti's (176 First St)

Morels: Amazing Foods (807 Washington St)

Moussaka: Periyali (35 W 20th St)

Mozzarella: Alleva Dairy (188 Grand Ave) and Melampo (105 Sullivan St)

Mozzarella and ricotta, homemade: Russo and Son Dairy Products (334 E 11th St)

Muffins: Between the Bread (141 E 56th St), Petak's (1244 Madison Ave), and Connecticut Muffin (206 Elizabeth St)

Muffin tops: Bloomingdale's Bakery (1000 Third Ave)

Mushrooms, wild: Grace's Market Place (1237 Third Ave)
Mutton chops: Keens (72 W 36th St)
Nachos: Benny's Burritos (93 Ave A)
Napoleon: Ecco (124 Chambers St)
Natural foods: Whole Foods in SoHo (117 Prince St)
Noodles, Chinese: Yat Gaw Min Company (100 Reade St)
Noodles, cold with hot sesame sauce: Sung Chu Mei (1367 First Ave)
Nuts: A. L. Bazzini Co. (339 Greenwich St)
Nuts and packaged dried fruits (great prices): J. Wolsk and Company
 (81 and 87 Ludlow St)
Oatmeal: Sarabeth's Kitchen (1295 Madison Ave)
Olives: International Grocery Store (529 Ninth Ave)
Omelettes: Romaine De Lyon (29 E 61st St)
Omelettes, French: Potbelly (92 Christopher St)
Onion rings: Palm (837 Second Ave)
Orange juice, fresh squeezed: hole-in-the-wall stand at 1428 Sixth Ave
Organic foods: Angelica's (147 First Ave, at E 9th St)
Organic produce: Bink & Bink (117 Perry St)
Oysters, Long Island: Cafe des Artistes (1 W 67th St)
Oyster stew: Grand Central Oyster Bar Restaurant (Grand Central
 Station)
Paella: Sevilla (62 Charles St)
Pancakes: Friend of a Farmer (77 Irving Pl) and Royal Canadian
 Pancake House (145 Hudson St)
Pasta: Todaro Brothers (555 Second Ave)
Pasta, angel hair: Contrapunto (1009 Third Ave) and Piemonte
 Homemade Ravioli Company (190 Grand St)
Pasta (inexpensive): La Marca (282 Third Ave)
Pasta, handmade egg: Balducci's (424 Sixth Ave)
Pasta to go: Primo Piatto (1498-B First Ave, at 78th St)
Pasta, Venetian: Remi (145 W 53rd St)
Pasticciotto: Siracusa (65 Fourth Ave)
Pastrami: Bernstein-on-Essex (135 Essex St) and Carnegie Delicatessen
 and Restaurant (854 Seventh Ave)
Pastries, Hungarian: Budapest Pastries (207 E 84th St) and Hungarian
 Pastry Shop (1030 Amsterdam Ave)
Pâté: Les Trois Petite Cochons (453 Greenwich St)
Pâté, chicken liver: Cafe de la Gare (143 Perry St)
Peanut butter: Country Life (48 Trinity Pl)
Peanuts, candied: A. L. Bazzini Co. (339 Greenwich St)
Pecan squares: Slice of Orange (987 Lexington Ave)
Penne with Prosciutto: Petak's (1244 Madison Ave)
Peppers, roasted: Rao's (455 E 114th St)
Peppers, stuffed: Bo Ky (80 Bayard St)
Pheasant: An American Place (2 Park Ave)
Pickles: Guss Pickles (35 Essex St)

Pie, apple: William Greenberg Jr. Desserts (912 Seventh Ave) and the Coach House (110 Waverly Pl)

Pie, caramel nut crunch: Houlihan's (729 Seventh Ave, at 49th St)

Pie, cheddar-crust apple: Little Pie Company of the Big Apple (424 W 43rd St)

Pie, chocolate pecan: Gindi Desserts (935 Broadway)

Pie, key lime: Little Pie Company (424 W 43rd St)

Pie, rum pecan: A Sweet Place (301 E 91st St)

Pie, shepherd's: Landmark Tavern (626 11th Ave)

Pie, sour-cream apple: Gindi Desserts (935 Broadway)

Pie, walnut sour-cream apple: Little Pie Company (424 W 43rd St)

Pies, pot: Alain's Cheese Please Deli (158 E 39th St)

Pig sandwich (pulled pork): Hard Rock Cafe (221 W 57th St)

Pig, suckling: Sabor (20 Cornelia St)

Pizza: John's Pizzeria (278 Bleecker St), Yellowfingers di Nuovo (200 E 60th St), Famous Ray's (465 Sixth Ave), and Fisher & Levy (875 Third Ave, at 53rd St)

Pizza, deep dish: PIZZAPIAZZA (785 Broadway)

Pizza, Sicilian: Sal's and Carmine Pizza (2533 Broadway)

Pizzas, designer: Paper Moon Milano (39 E 58th St)

Po' boys: Two Boots (37 Ave A)

Pommes frites: Cafe de Bruxelles (118 Greenwich Ave)

Popcorn: Creative Corn Co. (1275 Lexington Ave, bet 85th and 86th St)

Popcorn, gourmet: Nancy's Gourmet Popcorn (700 Third Ave) and Jack's Corn Crib (700 Third Ave)

Pork: Faicco's Pork Store (260 Bleecker St)

Pork, European-style cured: Salumeria Biellese (376 Eighth Ave)

Pork loin: Sabor (20 Cornelia St)

Potato chips, homemade: Amsterdam's Bar and Rotisserie (454 Broadway) and U.S. Chips (Grand Central Station)

Potato pancakes: Ideal Lunch and Bar (238 E 86th St)

Potato salad Nicoise: Manny Wolf's (145 E 49th St)

Potatoes, home fried: Ideal Lunch and Bar (238 E 86th St)

Pot-au-feu: La Grenouille (3 E 52nd St)

Pot pies: Alain's Cheese Please (158 E 39th St)

Pot roast: Cafe des Artistes (1 W 67th St)

Pretzels/cookies, chocolate, hand-dipped: Evelyn's Chocolates (4 John St, 9A Beaver St)

Prime rib: Smith & Wollensky (201 E 49th St)

Profiteroles: Chez Ma Tante (189 W 10th St)

Pudding, chocolate: Jim McMullen (1341 Third Ave)

Quiche Lorraine: Rene Pujol (321 W 51st St)

Rabbit stew: Cafe de la Gare (143 Perry St) and Lafayette (65 E 56th St)

Raspberry Charlotte: Dolci on Park Caffé (12 Park Ave)

Ravioli: Piemonte Homemade Ravioli Company (190 Grand St) and Di Palo Dairy Store (206 Grand St)

Ravioli, steamed Vietnamese: Indochine (430 Lafayette St)

Raw bar: Citarella Fish Company (2135 Broadway)

Relish, cranberry: Artichoke (968 Second Ave)

Ribs: Tony Roma's (400 E 57th St and other locations), Wylies (891 First Ave, at 53rd St), and Brother Jimmy's Bar-B-Q (1461 First Ave)

Ribs, beef: Sylvia's (328 Lenox Ave, at 126th St)

Rice pudding: Marti Kebab (228 E 24th St) and Chelsea Central (227 Tenth Ave)

Ring, apple: Lafayette (298 Bleecker St)

Rugelbach: Royale Pastry Shop (237 W 72nd St)

Salad bar: Miss Kim's (270 Park Ave)

Salads: Blazing Salads (228 W 4th St, 1135 First Ave)

Salad, seafood: Gotham Bar and Grill (12 E 12th St)

Salads, fresh: Courtyard Cafe (130 E 39th St) and the Salad Bowl (566 Seventh Ave)

Salmon, marinated: La Reserve (4 W 49th St)

Salmon mousse: Silver Palate (274 Columbus Ave)

Salmon, sandwich, smoked Norwegian: Peter Dent (120 Hudson St)

Salmon, smoked: Starfish Enterprises (233 Ninth Ave, at 24th St)

Salta in Bocca: Salta in Bocca (179 Madison Ave)

Sandwich, brisket: Second Avenue Kosher Delicatessen (156 Second Ave)

Sandwich, turkey: Viand Coffee Shop (673 Madison Ave)

Sandwiches: Donald Sacks (120 Prince St, 3 World Financial Ctr)

Sandwiches, Focaccia: Yellowfingers di Nuovo (200 E 60th St)

Sandwiches, Italian: Panini (365 E 62nd St)

Sandwiches, puff pastry: Dufour Pastry Kitchens (808 Washington St)

Sandwiches, tea: Mortimer's (1057 Lexington Ave)

Sauerkraut: Katz's Delicatessen (205 E Houston St)

Sausages: Kurowycky Meat Products (124 First Ave)

Sausage, French: P. Carnevale and Son (631 Ninth Ave)

Sausage, Hungarian: Tibor Meat Specialties (1508 Second Ave)

Scallops: Bouley (165 Duane St)

Schnecken: William Greenberg Jr. (1377 Third Ave, 1000 Madison Ave, 912 Seventh Ave)

Scones: Mangia (54 W 56th St)

Seafood dinners: Wilkinson's (1573 York Ave) and Le Bernardin (155 W 51st St)

Shrimp, blackened Louisiana: Four Seasons (99 E 52nd St)

Shrimp creole: Jezebel (630 Ninth Ave)

Shrimp, frozen: Hyfund Company (75 Mulberry St)

Smorgasbord plate: Aquavit (13 W 54th St)

Snacks, soups, sandwiches: Serendipity 3 (225 E 60th St)
Snails: Lutece (249 E 50th St)
Sole, Dover: Le Regence (37 E 64th St)
Sorbet: La Boite En Bois (75 W 68th St)
Souffles: La Côte Basque (5 E 55th St)
Souffle, chocolate cappuccino: Trumpet's (Grand Hyatt Hotel)
Soup, black bean: Coach House (110 Waverly Pl)
Soup, French onion: La Bonne Soupe (48 W 55th St)
Soup, Mandalay fish: Road to Mandalay (380 Broome St)
Soup, minestrone: Il Vagabondo (351 E 62nd St)
Soup, sorrel: The Box Tree (250 E 49th St)
Soup, tomato: Sarabeth's Kitchen (412 Amsterdam Ave, 1295 Madison
    Ave)
Soup, vegetable: Country Host (1435 Lexington Ave)
Soups, homemade: Kiev Restaurant (Second Ave and 7th St)
Southern-style food: Memphis (329 Columbus Ave)
Spareribs, Chinese: Fu's (1395 Second Ave)
Spices: Aphrodisia (282 Bleecker St)
Spices, Indian: Spice and Sweet Mahal (135 Lexington Ave)
Spinach pies, Greek: Poseidon Bakery (629 Ninth Ave)
Steak: Post House (28 E 63rd St)
Steak and fries: Le Steak (1089 Second Ave)
Steak, Cajun rib: Post House (28 E 63rd St)
Steak tartare: Voulez-Vous (1462 First Ave)
Strawberry shortcake, old-fashioned: An American Place (2 Park Ave)
Strudel: Mocca Hungarian (1588 Second Ave)
Sushi: Hatsuhana (17 E 48th St), Nippon (155 E 52nd St), and Akemi
    (1128 Third Ave, at 66th St)
Sweetbreads: Orso (322 W 46th St)
Sweet-potato fries: Trixie's (307 W 47th St)
Swordfish, grilled: Chez Ma Tante (189 W 10th St)
Tabbouleh: Benny's (321¹/₂ Amsterdam Ave, 37 Seventh Ave)
Tacos: Rosa Mexicano (1063 First Ave)
Tapas, Spanish: El Cid (322 W 15th St)
Tart, apple: Quatorze (240 W 14th St and 323 E 79th St)
Tarts and logs, stuffed puff pastry: Dufour Pastry Kitchen (808
    Washington St)
Tarts, coconut: Saint Honoré Bakery (28 Bowery)
Tartufo: Erminia (250 E 83rd St) and **Tartufo Gelato** (37-22 13th St)
Tea and coffee, iced: Henri's (357 Bleecker St)
Tempura: Mitsukoshi (461 Park Ave)
Tirami Sú ("Lift Me Up") dessert: Mezzogiorno (195 Spring St)
    and Biricchino (260 W 29th St)
Torte, delizia: Sant Ambroeus (1000 Madison Ave)
Torte, Viennese chocolate: Peacock Caffe (24 Greenwich Ave)
Trifle, English: John Clancy's (181 W 10th St, 206 E 63rd St)
Truffles: Gini Desserts (935 Broadway)

Truffles, champagne: Teuscher (25 E 61st St)
Truffles, chocolate: Rich Treats (18 W 55th St)
Truffles, Grand Marnier: Normandie Chocolat (338 E 116th St)
Truffle tart: Encore (141 Second Ave)
Tuna salad: Todaro Bros. (555 Second Ave)
Turnover, apple: La Boulangere (49 E 21st St)
Veal cutlet: Trastevere (309 E 83rd st)
Veal scaloppini: Zinno's (126 W 13th St)
Veal stew: Pierre au Tunnel (250 W 47th St)
Vegan baking: Whole Earth Bakery & Kitchen (70 Spring St)
Vegetable pâté sandwich: Lamston's (205 E 42nd St) and Fisher
    & Levy (1026 Second Ave)
Vegetable salads: Michelle's Kitchen (1392 Madison Ave)
Vegetables, Chinese: Sun Kwong Lee (85 Mulberry St)
Vegetable terrine: Montrachet (239 W Broadway)
Vegetarian items: Vegetarian's Paradise (144 W 4th St)
Vegetarian meals: Natural Gourmet Cookery School (48 W 21st St)
Venison: Chanterelle (2 Harrison St)
Vinegars: Marketplace (54 W 74th St)
Waffles: Berry's (180 Spring St)
Waffles, Belgian: Cafe Bruxelles (118 Greenwich Ave)
Whiskeys, malt: SoHo Wines and Spirits (461 W Broadway)
Wines, European: Quality House (2 Park Ave)
Wursts: Wurst (2832 Broadway)
Yogurt, frozen: Yogen Fruz (2151 Broadway)
Yogurt shake: TCBY (1452 Second Ave)
Zabaglione: Il Monello (1460 Second Ave) and Parioli Romanissimo
    (24 E 81st St)

Here's a New York recipe for egg cream, a unique New York specialty drink. It consists of one quart of milk, a bottle of seltzer water,
and two scoops of Fox syrup. You combine these ingredients and shake
them up. Actually, there is no egg and no cream in the drink!

Barbecues

Great barbecue spots are not a Manhattan specialty, but here are some
of the better ones:

Big Wong (67 Mott St): Chinese style.
Brother's Bar-B-Q (228 W Houston St): Smoked ribs.
Copeland's (547 W 145th St): Harlem setting.
Dallas BBQ (1265 Third Ave, 27 W 72nd St, 21 University Place,
    132 Second Ave, 315 Sixth Ave): Big and busy, but only fair in quality.
Rusty's (1271 Third Ave): All-American tasty baby back ribs.
Shun Lee Cafe (43 W 65th St): Classy Chinese.
Sylvia's (328 Lenox Ave, at 126th St): Reputation better than the food.

Before Theater

It is best to let your waiter know immediately that you are planning to go to theater so that service can be properly adjusted. Also, if it is raining, be sure to allow extra time for getting a taxi. Some restaurants have specially priced pre-theater dinners.

Alo Alo (1030 Third Ave, at 61st St)
American Festival Cafe (Rockefeller Center)
Andiamo (1991 Broadway, bet 67th and 68th St)
Antolotti's (337 E 49th, bet First and Second Ave)
Aquavit (13 W 54th St, bet Fifth and Sixth Ave)
Arqua (281 Church, at White St)
Barbetta (321 W 46th St, bet Eighth and Ninth Ave)
Cafe de Bruxelles (118 Greenwich Ave, at W 13th St)
Cafe Greco (1390 Second Ave, bet 71st and 72nd St)
Cameos (169 Columbus Ave, bet 67th and 68th St)
Carolina (355 W 46th St)
Darbar (44 W 56th St, bet Fifth and Sixth Ave)
Dawat (210 E 58th St)
Edwardian Room, Plaza Hotel (Fifth Ave and 59th St)
Four Seasons (99 E 52nd St)
Gino (780 Lexington Ave, bet 60th and 61st St)
Greene Street (101 Greene St, bet Spring and Prince St)
JW, Marriott Marquis Hotel (1535 Broadway, at Times Sq)
La Boite en Bois (75 W 68th St)
La Caravelle (33 W 55th St, bet Fifth and Sixth Ave)
Lafayette (Drake Swissotel, 65 E 56th St)
La Reserve (4 W 49th St)
Le Chantilly (106 E 57th, bet Lexington and Park Ave)
Marchi's (251 E 31st St)
Marie-Michelle (57 W 56th St, bet Fifth and Sixth Ave)
Olde Garden and Winery (15 W 29th St)
Orso (322 W 46th St, bet Eighth and Ninth Ave)
Rainbow Room (Rockefeller Center, bet 49th and 50th St, 65th floor)
San Domenico (240 Central Park S)
Symphony Cafe (950 Eighth Ave, at 56th St)
Tavern on the Green (Central Park W and 67th St)
Tropica (Pan Am building, 200 Park Ave, 45th St and Vanderbilt Ave)
Voulez-Vous (1462 First Ave at 76th St)

Breakfast

Doesn't anyone eat breakfast at home anymore? In Manhattan, the "power breakfast" has become a big thing. Even if you're not consummating a deal to take over General Motors, it's fun to watch the major players (and some minor leaguers who think they are) emptying brief-cases and making calls from portable telephones.

The action these days is centered around the **Plaza Hotel's Edwardian Room** (59th and Fifth Ave), the **Regency Hotel** (540 Park Ave), **"21"** (21 W 52nd St), the **Peninsula Hotel** (700 Fifth Ave, at 55th St), the **Carlyle Hotel** (35 E 76th St), **Cafe Pierre at the Pierre Hotel** (61st and Fifth Ave), the **Helmsley Palace's Trianon Room** (455 Madison Ave), and the **Grand Hyatt Hotel** (at Grand Central Station).

If people watching is secondary to solid fare to start the day, try **Chelsea Square Restaurant** (369 W 23rd St), **American Festival Cafe** (20 W 50th st), **Courtyard Cafe** (130 E 39th St), **Empire Diner** (210 10th Ave), **Sarabeth's Kitchen** (1295 Madison Ave, bet 92nd and 93rd, or 423 Amsterdam Ave, bet 80th and 81st). The **Cottonwood Cafe** (415 Bleecker St) features Grandma Bronson's buttermilk biscuits on weekends, while the **Cupping Room Cafe** (359 Broadway, bet Grand and Broome St) is the place to go for French toast. You might also try the **Pink Tea Cup** (42 Grove St), **Viand Coffee Shop** (300 E 86th St), the **Paris Commune** (411 Bleecker St, near Eighth Ave), **Delmonico's** (*way* downtown at 56 Beaver St), **Aggie's** in SoHo (146 W Houston St), **Carnegie Deli** in midtown (854 Seventh Ave, at 55th St), or **West Side Storey** (700 Columbus Ave, at 95th St) on the Upper West Side. Also, don't miss the blintzes at **B&H Dairy** (127 Second Ave, at St Mark's Pl) and the freshest orange juice in town at the tiny hole-in-the-wall stand at 1428 Sixth Ave (bet 58th St and Central Park S).

If price is no object, the breads and other temptations at Eli Zabar's **E.A.T.** (1064 Madison Ave) are as delicious as they are outlandishly priced. The bakery section at **Bloomingdale's** opens early; it's a great place to go at the start of the day for a large selection. Another good bet is the **Royal Canadian Pancake House and Restaurant** (145 Hudson at Canal St), where you can fill up on your choice of 53 varieties of pancakes. **EJ's Luncheonette** (433 Amsterdam, near 81st St) serves challah, **Friend of a Farmer** (77 Irving Pl) is great for a late pancake feast, and **Trixie's** (307 W 47th St) features bacon and grits. The **City Bakery** (22 E 17th St) offers whole-wheat turnovers with raspberry preserves and local farmstead yogurts.

Brunch

Personally, I don't care for the usual eggs-and-sausage brunch. I look for restaurants with broader and more appealing menus. The two classiest Sunday brunches are offered at the **Palm Court** at the Plaza Hotel (59th and Fifth Ave) and the **Grand Hyatt Hotel** (42nd St, near Grand Central Station). The entire Palm Court is opened up on Sunday to showcase a dazzling array of hot and cold dishes, seafood, salads, and fresh fruit, along with a dessert selection that can only be equaled at Gerry Frank's Konditorei in Salem, Oregon! The Grand Hyatt presents a superb brunch that includes just about anything you can think of presented in a most appetizing buffet. Also consider **Windows on the World** (World Trade Center), where the thrilling view enhances the good food; **Cafe des Artistes** (1 W 67th St), where both the ambiance and the food are classy; **Berry's** (180 Spring St) for Nova Scotia salmon; **Hurlingham's** at the New York Hilton; **Mortimer's** (1057 Lexington Ave, at 75th St) for people watching; **Aurora** (60 E 49th), where it's fun to choose great desserts from the rolling carts; or **Voulez-Vous** (1462 First Ave, at 76th St) for marvelous steak tartare. Other possibilities are the **Rainbow Room** (Rockefeller Center) for nostalgia; **Greene Street** (101 Greene St) for caviar; **Tavern on the Green** (Central Park, at W 67th) for entertaining your out-of-town guests; **Friend of a Farmer** (77 Irving Pl); the **Russian Tea Room** (150 W 57th), which is better than anything in Moscow; and the classy **Mark's** restaurant (25 E 77th St).

Burgers

Everyone has a nominee for best burger in town. I vote for **Jackson Hole Wyoming Burgers** (232 E 64th St, Third Ave and 35th St, and Second Ave and 84th St). These burgers are seven juicy ounces of sheer goodness. Runners-up include **Corner Bistro** (331 W 4th St), **Hamburger Harry's** (157 Chambers St, 145 W 45th St), **Hard Rock Cafe** (221 W 57th St), where the action is as tasty as the burgers, **Penguin Cafe** (581 Hudson St), **Taste of the Apple** (1000 Second Ave), **Diane's** (249 Columbus Ave), **Billy's** (948 First Ave), **Harper** (1303 Third Ave at 74th St), and **P. J. Clarke's** (915 Third Ave, at 55th St).

Cheap Eats

Today it is fashionable to seek out inexpensive places where you can get good food and good value. Here are some of the better deals in town!

Bella Donna (307 E 77th St)
Bernstein-on-Essex (135 Essex)
Buckaroo's Bar & Rotisserie (1431 First Ave, bet 74th and 75th St)
Cabana Carioca (123 W 45th St)
Cafe Lalo (201 W 83rd St)
Caffe Vivaldi (32 Jones St)
Carmine's (2450 Broadway, bet 90th and 91st St)
Chez Brigette (77 Greenwich Ave)
Christine's (438 Second Ave, 208 First Ave)
Coffee Shop (29 Union Sq W)
Corner Bistro (331 W 4th St)
Cottonwood Cafe (415 Bleecker St)
Cucina de Pesce (87 E 4th St)
Cucina Stagionale (275 Bleecker St)
Dallas BBQ (1265 Third Ave, at 73rd St)

Dining Commons, City University of New York Graduate Center (33 W 42nd St, 18th floor)
Ed Debevic's (661 Broadway, at Bond St)
Frank's (431 W 14th St)
Golden Unicorn (18 E Broadway)
Good Enough to Eat (483 Amsterdam Ave, bet 83rd and 84th St)
Hamburger Harry's (157 Chambers St)
John's Pizzeria (408 E 64th St, 278 Bleecker St)
Katz's Delicatessen (205 E Houston St)
La Bonne Soupe (48 W 55th St)
Les Poulets (27 E 21st St)
Lulu (430 Broome St)
Moondance Diner (Sixth Ave at Grand St)
Papaya King (179 E 86th St, 201 E 59th St)
The Pie (340 E 86th St, bet First Ave and Second Ave)
PIZZAPIAZZA (785 Broadway, at 10th St)
Rao's (455 E 114th St)
Ray's Pizza (465 Sixth Ave, at 11th St)
Royal Canadian Pancake House (145 Hudson St)
Saranac (1350 Madison Ave, at 95th St)
Second Avenue Kosher Delicatessen and Restaurant (156 Second Ave)
7th Regiment Mess Restaurant (Armory, Park Ave at 67th St, 4th floor)
Sevilla (62 Charles St)
Siu Lam Kung (18 Elizabeth St)
SoHo Kitchen and Bar (103 Greene St)
Spring Street Natural Restaurant (62 Spring St)
Sylvia's (328 Lenox Ave, bet 126th and 127th St)
Thai Express (1750 First Ave)
Veronica (240 W 38th St)
Veselka (144 Second Ave, at 9th St)
Wong Kee (113 Mott St)

Coffeehouses

No city in the world has as many colorful and comfortable coffeehouses as New York. You can relax and enjoy good company and drink at:

Aupetit Beurre (2737 Broadway)
Cafe Orlin (41 St. Mark's Pl)
Caffe Dante 79 MacDougal St)
Caffe Reggio (119 MacDougal St)
Caffe Vivaldi (32 Jones St, bet 4th and Bleecker St)
Cupping Room Cafe (359 W Broadway)
Pane & Cioccolato (10 Waverly Pl)
Sant Ambroeus (1000 Madison Ave, bet 77th and 78th St)
Veniero Pasticceria (342 E 11th St)
Veselka Coffee Shop (144 Second Ave)

Desserts

Want to give yourself a treat? New York combines the best of London, Paris, Rome, and all points in between! To really splurge, these are must-trys:

Cafe Lalo (201 W 83rd St): European-style cafe.
Caffe Bondi (7 W 20th St): Italian tortes.
Carnegie Deli (854 Seventh Ave): Everything here is big.
Delices de France (289 Madison Ave): The name says it all.
Dolci on Park Caffe (12 Park Ave): Undiscovered gem.
Eclair Pastry Shops (Grand Central Terminal, Herald Square, 54th St and First Ave, 141 W 72nd St): Good selection.
Ferrara (195 Mulberry): Italian gelati.
Gindi (935 Broadway): Great pastries.
Hard Rock Cafe (221 W 57th St): All-American treats.
Les Delices West (370 Columbus Ave, bet 77th and 78th St): Fine French pastries.
Madeline's (117 Prince St): End of a great meal.
Palm Court (Plaza Hotel): Vintage New York.
Pappa's Place (510 Sixth Ave): Ice cream plus.
Peppermint Park (1225 First Ave): Outrageous offerings.
Sant Ambroeus (1000 Madison Ave): Rich and classy.
Serendipity 3 (225 E 60th St): An institution for the young-at-heart.
Succes la Côte Basque (1032 Lexington Ave, Henri Bendel): Really successful for hunger curing pangs!
Zabar's Cafe (80th & Broadway): Big treats, low prices.

Most of these places also serve fine coffee, espresso, and cappuccino.

Dim Sum

Dim sum translates as tidbits or snacks, Chinese-style. You'd eat it on a daily basis in Chinatown or Hong Kong. In Southern China, for instance, dim sum is eaten while having tea. Dim sum includes all kinds of dumplings, a variety of noodle and rice dishes, and desserts. Some of the best are stuffed bean curds, Peking spareribs, shredded chicken rolls, egg custards, sesame shrimp toast, fried wontons, curry beef dumplings, beef balls, braised duck feet, and crab claws. Dim sum items are often wheeled to your table on carts, offering the diner an amazing array of choices

For the most authentic and delicious dim sum in New York, I recommend **Shun Lee Cafe** (43 W 65th St), **H.S.F.** (46 Bowery; 578 Second Ave, at 31st St), **Golden Unicorn** (18 E Broadway, at Catherine St), **China Royal** (17 Division St), **Sun Hop Shing Tea House** (21 Mott St), **King Fung** (20 Elizabeth St), and **Mandarin Court** (61 Mott St). The Golden Unicorn serves an especially appetizing presentation.

Diners

There are not many classic diners left in Manhattan, but the best survivors are **Empire Diner** (210 10th Ave, at 22nd St), **Moondance Diner** (Sixth Ave and Grand St), and **Market Diner** (43rd St and 11th Ave).

Dining Solo

Arizona 206 and Cafe (206 E 60th St)
The Ballroom (253 W 28th St)
Bellevues (496 Ninth Ave, bet 37th and 38th St)
Brasserie (100 E 53rd St)
Broadway Diner (590 Lexington Ave; 1726 Broadway, at 55th St)
Cafe des Sports (329 W 51st St)
Carnegie Deli (854 Seventh Ave, bet 54th and 55th St)
Chez Napoleon (365 W 50th St)
Coffee Shop (29 Union Sq W, at 16th St)
Ed Debevic's (661 Broadway, at Bond St)
Elephant & Castle (68 Greenwich St, Seventh Ave and 11th St)
Florent (69 Vansevoort, bet Washington and Greenwich St)
Ginger Man (51 W 64th St)
Grand Central Oyster Bar Restaurant (Grand Central Station)
Jackson Hole Wyoming Burgers (232 E 64th St; Third Ave, at 35th St; Second Ave, at 84th St)
La Bonne Soupe (48 W 55th St)
Lexington Avenue Grill (Loews Summit Hotel, 569 Lexington Ave, at 51st St)
Market Dining Rooms (World Trade Center)
Sarabeth's Kitchen (1295 Madison Ave, bet 92nd and 93rd St; 423 Amsterdam Ave, bet 80th and 81st St)
Second Avenue Kosher Delicatessen (156 Second Ave, at 10th St)
Stage Deli (834 Seventh Ave, bet 53rd and 54th St)
Trattoria Dell'Arte (900 Seventh Ave, bet 56th and 57th St)
Union Square Cafe (21 E 16th St, bet Fifth Ave and Union Sq W)
Viand Coffee Shop (300 E 86th St, 1011 Madison Ave, 637 Madison Ave)
Yellowfingers di Nuovo (200 E 60th St at Third Ave)

Don't Bothers

Too many restaurants spoil the real reason for coming: to get a good meal in a comfortable setting at a decent price. A perfect example is the **Chefs Cuisiniers Club** (36 E 22nd St), an inspiration of several three-star chefs who wanted a place where foodies could exchange news and views—and where the public would be welcome, also. Well, they succeeded in the kitchen, but that's all. One must push aside bar patrons to reach the dining room, where no one seems to be in charge. Amateur servers are dressed in blue jeans. Tables are so close together that conversation is all but impossible, and it makes no difference if you are in the smoking or nonsmoking section. The tables have paper covers. However, the limited lunch and dinner menus are priced right, and the portions are tremendous. If only those chefs lavished the same attention upon the front area of their establishment.

The point is, with so many great restaurant choices in Manhattan, why waste your time and money in poor or mediocre ones? Many on the following list are well-known and popular, but I feel you can get better value elsewhere.

Alexandra's: Sloppy sailing.
Algonquin Hotel: Old hotels never die, they just . . .
Angelo of Mulberry St.: The portrait of former prez Reagan is their only claim to fame.
Au Grenier Cafe: High hopes as you climb up; great disappointment on the way down.
Bahama Mama: Leave it to the kids.
Bice: Very "in," very noisy, very unimpressive.
Black Sheep: Once was fun, but that's history.
Cafe Crocodile: Too bad Andree took her name off.
Cafe de la Paix: Only thing worth watching is the other customers.
Cajun: The Southern accent has faded.
Camelback and Central: The street-sign decor is the most appealing aspect.
Carlyle: Social climbing can be very expensive.
Charley O's: The Benetton of the food scene.
Christ Cella: Forget about what you may have heard.
Columbus: He surely wouldn't have dined here.
Due: Noisy, frantic, and not worth the stress.
Elaine's: You gotta be kidding.
Eli Zabar's Cafe: Fantastic food, exorbitant prices.
El Teddy's: Only the desserts are worth the effort.
Ernie's: The pickup scene must be awfully good, though.
Gloucester House: Major setting, minor presentation.
Jockey Club: Way behind in the stretch.
Lello: A few smiles would help.
Le Veau d'Or: Heaven help the stranger.
Lexington Avenue Grill: Poor service.
Mamma Leone's: Tourissimo!
Memphis: I'd rather go South.
Mickey Mantle's: A strikeout.
Mon Cher Ton Ton: I don't understand this place.
Mortimer's: For the eyes only.
New York Deli: It was better as an automat.
Nusantara: Indonesia is a long way from here.
Old Homestead: "Old" is the best description.

Ottomanelli Cafe: Haven't they heard what happens to conglomerates?
Positano: Positively not up to the billing.
Ratner's: Why pay to get insulted?
Rosolio: Plain Jane ambiance and Plain Jane plates.
Rumpelmayer's: Badly faded.
Sardi's: Pretty sad.
Sfuzzi: What's all the "sfuss" about?
Shun Lee Dynasty: Time for a new emperor.
Sloppy Louie's: Lives up to the name.
SPQR: An insult to Rome.
Tennessee Mountain: Not much at the top.

Foreign Flavors

In response to suggestions from readers, I have tried to make this edition more convenient for those looking for restaurants in a specific part of town that serves a given foreign cuisine, and are, perhaps, open on Sundays. A special section combines information on the several hundred restaurants reviewed herein. You can easily scan the list and pick out an establishment that suits your needs. However, there are some unusual foreign flavors featured in restaurants that do not have write-ups. For those who may be interested, here are the best of the more exotic cuisines.

Burmese: Road to Mandalay (380 Broome St, bet Mulberry and Mott St)
Czech: Vasata (339 E 75th St, bet First and Second Ave)
Ethiopian: Zula (1260 Amsterdam Ave, at 122nd St)
German: Kleine Konditorei (234 E 86th St)
Greek: Periyali (35 W 20th St, bet Fifth and Sixth Ave)
Hungarian: Red Tulip (439 E 75th St, bet First and York Ave)
Irish: Neary's (358 E 57th St, bet First and Second Ave)
Japanese: ISO (175 Second Ave)
Malaysian: Malaysia Restaurant (48 Bowery)
Middle Eastern: Cafe Greco (1390 Second Ave, bet 71st and 72nd St) and Cleopatra's Needle (2485 Broadway, at 92nd St)
Peruvian: Peruvian Restaurant (688 Tenth Ave, bet 48th and 49th St)
Polish: Christine's (438 Second Ave, at 25th St; 208 First Ave, bet 12th and 13th St)
Russian: Russian Samovar (256 W 52nd St)
Tibetan: Tibetan Kitchen (444 Third Ave, bet 30th and 31st St)
Turkish: Anatolia (1422 Third Ave, bet 80th and 81st St)
Ukranian: Veselka (144 Second Ave, at 9th St)

Healthy Fare

Menu alert from the Mayo Clinic: If you are watching your diet, be cautious about menu items described as *au jus, in broth, cocktail sauce, tomato base, pickled,* or *smoked.* The experts also tell you to avoid the words *au gratin, basted, braised, buttered, buttery, casserole, creamed, crispy, fried, hash, hollandaise, butter sauce, cheese sauce, cream sauce, prime, sautéed, scalloped,* and *stewed.* My goodness, what's left to enjoy? More than you might think, and you can find healthy fare at the following restaurants, some of which have special menus.

Akbar (475 Park Ave, at 57th St): Indian.
Buckwheat and Alfalfa (182 Eighth Ave, bet 19th and 20th St)
Four Seasons (99 E 49th St, bet Park and Lexington Ave): Expensive.
Fraunces Tavern Restaurant (54 Pearl St): Historic.
Great American Health Bar (several locations throughout the city)
Health Pub (371 Second Ave, at 21st St)
Healthy Candle (Lexington Ave at 71st St)
Nosmo King (54 Varick St)
Salad Bowl (721 Lexington Ave, bet 57th and 58th St)
Saturnia (70 Park Ave)
Scarlatti (34 E 52nd St)
Spring Street Natural Restaurant (62 Spring St, at Lafayette St): Your best bet.
"21" (21 W 52nd St): For the health- and status-conscious.

Hotel Dining

One of the biggest changes on the restaurant circuit in Manhattan is the resurgence of hotel dining. No longer are these on-premises eateries just for the convenience of guests. Now they are, indeed, destinations for those who like a bit more atmosphere and a bit less trendy scene. Following are some of the best:

Algonquin (59 W 44th St): Rose Room, Oak Room. Evening cabaret.
Carlyle (35 E 76th St): Carlyle Restaurant. Features Bobby Short; very expensive.
Doral Court (130 E 39th St): Courtyard Cafe. Outdoors in summer.
Doral Park Avenue (70 Park Ave): Park Avenue Grill. American cuisine.
Doral Tuscany (116 E 39th St): Time & Again. Cozy, comfortable.
Drake Swissotel (440 Park Ave, at 56th St): Cafe Suisse, Restaurant Lafayette. Pricey.
Essex House (160 Central Park S): New opportunities.
Grand Hyatt (Grand Central Station and Park Ave): Sun Garden (nice setting), Trumpets (classy dining).
Helmsley Palace (455 Madison Ave, at 50th St): Le Trianon, Harry's New York Bar (for fun), Gold Room (for tea).
Hilton (1335 Sixth Ave, bet 53rd and 54th St): Grill 53 (steaks, chops), Cafe New York (snacks).
Holiday Inn Crowne Plaza (1605 Broadway, bet 48th and 49th St): Broadway Grill. Pre- or after-theater.

Inter-Continental (111 E 48th St): Barclay. American.

Kitano (66 Park Ave): Hakubai. Japanese.

Lowell (28 E 63rd St): Post House (meat and potatoes), Pembroke Room. Continental.

The Mark (25 E 77th, at Madison Ave): Mark's Restaurant. One of the very best.

Macklowe (145 W 44th St): New, classy.

Marriott Marquis (1535 Broadway, bet 45th and 46th St): four restaurants including The View. Top floor, revolving.

Mayfair Regent (610 Park Ave, at 65th St): Le Cirque. Society plus.

Omni Berkshire (21 E 52nd St): La Galerie. Country French.

Parker Meridien (118 W 57th St): Maurice. Brasserie.

Peninsula (700 Fifth Ave, at 55th St): Adrienne. Overlooks Fifth Avenue.

Pierre (61st St, at Fifth Ave): Cafe Pierre. Stately.

Plaza (768 Fifth Ave, at 59th St): Edwardian Room (overlooks Central Park), Palm Court (vintage New York), Oak Room (serious), Oyster Bar (seafood).

Plaza Athenee (37 E 64th St): Le Regence. Elegant.

Regency (540 Park Ave, at 61st St): 540 Park Ave Restaurant. Power scene.

Rihga Royal (151 W 54th St): Halcyon. Beautiful appointments.

Royalton (44 W 44th St): 44. Chic.

Sheraton Park Avenue (45 Park Ave, at 37th St): Russell's American Grill.

Sheraton Centre (Seventh Ave, at 52nd St): Rainier's Restaurant (good), Caffe Fontana (international).

St. Regis (Fifth Ave and 55th St): Lespinasse. Fine dining.

Stanhope (995 Fifth Ave): The Dining Room. French.

United Nations Plaza (44th St, at First Ave): Ambassador Grill. Sophisticated.

Vista International (3 World Trade Center): Greenhouse (casual). American Harvest (Yankee food).

Waldorf-Astoria (301 Park Ave, at 50th St): four restaurants, including Bull & Bear (British atmosphere), and Inagiku (Japanese).

Wales (1295 Madison Ave): Sarabeth's Kitchen. Delightful.

Westbury (840 Madison Ave, bet 69th and 70th St): Polo. Gracious.

Kosher

There will never be a shortage of pastrami or chicken soup in New York, but nowadays the kosher diner can sample a wider variety of flavors, from Afghan to Indian. Here's a partial list:

Bernstein-on-Essex (135 Essex St): Quintessential kosher deli. Hint: If you want to be "in," refer to Bernstein's-on-Essex as "Shmulk's."

Boychik's (19 W 45th St): Pasta, salads, and quick takeouts.

Cafe Masada (First Ave and 67th St): Israeli grill.

Cheers (120 W 41st St): The accent is Italian, the menu meaty.

Dairy Planet (182 Broadway): Health food, vegetarian.

Deli Kasbah (251 W 85th St): Grill, deli, and salad house.

Diva (306 E 81st St): Mainly Italian, dairy menu.

Eden Terrace (475 Park Ave S): Elegant deli and restaurant.

Galil (1252 Lexington Ave): Middle Eastern grill.

Gefen's (297 Seventh Ave): The dairy menu is a favorite with the "rag trade."

Goldie's (211 E 46th St): Crowded noontime deli.

Great American Health Bar (all over town): Vegetarian and dairy menu.

Jerusalem II (1375 Broadway): Pizza and falafel.

Kosher Delight (1365 Broadway): Kosher burger joint.

La Kasbah (70 W 71st St): Moroccan.

Levana (141 W 69th St): Outstanding European cuisine.

Lou G. Siegel (209 W 38th St): Businessman's delight.

Maccabeem (147 W 47th St): Chicken soup, etc., cafeteria-style.

Madras Place (104 Lexington Ave): Vegetarian South Indian.

Madras Woodlands (308 E 49th St): Indian vegetarian.

Mosha Peking (40 W 37th St): Elegant Chinese.

Naftali's (77 Fulton St): Continental meat and seafood.

Nanou (24 W 21st St): French kosher.

Verve Naturelle (157 W 57th St): California-style health food.

Late Hours

(See also "Manhattan at Night")
The city that never sleeps . . .

Never closes:
Brasserie (100 E 53rd St)
Empire Diner (210 Tenth Ave, at 22nd St)

Open until about six a.m.:
Coffee Shop (29 Union Sq W)

Open until about three a.m.:
Carnegie Deli (857 Seventh Ave, bet 54th and 55th St)
Hard Rock Cafe (221 W 57th St)
Lucky Strike (59 Grand St)
P.J. Clarke's (915 Third Ave, at 55th St)

Open until about two a.m.:
Chefs and Cuisiniers Club (36 E 22nd St)
Elaine's (1703 Second Ave, bet 88th and 89th St)

Telephone Bar and Grill (149 Second Ave, bet Ninth and Tenth St)
Wollensky's Grill (205 E 49th St, at Third Ave)

Open until about one a.m.:
Amsterdam's (454 Broadway, bet Grand and Howard St)
Ballroom (253 W 28th St)
Broome Street Bar (363 W Broadway)
Ciaobella (1311 Third Ave, at 75th St)
Delia's (197 E Third St)
Halycon (Righa Royal Hotel, 151 W 54th St)
I Tre Merli (463 W Broadway, bet Houston and Prince St)
Jackson Hole Wyoming Burgers (232 E 64th St; Third Ave, at 35th St; Second Ave, at 84th St)
J.G. Melon (340 Amsterdam Ave, at 76th St; 1291 Third Ave, at 74th St)
Mezzaluna (1295 Third Ave, bet 74th and 75th St)
Papaya King (179 E 86th St, at Third Ave; 201 E 59th St, at Third Ave)
Stage Deli (834 Seventh Ave, bet 53rd and 54th St)
Trattoria Dell'Arte (900 Seventh Ave, bet 56th and 57th St)
Veselka (144 Second Ave, at 9th St)
Walker's (16 N Moore, at Varick St)

Until midnight:
Algonquin Hotel (59 W 44th St)
Alo Alo (1030 Third Ave, at 61st St)
Bellevues (496 Ninth Ave, bet 37th and 38th St)
Bice (7 E 54th St)
Broadway Diner (590 Lexington Ave, at 52nd St; 1726 Broadway, at 55th St)
Cafe des Artistes (1 W 67th St)
Cameos (169 Columbus Ave, bet 67th and 68th St)
Chelsea Commons (242 Tenth Ave, at 24th St)
Chez Josephine (414 W 42nd St, bet Ninth and Tenth Ave)
Contrapunto (200 E 60th St, at Third Ave)
Docks (2427 Broadway, bet 89th and 90th St; 633 Third Ave, at 40th St)
Florent (69 Gansevoort St)
Fu's (1395 Second Ave, bet 72nd and 73rd St)
Girasole (151 E 82nd St)
Golden Unicorn (18 E Broadway)
Joe's Bar & Grill (142 W Tenth St, bet Greenwich Ave and Waverly Pl)
La Bonne Soupe (48 W 55th)
La Cité (120 W 51st St)
La Focaccia (51 Bank St)
Le Comptoir (227 E 67th St, bet Second and Third Ave)
Le Madri (168 W 18th St, at Seventh Ave)

Madeline's (177 Prince St, bet Thompson and Sullivan St)
Manhattan Chili Company (302 Bleecker St)
Manhattan Ocean Club (57 W 58th St)
Marylou's (21 W 9th St)
Metropolis Cafe (31 Union Sq W)
Mickey Mantle's (42 Central Park S)
Nicola's (146 E 84th St, bet Lexington and Third Ave)
Paper Moon Milano (39 E 58th St)
Plaza Hotel Oyster Bar (58th St, bet Fifth and Sixth Ave)
Post House (28 E 63rd St)
Primavera (1578 First Ave, at 82nd St)
Provence (38 MacDougal St)
Rose Cafe (24 Fifth Ave)
Royal Canadian Pancake House (145 Hudson St)
Serendipity 3 (225 E 60th St)
Sfuzzi (58 W 65th St)
SoHo Kitchen and Bar (103 Greene St)
Sylvia's (328 Lenox Ave, bet 126th and 127th St)
Trixie's (307 W 47th St)
"21" Club (21 W 52nd St)
Vince and Eddie's (70 W 68th St)
Voulez-Vous (1462 First Ave, at 76th St)
Yellowfingers di Nuovo (200 E 60th St, at Third Ave)
Zarela (953 Second Ave, bet 50th and 51st St)

Offbeat

Looking for a place that is just a bit different? Here are some ideas:

Acme Bar & Grill (9 Great Jones St, bet Lafayette St and Broadway): Swinging.
Afghan Kebab House (764 Ninth Ave, 1345 Second Ave): Kebabs.
Artie's Warehouse Restaurant (539 W 21st St): Warehouse setting.
Bellevues (496 Ninth Ave): Bistro.
Boathouse Cafe (Central Park Lake): Overlooks water.
Brother Jimmy's Bar-B-Q (1461 First Ave): Great ribs.
Buckaroo's (1431 First Ave, bet 74th and 75th St): Bar/rotisserie.
Canal Bar (511 Greenwich St): Friendly.
Coco Pazzo (23 E 74th St): Crazy chef!
Delia's AB 3 (197 E Third St): Alphabet land.
Ed Debevic's (661 Broadway at Bond St): Crazy 40s, 50s.
Florent (69 Gansevoort at Washington St): In the Meat District.
Frank's (431 W 14th St): Meat and potatoes.
Great Jones Street Cafe (54 Great Jones St at Bowery): Eclectic.

Khyber Pass (34 St Mark's Pl): Afghan.
Landmark Tavern (626 Eleventh Ave, at 46th St): Historic.
NoHo Star (330 Lafayette St): Diner.
Nosmo King (54 Varick St): Organic.
Rao's (455 E 114th St): Way uptown.
Red Tulip (439 E 75th St, bet First and York Ave): Hungarian.
Ruby's River Road Cafe (1754 Second Ave, bet 91st and 92nd St):
  Cajun.
Sabor (20 Cornelia St, at Sixth Ave): Cuban.
Sammy's Roumanian (157 Chrystie St): Lower East Side.
Seventh Regiment Mess (643 Park Ave, at 66th St): Unusual setting.
Sugar Reef (93 Second Ave, bet Fifth and Sixth St): Caribbean.
Sylvia's (328 Lenox Ave, bet 126th and 127th St): Soul food.
Trixie's (307 W 47th St): Southwestern.
Vasata (339 E 75th St, bet First and Second Ave): Czech.
Veselka Coffee Shop (144 Second Ave): Polish-Ukranian.

Old-Timers

How far back do you want to go?

1763: **Fraunces Tavern Restaurant** (54 Pearl St)
1836: **Delmonico's** (56 Beaver St)
1842: **Sweet's** (2 Fulton St)
1854: **McSorley's Old Ale House** (15 E 7th St)
1864: **Pete's Tavern** (129 E 18th St)
1865: **Landmark Tavern** (626 Eleventh Ave)
1868: **Old Homestead** (56 Ninth Ave)
1879: **Gage & Tollner** (372 Fulton St, Brooklyn)
1885: **Keens Chop House** (72 W 36th St)
1887: **Peter Luger** (178 Broadway, Brooklyn)
1889: **Harvey's Chelsea House** (108 W 18th St)
1890: **P.J. Clarke's** (915 Third Ave, at 55th St)
1905: **Ratner's** (138 Delancey St)
1906: **Barbetta** (321 W 46th St)
1912: **Frank's** (431 W 14th St)
      Olde Garden Cafe & Winery (15 W 29th St)
1913: **Grand Central Oyster Bar Restaurant** (Grand Central Station)
1914: **Cafe des Artistes** (1 W 67th St)
1920: **Ye Waverly Inn** (16 Bank St)
1922: **"21"** (21 W 52nd St)
1926: **Palm** (837 Second Ave)
      Russian Tea Room (150 W 57th St)
1927: **Minetta Tavern** (113 MacDougal St)

Outdoor Dining

A taste of the outdoors, either in a garden, patio, or on the sidewalk:

American Festival Cafe (Rockefeller Center)
Aureole (34 E 61st St)
Barolo (398 W Broadway)
Boathouse Cafe (Central Park Lake, Fifth Ave and 72nd St)
Caffe Dante (79 MacDougal St)
Chez Ma Tante (189 W 10th St, bet W 4th and Bleecker St)
Ciaobella (1311 Third Ave, at 75th St)
Coastal (300 Amsterdam Ave, at 74th St)
Courtyard Cafe (130 E 39th St)
Da Silvano (260 Sixth Ave, bet Bleecker and W Houston St)
Empire Diner (210 Tenth Ave, at 22nd St)
Gascogne (158 Eighth Ave, near 17th St)
Ginger Man (51 W 64th St)
La Bohème (24 Minetta Lane, bet W 3rd and Bleecker St)
La Goulue (28 E 70th St)
La Petite Ferme (973 Lexington Ave, at 70th St)
Le Madri (168 W 18th St)
Le Relais (712 Madison Ave, bet 63rd and 64th St)
Lox Around the Clock (676 Sixth Ave)
Manhattan Chili Co. (302 Bleecker St, near Seventh Ave)
Mezzogiorno (195 Spring, at Sullivan St)
Miracle Grill (112 First Ave, nr 7th St)
Mortimer's (1057 Lexington Ave, at 75th St)
Museum of Modern Art (11 W 53rd St)
One if By Land, Two if By Sea (17 Barrow St)
Pete's Tavern (129 E 18th St)
Provence (38 MacDougal St)
River Cafe (1 Water St, Brooklyn)
The Saloon (1920 Broadway, at 64th St)
Stanhope Hotel (995 Fifth Ave)
Summerhouse (50 E 86th St, bet Madison and Park Ave)
Sumptuary (400 Third Ave)
Tavern on the Green (Central Park, at W 67th St)
211 Restaurant (211 W Broadway)
White Horse Tavern (567 Hudson St)

Party Rooms

Most major hotels have private function rooms.
(See also special section on unusual party places.)

Akbar (475 Park Ave, bet 57th and 58th St; 256 E 49th St, bet Second and Third Ave)

An American Place (2 Park Ave, at 32nd St)
Barbetta (321 W 46th St)
Bouley (165 Duane St, bet Greenwich and Hudson St)
Brandywine (274 Third Ave, bet 21st and 22nd St)
Brasserie (100 E 53rd St, bet Lexington and Park Ave)
Coach House (110 Waverly Pl, bet Fifth and Sixth Ave)
Darbar (44 W 56th St)
Delmonico's (56 Beaver, at William St)
Four Seasons (99 E 52nd St)
Frank's (431 W 14th St, bet Ninth and Tenth Ave)
Fraunces Tavern Restaurant (54 Pearl St)
Ginger Man (51 W 64th St)
Harvey's Chelsea Restaurant (108 W 18th St, at Sixth Ave)
Hatsuhana (17 E 48th St)
Hudson River Club (World Financial Center)
Jim McMullen (1341 Third Ave, bet 76th and 77th St)
Keens Chop House (72 W 36th St)
La Grenouille (3 E 52nd St)
La Reserve (4 W 49th St)
Le Cirque (Mayfair Regent Hotel, 58 E 65th St)
Le Perigord (405 E 52nd St, east of First Ave)
Mondrian (7 E 59th St)
Montrachet (239 Broadway, bet Walker and White St)
One if By Land, Two if By Sea (17 Barrow St)
Palio (151 W 51st St, bet Sixth and Seventh Ave)
Palm (837 Second Ave, bet 44th and 45th St)
Periyali (35 W 20th St, bet Fifth and Sixth Ave)
Primavera (1578 First Ave, at 82nd St)
Rainbow Room (Rockefeller Center)
Russian Tea Room (150 W 57th St)
Sign of the Dove (1110 Third Ave, at 65th St)
Smith & Wollensky (201 E 49th St, at Third Ave)
Sparks (210 E 46th St, bet Second and Third Ave)
Tavern on the Green (Central Park, at W 67th St)
TriBeCa Grill (375 Greenwich, at Franklin St)
Windows on the World (World Trade Center)

People Watching

Bellini (777 Seventh Ave, bet 50th and 51st St)
Bice (7 E 54th St)
Bouley (165 Duane St, bet Greenwich and Hudson St)
Chefs & Cuisiniers Club (36 E 22nd St)
Ecco (124 Chambers St, bet W Broadway and Church)
Elaine's (1703 Second Ave, bet 88th and 89th St)
Florent (69 Gansevoort St, bet Washington and Greenwich St)

Four Seasons (99 E 52nd St, bet Park and Lexington Ave)
Gotham Bar & Grill (12 E 12th St, bet Fifth Ave and University Pl)
Harry Cipriani (Fifth Ave and E 59th St)
Jim McMullen (1341 Third Ave, bet 76th and 77th St)
La Grenouille (3 E 52nd St)
La Reserve (4 W 49th St)
Le Cirque (Mayfair Regent Hotel, 58 E 65th St)
Le Madri (168 W 18th St)
Mickey Mantle's (42 Central Park S)
Mortimer's (1057 Lexington Ave, at 75th St)
P.J. Clarke's (915 Third Ave, at 55th St)
Palio (151 W 51st St, bet Sixth and Seventh Ave)
Palm (837 Second Ave, bet 44th and 45th St)
Palm Court (Plaza Hotel, Fifth Ave and Central Park S)
Provence (38 MacDougal, at Prince St)
Rainbow Room (Rockefeller Center)
Russian Tea Room (150 W 57th St)
San Domenico (240 Central Park S)
Sette Mezzo (969 Lexington Ave, bet 70th and 71st St)
Tavern on the Green (Central Park W and 67th St)
Trattoria Dell'Arte (900 Seventh Ave, bet 56th and 57th St)
TriBeCa Grill (375 Greenwich, at Franklin St)
"21" Club (21 W 52nd St)

Personal Favorites

Everybody has a list of favorite places, and I am happy to share mine:

Andiamo (1991 Broadway, bet 67th and 68th St): Italian.
Bouley (165 Duane St, bet Greenwich and Hudson St): Class plus.
Cafe des Artistes (1 W 67th St): Restful.
Cafe des Sports (329 W 51st St): Homey French.
Carolina (355 W 46th St): Southern hospitality.
Coach House (110 Waverly Pl): Consistently good.
Edwardian Room (Plaza Hotel, 59th and Central Park S): Right on the park.
Gotham Bar & Grill (12 E 12th St): Darn good food.
Il Mulino (86 W 3rd St, bet Thompson and Sullivan St): Italian at its best.
Jackson Hole Wyoming Burgers (various locations): Simply the best.
La Bohème (24 Minetta Ln): Unpretentious.
La Grenouille (3 E 52nd St): Beautiful.
La Metairie (189 W 10th St, bet Bleecker and W 4th St): Cozy.
La Reserve (4 W 49th St): Perfection!
March (405 E 58th St, bet First Ave and Sutton Pl): Imaginative.
Mark's (Mark Hotel, 25 E 77th St): Classy.

Nick and Eddie's (203 Spring St): Lively.
One if By Land, Two if By Sea (17 Barrow St): Romantic.
Park Side (107-01 Corona Ave, Queens): Super dishes.
Primavera (1578 First Ave, at 82nd St): Superb service.
River Cafe (1 Water St, East River, Brooklyn): Oh, that view!
Terrace (Columbia University, 400 W 119th St): Great outlook.
Wong Kee (113 Mott St): Basic Chinatown.

Pizza

Everyone has a favorite pizza place. You can't go wrong with any of these:

Arturo's Pizzeria (106 Houston St)
Barocco (297 Church St)
Broadway Grill (Holiday Inn Crowne Plaza; 1605 Broadway, at 48th St)
Fisher & Levy (875 Third Ave, at 53rd St)
John's (278 Bleecker St, 408 E 64th St)
La Bohème (24 Minetta Lane)
Le Madri (168 W 8th St, at Seventh Ave)
Mezzogiorno (195 Spring St)
New Haven Pizza Co. (140 W 13th St)
Orso (322 W 46th St)
Patsy's Pizza (2287 First Ave, bet 117th and 118th St)
PIZZAPIAZZA (785 Broadway, at 10th St)
Sal's & Carmine's Pizza (2533 Broadway)
Trattoria Dell'Arte (900 Seventh Ave, bet 56th and 57th St)

Pubs

To feel the real flavor of New York, visit a pub on St. Patrick's Day. However, these spots feature good brew, good times, and good company every day of the year.

Billy's (948 First Ave, at 53rd St)
Chelsea Place (147 Eighth Ave, bet 17th and 18th St)
Great Jones Street Cafe (54 Great Jones St)
Jimmy Day's (186 W 4th St)
Joe's Bar & Grill (142 W 10th St)
Landmark Tavern (626 Eleventh Ave, at 46th St)
McSorley's Old Ale House (15 E 7th St, at Third Ave)
Peculier Pub (145 Bleecker St, corner of La Guardia Pl)
Pete's Tavern (66 Irving Pl): New York's oldest continuously operating pub.
P.J. Clarke's (915 Third Ave, at 55th St)
SoHo Kitchen and Bar (103 Greene St, bet Prince and Spring St)

Telephone Bar & Grill (149 Second Ave, bet 9th and 10th St)
White Horse Tavern (567 Hudson St)

Romantic

Some great places for hand holding (or whatever):

Barbetta (321 W 46th st)
Bouley (165 Duane St)
Cafe des Artistes (1 W 67th St)
Cafe Pierre (Pierre Hotel, 61st St and Fifth Ave)
Cafe Trevi (1570 First Ave)
Caffe Vivaldi (32 Jones St)
Chanterelle (2 Harrison St)
Chez Josephine (414 W 42nd St)
Four Seasons (99 E 52nd St)
Hudson River Club (World Financial Center)
La Bohème (24 Minetta Ln)
La Caravelle (33 W 55th St)
La Côte Basque (5 E 55th St)
La Grenouille (3 E 52nd St)
La Metairie (189 W 10th St)
La Petite Ferme (973 Lexington Ave, bet 70th and 71st St)
La Reserve (4 W 49th St)
Le Cirque (Mayfair Regent Hotel, 58 E 65th St)
Le Cygne (55 E 54th St)
Le Train Bleu (Bloomingdale's, 1000 Third Ave)
Mark's (Mark Hotel, 25 E 77th St)
One if By Land, Two if By Sea (17 Barrow St)
Palm Court and Edwardian Room (Plaza Hotel, Fifth Ave and Central Park S)
Paola's (347 E 85th St)
Parioli Romanissimo (24 E 81st St)
Pete's Tavern (129 E 18th St)
Provence (38 MacDougal St)
Rainbow Room (Rockefeller Center)
River Cafe (1 Water St, East River, Brooklyn)
Russian Tea Room (150 W 57th St)
Sign of the Dove (1110 Third Ave)
Tavern on the Green, Crystal Room (Central Park W and 67th St)
Terrace (400 W 119th St, Columbia University)
Time & Again (Doral Tuscany Hotel, 116 E 39th St)
Trastevere (155 E 84th St)
Vanessa (289 Bleecker St)
Windows on the World (1 World Trade Center)
World Yacht Cruises (Pier 62, W 23rd St and Hudson River)

Sandwiches

There are thousands (yes, thousands) of places that serve sandwiches in Manhattan, and most of them are pretty ordinary. But the following turn out exceptionally good combinations for eating in or taking out.

America (9-13 E 18th St)
Brasserie (100 E 53rd St)
Burke and Burke (2 E 23rd St)
Carnegie Deli (854 Second Ave, at 55th St)
Cleaver Company (229 W Broadway)
Delices de France (289 Madison Ave)
Donald Sacks (120 Prince St, World Financial Center)
Jerry's (101 Prince St)
Manganaro's Hero Boy (492 Ninth Ave, bet 37th and 38th St)
Peter Dent (120 Hudson St)
Small Feast (1173 Second Ave)
Telephone Bar and Grill (149 Second Ave)
Thorough Bread (450 Park Ave S, near 30th St)
Union Square Cafe (21 E 16th St)
Yellowfingers di Nuovo (200 E 60th St, at Third Ave)

Seafood

Coastal (300 Amsterdam Ave, at 74th St)
Dock's Oyster Bar (2427 Broadway, bet 89th and 90th St; 633 Third Ave, at 40th St)
Grand Central Oyster Bar Restaurant (Grand Central Station, E 42nd St)
Jane Street Seafood Cafe (31 Eighth Ave, at Jane St)
John Clancy's (206 E 63rd St, bet Second and Third Ave; 181 W 10th St, at Seventh Ave S)
King Crab (871 Eighth Ave, at 52nd St)
Le Bernardin (155 W 51st St)
Le Cirque (Mayfair Regent Hotel, 58 E 65th St)
Manhattan Ocean Club (57 W 58th St)
Maryland Crab House (237 Third Ave, bet 19th and 20th St)
Marylou's (21 W 9th St)
Oriental Town Seafood (14 Elizabeth St)
Primola (1226 Second Ave, bet 64th and 65th St)
Remi (145 W 53rd St, bet Sixth and Seventh Ave)
Sweets (2 Fulton St, South Street Seaport)
Tropica (Pan Am Building, 200 Park Ave)
Trumpet's (Grand Hyatt Hotel, 109 E 42nd St)
Wilkinson's (1573 York Ave, bet 83rd and 84th St)

Shopping Breaks

To replenish your energy (and take it easy on the credit cards for a few minutes), here are some good places to eat in the major Manhattan department stores:

Le Salon de Thé (second floor) at Henri Bendel. Be sure to notice the magnificent Lalique windows.
Le Cafe (women's store) at Barney's.
Cafe SFA (eighth floor) at Saks Fifth Avenue. This is a new one.
Cafe Vienna (seventh floor) and **Pasta and Cheese** (fifth floor) at Bergdorf-Goodman.
40 Carrots (lower level). **Le Train Bleu** (sixth floor), and **Showtime Cafe** (seventh floor) at Bloomingdale's.
Red Rose (sixth floor) and **Soup Bar** (tenth floor) at Lord & Taylor.
Cafe L'Etoile (balcony), the **Fountain** (fifth floor), and the **Patio** (eighth floor) at Macy's.

Steaks

Even though most of us have cut down on red meat, there's always a time when a really good steak hits the spot. For meat-and-potato lovers, here are the best steaks in town:

Ben Benson's (123 W 52nd St)
Frank's (431 W 14th St)
Gotham Bar & Grill (12 E 12th St)
Le Steak (1089 Second Ave)
Manhattan Cafe (1161 First Ave)
Palm and Palm Too (837 Second Ave, 840 Second Ave)
Pen and Pencil (205 E 45th St)
Peter Luger (178 Broadway, Brooklyn)
Pietro's (232 E 43rd St)
Post House (28 E 63rd St)
Smith & Wollensky (201 E 49th St)
Sparks (210 E 46th St)

Take-home

This volume features several sections on take-home possibilities. First, study the list of "Best Taste Treats" at the start of this set of listings; practically every item mentioned is available for take-home purchase. Then, look at the food section under "Delis, Catering, Food to Go" (not available in the pocket edition) for a complete listing of the best takeout places in town. The four major gourmet stores (**Balducci's**, 424 Sixth Ave, at Ninth St; **Dean and Deluca**, 560 Broadway, at Prince St;

Grace's Market Place, 1237 Third Ave, at 71st St; **Zabar's**, 2245 Broadway at 80th St) all have outstanding selections of dishes to go.

Teatime

The age-old custom of afternoon tea has returned with class to a number of Manhattan spots. Besides cream and sugar, proper accessories include a pitcher of hot water and a small silver strainer to catch the tea leaves. Most of these places have delicious calories to accompany your cup of tea:

Anglers and Writers (420 Hudson St)
Barclay Restaurant at the Hotel Inter-Continental (111 E 48th St)
Cafe SFA at Saks Fifth Avenue (611 Fifth Ave, at 50th St)
Danal (90 E 10th St). Different!
Gold Room at the Helmsley Palace (455 Madison Ave)
Gotham Lounge at the Peninsula Hotel (700 Fifth Ave, at 55th St)
Le Cafe at Barney's (Seventh Ave and 17th St)
Le Salon at the Stanhope (995 Fifth Ave, at 81st St)
Le Salon de Thé at Henri Bendel (712 Fifth Ave, near 56th St)
Le Train Bleu at Bloomingdale's (Third Ave and 59th St)
Les Delices Guy Pascal (939 First Ave, at 52nd St; 1231 Madison Ave, at 89th St)
Little Nell's Tea Room (343 E 85th St, bet First and Second Ave)
Mayfair Regent, lounge (610 Park Ave at 65th St)
Oak Room at the Algonquin Hotel (59 W 44th St)
Palm Court at the Plaza Hotel (Fifth Ave and 59th St)
Polo Lounge at the Westbury Hotel (Madison Ave at 69th St)
Rotunda at Hotel Pierre (2 E 61st St)
Sant Ambroeus (1000 Madison Ave, at 77th St)
Serendipity 3 (225 E 60th St)
Stone Room at the National Academy of Design (1083 Fifth Ave, at 89th St)
"21" (21 W 52nd St)
Waldorf-Astoria, (301 Park Ave, at 49th St)

Views

Contrary to the axiom that good food does not come with a good view, the food at all of these "rooms with a view" is very good.

American Festival Cafe (Rockefeller Plaza) From the sidelines of the skating rink, the art deco monuments of Rockefeller Plaza tower above you.
Boathouse Cafe (Central Park, East Side entrance) From lakeside, you get a you-are-there view of Central Park, and the city skyline looms above the treetops.

Rainbow Room (Rockefeller Center) This elegant and romantic perch provides a panoramic midtown view.

River Cafe (1 Water St, Brooklyn) A window seat gives you that famous view of the downtown skyline you've seen on post cards and in movies.

Terrace (400 W 119th St) The windows here show you what the city looks like from uptown.

The View (Marriott Marquis Hotel) You're high above Times Square—and revolving.

Windows on the World (World Trade Center, 107th floor) You can't dine and gaze from a higher point, unless you're in a plane.

Wine Bars

Manhattan's better-known wine bars include **Cafe Europa** and **La Brioche** (347 E 54th St), **Cellar in the Sky** (1 World Trade Center), **I Tre Merli** (463 W Broadway, bet Prince and Houston St) and **SoHo Kitchen and Bar** (103 Greene St, bet Prince and Spring St).

Young People's Choices

Many time the older folks have just as much fun as the kids at some of the trendier places in town. Here is a sample of places where children of all ages will have a ball:

America (9 E 18th St): Big place, big menu.

American Festival Cafe (20 W 50th St): Skating at Rockefeller Center.

Arizona 206 and Cafe (206 E 60th St): A taste of the southwest.

Bellevues (496 Ninth Ave, bet 37th and 38th St): Funky.

Boathouse Cafe (Central Park, E Park Dr and 72nd St): Overlooks Central Park lake.

Brother Jimmy's Bar-B-Q (1461 First Ave): Great ribs.

Carnegie Deli (854 Seventh Ave, bet 54th and 55th St): For big appetites.

Corner Bistro (331 W 4th St): Burgers deluxe.

Dallas BBQ (1265 Third Ave, at 73rd St; 27 W 72nd St; 21 University Pl): Texas-style.

Ed Debevic's (661 Broadway, at Bond St): What the 40s were like!

Food Fairs: Pier 17 (South Street Seaport), A&S Plaza (Herald Sq)

Gray's Papaya (2090 Broadway): Hot dogs and the trimmings.

Hamburger Harry's (157 Chambers St; 156 Seventh Ave; 145 W 45th): The name says it all.

Hard Rock Cafe (221 W 57th St): It's worth the battle.

Jackson Hole Wyoming Burgers (232 E 64th St; Third Ave, at 35th St; Second Ave, at 84th St): The best.

John's Pizzeria (408 E 64th St; 278 Bleecker St): Crispy and delicious.
Landmark Tavern (626 Eleventh Ave, at 46th St): Historic.
Lox Around the Clock (676 Sixth Ave): Action.
Mickey Mantle's (42 Central Park S): Jock hangout.
Moondance Diner (Sixth Ave at Grand St): Nostalgic.
Nice Restaurant (35 E Broadway; 64 Fulton St): It *is* nice.
Papaya King (179 E 86th St; 201 E 59th St): Stand-up dogs and drinks.
Pappa's Place (510 Sixth Ave, at 13th St): Treasure house for kids.
Peppermint Park Cafe (1225 First Ave, bet 66th and 67th St): Waffles, candies, ice creams, sandwiches, pastries, calories.
Pig Heaven (1540 Second Ave, bet 80th and 81st St): Chinese pig heaven.
Seventh Regiment Mess (643 Park Ave, at 66th St): A secret military winner!
Serendipity 3 (225 E 60th St): Very "in."
Tavern on the Green (Central Park, at W 67th St): Magical.
Tony Roma's (several locations): Great ribs and onion loaf.
Trixie's (307 W 47th, bet Eighth and Ninth Ave): Wacky.
Windows on the World (1 World Trade Center): Come here for the view.
Yellowfingers di Nuovo (200 E 60th St): Pizzalike breads.
Yellow Rose Cafe (450 Amsterdam Ave, at 82nd St): Southern-fried goodies.
Zarela (953 Second Ave, bet 50th and 51st St): South of the border.

Western

These places are a good distance from the Wild West, but they do their best to deliver a taste of cattle country! **Arizona 206 and Cafe** (206 E 60th St), **Border Cafe** (2637 Broadway, at 100th St), **Cadillac Bar** (15 W 21st St), **El Rio Grande** (Third Ave, bet 37th and 38th St), **Yellow Rose Cafe** (450 Amsterdam Ave, at 82nd St), and the **Mesa Grill** (102 Fifth Ave).

WHEN WAS THE FIRST DEPARTMENT STORE BUILT?

In 1848, the Marble Dry Goods Palace opened on Broadway in New York City. Its proprietor and developer was Alexander Turney Stewart, formerly a schoolmaster in Ireland. By the time of his death in 1876, the block-long store yielded annual earnings of $70 million.

ADAMS RIB (and CAFE)
1338 First Ave   535-2112
Lunch, Dinner: Daily; Brunch: Sun
Moderate

There just aren't many good roast-beef houses in New York, and this one has to be at the top of the list. The showpiece, of course, is Adams Rib. It is accompanied by wonderful Yorkshire pudding, a strong horseradish sauce, fresh broiled mushrooms, and a real Idaho baked potato (not the mushy foil-wrapped variety). Non-beef lovers can savor breast of chicken Milanese, shrimp scampi, or several other seafood dishes. They even bake their own bread, which leaves the place smelling like Grandma's kitchen. For lunch a roast beef-sandwich is served on toasted French bread with French fries, along with some great salads. The Garden of Eve salad is full of forbidden vegetables, or so they claim. Apricot torte or mud pie will finish filling you up. There is also a cafe serving lighter food. For those readers who have tried Lawry's Prime Rib in Los Angeles, which I think is terrific, this is the closest equivalent in New York.

ALISON ON DOMINICK STREET
38 Dominick St   727-1188
Dinner: Daily
Moderate to moderately expensive

This is no place to take your meat-and-potatoes friends! Dominick Street is not the easiest place to find, but just head toward the entrance to the Holland Tunnel and you won't be too far off. When you arrive, you'll find yourself in a long, narrow room, attractively understated, with pleasant background jazz keeping you company. By all means avoid being seated at the several tables in front of the bar; the scenery here is not conducive to pleasant eating. The two partners (Alison is one of them) came from Gotham Bar and Grill, and they brought along a considerable number of sophisticated ideas. The menu has unique southwestern France specialties. The entree choices read like a "chef de cuisine" tasting: lamb shank, rabbit stew, sauteed squab, striped bass antiboise. Each is served with unique accompaniments, such as diced turnips, garlic spinach, and deep-fried celery leaves. Get the picture? For starters, try the vegetable tart (eggplant, zucchini, tomatoes, and carmelized onions with basil and oil) and finish up with warm chocolate raspberry tart or three-layered sorbet. But don't try to duplicate the menu in your own kitchen; the old man would probably have to send out for pizza and french fries if you did!

AMERICA
9-13 E 18th St   505-2110
Lunch, Dinner: Daily; Brunch: Sat, Sun
Inexpensive to moderate

Only in New York could you find a place like this. It's big, big, big! The building is enormous—it used to be a carpet showroom. The bar is enormous—when it's full, it looks like a yuppie convention. The menu is enormous—not dozens, but hundreds of items. The portions are enormous. And the noise level is enormous when all 350 to 400 seats are filled. But the good news is that the tab is small. Well, where do you start? They have a dozen or so egg dishes and just as many omelets. There are delicious griddle cakes, including sweet-potato pancakes. Excellent side dishes range from "hash-slinger" potatoes to white-corn hush puppies to Boston brown bread and even Cincinnatis (shoestring French fries drenched in gravy). Appetizers run the gamut from New Orleans Cajun popcorn (deep-fried crawfish tails) to buffalo chicken wings (deep-fried and marinated) to New Mexican black-bean cakes to Oregon mushroom cakes—to which, as you'd expect, I am partial. There are several dozen main-course entrees, from American chop suey to New England roast turkey to shrimp jambalaya to South Carolina crab cakes and everything in between. Oh, and add hamburgers, chili, pasta, pizza, and absolutely the best sandwiches you can imagine. Then there are the desserts. Tennessee Black Bottom pie, Tollhouse cookies, Death by Chocolate, Key Lime mousse, New Orleans pralines—you name it, they've got it. Come on down, especially if you're escorting a group of youngsters.

AMERICAN FESTIVAL CAFE
20 W 50th St   246-6699
Lunch: Mon-Fri; Dinner: Daily; Brunch: Sat, Sun
Moderate

The big attraction here is the location. The ice-skating rink at Rockefeller Center is glamorous in summer or winter, and when you add the novelty of various ethnic promotions to the setting, the American Festival Cafe fills the bill as a unique New York attraction. There's always a lot going on at Rockefeller Center: entertainment, shopping, eating, and people watching. I'd say it's a must for any visitor to the city. The cafe serves good salads, sandwiches, and items from the charcoal grill. The chef's salad (greens, veal bacon, corncob ham, smoked turkey, peppered beef, and cheese) is delightful, as are the grilled lamb chops. For kids, the hamburgers are just right, and the desserts are unusually appetizing. Try the key lime pie, bread pudding with sour-mash whiskey sauce, or strawberry shortcake. A large selection of domestic and imported beers is also available.

AMERICAN HARVEST

New York Vista Hotel
3 World Trade Center   938-9100, 432-9334
Breakfast, Lunch: Mon-Fri
Moderate to expensive

I usually don't get excited about dining in hotel restaurants, because convenience is often their best quality. But this one is a bit different. Hilton International has done an excellent job. The décor is Early American; a selection of antiques enhances the ambiance. The restaurant is divided into three areas, and the tables are arranged far enough apart to create a very comfortable and pleasant dining experience. The menu changes, as the name implies, with each harvest. The vegetables and produce that are available in-season are prepared in a variety of ways. Order from an extensive à la carte menu or select lunch at a fixed price, with appetizer or soup or dessert, main course, and vegetables flans. For the main course, the seafood is excellent; sea trout, Florida pompano, and butterflied shrimp are among the best selections. I also recommend the stuffed lamb chops and the steaks. Make way for the dessert trolley! It's magnificent, laden with chocolate cheesecake, chocolate layer cake, maple-date pecan pie, and maple mousse loaf—all made in the hotel. The American Harvest is a delightful place to bring guests. It's well worth the trip downtown.

AN AMERICAN PLACE

2 Park Ave (at 32nd St)   684-2122
Lunch: Mon-Fri; Dinner: Mon-Sat
Moderately expensive to expensive

Larry Forgione, the owner-chef of An American Place, hopes that the third time is a charm. His quarters are in a location that has had two unhappy restaurant experiences. It is obvious that Larry is the expert in the kitchen, for there is no question about the quality and attractiveness of the food here. If I had guests from overseas, and I wanted to give them a quick, all-American taste experience, I'd bring them here. With lunch and dinner dishes featuring the best from across the land, Larry Forgione features such delicacies as Florida's Key West shrimp, Chicago stockyard chowder with white beans, fried New England Ipswich clams, and grilled Maine sea scallops. The dessert selections come wrapped in the old red, white, and blue: banana betty, apple pan dowdy, old-fashioned berry shortcake, domestic farmstead cheeses, and angel food chiffon. Forget about the unattractive atmosphere. Let the talented and polite personnel pamper you, and concentrate on some of the best food presentations in Manhattan.

ANDIAMO
1991 Broadway
(at 67th St, in the back of Cafe Bel Canto)   362-3315
Lunch: Mon-Fri; Dinner: Daily
Moderate

The old saying "If you have something good, people will find you" surely applies to Andiamo. Tucked away in the back of the popular Cafe Bel Canto in the Lincoln Center area, Andiamo is one of the most attractive and tasteful rooms in town. The airy bilevel restaurant is decorated with artwork from the personal collection of the owner, Lewis Futterman. The lighting is flattering, and the staff gives you a sincere and pleasant greeting. The selection of hot and cold openers includes marinated venison carpaccio and poached lobster. I'd suggest saving room for a pasta dish; the crabmeat tortelli in carrot butter sauce is one of the best. Larger portions of pasta are available as a main course, or you can feast upon grilled rack of lamb, grilled Norwegian salmon, and seared sea scallops. The portions are king-sized and expertly presented. Sheer artistry is the only way to describe the desserts. There is a layered mousse of chocolate and raspberry, homemade gelato in a choice of flavors, and a deep chocolate terrine with chocolate gelato. Andiamo is a fixture in the neighborhood.

ANTOLOTTI'S
337 E 49th St   688-6767
Lunch: Mon-Fri; Dinner: Daily
Moderate

When you've been successful in the same business for nearly four decades, you must be doing something right. And Antolotti's surely is. You can tell from the moment you enter: the greeting is pleasant, and the seating prompt and efficient. You have no sooner taken your place in the pleasant, compact room, decorated with an eclectic mix of pictures and memorabilia, than one of the crisply professional staff places excellent bread, healthy nibbles, and cole slaw in front of you. Then you're presented with a huge menu of Italian and continental choices. It seems impossible for a kitchen to do a dozen veal dishes so well, but they do. In addition, there are wonderful seafood items, from sole to lobster, chicken any way you want it, pork and lamb chops, steaks, and a wide choice of typical Italian dishes. The homemade manicotti, canelloni, and lasagna can't be beaten. All the dishes that are supposed to be served hot are steaming, and the cold ones taste as though they just came from the refrigerator. Nothing is cooked ahead of time. If you can muster up the appetite for spumoni or rum cake, more power to you. I chose the big iced dish of fresh fruit to finish the meal. Two generations of the Antolotti family are on the job: Dad is seated at a booth, keeping an eye on his success story, while his son tends bar and greets a host of regular customers who have been coming here for years. An attractive party room is also available.

AQUAVIT
13 W 54th St   307-7311
Lunch: Mon-Fri; Dinner: Mon-Sat
Cafe: Moderately expensive; Dining Room: Expensive

Just as you would expect from the organized and hospitable Scandinavians, Aquavit presents an attractive, wholesome background for some very tasty—and expensive—meals. The setting is also a feast for the eyes: you have a choice of eating upstairs in the moderately priced cafe, or in several areas downstairs, including an attractive covered patio with a waterfall. Here the diner looks eight stories skyward at an unusually attractive atrium. The meal starts with a healthy breadbasket, including delicious seven-grain bread. Upstairs, the Cafe offers appetizers heavy on the fish side: a herring plate, Scandinavian shrimp soup, and smoked Swedish salmon. Main course specialties include delicious Swedish meatballs, whole cold poached lobster, a typical smorgasbord plate, and Kaldolmar (Savoy cabbage rolls with ligonberry). Downstairs, hold on to your wallet for the three-course, price-fixed dinner. The first course features a choice of some ten items, including blinis, traditional gravlas, and marinated arctic venison. Then on to such second course entrees as poached halibut, turbot or salmon, fillet of veal and sweetbreads, and snow grouse (a real delight!). No ordinary dessert menu here. Choices include Swedish pancakes, Swedish blueberry pie, and a fabulous chocolate cake with burned almond crust. You will be impressed with the very polite and attractive ladies and gentlemen who guide you through this sumptuous banquet. They are as low-key as the prices are high.

ARIZONA 206 AND CAFE
206 E 60th St   838-0440
Lunch: Mon-Sat (Cafe Tues-Sat); Dinner: Daily
Moderate

This establishment has had several reincarnations, and the last one is certainly, well, different! The best of Southwest cuisine and atmosphere has been transported to Manhattan, cactus and all. The front area—a room for drinks and conversation, complete with a fireplace—is pleasant. There is a good-sized bar in the center of the restaurant, and there are tables for serious dining in the back. They've provided some benches with cushions for those who find the wooden fixtures uncomfortable. Arizona 206 is noisy and slightly disorganized—the help gets a bit frantic—but don't let that discourage you. Specialty items include barbecued foie gras with black pepper brioche, sautéed sweetwater prawns, and Black Angus fillet. Lighter dishes are offered at the adjoining cafe.

ARQUA
281 Church St 334-1888
Lunch: Mon-Fri; Dinner: Mon-Sat
Moderate

There are Italian restaurants of every size, price range, and specialty in almost every neighborhood of Manhattan. I sometimes wonder if there aren't more Italian restaurants in Manhattan than in all of Italy. So, to be outstanding in New York, an Italian restaurant must have something special going for it. Arqua is really special because the staff does things so plainly and simply. This is not a fancy, pricey restaurant of the moment. Arqua (named for a small city near Venice) is situated in an old warehouse with high ceilings, which adds to the noisy atmosphere. The folks who run this place are not fancy, either. It shows in the TLC they give all the patrons, and the food is exceptional. You can have your choice of any kind of pasta, marinated salmon, and ravioli with butternut squash. Squab and duck are specialties. There are also a number of excellent veal dishes. The flourless espresso chocolate cake is so good that I took some home to the bakers at my cake shop in Oregon.

ARTIE'S WAREHOUSE RESTAURANT
539 W 21st St 989-9500
Dinner: Tues-Sun; Brunch: Sun
Moderate

Some folks have told me that they are interested in really out-of-the-way places. Well, this one surely falls into that category. Artie's Warehouse Restaurant is located in a warehouse district, and it's actually part of a working warehouse. For a friendly greeting, prompt and efficient service, and good food at reasonable prices, I haven't found too many that beat it. And it certainly is different! Artie himself is a frustrated piano player, who entertains and tablehops. And he keeps a steady eye on the help; they're right on the job, providing informed, courteous service. Be sure to save room for the great homemade desserts. What an offering! Chocolate or orange cheesecake, chocolate mud cake, lemon mousse, chocolate mousse, pecan pie, and even marzipan-apricot cake. What a spot for relaxing and enjoying a leisurely dinner, topped off with such exotic drinks as amaretto coffee, an Irish Float, a Tipsy Monk, or an Angel Cloud. You'll have to go there to find out exactly what they are! There are a dozen different coffees on the menu. Dinner in a warehouse? Sure, but you don't have to wear your overalls.

AU CAFE DE BRUXELLES
118 Greenwich Ave   206-1830
Lunch: Tues-Sat; Dinner: Daily; Brunch: Sun
Moderate

One of the treats at a county fair is the Belgian waffles booth. There always seems to be a queue at that concession, and for good reason. In New York, you don't have to go to the county fair. Just make your way to the Village, where Thierry, the chef, and his wife, Patricia, set an informal table brimming with specialties from Belgium. The waffles are served with whipped cream and chocolate and strawberry sauce; they are a meal in themselves. But here I go talking about desserts before we've even started our meal. Hot chicken-liver custard in port wine sauce, homemade country pâté, and stuffed mussels with garlic (yes, heavy on the garlic) are some of the house hors d'oeuvres. Entree choices range from medallions of monkfish to dark Belgian beer stew, a house specialty, to several steak dishes. On certain nights, Belgian dishes like chicken waterzooi, Bruxelle bouillabaisse, and a very tasty choucroute (sauerkraut) dish are offered. They're also available anytime, if you give them adequate notice. But back to those desserts. If you don't try the waffles, at least sink your teeth into the tasty apple or apricot tarts made in Thierry's own kitchen.

AU TROQUET
328 W 12th St   924-3413
Dinner: Daily
Moderate

This is one of those difficult-to-find places in the Village. If you're arriving by taxi, allow extra time since most drivers will have trouble delivering you to the front door. And be sure you call for reservations; the place is small, and it is very popular with neighbors as well as knowledgeable people who have previously enjoyed Au Troquet's dining delights. This is a no-nonsense French country restaurant, where professional people prepare food professionally. Your plate looks like a colorful magazine ad—flamboyant in presentation—and it's especially good in the taste category. Au Troquet deserves special mention for its seasonings alone; they know how it's done. The soups are all delicious, as is the pâté de foie de canard. You can go on to filet of sole, grilled salmon, lobster, or a fabulous rabbit dish. There is almost always a fine selection of lamb dishes available. Homemade desserts include a great mousse and sorbets. This is the kind of place you want to go to when you feel like having a relaxed, cozy dinner for two. It will surely help cement that business relationship—or maybe even a more personal one!

AZZURRO

1625 Second Ave (at 84th St)   517-7068
Dinner: Daily
Moderate

I'd give this place an A-plus for their polite and well-informed help. What a joy it is to find a restaurant that has no affectations, no unnecessary waiting, and no maitre d' with permanently outstretched palm. Instead, you find really nice folks who want to make your dining experience a pleasant one. Azzurro is a tiny hole-in-the-wall with a dozen-plus tables, a tile floor, and a wholesome, informal atmosphere. Neither the waiters nor the customers are dressed up, but the food is! An absolutely marvelous fresh minestrone soup is great to start with, as is the mixed eggplant, Sicilian style. The linguini with tuna fish and the maccaruna chi sarde (bucatini with fresh sardines, raisins, pinoli nuts, and wild fennel) are outstanding. For heartier appetites, there are grilled items every day. The boys in the kitchen are evidently as talented as the ones out front. You'll have a great time and a great meal. Be sure to call for reservations; they are very busy.

BARBETTA

321 W 46th St (bet Eighth and Ninth Ave)   246-9171
Lunch, Dinner: Mon-Sat
Moderate to expensive

This is an elegant restaurant with Piemontese cuisine; Piemonte is located in the northern part of Italy, and the cuisine reflects that charming part of the country. You can dine here in European elegance. It is one of New York's oldest restaurants still owned by the family that founded it, and the family has been here for nearly eight decades. One of the special attractions about Barbetta is dining alfresco in the garden during the summer. There is an à la carte luncheon menu, as well as a before-theater dinner menu, which offers a fish specialty, baby salmon, and a number of other selections served expeditiously so that you can make the opening curtain. If you have more time and can enjoy a leisurely dinner, think about the minestrone soup, which is almost a meal in itself, ravioli that is made by hand, or the fabulous mushroom salad. Barbetta specializes in fish and game dishes that vary daily. If you're lucky enough to find squab on the menu, by all means try it. Other selections include veal kidneys, beef braised in red wine with polenta, or a delicious sirloin of beef. Desserts include several chocolate offerings and an assortment of cooked fruits, as well as one of the best crème caramels in the city. To be in business in the highly competitive restaurant field for such a long time, Barbetta's has to be doing something right—and they are.

BAROLO

398 W Broadway (bet Spring and Broome St)
226-1102
Lunch, Dinner: Daily
Moderate

This SoHo establishment must serve a lot of meals to keep its two inside rooms and adjoining garden busy! Featuring an Italian Piemontese menu, the kitchen is doing its share to accomplish that, but the front of the house has a long way to go. The menu is almost as big as the facility, with a large selection of soups, seafood appetizers, antipasti, pastas, and meat and fish entrees. Specialties like the Piemontese tagliolini and risotto or braised beef with Barolo wine sauce make for an exciting meal. But the service is confused and uninformed; maybe they should send the young, unseasoned staff back to Italy for a little schooling. But never mind if you are hungry. The end product is absolutely delicious, and a summer evening in the garden is magic—even if the ladies have a hard time navigating in the soft rocks. Eat up on your early courses, because the desserts are nothing special. Even the traditional Piemontese chocolate cake, *bonet,* is a disappointment.

BELLA DONNA

307 E 77th St (bet First and Second Ave)   535-2866
Lunch: Mon-Fri; Dinner: Daily; Brunch: Sat, Sun
Inexpensive

If every one of the 30 or so diners who crowd into this tiny Upper East Side trattoria were to order a different dish, there would still be a number to spare! The menu is more than complete, with a vast selection of salads, pastas, and pizzas (plus a number of specials each day). It is strictly "plain Jane" dining, with your next-door dining neighbors almost on top of you, but never mind. The portions are more than adequate, the quality excellent, and the prices unbelievably modest. No wonder there is a line outside most of the time, even in harsh weather. Homemade cakes, tarts, and tirami sú will finish a great meal. Free delivery service is offered.

BILLY'S

948 First Ave   355-8920, 753-1870
Lunch, Dinner: Daily
Moderate

If you like old-fashioned setups, complete with white tiled floors, checkered tablecloths, and a busy bar right in the center of the dining area, then Billy's is your kind of place. Established in 1870, this bustling pub-restaurant is a First Avenue institution, where the food is just as inviting as the atmosphere. It's been in the same family since opening day! No menus, just a blackboard listing steaks, scallops, chops, hamburgers, and the like. All are well prepared, with large portions accompanied by fair French fries or non-foil-wrapped baked potatoes. Cole slaw is served when you are seated. Oh, yes. The waiters are vintage New York. For example, when a party of four arrives, they'll ask, "Do you wish to sit together?" But they are efficient, pleasant guys. A word about the bread. The ethnic mix of the Big Apple makes for exceptional talent in baking, and you can take advantage of these fine breads at many restaurants like Billy's. Desserts include delicious ice cream, cheesecake, pies, and homemade rice pudding. Try the Irish coffee with real whipped cream to top it all off.

BISTRO-BORDEAUX
407 Eighth Ave   594-6305
Lunch: Mon-Fri; Dinner: Mon-Sat
Moderate

It's not easy to find a pleasant, reliable spot to eat in the Madison Square Garden area, but Bistro-Bordeaux, a delightful French restaurant, is a very satisfactory place for either a pre-Garden or after-Garden meal. Alan and Georges, who have had lots of experience in various New York restaurants, have put together an unpretentious, homey bistro with tasty and well-prepared food at reasonable prices. I was struck by how eager they and their staff are to provide for their guests. If there are any complaints, it's that the portions are too big. This is one place from which you can be sure you won't go away hungry. Escargots, pâté, smoked salmon—all are available for starters, along with fresh artichokes and fresh asparagus, if in season. The filet mignon is done to perfection, the grilled sole and grilled chicken are both delicious, and the escalope de veau is really special. The vegetables have a home-cooked flavor. Desserts seem a bit expensive compared to the rest of the dinner, but they're good. Of all the desserts (and there are nearly a dozen), the crème caramel is the best. Instead of wasting your money on junk-food places in and around Madison Square Garden, I suggest this bistro as a handy, satisfying alternative.

BOATHOUSE CAFE
Central Park   517-CAFE
Lunch, Dinner: Daily (May 1 - Nov 1)
Moderate

Central Park has come back to life, and the Boathouse Cafe is one of its best attractions. It's situated in a charming spot on the east side of the park, between the 72nd Street and 79th Street entrances; a free trolley brings patrons from the 72nd Street and Fifth

Avenue park entrance. The dockside has been partially tented, and authentic Venetian gondolas are available (by reservation) for rent, as are rowboats. The view is great, the setting couldn't be more romantic, and the food is tasty and well presented. The menu is Northern Italian, with a variety of pasta. There is a great private party area located in a landscaped English garden. What a spot to launch your hot new product!

BOULEY
165 Duane St   608-3852
Lunch: Mon-Fri; Dinner: Mon-Sat
Moderately expensive

One of the more exciting evenings I've spent in New York was with Bryan Miller (restaurant critic of the *New York Times*) the evening before his review was published giving Bouley four stars. Had he realized what this was going to mean to his restaurant, David Bouley would not have been able to function in his usual manner. The accolade was well deserved; this is a superb restaurant, romantic, delicious, professional. It is so romantic that I like to tell the story about a young lady who rushed into a New York store to get the latest edition of this book. She announced to the clerk that her boyfriend was going to propose very soon, and she wanted the most romantic place for the big event. She wanted my input. If I had spoken to her personally, I would have pointed her to 165 Duane Street! David, a most talented chef (who, by the way, has strong Oregon ties), has created a spacious and charming establishment. There are wonderful decorative touches, like the marvelously ornate doors and the beautiful Limoge china. Absolutely wonderful bread is served warm and fresh. Every item on the menu is served to perfection. And what a selection of desserts! The soufflés are a specialty, and so is the chocolate ganache terrine. You have to experience an evening here to be assured that there still are some true geniuses in the food business. David is one of them.

BRAVO GIANNI
230 E 63rd St   752-7272
Lunch: Mon-Fri; Dinner: Mon-Sat
Moderately expensive

Fans of Bravo Gianni—and there are many—may be upset that I'm mentioning it in this book. They want to keep it a secret. It's so nice and comfortable and the food is so good that they don't want it to become overcrowded and spoiled. But it doesn't look like there's any real danger of that happening, as long as Gianni himself is on the job. The room—not too large—is pleasantly appointed, with beautiful plants on every table; the intimate atmosphere makes it seem as though you're in your own private dining room. And what tastes await you there! You can't go wrong with any of the antipasto selections or soups. But do save room for the tortellini alla panna or the fettuccine con ricotta; no one does them better. I can recommend every dish on the menu, with top billing going to the fish dishes and the rack of lamb. Marvelous desserts, many of them made in-house, will surely tempt you. Legions of loyal customers come back again and again; it's easy to see why. But please, keep all of this to yourself!

BUCKAROO'S
1431 First Ave (at 74th St)   861-8844
Dinner: Daily; Brunch: Sun
Inexpensive

Upper East Siders need go no farther than 74th and First Avenue to find an informal, fun spot that is right in keeping with the trend toward good food at realistic prices. Buckaroo's has it all: pool in the back, a busy bar, comfortable tables inside and outside, and a menu that will appeal to the kids as well as their parents. Chicken dishes are a specialty; spit-roasted half chicken, marinated chicken skewers, hot and spicy chicken wings, grilled honey-mustard chicken breast, and the grilled chicken breast sourdough sandwich are all delicious. If you want something else, there are pastas, grilled salmon, and one of the best hamburger sandwiches in town. The Sunday brunch menu includes egg and omelette dishes. Wonderful homemade desserts (also at a reasonable tab) like triple chocolate-chip chocolate cake or hot apple brown betty with fresh whip cream will make you sit more comfortably in the saddle!

BUKHARA
148 E 48th St   838-1811
Lunch, Dinner: Daily
Moderate

Whether it is Seekh Kabob (minced lamb), Barah Kabob (lamb marinated in yogurt), or Kadak Reshmi Kabob (rolls of minced chicken with cashews), Bukhara does it up with style. With a background of Indian spice aroma, native music, and serving pieces with an authentic touch, you are put in the mood to enjoy delicious Indian dishes from the time you enter. The Indian Haute Cuisine includes a dozen entrees—not only the Kabobs but also marinated jumbo prawns, marinated leg of lamb, and marinated beef tenderloin. A special treat is a dish of whole trout spiced with yellow chilies, cooked in the clay oven. For the vegetarian diner, there are cottage-cheese kabobs, cauliflower seasoned with spices and glazed in the clay oven, and stuffed bell peppers roasted in the tandoor. And what a great selection of Indian breads; try the Bukhara bread basket, which includes an assortment. I'd skip the desserts and head for an ice-cream parlor to cool down the insides of a hot, but satisfied, mouth and tummy!

CABANA CARIOCA II
133 W 45th St (bet Sixth Ave and Broadway)
730-8375
Lunch, Dinner: Tues - Sat
Moderate

There are two Cabana Cariocas, located just several doors from each other. Make sure you go to the one at 133 West 45th Street, not the branch at 123 West 45th Street. The latter is unattractive, smelly, and generally unappetizing, while the former features the best Brazilian and Portuguese cuisine in the city. The atmosphere is homey, the waiters eager to explain their native dishes, and the portions huge. Wonderful homemade chicken soup, fried Portuguese sausage, or a Portuguese omelet will get you off to a good start. *Feijoada completa,* the Brazilian national dish, is a house favorite. Besides a large selection of seafood, steak, pork, veal, chicken, and liver dishes, there are several different specials every day. Of course, the black beans are a must, and they are delicious. The Cabana is a handy, sensibly priced place for lunch in midtown.

CAFE
210 Spring St (at Sixth Ave)   274-0505
Lunch, Dinner: Daily; Brunch: Sat, Sun
Moderate

The name and the decor may be simple, but the food is stylish, satisfying, and special. Lunch features salads and sandwiches with a distinctive French flavor, homemade pastas, coq au vin, and steak, salmon, and tuna from the grill. In the evening, try "Napoleon aux legumes" (vegetables, polenta, spinach, and roasted pepper with lentil sauce). The great warrior never had it so good! Or try Maine lobster with avocado, grapefruit, beets, and champagne vinaigrette. Roast rack of lamb, sautéed breast of duck, braised brass, and sautéed sweetbreads are other favorites. Finish your visit to France with a dish of the best crême brûlée you have ever tasted. When someone asks you if you have tried "the Cafe," make sure you ask them which one they mean. This one is the place with the easy name and the easy prices.

CAFE DES ARTISTES
1 W 67th St   TR7-3500
Lunch: Mon-Fri; Dinner: Daily; Brunch: Sat, Sun
Moderate

With Cafe Des Artistes, owner George Lang created an absolute masterpiece on the West Side, just off Central Park. It's truly a landmark. There are several different dining levels and some hidden tables, giving each diner the impression of being in a small, cozy establishment. Beautiful murals by Christy complement the charming décor, the personnel are wonderfully accommodating, and the food is absolutely delicious. Try the unusual Sunday brunch. Some of the mouth-watering selections include smoked salmon benedict, asparagus omelet, spicy Virginia crab cakes, and delicious stuffed French toast. Dinner appetizers include dill-marinated fish, duck or chicken liver, and a number of seafood items, like oysters, clams, and snails. For the main course, there is sea bass; grilled Coho salmon; broiled veal chops; pork, lamb, and beef dishes; and a pasta. By all means, don't overlook the desserts: such dandies as key lime pie, toasted almond cake, chestnut cream torte, and a great dessert platter that features a sample of each. This is a lovely, romantic place at any time, but I especially recommend it for an after-theater supper.

CAFE DES SPORTS
329 W 51st St   581-1283, 974-9052
Lunch: Mon-Fri; Dinner: Daily
Inexpensive

This is a cozy spot, with an intensely loyal following developed over many years of serving good, wholesome food in generous amounts at a reasonable price. The selections change daily, depending on what is available from the marketplaces. I have found the homemade sausage and the London broil to be exceptionally good values. Blue jeans and your most comfortable house dress are perfectly acceptable here. You'll smile along with the hospitable personnel, especially when they hand you a very realistic tab for a most satisfying meal.

CAFE EUROPA and LA BRIOCHE
347 E 54th St   755-0160
Lunch: Mon-Fri; Dinner: Mon-Sat
Moderate

A charming cafe. It gives you the feeling that you're walking in from the streets of Paris or Munich. I recommend it for either lunch or dinner. For lunch, you might be interested in the imperial sandwich (steak tartare with caviar, icy vodka, and beer), but my choice is the chicken brioche with fresh tarragon, celery, carrots, and mushrooms. It's a hefty portion and just right for a delightful lunch. The brioche offerings change from time to time, variously featuring curried beef, veal marengo, or shrimp and mushroom. The dinner menu is also varied, with entree selections ranging from chicken breast to beef stroganoff. There is a large selection of desserts, from chocolate mousse to lemon Bavarian cream or bananas with rum. Another dessert alternative is the French, English, or Italian cheese selection, served with fruit or nuts. There is an interesting combination of European and Oriental personnel in the kitchen and out front. It all adds up to a most pleasant dining experience.

CAFE UN DEUX TROIS
123 W 44th St   354-4148
Lunch: Mon-Fri; Dinner: Daily; Brunch: Sat, Sun
Moderate

Paper tablecloths and napkins may seem like a stingy way to dress a restaurant table, but at this bustling cafe, there's a reason. Two reasons, in fact. One is that it helps keep the tab down. The other is to provide drawing paper; crayons are furnished on every table. Doodling helps pass the time, and isn't it something you've always wanted to do since you were a kid? The surroundings (an old hotel lobby) are plain, but the location is handy if you're going to the theater. Service is very prompt and friendly, and prices are moderate. Though the menu is limited, each item is handled with obvious attention to quality and taste. Begin with a hearty onion soup, salade nicoise, or pâté de canard. Seafood en papillote is an excellent selection. This spot is popular with big names in the recording industry and young people. Maybe aspiring singers will be able to make the deal of their lives over a cup of cappuccino.

CAFFE DANTE
81 MacDougal St   982-5275
Inexpensive

If you are in the mood for a light lunch or supper, Mario Flotta will take good care of you at this busy, popular cafe, one of the oldest in the city. The simple menu features delicious, light Italian-style sandwiches, cold platters, and salads. The real treats are the fabulous Italian cake specialties, like Sacher Sant Ambroeus, ambrosia cake, zabaglione cake, and tirami sú. There are also dozens of Italian pastry items, and the homemade rum cake with gelati is heaven-sent. Speaking of gelati, no one does it better. They make their own, and the fresh fruit gelati is sensational. Of course, no session would be complete without espresso or cappuccino. You can have it any way you want, from Caffe Fantasia, an exotic combination of orange and chocolate and whipped cream, to Cappuccino Dante, a cinnamon and cocoa concoction. Through it all, Dante Aligheri, framed on the wall, is looking down upon you.

CAMEOS
169 Columbus Ave   874-2280
Lunch: Mon-Fri; Dinner: Daily; Brunch: Sat, Sun
Moderate to moderately expensive

Trendy restaurants come and go by the week on the Upper West Side, so it is important to know of a few that have been around for awhile, because they do things right consistently. Cameos is one of those places. It's good you'll have to use up a few calories climbing the stairs to this art deco room overlooking busy Columbus Avenue. You'll need to make extra room for the goodies you will find on the interesting and complete menu. Seafood lovers will feel right at home; a wide variety of fresh fish is available. Service is pleasant and professional, with jazz-piano music to accompany your meal. With the trend for more moderately priced meals taking hold, Cameos is bucking the tide. Better watch those dollar signs, my friends!

CANTON
45 Division St   226-4441, 226-0921
Lunch, Dinner: Wed-Sun
No credit cards
Moderate

For those in the know, Canton has been a favorite spot for some time. Why? The place is clean, and the personnel are friendly and very polite. But most of all, unlike so many Chinese restaurants, the cooking is done on an individual basis. It's almost like stepping into the kitchen of a Chinese family. Visit with the waiter and tell him the kind of Cantonese delicacies you wish to have. You will be delighted with the results! I would suggest the butterfly shrimp, the diced chicken with Chinese vegetables and mushrooms, or the fried young squab, Chinese style. All the seafood is fresh and tasty. So, gather up a group of friends for a special Chinese treat. You'll be pleased with the quality of your food *and* the moderate bill.

CARMINE'S
2450 Broadway (bet 90th and 91st St)   EN 2-2200
Dinner: Daily
American Express
Moderate

The first thing you want to do is round up at least six of your heavy-eating friends, call Carmine's for reservations, don't eat any lunch, and show up in loose clothing and famished. You won't be disappointed! Carmine presents Southern Italian family dining fare, with huge (and I mean *huge*) portions and the zesty seasonings that go along with the territory. Not only are the platters full, they are delicious. All of this, on top of a full house and reasonable prices, makes this one of the Upper West Side's real attractions. If you go with fewer than a half-dozen friends, my advice is to go early —the wait can be as long as an hour, as they will not reserve tables for smaller parties. The menu runs the gamut of pastas, chicken, veal, seafood, and some very tasty Italian appetizers. Oh, yes, there is no printed menu. Wall signs explain the offerings; take along your glasses if you really want to study the choices.

CARNEGIE DELICATESSEN AND RESTAURANT
854 Seventh Ave (at 55th St)   757-2245
Breakfast, Lunch, Dinner: Daily (6:40 a.m.-4 a.m.)
No credit cards
Moderate

There's no city on earth with delis like New York's, and the Carnegie is one of the best. Its location in the middle of the hotel district makes it perfect for midnight snacks. Everything is made on the premises, and Carnegie offers free delivery at any time between 7 a.m. and 3 a.m., if you're within a five-block radius. Where to start? Your favorite Jewish mother didn't make chicken soup better than the Carnegie's homemade variety. It's practically worth getting sick for! It comes with matzo balls, garden noodles, and fresh rice, fresh homemade kreplach, or real homemade kasha. And there's more: Great blintzes. Open sandwiches, hot and delicious. Ten different deli and egg sandwiches. A very juicy burger with all the trimmings. Lots of fish dishes, and corned beef and pastrami. A choice of egg dishes unequaled in New York. Salads. Side orders of everything from hot baked potatoes to potato pancakes. Outrageous cheesecake topped with strawberries, blueberries, pineapple, cherries, or just served plain. Desserts from A to Z —even Jell-O.

CHANTERELLE
2 Harrison St (at Hudson St)   966-6960
Lunch, Dinner: Tues-Sat
Expensive

It was only a matter of time before Karen and David Waltuck would have to move from their tiny SoHo restaurant on Grand Street. The place simply wasn't big enough to handle the legion of loyal customers who feel that Chanterelle is one of the better restaurants in New York. Well, the Waltucks moved to a space with a larger dining room (seats about 60), a bigger kitchen, and a cute after-dinner area. The setting is formal and attractive, with interesting high stamped-tin ceilings in the historic Mercantile Exchange Building in TriBeCa. The menu changes periodically, but that really isn't important since every dish is a masterful creation. With David in the kitchen, making good use of his marine biology background and preparing great fish and lobster dishes, and Karen out front pampering her guests, it is a good bet you won't even notice the size of the tab for the *prix fixe* dinner or the tasting menu.

CHELSEA CENTRAL
227 Tenth Ave 620-0230
Lunch: Mon-Fri; Dinner: Daily
Moderate

You're in for a real surprise at Chelsea Central. The tile floor, unimposing atmosphere, and paper tablecloths belie an establishment that turns out some of the best and most sophisticated food in Chelsea. Before you order a meal, be sure to receive a reading of the many specials offered by the well-trained and highly efficient staff. Butternut squash ravioli, grilled wild mushrooms, and backfin crab cakes are all delicious starters. Portions are very large. Great entrees include roast loin of pork, grilled Norwegian salmon, confit of duck or angel-hair pasta. The dessert presentations are a feast for the eye as well as the stomach; they look like they came from an artist's pallette, and all are made in-house.

CHELSEA PLACE
147 Eighth Ave (bet 17th and 18th St) 924-8413
Lunch: Mon-Fri; Dinner: Daily
Moderate

Chelsea Place is different—very different. I think the exact word is *eclectic*. You won't be impressed by the neighborhood or the rather disheveled antiques shop through which you enter. A door at the rear of the shop takes you into a noisy, crowded, smoke-filled bar, where the biggest challenge is elbowing through without Gertrude spilling her tray of drinks on you, or getting tangled up with the neighborhood's answer to Ginger Rogers and Fred Astaire as they wheel around the tiny dance floor. Down some stairs and through another room, you enter what looks like a maiden aunt's room, circa 1929: hanging plants, a strange collection of pictures, mismatched chairs, water fountains, ceiling fans—you name it, it's here. But you don't come to Chelsea Place for the décor; you come for the Italian food. And it's excellent. The menu includes traditional fare: baked manicotti, scampi alla Romana, and scaloppini francese. But don't look at the menu. Instead, listen to your waiter recite the list of daily specials, which include fish, poultry, and meat served with first-class vegetables. I recommend this eatery as a very unusual dining experience. It may look like it has been put together by the Marx Brothers, but the culinary satisfaction is strictly first-rate.

CHELSEA TRATTORIA ITALIANA
108 Eighth Ave 924-7786
Lunch: Mon-Fri; Dinner: Mon-Sat
Moderate

The Bitici brothers, the owners of the Chelsea Trattoria, are hard-working Italian boys who know how to make a restaurant tick, and the brother who personally takes care of it is a jewel. Working in the kitchen and out front, he runs a good show. The restaurant, complete with a tile floor and brick walls decked out with wine bottles, looks like the local trattoria in an Italian village. The whole place is friendly, unimposing, and bustling; it's definitely not a trendy, pricey Italian novelty. You come here for good, hearty Italian food, beautifully presented by professional waiters who haven't just graduated from high school. The menu runs the gamut from great soups and pasta to veal scaloppini, boneless breast of chicken sautéed in white wine, sausage, mushrooms, and garlic, bay scallops, scampi, and many daily specials. The dessert cart is gorgeous; you can't help bumping into it on your way in. It's loaded with goodies made in-house, including an incredible white and dark chocolate cake. Chelsea is sprouting many excellent eating spots, and this is one of the best. The folks here couldn't be more accommodating; they will even do their best for the drop-in diner. But I strongly suggest you make early reservations.

CHEZ JACQUELINE
72 MacDougal St   505-0727
Dinner: Daily
Moderate

If you dislike the frantic, one-upmanship dining so prevalent these days in Manhattan, then try this modest French bistro in the Village. The atmosphere is very relaxed. You can see cozy couples eating at the bar, or serene seniors holding hands at one of the small number of tables in this popular neighborhood restaurant. Fresh, large salads are a specialty, as well as country pâté, duck liver mousse, and mussels with garlic. Among the dozen items regularly available as entrees, house favorites are the broiled rack of lamb, chicken casserole, veal kidneys, veal sweetbreads, and a hearty beef stew in a red wine, tomato, and carrot sauce. The portions are very generous, and the young lovers like the fair prices. If you can manage a dessert, the crème brûlée or the white and dark chocolate mousse cake will convince you that the kitchen sure knows what it's doing.

CHEZ JOSEPHINE
414 W 42nd St   594-1925
Dinner: Mon-Sat
Moderate

Those who follow the entertainment business will remember the late Josephine Baker, who was the toast of Paris in the first quarter of this century. Well, one of her adopted children, Jean Claude, has kept the show-biz interest and added the food business to his accomplishments. He has created a first-class atmosphere, with sexy and attractive décor and delicious food to match. Chez Josephine is a haven for those who have made it, and those who wish they had—it is dining with theatrics, plus. This is a great place for a late-night, after-theater rendezvous. If Jean Claude settled down for a minute, you would find him fascinating company. The menu has French tones; however, it is really in the dessert category that the place shines. The warm apple and rhubarb cake is very special, as is the bombe pralinee. A private party room is available upstairs. The bistro is a charmer, and so is Jean Claude!

CHEZ MA TANTE
189 W 10th St   620-0223
Dinner: Daily; Brunch: Sun
Moderate

This Village cafe is small and unassuming, and you've probably never heard of it. Its main claim to fame is that it's next door to La Metairie, one of the Village's better known (and most expensive) dining spots. The difference between the two restaurants is in the price. Chez Ma Tante does an excellent job at a very reasonable tab. Friendly and cozy in the winter, this bistro opens onto the side-walk in summer. Two partners do the duties out front and in the kitchen, and they obviously do a consistently good job, since the place is filled with regular patrons. Hors d'oeuvres include duck liver pâté, fresh fish terrine on a bed of dill sauce, and a different pasta each day. Outstanding entrees are casserole of jumbo shrimp, "French's favorite dish" (steak, French fries, and green salad), and grilled Norwegian salmon in a cucumber sauce. Grilled swordfish is also a specialty of the house. The profiteroles topped with white and dark chocolate sauce (and served hot) is a delicious variation on this popular dish. As a matter of fact, all the desserts rate special mention: warm, fresh apple tarts, chocolate mousse torte, and raspberry or pecan sorbet. The partners' aunt must have been par-ticularly talented in the kitchen, and fortunately for us, they've in-vited us to have dinner with her in the Village.

CHEZ NAPOLEON
365 W 50th St   265-6980
Lunch: Mon-Fri; Dinner: Mon-Sat
Inexpensive to moderate

With all the problems of daily life, it's fun to go to a place where the atmosphere is cheerful. Chez Napoleon is that kind of place. The lady who owns it greets you like a long lost friend and seats you in a small, clean dining area. It's an old house—warm and cozy and obviously a neighborhood favorite for many years. The cooking is dependable and hearty. My top recommendations from the large menu are coquille St. Jacques, bouillabaisse (only served on weekends), rabbit with mustard sauce, and sweetbreads. Many of the desserts are homemade. But the big plus here is the freshness of the dishes and the gracious feeling of "We're glad to have you."

CHIN CHIN
216 E 49th St (bet Second and Third Ave)   888-4555
Lunch: Mon-Fri; Dinner: Daily
Moderate to moderately expensive

This is a very classy Chinese restaurant, and the ambiance and price reflect the superior style of Chinese cooking. There are two rooms, including a garden in back. The soups and barbecued spareribs are wonderful for starters. The Szechuan jumbo prawns are sensational. As a matter of fact, I'd concentrate on the seafood dishes; some of the other presentations are a bit bland. You might try the wonderful Peking duck dinner with your choice of soup, crispy duck skin with pancakes, fried rice, poached spinach, and homemade sorbet or ice cream. The menu is much the same for lunch or dinner. This is an excellent choice for a business lunch with a client who has a hankering for improving East-West relations.

CLAIRE
156 Seventh Ave (at 19th St)   255-1955
Lunch: Mon-Fri; Brunch: Sat-Sun; Dinner: Mon-Sun
Moderate

Key West may be a long way from Chelsea, but the owner of this bustling seafood emporium decided he wanted to make that move. Neighborhood regulars are glad he did! Don't come here unless you are in the mood for fish, although burgers and steaks are also on the menu. Appetizers include gravlax (fresh cured salmon), mussels, oysters, smoked trout, and fresh tuna. Hungry diners will enjoy the Fisherman's Harvest, which includes shrimp, mussels, scallops, and red snapper. Other entrees usually available are broiled fillet of flounder, tilefish, grouper, monkfish, or salmon. If you are a crawfish lover (like your author), the bayou crawfish patties are outstanding. Many other Southern-style fish dishes are featured as specials. The establishment has a professional air, with prompt and efficient service. As you might expect, key lime pie and Mississippi mud cake head up the dessert menu.

COACH HOUSE
110 Waverly Pl   777-0303, 777-0349
Dinner: Tues-Sun
Expensive

Don't believe all you read! For some perverse reason, when something is highly successful, there is always a chorus of detractors who want to shoot it down. For years the Coach House has been a popular and distinguished room in Manhattan. The quality of the food and service under the ever-watchful eye of the talented owner, Leon Lianides, was always top-notch, but some reviewers took shots at this Village institution. It was very unfair, in my opinion. I have dined here dozens of times, and each experience has been pleasant, satisfying, and a treat for my guests. Yes, there is a dress requirement—men must wear a coat and tie—but what's wrong with that? Believe me, though, you'll have to loosen that tie after a meal of black bean soup, rack of lamb, and a piece of famous flourless chocolate cake. I can think of few more attractive places to spend an evening, savoring a truly first-class dining experience.

COASTAL
300 Amsterdam Ave (at 74th St)   769-3988
Dinner: Daily; Brunch: Sun
Moderate

Like a number of establishments, Coastal has gone through an early-life crisis. At the start, it was a noisy, very "in" place where the circus atmosphere was secondary to the food. Well, that does not last long in today's environment. Coastal has now settled down to what it should be—an excellent neighborhood seafood house. Soundproofed ceiling tiles have been added, and the waiters now act like normal human beings. Coastal does well with their sauces. The cioppino conjures up images of Fisherman's Wharf in San Francisco: a great stew with jumbo shrimp, scallops, mussels, clams, and assorted fish served with buttered pasta. Fresh American regional pastas are offered every day. An extensive gourmet home-delivery menu is available. And in keeping with the times, a Coastal Cafe has opened at 1359 First Avenue (73rd St) with an eye to moderate prices.

COCONUT GRILL
1481 Second Ave (at 77th St)   772-6262
Lunch, Dinner: Daily; Brunch: Sun
Moderate

A lighthearted staff will serve you a delicious light meal in a light, pleasant atmosphere at this popular Upper East Side cafe. There are several different dining spaces, including an airy, glass-enclosed room that looks out on Second Avenue. A huge bar in the center of the cafe is teaming with girl talk and business chat from dusk to the wee hours, and the outside tables are a delight in nice weather. The menu at lunchtime ranges from fettucine to your choice of several salads to sandwiches or cold salmon. The shrimp salad with avocado and artichokes is a treat. For Sunday brunch, the usual fare is available, but the cinnamon-raisin-bread French toast is worthy of special mention, as are the delicious waffles served with your choice of apples and cinnamon, blueberries, strawberries, or maple syrup. At night you can feast upon Cajun fried chicken or steamed, seaweed-wrapped mahi-mahi, among other delights. Be sure to ask for the house chutney of tomato, mango, and cilantro, an unusual taste treat. Top all of this off with a French vanilla cheesecake in a raspberry sauce.

COCO PAZZO
23 E 74th St (just off Madison Ave)   794-0205
Breakfast, Lunch, Dinner: Daily
Moderate

Now this one is different! The owners of the very successful Le Madri have created an unusual operation in what once was Adams Rib and then Metro. This time it looks like a real winner will grace the room. They call the chef crazy, but I would call him talented. Starting at dawn, a great breakfast is offered at reasonable prices. It's European, American, Italian—and it's good. Wonderful home-made breads and preserves, eggs and pancakes, homemade waffles, Italian omelettes, and much more. Then on to lunch and dinner, with a decidedly Tuscan flavor. Some evenings the servings are à la carte, other times the Italian tradition of family-style dining takes over. And what dishes! The Tuscan bread soup is so delicious and filling it is worth a visit in itself. Then there is risotto or spaghetti with clams, mussels, scallops, and shrimp, all done in white wine and herbs. Fantastic. Other winners include lasagne (the real kind), grilled and roasted meats, spicy seafood stew, and roasted game birds. Save room for the pistaschio ice cream laced with chocolate sauce. If you have a party of three or four, the tab becomes even more reasonable for the amount of food offered.

COLORS
237 Park Ave (bet Park and Lexington Ave. at 46th St)
661-2000
Lunch, Dinner: Mon-Fri
Moderate

Note the address carefully; do not try to reach this place from the Park Avenue side, or you will have some difficulty! Colors is a sleeper. This is a great spot for a reasonably priced buffet (hot and cold) lunch served in the atrium cafe. Of course, you can also order your Italian specialties from the menu: seafood, chicken, veal, steaks, and all the rest. The antipasto and pasta selections are uniformly delicious, the service is extremely fast, and the personnel seem overjoyed you found the place! A nice touch: a dish of goat cheese is placed on your table at the start to get the juices flowing. All desserts, including the top-notch cheesecakes, are made in-house.

CONTRAPUNTO
1009 Third Ave (at 60th St)   751-8616
Lunch, Dinner: Daily
Moderate

The thing that struck me first about Contrapunto was the airiness and lightness of the dining room. It's located on the second floor of a busy corner building across the street from Bloomingdale's, with full-length windows allowing a view of the activity on Third Avenue. It's a delightful place for a delicious and different Italian lunch. For appetizers, you might have a salad Di Casa (seasonal greens with Tuscan olive oil) or Pinzimonio Caprese (tomatoes, sweet peppers, fresh fennel, and mozzarella with Tuscan olive oil). The pastas are unique! All the portions are a good size, and you will be impressed with the quality. If there is one drawback, it's that service is very slow; don't come here if you have an appointment within the hour. This place advertises itself as a pasta, wine, and gelati house, and it is just that. Be sure to save room for dessert; the chocolate cake is absolutely sinful. I also recommend that you try the chocolate, praline, or strawberry gelati.

CUCINA STAGIONALE
275 Bleecker St   924-2707
Lunch, Dinner: Daily
No credit cards
Inexpensive

When you serve good food at a small price, the word gets around. So it's no wonder there's a line in front of this small Village cafe almost any time of the day. Its name translates as "seasonal kitchen," and the seasonal specialties are real values, indeed. It's a bare-bones setup, with seating for only several dozen hungry folk. Service is impersonal and nonprofessional, but who cares at these prices. Innovative Italian cuisine is served here—tasty, attractive, and filling —and you can do very well on a slim budget. Appetizers include sun-dried beef on a bed of arugula, smoked salmon with endive and radiccio, and sautéed wild mushrooms. For a few pennies more, you can get a large dish of vegetarian lasagna, linguini, or ravioli. I'm constantly asked about inexpensive places that serve quality food; I have no hesitation in recommending this spot. But one word of warning: don't go if it's raining, because you'll probably have to wait to get seated, and the wait is outside.

DARBAR
44 W 56th St   4-DARBAR, 432-7227
Lunch, Dinner: Daily
Moderate

It's a joy to walk into a very appealing and well-designed restaurant where the tables are separated by partitions and one can really have a private conversation. Darbar is such a spot, and all of the staff wait on you in a quick and respectful manner, at the same time providing informed, efficient service and presenting fresh, attractive Indian dishes. A wonderful start for your meal would be the murgh pakoras, tender pieces of chicken sautéed in yogurt and Indian spices and batter-fried. Specialties from the charcoal clay oven are sizable in selection: chicken, prawns, and lamb. The tandoori prawns are my favorite. By all means, try some of the Indian breads. A real taste treat is the vegetarian paratha, unleavened whole wheat bread filled with vegetables and baked in the tandoor with butter. Rice dishes are excellent, and the desserts are exceptionally good. The chocolate cinnamon ice cream is worth the visit in itself. There is a buffet lunch daily.

DAWAT
210 E 58th St   355-7555
Lunch: Mon-Sat; Dinner: Daily
Moderate

Dawat is a quality operation. It serves tasty, reasonably priced Indian food in a refined atmosphere with superior service. There are a number of wonderful seafood choices, including a sensational shrimp entree cooked with herbs and spices. You'll also find chicken dishes, a number of goat and lamb offerings, and such vegetarian selections as homemade cheese cubes with delicious vegetables, eggplant with sweet-and-sour tamarind sauce, and stir-fried cauliflower with ginger and cumin seeds. One of the trademarks of an Indian restaurant is its bread, and Dawat is no exception. They do it to perfection. A number of different varieties are offered, and no meal is complete without trying a couple of them. Forget about the desserts here; they're nothing special.

DELIA'S AB3
197 E 3rd St (between Ave A and B)   254-9184
Dinner: Tues-Sat
Moderate

Feeling adventurous? Alphabet land is better known for drugs and other things than good dining, but here is an exception. By all means take a taxi to this establishment; walking and even taking a private car are not recommended. You will never know from the outside what awaits you as you enter through a curtain into a rather noisy, but clean and attractive restaurant *cum* bar *cum* dance spot (late on Friday and Saturday nights). But the food is the real surprise. Young, pleasant waiters (some with British accents) will lead you through a menu composed of such delicious appetizers as Delia's homemade savory mousse or an excellent homemade pâté. In keeping with the British flair, there is shepherd's pie, roasted

Cornish hen, and well-prepared fish dishes like poached salmon or brook trout as entrees. Save room for the wonderful Stilton cheese with port wine for dessert. If something lighter is desired, home-made sorbet is the answer. I did not meet Delia (if there is one), but she surely does great things in a less-than-great neighborhood. Oh yes, the folks here are very helpful about ensuring that you safely get in a cab for your trip home.

DELMONICO'S
56 Beaver St   422-4747
Breakfast, Lunch, Dinner: Mon-Fri
Moderate to expensive

Those who are familiar with the Wall Street area already know about Delmonico's. It has been a tradition for decades and is still a class act, resplendent with elegant furnishings and polite service well-honed from years of experience. Whether you're here for a "what's new in the market lunch" or for a social dinner, I heartily recommend this consistent, established institution. It's hard to pick out only a few specialties, but I would suggest the swordfish; the marvelous filet of sole glazed with white wine, mushrooms, and to-matoes; the boneless breast of chicken in brandy mustard sauce; or the mixed grill Delmonico (lamb chop, filet mignon, liver, and bacon). All of these should be at the top of anybody's list. And bit-ter chocolate with vanilla sauce is the Delmonico dessert showpiece.

DINING COMMONS
City of University of New York Graduate Center
33 W 42nd St (18th floor)   642-2013
Mon-Fri: 8-8
Inexpensive

This is definitely a find for those who don't mind cafeteria din-ing. Right in the center of town, on the top floor of City University Graduate Center, is a first-class all-day cafeteria that offers excel-lent food in nice surroundings at very reasonable prices. Continen-tal breakfasts, featuring muffins, danishes, croissants, bagels, and fruit, are available from 8 a.m. to 11 a.m. Lunch and dinner—deli sandwiches, salads, hot entrees with vegetables and potatoes, desserts and beverages—are available until 8 p.m. You can eat heartily for under $10; if a sandwich is all you want, the tab would be half that. Seating is available, but all items may be taken out. A full-service bar is adjacent to the Commons, which even offers a special catering menu with rock-bottom prices. The cafeteria is open to faculty, students, and the general public, with students get-ting a special discount upon presentation of CUNY identification cards. This is not your run-of-the-mill fast-food operation. Res-taurant Associates does a particularly good job in offering tasty and very adequate portions, without the fancy touches that cost extra bucks. A great midtown spot for groups, young people, singles, and people in a hurry.

DIVA
306 E 81st St   650-1928
Dinner: Sat-Thurs
Moderate

Several years ago, Lou Stuart turned the lower level of his townhouse into an Italian restaurant and named it Diva. Offering excellent Italian food in an elegant setting, complete with an antique Russian player-piano, was certainly a novel twist on a classic theme. But Stuart took an even more dramatic step toward distinguishing Diva from the numerous other Italian restaurants in the area. Diva went kosher! Since kosher food does not mix dairy and meat dishes, Diva was faced with giving up either its meat menu or its dessert menu. As one diner said, "Lou's desserts are fabulous, so he gladly sacrificed veal for cream filling." Today the menu is almost vegetarian: heavy on pasta and fish and excelling in desserts. (Diva could have made a go of it as a dessert house.) The appetizers include an exquisite marinated artichoke as big as a cabbage, fried red peppers, and broccoli salad with anchovies. There are two soups—a minestrone and a vegetable when I was there—and several salads. Portions are enormous, unlike the tab, which is quite reasonable. And you don't have to be kosher to like Diva.

DIVINO
1556 Second Ave (at 80th St)   861-1096
Lunch: Mon-Fri; Dinner: Daily
Moderate

Divino is a professional Northern Italian restaurant—professional service, professional cooking, professional supervision. It's always a thrill to watch a well-trained team in action, and Divino has one of the best in town. The owner is on the job, and the place is orchestrated with the baton of a master. The moment you enter (better make reservations), you notice an attractive and unusual bowl of relishes on the bar. Every sight and sense is a happy one, and there's plenty of good, hot, fresh Italian bread. To start, try the seafood salad or, if it's a cold evening, the *tortellini in brodo* (meat-filled pasta in broth). What a selection of pasta! Pasta stuffed with meat, spinach, and cheese; Genovese-style pasta in garlic and basil sauce; and pasta and seafood. Steamed clams, Italian-style bouilla-baisse, and scampi with tarragon are featured, but my prime choices are the veal chop Primavera or swordfish Divino. All entrees are served with fresh vegetables. Desserts are baked daily on the premises.

DOCKS

2427 Broadway	633 Third Ave
(bet 89th and 90th St)	(at 40th St)
724-5588	986-8080
Lunch: Mon-Sat; Dinner: Daily	Lunch: Mon-Fri; Dinner:
Moderate	Daily

For seafood lovers on the Upper West Side, I do not hesitate recommending that you sail right up Broadway to Docks' Oyster Bar and Seafood Grill. At both lunch and dinner, you can get fresh swordfish, lobster, tuna, Norwegian salmon, red snapper, and other seafood specials of the day. In the evening, you can enjoy a shell bar with four oyster varieties and three different selections of clams. All this comes with Docks' cole slaw and potatoes or vegetables. For a lighter meal, try the steamers in beer broth or the mussels in tomato and garlic. Delicious smoked fish, like sturgeon and whitefish, is available. Docks has a special New England clambake on Sunday and Monday nights. The lobster, in particular, is delicious and reasonably priced. Nothing fancy about the setting, but the personnel are helpful and accommodating. You can enjoy the same fare at Docks #2, on Third Avenue.

DUANE PARK CAFE
157 Duane St   732-5555
Lunch: Mon-Fri; Dinner: Mon-Sat
Moderate

More and more interesting places to dine are appearing in the TriBeCa area, and many are located on or near Duane Street. Some have revamped already existing operations that couldn't make the grade; Duane Park Cafe is one of them. Housed in the former Tapis Rouge, this nondescript room serves much better food than the décor would suggest. The menu is eclectic. There is a touch of Italian, a heavy emphasis on seafood, and a nod to Cajun influences. The dishes sparkle with interest, especially because of the tasty manner in which herbs are used. Even some of the delicious bread has herbal flavors; by the way, all the breads are made in-house. A selection of pasta is offered at all times. The desserts are also done on the premises, and show off the vivid imagination of the pastry chef. My top choice has to be the fallen apple soufflé.

ED DEBEVIC'S
661 Broadway (at Bond St)   982-6000
Mon-Thurs: 11 a.m.-midnight;
Fri, Sat: 11 a.m.-1 a.m.; Sun: 11 a.m.-11 p.m.
Inexpensive

What do "the Eccentric," "Bones," "R. J. Grunts," "the Pump Room," and "Ed Debevic's" have in common? Well, they are all run by a Chicago-based outfit called "Lettuce Entertain You." And entertain they do! The other restaurants are all in the Chicago area; this branch of Ed Debevic's is their first adventure in Manhattan. If the crowds of youngsters and oldsters (and all ages in between) is any indication, they are going to expand in a big way in Manhattan. The formula: color, excitement, noise, costumed help, solid Americana food, and low prices. There are three sections: a 1940s bar, a 1950s dining area, and a 1960s eating annex. The menu is heavy on burgers, sandwiches, barbecue items, and thick milkshakes. A salad bar is provided with the main entrees or can be a dish in itself. You won't go away feeling like you have had the greatest food in the world, but that is secondary to the atmosphere. If you have young people in tow, or if you just want to hang out at an establishment that pokes fun at itself (and everyone else), join the throngs at this only-in-America experience. (P.S. If you meet Ed, please give him my regards.)

EDWARDIAN ROOM
Plaza Hotel (Fifth Ave and Central Park S)
759-3000
Breakfast, Lunch, Dinner: Daily
Expensive

There are some New York experiences that one never forgets. I remember a magical evening in the Edwardian Room at the Plaza Hotel, overlooking the heart of New York at Fifth Avenue and Central Park. Outside, the streets and sidewalks were being dusted by a snowfall; inside, the tables sparkled with the finest silver, china, and glassware. The candles flickered, and the piano music provided the final romantic ingredient. This was years ago. Alas, the room has undergone many changes over a long period of time by a series of uncaring owners. Now the magic is back, and there just isn't another spot like it anywhere in New York. Hansom cabs sit outside your window, soft piano music soothes your nerves, and the kitchen is once again turning out superb cuisine in keeping with the room's history. This is the place to take your guests for that very special New York evening, to celebrate an engagement or important occasion. This is not just another hotel dining room! A talented young chef, Kerry Simon, takes care of just the Edwardian Room, and it shows. With gorgeous flowers and old-time waiters, along with an extensive dinner menu of continental favorites, who could ask for anything more?

ELDORADO PETIT
47 W 55th St (bet Fifth and Sixth Ave)   586-3434
Lunch: Mon-Fri; Dinner: Mon-Sat
Moderate to moderately expensive

At last there is a classy restaurant in Manhattan with a Spanish flavor. If time is important, forget about this place. . . . they act like they are in siesta land. Forget about the almost zombie-like greeting from some of those at the front office and the distracted service from the amateurish staff. The food is top-notch, though a bit on the overpriced side. This outlet is the first for the Barcelona-based chain in the United States, and they have designed a cold, stark setting. Warm up with pricey appetizers like seafood wrapped in cabbage or Maine lobster salad. On to Catalan favorites like braised rabbit in honey sauce and chicken and lobster ragout. Fabulous desserts make it all worthwhile! Catalan cream ice cream or glacéed fruit biscuit with Spanish brandy cream are excellent.

EL PARADOR
325 E 34th St (near First Ave)   679-6812
Lunch, Dinner: Daily
Moderate

When you have been in the restaurant business for over three decades in New York, you are obviously doing something customers like. El Parador is doing just that: serving delicious Mexican food in a fun atmosphere at down-to-earth prices. Besides all that, they are some of the nicest folks in the city. Warm nachos are put on the table the minute you arrive; from here you have a choice of specialties. There are tortillas, Spanish sausages, and pinto bean soup to start. Delicious shrimp and chicken dishes follow (the chicken wings are great). You can create your own tacos and tostaditas if you like. You'll probably want some tequila to make the evening complete. How do you drink it? Hold a wedge of lime or lemon in your left hand, then place a little salt in the well at the base of the thumb and index finger of the same hand. Then lick the salt, swallow some tequila, and suck the lemon or lime. Caramba!

ERMINIA
250 E 83rd St   879-4284
Dinner: Mon-Sat
American Express
Moderate

The Trastevere operation now has five branches, and Erminia, the smallest, is the jewel in the crown. It has about a dozen tables in a most pleasant and rather rustic atmosphere—just right for a leisurely, intimate dinner. I found it an absolutely charming spot with helpful personnel and outstanding food. To start, try the artichokes cooked in olive oil. In the pasta category, you can't go wrong with tender dumplings with potatoes and tomatoes or large noodles with ricotta cheese. The number of entrees is limited and all are grilled, but they are tasty and served with delicious vegetables. There is grilled chicken, various seafood items on a skewer, a special fish dish, and lamb or veal chops. Dessert selections vary daily.

EZE
254 W 23rd St   691-1140
Dinner: Tues-Sat
Expensive (almost!)

Gina Zarrilli, who spent time in the tiny French village of Eze, between Nice and Monte Carlo, has brought to New York a warm, inviting table of understated elegance. Nothing flashy or abrasive, just wonderful food served in a friendly ambiance. Gina is well suited for this achievement, having served her apprenticeship at Chanterelle, the Quilted Giraffe, and Roxanne's. The room is small, maybe a dozen tables, with a huge flower arrangement providing the only splash of color. The personnel seem almost elated to serve you. The bread is served warm and crusty. There's a wonderful choice of appetizers, like ravioli with Swiss chard and prosciutto, chicken livers with wild rice and pecans, or marinated trout. Loin of venison, whole red snapper with couscous, or rack of lamb are among the stars on the list of entrees. The coffee cake with ice cream and fig sauce or praline ice cream cake with chocolate sauce will make a trip to Body By Jake necessary in the morning. But that isn't the end. A wonderful assortment of pecan goodies, coconut tuiles, and candied grapefruit rind along with truffles is also placed before you. What a way to go!

FERRIER
29 E 65th St   772-9000
Mon-Sun: 12-12
Moderate

When you put together a cozy atmosphere, pleasant personnel, moderate prices, convenient hours, and good food, you obviously have a winning ticket. This is exactly what Alain Chevreux has done with this very busy bistro convenient to Upper East Side hotels. Chevreux got his start with Chez Ma Tante in the Village, and he has expanded the winning formula to Ferrier. There is a wide choice of hot and cold hors d'oeuvres, like sauteed Portuguese sardines, pâté of pork and chicken livers or carrot soup with basil (very good). On to pastas, several chicken dishes, wonderful seafood like grilled salmon in a light mustard sauce, and crispy roasted duck in an orange sauce with wild rice. There is a light menu in the late afternoon that offers salads, pâté and goodies like melted Swiss cheese and chicken on toast with french fries. And what a selection of homemade desserts! Feast on chocolate mousse cake, homemade sorbets, carmelized apple tart and profiteroles topped with white and dark chocolate sauce and served warm. A great place when the hunger pangs come at inconvenient hours!

FORTUNE GARDEN PAVILION
209 E 49th St   753-0101
Lunch: Mon-Fri; Dinner: Daily
Moderate

This is a garden delight. Make sure that you are seated upstairs, where the hanging plants and patio add to the charming, sophisticated atmosphere. Don't be in a rush at the Pavilion! All the Chinese food is cooked to order, and it's well worth the extra time. The help know what they're doing; be sure to confer with them so that you get exactly what you want. The appetizer selections are absolutely marvelous: barbecued spareribs, delicious crab meat and vegetables in lettuce leaf, steamed beef dumplings, and the best Shanghai chicken soup I've ever tasted. If you don't find what you want on the menu, check with the maitre d'. He'll be more than happy to have the staff prepare your choice. There are a number of hot and spicy items, like seafood sautéed in Hunan chili sauce, crab meat malay (crab meat braised with black and straw mushrooms), and a red snapper topped with a spicy Szechuan sauce. Milder offerings include ginger pineapple beef (marinated fillet of beef sautéed with pineapple, sweet ginger, and other vegetables), velvet chicken (shredded chicken sautéed in light egg-white sauce and served on spinach), and marinated medallions of pork.

FOUR SEASONS
99 E 52nd St   754-9494
Lunch: Mon-Fri; Dinner: Mon-Sat
Expensive

This is a Manhattan "must try." Nearly everything about this famous restaurant is special. The setting around the pool is spectacular. The tables are far enough apart to allow for private conversations. The huge menu changes with every season. The staff is very professional and well trained. Every dish is a masterpiece of presentation. The dessert selection is almost obscene, and the individual soufflés in coffee cups are something special. The grill room, outside the main dining hall, is the setting for more power lunches than are ever served at the White House. Take along a *Who's Who in New York* for lunch, and you'll be able to identify dozens of the country's top movers and shakers. It is a particular favorite for big names in the publishing world. If you really want to spend some bucks—and almost get your money's worth—you can't do better than Four Seasons.

FRANK'S
431 W 14th St   243-1349
Lunch: Mon-Fri; Dinner: Mon-Sat
Moderate

At lunch, this old-time spot is crowded with nearby butchers, sporting blood on their aprons and large stomachs to fill. If that kind of clientele doesn't bother you, come on down early. But dinner is really the best at Frank's, which is operated by five members of the Molinari family, the third generation in a business started in 1912. Reservations are difficult, especially on weekends (a week in advance is necessary), since they can take care of only 65 people. When cloths come out on the tables for dinner, the family chef (well trained at the now-defunct Brussels Restaurant) will offer you superb prime ribs of beef, fresh fish, great steaks, and pasta. The neighborhood is seamy, the desserts are ho-hum, and the ambiance is Pittsburgh diner, but the food is absolutely top-drawer.

FRANK'S TRATTORIA
371 First Ave (at 22nd St)   677-2991
Lunch, Dinner: Daily
Inexpensive

It's true in New York just as it is anywhere else in the country: no one knows the best inexpensive places to eat better than the local boys in blue. Manhattan's finest are some of the best customers of this modest trattoria, and it is easy to see why. The menu runs the gamut of Florentine dishes, each one prepared to order and each served piping hot. And so is the bread, which is always a good sign. There is a large seafood selection, and all the fish are first quality and very fresh. You can choose from over 20 different pizzas, and have them served whole or in individual pieces. Everyone here is very informal and friendly, and Jack, the boss, is delighted that the good word about his place has spread to others beyond the neighborhood regulars.

FRAUNCES TAVERN RESTAURANT
54 Pearl St   269-0144
Breakfast, Lunch, Dinner: Mon-Fri
Moderate

General George Washington is supposed to have said goodbye to his officers at a reception at Fraunces Tavern in 1783. General George obviously had good taste, if the tavern was as top-notch then as it is now. It's an inviting, historic spot serving authentic American fare in a charming part of lower Manhattan. The dining areas are spacious and comfortable, the service is very professional, the prices are reasonable, and the menu is sizable. One of the outstanding appetizers is a seafood sampler, consisting of fresh lump crab and Maine lobster meat, shrimp, oyster, and clams—a feast in itself. A specialty of the house is the baked chicken à la Washington (cubes of tender chicken and mushroom baked en casserole au gratin). Absolutely delicious. I'd suggest making a beeline here on Wednesdays for the Yankee pot roast with red cabbage and potato pancakes. On Tuesdays you can sample ales from around the world. And don't overlook dessert! The cheesecake, Georgia pecan pie, and chocolate mousse are well worth investigating. After your meal, go upstairs and visit the Fraunces Tavern Museum, one of the oldest museums in the city and a historic landmark. There you'll find exhibits focusing on eighteenth- and nineteenth-century life in America. The "long room" is especially well done. By the way, there's a breakfast menu offering a fine selection of omelets, eggs, fruit, and muffins. It's one of the best buys in New York.

GINO
780 Lexington Ave (at 61st St)   758-4466
Lunch, Dinner: Daily
Cash only
Moderate

As you look around the crowded dining room of this famous New York institution, you can tell immediately that the food is great. Why? Because this Italian restaurant is filled with native New Yorkers. You'll see no tourist buses stopping out front. The menu has been the same for years: a large selection of popular dishes (over 30 entrees), from antipasto to soup to pasta to fish. There are daily specials, of course, but you only have to taste such regulars as the linguini al pesto or the Italian sausages with peppers or scampis a la Gino, and you are hooked. Gino's staff has been there forever, taking care of patrons in an informed, fatherly manner. The best part of the whole experience comes when the tab is presented. East Side rents, as you know, are always climbing, but Gino has resisted the price bulges by taking cash only and by serving delicious food that keeps the tables full. No reservations, so come early and don't expect your waiter to know where Peoria is.

GIORDANO
409 W 39th St   947-9811
Lunch, Dinner: Mon-Sat
Moderate

When a restaurant has been in the same family for 30 years, it should be a fine-tuned establishment. And indeed, the Creglia family runs a first-rate operation at Giordano. An attractive bar greets you with trays of appetizers during the cocktail hour. There are several pleasant dining areas, including an outdoor patio. The cuisine is Northern Italian highlighted by such delicious pastas as fettuccine al fungetto, tortellini alla panna, fettuccine alfredo, or linguini al sugo. For entrees, I'd suggest the langostine alla mugnaia, an excellent seafood dish, or the calf's liver alla veneziana. A side order of fried zucchini or eggplant parmigiana tops off a superb meal. Although the food is excellent, I was most impressed with how comforting it is to have old-time waiters taking care of you; they sure know what they're doing. For no-nonsense Italian food at a reasonable price, you can't beat Giordano. A banquet room has been added.

GOLDEN UNICORN
18 E Broadway (at Catherine St)   941-0911
Lunch, Dinner, Dim Sum: Daily
Inexpensive

Spencer P.S. Chan presides over this bustling Hong Kong-style two-floor Chinese restaurant that serves delicious dim sum every day of the week. And besides the delicacies from the rolling carts, diners may choose from a wide variety of Cantonese dishes from the regular menu. Pan-fried noodle dishes, rice noodles, and noodles in soup are house specialties. Despite the size of the establishment (they can take care of over 400 diners at one time), you will be amazed at the fast service, the cleanliness, and most of all the price tag. This has to be one of the best values in Chinatown.

GOTHAM BAR AND RESTAURANT
12 E 12th St   620-4020
Lunch: Mon-Fri; Dinner: Daily
Moderately expensive

Yes, there is an afterlife! Your author (along with many others) had showered the original Gotham with some very unflattering words. What has happened in the past several years proves that restaurants may indeed go up the ladder, as well as the reverse. The Gotham today is well worth the sizable price tag. In a cavernous setting, anything but intimate, the high-ceilinged coldness is broken by direct lighting spots on each table. Beautiful orchid plants give a bit more color, but the real treat is the delicious food. Several wonderful salads, including a seafood presentation of squid, scallops, Japanese octopus, mussel and lobster in lemon and olive oil, will get you off to a good start. The entrees are uniformly appealing: beautifully seasoned, attractively presented, and obviously made from first-quality ingredients. The rack of lamb has to be one of the finest served in the city. A dozen homemade desserts, including such waist-busters as a peanut butter coupe (vanilla and peanut butter ice cream, nut brittle and milk chocolate sauce), raspberry gratin and a chocolate mousse filled with a coffee bean flavor, are expensive and exciting. Low-key personnel combined with a talented chef, Alfred Portale, make dining here a special experience.

GRAND CENTRAL OYSTER BAR RESTAURANT
Grand Central Station (lower level)   490-6650
Mon-Fri: 11:30-9:30
Moderate

If you are a native New Yorker, you know about the 75-year-old institution that is the Oyster Bar at Grand Central; it was once popular with commuters and residents. A midtown institution that was neglected for years, it is now restored and doing nicely, thank you. (They serve over 2,000 folks a day!) Located in the caverns of Grand Central, it is attractive, the young help most accommodating, and the drain on the pocketbook minimal. The menu boasts more than 90 seafood items (new, fresh entrees daily), a dozen different kinds of oysters, super oyster stew, clam chowder (Manhattan and New England), oyster pan roast, bouillabaisse, coquille St. Jacques, Maryland crab cakes, and marvelous homemade desserts.

GRAZIELLA
2 Bank St (at Greenwich Ave)   924-9450
Lunch: Mon-Fri; Dinner: Daily
Moderate

Since there are so many Italian restaurants, new and old, in Manhattan, they must be special to be included in this book. Graziella is very special in terms of value, cleanliness, ambiance, and service. The restaurant is a family affair: Graziella herself is out front, and her brothers are in the kitchen. Graziella is not the usual table-hopping proprietor, who constantly and insincerely asks, "Is everything all right?" Graziella's English has a lovely Spanish tilt to it, and she makes sure that everything is absolutely spotless and that place settings are arranged picture-perfect. The restaurant has less than 20 tables and is always booked with neighborhood regulars, so reservations are decidedly in order. Nonetheless, the atmosphere is casual and unhurried. Try a fabulous appetizer platter to start, then have your choice of a number of homemade pasta and veal dishes, boneless shell steak, breast of chicken, or grilled scampi. This is definitely a place for big appetites. Diet-conscious gourmets should head in the opposite direction and leave one of New York's best bargains to the real eaters in the family. By the way, Graziella's Bank Street entrance is just off Greenwich *Avenue,* not Greenwich Street.

GUIDO'S
511 Ninth Ave (at 39th St)   502-4842
Lunch: Mon-Fri; Dinner: Mon-Sat
No credit cards
Inexpensive

You might ask yourself what a nice person like you would be doing in the middle of Ninth Avenue having lunch in the back room of a macaroni factory? Well, this is no usual back room and no usual macaroni factory. Up front, as you walk in, you'll see a display of 23 brands of macaroni. That was the original business, but now it's just a sideline. The real draw is the smallish restaurant in the back, which is as busy as Times Square. Tom Scarola is the third-generation family member who runs this unusual operation. Whether you're coming for lunch or dinner, make sure you have a reservation; you might even rub shoulders with Olivia Newton-John, Robert de Niro, or other celebrities. Even if they're not there in person, their pictures (along with the blue checkered tablecloths and wine bottles on the ceiling) help create a special atmosphere at Guido's. You don't want to miss the shrimp francese, the veal sorrentino, or the house specialty, chicken alla Guido. The pasta is freshly made, authentic, inexpensive, and delicious. Finish with spumoni or rum cake, and you will have had a marvelous meal. Lunch specials include four different chicken, veal, and shrimp entrees, as well as linguini or spaghetti with all the trimmings.

HARD ROCK CAFE
221 W 57th St   459-9320
Sun-Thurs: 11:30 a.m.-2 a.m.;
Fri, Sat: 11:30 a.m.-4 a.m.
Inexpensive

This New York offshoot of the original and very successful Hard Rock, which opened in London in 1971, is a noisy, swinging hangout for the younger generation. Stop at the small counter as you enter and get one of the Hard Rock Cafe sweat shirts for your son or daughter, and your popularity rating at home will go up. The food is really good here. Specialties of the house include the Pig Sandwich (hickory-smoked pulled pork, served with cole slaw and French fries), barbecued chicken and pork ribs, a great BLT sandwich, and marvelous burgers and salads. But the real treats are from the fountain and dessert menu: homemade apple pie, hot-fudge brownies, homemade shortcakes, and absolutely outrageous sundaes and shakes. The multilevel cafe is decorated with artifacts of rock and pop culture (gold records, musical instruments once owned by famous stars, etc.), and the background music is just what you'd expect—loud rock and roll. But come on now, let your hair down and see how the other half has fun.

HARRY'S
The Woolworth Building
233 Broadway   513-0455
Lunch, Dinner: Mon-Fri
Moderate

Never mind that you're not a member of the Harvard or Yale Club, or that you don't have a gold pass to the private dining room of Citicorp or Chase Manhattan. Just head for the Woolworth Building, go down to the lower level, and you'll find a remarkable eating spot called Harry's. You would probably never know about it unless you work in one of the nearby offices—or read this book! What with all the wood and leather (a very masculine atmosphere), good food, and reasonable prices, it's a real find. Although dinner is served until 10:30 at night, this is basically a luncheon spot. Ladies are certainly welcome, but the clientele is predominantly male (the important-looking, three-piece-suit variety). While big deals are being made at the tables around you, you can feast on clams, smoked trout, marinated herring, and smoked sturgeon. Omelets and homemade pastas are available, as well as a number of selections from the cold buffet, including chicken-salad, sliced-turkey, and tuna-salad platters. There are also grilled items, cold sandwiches, seafood, and several specials each day. If you drop by on a Tuesday, try the braised sauerbraten, and if you visit on Friday, the boiled brisket of beef is outstanding. This is the ideal place to take business associates, who will be pleasantly surprised to learn about it. Harry's is open on weekends only for private events.

HARVEY'S CHELSEA HOUSE
108 W 18th St (at Sixth Ave)   243-5644
Lunch, Dinner: Daily; Brunch: Sun
Moderate

This historic house has been in operation since 1889, and the charm has increased every year. Recently owner Dick Harvey spruced up the inlaid-mahogany walls, the saloon clock, the cut-crystal cabinets, and the bar's brass rails. The place literally oozes atmosphere! The menu features typically American cuisine, served by serious waiters in a congenial atmosphere. Those dining alone will feel just as much at home as those in larger gatherings. A magnificent 44-foot-long bar graces the front room; quieter dining is available through the swinging doors in the back saloon. There are daily specials (like baby back ribs on Wednesday, weiner schnitzel on Thursday, and Beef Wellington on Saturday). Every day you can order delicious shepherd's pie, grilled medallions of venison, and great steaks. Upstairs newly remodeled private party rooms with fireplaces are available for groups from 10 to 150. Free delivery from a special menu is offered. And don't forget to leave room for the sensational chocolate mud cake!

HATSUHANA
17 E 48th St   355-3345
Lunch: Mon-Fri; Dinner: Mon-Sat
Moderate

Hatsuhana has deservedly become known as the best sushi house in Manhattan. One can sit at a table or at the bar and get equal attention from the informed help. There are several dozen choice appetizers, including broiled eel in cucumber wrap, steamed egg custard with shrimp, fish, and vegetables, squid mixed with Japanese apricots, and chopped fatty tuna with aged soybeans. Next, try the salmon teriyaki (fresh salmon grilled with teriyaki sauce) or any number of tuna or sushi dishes best described by the personnel. Forget about the desserts, and concentrate on the exotic offerings for your meal.

HUDSON RIVER CLUB
Lobby level, 4 World Financial Center   786-1500
Lunch: Mon-Fri; Dinner: Mon-Sat
Moderate to moderately expensive

How often can you dine with the Statue of Liberty in clear sight? The setting is magnificent: spacious, with high ceilings and a view of the river and yacht harbor. Nothing has been spared to make the destination (as difficult as it is to find) worth the trouble. Don't be put off by the word *Club*; the house is open to everyone, but it serves as a special place for residents of Battery Park City. The menu is strictly American, with an emphasis on food from the Hudson Valley. A special five-course dinner offers specialties from the area for every course. Luncheons feature excellent soups, several salads (like corn-crusted scallop or Maine lobster), and marvelous lighter dishes like a Hudson Canyon omelet or herbed free-range chicken. In the evening, they serve a large selection of seafood and house specialties like brandy-braised rabbit, roast squab, shank of veal, and Hudson Valley venison chop and loin. Desserts are a feast for the eye and the palate; warm sack of baked bananas or five-layer chocolate-chip sundae will knock your eyes out, as well as activate the arrow on your scales. This is a delightful place to entertain someone who has been "everywhere" in the Big Apple.

IL GIGLIO
81 Warren St (bet W Broadway and Greenwich St)
571-5555
Lunch, Dinner: Mon-Fri
Moderate

Il Mulino's "little brother" is doing well—so well, in fact, he might be even more handsome than his father! If you can find the place (the neighborhood is drab and dull, to say the least) you will be delighted to find a bright, clean, classy operation that serves absolutely great Northern Italian food. Smallness is a virture here, as the two dozen tables are looked after by a crew of highly trained, tuxedo-clad waiters, most of whom have been on the premises since its opening. The specials are almost as numerous as the menu items (be sure to ask for prices), and by all means take a look at the display of fresh fruits, desserts, and other goodies by the entrance way. The scampi and veal dishes are superb, and few places in TriBeCa (or elsewhere in Manhattan) do pasta any better. Moreover, all the desserts are made in house.

IL MULINO
86 W 3rd St (bet Sullivan and Thompson St)
673-3783
Lunch: Mon-Fri; Dinner: Mon-Sat
American Express
Moderately expensive

Never mind that you usually have to reserve a table a week or so in advance. Never mind that when you arrive it's always crowded, the noise level intolerable, and the waiters nearly knock you down as you stand waiting to be seated. It's all part of the ambiance of one of New York's best Italian restaurants. Your greeting is usually "Hi, Boss," which gives you the distinct impression that the staff is accustomed to catering to members of the, uh, "family." When your waiter finally comes around, he reels off the lengthy list of evening specials with glazed-over eyes and about as much interest as your kid would have while you recited your favorite Shakespeare sonnet. On the other hand, there is a beautiful, mouth-watering display of the daily specials on a huge table at the entrance. Once you're seated, your waiter delivers one antipasto after another to your table, while he talks you into ordering one of the fabulous veal dishes with portions plentiful enough to feed King Kong. The Dover sole is just as delicious and abundant. By the time you finish one of the luscious desserts, you'll know why every seat in the small, simple dining room is kept warm all evening. Il Mulino can become habit forming.

IL VAGABONDO
351 E 62nd St   832-9221
Lunch: Mon-Fri; Dinner: Daily
Inexpensive

One of the major airlines advertises with the phrase "doing what we do best." It could just as well be the motto of this bustling restaurant, which has been a favorite with knowledgeable New Yorkers for more than 20 years. The atmosphere is strictly old-timey, complete with checkered tablecloths, four busy rooms, and an even busier bar. No menus are offered; the pleasant but harried waiters reel off the regular items and the daily specials. Depending on when you go, you may have spaghetti or ravioli, an absolutely marvelous minestrone soup, chicken parmesan, prime rib steak, or sliced beef. I would also heartily recommend the Friday scampi or lobster special. There is no pretense in this place. It is a great spot for office parties and for folks with slim pocketbooks. You won't see Jackie O. here, but you'll see happy faces, compliments of a delicious meal and the extremely reasonable bill. Save room for the great bocce ball dessert (tartufo). Il Vagabondo, you see, is the only restaurant in New York with an indoor bocce court.

INDOCHINE
430 Lafayette St   505-5111
Dinner: Daily
Moderate

Indochinese cuisine has become very popular, which is probably due to the number of American military men who have spent time in that part of the world, as well as the number of talented chefs and cooks who have come to our country. Indochine is undoubtedly the best restaurant of its type in New York, and it's located right across the street from Joseph Papp's famous New York Public Theater. The staff is happy to explain the delicious exotic dishes they offer. Soups are a specialty of the house, and the best is the Pho: sliced filet of beef, rice noodles, and bean sprouts in broth. Several salads and appetizers are worth trying. One is called Bi Coun, steamed Vietnamese ravioli. Another delicious dish is Nhom Ban Kann, steamed shrimp served with fresh mint and red snapper in lemon juice. For entrees, I recommend the fresh filleted fish steamed in coconut milk with lemon grass and wrapped in banana leaf; the frog's legs in coconut milk; or Banh Hoi Bo Lui, a brochette of fillet of beef with lemon grass and angel hair noodles. Be brave and try one of these delicious dishes combined with sticky rice, Indochinese style. Such desserts as hazelnut mousse cake rate special mention. You'll understand why Phnom Penh was such a gourmet paradise in its heydey.

JACKSON HOLE WYOMING BURGERS

232 E 64th St	Third Ave at 35th St	Second Ave at 84th St
371-7187	679-3264	737-8788
Mon-Sat:	Mon-Sat:	Mon-Thurs:
10:30-1 a.m.;	10:30-1 a.m.;	10:30-1 a.m.;
Sun: 12-12	Sun: 12-12	Fri, Sat: 10:30-4 a.m.;
		Sun: 11-midnight
	No credit cards	
	Inexpensive	

You might think that a burger is a burger is a burger. But having done a burger taste test all over the city, I choose Jackson's as the best. Each one weighs in at seven juicy, delicious ounces. All ingredients are fresh, and the taste tells the story. You can get all types of hamburgers, along with great coffee and French fries. You can have a pizza burger, an alpine burger, an English burger, or maybe a Baldouney burger (mushrooms, fried onions, and American cheese)—or omelets, if you prefer. The atmosphere isn't fancy, but once you sink your teeth into a Jackson Hole burger accompanied by great onion rings and one of the homemade desserts, you'll see why I'm so enthusiastic.

JIM McMULLEN'S

1341 Third Ave (at 77th St)   861-4700
Lunch, Dinner: Daily
American Express
Moderate

I'm always a bit suspicious of a restaurant where the waiting line moves with irregular motion, and this is one spot where that happens. If the maitre d' or Jim McMullen knows you, or if your name is well-known, the wait is short. Otherwise, it's ridiculous. But people do wait, I guess, not only because it is chic to see and be seen here, but because the food is good and the prices are certainly right. Jim was a model, and the place is a favorite hangout for the famous and near-famous. The menu is unimaginative, with the usual appetizers. But I find the chicken pot pie worth the visit in itself. There is a good selection of fish dishes, including poached salmon and several steak offerings. The chocolate brownie pie is an A-1 dessert, and the hot fudge sundae is not the usual ice-cream store variety. There is also a private dining room (seating 30-50 guests) available for lunch or dinner. Now, a wine and spirit store at 1381 Third Avenue (288-2211) bears the McMullen name.

JOE'S
79 MacDougal St   473-8834
Lunch, Dinner: Wed-Mon
Moderate

Joe's belongs in the very good Italian category, not only for the quality of the food but also for the value you get from your dining dollar. Joe himself is on the job, as he has been for several decades, imparting Old World charm to this small Village establishment. His staff is also made up of experienced, efficient, no-nonsense old-timers. Spaghetti (in six different ways), baked ziti, linguini, and homemade egg noodles are all excellent starters. I'd stick to the veal scaloppini (fixed five different ways), the veal chops, or the veal cutlets for entrees. Shrimps and clams are featured, and the breast of chicken alla parmigiana is a winner. My favorite meal here is cannelloni served with great Italian bread and a very fresh salad "alla Joe's." A perfect meal at a tiny price. If the name of this place was Valentino's instead of Joe's, you'd pay double!

JOE'S BAR & GRILL
142 W 10th St   727-1785
Dinner: Mon-Sun; Lunch: Mon-Fri;
Jazz Brunch: Sat, Sun
Moderate

Just why so many eating places are called "Joe's" is still a mystery to me, but at least this one is not a pizza parlor. As a matter of fact, it is anything but a trendy restaurant in an area that is noted for that type of establishment. On a pretty little street in the Village, Joe's puts out excellent food at prices that make dining a pleasure. No wonder the place is nearly always packed to the rafters. I knew I was going to like it the minute I saw delicious cheese sticks at the bar, rather than the fattening and (usually) stale peanuts served elsewhere. You can dine here anyway you want. There are bar basics like great burgers, chicken club sandwiches, or a filet mignon sandwich served on garlic bread. Or there are salad plates, pastas, fresh fish dishes, omelets and "large plates" that would do credit to any restaurant. Sunday brunches have the usual fare, but one entree is a must: eggs in purgatory (baked with sausage in a spicy tomato sauce). Desserts are all done in Joe's kitchen (there really isn't a Joe, the place is owned by Kathy Wagner); I'll settle for the espresso crème brûlée!

JOHN CLANCY'S

181 W 10th St	206 E 63rd St (at Second Ave)
242-7350	752-6666
Dinner: Daily	Lunch: Mon-Fri; Dinner: Daily
Moderate	

It's always a bit dangerous when a successful restaurant expands; it's more difficult to maintain the hands-on operation. For years, John Clancy's was one of the better seafood houses in the Village, and now there is a branch uptown. The atmosphere in both is a bit stuffy—the staff is somewhat affected—but so far the same good food is served up in both places. Specialties of the house include a hearty fisherman's stew, lobster Americaine, and delicious barbequed jumbo shrimp. The mesquite-grilled items are very tasty, especially the swordfish teriyaki. Desserts always seem to go especially well after a seafood dinner, and all those at John Clancy's are homemade and delicious. There are usually several selections of outrageous chocolate items (like chocolate velvet cake), and the English trifle is first-rate.

JOHN'S PIZZERIA

278 Bleecker St   243-1680
Mon-Thurs: 11:30 a.m.11-30 p.m.; Fri, Sat: 11:30 a.m.-
    12:30 p.m.; Sun: 12-11:30 p.m.
No credit cards
Inexpensive

The boss here isn't even named John—he's Pete Castellotti, a.k.a. the Baron of Bleecker Street. Pete offers 55—count 'em— varieties of pizza, from cheese and tomatoes to a gourmet extravaganza of cheese, tomatoes, anchovies, sausage, peppers, meatballs, onions, and mushrooms. If spaghetti, cheese ravioli, or manicotti (all homemade) is your preference, this is also the place for you. The manicotti filled with ricotta and mozzarella cheese, covered with plain tomato sauce and served with great Italian bread will make even your Uncle Menachem a believer. The surroundings are shabby, the menus are shabby, the plates are shabby, and the neighborhood is shabby, *but* the pizzas are perfection.

JO-JO

160 E 64th St   223-5656
Lunch, Dinner: Daily
Moderate to moderately expensive

It is satisfying and fun to share in a real American success story. And this is one. For years Jean-Georges Vongeerichten presided over the outstanding kitchen at Lafayette, a four-star grand French dining establishment. Although only in his mid-30s, he decided that if he had to work so hard, he'd rather do it for himself. Jo-Jo is the result. It is a happy, classy, delicious establishment, with those extra touches that make dining a memorable experience. Unusual napkin rings. Wonderful warm bread. Pleasant and helpful waiters. A very classy lady maitre d'. There are only a half-dozen choices of appetizers, entrees, and desserts; every one is unique and tasty, beautifully presented. Rabbit, soup, or salad are among the choices to start; then move on to fish, lobster, chicken, lamb, or duck. Superb warm chocolate cake . . . brioche with carmelized apple is the way to finish. Upstairs is a charming room with fireplace for private entertaining or after-dinner drinks and conversation. Don't miss Jo-Jo!

KATZ'S DELICATESSEN
205 E Houston St (at Ludlow St)   254-2246
Sun-Thurs: 7 a.m.-11 p.m.; Fri, Sat: 7 a.m.-1 a.m.
No credit cards
Inexpensive

When you are down on the Lower East Side and need an extra big bite, try Katz's Delicatessen. It is a super place with some of the biggest and best sandwiches in town. The atmosphere goes along with the great food, and the prices are reasonable. You can go right up to the counter and order (it is fun watching the no-nonsense operators slicing and fixing), or sit at a table where a seasoned waiter will take excellent care of you. Try the dill pickles and the sauerkraut with your sandwich. Katz's is a perfect way to sample the unique "charm" of Lower East Side establishments. When you wait at a table for an hour, or discover that the salt and pepper containers are empty and the ketchup is missing, you'll know what I mean.

KEENS CHOP HOUSE
72 W 36th St   947-3636
Lunch: Mon-Fri; Dinner: Mon-Sat
Moderate

It seems that some of the best old restaurants in New York get lost in the shuffle. With glamorous new places opening every week and people always wanting to know which places are "in," we forget about the dependable restaurants that consistently do a good job. One of them is Keens Chop House, a unique New York institution. I can remember going there decades ago when those in the garment trade made Keens their lunch headquarters. This has not changed. Keens still has the same attractions: the bar reeks of atmosphere, and there are great party facilities and fine food to match. Keens opened in 1885 and has been a fixture in the Herald Square area ever since. For some time, it was a "gentlemen only" place, and although it still has a very masculine atmosphere, ladies now feel comfortable and welcome. Of course, the famous mutton chop with mint is the house specialty, but other delicious dishes include veal, steaks, lamb, and fish, and a special omelet of the day. For the light eater, especially at lunch, there are some great salads. There's a hearty, robust atmosphere about the place, and the waiters are the no-nonsense type. If you have a meat-and-potatoes lover in your party, this is the place to take him. Make sure you save a little room for the deep-dish apple pie.

KLEINE KONDITOREI
234 E 86th St   737-7130
Sun-Thurs: 11 a.m.-11 p.m.; Fri, Sat: 11 a.m.-midnight
Moderate

If you're in the mood for sauerbraten and potato dumplings and red cabbage, wiener schnitzel, goose, venison, steak, or an outrageously calorie-laden linzer torte, try Kleine Konditorei. It is one of the very few German restaurants worth visiting in New York; the cakes and pastries would do credit to the fine little pastry shops you find in Munich. East 86th Street is one of New York's most colorful areas, and a walk around the neighborhood (which you'll need after a stop here) is interesting. I recommend Kleine Konditorei for an after-the-show visit, or for a special lunch when a golden-brown German pancake sounds just right. There is also a bakery section for take-out orders.

LA BOHÈME
24 Minetta Lane (Sixth Ave bet W 3rd
   and Bleecker St)   473-6447
Dinner: Tues-Sun; Brunch (and full menu): Sun
Moderate

Pari Dulac likes people and food, and it shows. The part-Iranian, part-French hostess is right on the job in her cozy, informal Bohemian bistro, dispensing delicious edibles at moderate prices. The setting is on a quiet, charming street in the Village. When the front doors are open in the nice weather, you get the impression you are in a quaint European town. Inside, soothing music puts you in the mood to enjoy some of the best pizza you have ever tasted. In the back, an open kitchen puts out pasta, salads, and great French dishes done to perfection. On Sundays, you can't beat the Country French brunch or the unique omelet selection. Dessert specialties include tarts made in-house, as well as first-class chocolate mousse cake and lemon soufflé with raspberry sauce. Pari has been wise in using only the best ingredients in her dishes, and has resisted the temptation to raise prices to a point where value is questionable. Pari is part of a restaurant family; her husband runs the reincarnated Le Chantilly on East 57th Street.

LA BOITE EN BOIS
75 W 68th St   874-2705
Dinner: Daily
No credit cards
Moderate

This restaurant is packing them in every evening—for obvious reasons. The owner, an ex-chef, has hit upon that winning combination: delicious food, personal service, and moderate prices. The salads are unusual; the escargots aux champignons des bois is a great beginner. For an entree, I recommend the fillet of snapper, fricassee of chicken, or the escalope of veal. The intimate atmosphere allows you to become acquainted with your neighbor, if you so desire, and all the niceties of service are operative from start to finish. All the desserts are made in-house; I suggest choosing one of their sorbets. By all means, call for reservations, since the place is very small and very popular.

LA CARAVELLE
33 W 55th St (at Fifth Ave)   586-4252
Lunch: Mon-Fri; Dinner: Mon-Sat
Expensive

For years I enjoyed La Caravelle because it was a truly classic restaurant, in food, service, and ambiance. For a while, though, I felt it was going downhill, relying on past glory instead of keeping up with the times. True, if they knew you, the attention would be superb. But alas, if you were a stranger, it was another story altogether. Now things seem to have undergone a revival, and even the old décor, beautiful murals, flowers and all, have taken on a new life. The classic menu is still there, but now it de-emphasizes the heavier dishes of the past. As with so many new restaurants, concern for health is evident in a number of the menu selections. There is even a hint of Oriental influence in some of the preparations. If you are looking for an absolutely superb meal, I'd order the duck and finish off with one of La Caravelle's great soufflés.

LA CITÉ
120 W 51st St   956-7100
Mon-Fri: 12-10; Sat, Sun: 5-12
Grill: Daily, 11:30 a.m.-midnight
Moderate

When it comes to an authentic Parisian brasserie, New York does not have much of a selection. La Cité opened with much hype and fanfare, some deserved and some not. The result is a handy, fun, and crowded place for a midtown lunch. The choice is between a rather brash cafe and a more sedate (and less expensive) grill room. If the conversations are very personal or involve state secrets, this is hardly the spot to choose. But the menu is a complete one, and most dishes are done rather well. Best dishes are the warm chicken salad with artichoke and peppers, roast rack and loin of lamb, and the grilled lobster. Potato lovers will enjoy the choice of butter-mashed, french-fried, creamy potato gratin, mashed potatoes with herbs and diced ham or sautéed new potatoes with bacon, mushrooms and pearl onions. There are specials every day of the week; if you can make it on a Thursday, the roast loin of pork is worthwhile. Save some room for banana ice cream surrounded by chocolate mousse or for a great cappuccino mousse. The grill menu is a bit more traditional and masculine. A *prix fixe* menu (with champagne) is available.

LA COLOMBE D'OR
134 E 26th St   689-0666
Lunch: Mon-Fri; Dinner: Mon-Sat
Moderate

It's easy to see why La Colombe d'Or is always busy. They provide well-prepared meals at a reasonable price. The place has an intimate French provincial atmosphere, and the service is prompt and efficient. Take note of this spot, since there are not too many good eating establishments in this part of town. I'd suggest the super bouillabaisse maison for a very good lunch dish. I also recommend the pasta. For dinner, you might start with ratatouille or the snails with beets and Rhone wine. Then go on to the grilled chicken in red wine with olives and rosemary. A superb dish. Off the menu, Gâteau Victoire, their chocolate cake, is first-rate. One of the nicest features is the number of specialty coffees with cognac, Triple Sec, Calvados, or even Cafe Morello, with Kahlua, whipped cream, chocolate shavings, orange rindlets . . . *wow!* Let's start with coffee and dessert for a change!

LA CÔTE BASQUE
5 E 55th St   688-6525
Lunch, Dinner: Mon-Sat
Expensive

My uncle started taking me here 30 years ago. I remember thinking even then that it was a fantastic place to see, to be seen, and to enjoy. It still is. The beautiful people flock to this restaurant for fine French food, and if you're a gourmet, this is a spot you won't want to miss. The food is as tasty as the people watching is enthralling. And the elegant murals and flowers are matched by the elegant guests. Once in a while, we are all tempted to try some spectacular dish that we can't make at home. This is the place to go (with a very full wallet or the company credit card) when you have that desire. Specialties of the house include pepper steak, Dover sole, roast duck, sweetbreads, and quail. The appetizers, especially the smoked salmon, seafood casserole, and seasonal salads are among the best in the city. Save some room for raspberry soufflé or the out-of-this-world hazelnut daquoise. Note: La Côte Basque regulars get distinctly preferential treatment over newcomers.

LA FONDUE
43 W 55th St　　581-0820
Lunch, Dinner: Daily
No credit cards
Inexpensive

This business is an outgrowth of a cheese store that was founded in Greenwich Village over 25 years ago. La Fondue is always busy —a great spot for a quick snack, a good lunch, a no-frills dinner, or an after-theater repast. Because of its popularity, they have added more than 100 seats. My favorites for starters include onion soup, cheddar-cheese soup, or Swedish green-pea soup—all very well made and very filling. The specialty of the house for light snacks is a cheese and sausage board, featuring a great variety of imported cheeses and sausages from Denmark, Poland, the Netherlands, Spain, Norway, Austria, Switzerland, Germany, Italy, Hungary, and almost any other place you can think of. This attractive offering includes salad, bread, and relishes. You can also have fun with a prime filet mignon fondue or a genuine imported Swiss cheese fondue. There's even a Continental Cheese Tour, in which you get a fine selection of international cheeses, plus bread, fresh fruit, and crackers. I also recommend the Swiss chocolate fondue with fruit and fruit bread for dessert, or perhaps the banana fruit bread, rum raisin ice cream, and chocolate fondue sauce. This is a number-one spot, where your stomach will be satisfied and your pocketbook treated kindly.

LA GAULOISE
502 Sixth Ave (at 13th St)　　691-1363
Lunch, Dinner: Mon-Sat
Moderate

This unassuming French bistro could be turn-of-the-century San Francisco or present-day Paris. Simplicity in décor and in presentation is the secret of success at La Gauloise, where Village gourmets go when they want to get away from the trendy places. The folks who run the place fit right into the picture. No cutesy stuff here.

The salad selection is especially good; ravioli stuffed with lobster or shrimp and sole pâté are other good starters. The entrees include just about anything you want, from sweetbreads and duck breast to grilled seafood items, steaks, and chicken. Each dish comes with its own special accompaniment. For example, the roast veal tenderloin with asparagus ratatouille is a marvelous combination. The rice pudding with fruit for dessert will give you less of a guilt complex in the morning. So will the tab.

LA GRENOUILLE
3 E 52nd St (at Fifth Ave)   752-1495
Lunch, Dinner: Tues-Sat
Expensive

Giselle Masson and her son, Charles, have set their establishment apart. La Grenouille is one of those special places that one really has to see to believe. It's impossible to describe. The beautiful fresh flowers are but a clue to a unique, not-to-be-forgotten dining experience. The food is just as great as the atmosphere, and although the prices are high, it's worth every penny. The celebrity watching adds to the fun. The French menu is complete, the staff professional. Be sure to try their cold hors d'oeuvres; they're a specialty of the house, as are the clams and the Bayonne ham. Don't miss the soufflés for dessert—they're superb. The tables are very close together, but what difference does it make when the people at your elbows are so interesting?

LA LUNCHONETTE
130 Tenth Ave (at 18th St)   675-0342
Lunch: Mon-Fri; Dinner: Daily
No credit cards
Moderate

I've got news for readers who think that only fancy restaurants are included in this book. Of course, that is not true at all. Many of these restaurants are quite plain and inexpensive, but they serve good food at an attractive price. La Lunchonette definitely falls into the "unfancy" category. It's located in a rather run-down neighborhood of the city, and since it lacks an eye-catching sign out front, you're likely to pass La Lunchonette without a second look. But some distinctive and delicious things happen on the inside. In a space that looks as though it were decorated with objects that didn't sell at last year's church bazaar, Zoe Porte serves up some of the tastiest dishes around. The selection is sophisticated: you could have sweetbreads vinaigrette or lobster bisque to start, and go on to swordfish with capers and lemon butter, or a delicious gratinée of lobster, crab, and scallops. Part of the kitchen area is curtained off, but one can still see that really primitive equipment can turn out some of the best food. The talent lies with the user, and that's the case at this no-pretense bistro.

LA METAIRIE
189 W 10th St (bet W 4th and Bleecker St)
989-0343
Dinner: Daily
Moderate

La Metairie (it translates as small communal farm) has built its reputation through an owner who has given tender, loving care to this tiny hole-in-the-wall in the Village. The menu changes every three months, so I suggest you call ahead to see if your favorite is being featured that day, be it tripe, rabbit with mustard sauce, or bouillabaisse. The room accommodates only 22 people, the tables are close together, and the atmosphere extremely cozy and friendly. How they can operate in a thimble-size kitchen and produce such tasty morsels is a mystery, but the owner is carrying on a quality tradition.

LANDMARK TAVERN
626 11th Ave (at 46th St)   757-8595
Daily: Noon to midnight; Sun: Brunch

Landmark Tavern is open friendly hours for sandwich platters, a variety of salads, fresh seafood, steaks, and roast prime rib of beef. Blue plate specials have been added to the dinner menu. But the real treat here is Sunday brunch. A tradition in the city since 1868, the Tavern is not content to be a carbon copy of everyone else's fare. Indeed, the normal brunch items are available, but so is shepherd's pie (ground lamb sautéed with herbs), delicious lamb steaks, and English-style fish and chips. There is the added pleasure of sampling their famous soda bread (made fresh every hour) served with imported jams and marmalade. Homemade corned beef hash is a favorite. And those great homemade desserts will make you want to come back every Sunday: spiced apple cake, chocolate truffle pie, Landmark "little" cake, and cranberry almond torte. The bar is friendly here, the help is somewhat harried, and the atmosphere reeks of nostalgia. More important, the food is delicious and the prices are a bargain.

LA PETITE FERME
973 Lexington Ave (at 70th St)   249-3272
Lunch, Dinner: Mon-Sat
Moderate

La Petite Ferme was a very small spot down in the Village the first time I visited it. It has since grown to be a larger, fancier place on Lexington Avenue. The atmosphere is still intimate, and the same sort of menu (printed on a blackboard) is available to a large group of faithful customers. As the seating is quite limited, calling for reservations is a good idea. Without them, it is easier to get in during the early part of the dinner hour. The cuisine is French country style, and the featured entree selections are all tastefully prepared, whether it's poached bass, veal, sole, or whatever. I have to give high marks to their vegetables, because they don't overcook them. There is an attractive garden downstairs, and although the service is a little confusing (the kitchen is upstairs), the staff manages to do a very satisfactory job.

LA RESERVE
4 W 49th St   247-2993
Lunch, Dinner: Mon-Sat
Expensive

In every great city there are a very select few great places. Great hotels. Great stores. Great restaurants. In New York, La Reserve is one of them. The question I am asked most often is: "What is your favorite restaurant?" Without a hesitation, I answer "La Reserve." Why? First, because the host, Jean Louis Missud, is one of the most charming and talented gentlemen I have ever had the privilege of knowing. But this is only the start. The seductive ambiance, the beautifully prepared dishes, the gracious service, the feeling that you are a special guest—all of this combines to make a meal here an experience you will not forget. It would be impossible to list the best items on the menu. I would suggest you put yourself in the hands of Jean Louis (or one of his capable assistants) and let them prepare "the meal of a lifetime." A pre-theater dinner is available, and private party facilities are yours for the asking.

LA RIPAILLE
605 Hudson St (at W 12th St)   255-4406
Dinner: Mon-Sat
Moderate

There's a new menu every night at this small and romantic Parisian-style cafe, so call ahead to see what's available. I find it to be a cozy spot for an informal dinner. The tables are rickety, but the chef puts his heart into every dish. It is certainly worth a visit. Most entrees are done to perfection, the seafood is always fresh (seafood in puff pastry is a specialty), and they do an excellent job with sweetbreads and rabbit. White chocolate is a house favorite; at least half of the dessert offerings use chocolate as an ingredient. Proudly displayed at the front of the room are rave notices from a number of New York gourmets. They can add mine, too!

LATTANZI

361 W 46th St   315-0980
Lunch: Mon-Fri; Dinner: Mon-Sat
American Express
Moderate

There's something about West 46th Street, the so-called "restaurant row" in the Broadway theater district, that is unappealing. Sign after sign, one restaurant after another—one wonders how they all stay in business. Actually, they don't! The comings and goings are rapid, and many really don't deserve to stay around. One of the winners, however, is Lattanzi, owned by a family of the same name. It's warm and cozy, with attractive brick walls. Management and service are disorganized and amateurish, but that doesn't take away from the excellent pre-theater Italian dinner. The usual pasta and antipasto are available, but I'd like to call attention to the Capellini Primavera, a very fine spaghetti with vegetables that's truly delicious. Then there's a combination seafood dish (some squid with fresh tomato, garlic, peas, and basil) and some of the best veal scaloppini I've ever tasted. Lamb chops, swordfish, and scampi are also featured. There's nothing special about the desserts here; however, you can't go wrong with the Napoleon or tartufo. Don't waste your time with most of the other places on "restaurant row" (except Orso). Head toward Lattanzi (with advance reservations), and you won't go wrong.

LAURENT

109 E 56th St (at Park Ave)   753-2729
Lunch: Mon-Fri; Dinner: Mon-Sat
Expensive

Laurent serves excellent food, beautifully prepared and presented (their fruit tart is a work of art) by waiters in black tie. It's a quiet, elegant restaurant patronized by quiet, elegantly dressed diners—the sort of place to go for an intimate dinner *à deux,* or for discussing business over a lobster. The sort of restaurant, in short, that is favored by executives with company credit cards. The menu changes daily, according to the season's best produce. Thus, in spring, soft-shell crabs are offered, while later on, shad and shad roe are available. Year-round favorites are duckling served with orange sauce, and steak au poivre flambé a l'Armagnac. There are three private dining rooms, and the restaurant's wine cellars stock over 54,000 bottles of wine, including vintages old and rare enough to satisfy the most discriminating palates. A *prix fixe* menu is available. Quite a place!

LE BERNARDIN
155 W 51st St   489-1515
Lunch, Dinner: Mon-Sat
Very expensive

Le Bernardin is a magnificent restaurant, no *ands, ifs,* or *buts* about it. Well, there is one *but,* which I'll get to later. The room itself is tasteful and classy, with colorful fishing scenes adorning the walls. The service is friendly, unobtrusive, and highly professional, just as you'd expect from Maguy and Gilbert LeCoze. The seafood dishes are marvelously fresh, tasty, and superbly seasoned with just the right sauces. The bass, sea scallops, and warm lobster salad are terrific appetizers. Then you may feast upon sea scallops, halibut, salmon done several different ways, snapper, and at least four different lobster dishes. The dessert selection includes warm mousse of passion fruit with raspberry and caramel (this takes first place) and a number of ice creams and sorbets, my favorite being the bitter chocolate. Now for the *but.* And it is a big one. The prices are simply outrageous. The same quality dishes, served perhaps in a less impressive atmosphere, are available in several other Manhattan seafood houses at half the price. But there are always those who equate high prices with "*the* place to go," and as long as that is the case, places like Le Bernardin will prosper.

LE BIARRITZ
325 W 57th St (bet Eighth and Ninth Ave)   757-2390
Lunch: Mon-Fri; Dinner: Mon-Sat
Moderate

What a pleasure to be treated so pleasantly by everyone at a restaurant! This is the kind of homey place where the busboy "lets" you keep the knife from the first course to reuse with the entree. But then, you don't come here for the professional service or fancy trimmings. New York is full of "neighborhood" restaurants, and Le Biarritz is one of the best in that category. It seems like home every evening as the regulars take most of the seats in this warm, smallish eatery. The place has been in the same location and in the same hands for over 25 years. Gleaming copper makes any eating establishment look inviting, and here you can see a first-rate collection of beautiful French copper cooking and serving pieces. If you're in the mood for escargots to start, the chef knows how to prepare them well. Or maybe some real French onion soup or crepes à la Biarritz (stuffed with crab meat). You can't go wrong with either. Entrees range from frog's legs provençale to boeuf bourguignonne to filet de sole veronique. The menu includes all kinds of chicken, lamb, beef, veal, and fish dishes, each served with fresh vegetables. Although there are no unusual desserts, all of them are homemade and very tasty. The reasonably priced dinner includes soup, salad, and a choice of dessert. I recommend Le Biarritz if you are going to a Broadway show or an event in the Lincoln Center area.

LE BILBOQUET
25 E 63rd St   751-3036
Lunch, Dinner: Daily
American Express
Moderate

Philippe presides over this cozy Upper East Side Parisian sidewalk cafe as if it were his own backyard. The place isn't really much bigger than that, but in nice weather you can eat outside on the sidewalk. Philippe seems to know everyone; indeed, most of the loyal clientele live in the neighborhood. Nonetheless, hungry visitors looking for good, informal dining all day long will feel just as welcome. It's amazing that such a tiny kitchen can turn out such good food. The pâté and the terrine de saumon are both delicious appetizers. Le Bilboquet is best known for its salads; the niçoise and duck salad with mangoes are the best bets. Any one of the assorted tarts are excellent, but my favorite is the lemon. The chocolate gâteau is definitely waist expanding! Philippe's constant presence is surely the secret of Le Bilboquet's success.

LE CHANTILLY
106 E 57th St   751-2931
Lunch, Dinner: Mon-Sat
Expensive

Some years back, a meal at Le Chantilly was a special New York treat. But, alas, the restaurant went distinctly downhill until a talented, gracious gentleman by the name of Camille Dulac took the reins. With a superior knowledge of the kitchen and a natural understanding of the importance of the owner being on the job to watch the operation, Camille has brought back the charm and distinction of this beautiful room. Today one would be hard-pressed to find a better meal, despite the pricey tab, in a more attractive setting. Complementing the food and ambiance, the professional staff ensures that your dining experience is a special one. There is something very elegant about having the dishes served with those gleaming silver covers, and then having them all lifted simultaneously at the table. It's like the opening of gifts. Under those covers you'll find such delicious luncheon choices as duck confit with ginger, smoked salmon omelet, casserole of fish, and seafood with fennel. A large choice of hot and cold hors d'oeuvres is offered with the fixed-price luncheon: try the chicken sausage with truffles, cold poached salmon, or the delicious fresh vegetable soup. À la carte offerings are also available. For dinner, you can order à la carte as well, or go with the fixed-price menu. Special dinner treats include breast of squab, roast rack of lamb, and roast muscovy duck. The dessert cart groans with an eye-popping selection of goodies, any one of which will be a fitting end to a magnificent meal.

LE CIRQUE
58 E 65th (at Park Ave)   794-9292
Lunch, Dinner: Mon-Sat
Expensive

Sirio Maccioni is a legend in the restaurant world of New York, and well he should be. While many of the grand, old-time restaurants rest on their laurels, Sirio is innovative and ingenious. Above all, he's a showman. His magnificent restaurant is crowded to the gills with the famous and those who would like to be. Elegant food draws these elegant folk. It is a pleasure to watch as the superbly orchestrated staff makes sure that every person in the room feels that he or she is someone very special. Each dish, whether it's game, fish, or meat, comes with superb sauces, and is served in satisfying portions. The "must try" dishes are the sea scallops fantasy, the fettucine with truffles, and the creme brûlée. Take along your goldest credit card, and be prepared for an event that would restore anyone's faith in the concept of the United Nations: a great American restaurant, serving superb French food, and orchestrated by an Italian.

L'ECOLE
462 Broadway (at Grand St)   219-3300
Lunch: Mon-Fri; Dinner: Mon-Sat
Moderate

Class is in session in the kitchen at L'École, the dining room of the French Culinary Institute. The students, eager and excited, are preparing daily meals under the watchful eye of the dean of culinary studies, their head chef and his team. They are learning their lessons well. Out front, the neighborhood is hardly the most inviting, and the maitre d' adds little to the effort inside. The room itself is attractive enough, if you can keep your eyes at table height and forget about the tall, unattractive ceiling. But the meals here are a real bargain! Dinner consists of a five-course effort, including a choice of appetizers, a fish dish, the entree (several selections), a salad, and dessert. It is obvious that the instructors are watching things very carefully, for each dish is presented beautifully, is served hot (or cold, as called for), and is uniformly delicious. Because there is a limited menu, the would-be chefs are able to concentrate on a few dishes. Semiprofessional waiters serve you at a leisurely pace; don't come here if you are in a hurry. The price is right, and the school cafeteria you remember from years back was never this good!

LE CYGNE
55 E 54th St   759-5941
Lunch: Mon-Fri; Dinner: Mon-Sat
Expensive

A most appealing ambiance combined with a very professional kitchen is really all that needs to be said about Le Cygne. This spot is one that you will not want to miss, but make sure it's saved for a great occasion or when you're dining on an expense account. The whole setting is comfortable, relaxing, and appealing. To begin your meal, how about Maine scallops in a wine and saffron sauce, or perhaps artichoke hearts with sweetbreads, mushrooms, and truffle sauce? And what a selection for the main course: frog's legs sautéed in garlic butter; snails with wild mushrooms; braised squab with olives, mushrooms, and artichokes; breast of duck in honey-vinegar sauce; and absolutely sensational braised sweetbreads with Chanterelle mushrooms. Meals run a hefty *prix fixe* tab, but it's well worth it. There are specialties of the house every day, and private dining facilities are available.

LE MADRI
168 W 18th St (at Seventh Ave)   727-8022
Lunch: Mon-Fri; Dinner: Daily
Moderate

Pino Luongo's mother would be very proud of him. He has created a great restaurant ("the Mother") busy and exciting as it should be, because he is serving first-class fare. The fact that he is personally on the job adds to what is surely one of the more pleasant new places in Manhattan. The site used to be the stables for Macy's and later a warehouse of Barney's. Today it is a charming establishment, with a delightful garden patio for warm evening meals and an appetizing interior, including a fabulous fresh vegetable and cheese display as you enter. The staff fits right into the ambiance, many of them bearing authentic Italian accents and native words of advice on the varied menu. Wonderful Italian bread gets you started, or you can have a Tuscan bread salad, if you desire. On to pastas, pizzas, or grilled and marinated vegetables. The place is spotless, noisy, colorful, and fun: although the youngish clientele is enough to keep you amused and intrigued, the food is the big draw here. Pino's dream of Italian Renaissance dining will continue to be a winner. . . . that is, if he doesn't forget the special lessons his mother taught him in the kitchen at home!

LE PISTOU
134 E 61st St (bet Lexington and Park Ave)   838-7987
Lunch: Mon-Sat; Dinner: Daily
Moderate

The accent is unmistakenly French at this East Side bistro. Conceived by the folks at La Côte Basque, Le Pistou is an ideal resting and feasting place for those who are starting or finishing their shopping expeditions. Loud French music pervades the atmosphere; this is probably all for the best, as many tables are too close together for intimate conversation. The place is spotlessly clean, the décor features dozens of beautiful French puppets, and the personnel are gracious in the extreme. What's more, the food matches the surroundings. Norwegian smoked salmon, baby artichokes in olive oil, and garlic sausage in crust are all presented in an appetizing manner. Main course favorites include breast of capon, veal scallopine, and a wonderful lamb stew with vegetables. The desserts are also first class. From the time the wonderful warm bread arrives at your table to the final cup of delicious cappuccino, you are going to have a very pleasant French outing.

LE REFUGE
166 E 82nd St (bet Third and Lexington Ave)
861-4505
Lunch, Dinner: Daily
No credit cards
Moderate (overpriced desserts)

In any city other than New York this would be one of the hottest restaurants in town. But aside from the folks in the neighborhood, nobody seems to have heard of Le Refuge, a charming, three-room French country inn that offers excellent food, professional service, and delightful surroundings. The front room (for nonsmokers) is cozy and comfortable, and the back two sections provide nice views and pleasant accommodations. This is another house where the owner is the chef, and as usual, it shows in the professionalism of the presentations. To start, I suggest the excellent salads, carpaccio, or raviolis langonstine. Then you have your choice of three seafood, three poultry, and three meat entrees. The Norwegian salmon with caviar is superb. Desserts are very special in taste and price. Creme brûlée, a flourless chocolate gâteau, and the poached pear with white and dark chocolate sauce are winners. Seek Le Refuge, and be prepared for a very special evening.

LE RÉGENCE

37 E 64th St   734-9100
Lunch, Dinner: Daily; Brunch: Sun
Expensive

Hotel Plaza Athénée is well-known in Paris; now there is a New York version with a very classy restaurant. Not only is the setting understated and immensely attractive, but the tables are even far enough apart to have a private conversation. The presentation is outstanding, and the food is superb! One of the most impressive points of Le Régence is that the personnel are not impressed with their own importance. The waiters and maitre d' are pleasantly accommodating, hard working, and well informed. Other expensive New York restaurants, take note; it can be done. This spot is suitable for either lunch or dinner. You can't go wrong with any of the selections, but a few favorites stand out. Since it's mainly a seafood house, I strongly recommend the Dover sole filets in champagne sauce, the lobster ravioli, and the braised striped bass in a marvelous wine sauce. The luncheon salads are magnificent; a real treat is the sliced chicken breast salad with hazelnuts. It's so inviting to look at, you hate to eat it! Even mundane French-fried potatoes are done to perfection. And don't overlook the meat entrees, like the veal chops and the delicious steaks. The famous French family of restaurateurs, the Rostangs, supervise this fine operation.

LES HALLES

411 Park Ave South (bet 28th and 29th St)   679-4111
Daily: Noon to midnight
Moderate

Les Halles has struck a responsive note on the New York restaurant stage. Perhaps it is because France remains the romantic scene to many gourmets or that bistros have become the "in" thing in Manhattan. But most probably it is because this establishment provides most of the necessary ingredients in today's restaurant sweepstakes: tasty food in an appealing atmosphere at reasonable prices. Les Halles is no place for those who want a quiet, leisurely meal. Specialties like blood sausage with apples, lamb stew, or fillet of beef are served in hefty portions, with a fresh salad and delicious French fries on the side. Harried waiters try their level best to be polite and helpful, but they are not always successful as tables turn over more rapidly than at most fast food outlets. If a week in Paris is more of a dream than a reality, you might settle for snails, onion soup, and classic cassoulet at this busy establishment. Unless you are big in the tart department, the dessert selection is a major disappointment. P.S. An attractive butcher shop is at your service right by the front door!

LES PLEIADES
20 E 76th St   535-7230
Lunch, Dinner: Mon-Sat
Moderate to expensive

What a well-organized restaurant this is! It's obvious that the folks here know the ins and outs of the business—another case of the management being on the job. I have seldom encountered a restaurant with better trained, more courteous personnel. From the time you call to make a reservation to your farewell at the door, your host, captain, waiter, and busboy—everyone—give the impression that they know what they're doing and that they're pleased to serve you. The clientele are strictly Upper East Side matrons and their husbands, or perhaps their middle-aged sons and daughters taking the "old folks" out to dinner. But what a nice, comfortable place to do so! The food is excellent, the atmosphere is charming, and the entire evening can be a most satisfactory experience. Many of the hors d'oeuvres are displayed at an attractive table near the entrance, and the choices are numerous: coquilles au safran, sardines a l'Huile, le saumon fume, a great lobster salad, and so on. For entrees, try the coquilles St. Jacques with white wine and saffron, or the frog's legs sautéed with garlic. Specialties of the house include sweetbreads, rack of lamb, and broiled Dover sole. If you feel really hungry, tell them at the start that you'd like one of their soufflés for dessert—either the Grand Marnier or the chocolate.

LE TRAIN BLEU
1000 Third Ave (Bloomingdale's, 6th floor)
705-2100
Lunch, Brunch: Mon-Sat; Afternoon snacks: Mon-Fri;
Dinner: Thurs
Moderate

All aboard! Those who are old enough to remember when eating on a train was elegant and fun can relive a bit of that experience on the sixth floor of Bloomies, at the end of the "Main Course" housewares area. You are seated in a mock dining car, with authentic atmosphere and accessories. The view through the windows, however, does not change. The menu is unusual and well done. You can dine lightly or with gusto on salads (there's one with goat cheese), pasta, or omelets. An especially tasty dish is the onion soup with croutons. Very rich desserts will fortify you for additional use of your plastic card: crème brûlée, pecan tarts and chocolate ganache cake are just a few examples. Le Train Bleu is available for private receptions and dinners, and it features one of the most extensive wine lists of any department-store restaurant. But what else would you expect from the ever-innovative folks at Bloomingdale's.

LION'S ROCK

316 E 77th St   988-3610
Dinner: Daily; Brunch: Sat (Spring, Summer), Sun
Moderate

More than 100 years ago, Jones Wood was a favorite picnic spot for New Yorkers. Part of an estate owned by Bishop Samuel Provost, it was distinguished by its outcroppings of red granite, which made it a popular place for romantic trysts. Today, the Lion's Rock restaurant operates in the same area, and it even has one of those large slabs of red granite in its backyard. It's a particularly delightful place in nice weather because of its sizable outdoor patio and beer garden, where cool water trickles down the rock. When it snows, the patio becomes a winter wonderland. The restaurant uses natural fresh herbs, no frozen foods, and no artificial flavorings. The menu includes hot and cold hors d'oeuvres. I was particularly impressed with the chicken pecan and duck. The brunch menu is an unusual one, with selections ranging from chilled strawberry soup to whole-wheat pancakes. For dessert, try the bread pudding, apple crisp, or the homemade sorbets. The excellent food and the atmosphere setting make Lion's Rock a unique Upper East Side dining experience.

LITTLE NELL'S TEA ROOM

343 E 85th St (bet First and Second Ave)
772-2046
Lunch: Mon-Fri; Dinner: Daily; Tea: Daily;
Brunch: Sat, Sun
Moderate

Little Nell is really Judy Nell Pickens, whose mother is also Nell. So it is only natural that she should be intrigued with Nell of Dickens' Old Curiosity Shop fame. Nell's cozy restaurant features Dickens on the wall, eclectic English memorabilia throughout, and especially friendly people who seem to be having a wonderful time serving you. There are two small rooms, with a kitchen in between. Try to be seated in the room to your left as you enter; it is brighter and more attractive. The food goes along with the surroundings: hearty but not fancy, served with tender loving care, and sure to satisfy. For lunch there are salads, pasta, and light entrees. Afternoon teas are very popular with homemade goodies. They feature a harpist on Sunday afternoon from three to five p.m. Dinners feature grilled Cornish hen and grilled marinated swordfish, along with a wonderful chicken breast sautéed with apple Calvados sauce. The brunches are a neighborhood favorite, offering melt-in-your-mouth buttermilk waffles topped with fresh fruit and potato pancakes with scallions and sautéed mushrooms. Nell and her associates seem intent to make Dickens come to life with fond memories of friends, food, and fun.

LOLA

30 W 22nd St (bet Fifth and Sixth Ave)   675-6700
Lunch: Mon-Fri; Dinner: Daily
Moderate

This is no place for those with claustrophobia, hearing aids, small stomachs, or headaches. Sexy and super-charged Lola has found the right combination: a jumping establishment with great music that is noisy and crowded and features delicious food. The decibel level can become intolerable, the quantity of food on your platter may seem so big it will almost turn you off, and the entertainment is so exciting that eating is almost secondary. But don't worry. When you finally get down to that Southern fried chicken or some super-tasty Caribbean-flavored food, you won't be disappointed. Lola makes sure, personally, that everyone has a great time. She even provides a gospel dinner on Sunday night!

LOTUS BLOSSOM

319 Greenwich St   219-0005
Lunch, Dinner: Daily
Moderate

In an area of TriBeCa that has come to life with several attractive new residential buildings, a new school, and a number of first-class restaurants, Lotus Blossom stands out as the best choice for true Cantonese-style Chinese food. The room is immaculate and comfortable, the personnel friendly and efficient, and all the food fresh, with no MSG used. Besides the usual selection found in a Chinese restaurant, Lotus Blossom offers superb Hakka specialties such as stuffed eggplant, Hakka scallops, and salt-baked gray sole with hot pepper. Other specialties of the house include Beijing duck (served in two courses) wrapped in homemade pancakes; crispy steak; shredded chicken and beef tenderloin served in a taro nest; and seafood with vegetables also served in a taro basket. The atmosphere is rather elegant for a moderately priced Chinese establishment; there is a noticeable absence of the usual noise and confusion. Free delivery service from the wide-ranging menu is available, and they cater any event (up to 150 people).

LOU G. SIEGEL

209 W 38th St   921-4433
Sun-Thurs: 11:30-10; Fri: 11:30-3
Moderate

Lou G. Siegel has been around longer than most New Yorkers can remember. It opened its doors in 1917, and customers have been pushing through them ever since. Its reputation—of which it is well aware ("The best-known kosher restaurant in the world," says Siegel's Eddie Share)—is based mostly on their cold cuts, especially the pastrami. Workers in the garment district fill the place during lunch and dinner hours. Remember that, and schedule your visit for an early lunch or a "white tablecloth" dinner.

L'OUSTRALET
448 E 79th   249-4920
Dinner: Mon-Sat
Moderate

If you are tired of the "in" places, try this one! Owner André Campana is the maitre d', the bartender, the captain, the waiter, and the cashier. Oh yes, he does have help both out front and in the kitchen, but the charm of this small, cozy establishment is that there is absolutely no hype. The service is friendly and quick, the food is absolutely first-rate, the price is right, and you can come as you are. Why a place like this is not crowded to the gills is beyond me, for you can't find a better all-around value on the Upper East Side. From the start, when warm bread is placed before you, to the tasty salads and soups and the delicious entrees (like rack of lamb, sweetbreads, and baked salmon) everything is done with tender loving care in the kitchen. French house specialties like choucroute, couscous, and coq au vin are available. A baked-to-order apple tart will send you away with smiles. That André sure earns his board and keep!

LUTÈCE
249 E 50th St (bet Second and Third Ave)   752-2225
Lunch: Tues-Fri; Dinner: Mon-Sat
Expensive

The standard by which so many of the restaurants in Manhattan are judged is Lutèce. It's so high-toned that there aren't even prices on the menu. Almost every restaurant guide lists it as number one. I'm not sure it's that, but certainly the chefs are masters, and the service is impeccable. The owner, Andre Soltner, has received many awards, and they're well deserved. Lutèce is housed in a former brownstone that's tastefully decorated with handsome furnishings and shimmering tableware. An indoor garden at the back adds to the charm. The restaurant also features three great *s*'s—soups, snails, and sauces. All of them are about the best in New York. Try the saumon à la mousse de moutarde or the carré de agneau caramelisé. But be prepared for less than great service if they don't know you. Nonetheless, you can't beat Lutèce. Considering their prices, ask if you can take home the beautiful menu as a souvenir!

MADELINE'S
117 Prince St   477-2788
Breakfast, Lunch, Dinner: Tues-Sun
Moderate

Madeline Lanciani was a part of the famed Patisserie Lanciani, one of New York's best. Now she has brought that expertise to Madeline's where she has expanded the treats to include an excellent selection for any meal of the day. Appetizers range from barbecued quail to pan-fried oysters; wonderful pastas looking like a page from an Italian cookbook; entrees like fricassee of lobster and lotte or pan-roasted game hen with matzoh dumplings. A special chef's five-course tasting menu is available. But oh, those desserts; not less than 13 are offered. Each one is a feast for the eyes and the palate. Take your pick: raspberry Bavarian, old-fashioned bread pudding, chocolate cake and bittersweet chocolate mousse, pistachio Amaretto cake, chocolate almond torte, mocha and bittersweet chocolate seven-layer torte. You get the picture. All of this comes for a fraction of what you would pay uptown at a classy operation. Yes, these people know what they are doing—from the end of the meal to the start!

MANHATTAN CAFE
1161 First Ave (at 64th St)   888-6556
Lunch: Mon-Fri; Dinner: Daily; Brunch: Sat, Sun
Moderate to expensive

New York does not have all that many classy steakhouses, although several have opened in recent years. Manhattan Cafe is one of them, and it is indeed an attractive, pleasant place to dine. Start with the shrimp, the lump of crab meat, or even the overpriced Nova Scotia salmon. The steaks are large and delicious, as are the lamb chops and prime rib. Even the seafood, especially the filet of sole, is worth trying. A number of veal dishes are available, with the veal piccata being particularly good. Accompany your choice with the excellent cottage fried potatoes. For dessert, the tartufo equals any I've tasted in Italy (except for Tre Scalini's in Rome), and the cheesecake absolutely melts in your mouth. This polished establishment is an excellent place for an expense-account outing.

MARCH
405 E 58th st (bet First Ave and Sutton Place)
838-9393
Lunch: Wed-Thurs; Dinner: Mon-Sat
Expensive

I usually shy away from restaurants with fixed-price menus, because I believe in many cases you do not get true value. This is definitely *not* the case at March. As a matter of fact, I would sug-

gest that you allocate eight nights to visit this outstanding operation. In that way, you could taste every one of the eight appetizers,
entrees, and desserts offered on the unusual menu. Chef Wayne
Nish and host Joe Scalice have their separate responsibilities honed
to excellence, and it shows in the service and food. Each dish has a
special feature, like rabbit sausage with savory bread pudding, rack
of lamb with herbed crust and gnocchi, seared beef with warm
potato salad and miso. And what desserts! Vanilla custard with
raspberries, warm chocolate cake with pear sauce and soft caramel,
mascarpone chibouste with chocolate macaroon and espresso
sauce; get the picture? Actually, you'll get more than a picture
here; you'll get your $45 *prix fixe* money's worth!

MARCHI'S
251 E 31st St   679-2494
Dinner: Mon-Sat
Moderate

It's amazing that I didn't discover this place earlier. It must be
one of the best-kept secrets in New York. Indeed, there's no sign
out front, but Marchi's has been a New York fixture since 1930,
when it was established by the Marchi family in an attractive brownstone townhouse. The Marchis, joined by their three sons, are still
on hand, giving a homey flavor to the restaurant's three dining
rooms and garden patio (a great spot for a private dinner). It's almost like going for dinner at your favorite Italian family's house,
especially since there are no menus. Be sure you have a hearty appetite when you arrive, so you can take full advantage of a superb
feast. The first course is a platter of antipasto, including radishes,
finocchio, and Genoa salami, plus a salad of tuna fish, olives, and
red cabbage. The second is an absolutely delicious homemade lasagne. The third is either crispy deep-fried fish or sautéed chicken
livers; the side orders of cold beets and string beans are light and
tempting. The entree is delicious roast chicken and roast veal served
with fresh mushrooms and a tossed salad. For dessert, there is a
healthy bowl of fresh fruit, cheese, a lemon fritter, and sensational
Crostoli (crisp fried twists sprinkled with powdered sugar). The
price tag is decidedly *under*whelming. Come to Marchi's for a unique, leisurely meal—and an evening you will long remember.

MARK'S RESTAURANT
25 E 77th St (bet Fifth and Madison Ave)   744-4300
Lunch, Dinner: Daily; Brunch: Sun
Moderately expensive

In a setting that will remind you of an English club, one can enjoy a delicious dinner with refined service and no distractions to take
away from a very pleasant meal. The appetizers are heavy in the
seafood area: oysters, scallops, red snapper, salmon, and prawns

are all uniquely presented. Main course possibilities run the gamut
from staples like filet mignon and roast rack of lamb to more exotic
dishes like lobster baked potato or red snapper on eggplant caviar.
Desserts are all made in-house and feature great possibilities like
profiteroles with three different kinds of ice cream. Beautiful
flowers, nice wood tables, gorgeous china and informed servers
complete what is one of the most satisfying dining experiences on
the Upper East Side.

MARYLOU'S

21 W 9th St   533-0012
Lunch: Mon-Fri; Dinner: Daily; Brunch: Sun
Moderate

Marylou owns a fish store in the Village, so it's only natural that
she would want to see her product served in an appealing manner.
She has done just that at Marylou's, also in the Village. There are
several rooms—some with fireplaces, some with books—all very
cozy. Not-too-close tables help set the stage. For starters, there's
quite a selection of fish dishes, including cold mussel salad, smoked
trout, and great chowders. The entree menu is large, including
many things other than fish, although they are the specialties. Of
particular note are the broiled filet of sole, the seafood brochette,
the trout almondine, and mesquite-grilled jumbo shrimp. Inas-
much as Marylou has a number of special fresh fish items in her
market, the menu reflects these daily specials. Before you order,
make sure you ask about them. For those not wanting fish, the
chicken pot pie is scrumptious, and the steak Madagascar is equally
good. All the entrees are served with rice or potatoes and a vegetable. All desserts are homemade! After a most satisfying meal, try
the lemon or raspberry mousse or the special chocolate plate featuring all sorts of goodies! I was very impressed with the efficient and
friendly but not overbearing help, the reasonable prices, and the
delicious food. This is definitely one of the Village's better spots.

McSORLEY'S OLD ALE HOUSE

15 E 7th St (at Third Ave)   473-8800
Mon-Fri: 11-midnight; Sat: noon-midnight;
Sun: 1-midnight
No credit cards
Inexpensive

If it's local color you want, you've got to visit McSorley's Old
Ale House. Established in 1854, it's one of the original pubs of
New York. Abe Lincoln, the Roosevelts, and John Kennedy have
guzzled here. It's certainly not on the beaten track, but the atmosphere is terrific, and the ale is great. One can conjure up visions of
all the good times spent in this old watering hole. It completely

lacks the pretentiousness of so many New York eating places. The sawdust on the floor completes the picture of the classic spot to take your drinking buddy. And now, after all these years, women are welcome. The menu is limited and secondary to the ales, but hearty sandwiches, cheese platters, and burgers are available. Put on your jeans, take a stroll down to old New York, and listen while you sip. Everyone in the place is a character—except you, of course.

MESA GRILL
102 Fifth Ave (near 15th St)   807-7400
Lunch: Mon-Fri; Dinner: Mon-Sat
Moderate

Sometimes restaurants are included in guidebooks because everyone is talking about them, not necessarily because of their appealing atmosphere or great food. This is certainly the reason for the inclusion of the Mesa Grill in this volume! The décor and the color scheme could hardly be more unattractive. The bistro's noise level is absolutely intolerable; pleasant conversation is virtually impossible. This would definitely not be my choice for a relaxing, intimate meal. However, if you concentrate on the food, and if you like good, hot dishes, you'll do well here. The salads are delicious; entrees like red snapper roasted in banana leaves and grilled chicken breast with corn and grilled pepper relish will wake up any appetite. For those who want to be a part of the New York scene and don't really care about decibels and heartburn, put on your cowboy boots and saddle up!

MEZZOGIORNO
195 Spring St   334-2112
Lunch, Dinner: Daily
Moderate

Florence, Italy, is one of the most charming places to visit, not only for its abundance of great art, but for the wonderful small restaurants you find on every street. Mezzogiorno, a Florence-style trattoria in New York, is located in what used to be the SoHo Charcuterie. It certainly adds a tasty new dimension to the SoHo area. The place is busy and noisy; the tables are so close together that a private conversation is impossible. The décor is best described as "modern Florence"; check out the unusual writing on the ceiling. Better yet, keep your eyes on the food. The salad selection is outstanding, and all of them are delicious and unusual. Fine entrees of linguini, fettuccine, and ravioli are available, as well as some tasty veal and steak dishes. Mezzogiorno is already famous for the pizzas it serves during the noon hour and in the evening. You'll find all the necessary ingredients here for a wonderful make-believe evening in Florence.

MICHAEL'S
24 W 55th St (bet Fifth and Sixth Ave)   767-0555
Breakfast: Mon-Fri; Lunch, Dinner: Daily
Moderately expensive

Michael McCarty has brought his recipe for success from Santa Monica, California, to the Big Apple. There is something very appetizing about this place, from the minute you walk in until you finish the spectacular "Heath Bar" dessert (caramel custard torte with layers of caramel and chocolate, topped with caramel mousse and wrapped in bittersweet chocolate). The menu is essentially light California fare, with starters like oysters on the half shell, air-dried beef, and delicious fettucine. One could make a whole meal of a salad; I found the Maine lobster with avocado and onions to be a winner. Main courses run the gamut from poached eggs and Iowa bacon to scallops and swordfish. More adventurous dishes might be quail or animal-farm duck with Grand Marnier. The steak and french fries are perfection. Besides the Heath Bar for dessert, there is carmelized walnut torte and a wonderful raspberry mousse cake. The only downside is the rude practice of adding a 15 percent service charge for all food and beverage items. What does T.I.P. stand for, Michael?

MINETTA TAVERN
113 MacDougal St   475-3850
Lunch, Dinner: Daily
Moderate

Do you want to take your kids or guests to a Village restaurant where the coat-and-tie, meat-and-potatoes set will feel comfortable? Well, Minetta Tavern, established in 1937 and serving excellent food to generations of the famous and not so famous, is the place to go. Located on the spot where the Minetta Brook wandered through Manhattan in the very early days, this Tavern was made famous by Eddie "Minetta" Sieveri, a friend of many of the sports and stage stars of yesteryear. Dozens of old pictures adorn the walls of this intimate, scrupulously clean tavern, where professional personnel serve no-nonsense Italian food at attractive prices. Stuffed mushrooms, baked clams, or the traditional spinach and egg soup are good ways to get the juices flowing. Follow that up with the pasta with red lettuce and shrimp or perhaps Branzino, a great combination of sea bass, onions, vinegar, tomato cubes, and white wine. If you'd like something a bit heftier, grilled Cornish game hen and steaks are also available. The almond cake would make a wonderful cap to a satisfying meal. By the way, if you have to wait, the bar stools at the Minetta have to be the most comfortable in New York.

MME. ROMAINE DE LYON
29 E 61st St (at Madison Ave)   758-2422
Lunch: Daily; Dinner: Mon-Fri
Moderate

The best omelets in New York are served at Mme. Romaine's. If you can't find what you want from their 545 varieties, it probably doesn't exist. How about a lobster, spinach, or chicken omelet? They will make any combination you want. When you're in the mood for a light lunch or dinner, this is the place to go. If omelets are not your bag, you might try the chef salad or the smoked salmon, and at dinnertime, duck, chicken, calf's liver, and veal dishes are available.

MONDRIAN
7 E 59th St (near Fifth Ave)   935-3434
Lunch: Mon-Fri; Dinner: Mon-Sat
Expensive

For awhile it looked like this attractive house might be one of the casualties of the trend away from pricey eating establishments. Then some new blood was infused in the kitchen, and things rapidly changed for the better. One doesn't mind paying top price for a meal from time to time if there is true excellence, and it can now be safely said that Mondrian presents some outstanding dishes. Lobster and artichoke salad is a great appetizer. Every entree, from roast venison to roasted salmon, is appealing! Chocolate lovers can order a tasting of chocolate dessert items or the chocolate ganache cake with bay leaf syrup, which will put you completely at ease after a very special evening's experience. Business accounts might ease the blow for the hefty tab!

MONTRACHET
239 W Broadway   219-2777
Lunch: Fri; Dinner: Mon-Sat
American Express
Moderately expensive

The TriBeCa area is not picturesque, but it is thriving, and exciting places like Montrachet make it a very appealing place to visit. Once inside Montrachet, the feeling of drabness dissipates. The staff used to wear awful black outfits, but that has changed. Now you can concentrate, undistracted, on a fine array of seafood, game, and meat prepared to perfection by the restaurant's latest super chef, Debra Ponzek. One of her predecessors, David Bouley, was so good that he has gone on to open his own successful restaurant. The menu changes regularly, with exciting new things done with fresh produce. If you are lucky enough to find a bouillabaisse dish on the menu, go for it. Roast pheasant, roast chicken, and roast duck are outstanding choices, and Debra does lobster dishes to perfection. The presentation is half the fun, and the three simply decorated rooms do not detract from the main reason you are there: good eating. The desserts have finally come up to par with the rest of the menu, with soufflés at the top of the list. Having tasted many crème brûlée dishes, I can say with authority that Montrachet's is one of the best.

MOONDANCE DINER
Sixth Ave at Grand St   226-1191
Sun-Thurs: 8:30 a.m.-midnight;
Fri, Sat: 24 hours
No credit cards
Moderate

Remember that old song: "Dinner in the diner, nothing could be finer." Well, of course it *could* be finer than the Moondance, but it would surely cost you a heck of a lot more, and I'm not sure the quality would be any better. Larry Panish, a graduate of the Culinary Institute of America, turned an old greasy-spoon diner into a spotless, efficient operation that serves absolutely first-class "simple" food at a price anyone can afford. There is the usual counter and about a dozen tables; what isn't usual is the great taste of wholesome salads and sandwiches for lunch and the gourmet-style chicken, steak, and what-have-you for dinner. The help is extra polite; the plates are balanced and attractive. Specialties include great onion rings, outstanding chili, and homemade apple pie. Daily specials are listed on the blackboard, and take-out orders are available. Drop by for breakfast, and you'll be starting the day out right! Larry's Lox Around the Clock (676 Sixth Ave) is equally well operated. Note the extended weekend hours!

NANOU
24 E 21st St   505-5252
Lunch: Mon-Thurs; Dinner: Sun-Thurs, Sat in winter
Moderate to moderately expensive

Very fine French Mediterranean cuisine is served in this kosher house at prices that are not out of line with the quality offered. Excellent salads, soups and omelets are almost meals in themselves. Entree selections include chicken, cold poached salmon, roast duckling, and steaks. The side dish of sautéed potatoes and onions is very special. Whether you are interested in a top-notch kosher restaurant, or just some really excellent food, Nanou is a good choice. The setting is rather stark, but the friendly personnel make up for the chilly surroundings.

NICK AMD EDDIE
203 Spring St (at Sullivan St)   219-9090
Lunch, dinner: Daily
Moderate

This place is so popular it looks like the only ones missing are Nick and Eddie themselves. It turns our that the place was named for two kids in the neighborhood. It is easy to understand the popularity: good food in a hearty atmosphere at reasonable prices. If there is one word to describe the plates, it is *wholesome*. There are no affectations with the menu or the service, everything is just what you would want to be served at home. Potato pancakes and apple compote or an ice-cold salad make good starters. The salads, especially, are tasty and filling. Main courses include burgers, a number of grilled fish dishes (salmon, catfish, red trout, shrimp), or tender steaks with real mashed potatoes and well-cooked veggies. The banana bread with ice cream and hot fudge is the best dessert. Better call ahead for reservations, for at these prices word is sure to get around!

OLD DENMARK
133 E 65th St (at Lexington Ave)   744-2533
Mon-Sat: 9-5:30
No credit cards
Inexpensive to moderate

Old Denmark is really a gourmet food shop, but it is also a good spot to go for a light, quick, different kind of lunch. And if you are keen on Scandinavian food items, you can stock up here. There is no menu, but you have your choice of assorted salads and appetizers, tasty breads, and cakes. Old Denmark is very handy when you are out shopping and don't want anything too heavy. The personnel are particularly helpful.

OLDE GARDEN CAFE & WINERY
15 W 29th St   532-8323
Lunch: Mon-Fri; Dinner: Mon-Sat
Inexpensive to moderate

So you're all worn-out after pushing through the crowds at Macy's or shopping the discount photo stores, or maybe you just got off the train at Penn Station. Whatever the case, it's an easy walk to the Olde Garden Cafe & Winery on West 29th Street, an enchanting place established in 1912. It was originally an antiques shop that offered tea and sandwiches to its customers. Folks liked the eats so well that the owners decided to give up the antiques and concentrate on the treats. An open garden in the back has now been covered. The restaurant encompasses several warm and attractive rooms with wooden floors and partial brick walls. A smattering of antiques are still around, and the comfortable captain's chairs and wooden tables add to the inviting ambiance. This is a great place for lunch. All kinds of salads are offered: diced chicken platter, Olde Garden Club salad, or the executive salad bowl with Swiss cheese, ham, shrimp, and anchovy and herb dressing. Entree selections include ocean sole, sea scallops, wiener schnitzel, Western prime rib of beef, eggs Benedict, and several different kinds of omelets. All entrees are served with potato and garden vegetables. Reasonably priced desserts include a wonderful apple strudel and freshly baked pies. This is a great spot for a leisurely lunch, particularly with friends from out of town.

107 WEST
2787 Broadway (at 107th St)   864-1555
Dinner: Daily; Brunch: Sun
Moderate

107 West is attractive and clean, with a pleasant glassed-in sidewalk area. The menu definitely has a Southern accent. Buffalo chicken wings, Louisiana crab cakes, Cajun popcorn, and the like are offered as appetizers for such entrees as hickory-smoked ribs, crispy Southern fried chicken with mashed potatoes, jambalaya, and Mississippi Delta catfish. There are side orders of Southern favorites, like fried bananas and Cajun rice. Pasta is also available. The menu is interesting, the service is prompt and pleasant, and the price is right. Y'all come!

ONE IF BY LAND, TWO IF BY SEA
17 Barrow St (bet Seventh Ave and W 4th St)
228-0822
Dinner: Daily
Expensive

Finding this place is a bit of a challenge, but what a reward when you do! The building that was once Aaron Burr's old carriage house is truly unique, and the atmosphere is warm and friendly. One if By Land is especially popular with young people, who appreciate the romantic ambiance, as well as the extraordinarily good food. Make reservations before coming down, and allow yourself enough time to find Barrow Street (one of the Village's most charming yet hard-to-find side streets) and the restaurant (there's no sign out front), so that you'll have a few minutes to enjoy a drink at the spacious bar by the fireplace. Try to get a table on the balcony level; it's especially romantic. As for dinner, the roast rack of lamb, Long Island duckling, grilled filet mignon, and beef Wellington are all excellent. Dessert is an ever-changing selection of delicious homemade goodies.

ORSO
322 W 46th St   489-7212
Mon, Tues, Thurs, Fri, Sun: 1-11:45;
Wed, Sat: 11:30 a.m.-11:45 p.m.
Moderate

This restaurant features the same menu all day, which is great for those with unusual dining hours and handy for those going to the theater. Orso is one of the most popular places on midtown's "restaurant row," so if you're thinking about a six o'clock dinner, be sure to make reservations. The smallish room is cozy and comfortable and watched over by a portrait of Orso, a Venetian dog who's the mascot for this no-nonsense Italian bistro. The kitchen is open in the back and visible to the diners; you can see for yourself just how experienced the staff is. The menu includes many good appetizers, like grilled shrimp, cold roast veal, and fried artichokes. A number of pizzas and some excellent pasta dishes are also offered. For an entree, you can't go wrong with the lamb sausage or the veal shank. The truffle gelato, one of many homemade desserts, could finish off a great meal.

PALM
837 Second Ave (at 44th St)
687-2953

PALM TOO
840 Second Ave (at 44th St)
697-5198

Lunch: Mon-Fri; Dinner: Mon-Sat
Expensive

Steak and lobster lovers in Manhattan have a special place in their hearts for the Palm and Palm Too. These two restaurants are located across the street from each other, and both have much the same atmosphere. The waiters will tell you what's available—there is no printed menu. They're noted for huge, delicious steaks, chops, and lobsters, but don't miss the Palm fries—homemade potato chips. They're the best. Or try a combination order of fries and great onion rings. It's an earthy spot, so I wouldn't get too dressed up. There is sawdust on the floor, thick tobacco and grease smoke in the air, and outrageous caricatures on the dirty walls. You are only part of the passing scene to the indolent waiters, but come early (it's usually crowded) and enjoy the good bread, an excellent salad, and the expensive entrees. You won't forget it.

PAMIR
1437 Second Ave (bet 74th and 75th St)   734-3791
Dinner: Tues-Sun
Inexpensive

You probably don't have Afghanistan at the top of your list of countries to visit, but this Afghan restaurant definitely should be. The room is small, the personnel refreshingly low-key, modest, and friendly, and the food different enough to make an evening here a novel experience. Turnovers are an Afghan specialty, and Pamir offers several: one stuffed with scallions, herbs, and spices; another stuffed with potato, ground beef, and spices. If you like extra-spicy food (like that served in the native country), they will gladly oblige, but you needn't worry if that is not to your liking. And the Afghan bread! It's great, and you get it with each entree. Lamb is the order of the day: seasoned lamb with rice, almonds, and pistachios; chunks of lamb in an onion- and garlic-flavored spinach sauce; lamb and eggplant cooked with tomatoes, onions, and spices; lamb on a skewer, marinated in spices; lamb chops broiled on a skewer— all worth a try. The best choice, however, is Pamir kabab: four different kinds of kabab on skewers, broiled with vegetables and served with brown rice. Several vegetarian dishes are also available. Eat heartily from the start, because the desserts are zilch. The folks here are so unpretentious, the desire to please so sincere, and the prices so modest that this just has to be one of the best ethnic-restaurant choices.

PAOLA'S
347 E 85th St   794-1890
Dinner: Daily
American Express
Moderate

One of the pleasures of writing a book such as this is getting the opportunity to visit with readers who have a special question or an unusual need. Several times young ladies have called asking me to suggest a place to take their boyfriends for a cozy and romantic evening. One young lady even called the next day to tell me it had worked: the young man proposed! Paola's, a tiny hole-in-the-wall, is a prime spot for such an evening. The only problem might be that you'll have an audience for the proposal, since the room has just ten tables and it gets crowded and intimate. But no matter. The Italian home cooking is first-class. Paola is in the kitchen taking care of the food. Great homemade pasta, superb veal dishes, and tasty hot vegetables (like grilled radicchio) are house specialties. Take along a Velamint if romance is in the air, because they don't use garlic sparingly. The folks here are pleasant and informal, the mirrors reflect the warmth and flicker of the candles, and the lady of the house will charm any guest. To top off the reasonably priced dinner, in the nice weather, try a dish of espresso ice cream, so creamy and rich. There are dozens of small Italian restaurants going in and out of business almost weekly on the Upper East Side, but Paola's is here to stay.

PAPER MOON MILANO
39 E 58th St   758-8600
Lunch: Mon-Sat; Dinner: Mon-Sat
Moderate

This offshoot of the well-known Milan house bills itself as a "restaurant-pizzeria." It does a good job in both classifications. In a high-rent area, the atmosphere is friendly and casual; patrons in jeans and sportswear will feel perfectly comfortable. Décor is simple and appealing. The harried help tries its best to be accommodating, although most of them seem to be having a Maalox moment! Try the assorted appetizers from the attractive buffet to start; they look and taste delicious. A fine selection of salads and pastas is offered, each presented with a finesse that comes from years of experience in Italy. The full menu includes fish, meat, and poultry dishes, as well as several carpaccio dishes (thin slices of raw beef with various toppings). But you will be missing something special if you don't try the pizzas. A talented young Italian pizza chef turns out some of the lightest, tastiest combinations you have ever savored. They are a meal in themselves. A refreshing dish of gelati will top off a wonderful meal. The place is a winner.

PAPPA'S PLACE
510 Sixth Ave (at 13th St)   924-3799
Breakfast, Lunch, Dinner: Daily
Moderate

Pappa has gone wild. Under one roof, he has assembled a treasure house for kids. Appetizers and soups and snacks. Big burgers with all the trimmings. Delicious sandwiches with homemade fillings. Healthy salads and cold plates. Tasty entrees like lasagna and pot pies. Quiches and individual pizzas. Brunch items like blintzes and pancakes and omelets and waffles that are served all day, every day. But the real eye-openers are in the sweets departments. Candy jars line the walls. Next to these temptations are dozens of different kinds of ice creams, including the less caloric varieties. Wash all this down with a selection of international cappuccinos and coffees. How's this for a teaser: the Kahlua momma, a magnificent dish of mocha chip and vanilla ice cream with chocolate syrup, Kahlua, whipped cream, and ground coffee beans. Let's go!

PARIOLI ROMANISSIMO
24 E 81st St   288-2391
Dinner: Mon-Sat
Expensive

When you pay these prices, you want class and great food. You get both in abundance at Parioli. Outstandingly helpful personnel serve you in a rather intimate room (or garden area) on tables appointed with Tiffany-style china, glassware, and silver. Save your appetite, even if that means passing up the Macadamian nuts at the bar! Instead, feast upon scampi or some delicious pasta, like trevette or fettuccine alfredo. Appetizer selections change with every season. And what a selection of veal dishes. Each one is a treat in itself. Choose from sautéed veal, breaded veal chops, rolled veal scallopine, filet of veal, or rack of veal. Of course, game, chicken, beef, and steak dishes are also offered, with superbly done (and very expensive) vegetables as side orders. The zabaglione is marvelous, and the chocolate cake—a bittersweet and brownie delight—is not only sinful, it's downright exciting! The cheese cart is also sensational.

PARIS COMMUNE
411 Bleecker St   929-0509
Dinner: Daily; Brunch: Sat, Sun
Moderate

Tony and Ari operate this small, charming Greenwich Village bistro. It is a neighborhood gathering place, and each evening the rooms fill up quickly with regulars. The food is absolutely first-rate, with prices no one could possibly complain about. There are just a dozen tables, each one promptly served by attentive, friendly waiters. Even the owners take orders, bus dishes, and help with all those important little things that make dining a pleasure. At noon on Saturday and Sunday, a super brunch features the best French toast anywhere, along with cereals, eggs, omelets, English muffins, and pomme frits. The delicious omelets include cheddar cheese and bacon, apples and Jarlsberg cheese, and marinated artichoke hearts and mozzarella. On the regular dining menu, which changes seasonally, there is always a good selection of soups, salads, and poultry, meat, and fish entrees. The mustard grilled chicken is a house favorite. The dessert course is a must; their own cheesecakes come in a variety of flavors. They manage to make the chocolate-chip bundt cake, served with mounds of whipped cream, seem so light that you won't realize how much you've sinned. Join the community at the Paris Commune. It's a real Village find.

PARK BISTRO
414 Park Ave S (bet 28th and 29th St)   689-1360
Lunch: Mon-Fri; Dinner: Mon-Sun
Moderate

This is a bistro you will want to visit over and over again. Some of the folks from the short-lived Maxim's Hotel moved downtown to take over this small, homey dining room, which specializes in cuisine from the Provence region of France. It's a jewel. From the start, when warm and tasty bread is placed before you, to the finishing touches of rich and luscious homemade desserts (like crème brûlée, gâteau basque, tortes, and a sinful chocolate gâteau), you are surrounded by attentive service and magnificent food. Don't miss the shellfish soup at the start. The entrees include fresh codfish, skate fish, and lobster, all presented with tasty and attractive side dishes.

PARKSIDE
107-01 Corona Ave (at 51st Ave and 108th St,
Corona, Queens)   (718) 271-9274
Lunch, Dinner: Daily
Moderate

You want to show that person who "knows everything about New York" something he or she doesn't know? You want to eat on your way to or from LaGuardia or Kennedy airport? You want a special meal in an unusual setting? Well, any of the above is an excellent reason to visit Parkside, in Queens. Yes, I know this is a book on Manhattan, but this place is worth making an exception. Ed D'Angelo runs a first-class, spotlessly clean restaurant that serves wonderful Italian food at prices that make most New York restaurateurs look like highway robbers. Start with garlic bread and then choose from two dozen different kinds of pasta and an opulent array of fish, steak, veal, and poultry dishes. The meat is all prime cut—nothing frozen here. You'll also find polite, knowledgeable waiters in an informal atmosphere. Get a table in the garden room, eat until your heart's content, and be amazed when you see the tab. You'll see why Parkside is so exceptional.

PATSY'S
236 W 56th St (bet Broadway and Eighth Ave)
247-3491
Lunch, Dinner: Daily
Moderate

For half a century, the Scognamillo family has operated this popular eatery specializing in Neapolitan cuisine. At the moment, son is taking care of the front of the house, and grandson is following the family tradition in the kitchen. "Patsy" was an immigrant gentleman chef whose nickname was soon attached to a New York tradition that has now grown into a two-level restaurant, each floor with its own cozy atmosphere and convenient kitchen. The family makes sure that every guest is treated as if they were in a private home; courtesy and concern are the name of the game here. A full Italian menu is available, with numerous specials that include a different soup and seafood entree each day. If you can't find what you like among the two dozen pasta choices, you are in deep trouble!

PEPPERMINT PARK CAFE AND BAKERY
1225 First Ave (bet 66th and 67th St)
288-5054 (cafe); 288-5415 (candy)
Lunch, Dinner: Daily (open late)
Moderate

There are a number of excellent reasons to visit Peppermint Park: if you want a light meal, if you're a dessert lover, if you want to eat after a show, if you've got the kids with you, or if you simply prefer informal restaurants with carnival-like atmosphere. For sustenance, there are fantastic crepes, like the Crepe Train Robbery (creamed spinach with your choice of sharp cheddar or Roquefort cheese) or Crepe Canaveral—they say it blasts your spirits into orbit. Another good combination: fresh mushrooms, sautéed onions, melted Gruyère, and blended herbs. Several dessert crepes are also available, like the one with maple syrup, melted butter, and powdered sugar. There are all kinds of Belgian waffle concoctions and a few quiches. The big news, though, is the fantastic selection of homemade ice creams (from mocha chip—number one for me—to rum raisin and black raspberry), several sherbets and sorbets, big banana splits, really thick shakes, yogurts, a selection of ten toppings—among them, walnuts in syrup, crushed cherries, and hot butterscotch—and an array of pastries, cakes, and cookies you won't believe, all made with fresh eggs.

PIETRO'S
232 E 43rd St   682-9760
Lunch: Mon-Fri; Dinner: Mon-Sat
Expensive

Pietro's Restaurant is a steakhouse with Northern Italian cuisine; everything is cooked to order. The menu features steaks and chops, seafood, chicken, and an enormous selection of veal. Tell your companion not to bother getting dressed up. Bring your appetite, though, because the portions are huge. Although steaks are the best known of Pietro's dishes, you will also find eight chicken dishes and ten veal selections (marsala, cacciatore, scallopine, piccata, francaise, etc.). And for meat-and-potato lovers, there are eight different potato dishes. Prices border on expensive, and the service is boisterous, but you'll certainly get your money's worth.

PIG HEAVEN
1540 Second Ave (bet 80th and 81st St)   PIG-4333
Lunch, Dinner: Daily
Moderate

This one may be a forerunner of things to come in Peking! The look is French country, the food is Chinese delicious, the pigs are everywhere. You'd never know you were in a Chinese restaurant, judging from the wood-covered walls and the fresh flowers. This is one of David Keh's operations; he owns and operates a number of Chinese eating spots in Manhattan. The menu offers many hot and cold pork dishes, the best of which are the spring rolls and steamed little dumplings in a basket. The barbecued spareribs are also super. Other winners include beef with snow peas, and flattened shrimp in shells with hot pepper sauce. A number of dishes are very spicy, so be prepared. You can look in through a glass window at the kitchen and see the various items being prepared for both in-house consumption and orders to go. And hallelujah! Finally, someone got smart about desserts in a Chinese restaurant. Instead of the limited selection offered in most, here you can enjoy American apple pie, Peking snow balls, and a sensational frozen praline mousse.

PINOCCHIO
170 E 81st St   650-1513, 879-0752
Lunch: Tues-Sat; Dinner: Daily
American Express
Moderate

Pinocchio is off the beaten path: a small and inexpensive restaurant that serves the kind of Italian food Geppetto's grandmother used to make. You won't find the menu limited to spaghetti and pizza. Pinocchio specializes in regional Italian cooking, and if you're puzzled about what to order, the friendly waiters are happy to advise. And, unlike too many restaurants, families are welcome here, perhaps because it's a family-run place. Sal Petrillo and his four children do the honors. Small parties are also treated well. What a difference a little personal attention can make! Some of the classier restaurants downtown could learn a lesson from Pinocchio's.

PIZZAPIAZZA
785 Broadway (at 10th St)   505-0977
Lunch, Dinner: Daily
Inexpensive

Does deep-dish pizza sound good to you? Go to PIZZAPIAZZA in a hurry. Their pizza comes in three sizes, all made to order and absolutely chockablock full of cheeses, vegetables, and meats. All are prepared without any preservatives. If you're a crust lover like I am, you'll definitely like these. The pizzas are served piping hot, and they look as good as they taste. There is a choice of over a dozen possibilities, from chicken Mexicana to Piazza pepperoni to

Cajun or Hawaiian pizza and the ultimate Piazza special, which includes bacon, sweet sausage, sliced mushrooms, broccoli, pepperoni, onions, artichoke hearts, roasted garlic, tomato sauce, and three cheeses. Get the picture? Forget about the burgers and chili; concentrate on the absolutely super specialty of the house. If you have any room left for dessert, you might ask for the Bailey's Bombe: coffee ice cream with Irish cream liqueur and chocolate coffee beans. Takeout and delivery are also available.

PLAZA HOTEL PALM COURT
59th St at Fifth Ave   759-3000
Breakfast, Lunch: Mon-Sat; Tea, Supper: Daily;
Brunch: Sun
Moderate

If just one place in the city could be singled out as the embodiment of all that folks dream of as the New York of yesteryear—romantic and carefree, delicious and proper—it would have to be the Palm Court at the Plaza Hotel. The great and near-great have laughed and loved here with the likes of Eloise and Auntie and Uncle, creating thousands of memories of special times. You can enjoy breakfasts, luncheon quiches, salads, wonderful teas with tea sandwiches, and caloric goodies, all to the accompaniment of classic piano and violin music. There are also supper snacks, seafood salads, assorted smoked fish, and the unusual sandwiches and pastries. The fabulous Sunday buffet, the largest and most glamorous in the city, is a popular New York tradition; you see many three-generation families showing the young ones where they used to go in the "good old days." A real treat, day or night, and a must for the New York visitor.

POLO
Westbury Hotel (Madison Ave at 69th St)   439-4835
Breakfast, Lunch, Dinner: Daily; Tea: Sat, Sun
Moderately expensive

Ralph Lauren has made the word *polo* synonymous with what's fashionable and in good taste. The Polo Restaurant, located just three blocks down the street from Ralph's magnificent Rhinelander mansion store, captures the caché of its name. In an intimate hotel dining room, with tables far enough apart to make it comfortable and personal, you can enjoy a "power" breakfast, a pricey but delicious lunch, or a dinner in just the right setting for the 40th wedding anniversary of your in-laws. The guests and staff are on their very best behavior, the room is bathed in piano melodies, and the dishes are served in a flurry of polished silver covers. Under them you find delicacies such as seared Atlantic salmon, the special house dish. Save some appetite for the most creamy and delectable chocolate mousse cake imaginable; it's so light you can't believe it hides so many calories. This restaurant, like the stock market, has its ups and downs, but the current outlook is bullish.

POST HOUSE
28 E 63rd St   935-2888
Lunch: Mon-Fri; Dinner: Daily
Moderate to expensive

The best way to describe the Post House would be as a social and political "in" hangout on East 63rd Street, which serves excellent food in comfortable surroundings. The guest list usually includes many well-known names and easily recognizable faces. They are attracted, of course, by the fact that this spot has been written up favorably in the gossip columns. Hors d'oeuvres like crab-meat cocktail, lobster cocktail, and stone crabs are available in season, but the major draws are steak and lobster. Prices for the latter two entrees are definitely not in the moderate category; ditto for lamb chops. However, the quality is excellent, and the cottage fries, fried zucchini, hashed browns, and onion rings are superb. Save room for the white chocolate mousse with raspberry sauce. If you can walk out of the place under your own steam after all this, you're doing well! The Post House is not as earthy as the Palm or as masculine as Christ Cella, but it is a fitting spot to take your favorite lady for a hearty dining experience.

PRIMAVERA
1578 First Ave (at 82nd St)   861-8608
Dinner: Daily
Expensive

There are hundreds of Italian restaurants in Manhattan. When I'm asked which is the greatest, my answer is always Primavera. So many times an establishment reflects a proprietor's personality and talent; nowhere is this more apparent than at Primavera. Nicola Civetta, the owner, is the epitome of class. He knows how to greet you, how to make you feel at home, and how to present a superb Italian meal. Don't go if you're in a hurry, though. This place is for relaxed dining. I could wax eloquently with descriptions of the dishes, but enough said: you can't go wrong, no matter what you order. Let Nicola choose for you, as there are specials every day. To top it all off, they have one of the most beautiful desserts anywhere: a gorgeous platter of seasonal fruit that looks too beautiful to eat. Primavera is always busy, so reservations are a must. If Primavera is not as good as any place you've dined at in Italy, I'd be very surprised.

PROVENCE
38 MacDougal St (at Prince and Houston St)
475-7500
Lunch, Dinner: Daily
Moderate

Provence, of course, is a region of France, where some of the world's best cuisine originated. A bit of that area has been transported to New York's Greenwich Village. Large windows in the front offer a not terribly exciting view of MacDougal Street, but it is exciting inside, where bustling waiters are busy coping with large, hungry crowds. To tell you the truth, I was surprised at how good the food was, when I discovered the owner was formerly of Régines, a place never known for its professionalism. However, he must have discovered what *not* to do, for Provence serves delicious food in very sizable portions and in a most attractive manner at a reasonable price. For starters, try scallops baked in their shell with vegetables or homemade pâté. A tasty fish soup is a treat and a specialty of the Provence region. Roast lamb, poached fish, baby roasted chicken, and rabbit are specialties. By all means, get a side order of French fries. They're good and not greasy, just like the ones you had in that little French bistro on your last trip to Europe. If you can make it on a Friday, there's a wonderful bouillabaisse, and on Sundays couscous is featured. Leave room for a great sorbet for dessert.

QUATORZE
240 W 14th St   206-7006

QUATORZE BIS
323 E 79th St.   535-1414
Lunch: Tues-Sun; Dinner: Daily
American Express
Moderate

The genius of the two Quatorze restaurants is their simplicity. They have a limited menu, with quality food and professional service. The portions are enormous; for friends with large appetites this is a good bet. For lunch, a great offering of soups and sandwiches. For dinner, the choucroute garnie is a specialty. Other choices include braised duck, grilled salmon, seafood ragout, and sautéed brook trout. Their specialty dessert, the chocolate regal, is superb. Both outlets serve the identical menu, and both houses are attractive and comfortable.

QUILTED GIRAFFE
550 Madison Ave (at 55th St)   593-1221
Lunch: Tues-Fri; Dinner: Tues-Sat
Expensive to very expensive

We all have our favorite animals, and I've always been fascinated with the giraffe because it's so haughty and rare. That description also fits this restaurant; it is indeed unusual and rare, and it can certainly be a bit haughty. When a restaurant reaches the four-star category, it has to be good, and the Quilted Giraffe is just that. Susan and Barry Wine have put together a superb dining spot. The fixed-price dinner (believe me, it's not inexpensive) is something you'll long remember. The dishes are unusual, to say the least. Specialties include lobster and truffles in tomato bouillon, caviar beggar's purses, and confit of duck. Each one is presented in a kingly manner. There's a fabulous selection of cheeses and such desserts as spice cake with warm pear and caramel sauce, chocolate soufflé with espresso ice cream, apple tarts with cinnamon ice cream (absolutely delicious), and fresh fruit sorbets in cranberry soup. Or you might want to try the "grand dessert," which features samples of many of the offerings. Barry and Susan are to be congratulated. They set out to carve a special niche in Manhattan dining, and they've succeeded in spades.

RAINBOW ROOM
30 Rockefeller Plaza (65th floor)   632-5000
Dinner: Tues-Sun
Expensive

On October 3rd, 1934, the Rainbow Room opened atop Rockefeller Center, giving New Yorkers and visitors a thrill to be found nowhere else. The lights of the city below were vibrant and visible from the opulent room, where famous chefs and famous bands worked to make the evening a very special event. On December 29th, 1987, that scene was re-created when a spectacular new two-floor facility, redone by the Rockefellers at a cost of $20 million, opened on the same site. Joe Baum has turned the 64th and 65th floors into a magnificent private club during the day and a great dining and dancing spot in the evening. The Rainbow Room, a two-story, glass-enclosed jewel, is the showpiece of the new layout. Smartly uniformed personnel serve gourmet food to the accompaniment of a 12-piece dance band. The Rainbow Promenade is a smaller room, with cozy tables and light meals. Rainbow and Stars is the dining and supper club, which features live cabaret entertainment. Views from all rooms are spectacular, but the one facing directly north to Central Park is breathtaking. The views inside the rooms aren't so bad either; a million-dollar collection of 40 pieces of modern American art adorn the walls. An evening of being pampered and spoiled by Joe Baum and his professional crew is certain to be quite an occasion for even the most jaded diner. The Rainbow also offers party and banquet facilities.

RAO'S
455 E 114th St 534-9625
Dinner: Mon-Fri
No credit cards
Inexpensive

What are you doing for dinner three months from tonight? Sound ridiculous? Not really, if you want to go to Rao's, an intimate, old-time (1896) Italian-type restaurant run by an aunt and an uncle in the kitchen and a nephew named Frank out front. The regulars know it, and the place is crowded all the time for two very good reasons: the food is great, and the prices are ridiculously low. Don't walk, but don't take your car either. Take a taxi and get out in front of the restaurant. When you're ready to leave, have Frank call a local taxi service to pick you up and deliver you to your home or hotel. (A sizable tip to the driver will be necessary for this.) Frank is a gregarious and charming host, who makes you feel right at home; he'll even sit with you at your table while you order. Be prepared for leisurely dining; while you're waiting, enjoy the excellent bread and warm atmosphere. Among the offerings that are especially tasty, I enjoyed the pasta and piseli (with peas). The veal marsala and veal piccata are excellent choices, as well as any number of shrimp dishes. Believe it or not, the Southern fried chicken is absolutely superb; it would be my number-one choice. Don't miss this spot in Spanish Harlem. Hint: Try just appearing unannounced at the door. Tables are often available on the spur of the moment.

RAOUL'S
180 Prince St 966-3518
Dinner: Daily
Moderate

The dining-out scene in SoHo has certainly changed for the better. Now there are dozens of good places to eat in this colorful area, and Raoul's is one of the best. The long, narrow restaurant used to be an old saloon. There are paper tablecloths and funky walls covered with a mishmash of posters, pictures, and calendars of every description. No menu is presented; you read the day's selections from the blackboard. The bistro atmosphere is neighborly, friendly, and intimate, the prices moderate, and the service attentive. The trendy clientele runs the gamut from jeans to mink. The house specialties are the steak au poivre and the rack of lamb. Don't pass up the sensational sweetbreads in homemade mayonnaise as an appetizer.

(THE FAMOUS) RAY'S PIZZA OF GREENWICH VILLAGE

465 Sixth Ave (at 11th St)   243-2253
Sun-Thurs: 11 a.m.-2 a.m.; Fri, Sat: 11 a.m.-3 a.m.
No credit cards
Inexpensive

There is an untold number of pizzerias in New York, and you can smell many of them blocks away! But none of them is really distinguished, except a special place called Ray's Pizza, located in the Village. It's a busy parlor, serving over 2,000 customers a day. The pizzas are super. Because Ray's is so busy, you don't have to worry about the slice being stale; of course, you can buy a whole pizza. And why not try one of the Sicilian squares or the Neapolitan wedges for a change? Unusual toppings are available, and I guarantee this place is the ultimate for the pizza crowd in the Big Apple. They even offer the "Famous Slice," a slice of pizza with *all* the toppings on it. Calzones and baby pizzas are new arrivals. Note: This may be fast food, but there's usually a long, slow waiting line. Free delivery is available (243-3010).

REMI

1325 Sixth Ave (53rd St bet Sixth and Seventh Ave)
581-4242
Lunch: Mon-Fri; Dinner: Daily
Moderate

When Remi closed on the Upper East Side, many of those who were loyal fans felt like they had lost a real friend. Alas, not to worry. Remi has reopened in a spectacular space in midtown, handy to hotels and theaters. In an unusually long room, dominated by a dramatic 120-foot Venetian wall painting by artist Paulin Paris, the food is as soaring as the setting. In the nice weather, doors open up and diners can enjoy tables in the adjoining passageway. Waiters, chairs, and wall fabrics all match in attractive stripes. The menu is much the same as the original house. Antipasti like smoked goose prosciutto or roasted quail wrapped in bacon will get you off to a delicious start. The main dishes are not the usual variety; the spaghetti, linguine, or ravioli can match any house in Venice. Of course, there are fish and meat dishes for the more timid. The apple strudel with ice cream topped with caramel sauce is enough to make anyone feel guilty. Being a gelato lover myself, I found the homemade cappuccino flavor sensational. Paddle on down (Remi means "oar") for a first-class experience!

RENÉ PUJOL
321 W 51st St   246-3023
Lunch: Mon-Fri; Dinner: Mon-Sat
Moderate

This very attractive French restaurant is an ideal spot for a pre-theater dinner. It's always busy, and it's obvious that a large number of the customers are regular patrons, which always speaks well for a restaurant. One of the reasons this is such a successful operation is that it's a family enterprise. The owner is on the job. Housed in an old brownstone, the restaurant has two warmly decorated, cozy, and comfortable dining rooms, complete with a working fireplace in the winter. There are private party rooms upstairs, and they are attractive, too. The menu is vintage French.

RESTAURANT FLORENT
69 Gansevoort St (bet Washington and Greenwich St)
989-5779
Open 24 hours
No credit cards
Moderate

When you have something good, people will find you no matter where you are. A case in point: Restaurant Florent, a run-of-the-mill diner transformed into a chic, popular restaurant, is located—of all places—in the heart of the seamy meat-packing district on the Lower West Side. This noisy, busy French bistro never closes, and the level of activity seems to increase by the hour in the evening. The menu is simple, and perhaps that is one of the keys to its success. Escargot, pâté, sautéed calf's brains, coho salmon, and grilled chicken are all good choices. And it's a great place for people watching, New York style.

RESTAURANT RAPHAEL
33 W 54th St   582-8993
Lunch: Mon-Fri; Dinner: Mon-Sat
Expensive

Expensive, but worth it. This classy, intimate, French restaurant, which does a few things very well, is for the serious diner. Tasty smoked salmon, ravioli de St. Jacques, or duck salad will get you off to a great start. Main courses of pigeon, lamb, veal, and duck are served imaginatively with superb seasonings and sauces. There is no on-the-job training for the servers; they all know what is expected in a first-class operation. Take your time, savor the taste of classic French cooking, and finish with a chocolate mousse that is as rich and delicious as any you have ever tasted.

RIVER CAFE
1 Water St (Brooklyn)   (718) 522-5200
Lunch, Dinner: Daily
Moderately expensive

The River Cafe isn't in Manhattan. It's in Brooklyn, but it *overlooks* Manhattan. And that's the reason to come here. The view from the window tables (be sure to ask for one) is fantastic, awesome, unequaled, romantic—you name it. There's no other skyline like it in the world. And so, just across the East River, in the shadow of the Brooklyn Bridge, the River Cafe remains an extremely popular place. Be sure to call at least a week in advance to make reservations. This is a true, Yankee, flag-waving restaurant that's proud of its American cuisine. But there's no point in describing the dishes in detail, since you'll be looking out the window more than down at your plate. The seafood, lamb, and game entrees are particularly good. And the desserts are uniformly rich and fresh. You won't forget to hold hands at this romantic spot—once you've made the trek across the bridge.

ROSE CAFE
24 Fifth Ave (at 9th St)   260-4118
Lunch: Mon-Fri; Dinner: Mon-Sun; Brunch: Sat-Sun
Moderate

This address is a jinx! At least it has been in the past, with all kinds of operations that were medicore at best. The last one, Mosaico, was a near disaster. But now Richard Krause, the former chef at Melrose, has opened up a moderately priced cafe in a neighborhood that is sorely in need of such a place. Wisely, Krause is setting his sights on the neighborhood regulars, but visitors from other parts of the Big Apple scene will be pleased with the friendly greeting, moderate prices, and tasty dishes. Don't waste a second before ordering the crisp potato pancakes with créme fraiche and caviar or the roasted red pepper and corn crab cakes. If Krause can keep his help smiling and his hand in the kitchen (at which he is good), #24 may lose that sad reputation.

THE RUSSIAN TEA ROOM
150 W 57th St (at Seventh Ave)   265-0947
Lunch, Dinner: Daily; Brunch: Sat, Sun
Moderate

Believe me, the food (and the ambiance) here are a lot better than you'll find anywhere in Moscow! The Russian Tea Room is a popular place with Manhattan socialites and showbiz people. Unless you specially request a table in the main room (sort of a Grand Central Station for celebrities), you'll be seated in Siberia, way back from the line of action. Assuming you're coming here to fill your mouth as well as your eyes, note that the specialties on the à la carte menu are eggplant à la Russe, blinchiki with cheese and sour cream, and shashlik Caucasian. Or there's hot and cold borscht, cream of spinach soup, caviar, and meats grilled with a Russian flair. And check out the décor! It's kitsch with class. Any other restaurant looking like this would be laughed out of business, but the Tea Room is an institution. Look for the cute little building that refuses to be gobbled up by all the high-rises springing up around it. A banquet room is also available. There is a cabaret on Sunday evenings.

RUSTY'S
1271 Third Ave (at 73rd St)   861-4518
Lunch, Brunch: Sat, Sun; Dinner: Daily
Moderate

There is only one way to describe this restaurant: it's all-American. The menu is all-American, the help is all-American, the customers are all-American. It is as red, white, and blue as apple pie. Don't get too dressed up to come here, or you'll feel out of place. A great starter is the Grand Slam Salad, made up of everything you could put in a salad bowl: ham, cheese, tomato, black olives, cucumbers, shrimp, eggs, etc. You name it, it's there. The French onion soup is another winner. The specialty of the house is the rack of ribs: whole baby back ribs marinated and cooked with barbecue sauce. Other winning entrees are the seafood New Orleans (a blend of lobsters, shrimp, clams, mussels, and scallops simmered in red wine, garlic, tomatoes, and a special seafood sauce) and the Louisiana chili topped with onion, mild cheddar cheese, and grilled franks. All entrees are served with bayou rice. The portions are for hearty eaters. (This could be why the place is always filled.) Note to Rusty's: take the foil off your baked potatoes.

SABOR
20 Cornelia St (west of Sixth Ave)   243-9579
Dinner: Daily
Moderate

Don't expect anything fancy at Sabor, and don't come with a sensitive tummy. But if you're out for an adventure and some really good Cuban food, then head down to what has become one of Manhattan's best Cuban restaurants. I'm not well versed in this kind of food, but I found the apervitos—like the chilled cooked pickled fish with vegetables and the Caribbean root vegetable puréed with garlic and parsley—delicious and unusual. In the fish category, the best dish is the Zarzuela de Mariscos (clams, shrimps, mussels, scallops, and calamaries in a tomato sauce); it's a whole meal in itself. The most popular meat dishes are Carne Estofada (pot roast stuffed with chorizo, olives, capers, raisins, and prunes) and Ropa Vieja (flank steak seasoned with tomato sauce, cloves, and cinnamon). I'm told that a Cuban dinner wouldn't be complete without key lime pie or Coco Quemado (warm baked coconut with sherry and cinnamon), and both are good here. Delicious frozen drinks are also available.

SANDRO'S
420 E 59th St   355-5150
Dinner: Mon-Sun
Moderate

Don't waste any time in getting over to the far end of East 59th Street to try Sandro's. The dining room is not too large, but it's big enough to feel comfortable. Tile floors and unusually attractive serving pieces give it a clean, crisp look. The big winners, however, are the efficient service and the absolutely delicious food. You'll be impressed at how quick, helpful, and professional the service is, and it's done in a very unobtrusive way. There's nothing like good fresh warm Italian bread, and they serve it here. The homemade ravioli with sea urchin in a sauce of baby scallops and the fried ricotta with tomato sauce are sensational starters. There are a number of fish specialties; I especially enjoyed the striped bass with artichokes. Other worthwhile entrees include the veal scaloppine (any way you want it), tripe, and a very tasty sirloin of beef. A most unusual cart with a large selection of dressings is not only attractive to look at but also helps make a very delicious salad dish. Top off the meal with some of Sandro's own gelati and very rich espresso, and you'll be talking for days about what a pleasant evening you had. Sandro's is a classy operation in every sense of the word.

SARABETH'S KITCHEN

423 Amsterdam Ave (at 80th St)	1295 Madison Ave (at 92nd St)
496-6280	410-7335
Breakfast, Lunch, Dinner: Daily	Breakfast, Lunch, Dinner: Daily

Moderate

Swinging, it is not. Reliable, it is. One is reminded of the better English tearooms when visiting either of Sarabeth's two locations. The East Side location has been considerably expanded; it now has a bar. The big draw is the homemade quality of all the dishes, including the baked items and the excellent desserts. They also make gourmet preserves and sell them nationally. Menu choices include excellent omelets for breakfast, a fine assortment of light items for lunch, and fish, game, or meat dishes for dinner. Service is rapid and courteous. This would be an ideal place to take your mother-in-law. P.S. The chocolate truffle cake, lemon soufflé, and cinnamon apple ice cream with macadamia nuts are outrageous.

SARANAC
1350 Madison Ave (at 95th St)   289-9600
Lunch: Mon-Fri; Dinner: Mon-Sun; Brunch: Sat-Sun
American Express
Inexpensive to moderate

A fun, rustic, inexpensive place to dine on upper Madison Avenue that serves good food? Too good to be true? No sir, just head to Saranac, a casual bistro with a high noise level, wooden tables, and an atmosphere reminiscent of a dining lodge at lakeside in your favorite mountain resort. Everything is informal and homey, with the young staff bustling full-tilt to keep the waiting line moving. Black bean chili, shrimp bisque, and fried calamari will get you off to a good start. The cobb salad and hamburgers are house favorites. The "Senior Executive" burger combines cheese, bacon, avocado, and sautéed onions. A good selection of sandwiches is offered, including a real old-fashioned turkey club on white toast. For heartier appetites, there is a selection of crab cakes, salmon steak, wonderful crispy Kansas City fried chicken (served with fried onion mashers), and grilled weiners with brown-sugar baked beans. The kids will love it, and so will you. Oh yes, don't miss the chocolate mud pie for dessert!

SATURNIA
70 Park Ave (at 38th St)   983-3333
Breakfast: Daily; Lunch: Mon-Fri;
Dinner: Mon-Sat; Brunch: Sun
Moderate

For those who count calories and fat, Saturnia is ideal. Beside each appetizer and entree selection, the exact amounts are listed for you. Saturnia is cool and comfortable, with an air of freshness about it. Don't expect to find highly seasoned food here; everything is relatively simple but delicious. The appetizers (none of which have over 182 calories) include soups, salads, pasta, pizza, and seafood items. Usually, fresh fish dishes are available as entrees, in addition to a nice selection of meat. Amazingly, all of the entree items are 400 calories or less. If you are watching your diet that closely, forget about dessert! A three-course fixed-price menu is available.

SCALETTA
50 W 77th St   769-9191
Dinner: Mon-Sun
Moderate

Finding an excellent downstairs restaurant on the Upper West Side is truly unusual, but Scaletta is such a place! It is really located in a basement, but you would never know it. The room is airy and pleasant, the tables are far enough apart to permit comfortable conversations, the service is highly efficient and professional, and the food is very appealing. The well-trained staff will not leave an empty glass or dirty plate on your table. The menu is mostly typical Italian, heavy on the pastas. All may be ordered in half portions, and all are equally delicious. The scampi entree was one of the best I have ever tasted, tender and well seasoned. However, the rolling dessert cart looks better than it tastes.

SCARLATTI
34 E 52nd St   753-2444
Dinner: Mon-Sat
Moderately expensive

The rave reviews that this house has received are well deserved. The ambiance is totally top-drawer; one would feel out of place here if one didn't put on the best bib and tucker. Tables are far enough apart to allow for pleasant, private dining. The waiters act as if they're prime candidates for a stress clinic, so service can be hectic. But the food is excellent. Scarlatti reminds me of Sans Souci in Rome, which is a real compliment. One of the nicest ways to start your meal is to order a selection of antipasto; the house serves each person a small portion of a number of delicious dishes. The outstanding entrees are the striped bass in wine; scampi baked in mozzarella; broiled calf's liver; and stuffed veal chops. The servings are just right, and the presentation is superb. A low-cholesterol menu is also available. But try to order a decent Italian dessert, and they act as if they don't even know what tartufo is!

SECOND AVENUE KOSHER DELICATESSEN AND RESTAURANT
156 Second Ave (at 10th St)   677-0606
Daily: 5:30 a.m.-midnight (Fri, Sat until 2 a.m.)
American Express
Inexpensive

You've heard of the great New York delicatessens; now you should try one of the really authentic ones located in a historic area of the city, the East Village. From the traditional K's—knishes, kasha varnishkes (buckwheat groats with pasta), and kugel—to boiled beef or chicken in the pot (with noodles, carrots, and matzo balls), no one does it quite like the Lebewohl family. The selections are enormous. Homemade soups, three-decker sandwiches (the tongue or the hot corned beef is sensational), deli platters, complete dinners—you name it, they've got it. The smell is overwhelmingly appetizing, the atmosphere is "caring Jewish mother," and they don't mind if you want to take your meal with you instead of dining in the colorful back room. Don't leave without trying chopped liver or warm apple strudel. Then break out the Alka-Seltzer.

SERENDIPITY 3
225 E 60th St   838-3531
Sun-Thurs: 11:30 a.m.-12:30 a.m.;
Fri: 11:30 a.m.-1 a.m.; Sat: 11:30 a.m.-2 a.m.
Moderate

For decades, Serendipity 3 has been the "in" place for youngsters and the young at heart, offering the most trendy food and gifts in an atmosphere of nostalgia. The restaurant is housed in a quaint, two-floor brownstone. While folks wait to grab one of the busy tables, they can browse through the eclectic selection of goodies, gifts, books, clothing, and accessories. The tummy gets satisfied with tasty selections from the light menu of sandwiches, sundaes, salads, and pasta. Serendipity has been at the forefront of style for nearly 40 years. How do they do it? By constantly changing much of its merchandise while maintaining the charm and décor of an old-fashioned ice cream parlor.

SETTE MEZZO
969 Lexington Ave (at 70th St)   472-0400
Lunch, Dinner: Daily
Cash only
Moderate

It's small, professional, and very busy. There are no affectations at Sette Mezzo in décor, service, or food preparation. This is strictly a business operation, with the emphasis where it should be: on serving good food at a reasonable price. Don't worry about wearing your best gown or a suit and tie; many diners are informally dressed, enjoying a variety of Italian dishes done to perfection. At noon the menu is tilted towards lighter pastas and salads. In the evening, all of the grilled items are excellent. Fresh seafood is a specialty. Ask about the special pasta dishes; some of the combinations are marvelous. For more traditional Italian plates, try the breaded rack of veal, stuffed baked chicken, grilled boneless quail, or fried calamari and shrimp. All of the desserts are made in-house. They include several caloric cakes, tasty lemon tarts, sherbets and ice cream, and (take it from an expert) one of the best tartufos you've ever sinned over.

SHELBY
967 Lexington Ave (bet 70th and 71st St)   988-4624
Lunch: Mon-Fri; Dinner: Daily; Brunch: Sat, Sun
Moderate

A little bit of Tennessee has been moved to Manhattan's Upper East Side! The owner of Shelby hails from the Memphis area, which happens to be in Shelby County, Tennessee (thus the name). The Southern influence is obvious in much of the cooking. Shelby has become a very popular business restaurant for lunch and a neighborhood watering (and eating) place for dinner. Friendly, intimate, and professional would best describe this establishment. With Chip, the owner, overseeing his crew, it is obvious that these folks deserve the success they are having. A bit of Italy creeps into the menu with the delicious pastas, while the Southern accent is apparent in the roast pecan smoked pork chops. The roast baby lamb chops are superb. An attractive and refreshing dessert, fresh fruit in a nut-lace cookie, deserves special mention.

SHINWA
645 Fifth Ave (at 51st St)   644-7400
Lunch, Dinner: Mon-Sat
Moderate to moderately expensive

If you're looking for a classy, authentic Japanese restaurant, look no further. Shinwa, in the midtown high-rent district, offers a full menu of traditional Japanese dishes, served beautifully in an understated atmosphere that puts the emphasis on food. Each course is brought to your table on a tray; the presentation is a feast of color and flavor. As much as I dislike the typical Japanese "picture menu," it does give you a good idea of what to expect. There are literally dozens of appetizers from sushi and tempura to more exotic dishes like eel and cucumber with vinegared rice or preserved squid. Entrees include tempura zen with seasonal appetizers; sashimi zen, with appetizers, vegetable soup, and ice cream; unagi zen, with a choice of kabayaki and rice; and una jue, with eel. My favorite is Shabu Shabu, sliced prime rib of beef, which you dip and cook to your liking in a boiling broth. There are two kinds of noodle dishes, one made from wheat flour and one from buckwheat flour. If you can find room at the end of the meal, you might try seaweed, codfish, or cooked squid in a dish called Chazuke, which is served with green tea and white rice. The green-tea ice cream is also fabulous. If you want to sample and savor the flavors of Japan, this is one of the best places to do it.

SHUN LEE CAFE
43 W 65th St   769-3888
Lunch: Sat, Sun; Dinner: Daily
Moderate

Dim sum and street-food combinations are served in an informal setting, adjoining Shun Lee West, an old and excellent West Side Chinese restaurant. A large selection of special items is offered by a waiter who comes to your table with a rolling cart and describes the various goodies. The offerings are different from time to time, but don't miss the stuffed crab claws if they are available. Go on to the street-food items: delicious roast pork, barbecued spareribs, a large selection of soups and noodle and rice dishes, and a menu full of both mild and hot, spicy entrees. The sautéed prawns with ginger and the boneless duckling with walnut sauce are great choices. A vegetarian dish of shredded Chinese vegetables is cooked with rice noodles and served with a pancake (like Moo Shu pork but without the meat). It's a fun place, where you can try some unusual and delicious Chinese dishes. The adjoining Shun Lee West restaurant is equally good for heartier appetites. Some of the best Chinese food in Manhattan is served here, like Moo Shu pork that you will never forget. If you come with a crowd, family style dining is available. Prices are a bit higher in the restaurant than in the cafe.

SIRACUSA
65 Fourth Ave (near 10th St)   254-1940
Lunch: Mon-Fri; Dinner: Mon-Sat
Moderate

First, carefully note the address, because it is not the easiest find. But once there, you will be enchanted with the small, unpretentious place the Cammarata family operates with tender, loving care. Several dozen tables are nestled in the cozy backroom of a takeout establishment long known for great pasta and super gelati. It still is, only now the menu has been expanded to include such mouth-watering favorites as spaghetti with sardines, raisins and pinenuts, curri curri (pasta with tomato sauce), and several linguine dishes. To moisten the palate, ask for a tray of appetizers from the ever-changing display. To finish off what may well be one of the best Sicilian meals you have ever had, the caffé gelato is simply out-of-this-world. In the summertime, Gelateria Siracusa (next door) is available for snacking.

SISTINA
1555 Second Ave (at 80th St)   861-7660
Lunch: Mon-Fri; Dinner: Daily
Moderate

Don't come here expecting beautiful decorations and extravagant surroundings. One comes to Sistina for the food, and it can't be beat. Four brothers run this outstanding Italian restaurant; one is in the kitchen, the others are out front. The only decoration is a picture of its namesake, the Sistine Chapel, on the wall. The specialty of the house is seafood; both the Mediterranean red snapper and the salmon are excellent dishes. There are also the usual choices of pasta, veal, and chicken, as well as a number of daily specials. The philosophy of this family operation is that the joy is in the eating, not the surroundings, and for that they get top marks.

SMITH AND WOLLENSKY
797 Third Avenue (at 49th St)   753-1530
Lunch: Mon-Fri; Dinner: Daily
Moderate to moderately expensive

This is a big place for big appetites. If you have teenagers or some college friends who you want to treat to a special meal, I can't think of a better place. Fancy and elite, it is not. Hearty, fun, and satisfying, it is. It has two floors of facilities, nicely divided to give it a comfortable and rather masculine atmosphere. There is no shortage of help; lots of bright, young men eager to help you—a bit of a contrast to the older, disinterested waiters at the Palm and Palm Too. The bread is varied, tasty, and warm. The lobster cocktail, though expensive, is the best in New York. The big sellers among the entrees are the steaks, prime ribs of beef, lamb chops, and lobster. On the side, you don't want to miss the cottage fries, onion rings, and fried zucchini. A word about the baked potatoes: they don't use foil—*three cheers!* And a couple of words about the desserts: the pignola nut cake is super, and the hot deep-dish apple pie with vanilla sauce can top off a great dinner.

SOHO KITCHEN AND BAR
103 Greene St   925-1866
Lunch, Dinner: Daily
Inexpensive to moderate

With over 100 wines by the glass and 14 different cold draft beers, this is one of the busiest bar and restaurant scenes in the lower canyons of Manhattan. But it is not only in the liquid department that the SoHo Kitchen shines. Besides soups, salads and pastas, there are great hamburgers and omelets. A delicious fruit and cheese plate is a welcome change from heavy eating. The real treat here is the pizza, each made with its own homemade pizza dough. You can choose from wild mushroom, smoked chicken, pesto, vegetarian, or a fantastic Italian combination of sausage, roasted peppers, grilled eggplant, mozzarella, and provolone cheese. Prices are amazingly reasonable. A good place for the casual encounter.

SPARKS
210 E 46th St   687-4855
Lunch: Mon-Fri; Dinner: Mon-Sat
Moderately expensive

You come here to eat, period. Don't expect classy ambiance or service, but this is a well-seasoned and very popular beef restaurant. For years, businessmen have made an evening at Sparks a must, and the house has not let time erode its reputation. In the meat category, you can choose from veal and lamb chops, beef scaloppine, and medallions of beef, as well as a half dozen steak items, like steak fromage (with Roquefort cheese), prime sirloin, sliced steak with sautéed onions and peppers, and top-of-the-line filet mignon. Seafood dishes are another specialty; the rainbow trout, fillet of tuna, and halibut steak are as good as you'll find in most seafood houses. The lobsters are enormous, delicious, and expensive. You might want to skip the appetizers and dessert, and concentrate on the main dish.

SPRING STREET NATURAL RESTAURANT
62 Spring St (at Lafayette St)   966-0290
Lunch, Dinner: Daily
Inexpensive

With all the interest these days in healthy eating, I am constantly asked to recommend a good "all-natural" restaurant. Spring Street has been in business since 1973, and it serves only fresh, whole, unprocessed foods cooked to order. No canned items are used, and great emphasis is put on whole foods. Lunch includes sandwiches, eggs, and salads, plus blackboard specials of the day. For dinner, you can dine well on a large selection of salads, pasta, seafood, and chicken. With all the calories that you'll be saving, splurge on a no-sugar apple pie, Manhattan mud cake, or lime cheesecake for dessert. It's a neighborhood tradition!

STEPHANIE'S
994 First Ave (bet 54th and 55th St)   753-0520
Lunch: Mon-Fri; Dinner: Daily; Brunch: Sat, Sun
Moderate

If you are tired of the noisy, trendy restaurants, then I suggest you consider Stephanie's, a simple, spotless neighborhood establishment that turns out excellent food at modest prices. Stephanie's is owned by three partners, including the daughter of Joan Bennett, the actress, so the place has a theatrical clientele. The menu changes daily, but it usually includes such popular dishes as grilled Gulf prawns, sautéed soft-shell crabs, and roast duck. Sunday brunch favorites recommended by the regulars are Irish soda bread French toast, toasted wild mushroom sandwiches, and homemade biscuits and muffins. An especially large selections of beers is available.

TABLE D'HOTE
44 E 92nd St   348-8125
Lunch: Daily; Dinner: Mon-Sun; Brunch: Sun
No credit cards
Moderate

Here are the rules: (1) You call and leave a message on the Table d'Hote answering machine, telling them how many are in your party and when you want to dine. (2) They call back and tell you whether they have space. If they do, they will ask that you confirm the day of the booking and then read you the menu. And what do you experience when you finally get there? An absolutely delightful four-course, home-cooked meal at a reasonable price. It's served in an unpretentious storefront cafe at a leisurely pace by the friendly, charming owners. The tables, chairs, and china are definitely mix-and-unmatch, but you won't care a bit. It's part of the charm. The menu changes weekly; each of the four entrees seems like it just came from your mother's kitchen. For a delicious casual meal where substance is more important than style, try this little-known winner. Table d'Hote can only take care of about 25 guests, so you had better book your table early. Sunday brunch is a new addition, featuring tasty selections like salmon fillet, salt-roasted shrimp, and pan-grilled chicken breast.

TAVERN ON THE GREEN
Central Park (at W 67th St)   873-3200
Lunch, Dinner: Daily
Moderate to moderately expensive

The setting here is absolutely magical. In the evening, with the trees aglow with small lights, it is New York at its very best! Be sure you ask for seating in the Crystal Room; it is a wonderful setting for a party for your kids or a special evening with the folks from out of town. The cuisine is continental; translated, that means good, solid food—what you would expect from a place as large and as busy as this one. The service can be a bit distracted, but don't let that keep you from a visit to one of New York's "musts."

TERRACE
400 W 119th St   666-9490
Lunch: Tues-Fri; Dinner: Tues-Sat
Moderate

You'll have to go a bit out of your way to visit the Terrace Restaurant, but I assure you it's well worth the time. The Terrace is located on the roof of a Columbia University building, providing a superb view of Manhattan. Try to reserve a table by the window. In the evening, it's absolutely enchanting. You'll be impressed by the classy atmosphere, the beautiful table settings (attractive china, candlelight, and a single red rose), and the soft dinner music. The tables are spaced nicely apart, giving one a chance to talk confidentially. Indeed, if there's one word that describes this operation, it's *style*. The Terrace has it in spades! The food is as good as the atmosphere. The menu is modern French. Special services include free valet parking.

TIME & AGAIN
116 E 39th St   685-8887
Lunch, Dinner: Mon-Sat
Moderate to moderately expensive

Warm, elegant, friendly, and decidedly upscale—that's Time & Again. Located in the Doral Tuscany Hotel, the restaurant features new American cuisine with a European flavor. The chef, Larry Bird, brings flair and excitement to his work. When you arrive, you're greeted by exceptionally polite folks and seated in a room where the tables are nicely spaced apart. The menu offers a selection of eight to ten starters; I recommend the spicy crab cakes. Then try the excellent lobster, tasty roast breast of chicken, fillet of salmon, or seared loin of lamb. Most of the entrees come with fresh veggies and light sauces. The desserts are a bit high priced, but they're delicious. The chocolate terrine with bits of orange is my top choice. This place first gained a good reputation with the locals, but the word is spreading.

TOMMY TANG'S
323 Greenwich St   334-9190
Lunch: Mon-Fri; Dinner: Mon-Sat
Moderate

Because of the reasonable prices and unique flavors of Thai food, Thai restaurants are flourishing all over New York. Tommy Tang's is one of the very best. (There's also a branch in Hollywood, California.) At Tommy Tang's, the servings are smaller than usual so that each member of your party can taste a number of specialties served family style. (If you prefer regular individual servings, they are available, of course.) Another nice feature is that the menu indicates whether a dish is spicy, very spicy, or very, very spicy, so that you know what you're in for. You could make a meal just from the appetizers: won tons stuffed with chicken, potatoes, and sweet peas; egg rolls; angel wings (chicken wings stuffed with mushrooms, noodles, and bamboo shoots); or "Nam," a very spicy blend of chicken, chili, ginger, onion, and lime juice. A full selection of salads, soups, and meat dishes with veggies is featured, as well as a number of noodle, curry, and rice specialties. The best choices are barbecued beef (great!), blackened chili fish, and "the original Tommy duck."

TRASTEVERE
309 E 83rd St   734-6343
Dinner: Daily
American Express
Moderate

This is one of my favorites. The atmosphere reminds me of the Italian countryside. The room is very small (about a dozen tables), and the décor is far from glamorous. But the food preparation is very professional. The brochette of cheese and prosciutto with anchovy sauce, the mussels in light tomato sauce, the pasta la spaghettini and vegetables, or the fettucine with peas, prosciutto, mushroom, and cream—all are sensational! Also first-rate are sizable offerings of various chicken dishes, the rack of veal breaded with tomato salad on top, and the fillet of sole with mushrooms, scallions, and wine. And be sure to save a bit of room for the Napoleon dessert or the chocolate cartufel. You can tell a lot about a restaurant by the little things, and these people obviously know what they are doing. The glassware literally gleams, the bread is warm and delicious, the vegetables are fresh, and their seasonings have just the right amount of garlic to be tasty without being offensive. And the waiters are well-informed and friendly. It's a good idea to call early for reservations, since the place is always busy.

TRATTORIA DELL'ARTE
900 Seventh Ave (at 57th St)   245-9800
Lunch: Mon-Fri; Dinner: Daily; Brunch: Sat, Sun
Moderate

Just because you don't hear a lot about a restaurant doesn't mean that it isn't of star quality. This is the case with Trattoria Dell'Arte, a bustling spot just across the street from Carnegie Hall. The natives surely know about it, as the place is bursting at the seams every evening. A casual cafe is at the front, seats are available at the antipasto bar in the center, and the dining room is in the rear. One would be hard-pressed to name any place at any price with tastier Italian food than is served here. The antipasto selection is large, fresh and inviting; you can have your choice of a platter with various accompaniments. There are daily specials, ranging from crispy roasted duck on Mondays to stracotto (delicious Italian pot roast) on Sundays. Everyday there are superb pasta dishes (try the fettuccine with shrimp and artichokes), grilled fish and meats, focaccia sandwiches, and salads. Wonderful pizzas are available every day but Monday; the *pizzaiolo* takes that as his rest day. Chocolate macademia torte or raspberry zabaglione Napoleon will finish off a very special meal. The atmosphere and personnel are warm and pleasant; I recommend this place without reservation (although you'd better have one if you want to sit in the dining room).

TRIBECA GRILL
375 Greenwich St (at Franklin St)   941-3900
Lunch: Sun-Fri; Dinner: Daily
Moderate

There are dangers when a restaurant gets overhyped; the expectations never quite are satisfied. When Robert De Niro pulled out all the stops to insure that every foodie in the world knew about this new establishment, the crowds descended like locusts. Fortunately, professional operator Drew Nieporent (of Montrachet fame) was on hand to see that things didn't fall apart during a turbulent opening. The Tribeca Grill has now settled down into a fun and worthwhile place to dine. The setting is a huge old coffee roasting house in a decidedly unglamorous neighborhood. The Grill, however, has style and substance; a spacious bar and lots of tables downstairs, a large private party room and fabulous private screening room upstairs. With all the talent in the food department, I still cannot understand why Nieporent doesn't dress his staff in a more classy way. The black outfits at Montrachet were bad enough, but the dingy, drab garb here is pathetic. But on to the food, which is wholesome and delicious. Excellent salads, fresh fish with your choice of preparation (grilled, roasted, or sautéed), grilled calves liver, and rack of veal are all first-rate. And imagine a dinner house with a really good stuffed baked potato! I'd settle for an extra bite of any of the potato dishes (there are potato pancakes as well) rather than the rather humdrum desserts.

TROPICA
200 Park Ave (Pan-Am Bldg)   867-6767
Lunch, Dinner: Mon-Fri
Moderate

Hidden away in the bowels of the Pan-Am Building is this bright, charming Caribbean seafood house that serves as a drinking and eating headquarters for the hordes who work in that edifice. But others are finding their way to this excellent relative newcomer on the Manhattan horizon. You won't find the usual seafood appetizers here. Instead, the offerings include oysters baked with cornbread and bacon, kiwi mussels, and a delicious black bean and sausage soup. There are daily grilled fish specials, fresh, and tasty. You can choose from salmon, swordfish, frog's legs and such oddities as doctor fish and John Dory! For an absolutely delicious entree, try the tamarind BBQ shrimp. Other main plates and specialities include crab cakes, roasted monkfish, and sea scallops steamed in banana leaf. Non-seafood lovers will find chicken or steak. The Valencia orange flan wins the dessert sweepstakes. If a busy bar is your bag, you might want to arrive a bit early and join the throng here.

TRUMPET'S

Grand Hyatt Hotel
109 E 42nd St   883-1234
Lunch: Mon-Fri; Dinner: Mon-Sat
Moderately expensive to expensive

How about a place where you can really have a private, intimate conversation? This superb dining attraction is an absolute must! These may sound like strong words of praise for a hotel restaurant, but the Grand Hyatt has done an outstanding job. A very attractive room outfitted with beautiful appointments and staffed with courteous, well-trained personnel is certainly the right setting for an immensely satisfying dining experience. There are many special offerings, such as grilled veal carpacio with flaked tuna and lamb chops with braised eggplant. Since Trumpet's prepares seafood dishes particularly well, I recommend any of them. The roast monkfish is very special! There's also a fine selection of chicken, veal, lamb, and beef dishes. It's not too often you can get a superb Grand Marnier or chocolate chip soufflé (order these when you order the rest of your dinner); either would top off a memorable evening.

238 MADISON BISTRO

238 Madison Ave (bet 37th and 38th Ave)   447-1919
Lunch, Mon-Fri; Dinner: Daily
Moderate

This is a happy stop for a pleasant luncheon interlude while you are in midtown Manhattan. Neighbors have discovered the excellent food and prompt service; the place is crowded for lunch, but it also provides unhurried dinners. Salads, like roast chicken with citrus fruits or steak tartare are full meals in themselves. Assorted pastas are presented in a most appealing manner. Entrees include mixed grilled seafood, marinated grilled leg of lamb, grilled veal chop, and roast herb chicken with the most delicious mashed potatoes you have tasted in a long time. Homemade ice creams and sorbets provide a nice finish.

UNION SQUARE CAFE

21 E 16th St   243-4020
Lunch, Dinner: Mon-Sat
Moderate

Maybe restaurant operators really do read this book! In previous editions, I had recommended this interesting cafe but complained of the noisy downstairs dining room and the "funny food" that seemed a bit too offbeat and pretentious for my taste. Well, lo and behold! The Union Square Cafe has simplified its presentation and even soundproofed the room. Thank you! Now the chef is offering delicious Italian and French dishes that most of us know how to enjoy. Still, I prefer the grilled offerings, like smoked shell steak, marinated fillet mignon of tuna, and fillet of salmon. The hot garlic potato chips are extra special.

UNITED NATIONS DELEGATES' DINING ROOM
United Nations Headquarters
First Ave and 42nd St   963-7626
Lunch: Mon-Fri
Moderate

Don't let the name put you off! The public can eat here, and enjoy a special international atmosphere, with conversations at the adjoining tables being conducted in almost every conceivable language. The setting is charming, overlooking a patio and the river. The room is large and airy, the service polite and informed. Although there is a large selection of appetizers, soups, salads, entrees and desserts on the regular menu, by far the best deal here is the Delegate's Buffet. A huge table of salads, baked specialties, seafoods, roasts, vegetables, cheeses, desserts, and fruits await the hungry noontime diner. (The room is used for private gatherings in the evening.) There isn't a more appetizing complete daily buffet table in New York than this one, and all the dishes are attractively presented and very tasty. After a tour of the United Nations building, this is a great place to relax with friends and figure out how *you* would change the course of world affairs!

VERONICA
240 W 38th St   764-4770
Breakfast, Lunch: Mon-Fri
Inexpensive to moderate

A friend who works in the garment district told me about a fantastic Italian restaurant in his area, but he wouldn't give me the exact location or the name (he did hint that it was a woman's name) because he was afraid I'd put it in my book and spoil his secret. He didn't want to battle crowds. As you can imagine, this was enough to pique my interest, so I did some investigating. The restaurant in question turned out to be Veronica, a tiny place in the heart of the garment district, and it's only open for breakfast and lunch. Well-known by neighborhood workers, it is one of the busiest spots in town at lunchtime. This marvelous cafeteria-style restaurant serves sensational home-cooked food, and it's run by three amusing sons. What wonders they serve up! There is a marvelous veal piccata, mouth-watering homemade lasagna, delicious tortellini, and chicken salad. Other favorites are the pasta primavera and the chicken florentina (breast of chicken with creamed spinach, prosciutto, mozzarella, and mushrooms in cream sauce). Fortunately, as you enter the cafeteria line, there are signs with prices and descriptions of the daily specials, because once your eyes focus on the most appetizing dishes this side of Florence, you'll have a hard time making a decision. The clientele is sophisticated, and the atmosphere is informal and homey. Don't forget to try the homemade cheesecakes. Most of the food is available for takeout, for individual orders, or for parties and special occasions.

THE VIEW
Marriott Marquis Hotel
1535 Broadway (Times Square)   398-1900
Dinner: Daily; Brunch: Sun
Moderate to moderately expensive

Many restaurant reviewers say that you should avoid: (1) hotel restaurants, (2) restaurants on the top floors of buildings, and (3) restaurants that revolve. Well, I found a place that falls into all three categories, but it's a must *not* to avoid! I recommend brunch or dinner at the View, the revolving rooftop dining room in the Marriott Marquis Hotel on Times Square. Be sure to get a table by the window, of course. It's popular with businessmen and theatergoers, so be sure to call for reservations and come early. There's a pretheater *prix fixe* dinner menu with four courses. In the evening, there are several menus: American, Italian, and French. It's a good choice from any point of view.

VILLAGE ATELIER
436 Hudson St (corner of Morton St)   989-1363
Lunch: Mon-Fri; Dinner: Mon-Sat
American Express
Moderate

We all know of friends whose cooking is so good that we are excited when a dinner invitation arrives. (Alas, we also know of some whose table is so unappetizing that we dread to accept their hospitality!) The Village Atelier falls in the former category; it is like a good neighbor whose kitchen produces some of the best dishes around! Just 12 eclectic tables make up this cozy establishment, many of them showing off handsome wooden tops. If you are coming from uptown, you'll be good and hungry by the time you get here, because the one-way street pattern makes it almost impossible to reach! It is well worth the trouble. Each one of the dishes here tastes like it was cooked just for you, fresh and cool when it should be, well seasoned and warm when called for. Each day a special soup dish is offered, along with a wide selection of salads, fish, and unusual appetizers (like curry grilled lamb sausage with ratatouille). The roast stuffed poussin (baby chicken) is the best I have ever tasted: it is smothered with montmorency cherry and maple glaze. Of course, there are scallops and cod and paillard of veal and ribeye of beef and just about anything else that you might want. Feast well on your main course; the dessert selection hardly befits this fine establishment. Take a look at the cozy bar at the back of the room; it is just like one you would like to have in your own home!

VINCE & EDDIE'S
70 W 68th St   721-0068
Lunch: Mon-Sat; Dinner: Daily; Brunch: Sun
Moderate

The name "Eddie" is almost as popular as "Joe" when it comes to naming Manhattan eateries. This time Eddie (and Vince) have taken rooms that housed several now-deceased operations, and again have created in the small quarters a homey, well-priced bistro that is at once charming and professional. I have a problem with the long, narrow quarters, as you must pass by the rest rooms and the kitchen to reach the rear dining room and garden. But never mind. The cozy fireplace near the entrance will make you feel wanted, even if the help seem a little overpowered by their attentive customers. The menu selections can please most any taste; nothing fancy, just good home-cooking. Let's hope that 70 W 68th does not go through any more reincarnations. I like this one the way it is!

VIVOLO
140 E 74th St   737-3533
Lunch: Mon-Fri; Dinner: Mon-Sat
Moderate

An old townhouse converted into a charming two-story, moderately priced Italian restaurant has become a neighborhood favorite. There are cozy fireplaces on both levels, but the second floor is reserved exclusively for nonsmokers. Consistency is the name of the game here. You know that whatever dish you order will be presented in a professional manner every time you visit. Other restaurants could learn about daily specials from Vivolo! They print the list of specials each day and include it with the regular menu, so that the waiters don't have to stumble through a bad recitation. Menu choices run the gamut of unusual antipasti: carpaccio, baked clams, cold seafood salad, and mussels in tomato sauce. A complete selection of pasta, from angel hair with fresh vegetables to spinach with bacon, onion, and tomato, is available daily. The tortellini and linguini are done with true Italian flair. Popular entrees are the broiled shrimp, stuffed veal chops, scaloppine in lemon and butter, and breast of chicken with artichokes and mushrooms. For a different dessert, try the cannoli alla Vivolo, a pastry filled with ricotta cream. And don't be surprised if Paul Newman or Robert Redford is seated next to you.

VOULEZ-VOUS
1462 First Ave (at 76th St)   249-1776
Lunch: Mon-Fri; Dinner: Mon-Sun; Brunch: Sun
Moderate

Jacques Rameker makes sure his guests are well taken care of from the time they enter his premises to the moment they leave (stuffed and satisfied). Voulez-Vous is surely one of the best French bistros in town! I was particularly impressed with the natural manner of the staff; they all go out of their way to make diners feel right at home, with absolutely no posturing. A pre-theater *prix fixe* dinner is offered in the early evening (from 5:15 to 6:30 p.m.). It's a real three-course bargain with a number of selections from the regular menu. Every day is a special day here: Monday is rabbit, Tuesday is Onglet à l'echalotte, Wednesday is couscous royal, Thursday is Navarin d'Agneau, Friday is bouillabaisse and roasted leg of lamb, and Saturday and Sunday are roasted rack of veal and choucroute du Pecheur. Monday night is soufflé time; be sure to order as you sit down, as the preparation takes a bit of time. The attractively priced Sunday brunch is a bonanza, including fresh orange juice (or something a bit heavier); soup, salad, canape of eggplant caviar, or melon, and then a treasure trove of appetizing main dishes. These include cheese soufflé, steak tartare with sautéed potatoes, mesquite-grilled chicken glazed with ginger and orange mustard, cold poached salmon, and a large list of other delicacies. The dessert selection is fabulous. Don't skip the cappuccino frozen soufflé: Voulez-Vous!

WEST SIDE STOREY
700 Columbus Ave (at 95th St)   749-1900
Daily: 7 a.m.-11 p.m.
Moderate

This is not a fancy place, but if you're looking for a wholesome, delicious, and inexpensive meal, you'll find it here. The breakfast plates include French toast and flapjacks with delicious whipped butter and Vermont maple syrup. In fact, walnut apple flapjacks are the specialty of the house. You also have your choice of Vermont cheddar cheese omelets; country cream cheese and parsley omelets; herb omelets; ham, green pepper, and onion omelets; or nova and cream cheese omelets. All the eggs and omelets are served with home fries and toast; you can also get sweet breakfast pastries.

(If you're not an early riser, you'll be happy to note that breakfast is served late.) The salads are equally great. The West Side chef's salad is a delicious combination of cold meats, cheese, bean sprouts, cherry tomatoes, seasonal vegetables, herbs, and an artichoke heart—and you won't believe the very moderate price. All the salad bowls are served with fresh bread and whipped butter. And what a selection of sandwiches! You name it, and they'll make it. You also have your choice of breads. Hot dishes include quiche, grilled hamburgers, chili, hot roast beef, and hot turkey. And the small fry can dine for pennies (almost!) on frankfurters and beans or spaghetti and meatballs. It's easy to see why this is such a popular spot for quick dining.

WILKINSON'S
1573 York Ave (bet 83rd and 84th St)   535-5454
Dinner: Daily
Moderate to expensive

Everything looks good at Wilkinson's! The people look good because the lighting is very flattering. The pink tones make the diners look as though they've just returned from a holiday in the sun. The food looks good because it really is! This is a delightful, intimate seafood cafe. It does not pretend to be everything to everybody, but does particularly well with a somewhat limited menu. The appetizer dishes are unique. My favorite is the cured Norwegian salmon. For an entree, don't miss the fresh lump crab cakes with wild rice. Other possibilities are the broiled swordfish and the tuna with tomato sauce. As a thoughtful gesture, no cigars or pipes are allowed in the main dining area, so you can enjoy such delicious desserts as chocolate mousse cake or the carmelized apple tart without distraction.

WINDOWS ON THE WORLD
1 World Trade Center   938-1111
Dinner: Daily; Buffet: Sat, Sun; Brunch: Sun
Expensive

Windows on the World, on top of the World Trade Center, features one of the most spectacular views in all the world. It's worth going up just to see the great panorama from the 107th floor. (You can't wear jeans.) You need reservations for the restaurant, but I recommend that you *don't* stay for dinner—the food is not all that great. If you do decide to eat, I suggest the grand buffet table on weekends, which is attractive and reasonably priced. There is a super dessert selection, which includes chocolate Sabayon cake, warm apple tarts, and white chocolate mousse. Or you might have cocktails and some hors d'oeuvres in the Hors d'Oeuvrerie. Music and dancing start at 7:30 p.m. A "sunset supper" is served early in the evening at a reduced price. On Sundays, dancing starts at 4 p.m. and continues until 9 p.m. Also available is the Cellar in the Sky, where a preset menu (it changes every two weeks) features a seven-course dinner with five wines at an appropriate sky-high price.

WOO CHON RESTAURANT
8 W 36th St (off Fifth Ave)   695-0676
Daily: 24 hours
Moderate

Sparkling clean, friendly, and inviting would be the best adjectives to describe this Korean restaurant, which has thrown away the keys to its front door. For a group dinner, order a variety of beef, pork, or shrimp dishes and have fun broiling them right at your table. All of the accompanied dishes add a special touch to your meal. Besides the marinated barbecue items, there are such tasty delights as Oriental noodles and veggies, Chinese herbs and rice served in beef broth, a variety of noodle dishes, and dozens of other Far Eastern treats. If you are unfamiliar with Korean food, the helpful personnel will do their best to explain what you are eating . . . and how you should eat it! Woo Chon is a fun experience for a different style of dining.

WOO LAE OAK OF SEOUL
77 W 46th St   869-9958
Lunch, Dinner: Daily
Moderate

If you've had the opportunity to visit Korea, you've undoubtedly enjoyed Korean barbecue, certainly one of that country's tastier delights. In New York, there's an outstanding version of the real thing, brought to you by an establishment that's been in business for nearly a half century, Woo Lae Oak. One word of warning: many items are very hot and spicy, so order carefully. A delicious appetizer is sewu tuigim (deep-fried shrimp and vegetables). Of course, the big attraction is the authentic Korean barbecue. The meat, broiled right at your table, is marinated in a special sauce and served with rice, soup, and vegetables. Choice of meat includes sliced beef, short rib cubes, sliced chicken, beef tongue, beef liver, beef heart, beef tripe, and sliced pork. Hot pot casserole is also cooked at your table and served with rice and vegetables, as well as your choice of sliced beef, shrimp, fish, or chicken. A large assortment of rice dishes, porridge, and noodles is available. Reservations are a necessity for large groups; be prepared to wait if you arrive with a small party at regular dining hours. Service is rapid, but don't rush through your meal. Take time to savor that barbecue.

WYLIE'S RIBS AND COMPANY
891 First Ave (at 50th St)   751-0700
Daily: 11:30 a.m.-midnight
Moderate

Finding a convenient, pleasant, not-too-crowded spot that serves great food at a reasonable price is not always easy. If you like Texas-style barbecued chicken and ribs, Wylie's is the best in this department, offering ample platters of the tastiest, crispiest back ribs you have ever gotten all over your fingers—and some of the tenderest Northern fried chicken available. I suggest the combination dish served with excellent steak fries and cole slaw. Of course, you can also get half-pound burgers, barbecued beef sandwiches, salads, chili, and a very special brick onion loaf. The dinner menu leans more toward steak and fish, in addition to their famous ribs. The atmosphere is informal, the service efficient. Early evening hours are the least hectic.

YELLOWFINGERS DI NUOVO
200 E 60th St   751-8615
Lunch, Dinner: Daily
Moderate

Yellowfingers was reconceived with a wonderful idea called "fa vecchia." The name comes from "faccia vecchia," which was used in the past for pizzalike breads baked without a topping. Yellowfingers has put together absolutely delicious fa vecchia combinations, like the one baked with fresh tomato and buffalo mozzarella and the one baked with potatoes, pancetta, and rosemary (my favorite). You can also order them garnished with such items as prosciutto, braised onion, and parsley. They are crusty, but not too filling—just right for a unique lunchtime meal. If this kind of pizza is not to your liking, there are plenty of excellent salads, the best being the rosemary-roasted chicken salad with sweet peppers, pine nuts, and greens. The focaccia farcita sandwich (grilled eggplant, mozzarella, roasted peppers, basil, capers, and gremolata) is worth a try. For more substantial appetites, there's a house-ground hamburger on grilled focaccia. Various homemade desserts are usually available. This place is noisy, fun, handy, and moderately priced— a great addition to New York's Upper East Side lunch scene.

YELLOW ROSE CAFE
450 Amsterdam Ave (at 82nd St)   595-8760
Lunch, Dinner: Daily; Brunch: Sat, Sun
Inexpensive

Barbara Clifford of Fort Worth, Texas, has transplanted Texas-style chicken-fried steak, Southern fried chicken, smothered pork chops, and El Paso cheese enchiladas to her 12-table Upper West Side cafe. Accompanied by buttermilk biscuits, red chili, real mashed potatoes, and home-grown vegetables from her father's garden in Texas, Barbara's portions are huge, delicious, and incredibly inexpensive. The cafe is cactus filled, homey, and very busy. Strawberry rhubarb pie, pecan pie, or sweet potato pie will top off a great meal during the week or a hearty country brunch on weekends. Look for the unique Western bar next door.

YE WAVERLY INN
16 Bank St   929-4377
Lunch: Mon-Fri; Dinner: Daily; Brunch: Sat, Sun
Moderate

English food is not very fancy, but English pubs do have atmosphere, and they do some things quite well. In the Village there's Ye Waverly Inn, a picturesque pub in confined quarters, which dates from the early part of the century. There are four rooms and an outside eating area with adequate though uncomfortable furnishings, but the atmosphere is truly delightful. One is certain the food is good, because the place is always crowded and there are a number of famous folk who often dine here. If all this is not reason enough to go to the Inn, their chicken pot pie should be. It is absolutely one of the best I have ever eaten. Other possibilities would be the sautéed calf's liver, barbecued rack of ribs, boiled beef and horseradish sauce, or the boneless chicken breast. Before the main course, try the fresh fruit and cheese, French-fried eggplant, or a delicious fresh vegetable marinade. For the light eater, I suggest the smoked brook trout or the quiche and Waldorf salad. The dessert selection is excellent, especially the tasty pecan pie. I can see why legions of Village regulars flock here, and you will, too.

ZARELA
953 Second Ave (bet 50th and 51st St)   644-6740
Lunch: Mon-Fri; Dinner: Daily
Moderate

If you really want the very best Mexican meal in New York, you should get yourself invited to the home of Zarela Martinez. Failing that, the next best thing is to head for her charming and busy restaurant, a two-story building on Second Avenue. Don't let them seat you downstairs, because the second-floor dining room, complete with a fireplace, is much more quaint and colorful. You'll understand how Zarela has earned her reputation for the best south-of-the-border cuisine when you taste her antojitos, which include a wonderful poblano chile stuffed with chicken and dried fruit, rolled fried-chicken tacos, and fried calamari in a spicy sauce. And there is so much more: such seafood dishes as shrimp sautéed in a spicy jalapeno sauce and grill-smoked salmon; several chicken dishes and a grilled duck breast with peanut and pumpkin seed sauce; delicious meat entrees, like the jalisco-style pork and hominy stew; and a great selection of Mexican side dishes, from refried black beans to golden fried cauliflower to fried plantain slices with mole sauce. Even the desserts are special. The chocolate crepes are heaven-sent. But if you're going Mexican all the way, try the Mexican fruit bread pudding with applejack brandy butter sauce or the banana, pineapple, and peach jam cake.

WHAT ARE THE FIVE TALLEST BUILDINGS IN NEW YORK CITY?

World Trade Center	1,350 feet high, 110 stories
Empire State Building	1,250 feet high, 102 stories (with the 164 foot television tower included, it is 1,414 feet high)
Chrysler Building	1,046 feet high, 77 stories
AT&T Building	950 feet high, 67 stories
40 Wall Tower	929 feet high, 71 stories

(Sears Tower/**Chicago**) 1,454 feet high, 110 stories

III. Where to Find It: Special Activities, Experiences, and Tours for Residents and Visitors

Ultimate Lower East Side Shopping Experience

First a little history is in order. When the vast hordes of immigrants passed Ellis Island, they were often financially and emotionally wiped out. As a result, the vanguard settled in the first residential neighborhood they came upon, and their relatives followed suit. The first such neighborhoods, in modern times, were Little Italy, Chinatown, and the area known as the Lower East Side. Unlike immigrant areas in other cities, this was *never* the nice section of town. *The Seaport Experience* points out that "Five Corners" (the current site of 1 Police Plaza) was a murderer's row so infamous that residents preferred to sleep on the docks.

Over the years, the residents moved out to make room for succeeding waves of newcomers. (The Lower East Side Tenement Museum researched the residents of its buildings, which had been erected in 1865 but abandoned by 1935. They found that thousands had lived there in a 70-year span, with the average stay less than five years.) Yiddish, Chinese, Spanish, Italian, Ukrainian, Russian, and Greek were but a few languages spoken here.

No matter what the wave, the next generation rarely stayed in the neighborhood. (There are exceptions. Chinatown and Little Italy will probably still be there at the millennium.) But as they moved up and out, they still returned to shop the East Side for bargains and excellence. It is not an uncommon sight today to see a limo with Connecticut plates pull up in front of a pickle stand, or three coeds with Harvard sweat shirts and notebooks stopping in Chinatown for a home-cooked lunch. The San Gennaro festival brings everyone of Italian descent to five square blocks around Mulberry Street.

The original method of merchandising was via pushcarts. In the 1930s the pushcarts were "organized" and sent indoors to the city markets (which still exist). The more successful ones graduated to stores, usually along Orchard Street. And though many of the stores claim a pedigree older than that of Bloomingdale's (and they'd be right!), most of the proprietors reflect the changing ethnic scene, as does their merchandise.

I've been observing the scene for years, but in the last few the area has changed with dizzying speed. Old Jewish owners gave way to Hispanics, who gave way to Israelis. Chinatown now extends well into several synagogues and Grand Street. The delis that made your mouth water are now Spanish pizzerias, and many of the old landmarks are gone altogether (Bell Yarn, M&M Shoes, Guss Pickles). Although the places are gone, the customs and mores remain. M&M and Bell had the distinction of topping our "rudest" and "nastiest" lists every year they existed. We kept them in because they were the best and cheapest in the city. Manners have been tempered, but only slightly. (No one else could ever aspire to such rudeness!) Nowadays, Guss's successor takes Visa and Mastercard. And they are quite friendly. But the bargains aren't as good.

This doesn't mean you shouldn't take a Sunday off and go down there. "List price" is the starting point for negotiations on any item you want. If you're from abroad, you'll find a selection of adapters, converters, and foreign currency appliances when no one else knows what you're talking about. If there is new audio equipment out, the stores down here will have it faster and cheaper than anyone else. For designer clothing, shoes, and leather goods, it's the same story. And Grand Street, between Allen and Essex, is a permanent White Sale.

Some caveats: Take a cab! Do *not* use local subways, especially on the way back. There are a lot worse neighborhoods, but don't trust anyone you meet on the street or check over merchandise offerings in the park. Don't flaunt large amounts of cash. Stop for a bit to eat *before* you shop, so you don't have to put shopping bags down beside your seat. And forget your Sunday manners down here. You're in for a long wait if you let that little old lady go before you. She and her sisters have very sharp elbows (and tongues to match) and can take care of themselves! There is a municipal garage between Essex and Ludlow above Delancey. It's your only prayer of finding a parking space. On Sunday, the line is usually on Ludlow. When you see how long it is, you'll understand why we suggest taking a cab or having one person in your party stay with the car. Remember, most of these stores are closed on Saturday, and they're empty during the week. Sundays are so busy that Orchard Street is a closed pedestrian mall.

For the past 20 years I have made a practice of exploring the Lower East Side nearly every month. I feel that I know the territory almost as well as the local inhabitants. I share with you below the very best shopping bargains, considering quality and price, in nearly every category. The best food in the area is also listed (restaurants, however, are listed in the restaurant section). For the most fun, take your excursion on a Sunday.

Begin your stroll at Houston and Orchard Streets:

M. Friedlich (196 Orchard St): European sportswear and knits. Disinterested help. Don't miss the basement area.

Shulie's (175 Orchard St): Great shopping for Tahari fans. Up-to-date styles, good prices.

Beckenstein (men's, 121 Orchard St; ladies', 125 Orchard St; home, 130 Orchard St): The ultimate in fabrics for family and home. Accessory items are available at the ladies' store, decorating service at the home store. Best selection in city.

Breakaway Fashions (125 Orchard St): Good buys on designer and brand-name sportswear.

Fine & Klein (119 Orchard St): Simply the best there is in Manhattan for bags and leather goods at great prices. Many top designer pieces at sizable discounts.

Lea's (119 Orchard St, upstairs): Real bargains on ladies' better dresses and sportswear, particularly Albert Nippon and Louis Féraud (a third off on both).

Lace Up (110 Orchard St): Trendy footwear at good savings, featuring Mephisto among others. Real bargains if you are a good shopper.

Klein's of Monticello (105 Orchard St): Deep discounts on 30-40 top women's designer's items; usually at least 25% off. Also men's cashmere sweaters at bargain prices.

Forman's (plus sizes, 78 Orchard St; designer clothes, 82 Orchard St; petite sizes, 94 Orchard St): Well-known discount prices on new fashions for the ladies. Be sure to check downstairs departments.

Ted's Fine Clothing (83 Orchard St): A good place to pick up Adolfo and Pierre Cardin tuxedo shirts at discount, plus 20% off on After Six, Dior, and Bill Blass tuxedos.

Louis Chock (74 Orchard St): Undergarments, loungewear, and hosiery at worthwhile savings. A good place to stock up.

A. W. Kaufman (73 Orchard St): Ditto.

Fomo (61 Orchard St): Michael Klein's great handbag and leather outlet, with great prices to boot, plus active sportswear at discount.

Penn Garden (58 Orchard St): Men should not miss the outstanding values on Oleg Cassini, Hathaway, Pierre Cardin, Dior, and Pierre Balmain dress shirts.

Goldman & Cohen (55 Orchard St): Ladies' undergarments, robes, lingerie, and loungewear at least 25% off, but be sure you know what you want!

Pan Am Menswear (50 Orchard St): Brand-name men's designer suits at discount. Good quality, but service and ambiance leave something to be desired.

Charles Weiss & Son (38 Orchard St and 331 Grand St): Excellent selection and outstanding bargains in ladies' undergarments.

Next move on to Grand Street, and check out the following:

Kaufman Electrical Appliances (365 Grand St): Mr. Kaufman himself will be at the door with an unusually friendly Lower East Side greeting. Inside the tiny store you'll find reduced prices on all kinds of appliances, pens, cameras, and the like. One of the oldest electronics outlets in the city, it is still one of the best when it comes to bargains.

East Side Gifts and Dinnerware (351 Grand St): A treasure trove of bargains in top-quality gift items from Baccarat, Daum, Orrefors, Lalique, Christoffle, Royal Doulton, Wedgewood, Fitz & Floyd, Haviland, Hutchenreuter, and many others. Don't be put off by the crowded appearance!

Sun Ray Yarns (349 Grand St): Great savings for the knitter.

Grand Sterling Silver Co. (345 Grand St): A dazzling display of silver at substantial savings.

Rice & Breskin (323 Grand St): Why pay more for infants' and children's wear when you can get it here at big savings?

Leslie's Bootery (319 Grand St and 65 Orchard St): Top quality men's and women's shoes at savings. Many designer names in the large stock.

Fishkin (314 and 318 Grand St): Ladies' designer clothes and shoes at worthwhile savings. Be sure to check out both stores.

Goldman's (315 Grand St): China, crystal, flatware, clocks, and figurines from every top name in the business, including Lenox, Noritake, Mikasa, Rosenthal, Reed & Barton, Bing & Grondahl, Orrefors, Spode, and Royal Worcester, all at discount. Especially good savings (30% off) on a big selection of Lladro.

Ezra Cohen (307 Grand St): New York's best in all manner of domestics, including sheets, towels, bedspreads, bathroom rugs, pillows, comforters, and drapes, all top-quality designer names at real savings. Absolutely reliable in every respect.

On the adjacent side streets you will find more bargains:

J. Schachter (85 Ludlow St): For decades, the ultimate in bedding items; you can coordinate entire bedroom ensembles. Custom work is outstanding.

Bondy (40 Canal St): Electronics bargains amid the clutter.

Dembitzer (5 Essex St): Same story.

Montgomery Stationery (9½ Essex St): Stationery items at discount, including Mont Blanc pens, Rolodex, and most everything else you need for the office or home.

Allen Tie Center (146 Allen): My favorite tie store folded, as have most stores along this street, but Allen is the place to go to save big bucks on silk neckwear.

Lanac (73 Canal St): The name is Canal spelled backwards, but the savings are very forward on all kinds of gift items and tableware for the home. A good place to come for wedding and holiday gifts, and to replace pieces that Junior broke.

Vicmarr (88 Delancey St): Audio equipment, televisions and cameras at bargain prices. Take along someone who knows electronic items, as the help seems somewhat distracted.

After all this, you are probably ready to think of your stomach, too! The best in the area:

Russ & Daughters (179 E Houston St): For generations, the ultimate in appetizers, candy, and the like. Top quality, nice people, vast selection. Don't have a party without checking out this place.

Moishe's Bakery (181 E Houston St): Next door to Russ. Crowded, disinterested help, but features wonderful Old World bread and bakery items.

Yonah Schimmel (137 E Houston St): The traditional place for knishes.

Bernstein-on-Essex (135 Essex St): Deli items and kosher Chinese food. Forget about the surroundings.

Lucky China Lei Bakery (280 Grand St): Large selection of delicious Chinese bakery items.

The Sweet Life (63 Hester St): Amazing! A wonderfully clean store in a dirty neighborhood, very polite people in a rude district, fabulous candy and nut selection at super prices. Don't miss it!

Gertel's Bake Shop (53 Hester St): Superb cakes and bakery items to eat in or take out. (I suggest the latter.) The help never smiles, but this is absolutely the best quality. Don't miss the blackout cake!

Kossar's (367 Grand St): The bialys don't come any fresher or better.

Tours, Activities

ADVENTURE ON A SHOESTRING
300 W 53rd St   265-2663

Started as a lark by Howard Goldberg over two decades ago, Adventure on a Shoestring has evolved into the perfect city tour. Its title is self-explanatory: it promises and delivers an offbeat view of New York, and the price is easy on the wallet. How do they do it? There's an annual membership fee that entitles members to discount rates on each trip. Advance notice of trips is published in a newsletter, which is also sent to nonmembers who request it. Tourists and nonmembers can join the tours at a higher rate.

ART HORIZONS INTERNATIONAL
14 E 63rd St   888-2299

Art Horizons tours cover art, architecture, performing arts, culinary arts, fashion, and design. They can be arranged for individuals or groups, the latter usually for a specific exhibit. The guides are especially well qualified, and if you hook up with a group tour, the rates are very reasonable. Either way, you'll be getting a backstage view of city art not available elsewhere. The Horizons staff will introduce you to artists' lofts, gallery directors, and museum curators. Art Horizons also offers the more typical tour features—yacht trips, tours by helicopter, and the like.

BACKSTAGE ON BROADWAY
228 W 47th St (Suite 346)   575-8065

This tour offers a look at a Broadway that regular theater patrons miss. The tour is reasonably priced, with reduced rates for students and senior citizens, and includes an explanation of how a play is technically produced. The lecture is illustrated by taking you backstage. Often, you'll get a chance to meet and chat with theater people; stage managers, actors, and technical designers describe what they do as you're guided among the props and sets. You'll get a full understanding of how a play develops, from script to opening night. Reservations are required; this lets you learn, in advance, who will be your guide. Individuals can be confirmed only one week prior to the date of the tour. But don't miss it. It's very good!

BROOKS COUNTRY CYCLING AND HIKING TOURS
140 W 83rd St (bet Columbus and Amsterdam Ave)
874-5151
Mon-Fri: 9:30-5

Country Cycling offers walking and cycling tours, which range from quiet one-day rides to nine-day European tours. They are geared to the participant's ability, be it a neophyte or a professional. Rental equipment is available, and Country Cycling can arrange group tours, customized tours, and specific treks for visitors with special interests. Some of the more tasty possibilities are daytrips to Dutchess County strawberry fields and apple orchards, Connecticut raspberry fields, and New York wine country. A support vehicle is used on all tours to transport luggage or to provide any kind of emergency assistance.

CHINATOWN WALKING TOURS
70 Mulberry St (2nd floor)
619-4785

This group offers two tours daily, at ten a.m. and one p.m. Each lasts 90 minutes and shows the development of Chinatown. Highlights include food stores, restaurants, and historic sites, as well as many places that the average tourist never gets to see. Reservations are required for weekend tours.

CIRCLE LINE SIGHTSEEING YACHTS
Pier 83 (at 43rd St)   563-3200
Daily: mid-March through Dec

The Circle Line boats cruise Manhattan's waters for three hours. Along the way, sights are pointed out and explained. Unless there's a snowstorm, you can count on having a pleasant trip. Cynics who are too blasé to be moved by the city skyline (and you'd have to be pretty hard-nosed) amuse themselves by listening for mistakes in the guide's pat spiel and loudly correcting him. Keep an ear cocked for a New York-wise skeptic. Groups can avail themselves of the Circle Line package tours, which are all-inclusive tours of the city on land. They include Broadway shows, restaurants, sightseeing, and all the major tourist spots.

DAILEY-THORP CULTURAL TOURS
330 W 58th St (bet Eighth and Ninth Ave)   307-1555
Mon-Fri: 9-5:30

Dailey-Thorp works with the Metropolitan Opera Guild, organizing cultural tours around the world. At its home base in New York, Dailey-Thorp offers special tour packages to the Met. Most of the tours center around weekends, the exceptions being the opening night and opening week of the opera season. They include hotel accommodations (usually at the Pierre), center orchestra seats at the opera, transportation, meals, an experienced tour escort, and guided tours through cultural sights, such as the Metropolitan Museum of Art and the Museum of Modern Art. There are similar arrangements for the New York City Opera, the New York Philharmonic, and Carnegie Hall. And for New Yorkers who wish to expand their horizons, there are East Coast, North America, and worldwide opera-based tours. You could sing an aria about the smoothness and efficiency of this operation.

DISCOVER NEW YORK
The Municipal Art Society
457 Madison Ave   935-3960

The Municipal Art Society conducts several tours, but the most famous is the tour of Grand Central Station, which departs every

Wednesday afternoon at 12:30. Participants meet in the grand terminal lobby. The hour-long tour is free (yes, free!), and no reservations are needed. On spring and summer weekends, the society sponsors walking tours at nominal fees. They run about three hours each and cover historic buildings and districts.

DOORWAY TO DESIGN
1441 Broadway (Suite 338)   221-1111

In special tours organized by Sheila Sperber, you can go behind the scenes in the world of interior design, visit auction galleries and museums, meet artists and craftspeople, discuss the latest styles with fashion makers, and visit antique dealers. These tours can be arranged for any time of the day, can last for several hours or several days, and can be designed for any size group. In one of the most popular tours, you visit private homes in the colorful Greenwich Village area. Advance reservations are necessary.

FEDERAL RESERVE BANK
33 Liberty St   720-6130

Here is your chance to see big bucks being counted. You'll also see a historical coin and currency exhibit and the gold vault that houses the largest collection of gold in the free world. Tours are available four times daily, at 10:30 a.m., 11:30 a.m., 1:30 p.m., and 2:30 p.m., Monday through Friday. Tours last one hour, and a minimum of one-week advance notice for reservations is required.

FULTON FISH MARKET TOUR
17 Fulton Fish Market   962-1608

This is a really smelly tour! Only kidding, of course. It really is one of the most fascinating tours in New York. The Market, which has been in existence since 1831, is the largest of its kind in North America. There are over 75 wholesalers, who sell about 90 million pounds of fish each year. The market opens to buyers at three a.m. on Monday and at four a.m. Tuesday through Friday. It closes down around eight a.m. so that the owners of Manhattan's best restaurants can have fresh produce for the day. Tours cost about $10 per person (for three people or more).

GRACIE MANSION TOUR
East End Ave at 88th St   570-4751
Wed: 10 and 11 a.m., 1 and 2 p.m.

The tour of the newly renovated mayor's home only began in recent years, and since it's the first time in history that Hizzoner's home has been open to the public, business is brisk. Reservations must be obtained by writing or calling the tour director. Since the tour is held only one day a week, an out-of-towner doesn't have much chance to catch one of the hourly tours, but it's worth a try if you're good at planning ahead. Gracie Mansion remains (as it was when the Gracie family owned it) one of the choicest parcels of real estate on the Upper East Side. The view of the East River and the Fire Boat Station is terrific, and the house is magnificent. Call for information about special two-hour group tours of 35-50, available on Mondays and Tuesdays.

HARLEM RENAISSANCE TOURS
2130 First Ave (at 110th St, Suite 1601)   722-9534

Harlem Renaissance Tour personnel know Harlem as only people who live there can. They conduct busloads of visitors through the Harlem Jazz Festival, the Black Theater Festival, and Harlem Week, as well as specialized tours of shows and other cultural events.

HARLEM SPIRITUALS
1697 Broadway (Suite 900)   302-2594

Muriel Samama, the president of this novel operation, offers a wide variety of programs. There are spirituals and gospel on Sunday, gospel on Wednesday, and many other facets of Harlem (with lunch) on Thursdays. A great soul food and jazz tour is offered on Thursday, Friday, and Saturday evenings.

INSIDE NEW YORK
203 E 72nd St   861-0709

New York here means the fashion industry, and the folks at Inside New York aim to show visitors a behind-the scenes look at the fashion, art, and interior design industries in the city. Group tours (15 or more) can be formal affairs or especially designed to gain entrance into wholesale lofts for shopping or shows. There are half-day and all-day tours, and the group tours are quite reasonable.

ISLAND HELICOPTER
34th St Heliport, at the East River   683-4575

Daily, from 9 to 9 (9-6 in January, February, and March), Island Helicopter offers a number of different sightseeing tours. The simplest is a short flight over lower and midtown Manhattan. The more complex go as far as incorporating bus and boat transportation into two-day trips.

LOU SINGER TOURS
130 St Edward's St, Brooklyn   (718) 875-9084

For years, we heard about Lou Singer's tours, but we used to exclude him because he was based in Brooklyn. Now Lou has become synonymous with the "noshing tour" of New York, and no one does it better. (That may have been another reason to leave him out. We harbored notions of doing it ourselves. Now we know better.) Although Singer can arrange the usual behind-the-scenes tours, his specialty is the gastronomic tour, which makes stops in the Lower East Side, Little Ukraine, and Brooklyn.

MANHATTAN NEIGHBORHOOD TROLLEY
180 Eldridge St (bet Delancey and Rivington St)
677-7268
Daily: noon-5 p.m. (April-Oct)

Clang, clang, clang goes the trolley! Only this time it is a bright red-and-green air-conditioned job that will take you on a one-hour sightseeing tour of Lower Manhattan. Departures are from the South Street Seaport (South St and Fulton St), and passengers may get off or on at any of the scheduled stops and reboard at no extra cost. Communities visited include the Seaport, Battery Park, World Trade Center, World Financial Center, City Hall, Chinatown, Little Italy, and the fabulous Lower East Side bargain shopping area.

METROPOLITAN OPERA TOURS
70 Lincoln Center Plaza   769-7000

Here is an exciting chance to see what goes on backstage! Monday through Saturday, the Metropolitan Opera Guild gives inside tours of the Met in Lincoln Center for a nominal fee. Please note that advance reservations are essential.

NBC STUDIO TOUR
30 Rockefeller Center   664-7174

This is the only tour of a working television facility in New York. Prices are reasonable, and group reservations are available in advance for parties of ten or more. Tours leave every 15 minutes between 9:30 and 4:30. Sunday tours are available from early April through Labor Day.

NEW YORK STOCK EXCHANGE
20 Broad St   656-5168
Mon-Fri: 9:15-4

The New York Stock Exchange is a vital part of the business life of the city and a fascinating place to take a self-guided tour. Tickets for the tour are issued on the same day only, and it is suggested you arrive as early as possible in the morning to secure reservations for that day. By noon, most available space is gone. Highlights include a multi-image video, a demonstration of how space-age technology supports trading, and a multilingual explanation of the trading process from the gallery overlooking the world-famous trading floor.

OLD MERCHANT'S HOUSE
29 E 4th St   777-1089
Sun: 1-4, and by appointment

If you love Victorian homes, don't miss this one. It is one of the finest examples of Greek Revival architecture in the United States. A row house built in 1832, the historic landmark is a time capsule of nineteenth-century life in New York, as reflected in the original textiles, furniture, and decorative arts. Group tours for 20 or more are available; call between 9:15 and 5.

PARK RANGER TOURS
New York City Department of Parks and Recreation
427-4040

The Urban Park Rangers (for real!) guide free tours every Sunday at two p.m. in Central Park and other parks around the city. Some of the tours point out which herbs and plants are edible and offer other information on the local flora and fauna. All of the tours are very interesting. Afterward, you're much more inclined to contribute to the park projects that invite your financial support.

RADIO CITY MUSIC HALL
Rockefeller Center, 50th St and Sixth Ave   632-4041

More interesting than the stage show at Radio City is the behind-the-scenes tour, which is conducted every 45 minutes from ten a.m. to 4:45 p.m. Monday through Saturday (Sunday, 11-4:45). The hour-long tour includes a view of the world's largest organ, the "Mighty Wurlitzer," the underground hydraulic system, the costume department, the famous Rockettes' rehearsal room (if not in use), and the world-renowned art deco bathrooms. Note: Rockefeller Center has a self-guided walking tour of the complex. Maps are available throughout the complex.

RIVER-TO-RIVER DOWNTOWN WALKING TOURS
375 South End Ave (nr Liberty St)   321-2823
Times suited to client's request

Ruth Alscher-Green is just the person to call if you want a personalized tour of some of the great sights and sounds of Manhattan. Her service is mainly oriented to single parties, families, or small groups; she can provide a much more interesting experience than those offered by large tour groups. Ruth is a unique and colorful personality who will tailor your tour by personal prearranged visit, telephone, or mail.

SCHAPIRO'S WINERY
126 Rivington St   674-4404

Schapiro's is one of only two wineries in the city that are open on Sunday. (The other is Kedem, a block away on Ludlow, but they don't give tours.) They're kosher wineries and, as such, are closed on Saturday. In this cavernous space beneath the streets of the Lower East Side, barrels and barrels of kosher wine are aged and produced. (It was here I learned that Oregon is prized for its blackberries.) The tour is absolutely fascinating—and free. They give samples.

SHORT LINE TOURS
166 W 46th St   354-5122

The conventional bus tour of the city that Short Line offers is anything but conventional. For one thing, there is not one but eight different tour itineraries, and the line utilizes bus, boat, and helicopter to see it all. Along the way, tourists can visit Harlem, Grant's Tomb, the United Nations, the Empire State Building, Chinatown, the Statue of Liberty, Ellis Island, the South Street Seaport, the World Trade Center, and much, much more. Of course, that requires taking all eight tours (some of which are combinations of single tours) and probably much more time than the average tourist has, but there is no better way to get a well-documented orientation to the city. All tours leave from the Times Square headquarters and range from two hours in length to the all-day Big Apple Tour. Though they are more frequent in warm weather, they run all year. Incidentally, New Yorkers *never* take these tours. So, one trip could make a visitor more knowledgeable about the city than the residents, and you can do it in the lap of luxury, traveling in glass-roofed, air-conditioned buses.

SIDEWALKS OF NEW YORK
517-0201
Tours: Sat: 2 and 6 p.m.; Sun: 2 p.m.

Sam Stafford offers unusual and offbeat walking tours of Manhattan. Among the special experiences are a visit to neighborhoods where celebrities reside, a look at some of New York's most notorious crime scenes, an East Side tour of Jackie Onassis' favorite spots, a visit to some of the oldest and most historic bars and taverns in Greenwich Village, and an exciting "Mafia" tour of New York City. Customized private tours and group tours are available with advance notice. There is even a floral delivery and photographic service of local movie stars' grave sites!

VIEWPOINT INTERNATIONAL
1414 Sixth Ave (at 58th St)   355-1055

Viewpoint International organizes events, programs, and tours of New York. Its clients include corporations, associations, incentive travel groups, nonprofit organizations, and ordinary visitors to New York. The company's partners, Margaret Gins and Allyn Simmons, and their crew have done it all, from two presidential events to Grammy Award galas to centennial events for 15,000. On a smaller scale, they do block parties, black-tie events, complete city tours (with native-language guides), and anything that will make a New York visit easier on the planners and more fun for the participants. The Viewpoint folks are true professionals and are completely reliable. Since they have a working relationship with travel agents all over the world, they're able to map out a special New York experience for anyone.

IS IT TRUE THAT MANHATTAN ISLAND WAS BOUGHT FROM THE INDIANS FOR $24?

What Peter Minuit gave the Manhattan tribe was a package of trinkets and cloth valued at 60 guilders — roughly equivalent to $24.

IV. Where to Eat It: New York's Best Food Shops

Bakery Goods

A. ORWASHER BAKERY
308 E 78th St (nr Second Ave)   288-6569
Mon-Sat: 7-7

This family business has been in existence for over 75 years, and many of their breads are family recipes handed down from father to son. You'll find Old World breads that used to exist in the local immigrant bakeries and have become extremely rare. Over 30 varieties are always available. Hearth-baked in brick ovens and made with natural ingredients, the breads come in a marvelous array of shapes and sizes—triple twists, cornucopias, and hearts, just to name a few. (I've seen their ovens; they're the real thing.) Be sure to sample the onion boards and cinnamon raisin bread and the challah, available on Fridays. It's almost as good as the home-baked variety. Best of all is their raisin pumpernickel, which comes in small rolls or loaves. When warm, it's moist, delicious, and sensational.

A. ZITO AND SON'S BAKERY
259 Bleecker St (bet Sixth and Seventh Ave)   929-6139
Mon-Sat: 6 a.m.-6:30 p.m.; Sun: 6-1

Those in the know, know Zito's. They flock here at sunrise to buy bread straight from the oven. Among Zito's fans are Frank Sinatra and numerous Village residents. They love Zito's because the bread crust is crunchy perfection, a sharp contrast to the soft, delicate inside. Two of the best sellers are the whole wheat loaf and the Sicilian loaf. Anthony John Zito is proudest of the house specialties: Italian, whole wheat, and white breads. The latter two come in sizes of 4, 7, and 13 ounces.

BONTE PATISSERIE
1316 Third Ave (bet 75th and 76th St)   535-2360
Mon-Sat: 9-6:30; closed Aug

Mrs. Bonte serves a delicious line of pastries and cakes. The style is decidedly French, but the taste has earned universal appreciation. The pastry is flaky smooth, the chocolates creamy satin, and the croissants and éclairs—well, they're perfection. Mrs. Bonte personally supervises the operation, and everything sold here bears her hallmark—that of a tremendously accomplished pastry chef. And her husband is just as talented.

BREAD SHOP
3139 Broadway (at La Salle St)   666-4343
Daily: 8 a.m.-9 p.m.

This tiny, out-of-the-way bakery, under the tracks at 123rd Street, supplies some of the best handmade, untainted-by-preservatives bread in the city. Their customers are mostly local stores and New York's better food shops, but if you arrive between 10 a.m. and 3 p.m., one of the house specialties will be available fresh from the oven. (A gastronomic treat unique to New York is walking into the neighborhood bagel shop and sampling "whatever's hot.") Jenny Buchanan and Jim Fitzer, who run the shop, are big on healthy breads and natural ingredients, so the bread here is not only delicious but good for you.

BUDAPEST PASTRY
207 E 84th St (bet Second and Third Ave)   628-0721
Mon-Sat: 7:30-7:30; Sun: 9:30-5:30

In 1985, Al Maghrebi, a Syrian baker, bought Budapest Pastry from its Hungarian owners. The resulting mixture of baking styles was a success. Of course, they had a few things in common. The Hungarians stuff the thin, flaky babka, strudel, and baklava dough with cabbage or apples, while Middle Easterners stuff the same kinds of dough with spinach or eggplant. They also make cakes for birthdays and other personalized cakes. Nowadays, the bakery resounds with a mix of Syrian bakers, Hungarian pastry lovers, and all kinds of falafel fans who come together to form a model of foreign relations the UN would envy.

CAFE LALO
201 W 83rd St (at Amsterdam Ave)   496-6031
Mon-Tues: noon-1 a.m.; Wed-Thurs: noon-2 a.m.;
Sat: 11 a.m.-3 a.m.; Sun: 11 a.m.-1 a.m.

You will think you are in a fine European pastry shop as you enjoy fine cappuccino, espresso, cordials, and a large selection of delicious desserts. I know good cakes and pastries and can say with all honesty these are some of the best. Yogurt and ice cream are available, and soothing music makes every calorie easier to accept!

CAKES BY CLIFF
529 E 6th St (bet Ave A and Ave B)   777-9253
Usually available: 9-8

As this is not a regular retail business, Cliff Simon can be hard to reach, but it is worth the effort. Imagine a seven-foot-high spiral anniversary cake! It's not too tall an order for Cliff, who designs each cake to meet a customer's special needs. He was trained in the theater, lighting design, and graphics. Combined with his love of baking, this has resulted in big names like the late Malcolm Forbes, Madonna, and Diana Ross calling for his special talents. His prices are not in the supermarket bakery category, but then greatness doesn't come cheaply, does it?

CHELSEA BAKING COMPANY
259 W 19th St (bet Seventh and Eighth Ave)   242-7692
Daily: 7-7

The Chelsea Baking Company is a wholesale source for restaurants, caterers and gourmet stores, but it's also open to retail customers who call in advance. We rate David Talbot's deep-dish apple pie the very best in New York. The food is now divided into three separate lists to accommodate the wholesale customer. The top is the "Signature" line, which, Talbot says, offers the finest ingredients, style, and presentation available. Layer-cake and breakfast lines feature a renowned cheesecake, a Mandarin cream cake, a real key lime pie, and all-butter Danishes and croissants. Chelsea Baking also specializes in custom orders; you can get an absolutely superb wedding cake, birthday cakes, or other special occasion cakes all made to order.

CREATIVE CAKES
400 E 74th St (at First Ave)   794-9811
Tues-Fri: 8-4:30; Sat: 9-11

Being in the "creative cake" business myself, I know about the fun involved in making all kinds of unusual concoctions. Creative Cakes knows how to have fun, using fine ingredients and ingenious patterns. Famous and not-so-famous cake lovers are fans of the fudgy chocolate with frosted buttercream icing and the sensational designs. Bill Schultz, the boss, has designed Bella Abzug's hat (on a platter, of course) and has even made a copy of the U.S. Customs House for a Fourth of July celebration. Prices are reasonable, and the results are sure to be the conversation piece at any party.

DUFOUR PASTRY KITCHENS
808 Washington St   929-2800
Mon-Fri: 7-5; call for Sat hours

The location is not the handiest. The air is full of pastry dough, so you shouldn't wear your best black outfit. And all items are frozen, so you'll have to bake them yourself (instructions included). But these are the only drawbacks! You'll find delicious and creative pastry items of high quality at sensible prices at Dufour, which counts many fancy uptown restaurants among its regular customers. Chocolate and regular puff pastry dough is available in sheets and in bulk. Wonderful hors d'oeuvres can be ordered in quantity: puff pastry logs, mini quiches, tart shells, and bite-size, hand-filled "party lites" in flavors like fresh mushroom pâté, Swiss and spinach, Southwestern black bean, smoked salmon, Caribbean pâté, and Indian curry. Try the apple and spice turnovers for desserts. Great lunch puffs—chili with fresh vegetables, tuna melt, smoked salmon, broccoli-spinach gratin, and more—provide a satisfying and light meal. And all ingredients are natural.

ECCE PANIS
1120 Third Ave (bet 65th and 66th St)   535-2099
Mon-Fri: 10-7; Sat, Sun: 10-6

Evelina, the boss, says that bread is their passion, and it shows. The varieties are creative, to say the least. You have to come and take a look, then (on weekends) take home a loaf of chocolate bread! Breads include dark and light sourdough, neo-Tuscan, whole-wheat currant, double walnut, Sunday raisin, and more. Unusual gift baskets are a specialty.

EROTIC BAKER
582 Amsterdam Ave (bet 88th and 89th St)   362-7557
Tues-Thurs: 11-7; Fri, Sat: 11-8

In keeping with the spirit of the times, this shop is not as erotic as it used to be. Yes, they still make and stock X-rated cookies, cakes, and chocolates, but now they also make cakes for advertisers, like the picture of a Pavarotti album cover for a radio station. Well, as long as they don't mix up the deliveries, everything should be okay. I'd hate to think what would happen if they sent out the wrong kind of cake!

FERRARA PASTRIES
195 Grand St (bet Mott and Mulberry St)   226-6150
Daily: 8 a.m.-midnight

This big store in Little Italy is probably one of the largest (geographically speaking) "little grocery stores" in the world. Undoubtedly, the business must deal in wholesale imports and several other business ventures, but it is easy (and nice) to believe that the sheer perfection of their confections and groceries can support the whole business. Certainly, the atmosphere here would never reveal that this is anything but a very efficiently run Italian grocery store. Their Old World caffé is famous for its 21 varieties of pastry, ice cream, and coffee.

G&M PASTRIES
1006 Madison Ave (bet 77th and 78th St)   288-4424
Mon-Sat: 8-7; Sun: 8-6

In a neighborhood where everything is chic, elegant, and classic, G&M survives on its reputation as a small immigrant bake shop that turns out pastry best described as homemade in style. (Frank Gattnig, an Austrian immigrant, started G&M in 1958). As in any local apartment building, there are accents of Jewish, Italian, French, and German, in addition to Gattnig's native Austrian, in the shop's doughnuts, tortes, Danish, marzipan, and creamy cakes.

GERTELS
53 Hester St   982-3250
Sun-Thurs: 7-5:30; Fri: 7-2

The customers who come here are almost evenly divided between those who call this place Ger-tells (accent on the last syllable) and those who call it Girtils (as in girdles), but all agree that the cakes and breads store are among the best in New York. (They will ship anywhere in the United States.) Locals seem to prefer the traditional babkas, strudels, and kuchens, but I find the chocolate rolls and chiffon blackout cake to be outstanding. For those who want to sample the wares, there are tables where customers can enjoy baked goods, coffee, or a light lunch. From the regulars at these tables, one can glean the choicest shopping tidbits on the Lower East Side. A final tip: every Thursday and Friday, Gertels makes a potato kugel that is unexcelled. People have come all the way from California for a Thursday kugel. During a slow week, you can occasionally find one left over on a Sunday. It's good then, too.

GLASER'S BAKE SHOP
1670 First Ave (bet 87th and 88th St)   289-2562
Tues-Sat: 7-7; Sun: 7-4
Closed July and half of Aug

If it's Sunday, it won't be hard to find Glaser's: the line frequently spills outside as people queue up to buy the Glaser family's fresh cakes and baked goods. And *one* isn't enough of anything here. Customers always walk out with arms full of bulging packages. The Glasers run their shop as a family business and pride themselves on their breads, cakes, cookies, (especially birthday party), and wedding cakes. Try their chocolate chip cookie!

GROSSINGER'S UPTOWN
570 Columbus Ave (at 88th St)   874-6996
Mon-Fri: 8-6; Sun: 9-5

Grossinger's was once known as Grossinger's on Columbus Avenue, when that street was plain and drab, a far cry from today's trendy boulevard. Since 1935 Grossinger's has also been known for top quality cheesecakes and ice cream cakes—and a great homey aroma. The uptown operation is the only kosher shop on Columbus Avenue.

H&H BAGEL
2239 Broadway (at 80th St)   595-8000
Daily: 24 hours

H&H starts baking fresh bagels at two a.m., an hour at which you can get a piping hot bagel without having to wait on H&H's long daytime line. But the biggest plus is that you can satisfy your bagel craving at *any* hour of the day or night at H&H. Another only-in-New-York special. They are the best in Manhattan.

KOSSAR'S BIALYSTOKER
KUCHEN BAKERY
367 Grand St   473-4810, 674-9747
Daily: 24 hours

Tradition has it that the bialy derives its name from Bialystoker, where they were first made. Kossar's brought the recipe over from Europe almost a century ago, but the bialys, bagels, horns, and onion boards are as fresh as the latest batch from the oven. The taste is Old World, and those who have never had one should try these authentic versions first.

LET THEM EAT CAKE
287 Hudson St (at Spring St)   989-4970
Mon-Fri: 8-5

Primarily a wholesale bakery specializing in gourmet desserts, Let Them Eat Cake is not above offering the house quiches, nut loaves, or cakes to the public. All of them are unusually good, which makes it easy for caterers and restaurants to pass them off as their own. The quiches are made to order and—wonder of wonders!—never frozen. Better still, they're interesting and different, aside from the obligatory quiche Lorraine. Perhaps by the eighteenth edition of this book, the quiche craze will have peaked in New York, but in the meantime, try the broccoli-cheddar, spinach, and mushroom varieties. They are among the very best. The cakes and pies reflect the health-food consciousness of the neighborhood. Chelsea carrot cake (from a shop in SoHo) is but one of the examples of this, but any bakery that offers zucchini, date-nut, and banana-nut loaves as one quarter of the total offerings from the oven is big on health. In any case, the black-velvet chocolate chip fudge cake or the black-satin chocolate cake won't do a thing for the waistline, but they're sure to please the palate. Cakes are available in catering sizes as well as smaller sizes suitable, as they say, for resale. They are also available by the slice for on-the-spot consumption. Perhaps *that's* the best way to pick your favorite.

LITTLE PIE COMPANY
424 W 43rd St (at Ninth Ave)   736-4780
Mon-Fri: 8-7:30; Sat: 10-8; Sun: noon-5

Former actor Arnold Wilkerson started baking apple pastries for restaurants and food stores when he was working in his own kitchen. Now he and Michael Deraney operate a unique attraction—a shop that makes handmade pies and cakes using different fresh seasonal fruits. Although they specialize in apple pie (available every season), they also make fresh peach, cherry, blueberry, and other all-American fruit pie favorites. Stop by for a hot slice of pie à la mode, along with some delicious cider. Yankee Doodle never had it so good!

MOISHE'S BAKERY
181 E Houston St (bet Orchard and Allen St)   475-9624
Sun-Thurs: 7-6; Fri: 7-4

115 Second Ave 505-8555
Sun-Thurs: 7 a.m.-8:30 p.m.; Fri: 7-5

Jewish bakery specials are legendary, and they are done to perfection at Moishe's. The corn bread is prepared exactly as it was in the old country and as it should be now. The pumpernickel is dark and moist, and the ryes are, well, simply scrumptious. The house specialty is the black Russian pumpernickel, which probably cannot be bested in an old-fashioned bakery in Russia. But by no means should you ignore the cakes and pies. Owners Mordechai and Hymie are charming and eager to please, and they have one of the best bakeries in the city. There is the usual complement of bagels, bialys, cakes, and pastries. Most of all, try the challah on Thursday and Friday; Moishe produces the best. The chocolate layer cakes are also superb.

NEW FIRST AVENUE BAKERY
121 First Ave (at 7th St)   674-5699
Mon-Sat: 6 a.m.-7 p.m.

This is an old-fashioned bakery with one of the best reputations in town. The diverse ethnic makeup of the neighborhood is reflected in the variety of breads made here, and the quality is endorsed by the local natives from Italy, Poland, the Ukraine, and Russia, who claim the bread tastes as good as grandma's, if not great-grandma's. I don't know what to recommend most! The pumpernickel is dark and moist. It tastes nothing like the commercial variety. The babka smells and is irresistible. And the Italian breads are authentic enough to include a pizza dough. The Jewish contingent is represented by bagels and bialys, and each group thinks that New First Avenue is *their* bakery. Is there a higher compliment?

PALERMO BAKERY
213 First Ave (bet 12th and 13th St)   254-4139
Mon-Sat: 7-7; Sun: 7-3

A made-in-the-back specialty is featured here each day. One of the best is the pork bread—huge slices of pork inside a delicate dough, topped with a crackling crust. Palermo Bakery routinely produces bread in the most unusual and contorted shapes you can imagine, and they taste wonderful. Some of the exotic breads include the prosciutto bread, which contains bits of Italian salami, ham, and Lucatelli cheese. Then there's the French-style butter cookies, Friselli and breadsticks, challah and babka. Don't miss this one. It's a very inexpensive gourmet tour of the Old World.

PATISSERIE LANCIANI
271 W 4th St (bet Perry and W 11th St)   929-0739
Mon: 8 a.m.-9 p.m.; Tues-Thurs: 8 a.m.-11 p.m.;
Fri, Sat: 8 a.m.-midnight; Sun: 8 a.m.-10 p.m.

Patisserie Lanciani isn't terribly impressive; in fact, it seems a bit pretentious, until you get a look at the cakes and pastries. After that sight, even the extensive credentials of Joseph Lanciani are superfluous. For those who haven't yet observed the delicacies at Patisserie Lanciani, a quick résumé is in order. For starters, you have certainly seen Joseph's work. While chief pastry chef at the Plaza (enough of a recommendation in itself), he was the creator of Julie Nixon's wedding cake. He is also a certified expert in spun-sugar creations, and is probably the best pastry baker in the city. Results of this experience can now be sampled firsthand in Lanciani's own shop. The cakes, pastries, tortes, mousses, and breads defy description, and for the impatient, there are tables.

POSEIDON GREEK BAKERY
629 Ninth Ave (bet 44th and 45th St)   757-6173
Tues-Sat: 9-7; Sun: 10-4

Poseidon is a family-run bakery that endlessly and effortlessly produces Greek specialties. There's tremendous pride here. When a customer peers over the counter and asks, "What is that?" the response is usually a long description and sometimes an invitation to take a taste. There is homemade baklava, strudel, kataif, trigona, tiropita (cheese pie), spanakopita (spinach pie), sargli, and phyllo. Poseidon was founded in 1922 by super Greek baker Demetrios Anagnostou. Today it is still run by his family—grandsons John and Anthony Fable—to the same exacting standards. Poseidon's specialty is phyllo pastry, which is world renowned. Any and all Greek specialties using phyllo are turned out here.

RIGO HUNGARIAN VIENNESE PASTRY
318 E 78th St (bet First and Second Ave)   988-0052
Tues-Sat: 8-6; Sun: 9-4; closed Aug

Many European-type pastry shops have products that look great, but when you taste them, it's a different story. Not this one. Delicious homemade strudels, sacher torte, petit fours, linzer tortes, coffee cakes, and cookies of all kinds are first-rate. No preservatives are used. Wedding and birthday cakes are a specialty.

STREIT MATZOTH COMPANY
150 Rivington St   475-7000
Sun-Thurs: 9-5

Matzoth, for the uninitiated, is a thin waferlike square cracker, which, according to tradition, came out of Egypt with Moses and the children of Israel when they had to flee so swiftly that there was no time to let the bread rise. Through the years, matzoth was restricted to the time around Passover, and even when matzoth production became automated, business shut down for a good deal of the year. But not today and not in New York. In a small building with a Puerto Rican mural stretching the length of one side, Streit's matzoth factory pours forth matzoth throughout the year, pausing only on Saturday, Jewish holidays, and to clean the machines. Streit's factory not only allows a peek at the actual production—which is fascinating because it is both mechanized and extremely primitive at the same time—it also sells matzoth to the general public. It is baked in enormous thin sheets that are later broken up. The matzoth is so fresh that if you ask for a batch that happens to be baking at the moment, they will often break it off the production line for you.

SYLVIA WEINSTOCK CAKES
273 Church St (bet Franklin and White St)   925-6698
Mon-Fri: 9-6

Sylvia Weinstock has been in the cake business for over a decade, so she knows how to satisfy customers who want the very best. Her trademark is her floral decorations; they are almost lifelike! Although weddings are her specialty, she will produce a master-piece for any occasion (at a price, of course). The next time you are interviewed by Barbara Walters, ask her about Sylvia. She made Walters' wedding cake!

VESUVIO BAKERY
160 Prince St (bet W Broadway and Thompson St)
925-8248
Mon-Sat: 7-7

Tony Dapolito was born, bred (no pun intended), and nurtured in his family's store in SoHo. In all that time, the family's expertise in baking grew along with the bakery's claim to fame as SoHo's common green. When not manning the ovens, Tony serves stints on the community planning board, and disperses SoHo lore to customers. Visitors unaware of Dapolito's status (it doesn't remain a secret long) come for the bread, biscuits, and rolls. They all have a reputation that reaches far beyond SoHo. After all, it isn't every commercial bakery that eschews sugar, shortening, and preservatives and still manages to produce the tastiest Italian bread around. Try the biscotti, the pepper biscuits, or the whole wheat brick-oven-baked bread. And if you have *any* questions about the bread or SoHo, ask Tony. He can supply you with a slice of SoHo life, so to speak.

YONAH SCHIMMEL
137 E Houston St   477-2858
Daily: 8-6

Yonah Schimmel has been selling the perfect knish for so long that his name is legendary, and national magazines have written articles about him. Schimmel started out dispensing knishes among the pushcarts of the Lower East Side, and a Yonah Schimmel knish is still a unique experience. It doesn't, incidentally, look or taste anything like the mass-produced things sold in supermarkets, at lunch stands, or at New York ballgames. A Yonah Schimmel knish has a very thin, flaky crust—almost like strudel dough— surrounding a hot, moist filling. The best-selling filling is potato, but there is also kasha (buckwheat), spinach, and a half-dozen others, not including meat. No two knishes come out exactly alike since each is handmade, but if a particular batch is not up to par, the man behind the counter won't sell it.

Beverages

RIVERSIDE BEER AND SODA DISTRIBUTORS
2331 Twelfth Ave   234-3884
Mon-Sat: 9-6

Run by Hector Borrero, this place mainly supplies wholesalers and large retail orders, but he's not averse to serving retail customers. The only reason most orders aren't small is because once you've shlepped up there, you might as well take advantage of the good discount. He guarantees that his prices are at least as low as any supermarket. Because Borrero's store already offers merchandise at a discount, he doesn't have sales.

SERRANO
511 W 23rd Ave   243-6559
Mon-Sat: 9-5

Serrano is a wholesale beer and soda distributor, and while they happily deal with retail customers, trust them when they tell you that most of their business is wholesale. But that doesn't mean that those who shop on the premises aren't afforded the same excellent prices and service. For those in the neighborhood, Serrano should be a must for all soda and beer needs. Outside the area, unless there's a great love of lugging bottles, Serrano will probably only be a good bet for parties—large, thirsty parties.

British

MYERS OF KESWICK
634 Hudson St (bet Horatio and Jane St)   691-4194
Mon-Fri: 10-7; Sat: 10-6; Sun: noon-5
(except July, Aug)

In case you haven't noticed, the British are coming—again! According to the British Information Services, the number of expatriate Brits in the city has topped 100,000. Two of them, Peter and Irene Myers, are now doing with English food what Burberry, Church, and Laura Ashley have done with English clothing. They've made it possible for you to visit "the village grocer" for imported staples and fresh, home-baked items that you'd swear came from a kitchen in SoHo—the London neighborhood, not the one downtown below Houston Street. Among the tins, a shopper can find Heinz treacle sponge pudding, trifle mix, ribena, mushy peas, Smarties, Quality Street toffee, lemon barley water, chutneys, jams and preserves, and all the major English teas. The fresh goods include sausage rolls, kidney pie, Scotch eggs, Aberdeen kippers, and sides of salmon. There are also cheeses (the double Gloucester is outstanding!) and chocolates. For Anglophiles and expatriates alike, Myers of Keswick is a *luverly* treat.

Candy

CHOCOLATE PHOTOS/
CHOCOLATE CROSSWORDS
637 W 27th St (9th Floor)   714-1880
Mon-Fri: 9-6

Chocolate Photos was founded on the premise that nearly anything can be created in chocolate . . . and taste good, too. Unique items are ideal for gifts of all kinds, company logos, and you-name-it novelties. They are all custom-molded chocolate, with a minimum of 100 units packaged per order. The newest item is "Chocolate Crosswords" . . . chocolate letters and numbers on a board to spell out any message.

ECONOMY CANDY
108 Rivington St   254-1531
Sun-Fri: 8-6; Sat: 10-5

The same family of owners, who have been selling everything from penny candies to beautiful gourmet gift baskets since 1937, are still on the job. What a selection of dried fruits, nuts, candies, coffees, teas, jams, spices, cookies, crackers, and chocolates! The best part, of course, is the price. You can get gourmet items like caviars and pâtés without exceeding your party budget. Mail orders are filled efficiently and promptly.

ELK CANDY COMPANY
240 E 86th St   650-1177
Mon-Sat: 9-6:45; Sun: 10-5:45

Elk Candy Company is a glorious kingdom of chocolate. There's a royal selection; every conceivable kind of chocolate can be bought in at least two different forms. It's one sure place to find the old-fashioned European chocolate specialties. Elk Candy is known locally as a haven for the marzipan lover. Think of marzipan in all the configurations of your childhood fantasies, and you'll find it here. If you don't favor marzipan, then sink into the Florentines—thin chocolate layered over cream, fruit, nuts, honey, butter, and who knows what else. If that's not a hit, the little "Cats' Tongues" chocolate bars are bound to be. It's hard to select a favorite, but the most commonly heard comment is "Gee, I haven't had that in *years.*"

LA MAISON DU CHOCOLAT
25 E 73rd St (bet Fifth and Madison Ave)   744-7117
Mon-Sat: 10-6

What a place! Under one roof there are 34 delicious variations of light and dark chocolates. There are French truffles, plain and fancy champagnes, orangettes, coffee beans, chocolate-covered almonds, caramels, candied chestnuts, and fruit paste. Everything is made in Paris; this is the first store outside of France. Prices are not in the candy bar class, but then neither are exotic flavors like September raspberries, freshly grated ginger root, raisins flamed in rum, marzipan with pistachio and kirsh, and caramel butter. What a way to go!

LI-LAC CANDY SHOP
120 Christopher St (at Bleecker St)   242-7374
Mon-Sat: 10-8; Sun: 12-8

Since 1923, Li-Lac has been *the* source for fine chocolate in the Village. The most delicious creation is Li-Lac's own chocolate fudge, which is made fresh every day. If you tire of the chocolate, there is maple walnut, which is every bit as good. And there is much more: pralines, mousses, French rolls, nuts, dried fruits, hand- dipped chocolates, and so on.

MONDEL CHOCOLATES
2913 Broadway (at W 114th St)   864-2111
Daily: 11-6:30 (summer hours vary)

Mondel has been a tasty word in the neighborhood for about a half century. It was founded by present owner Florence Mondel's father. Fans of Mondel include the Columbia University community. The wonderful homemade chocolate-covered ginger, orange peel, nut barks, and turtles are special winners. There is also a dietetic chocolate line.

NEUCHATEL CHOCOLATES
Plaza Hotel   751-7742   60 Wall St   480-3766
Daily: 9-9   Mon-Fri: 9-6

Neuchatel Chocolates is a class act. And you pay for it. Of course, Neuchatel offers a discount for orders of over $1,000. And it's easy to earn that discount. To create the finest Swiss chocolate from family recipes, the chocolates are prepared by hand with natural ingredients. The taste has been likened to velvety silk. There are 70 varieties of chocolate, with the house specialty being handmade truffles. But that shouldn't keep anyone from trying the marzipan and the pralines with fruit or nuts. Neuchatel's origins are Swiss, but perhaps its greatest virtue is that there is no pretension of "flown-in daily" routines. Rather, the original recipes are re-created afresh in New York.

NEUHAUS CHOCOLATES
Saks Fifth Avenue
611 Fifth Ave (at 50th St)   753-4000
Mon-Wed, Fri, Sat: 10-6; Thurs: 10-8

The same year (1857) that my great-grandfather started his one-man store on the riverfront in Portland, Jean Neuhaus settled in Belgium and established a pharmacy and confectionery shop. Succeeding generations of his family have produced some of the finest handcrafted, enrobed, and molded-design bittersweet and milk chocolates in the world. They are still imported from Belgium. The showpiece is the Astrid Praline, named after the beloved late Queen of Belgium; it is a sugar-glazed butter delight!

ROCKY MOUNTAIN
CHOCOLATE FACTORY
11 Fulton St (South Street Seaport, Fulton Market)
393-1270
Daily: 10-9; Summer: 10-10

What is a store called ''Rocky Mountain'' doing in a place like the South Street Seaport? Believe it or not, the answer is simple. The first Rocky Mountain Chocolate Factory was started high in the Rocky Mountains in a town called Durango. Each batch of chocolate was handmade and hand-dipped according to generations-old recipes. Word soon spread, and within a very short time, the concept was franchised across the country. But the popularity hasn't had a bad effect on the quality of the chocolate. Forty percent of it is made on the premises, and it still meets the standards established in Durango. What to try? The chocolates should be your top choices, especially the fudge and truffles. But in season don't miss the dipped fresh fruit, the glazed fruit, the blueberry and raspberry clusters, and the candy or caramel apples. Your teeth squeak just thinking about it. And the fudge is available in a slew of exotic flavors, from Irish Cream to coffee crunch.

TEUSCHER CHOCOLATES
OF SWITZERLAND
25 E 61st St (at Madison Ave)   751-8482
Mon-Sat: 10-6

620 Fifth Ave (Rockefeller Center)   246-4416
Mon-Sat: 10-6; Thurs: 10-7:30

If there were an award for the most elegant chocolate shop, it would have to go to Teuscher's. Theirs are not just chocolates; they're imported works of art. Bernard Bloom, who owns these Teuscher stores, imports chocolates once a week from Switzerland. The chocolates are packed into handmade boxes so stunning that they add to the décor of many a customer's home. The truffles are almost obscenely good. The champagne truffle has a tiny dot of champagne cream in the center that lifts it to the super class. The same is true of the cocoa, nougat, buttercrunch, muscat, orange, and almond truffles, each of which has its own little surprise. Truffles are the stars here, but Teuscher's marzipan, praline chocolates, and mints (shaped like sea creatures) are of similar quality.

Cheese

ALLEVA DAIRY
188 Grand St (at Mulberry St)   226-7990
Mon-Sat: 8:30-6; Sun: 8:30-3

Alleva, founded in 1892, is the oldest Italian cheese store in America. The Alleva family has operated the business since the start, always maintaining meticulous high standards. Robert Alleva is the current boss, overseeing the production of over 4,000 pounds of fresh cheese a week: parmigiano, fraschi, manteche, scamoize, and provole affumicale. The ricotta is superb, and the mozzarella tastes like it was just made on some little side street in Florence.

BEN'S CHEESE SHOP
181 E Houston St (bet Allen and Orchard St)   254-8290
Sun-Thurs: 8:15-5:30; Fri: 8:15-3:30

About half of the varieties of cheese sold here are made in the back of the shop. The locals swear by the farmer's cheese in any of its forms. Some favorites include the homemade farmer's cheese embedded with such tasty ingredients as strawberries, scallions, raisins, pineapple, and—my personal favorites—almonds and pistachios. Don't miss the baked farmer's cheese. There is cream cheese also!

CHEESE OF ALL NATIONS
153 Chambers St (bet W Broadway and Greenwich St)
732-0752
Mon-Sat: 8-5:30

Cheese of All Nations is a gastronomic United Nations, a cheese-of-the-month clubhouse, a wholesale supplier to stores and restaurants, a gourmet catering service, a custom cheese spread manufacturer, and on and on. In short, cheese is a way of life here. The five floors of the shop are constantly engaged in various aspects of cheese production. The store has a worldwide business, which for nearly a half century has created, packaged, and shipped more than 1,000 varieties of cheese. That statistic gives the store the distinction of having the world's largest selection of cheese, and the sheer magnitude of it all is amazing. For example, there are 66 different kinds of cheese spreads listed in the catalog. Prices for the spreads, as well as everything else, are supposed to be among the city's lowest. Be prepared: this place is *always* crowded!

EAST VILLAGE CHEESE
34 Third Ave (bet 9th and 10th St)　477-2601
Mon-Fri: 9-6:30; Sat, Sun: 9-5:30

Value is the name of the game here. For years, this store has prided itself on selling cheese at just about the lowest prices in town. Now in larger quarters, they claim the same for bean coffee, fresh pasta, extra virgin olive oil, quiche, pâté, and a wide selection of fresh bread. An added reason to shop here: this is *not* a self-service operation!

IDEAL CHEESE SHOP
1205 Second Ave (at 63rd St)　688-7579
Mon-Fri: 9-6:30; Sat: 9-6

There are cheese shops, and there are *real* cheese shops. Ideal is the latter. The selection and quality is equal to any in the city. Besides taking care of the daily needs of their individual customers, they also supply many hotels and restaurants. Cheese, like wine, is an area where special advice is helpful, and the folks at Ideal are eager to share their expertise. If you are looking for a special food gift item, let them fix up a basket of unusual cheeses, pâtés, and gourmet coffees. And here is a health note: they carry a large selection of low-cholesterol and low-fat cheeses.

Chinese

CHINESE AMERICAN EMPORIUM
19 Pell St　577-8882
Daily: 9:30-8

You can't find a more authentic source for Chinese food than this one, not even in Peking, and the proprietors speak English. What's more, unlike some of their competitors, Michael Chan and his staff are happy to explain what some of the more exotic items are or to give the exact instructions on how to make your favorite takeout dish at home. Located in Chinatown, the store specializes in the ingredients for Szechuan and Hunan food. But there's an ample selection of Korean food, too, and even Japanese and American goods. The latter are mostly ingredients that don't travel well. Nearly everything else in the shop is imported. Ginseng root, for example, comes from China and Korea. It would be difficult to count all the different tastes or catalog all the unfamiliar items found here. In short, this is a great source for really authentic ingredients for Oriental cooking at great prices.

CHINESE AMERICAN TRADING COMPANY
91 Mulberry St (at Canal St)   267-5224
Daily: 9-8

If an authentic Chinese dinner is on your menu, there may be no better source than this store in Chinatown. Let it be a warning (or a good sign, depending upon your point of view) that Chinese American Trading boasts that 95 percent of its business is conducted with the Chinese community. In any case, there is an open and friendly attitude here, and great care is taken to introduce you to the wide variety of imported Oriental foodstuffs.

FUNG WONG BAKERY
30 Mott St   267-4037
Daily: 7 a.m.-9:30 p.m.

Fung Wong is the real thing, and everyone from the local Chinatown residents to the city's gourmands extol its virtues. The pastries and baked goods are traditional, authentic, and downright delicious; flavor is not compromised to appeal to Western taste. The bakery features a tremendous variety (enough so that Fung Wong sells wholesale all over town), and it has the distinction of being the oldest and largest "real" Chinese bakery. In surveys, Fung Wong is rated number one, and a visit is the surest way to see why.

KAM MAN FOOD PRODUCTS
200 Canal St (bet Mott and Mulberry St)   571-0330
Daily: 9-9

A trip to Kam Man is cheaper than one to China, and there's very little available over seas that Kam Man doesn't have here. It's the largest Oriental grocery store on the East Coast. Even native Chinese will feel at home in this shop, where you can find every possible ingredient for a Chinese meal. Speaking Chinese is not a requirement for shopping at Kam Man—some of the best English in Chinatown is spoken by the people who work here, and the amenities are totally familiar to those who patronize the city's other gourmet delis and supermarkets. The difference is that at Kam Man the shopping carts wheel past produce displays of water chestnuts, bok choy, winter melon, and tofu; 50 other types of delicacies (like shark's fin); and butcher and fish counters offering duck, sausages, pork dumplings, and shrimp. Desserts and tea (and *more* tea) round out the selection, and the prices for all of this—even American tangerines and oranges—are the least expensive anywhere.

LUNG FONG CHINESE BAKERY
41 Mott St   233-7447
Daily: 7:30 a.m.-9 p.m.

English is definitely a foreign language here, but you can place your order simply by pointing to the authentic Chinese cookies and pastries of your choice. Molded cookies are in abundance, as are rice cakes and pastries covered with sesame or lotus seeds—or perhaps it's something else. The truth is, these are not your every-day fortune cookies; they defy description. Nevertheless, it's all authentic, and none of it is ordinary. Don't bother asking how anything tastes, because Lung Fong's explanation is liable to be: "Is good. Is good." And it is.

QUON JAN MEAT PRODUCTS
79 Chrystie St (bet Hester and Grand St)   925-5175
Daily: 10-7

William Chan, one of Quon Jan's owners, studied Chinese cook-ing in Hong Kong, and he devoted two years solely to seasoning and cooking barbecued meats. He is just as meticulous with his staff, making sure that his store is the best Chinese barbecue place in the city. And it is. (*The Daily News* concurs.) Although it is just outside of Chinatown, even by the standards of the ever-expanding borders. Oriental is definitely the theme; most of the business is conducted either in Chinese or sign language. But sign away. Prices are reasonable, and the taste is authentic and delicious. The best seller is the Mandarin duck, but don't overlook the pork, sausages, or roast chicken. They are equally excellent and exotic.

Coffee, Tea

BELL-BATES
107 W Broadway (at Reade St)   267-4300
Mon-Wed: 9:30-6; Thurs, Fri: 9:30-6:30; Sat: 11-5

Bell-Bates is a caffeine emporium, specializing in all matters of tea and coffee for the retail customer. Their selection is extensive, and the prices are competitive. Bell-Bates considers itself a com-plete food center, stocking health food, vitamins, nuts, dried fruit, spices, herbs, and gourmet food, along with the freshly ground cof-fees and teas. Ask for Mrs. Sayage. She's marvelous.

CAFFE ROMA
385 Broome St   226-8413
Sun-Thurs: 8-midnight; Fri, Sat: 8-1 a.m.

Caffe Roma serves some of the best espresso this side of the Atlantic. To accompany the espresso, you can get such traditional Italian dishes as spumone, gelati, cremolate, cannoli, deep-dish Italian cheesecake, and all kinds of super pastries. Custom- designed cakes are made for all occasions. The atmosphere is Old World, complete with marble tiled floor and colorful oil paintings. The cappuccino made from freshly roasted beans is another reason this spot is so popular.

CAFFE REGGIO
119 MacDougal St   475-9557
Sun-Thurs: 10 a.m.-2 a.m.; Fri, Sat: 10 a.m.-4 a.m.

The owner of Caffe Reggio claims that cappuccino was introduced to this country by a former owner of the same Caffe Reggio. Could be, and this place has other ties with times past. Over 80 pieces of Italian art fill the cafe, and some of them date back to the Renaissance. The staff will be happy to identify the more important works for you. And if you're interested, they'll even tell you the history of the neighborhood. (Louisa May Alcott lived across the street, near the spot where Jo meets the professor in *Little Women*.) Nonetheless, this place wouldn't last two minutes unless the food was good, and in the past 60 years, it's only improved. This isn't the place you want to go to for a seven-course meal, but it's great for a snack. Breakfasts and lunches are served until seven p.m. Hot beverages, tea, and Italian soft drinks are refreshing specialties (the espresso machine is the room's distinctive centerpiece). The management encourages you to eat a pastry with your cappuccino. And nobody minds if you spend hours at the table, nursing one cup.

THE COFFEE GRINDER
348 E 66th St (bet First and Second Ave)   737-3490
Mon, Fri: 11-7; Tues, Wed, Thurs: 9-7; Sat: 9:30-6

If it has anything to do with coffee or tea, you can find it here. There is an excellent selection of custom-blended coffees and teas and coffee makers. They will also do gourmet gift baskets for the coffee lover.

EMPIRE COFFEE AND TEA COMPANY
592 Ninth Ave   586-1717
Mon-Fri: 8:30-7; Sat: 9-6:30

Midtown java lovers have all wandered in here at one time or another. There is an enormous selection of coffee (75 different beans), decaffeinated coffees, teas, and herbs. Because of the aroma and array of the bins, making solo choices is almost impossible. Empire's personnel are very helpful, but perhaps most helpful of all is a perusal of their free mail-order catalog *before* entering the shop. Dave Mottel pointed out that fresh coffee beans and tea leaves are available in bulk, along with fresh peanut butter and spices. Everything is sold loose and can be freshly ground. Empire also has a small selection of appliances.

McNULTY'S TEA AND COFFEE COMPANY
109 Christopher St (bet Bleecker and Hudson St)
242-5351
Mon-Sat: 10-9; Sun: 1-7:30

McNulty's has been supplying choosy New Yorkers with their coffees and teas since 1895. Over the years, they have developed a complete line that includes spice and herb teas and coffee blends ground to order. They have a reputation for personalized, gourmet coffee blends, and they work hard to maintain it. That reputation is hard on the pocketbook, but a number of their blends are unique, and the personal service is quite valuable. McNulty's maintains an extensive file on their customers' special coffee blends.

M. ROHRS
1692 Second Ave (bet 87th and 88th St)   427-8319
Mon-Fri: 10-6:30; Sat: 9-5

Dennis Smith owned a candy store in Manhattan before he bought M. Rohrs, which was established in 1896. The tradeoff of candy for coffee beans was primarily for better working hours, but Smith is always on the premises long before the store opens and stays long after it closes. Does he use his coffee to keep him awake? He's not telling. But he is willing to expound on the various types of beans and teas that the store stocks. And his guidance is needed. There are hundreds of varieties of tea, coffee, coffee beans, and honey in the store, as well as accessories. While not a coffee shop, it is possible to get a cup of coffee and sample the wares. And incidentally, despite all that coffee, Smith is one of the most relaxed proprietors in the city. So either he doesn't drink coffee or he's right when he says that all the studies on caffeine don't amount to a hill of beans.

PORTO RICO IMPORTING COMPANY
201 Bleecker St   477-5421
Mon-Sat: 9:30-9

In 1907, Peter Longo's family started a small coffee business in the Village. Primarily importers and wholesalers, they were soon being pressured to serve the local community around them, so they opened a small storefront as well. That storefront gained a reputation for having the best and freshest coffee available and developed a loyal corps of customers. Since much of the surrounding neighborhood consisted of Village Italians, the Longo family reciprocated the neighborhood loyalty by specializing in Italian espressos and cappuccinos as well as "health" and medicinal teas. Dispensed along with such teas are folk remedies and advice to help mend whatever ails you. The store remains true to its tradition, and Peter added a coffee bar. Now it is possible to sit and sip 60 various coffees and 120 loose teas while listening to the folklore or trying to select the best from the bins. (Hint: The inexpensive house blends are every bit as good as some of the more expensive coffees.)

SCHAPIRA COFFEE COMPANY
117 W 10th St   675-3733
Mon-Fri: 9-6:30; Sat: 9-5

Schapira, also known as the Flavor Cup Shop, has been run by the same family since 1903. Joel and Karl Schapira and Ron Bowen, who run the business now, offer advice on tea or coffee selections to any customer who asks. Many coffee shops disdain tea, but Schapira is fair to connoisseurs of both and is equally knowledgeable in either field. So secure are they in both knowledge and reputation that they will happily send you a mail-order price list and tuck in answers to any questions you might have as well. (Hint: Try Flavor Cup's own brand of tea or coffee.) Coffee is roasted every morning on the premises and is available in bulk, in bean form, or ground to personal specifications. Tea is sold similarly (in bulk or bags). There are also coffee- and tea-brewing accessories.

Dairy Products

HARRY WILS & CO
182 Duane St   431-9731
Mon-Fri: 6-3

For nearly three-quarters of a century and through three generations, this venerable outfit has been supplying the food needs of the better restaurants of New York. Butter, cheese, and eggs are the mainstays of the business, and they are sold in quantity to commercial buyers. But here is an inside hint: The individual customer will probably not be turned away for orders of a reasonable amount of cheese or butter. For eggs, you would have to want at least 15 dozen. The quality and the prices can't be beat!

Delis, Catering, Food to Go

AMAZING FOODS
807 Washington St   645-4166
Wed, Fri: 11-5; Sat: 10-3

Put on your walking shoes, double-check the irregular business hours above, and get going to this amazing food operation. In a most unlikely neighborhood of warehouses and trucks, you will find one of the city's best selections of salad-size produce items.

Well-known restaurants like Gotham Bar and Grill, Le Bernardin, and Sistina come here to buy miniature baby carrots, turnips, corn, artichokes, and the like. Also available are baby salads, mixed, red and green oak, bibb, arugula, and many more varieties. Fresh seafood and shellfish like Belon oysters, scallops, tuna, swordfish, Atlantic and Norwegian salmon, and free-range chicken are available at the same prices restaurants pay. You cannot find better price, quality, and selection. Ask for Pat Cummings, and tell him I sent you.

BALDUCCI'S
424 Sixth Ave (at 9th St)   673-2600
Daily: 7 a.m.-8:30 p.m.

No visit to the Village is complete without a stop at Balducci's, one of the premier food emporiums in the city. When Balducci's opened in Greenwich Village as a greengrocer in 1947, Mom and Pop tended a single cast-iron register, answered questions, serviced customers, and kept pencil accounts for their neighbors. To this day you will see members of the family in the store helping customers. Under one roof they sell nearly everything: coffee, pastries, fine cheese, smoked salmon, fresh pasta, aged beef, hearth-baked breads, prepared entrees, and the largest selection of quality produce in the city. They produce many traditional specialties, like focaccia, fresh-cut pasta and ravioli, sauces, taralli, country breads, and fresh fruit tarts. Special services include personal shopping, catering, gift baskets, and seasonal catalogs from which you can order many Italian home-cooked specials to be sent anywhere in the country. Free delivery is available between Houston, 15th Street, and Broadway to West Street. Half the fun of shopping at Balducci's is the crowded aisles and the family atmosphere; Village residents and city-wide fans jostle for space in this yummy emporium.

BARNEY GREENGRASS
541 Amsterdam Ave (bet 86th and 87th St)   724-4707
Tues-Sat: 8:30-5:45; Sun: 8:30-5
Closed Passover and first three weeks in Aug

Barney Greengrass is synonymous with sturgeon to New Yorkers, which is as it should be for a family business located at the same place since 1929. Barney has been succeeded by his son, Moe, and Moe's son, Gary (daughter-in-law Shirley is there, too), but the same quality of gourmet smoked fish is still sold over the neighborhood counters just as it was in Barney's day. The Greengrasses lay claim to the title of "sturgeon king," and there are few who would dispute it. While sturgeon is king here, Barney Greengrass also has a school of other smoked-fish delicacies. (And he could start a school on preparing and selling them.) There is Nova Scotia salmon, belly lox, white fish, caviar, and pickled herring in the fish lines. The dairy-deli line—including vegetable cream cheese, home-made salads and borscht, and a smashing Nova Scotia salmon with scrambled eggs and onions—is world renowned. In fact, because so many customers couldn't wait to get home to unwrap their pack-ages, Greengrass started a restaurant next door. Devotees claim that the Greengrass brunch is the example *par excellence* of what brunch should be. And after all, how could it be otherwise when the kitchen, which is just a step away, has been producing the ideal brunch menu for more than 60 years?

BENNIE'S
321½ Amsterdam Ave (at 75th St)   874-3032
Daily: 8 a.m.-10 p.m.

Bennie's was founded by Dr. Bennie, a Lebanese plastic surgeon, with his partner and compatriot, a pediatrician. And while a take-out food business wouldn't usually hold a candle to a medical career, here it's a tossup. And that's a pun. Bennie's, you see, specializes in salads, and they're among the best anywhere. Homage is paid to the Lebanese roots with the best tabbouleh in the city (it may also be the cheapest) and a plate that speaks with a definite Middle Eastern and European accent. The health aspect is not ignored either. Besides three sensational chicken salads, Ben-nie's boasts the biggest selection of vegetarian foods in the neighborhood. A prime example is the Muda-data (a salad of rice, onions, and lentils), and it, too, is reasonably priced and excellent. If you see Dr. Bennie, he may tell you business is healthy. Don't be surprised if he doesn't say anything, though. English is not spoken fluently here, but with all these goodies, who cares?

BURKE AND BURKE
Various locations throughout Manhattan (call for the closest one)
593-2488
Hours vary

Billed as "New York's fanciest food store," Burke is literally on the spot when there is a need for elegant food or snacks. Each store features a line of fine foods (with an accent on English candy and food products), gift baskets, chocolates, desserts, catering, and imported foods. Those on a lunch break can find sandwiches and food platters, the "Ploughman's Lunch" in two varieties, and a choice of hot dishes. There are also dozens of house specialties, most of which match the shop's aim to "bring together the very best of the Old World and the New." There is a delivery service for getting the goodies to customers with efficiency.

CANARD AND COMPANY
1292 Madison Ave (at 92nd St)   722-1046
Daily: 7 a.m.-9 p.m.

It seems as though you are in a rural country store when you step inside Canard and Company. The atmosphere is homey, and the personnel are eager to show you the fabulous selection of prepared gourmet foods, specialty jams and jellies, rich desserts, custom gift baskets, fine candy, and some of the best sandwiches to be found in Manhattan. Also available are the finest Beluga and Ossetra caviars and smoked salmon. Catering is a specialty here. No big-time hustle-and-bustle; it's a truly enjoyable shopping experience.

CAVIARTERIA
29 E 60th St   759-7410, 1-800-4-CAVIAR
Mon-Sat: 9-6

Caviarteria operates out of a small store, which is sufficient since most of the business is done by phone or by mail. Because of the wholesale business, prices are as reasonable as prices for caviar can be, and the quality is top-notch. The staff is very friendly and helpful, and they assure safe delivery (shipping on ice) anywhere. Caviarteria also stocks pâté de foie gras and Scotch and Swedish smoked salmon.

CHARLOTTE'S
146 Chambers St (bet Greenwich St and W Broadway)
732-7939
Mon-Fri: 10-6

Charlotte's has developed an outstanding reputation for quality catering. Their cast of customers is pretty heady: Chanel, Lincoln Center, Harry Winston, Sotheby's. Theirs is a full-service catering business, from the menu and the tablecloths to the waiter's outfits. For cocktail or wedding receptions, dinner dances, teas, luncheons, or dinners, let the chef do something really exciting. How about blue corn tortilla chips with caviar, cold smoked salmon on rondel of bread, or poached oysters with spinach and bourbon sauce?

CHELSEA FOODS
198 Eighth Ave (at 20th St)   691-3948
Mon-Fri: 9-9; Sat, Sun: 9-8

The Upper West Side has Zabar's. The Village has Balducci's. The Upper East Side has Grace's Marketplace. SoHo has Dean & Deluca. And Chelsea has its own gourmet emporium—Chelsea Foods. The owner is a neighborhood resident who combines a love of the area with the experience and skill necessary to run a really first-rate establishment. Catering is also available.

DEAN & DELUCA
560 Broadway (at Prince St)   431-1691
Mon-Sat: 10-7; Sun: 10-6

It was only a matter of time until Dean & Deluca had to move out of their historic location on Prince Street (which is now a cafe). The counters and aisles were just too filled with tempting items and busy customers. The solution was the opening of a store almost four times as large as the original. And what a place! There are packaged food items, gourmet takeout selections, fish, meat, chicken, pastries, vegetables, bread, coffee, desserts—you name it, and Dean & Deluca has it in quantity. There is a special kitchen for catering, and they can make any occasion something special. A popular espresso and cappuccino bar greets you at the door. Professional kitchen equipment and supplies are available to both wholesale and retail customers. And prices are competitive in most cases, although this is not the place to bargain-shop.

DELMONICO GOURMET FOOD MARKET
55 E 59th St (bet Park and Madison Ave)   751-5559
Daily: 24 hours

This is a very handy stop in an area that does not have a wide choice of gourmet food operations. In one stop, you can find deli items, gourmet breads and coffees, candies, cheeses, and a hot and cold salad bar. A breakfast menu is featured; at noontime a great selection of sandwiches is available, and an authentic French charcuterie is first-class. They do special catering, charge accounts are welcomed, and free delivery (with a minimum order) is offered in a ten-block radius. There is an indoor seating area, and in warm weather outside tables are pleasant.

DONALD SACKS

120 Prince St	220 Vesey St
(at Wooster St)	(World Financial Center)
226-0165	619-4600
Mon-Fri: 8-6; Sat,	Mon-Fri: 11-10; Sat,
Sun: 10-6	Sun: 11-6

For years Donald Sacks had been famous in SoHo for huge sandwiches, home-style soups, salads, stews, and desserts for take-out. You can munch there if you want, but the quarters are a bit cramped. There is also a delivery service. Now Sacks has gone bigtime with a bistro operation in the World Financial Center. Home-style cooking is featured in a large restaurant with bar, takeout service, catering, plus all the goodies from the original SoHo location. The desserts (especially the tarts) are special, but the rest is pretty ordinary. Bigger is not necessarily better, Donald.

FAIRWAY
2127 Broadway (at 74th St)   595-1888
Mon-Fri: 7 a.m.-midnight; Sat, Sun: 7 a.m.-11 p.m.

When you take care of over 50,000 customers a week, you must be doing something right. Fairway is a West Side institution originally known for its fresh fruit and vegetables. But now it has so much more: pasta, cheese, bread, and all kinds of deli items. They offer 30 varieties of olive oil, for example. Fairway has carved out its own niche in the food business, leaving the household items to their busy and aggressive neighbor, Zabar's. Fairway operates its own farm on Long Island, and they have developed relationships with the best produce dealers throughout the state, which has enabled them to capitalize on the trend for healthier items on the dinner table. There is no place like Zabar's for prepared food, but if you want to prepare it yourself, start with the ingredients at Fairway. Prices are right at both places.

FINE & SCHAPIRO
138 W 72nd St   877-2874, 877-2721
Daily: 9 a.m.-10 p.m.

Ostensibly a kosher delicatessen and restaurant, Fine & Schapiro offers some of the best dinners for at-home consumption in the city. Perhaps because of their uptown location, or perhaps merely as homage to the quality of their foods, they modestly term themselves "the Rolls-Royce of delicatessens." That description is cited here only because it is very apt. Fine & Schapiro dispenses a complete line of cold cuts, hot and cold hors d'oeuvres, Chinese delicacies, catering platters, and magnificent sandwiches. Everything that issues from Fine & Schapiro is perfectly cooked and artistically arranged. The sandwiches are masterpieces; it seems a shame to eat them, but the aroma and taste are irresistible. Chicken in the pot and stuffed cabbage are two of their best items.

FISHER & LEVY
875 Third Ave (at 53rd St; concourse level) 832-3880
Mon-Fri: 9-6 (call before 3 p.m. for dinner orders)

This is a quality operation, from taking care of big parties to providing pizza for a solitary dinner. Fisher and Levy begin the day with delicious breakfast items, which can be delivered to home or office (just as other food items can). Delivery hours throughout Midtown and Wall Street are seven a.m. to six p.m., Monday through Friday. Besides delicious pizzas, menu selections include a wide assortment of sandwiches and salads, great desserts, and appetizer platters for every kind of occasion. Special low-cholesterol items are available. Chip Fisher and Doug Levy have put together what may well be the best catering operation in the city.

FRASER MORRIS FINE FOODS
931 Madison Ave (at 74th St)   288-2727
Mon-Sat: 8:30-7; Sun: 10-5 (closed in summer)

1264 Third Ave (at 73rd St)   288-7716
Mon-Fri: 9-6; Sat: 9-5

Fraser Morris was a gourmet-to-go source eons before the neighborhood knew there was such a thing, and certainly long before the Upper East Side became the center of all such operations. The result was a carriage-trade store offering gourmet delicacies at not-inconsiderable prices. With a monopoly on virtually the whole idea, Fraser Morris was the definitive such stop and set the standard for the breed. But the changing neighborhood has wrought changes in Fraser Morris. First, the business moved to a cleaner, more modern store, and then, as a sure sign of success, it opened a second branch. These days the gourmet shop still stocks the finest fruit, cheese (500 different kinds), candy, chocolate, delicatessen (imported sliced ham and pâté de foie gras—not chopped liver!), quiche, canned gourmet items, ice cream, cheesecake, caviar, and coffee beans. You get the idea. A catering department offers such delicacies as salmon and crown roast of lamb. A bakery department features fruit tarts, Hungarian pastry, scones, and an international variety of goodies. And finally, for the true gourmet-to-go, there's a sandwich department. This is an old spot that has gracefully and successfully entered the modern age.

GINDI DESSERTS
935 Broadway (bet 21st and 22nd Sts)   505-5502
Mon-Fri: 8 a.m.-9 p.m.; Sat: 10:30-6; Sun: 11-5

What started as a small bakery in 1982 has grown into a very popular and delicious full service cafe in the historic Flatiron District. Francine Gindi, the founder and owner, was diagnosed with lupus, and thus developed a real interest in healthy foods. She instituted a menu that features items with no preservatives and was among the first to promote sugar-free muffins, pies, and cakes. A popular "grain of the day" menu is available. Besides the good eats, there is an in-store recycling program, inexpensive flatware for sale, a free-will donation canister, and unbleached paper shopping bags. And listen to this dessert menu: chocolate chocolate-chip cake, chocolate mocha layer cake, chocolate raspberry layer cake, chocolate truffle cake, white chocolate chip cake (this is a chocoholic's dream place, obviously!), lemon raspberry and apricot brandy cakes. The cafe is a bustling sit-down, takeout, or delivery beauty that serves healthy fare at very healthy prices. Quite an establishment!

GOOD & PLENTY TO GO
410 W 43rd St (bet Ninth and Tenth Ave)   268-4385
Mon-Fri: 8-8; Sat: 10-6; Sun: 8-4

Right in the center of things is this first-class gourmet store, featuring homemade brownies and cookies, fresh baked breads, meat entrees, healthy veggies and salads, and delicious pasta dishes. Outdoor seating is available in the nice weather, and catering for home and office parties is a specialty.

GRACE'S MARKETPLACE
1237 Third Ave (at 71st St)   737-0600
Mon-Sat: 7 a.m.-8:30 p.m.; Sun: 8-7

The Upper East Side finally has a first-class food store. You cannot find a better assortment of fine fruits and vegetables, cheese, gourmet takeout dishes, candy, bakery, and everyday items than the one at this enticing and appetizing emporium. The quality is first-rate, the selection almost overpowering. The displays seduce you into that "I want one of each" frame of mind. Grace and her family have deep roots in the food business in Manhattan, and her contacts and experience show in every phase of this outstanding operation.

GREAT PERFORMANCES CATERERS
125 Crosby St
219-2800 (catering), 925-9090 (personnel)
Daily: 9-5 (phone orders only)

Liz Neumark, the owner of Great Performances, should know the business from the bottom up. She is a former photographer who supported herself by working as a waitress in a help-for-hire agency. She soon realized that there were quite a number of moonlighting artists in the city, so she decided to organize her own agency, which supplies New Yorkers with party help from the city's artistic community. Her company is a full-service caterer, handling all kinds of affairs, from small dinner parties to gala dinners for thousands of people. The permanent staff includes party planners, an executive chef, and a professional kitchen crew. The party planners will arrange all the details of your event and provide the necessary personnel. (Corporate clients include many top names, like AT&T, Coca-Cola, and American Express.) Their personnel know the Heimlich maneuver (in case of choking), they study fire-evacuation procedures, and each carries a "survival kit," which includes such tools of the trade as aspirin, Band-Aids, a corkscrew, and even a coffee measure. The folks at Great Performances are the kind you want to have around. Good show!

HALE & HEARTY
849 Lexington Ave (bet 64th and 65th St)   517-7600
Mon-Fri: 8-8; Sat: 11-6

For those who look closely at the scale and the mirror each morning, here is the answer to your needs. Hale and Hearty offers soups, salads, sandwiches, pastas, entrees, side dishes, and desserts low in cholesterol, fat, and sodium. Their desserts taste great even though they are made without butter, egg yolks, and cream! Local delivery service is available.

H&H BAGELS EAST
1551 Second Ave (bet 80th and 81st St)   734-7441
Daily: 24 hours

The initials H&H have long been synonymous with the best bagels on New York's Upper West Side. Now East Siders can feast upon this fresh, delicious New York specialty, along with a choice of homemade croissants, pastries, super sandwiches, tasty salads, salmon, lox, and sturgeon. Homemade pickled herring is another specialty. Although this is mainly a takeout operation, there are a few tables for those who just can't wait to start noshing.

INDIANA MARKET & CATERING
80 Second Ave (at 5th St)   505-7290
Mon-Sat: 8 a.m.-9:30 p.m.; Sun: 11-8:30
(closed Sun in Aug)

Indiana offers a full-service catering operation, complete from box lunches to fancy banquets. They will take care of staffing, rentals, insurance, unique party sites, music, photography, flowers, and all the incidentals that are so important for a first-class affair. The staff is very cordial, responsive, and personally interested in every customer.

INTERNATIONAL GROCERIES AND MEAT MARKET
529 Ninth Ave (bet 39th and 40th St)   279-5514
Mon-Sat: 8-6

Ninth Avenue is one great wholesale market of international cookery, resplendent with exotic spices. So what would an international market on Ninth Avenue be if not a retailer of exotic spices at wholesale prices? The International Groceries and Meat Market is that, but it is also an excellent source for the rudiments on which to sprinkle the spices. The setup complements the whole aspect of the operation. Translated, this means that the neat glass jars that display food in other such places are replaced here by huge, open burlap bags. This may be disconcerting for some, but be willing to sacrifice the frills for some of the best prices in town and the assurance that the turnover is high enough to keep things fresh. The meat market is really something else. It's a gourmet market for aficionados of baby lamb and kid. It comes seasoned, prepared, and sliced. If you're unsure about what to do with it, ask!

LA FONTANELLA
1304 Second Ave (bet 68th and 69th St)   988-4778
Mon-Sat: 11-7; Sun: 2-7

Nelly de Oppes came from Argentina to open La Fontanella over 25 years ago. She is a caterer who can take care of any kind of gathering, but her specialty is intimate, formal dinners. She also likes to do buffets, cocktail parties, afternoon teas, wedding breakfasts, and corporate or club luncheons. The accent on her menu is decidedly Spanish, but she is equally, if not more, expert with French and Italian cuisine. Casseroles, quiches, soups, and empanadas are all available on 24-hour notice for reheating at home. The menu for more formal dinners is extensive and à la carte. La Fontanella doesn't care if you order for two or two thousand people. With sufficient advance notice, any combination on the incredible menu can be had. There is even delivery service.

MAIN COURSE CATERING
1608 Third Ave (at 90th St)   860-4440
Daily: 10-9

Beverly Fetner has a great background for running one of the best catering establishments in the city. She has traveled extensively, is trained as a culinary arts and pastry chef in the classical French manner, and as manager of the Faculty House at Columbia University turned a floundering outfit into a flourishing one with a membership of 3,000. Main Course has a full menu for takeout and does off-premises catering with an international flair. Services include party rentals, deliveries, special corporate lunches, and a huge selection of canapes and hors d'oeuvres.

MAISON GLASS DELICACIES
111 E 58th St (bet Lexington and Park Ave)   755-3316
Mon-Sat: 9-6; closed Sat in July, Aug

This is *the* source of gourmet supplies for New Yorkers in the know, and it has been since it was founded by Ernest Glass in 1902. Nowadays, the store is run by Marvin Goldsmith, who has only enhanced the mystique. The house specialties are caviar, foie gras, truffles, Virginia ham, smoked salmon, freshly roasted nuts and coffee, fine chocolates and candies, teas, herbs, spices, oils, vinegars, and jams. Goldsmith says that they have the largest selection of imported and domestic delicacies in the country and possibly the world. In addition to catering, there are gift baskets, package deliveries, and a catalog for gourmet subscribers.

MAMA LEAH'S
431 Amsterdam Ave (bet 80th and 81st St)   769-3355
Daily: 11:30-9:30

Upper West Siders can now treat themselves to some wonderful non-kosher Jewish-American home cooking straight from Mama Leah's kitchen. And you don't have to leave home to take advantage of the goodies; Mama delivers from 70th to 90th Streets and from Central Park to Riverside Drive on the West Side. In addition, she runs a restaurant and blintzeria (1400 First Ave, bet 74th and 75th St) on the East Side. You can order adult and children's dinners, or by the pound or the portion. Specialties include chicken in the pot, roast turkey, pot roast, and brisket. Potato latkes are always available. Mama features cooked and uncooked homemade blintzes in half a dozen flavors and, of course, chicken soup with matzo balls that is out-of-this-world.

MANGIA
54 W 56th St (bet Fifth and Sixth Ave)   582-3061
Mon-Thurs: 7:30-6:30; Fri: 7:30-6; Sat: 9-5
   (closed in summer)

16 E 48th St   754-7600
Mon-Fri: 7:30-6; Sat: 10-5

Joanna Cottrell and Sasha Muniak are a husband-and-wife team of artists. Joanna worked with food, and Sasha played the violin. Together, they became Mangia, which just may be the best, most epicurean gourmet takeout place and catering outfit on the island of Manhattan. And that's saying a lot. Joanna suggests using Mangia's wares to stock a picnic in Central Park (fortunately, you won't have to carry the brimming basket too far) or to take a couple of meals aboard an airplane. If it's a transatlantic flight, many of the ingredients in your lunch may be making a return trip. Cheeses are flown in weekly from France, Italy, and England. Baked goods are homemade in English and Colonial styles. There are more scones and Dundee cakes than can be counted, and all sandwiches are made with sourdough breads. The fresh salads, like everything else in the store, are brought in or made in the shop daily. Mangia is a joy. It's a super source for an impromptu picnic, and even if it's the middle of a blizzard, Mangia will deliver.

MISS GRIMBLE
909 E 135th St   665-CAKE
Mon-Fri: 7-2

Old-time New Yorkers drool when they hear the name "Miss Grimble." Long famous for the goodies at her cafe, she now operates uptown with the same delectables, priced a bit above wholesale. There are great cheesecakes made without preservatives or fillers (classic vanilla, chocolate chip, marble, raspberry marble, chocolate, strawberry, and orange), wonderful pies (chocolate pecan, apple, apple crumb, key lime, French open apple) and more. Don't leave without sampling the double chocolate fudge cake. It's worth the trip!

M. SCHACHT OF SECOND AVENUE GOURMET DELI
99 Second Ave (at Sixth St)   420-8219
Daily: 7 a.m.-12 a.m.

This is a self-professed "old-time Lower East Side appetizing store," which is almost totally unknown outside the neighborhood or among noncaterers. Without a doubt, some of the best smoked fish anywhere is served here, New York-style. The emphasis is on salmon, salads, gourmet deli, and any elegant fish. Schacht's slices it, platters it, smokes it, caters it, and even ships it worldwide. A really unique item is a Scotch salmon presented on a board with a knife and instructions for slicing. It makes an impressive gift and a mouth-watering centerpiece. Those lucky enough to drop in at Schacht's can sample all kinds of fish, cheese, caviar, and gourmet delicatessen meat.

NEUMAN AND BOGDONOFF
1385 Third Ave (bet 78th and 79th St)   861-0303
Mon-Sat: 7:30-7

Neuman is Paul Neuman, son of the owner of Rosedale Fish Market, and Bogdonoff is Paul's wife, Stacy. Together, they have married the showpiece salads that distinguished Rosedale from other fish stores to other elegant dishes, and they've created a stylish and trendy catering firm. With a fresh wholesale source for seafood, the menu frankly admits a bias to fish and fish dishes. So, there's shrimp mousse, smoked trout, and some of the best seafood salads in the city. If you can't get down to Neuman and Bogdonoff, Paul still prepares food for the Rosedale store. But where Rosedale is a fish-market-cum-takeout-salad spot, Neuman and Bogdonoff is a caterer with a specialty in seafood. So, the lobster can be accompanied by Cornish hens, ribs, or Paul's special citrus chicken. And vegetarians can pick from a half-dozen vegetable salads or a roasted eggplant in a yummy sauce. In fact, the sauces deserve their own mention. Any fish store maintains a good stock recipe, and Rosedale is no exception. At Neuman and Bogdonoff, stocks of both fish and beef can be purchased as a meal. Fresh baked pastries are also available.

PETAK'S
1244 Madison Ave (bet 89th and 90th St)   722-7711
Daily: 7:30 a.m.-8 p.m.; Sun: 9-8

58 Pearl St   558-6000
Mon-Fri: 7:30-5

Richard Petak, third-generation member of a family that has owned appetizing businesses in the South Bronx and later New Jersey, has now made the leap to New York, offering the first "appy shop" the Carnegie Hill neighborhood has had in a long time. (As housing has gotten scarcer, Carnegie Hill has emerged as a prime neighborhood. Ten years ago, it was the outskirts of Spanish Harlem.) In any event, no neighborhood could be assessed as truly having arrived without a gourmet takeout shop, and now Petak's (both corporately and personally) fills that need. So there are the "appy" standbys, such as salads (60 of them), corned beef, pastrami, smoked fish, and all sorts of takeout foods. The stores offer full corporate catering, quarter-pound containers of potato salad, gift baskets, picnic hampers, and box lunches. And don't forget the sesame snow peas, baked salmon salad, cheeses, vinegars, oils, preserves, breads, and other staples of gourmet food emporiums. In short, Petak's prepares food as mother never did—unless mother was a patron of Petak's in the South Bronx or Fairlawn, New Jersey.

PIATTI PRONTI
34 W 56th St (bet Fifth and Sixth Ave)   315-4800
Mon-Fri: 8-5; Sat: 11-5

If you are staying in a hotel in midtown or live nearby, note this phone number. This is the greatest alternative to room service in the city, and it's cheaper, to boot! At Piatti Pronti, you'll find an outstanding fresh salad bar, gourmet pizzas, dozens of pasta dishes, and a daily breakfast special. I recommend any of them for a quick, wholesome meal at a small price, but since they do corporate catering *(on one hour's notice!)* and delivery, they should be first and foremost considered an alternative to cooking at home. They are faster, better, and cheaper (even counting the tip!). Incidentally, David Snedden, one of the owners of Piatti Pronti, is also a co-owner of Fairway Fruits and Vegetables, one of the city's best markets. Fairway supplies the ingredients for the shop, as well as for restaurants around town owned by the other partners.

PRANZO
1500 Second Ave (at 78th St)   439-7777
Mon-Sat: 7:30 a.m.-10 p.m.; Sun: 9:30-9

Besides the delicious food, there are two special reasons to shop at Pranzo: the extended operating hours, offering the convenience of fulfilling your needs at almost any hour, and the free delivery service, from East 57th to East 96th Streets, and from the East River to Fifth Avenue. Prices are not inexpensive, but the quality is apparent in the wide selection of appetizers, like roasted sweet peppers and spicy chicken wings, pasta like meatless lasagna and homemade pizzas, salads in a dozen varieties, and tasty side dishes like stuffed potatoes and oven-roasted mushrooms. Entrees that will take care of that special dinner include stuffed chicken breast, filet mignon, and shepherd's pie.

RUSS & DAUGHTERS
179 E Houston St   475-4880
Daily: 9-7

A family business for several generations, Russ & Daughters has been a renowned New York shop since it first opened its doors. There are nuts, dried fruits, pâté de foie gras, lake sturgeon, pickled herring, Gaspe salmon sliced and replaced on the skin, and a number of fancy fish dishes, including caviar, smoked fish, sable, and herring. Russ & Daughters has a reputation for serving only the very best. Caviar alone comes in five different varieties, all of which are sold at low prices. They sell both wholesale and over the counter, and many a Lower East Side shopping trip ends with a stop at Russ & Daughters. Their chocolates are premium quality. They also ship anywhere. If I were to give a five-star rating, this shop would qualify. It is clean, first-rate, and friendly—what more could you ask?

SALUMERIA BIELLESE
376-378 Eighth Ave (at 29th St)   736-7376
Mon-Sat: 7-6

This Italian-owned grocery store is the best—and the only—French charcuterie in the city. If that isn't contradiction enough, get this: The loyal lunchtime crowd thinks it's dining at a hero shop when it's really enjoying the fruits of a kitchen that serves many good restaurants in the city. To understand how all this came about, a lesson in New York City geography is necessary. In 1945, when Ugo Buzzio (his son Marc is one of four partners who run the business today) and Joseph Nello came to this country from the Piedmontese city of Biella, they opened a shop a block away from the current one in the immigrant neighborhood called Hell's Kitchen. (Today, it's gentrified and known as Clinton.) The two partners almost immediately began producing French charcuterie. Word spread rapidly among the chefs of the city's restaurants that Salumeria Biellese was producing a quality product that could not be duplicated anywhere. Friendly service is not a trademark here, however.

SANDWICH HOUSE
58 Greenwich Ave 675-5211
Daily: 8-6

Sometimes just a sandwich will fill the bill. Maybe it's for lunch at the office. Maybe for a picnic. Whatever. This place offers some of the "best dressed" sandwiches in town. You have your choice of many different kinds of bread, fresh homemade dressings, and delicious ingredients. There's a vegetarian sandwich, several made with prosciutto and different kinds of cheese, and a super low-calorie turkey-breast special. You can get freshly squeezed juice, plus a number of salad and dessert possibilities, all at such a low price you will think you've gone to sandwich heaven.

SARGE'S
548 Third Ave (bet 36th and 37th St)   679-0442
Daily: 24 hours

It ain't fancy, but Sarge's could feed an army, and there's much to be said for the taste, quality, and price. Sarge's can cater everything from hot dogs to a hot or cold buffet for almost any number of people. Prices are gauged by the number of people and type of food, but there are several package deals, and all of them are remarkably reasonable. Even one of the more expensive buffets—the deluxe smoked-fish version—runs about $15 per person, and that includes cream cheese and bagels, as well as sturgeon, sable, and stuffed smoked whitefish. Sarge's also caters deli items and has an excellent selection of cold hors d'oeuvres platters, which offer everything from canapes of caviar, sturgeon, and Nova Scotia salmon to shrimp cocktails. And to make the party complete, Sarge's can supply serving pieces, condiments, and serving staff. My favorite is the guy who slices hot pastrami in front of the guests. The carver, cutting board, knife, pastrami, warming oven, and table can all be obtained from Sarge's.

THE SILVER PALATE
274 Columbus Ave (nr 73rd Street)   799-6340
Mon-Fri: 7 a.m.-9:30 p.m.; Sat-Sun: 7:30 a.m.-9:00 p.m.

There are picnic baskets, and then there are *picnic baskets*. The Silver Palate gourmet gift baskets are of a caliber that has prompted stores like Bloomingdale's to feature them in their gourmet sections. You can go directly to the source and have the

Silver Palate prepare anything from a light picnic lunch to a full-course meal or decadent dessert. The baskets can be filled with such gourmet specialties as mousses, pâtés, imported cheeses, and fresh homemade desserts. A professionally made basket from the Silver Palate will be a perfect fit for any occasion. The owners pride themselves on the reputation of its gourmet shop, a reputation built on the unique takeout food, gift baskets, and their own bottled mustards, chutneys, salad splashes, toppings, etc. Moreover, the Silver Palate offers fine foodstuffs at good prices. They also have a catering department that will handle anything from a basket for two to a splendid sit-down dinner for 2000.

SUSAN SIMON
32 E 2nd St   777-0080

Susan Simon knows her way around the catering business. Before opening her own shop in this unlikely location, she worked for a major catering house to learn the trade. This background, plus her worldwide travels, has enabled Susan to offer a distinctive array of unusual dishes for the private or corporate client. She can provide a simple luncheon or picnic, a fancy sit-down dinner, or a business cocktail party that features the romance of Thailand.

TAYLOR'S PREPARED FOODS AND BAKE SHOP
523 Hudson St (bet W 10th and Charles St)   645-8200
Mon-Thurs: 6 a.m.-8 p.m.; Fri: 6 a.m.-10 p.m.;
    Sat: 8 a.m.-9 p.m.; Sun: 8-8

This is a very cheery country store in the West Village. It is like visiting your neighbor's home and finding warm hospitality. They sell delicious pies and cakes; specialty baked items like scones, muffins, and bagles; assorted salads; and hot takeout entrees. Breakfasts are a specialty. A catering service for both informal and elegant affairs is available, and production companies may pick up their items as early as needed.

TODARO BROTHERS
555 Second Ave (bet 30th and 31st St)   532-0633
Mon-Sat: 7:30 a.m.-9 p.m.; Sun: 8-8

Don't come here if you're ravenous or on a diet, because Todaro carries the very best in imported and domestic gourmet food. Just about everything here is irresistible and will wreak havoc with pocketbook and diet alike. There is imported stuffed pasta, pâté, jams, cheeses, homemade sausages, and a half-dozen gourmet items, all top quality. Todaro even stocks fresh truffles, a delicacy seldom seen this side of a haughty restaurant. And then there are the chocolates. Lucien Todaro imports the very best from Europe.

The *Daily News* rated Todaro's tuna fish salad the best in the city, and our own survey gave them a top award for heros. When a gourmet shop is the best in mundane efforts such as heros and tuna salad, that gives a good indication of the quality of its more exotic items.

WORD OF MOUTH
1012 Lexington Ave (bet 72nd and 73rd St)   734-9483
Mon-Fri: 10-7; Sat: 10-6; Sun: 11:30-5:30
Closed Sun in Aug

The history of Word of Mouth is actually the gastronomic history of Manhattan—or at least the Upper East Side of it. When Christi Finch (an Oregonian—they pop up everywhere!) opened her original tiny shop in 1976, she was one of the very first establishments to offer home-style prepared foods for at-home or picnic use. Success was almost instantaneous, and by 1979 the shop had moved around the corner and became incorporated. Today, she enjoys a reputation as one of the finest sources for pasta, soups, vegetable salads, quiches, baked goods, and specialty meat dishes. The aim is still the same, however. Nothing is catered per se (although Word of Mouth does work with professional and amateur caterers), and everything is geared for at-home consumption. There is no ethnic orientation, though there are worldwide influences, and the style is still home-style cooking that makes use of the very finest ingredients. As Word of Mouth adds staff, they add new specialties, but the aim is always to make everything look as though it just came from the customer's kitchen—and that usually means the kitchen of an epicurean.

ZABAR'S
2245 Broadway (at 80th St)   787-2000
Mon-Fri: 8-7:30; Sat: 8 a.m.-midnight; Sun: 9-6
Mezzanine: 9-6 daily

"We need more croissants in the bakery section," announces Scott over the loudspeaker system in this busy and unique gourmet, appetizer, and housewares shop. It is no wonder that they have sold out of croissants, as the traffic at Zabar's is like no other place in Manhattan. But then, Zabar's is not just another food emporium; it is a New York institution. Don't expect neat aisles and fancy fixtures. That is not the way the store is merchandised by one of the last of the real hands-on operators, Murray Klein. The genius of the place is that it is like a permanent carnival. However, this carnival features top-quality food items in every category, with broad selections and enormous quantities, at what are arguably the best prices in the city. You can find a huge selection of bakery goods, candy bargains you won't believe (they buy in large lots), every kind of cheese you could ask for, an appetizer section that has to be the busiest in the city, and a coffee department that sells more than any other store in the country. In between, there are all the staple grocery items, pots and pans hanging from the ceiling, and aisles stacked high with daily specials and demonstrations. Upstairs you will find the city's best bargains on housewares—everything from toasters to ice cream machines to carving knives. Next door is an informal cafe where weary shoppers can be refreshed with orange juice, coffee, yogurt, and baked delicacies. For real New Yorkers, a visit here is a normal routine; for visitors, don't leave the Big Apple without a look!

Fruits, Vegetables

GREENMARKET
Office: 130 E 16th St   477-3220

The city sponsors open-air markets in various city neighborhoods. Since there's no overhead, their prices are cheaper than a supermarket's, and the produce is sold fresh from the farm by the farmers who grow it. One of Greenmarket's drawbacks, however, is that there are no stockrooms to supplement the farmer's supply. When the truckbeds are empty, the farmers close shop. So you have to get there early. Another problem is that Greenmarket isn't well organized. But for farm-fresh produce at super prices, it pays to put up with a little inconvenience. These markets are A-1. Some are open year-round, others just during the summer and fall; it is best to call for exact hours.

LA MARQUETA
Park Ave (under the tracks from 110th to 116th St)

Tucked under the train tracks in Harlem, this is one of the most fabulous shopping places in the city. La Marqueta is famous, and the early-morning babble of voices here is proof that its customers are not only the local residents of Spanish Harlem. Although the accent is definitely South American, there is nothing that isn't sold here. Each building contains several individual businesses that hawk whatever is fresh and reasonable that day. Lest you think that means 600 booths of Florida oranges, each building has a few stalls that provide really exotic produce. Some of the latter include collard greens, breadfruit, celery root, plantains, and Jamaican spice bread. If you can surmount the language barrier and show some curiosity, the merchants are eager to share recipes with you. It's a friendly, informal place. Once in a while, a squawking chicken can be seen among the stalls of papayas, mangoes, and peppers.

Gift Baskets

MANHATTAN FRUITIER
210 E 6th St (at Third Ave)   260-2280
Mon-Fri: 9-5:30; Sat: 9-1 (closed Sat in summer)

Most fruit baskets are pretty bad, but this outfit makes some great-looking (and great-tasting) masterpieces using fresh seasonal and exotic fruits exclusively. And you can add comestibles, such as hand-rolled cheddar cheese sticks, biscotti, and individually wrapped chocolates. Locally handmade truffles and flowers are also available for inclusion. Hand-delivery charges in Manhattan are very reasonable.

SANDLER'S
245-3112, 1-800-75-FRUIT
Daily: 9-6

Sandler's is a key source for scrumptious candies, delicacies, and some of the best chocolate chip cookies in New York. But Sandler's is best known for its gift baskets, which are perfect for any number of occasions. No one does it better!

Health Foods

COMMODITIES
117 Hudson St (at N Moore St)   334-8330
Daily: 10-8

Commodities is the largest natural-food store within a 100-mile radius, according to the store's staff. In addition, they are considered the best by virtually everyone in the health-food market. Their produce is of excellent quality, and the prices are comparable to those of local supermarkets. They earned that "largest" reputation with a very well-rounded stock of canned and processed health foods, including vegetable and meat substitutes and a full line of health-food products. They are able to serve everyone from macrobiotics to those who are only marginally interested in chemically free food. The staff is helpful without being fanatical, and the store is so large that you might assume it is just another grocery. It isn't. Commodities is the very best.

DOWN TO EARTH
33 Seventh Ave (bet 12th and 13th St)   924-2711
Mon-Fri: 9:30-9:30, Sat: 10-8:30; Sun: 11-8:30

This is probably the Village's most complete, best run, and most appealing health-food store. Look over the vitamins, packaged health foods, vegetables, frozen meats, cheeses, and sprouts. All are top quality. The takeout sandwiches are filling and wholesome. And they have also made their price structure more competitive.

EARTH'S HARVEST TRADING COMPANY
700 Columbus Ave (bet 94th and 95th St)   864-1379
Mon-Fri: 9:30-7:30; Sat, Sun: 10-6

This is really a natural-foods supermarket. With all the emphasis these days on healthy eating and healthy looks, you can take care of both in the aisles of this fascinating store. There is organic produce, herbs by the hundreds, a vast selection of organic and natural grocery items, color- and preservative-free cheeses, and a juice bar and deli for a quick, healthy snack. And to make sure you radiate that natural look, a full supply of natural cosmetics is available.

GOOD EARTH FOODS
1334 First Ave (bet 71st and 72nd St)   472-9055
Mon, Wed, Thurs: 10-7; Tues, Fri: 10-8; Sat: 10-6

167 Amsterdam Ave (at 68th St)   496-1616
Mon-Fri: 9:30-7:30; Sat: 9:30-6:30; Sun: 12-6

The Good Earth has the reputation of being the finest and best-stocked health-food store in New York—and one of the most expensive. The very helpful and knowledgeable sales personnel will vehemently deny that they are overpriced, but a quick comparison of prices will show that they are, just as surely as a quick visit will confirm their reputation for having one of the largest and freshest stocks. In addition to their enormous selection, the Good Earth offers delivery anywhere within the city, which is further proof that they are not in the reasonable class. On the other hand, one-stop shopping is easy to do here.

INTEGRAL YOGA NATURAL FOODS
229 W 13th St (bet Seventh and Eighth Ave)   243-2642
Mon-Fri: 10-9:30; Sat: 10-8:30; Sun: 12-6:30

Selection, quality, and health are the order of the day in this clean, attractive shop, which features a complete assortment of natural foods. Vegetarian items, packaged groceries, organic produce, bulk foods, juice bar, salad bar, deli, and baked items are all available at reasonable prices for the health-conscious shopper. They are located in the same building as a yoga center that offers classes in yoga, meditation, and philosophy.

Hungarian

PAPRIKAS WEISS, IMPORTERS
1546 Second Ave (bet 80th and 81st St)
288-6117, 288-6903, FAX: 212/734-5120
Mon-Fri: 9-7; Sat: 9-6

Paprikas Weiss is approaching a century of operation, and it is still a family owned and operated business. Paprika, spices, and

Hungarian staples built this business, but this fine store now offers, in addition, a complete line of coffee and tea, pâtés, foie gras, pastries, imported candies, pastas, and other specialties. Many professional cooks use this store as a source, as they carry imported items from France, Italy, Spain, China, India, and South America, as well as the Hungarian basics. If you are in the market for old-fashioned meat grinders, nut grinders, and poppy-seed mills (as well as the ground poppy-seed itself), this is a good place to look. A catalog is available at a moderate price.

Ice Cream

CHELSEA ICE
259 W 19th St (bet Seventh and Eighth Ave)   242-7692
Daily: 7-7

For a time you had to go to an expensive restaurant or eat in an executive dining room to enjoy top-quality sorbet, gelato, ice cream, and frozen desserts from this outfit. Now all you have to do is go to West 19th Street for such special flavors as espresso, white chocolate, cassis, passion fruit, and champagne. It is a good idea to call ahead, as they mainly deal with the trade.

MINTER'S ICE CREAM KITCHEN
Pier 17, South Street Seaport   (608-2037)
4 World Financial Center   (945-4455)
Open daily during Seaport and Center hours

Minter's Kitchen became famous dispensing ice cream mixes—combinations of any of 16 homemade ice cream flavors sprinkled with any of over 20 assorted candies, cookies, fresh fruits, and nuts. They are kneaded on a marble slab and dispensed as ice cream scoops, sundaes, milk shakes, malts, and ice cream sodas. At the new World Financial Center location, the concept has been expanded. They serve a variety of all-natural treats made on the premises. These include yogurt shakes, smoothies, salads, bakery items, and Belgian waffles. The Belgian waffle sundae is outrageous!

PRAVINIE GOURMET ICE CREAM
27 St Marks Pl (8th St, bet Second and Third Ave)
673-5948

193 Bleecker St (bet MacDougal St and Sixth Ave)
475-1968
Mon-Fri: noon-midnight; Sat, Sun: noon-1 a.m.

Pravinie offers "gourmet ice cream" and much, much more, none of which will reduce the waistline. But the calories are well worth it. Ice cream comes in over 30 exotic flavors, both American and Oriental. Pravinie, dedicated to sweet indulgence, also offers tofutti (in unusual-for-tofutti flavors, of course), cookies, Vitari (Fruitäge), and frozen yogurt. The locals claim that Pravinie offers the best milkshake in town. Needless to say, their help looks as if they never eat the goodies. Or maybe this stuff isn't as fattening as it looks.

Indian

KALPANA
2528 Broadway (at 95th St)   663-4190
Mon-Sat: 1-8:30 p.m.

Kalpana is a tiny neighborhood store with an excellent reputation among Indians. Owners Urmilla and Tony Maharaj (Indians from Trinidad) supply the Upper West Side with a variety of Caribbean products by way of Trinidad, Jamaica, and England. They even have Indonesian groceries. Urmilla doesn't mind giving recipes and instructions for the unusual products the store sells. Kalpana also has a catering service.

K. KALUSTYAN
123 Lexington Ave (bet 28th and 29th St)   685-3451
Daily: 10-8

In 1944, Kalustyan opened as an Indian spice store at its present location. After all this time, Kalustyan is still a great spot. Everything is sold in bins or bales rather than prepackaged containers, and everything is available in bulk or wholesale sizes for retail customers. The difference in cost, flavor, and freshness compared to that of regular grocery stores is extraordinary, and the best indication of the latter two points is a simple whiff of the store's aroma. Kalustyan is not strictly an Indian store, but rather an "Orient export trading corporation" with a specialty in Middle Eastern and Indian items.

Italian

ITALIAN FOOD CENTER
186 Grand St (at Mulberry St)   925-2954
Daily: 8-7

Joseph De Mattia, the Italian Food Center's proprietor, serves a tantalizing array of Italian food that's a credit to his prime location in the heart of Little Italy. The Food Center is truly that: it stocks fresh and cured Italian meats and cheeses, delicious fresh-baked breads, Italian-American cold cuts, Italian salads, delicacies, groceries, and dry goods. If it's Italian, it's here.

MELAMPO
105 Sullivan St (bet Spring and Prince St)   334-9530
Mon-Sat: 11-8

In a tiny store not much bigger than an oversized closet, Melampo manages to display a large variety of the best in Italian food items. The specialty, however, is *the* sandwich. This is the place to go for some super special combinations, like Battigota (salami, provolone), Ruben (prosciutto, provolone), Cristina (mozzarella, artichoke), and Alessandro (tuna, peppers, bel paese). All sandwiches are served on individual-sized white or whole wheat loaves of bread. A treat you'll never forget: the Bombolo Tricolore. It is made of fresh mozzarella, Jersey tomato, basil, and a special dressing, and is served on Focaccia bread. Yum, yum.

Japanese

KATAGIRI AND COMPANY
224 E 59th St (bet Second and Third Ave)   755-3566
Mon-Sat: 10-7; Sun: 11-6

Planning a Japanese dinner? Do you have some important clients from across the Pacific that you would like to impress with a sushi party? Katagiri features all kinds of Japanese food, sushi ingredients, and utensils.They also provide wholesale items for major hotels and restaurants. You can get some great party ideas from the helpful personnel here, and the prices are more reasonable than in Tokyo.

Kosher

LEIBEL'S KOSHER SPECIALTIES
39 Essex St   AL4-0335
Sun-Thurs: 9:30-6:30; Fri: 9:30-1

A handy place to buy all of your kosher food items, including cheese, fish, jams, and frozen goods. Almost every kosher specialty is available at this personable family-operated store on the Lower East Side. Prices reflect the neighborhood; translated, that means there are bargains by the dozen.

SIEGEL'S KOSHER DELI AND RESTAURANTS
1435 Second Ave (bet 74th and 75th St)   288-2094

1646 Second Ave (bet 85th and 86th St)   288-3632
Mon-Thurs: 11-10; Fri-Sun: 10-10

If you are looking for a top kosher deli and gourmet appetizer store on the Upper East Side, you can't do better than Siegel's. Not only do they keep long hours (Sundays, too), but they also deliver from 10-9. Featured here are fresh, decorated turkey dishes; over-stuffed sandwich platters; barbecue, roasted, and fried chicken platters; hors d'oeuvre selections; smoked fish platters; fresh baked breads and salad trays; and a large selection of cakes, cookies, and fresh fruit platters. The number of selections is awesome, with nearly two dozen sandwiches on the menu, ten different soups, dozens of salads, and side dishes ranging from potato and meat knishes to kugel and kishka.

Liquor, Wine

CROSSROADS WINES AND LIQUORS
55 W 14th St (at Sixth Ave)   924-3060
Mon-Sat: 9-9

This store may have the best selection of wine (over 3,000 different kinds) in the city, featuring a complete selection from all the great wine-producing countries. There are rare, unique, and exotic liquors as well. "Insider special" mailings every month or two are also available. Crossroads will special-order items, deliver, and help in party and menu planning. Finally, they are not in a snobby neighborhood, and their prices are as low as their attitude is low-key.

FAIRFAX LIQUOR
211 E 66th St   734-6871
Mon-Sat: 10-8

Since you can't pick a liquor supplier by price (although Fairfax promises that their markup is 12 percent, the absolute minimum allowed by law), you might as well pick one by the company it keeps and the service it offers. You'd be hard-pressed to beat this store on either count. The selection is vast, there's hardly a vintage that's not represented, and the price is guaranteed to be the lowest in town. And Fairfax claims to supply David Rockefeller, Richard Nixon, and Ronald Reagan, among others. This is the place to go if you want to be able to place a bottle on the table and say, "Oh, the Rockefellers recommend this label."

GARNET LIQUORS
929 Lexington Ave (bet 68th and 69th St)
772-3211 or 800-USA-VINO (out of state)
Mon-Sat: 9-9

Don't you love that "800" number? You'll love Garnet's prices even more. This may be the most inexpensive place in the city for specialty wines. So if you're in the market for champagne, bordeaux, burgundy, or imported wine, check out the prices here first.

And they're equally good on other wines and liquors. This is a first choice for choice spirits.

K&D FINE WINES AND SPIRITS
1366 Madison Ave (bet 95th and 96th St)   289-1818
Mon-Sat: 9 a.m.-10 p.m.

On the Upper East Side, K&D is an excellent wine and spirit supermarket. There are hundreds of choices of top brands and top wines, with prices that are more than competitive. Major ads in the local newspapers occasionally highlight K&D's special bargains, but even on a regular basis the values here are outstanding.

MORRELL AND COMPANY
535 Madison Ave (bet 54th and 55th St)   688-9370
Mon-Fri: 9-7; Sat: 9:30-6:30

The charming and well-informed Peter Morrell is the wine adviser at this small, jam-packed store, which has every possible type of wine and liquor. The stock is really overwhelming; since there isn't room for displaying everything, a good portion is kept in the wine cellar. All of it is easily accessible, however, and the Morrell staff is knowledgeable and quite amenable to helping you find the right thing. The stock consists of spirits, including brandy liqueurs, and many vintages of wines, from rare and old to young and inexpensive.

QUALITY HOUSE
2 Park Ave (bet 32nd and 33rd St)   532-2944, 532-2945
Mon-Fri: 9-6:30; Sat: 9-3; closed Sat in July, Aug

This wine and liquor store is very aptly named, since it has the most extensive varieties of French wine in the city, an equally valued assortment of domestic and Italian wines. Germany, Spain, and Portugal. Oenologist Willie Gluckstern says that Quality House's owner, Bernie Freyden, and his son Gary have the best wine palates in the city. They have wines in all price ranges, but don't look for bargains. The name is Quality, and you pay for it.

SOHO WINES AND SPIRITS
461 W Broadway (bet Prince and Houston St)   777-4332
Mon-Thurs: 10-8; Fri, Sat: 10-9

Stephen Masullo's father ran a neighborhood liquor store on Spring Street for over 25 years. When his local neighborhood evolved into the SoHo of today, his sons expanded the business and opened a stylish SoHo establishment for wine. The shop is lofty. In fact, it looks more like an art gallery than a wine shop. The various bottles are "tastefully displayed" (Stephen's words), with classical music playing in the background. Every advantage is made of the enormous floor space, and Stephen boasts that SoHo Wines also has one of the largest selections of single malt Scotch whiskeys in New York. Again, in keeping with the neighborhood, SoHo Wines and Spirits offers several unique services. Among them are party planning, wine-cellar advice, and specialty items of interest to the neighborhood. Note that this is *not* a liquor store (as Mr. Masullo Sr.'s was), but a wine and spirits shop.

WILLIAM SOKOLIN
178 Madison Ave (bet 33rd and 34th St)
684-3827 FAX: 212/873-0552
Mon-Fri: 9:30-6:30; Sat: 10-5:30

This is a unique wine store, featuring a huge inventory of fine wines at attractive prices. They also have a special program for storing wine in climate-controlled conditions in Bordeaux; they offer this service free for four years. (You can also opt to have your wines shipped to the United States or Moscow!) Many of these wines are tradable, and they offer that service, too. They have been in the wine business since 1934, claim to have a $20 million cellar, and are constantly making new discoveries. They will show you the best domestic and imported brands (especially whites), evaluate your rare wine cellar, and arrange for you to attend a tasting.

YORKVILLE WINE AND LIQUOR
1393 Third Ave (at 79th St)   288-6671
Mon-Sat: 9:30 a.m.-10 p.m.

This fair-sized store has carved out a niche for itself as the very best source for kosher wines and liquors. The selection is incredible; they are frequently the first to introduce a new label or variety of wine. They are a good source (with very good prices) for non-kosher wines as well. Hungarian wines and spirits are a specialty.

Meat, Poultry

BASIOR-SCHWARTZ MEAT PRODUCTS
421-423 W 14th St (bet Ninth and Tenth Ave)   929-5368
Mon-Fri: 5 a.m.-10:30 a.m.

The hours are unusual and the neighborhood is not the best, but Basior-Schwartz is the heart of the wholesale meat district, and that alone is enough to recommend a visit. This is a wholesaler who sells retail customers prime meat, cheese, frozen poultry, and gourmet products at the same prices it charges its regular wholesale customers—hotels and restaurants. Although this had been one of the worst-kept secrets among New York hostesses for years, there have been only minor concessions to the retail trade. The hours are more reasonable than they've been in the past, but the big change has been an additional selection of smoked fish, imported and domestic cheese, and gourmet items that are obviously geared to individual customers. They have even added dried fruits and nuts. But the tradition for freshness and quality remains, and the prices are literally fractions of those uptown. Sure, you may have to get up early and lug your purchases home by public transportation (it's difficult to find parking spaces here), but that's a small inconvenience for some big savings. Basior-Schwartz may well be the main source in the city for meats, cheese, gourmet fish, and appetizing prices, and now that they carry eggs, butter, and grocery items, you may not need to go to a supermarket again.

CITY WHOLESALE MEATS
305 E 85th St (bet First and Second Ave)   879-4241
Mon-Fri: 6-3

The name and the hours are indicative of the wholesale aspects of this business. The many services offered belie the fact that this is a briskly professional place, but the result is that the individual retail customer at City Wholesale Meats receive the same quality and price that is available to hotels and restaurants. Personalized services include delivery, freezer wrapping, and cutting to order. This may be the only such place in the neighborhood that precludes a trek down to the more traditionally wholesale areas of the city.

FAICCO'S PORK STORE
260 Bleecker St (at Sixth Ave)   243-1974
Tues-Sat: 8-6; Fri: 8-7; Sun: 9-2

An Italian institution, Faicco's has delectable dried pepperoni, cuts of pork, and fresh-frying sweet and hot sausage in two varieties. They also sell an equally good cut for barbecue and an oven-ready rolled leg of stuffed pork. The latter, a house specialty, is locally famous. Note Faicco's full name: the shop really specializes in sausage and cold cuts rather than meats. There is no veal or lamb—and no steaks. If you're into Italian-style deli, try Faicco's first. And if you're a lazy cook, take home some ready-to-heat chicken rollettes: breast of chicken rolled around cheese and then dipped in a crunchy coating. It's the perfect introduction to Faicco's specialties. Already prepared hot foods to take home, like eggplant parmesan and veal marsala, are also available.

H. OPPENHEIMER
2606 Broadway (bet 98th and 99th St)
662-0246, 662-0690
Mon-Sat: 8-6:55

Oppenheimer is one of the first names mentioned for prime meats in New York. Harry Oppenheimer has run the same meticulous shop for over 40 years. It's an old-fashioned butcher shop with the kind of service that used to be expected (and supermarkets never had). The supermarkets never had this quality, either. There's milk-fed veal, fresh poultry, and game. All of it is sold at competitive prices. Oppenheimer is so reliable and trustworthy that over half his customers never even bother to visit the shop in person; they leave the choices and cuts for their dinners in his capable hands.

JEFFERSON MARKET
455 Sixth Ave (at 10th St)   675-2277
Mon-Sat: 8 a.m.-9 p.m.; Sun: 9-8

Quality is the byword here. Originally just a meat and poultry market, Jefferson has expanded into an outstanding full-line store. Second-generation family management ensures hands-on attention to service. Prime meats, fresh fish, select produce, fancy groceries, Bell and Evans chicken, and fresh salads are all tempting. If you don't feel like cooking dinner, come by Jefferson and let Louis Montuori send you home with some delicious hot or cold prepared foods.

KUROWYCKY MEAT PRODUCTS
124 First Ave (bet 7th and 8th St)   477-0344
Mon-Sat: 8-6; closed Mon in July, Aug

Erast Kurowycky came to New York from the Ukraine in 1954. He opened this tiny shop in the same year, and almost immediately it became a mecca and bargain spot for the city's Poles, Germans, Hungarians, Russians, Lithuanians, and Ukrainians. Many of these nationalities still harbor centuries-old grudges, but they all come to Kurowycky's, where they agree on at least two things—the meats are the finest, and the prices are the best available. Erast's son, Jaroslaw ("Jerry"), runs the shop he grew up in, and he maintains the same traditions and recipes his father handed down. Come and taste the thick black bread, sausages, and ham (ask Jerry for a sample). Hams, sausages, meat loaves, and breads are sold ready to eat, as well as in various stages of preparation. There are also condiments, including a homemade Polish mustard, honey (imported directly from Poland), sauerkraut, and a half-dozen other Ukrainian specialties imported or reproduced from the area. On any given day, Kurowycky plays host to native sons coming "home," second generations being introduced to the old-country flavor, and foreigners seeking the real stuff. Jerry treats them all courteously and efficiently, and they all come back for more.

M. LOBEL AND SONS
1096 Madison Ave (bet 82nd and 83rd St)   737-1373
Mon-Sat: 9-6; closed Sat in summer

Lobel's has periodic sales on some of the best cuts of meat in town. Because of Lobel's excellent service and reasonable prices, there are few human carnivores in Manhattan who haven't heard of the shop. It has published four meat cookbooks, and the staff is always willing to explain the best use for each cut. It's hard to go wrong here, since the store carries nothing but the best.

OTTOMANELLI'S MEAT MARKET
285 Bleecker St (bet Seventh Ave and Jones St)   675-4217
Mon-Fri: 8-6:30; Sat: 7-6

The standard variety here is rare gourmet fare. Among the regular weekly stock are such meats as boar's head, whole baby lambs, game rabbits, and pheasant. This is *not* a place to act young and naive. Quality is good, but being served by the right person can make the difference between a good cut and an excellent cut. Other family members run similar operations in other sections of town, but this is the original store, and it's noteworthy. They gained their reputation by offering full butcher services and a top-notch selection of prime meats, game, prime-aged steaks, and milk-fed veal. The latter is available as prepared Italian roast, chops, and steaks, and its preparation by the Ottomanellis makes it unique. Best of all, they will sell it by the piece for a quick meal at home.

PREMIER VEAL
555 West St (off the West Side Hwy, two blocks south
    of 14th St)   243-3170
Mon-Fri: 5 a.m.-1 p.m.

Mark Hirschorn worked in various jobs in the restaurant business from Albany to Aspen before deciding to join the family wholesale veal distribution center. As a result, he is better attuned to the needs of both wholesale and retail customers than most such distributors. Or, as he says, he's been on both sides of the counter. This translates as a wholesaler who has a good eye for what sells in restaurants and institutions and who has a business that is friendlier than most to small, individual orders. Premier Veal offers veal stew, Italian cutlets, shoulder or leg roasts, and veal pockets for stuffing, at wholesale prices with no minimum order. Of course, if you're going to make a trip to West Street, it might be economical to make the order as large as possible. Hirschorn suggests that three or four customers get together to order a few loins. Less than that leaves too much waste and is not profitable for him or the customer. A loin weighing 26 pounds breaks down to 16 or 24 steaks and chops, and the price is a fraction of that at a butcher shop.

SCHALLER & WEBER
1654 Second Ave (bet 85th and 86th St)   879-3047
Mon-Fri: 9-6; Sat: 8:30-6

Once you've been in this store, the image will stay with you for a long time because of the sheer magnitude of cold cuts on display. The store is simply incredible. It is a Babes in Toyland for delicatessen lovers, and there is not a wall or a nook that is not covered with an assortment of deli meats. Besides a line of delicatessen items so complete it is hard to believe one store could assemble it, Schaller & Weber also occasionally stocks game and poultry, and they claim that they are a regular butcher shop as well. Try the sausage and pork. They will bake, prepare, smoke, or roll it for you, and that's just the beginning.

WASHINGTON BEEF COMPANY
573 Ninth Ave (at 41st St)   563-0200
Tues-Sat: 7-5:30

Washington Beef claims to be the nation's largest meat distributor. They regularly feature New York shells, filet mignon, and beef ribs. The retail store is touted as operating by exactly the same rules as the wholesale operation, but they will also cut meat, sell by the pound rather than the side, and individually wrap it all up. Prices are guaranteed to be the city's lowest, and the quality is good. But there are disadvantages. Washington Beef is *huge*. As a result, the service is brusque and professional, offered on a "take it or leave it, there are others behind you" basis. An attempt to find guidance and recipe suggestions would be a joke. They will cut to order, but lines can be staggeringly long. To sum it up: the prices are fantastic, the quality good. If those are your main criteria, join the crowd.

YORKVILLE PACKING HOUSE
1560 Second Ave (at 81st St)   628-5147
Mon-Sat: 7-6; Sun: 11-5

Yorkville used to be a bastion of Eastern European ethnicity and culture before it became the Upper East Side's swinging singles playground. Here and there, remnants of the previous Old World society remain, and within a four-block stretch on Second Avenue, there are three Hungarian butchers, each of whom offers the best in Hungarian provisions. Yorkville Packing House is patronized by Hungarian-speaking little old ladies in black, as well as some of the city's greatest gourmands. And the reason is simple: except for its neighbors, these prepared meats are available nowhere else in the city and possibly nowhere else on the continent. The shop offers almost 40 different kinds of salami. And that's just for starters.

Goose is a mainstay of Hungarian cuisine, so there is goose liverwurst, smoked goose, and goose liver. Fried bacon bits and bacon fried with paprika (another Hungarian staple) are other offerings. Ready for on-the-spot consumption is a selection of preserves, jams, jellies, prepared delicacies, and breads. (Hungarian bread, natch! Try the potato or corn breads.) All of it is authentic.

Middle Eastern

TASHJIAN'S
123 Lexington Ave (bet 28th and 29th St)
683-8458, 685-3451
Mon-Sat: 10-8; Sun: 11-7

One of the oldest food stores in the city (founded over a century ago), Tashjian is Armenian in origin, but it's been in the melting pot long enough to encompass all of the Middle East (Indian, Pakistani, and Bangladesh items). The shelves are jammed with all kinds of groceries and foodstuffs, and the counters display appetizers. There's even a catering service. Tashjian claims to be an importing business as well, and it would have to be to get some of the items it stocks.

Nuts

KADOURI IMPORT
51 Hester St (at Essex St)   677-5441
Sun-Fri: 9-5

Kadouri is a wholesale-retail store, operating out of burlap bags. Everything here is natural and healthful. The main staples are nuts and dried fruits. The almonds and their derivatives are especially good. Kadouri carries spices as well, but only the more popular varieties. Still, they are extremely fresh, and prices are wholesale, no matter how small the purchase.

YES INTERNATIONAL FOOD COMPANY
165 Church St (at Reade St)   227-4695
Daily: 9-7

Yes is a Middle Eastern food shop, but it's the nuts that attract their clientele. The nuts are freshly roasted and simply sensational. As a staff member said, "We're nuts about nuts." Also check out the dried fruits and confections, though nothing compares with those nuts.

Pasta

RAFFETTO'S CORPORATION
144 W Houston St (bet Sullivan and MacDougal St)
777-1261
Tues-Sat: 8-6

You could go for pasta at a gourmet place or you could go straight to the source. Raffetto's is the source and has been since 1906. Since that time, they have made all kinds of pasta and stuffing. Though most of the business is wholesale, Raffetto's will dispense fresh noodles, ravioli, tortellini, manicotti, gnocchi, fettuccine, and spinach fettuccine to anyone, with no minimum order. Variations on the theme include Genoa-style ravioli with meat and spinach, Naples-style with cheese, and a nongeographic cheese-and-spinach ravioli. Sauces (seven kinds), daily fresh bread, and bargain-priced olive oils and vinegars are featured here. Prices generally reflect the fact that this is indeed *the* source.

Pickles

GUSS PICKLES
35 Essex St (bet Grand and Hester St)   254-4477
Sun-Thurs: 10-6; Fri: 10-3

The legendary rival businesses that started decades ago with Guss and Hollander each dispensing pickles, tomatoes, sauerkraut, pickled peppers, and watermelon rinds from barrels on the sidewalk has since merged into one business that operates at Hollander's store. Pickles still come sour or half sour, with a half-dozen gradations in between, and the business is still conducted out on the street, with the "stock" taking up the interior of the store. Beyond the barrels outside, customers can actually glimpse a semblance of order and even a refrigerator inside. That refrigerator is stocked with such items as watermelon rind (in season), hot peppers, horseradish, sauerkraut, and even whole pickled melons. But what's really important to remember is that this enterprise is still the best place in the world for fresh-from-the-barrel pickles. New: pickled celery and pickled carrots!

Seafood

CATALANO'S FRESH FISH
1652 Second Ave (at 86th St)   628-9608
Mon-Fri: 9-7; Sat: 9-6

Add youth, consumer interest, and healthy eating to the ancient craft of the fishmonger, and you have Catalano's Fresh Fish market. Owner Joe Catalano is a rare blend of concern, knowledge, and youth. His customers—including many local restaurants —rely on him, as often as not, to select the best items for the dinner menu. And this he does with a careful eye toward health, price, and cookery. He feels strongly that a fish store should not be intimidating and that the only way to get new customers is to educate them. Catalano's also has a good selection of poached fish and super fish cakes. On cold, wintry days, don't miss the Manhattan clam chowder. Joe Catalano is too young to have concocted the recipe, but he deserves credit for the abundance of clam, ham chunks, and vegetables that go into it.

CENTRAL FISH COMPANY
527 Ninth Ave (bet 39th and 40th St)   279-2317
Mon-Sat: 7:30-6:30

Central doesn't look like much from the outside, but the stock is so vast that it's easier to list what is *not* available than what is. They have 35 different species in stock at any given time, including fresh imported sardines from Portugal and live carp. Conducting customers through this whale of a selection are some of the friendliest and most knowledgeable salespeople I've encountered anywhere. Louis and Anthony Riccoborno and Calogero Olivri are skillful guides, who also clean and fillet fish. They stock fresh and frozen fish and seafood products. There are fish that even the most devoted seafood lover would have trouble identifying, and the prices are among the most reasonable in town.

CITARELLA FISH
2135 Broadway (at 75th St)   874-0383
Mon-Sat: 8:30-7; Sun: 10-6

The raw bar is the big hit here. It features oysters, clams, and prepared foods for lunch or dinner. The way Citarella's fish are artfully displayed in the windows gives a hint of the shop's vast selection and fine quality. Take home the delicious salads and fish dishes for that special nautical-theme dinner.

LEONARD'S FISH MARKET
1241 Third Ave (bet 71st and 72nd St)   744-2600
Mon-Fri: 8-7; Sat: 8-6; Sun: 12-6

Leonard's, a family-owned business since 1905, is operated by three family members with the same exacting standards that the store has maintained throughout the years. It's a neighborhood store that gears its selection to the neighborhood's menus. Thus, the better, smaller portioned seafoods are always in stock. There are sea trout, oysters, crabs, haddock, scampi, striped bass, halibut, salmon, live lobster, and squid. The latter is usually purchased by people who know what they are doing, but if they don't, one of the Leonards is happy to assist. They also run daily specials on whatever happens to have been a good buy that day at the Fulton Market. This is not to say that Leonard's is a bargain establishment. Decidedly not. Leonard's is class all the way. And their takeout seafood department includes codfish cakes, deviled crabs and lobsters, and a super Manhattan clam chowder. Leonard's also carries a full range of imported appetizers. Yes, there is caviar, and you can also find filet mignon, smoked meats and fish, and canned delicacies. Barbecued poultry, cooked and prepared foods, and prime meats round out Leonard's selection.

MURRAY'S STURGEON SHOP
2429 Broadway (bet 89th and 90th St)   724-2650
Tues-Fri, Sun: 8-7; Sat: 8-8; Sun in July, Aug: 8-2

The reason Ira Goller is the owner of a place called Murray's Sturgeon Shop is that he bought Murray's several years ago. That is of interest to every appetizer lover in New York, because Murray's is the definitive place to buy fancy and smoked fish, dispensing the finest in appetizing products. There is sturgeon, Eastern and Norwegian salmon, whitefish, kippered salmon, sable butterfish, pickled herring, schmaltz herring, and caviar. Quality is magnificent and prices are fair.

ROSEDALE FISH AND OYSTER MARKET
1129 Lexington Ave (at 79th St)
861-4323, 288-5013, 734-3767
Mon-Sat: 8-6

Rosedale has quality seafood in good supply at all times. In addition, there is a selection of takeout fish dishes and salads that are tasty, unusual, and noteworthy. All are individually prepared for each customer. They are not inexpensive; their high quality is accompanied by equally high prices. But according to many of the city's restaurants and caterers, they are the best fish source in New York. (They don't want people to know that, however!) Free delivery is offered.

Spices

ANGELICA'S TRADITIONAL HERBS & FOODS
147 First Ave (at Ninth St)   677-1549
Mon-Sat: 10-7:45; Sun: 11-6:45

Because of its location in the East Village, Angelica's scent is heavily organic and home-remedy medicinal. The shop caters to the locals who want fresh, high-grade spices, teas, and coffees, but the bulk of the business is in dispensing medicinal herbs, organic food, and related books to a trendier clientele. They claim to be the largest and best-stocked herb retailer in the country. Special features include an organic-food department and an organic deli.

APHRODISIA
282 Bleecker St (at Seventh Ave)   989-6440
Mon-Sat: 11-7; Sun: 12-5; closed Sun in summer

Aphrodisia is stocked from floor to ceiling with nearly every herb and spice that exists. All 700 of them are neatly displayed in glass jars. Some of the teas, potpourri, dried flowers, and oils are really not what one would expect. The general accent is on occult and folk remedies, but all the ingredients for ethnic cooking can be found here. Prices depend upon the scarcity of the spice. Aphrodisia conducts a mail-order business via their catalog, which is available for a minimal fee.

MEADOWSWEET HERBAL APOTHECARY
77 E 4th St (bet Second and Third Ave)   254-2870
Tues-Sat: 12-7; closed Aug

Arcus and Dorothy Flynn believe in the power of herbs and herbal medicine. They offer a complete assortment of their own mixtures, oils, ointments, medicines, and formulas to aid a variety of ailments from alcoholism to tranquilizer addiction. In addition to herbal remedies, they have expanded their gift department to include potpourri, unusual incense, incense burners, candles, dream pillows, smudge sticks, hanging stained-glass pieces, musical tapes, massage oils, crystals, and crystal jewelry. The folks here like to share their own experiences, which helps to make any visit particularly interesting.

SPICE & SWEET MAHAL
135 Lexington Ave (cor 29th St)   683-0900
Mon-Sat: 10-8; Sun: 11-6

Want to spice things up? This is the place to start! Spice and Sweet imports spices, pickles, and lentils from India, Pakistan, and Bangladesh. They also manufacture Indian sweets and breads.

WHAT WAS THE TIN PAN ALLEY?

The birthplace of much of twentieth-century popular music, where songwriters plied their trade, actually had two locations — both in New York City. The first Tin Pan Alley section sprang up around Fourteenth Street; the second was in the Times Square area.

V. Where to Find It: New York's Best Services

Airline Tickets

Discounted air tickets may be available from **Hurturk Travel and Tours** (509 Madison Ave, at 53rd St, 750-1170, daily: 10-6) and **Up and Away Travel** (141 E 44th St, at Lexington Ave, Suite 403, 972-2345, daily: 9-7). Both have been recommended by responsible agencies.

MOMENT'S NOTICE
425 Madison Ave (at 49th St)   486-0500
Daily: 9-5:30

Moment's Notice is the place to call for last-minute travel arrangements. They are a clearinghouse for a number of leading tour operators, airlines, and cruise lines that are often faced with undersold or canceled bookings. This outfit provides sizable discounts on all types of vacation destinations, including European air tickets, Caribbean packages, and international cruises. Discounts are offered for travel within 30 days prior to departure. Membership is required. Moment's Notice is not some new fly-by-night outfit; they have been in the travel business for over 30 years.

Animal Services

ANIMAL MEDICAL CENTER
510 E 62nd St (bet FDR Dr and York Ave)   838-8100
Daily: 24 hours

If your pet should become ill in New York, try the Animal Medical Center first. This nonprofit organization handles all kinds of veterinary work reasonably and competently with board-certified specialists. The care here is far better than it is anywhere else in the city. They suggest you call for an appointment. Emergency care costs more.

CAROLE WILBOURN
299 W 12th St   741-0397
Mon-Sat: 9-6

Carole is an internationally known cat therapist who has the answer to most of your cat problems. She writes a monthly column for *Cat Fancy* magazine, and seems to have a special way with her furry patients. Carole makes house calls from coast-to-coast and can take care of many cat problems with just one session and a follow-up phone call. She also does consultations by phone.

THE FAMILY DOG
207 W 75th St (bet Broadway and Amsterdam Ave)
873-9630
Mon-Sat: 9-5 (in-home visits evenings and weekends)

Brian Kilcommons and Sarah Wilson operate an unusual service: they help dogs adapt to life in the Big Apple! (Now, if they would only take on the same assignment with us humans, their business would increase many fold!) Canines of all ages come here for training; it is the largest indoor dog-training facility in Manhattan. There are individual classes as well as group sessions, and boarding is also available. If you need information about veterinarians, walkers, groomers, boarding facilities, or pet supply stores, Brian and Sarah are an excellent source.

FIELDSTON PETS
796-4541
Mon-Sat: 9-7

Bash Dibra, a friendly, zeppelin-shaped man who was born in Albania, is an "animal behaviorist." Have you ever met one of those before? Or has your dog? Well, if your pet has bad manners, Bash is the person to teach you and your dog how to behave. This gentlemen identifies himself as "dog trainer to the stars"; would you believe that he got his start in a Yugoslavian camp where he and his family were interned after fleeing their native country? There, five-year-old Bash befriended the attack dogs!

LE CHIEN DOG SALON
1461A First Ave (at 76th St)   861-8100
Mon-Fri: 8:30-7; Sat: 9-7

Now note this: all dogs and cats at this establishment drink and are bathed in chlorine and bacteria-free water. How many of us can make that same claim? Dresses. Coats. Sweaters. 14-karat gold identification tags. Cultured pearls. Mink coats. Special brand-name perfumes. Lisa Gilford runs this classy establishment as an elegant spa for small and large breeds—sort of a finishing school for the canine set! A separate business grooms and trains cats and dogs, and boarding is provided for some breeds.

MANHATTAN PET HOTEL
312 E 95th St (bet First and Second Ave)   831-2900
Mon-Fri: 7-6:30; Sat: 8-4:30

This place sounds so good you may want to check in yourself! It's the only venture in Manhattan that boards pets as a primary business. They use the best commercial foods available, have separate exercise areas for cats to sun and play (and scratch), and have luxury suites for those cats and dogs that are used to living in Trump Tower. Services include pickup and delivery, air-travel arrangements, provision for medications, and dog and cat grooming. There's even a checkout time for their guests.

PET CARE NETWORK
251 E 32nd St (at Second Ave)   889-0756
Daily: 9 a.m.-9:30 p.m.

No need to worry if Fido or Linda Louise is going to be left behind while you vacation or go away for a weekend. Whether it's a cat, dog, bird, or bunny, Evelyn McCabe and her crew of pet-sitters can take care of your loved one. They have 20 locations around the city, and they will also come to your residence for service. All personnel are bonded, love animals, and have excellent references. No cages, please, and one pet or set of pets at a time per location. These folks will walk, feed, pick up, and deliver your pet. They will also provide transportation and veterinarian care, and they are available around the clock. Dustin Hoffman swears by them, and so will your lonesome partner.

Antique Repair

MICHAEL J. DOTZEL AND SON
402 E 63rd St (at York Ave)   838-2890
Mon-Fri: 8-4:30

Dotzel specializes in the repair and maintenance of antiques, so nothing will be done to your precious heirlooms that will hurt their intrinsic value. Dotzel won't touch modern pieces or inferior antiques, but if your antique is made out of metal and needs repair, he's the man for the job. He spends a lot of time and pays close attention to detail, and he will hand-forge or personally hammer metal work, including brass. If an item has lost a part, he can re-create it. One thing is certain: when the job's finished, your piece will be as good as new. Dotzel also does stripping and replating, although he feels it isn't always good for an antique. He'll probably try to talk you out of it.

SANO STUDIO
767 Lexington Ave (at 60th St, Room 403)   759-6131
Mon-Fri: 10-5; closed Aug

Mrs. J. Baran presides over this fourth-floor antique repair shop, and she has an eye for excellence. That eye is focused on the quality of the workmanship and the quality of the goods brought here to be repaired. Both must be the best. Sano limits herself to repairing porcelain, pottery, ivory, and tortoise-shell works and antiques. While Hess (see Hess Restorations, under "China and Glassware Repair") repairs everything, Sano is a specialist. As a result, both stores have their loyal adherents. Some customers like being able to bring a hodgepodge of broken items to one repair shop. Others prefer the feeling of security you get with specialized service. Either way, it's safe to say it's a matter of opinion.

Art Services

ELI WILNER & COMPANY
1525 York Ave (bet 80th and 81st St)   744-6521
Mon-Fri: 9:30-5:30; Sat: by appointment

Eli Wilner runs two separate businesses. The first one offers the unique service of positioning, grouping, and hanging artwork—a real art in itself. But his main business is period (or antique) framing, mirror framing, and framing restoration. He keeps two thousand nineteenth-century and early twentieth-century American and European frames in stock, and he can locate any given size or style with advance notice. Wilner is a handy guy to call in, especially when you and your partner are discussing what to do with the treasure your mother-in-law just gave you. His most recent frame exhibitions at the Metropolitan Museum and the Parrish Museum met with great success.

A. I. FRIEDMAN
25 W 45th St   243-9000
Mon-Fri: 9-5:45

Ready Frames does custom framing, but those who want to do it themselves can take advantage of one of the largest stocks of ready-made frames in the city at A. I. Friedman. Nearly all are sold at discount. In addition to fully assembled frames, there are ones that can be put together and come equipped with glass and/or mats.

GUTTMANN PICTURE FRAME ASSOCIATES
180 E 73rd St (bet Lexington and Third Ave)
744-8600
Mon-Thurs: 9-5; Fri: 9-2

Though the Guttmanns have worked on frames for some of the nation's finest museums, including the Metropolitan, they stand apart from other first-class artisans in that they are not snobby or picky about what work they will take. They will restore, regild, or replace any type of picture frame, and while they are masters at working with masterpieces, they are equally at home restoring or framing a Polaroid snapshot. Even better, the Guttmanns are not only willing to work on cheaper pieces, they are among the few experts who don't price themselves out of the market. When you bring a worn-out frame to them, they will graciously tell you exactly what it will cost to fix it.

JINPRA NEW YORK PICTURE FRAMING
1208 Lexington Ave (at 82nd St)   988-3903
Wed, Thurs: 12-7; Fri, Sat: 12-8; Sun: 12-5

The proprietor of Jinpra New York Picture Framing has the intriguing name of Wellington Chiang, and his service is as unique as his name. Jinpra handles art services (cleaning, restoration, and gilding) in general, and picture framing in particular. Chiang makes the high-quality frames himself, and they often outshine the pictures they frame. Chiang's artistry is evident in every piece he creates. His frames are the perfect complement to great artwork. They will frame lesser works as well, but because of the price and the fine workmanship, it would be a waste.

JULIUS LOWY FRAME AND RESTORING COMPANY
28 West End Ave   586-2050
Mon-Fri: 9-5

There are many firms in the city that specialize in art restoration and framing, but this is the definitive place for both services. Julius Lowy's seems to have no space that isn't heaped with frames, and many look as though they've been there since the place opened 80 years ago. It's obvious that any kind of frame could be unearthed somewhere on their two floors. This means there is no framing job that Laurence Shar of Julius Lowy's cannot do, and the shop's clients include the Metropolitan Museum of Art and the White House. As a byproduct of having done some really odd jobs, a sideline was developed in art restoration, antique-frame reproduction, and frame rearrangement. (Rearrangement means enlarging or reducing existing frames to match new artwork.) All of this work is done impeccably. Prices are not as high as might be expected, and brand-new custom-made frames are available.

Babysitters

BABYSITTERS GUILD
60 E 42nd St (Suite 912)   682-0227
Daily: 9-9

Established in 1940, the Babysitters Guild charges high rates, but their professional reputation commends them. All of their sitters have passed rigorous scrutiny, and only the most capable are sent out on jobs. There is a four-hour minimum here, but as members of the New York Convention and Visitors Bureau, they will sometimes relax the rule for tourists. Among their sitters, 16 languages are spoken.

BARNARD COLLEGE BABYSITTING SERVICE
606 W 120th St (Milbank Hall, Room 12)   854-2035
Mon-Fri: 10-5

Barnard College, the undergraduate women's college of Columbia University, has—counting instructors and graduate students—an unusually large number of kids following their parents around campus. To keep them out of their folks' hair, the Barnard Babysitting Service was started by the Office of Career Services. The service is a nonprofit organization, wholly run by students who become mother's helpers (usually, room and board are exchanged for babysitting services) and full-time or one-time babysitters. Most of the young women prefer one-time or occasional babysitting arrangements, though.

C.A.S.H./STUDENT EMPLOYMENT OFFICE
21 Washington Pl (at Greene St, 3rd floor)
New York University   998-4433
Mon-Fri: 9-5

New York University has always been known for its free and easy attitude (perhaps because of its Village location). Its babysitting service is no different, and it's certainly refreshing after the list of restrictions imposed elsewhere. At NYU, rates are reasonable, with no minimum fees. Rates are negotiated between parents and students. With such a large student body, there is usually someone willing to sit, even on short notice. No further commitment is necessary. C.A.S.H. combines all the student employment offices, so this is also the place to hire student bartenders, tutors, housesitters, and odd jobbers.

Beauty Care and Consultation

BORJA AND PAUL
805 Madison Ave (at 67th St)   734-0477
Mon: 9-5; Tues, Wed, Fri, Sat: 9-5:30; Thurs: 9-7

Pierre Henri, formerly of Saks, is in residence here on Tuesday, Wednesday, and Thursday, from 9 to 3:30. Though the other operators are good, Pierre is exceptional. He has a long list of clients who follow him wherever he moves. Indeed, this shop relies on steady clients. The service is courteous and old-fashioned, but the cuts are stylish and up-to-date—to a point. "Our makeup girl does elegant, chic makeup to complement our hair coloring," said one operator. "*That*, by the way, is natural coloring. We're not into the punk-rock look." The salon also does manicures, haircuts, setting, and pedicures—everything you'd expect from a traditional salon.

ESTEEM
201 E 69th St   744-4660
Mon-Fri: 10-5

This is truly a service company. Esteem markets a line of cosmetics used as concealers, including eye shadows, alcohol-free shampoo, allergy-free foundations, color cosmetics, and skin-care products. Their use is primarily for those with facial disfigurements, but they also work on varicose veins, age spots, stretch marks, and even body scars. The products are waterproof and unusually long-lasting, so a client doesn't have to worry if he or she is caught in a rainstorm. At Esteem, appointments are required, and during the consultation a company representative will give a personalized analysis. Esteem also markets its products through medical offices and gives free consultations to patients at various area hospitals. The makeup is often the most important aspect in a patient's recovery. Cosmetic therapy really does mitigate scars and birthmarks, and helps people live normal lives.

JOSEPH MARTIN
717 Madison Ave (bet 63rd and 64th St)   838-3150
Mon, Tues, Fri, Sat: 9-5; Wed, Thurs: 9-7

Often there is need for beauty care in a home, apartment, or hotel. For older folks, individuals who are ill, or if time is a problem, Joseph Martin will do services on an out-call basis. Hair coloring, nail care, cutting, and makeup are available, but of course you will pay extra away from the premises.

KENNETH

301 Park Ave (2nd floor)   Waldorf-Astoria Hotel
752-1800
Mon-Sat: 9-7 (Wed until 9)

You will remember that Kenneth was *the* hairdresser at the White House in the Kennedy years. He is still considered one of the best, and now anyone can make an appointment with Kenneth himself. Although he books three to four weeks in advance, it's possible to get an appointment with one of his associates the same day that you call. Some staff members will make appointments as early as eight a.m. They do everything from leg waxing to hair dying. Men may take advantage of all the services of the salon in privacy, and a Kenneth for Kids is available.

LESLIE BLANCHARD

19 E 62nd St (at Madison Ave)   421-4564
Tues, Wed, Fri, Sat: 9-5; Thurs: 12-8

The Private World of Leslie Blanchard (that's the shop's official name, not just flowery writing) offers everything for beauty preparation. The Blanchard salon does haircutting, styling, and makeup, and has been known to do complete make-overs. Blanchard is best known for its coloring techniques. Anyone in New York who wants the best uses Blanchard.

LINDA TAM BEAUTY SALON

680 Fifth Ave (2nd floor)   757-2555
Mon-Wed, Fri, Sat: 8-7; Thurs: 8-8

The specialty here is hair coloring. Linda Tam, a native of China, has been working in this field for over a quarter of a century, and she has assembled a staff of experts who give full service to both men and women. Private rooms and the latest in specialized machines are available.

MAKE-UP CENTER

150 W 55th St (bet Sixth and Seventh Ave)   977-9494
Mon-Wed, Fri: 10-6; Thurs: 10-8; Sat: 10-5

The purveyors of Allure cosmetics for over two decades, the Make-Up Center counts everyone from teenage girls to the rock group Kiss among its clientele. What makes that range interesting is the Center's credo that makeup should be natural and easy to apply and not wash away at night. "Well and good for the 13-year-olds," you say. "But Kiss?" The answer is simple. The Center is set up along parallel lines to serve stage stars, formal events (such as weddings), and everyday folks. All of it is individually geared to customer and lifestyle and packaged with instructions on how to achieve the look at home. Private one-hour sessions that feature the latest makeup techniques are tailored to the customer for around $25. It may well be the best bargain in town, for in addition to the personalized expertise, the lesson is given with the expectation that the client won't be back for quite a while, and there's only minimal pressure for you to buy Allure cosmetics. Lessons can even be videotaped and purchased.

NAILS DESIGN BY RELLY
1104 Lexington Ave (bet 77th and 78th St)   535-5333
Mon-Sat: 9:30-8

Take your malnutritioned nails to Nails Design for a healthy transformation. Cornecia Margaret Evans will create beautiful plastic or paper nail wrapping, all the while making sure you end up with healthy nails (your own) in the long run. TLC is regularly administered to help a client maintain healthy nails. While you're there, you may want to try the body-waxing and eyelash-tinting services, or a facial.

NARDI SALON
143 E 57th St (bet Lexington and Third Ave)
421-4810
Mon-Fri: 9:30-5:30; Sat: 9:30-4:30

Vincent and Fred Nardi wrote a book called *How to Do Your Hair Like a Pro,* and their two salons (only one is in Manhattan) prove they live up to that title. These are full-service salons: they handle the client from head (hair styling, cutting, perming, coloring, etc.) to toe (pedicures), with makeup (classes and demonstrations, as well as application), waxing, and accessory products. The aim is a total look, but it is a look less known for its professional gloss than its ability to be *almost* re-created by the client at home. Nardi even has services for men and children. All of this is well worth paying for, but those who wish to avoid 57th Street prices can do so by attending the six p.m. classes on Tuesday and Wednesday evenings. At that time, free haircuts by students are offered.

Bookbinding

TECHNICAL LIBRARY SERVICE
213 W 35th St   736-7744
Mon-Fri: 9-11:30, 1-5

Here you'll find tools, supplies, equipment, and books for artists, restorers, collectors, bookbinders, museums, archives, libraries, calligraphers, and retail customers. Elaine Haas presides over a wealth of services for bibliophiles. Should a book be in need of repair and you want to attempt it yourself, there is no better place to take it.

After all, if Haas can service professional book repairers, she can certainly help amateurs. The attitude here is briskly professional.

WEITZ, WEITZ & COLEMAN
1377 Lexington Ave (bet 90th and 91st St)
831-2213
Mon-Fri: 10-6; Sat: 12-3

Weitz is a highly respected name in the rare-book field in New York. Leo Weitz began a rare-book business in New York in 1908, becoming so well known that he did work for the Rockefellers, DuPonts, Firestones, and other well-known families. Today son Herbert Weitz and his partner, Elspeth Coleman, continue the tradition of fine bookbinding. Weitz and Coleman restore and rebind books and family heirlooms. They also design and create albums, guest books, archival boxes, presentation folders, and special gift books. Coleman's specialty is custom-designing to clients' specifications. Weitz and Coleman also buy and sell very rare books.

Calligraphy

CALLIGRAPHY STUDIOS
106 Franklin St (bet Church St and W Broadway)
226-4056
By appointment

Nothing sets off a card or a letter like calligraphy. Many claim to be experts, but if you want some really first-class work, let Linda Stein and her crew customize your order. She is able to do work in any language you desire.

Camping Equipment Repair

DOWN EAST
73 Spring St   925-2632
Mon-Fri: 11-6

Owner Leon Greenman provides a phenomenal range of services to outdoors people. He started Down East as a service center for hiking, camping, and outdoor equipment. He has excellent credentials, having been the proprietor of another camping equipment store and a veteran of years of hiking, camping, and trailblazing. During those years, he came to recognize the lack of service centers for camping equipment, and when he was ready to run a store again, Down East was the result. This store is a godsend for campers. It offers guidebooks, hiking maps, and USGS topoggraphic maps. Outdoor gear can be modified, repaired, and customized.

Carpentry

WOODSMITH'S STUDIO
525 W 26th St   879-4300
Mon-Fri: 9:30-4:30

Eric Gaathje ran a carpentry business-cum-woodworking school until he was forced to move when his old location was demolished. Instead of merely relocating, Gaathje reappraised the entire operation, and when he went back into business, he stressed those aspects of the craft that most appealed to him. So nowadays Gaathje is spending his time on custom cabinetry, particularly bookcases, wall units, tables, and even turnings and carvings.

Carriages

CHATEAU STABLES/CHATEAU THEATRICAL ANIMALS
608 W 48th St   246-0520
Daily: 9-5

How would you like to arrive at your next dinner party in a horse-drawn carriage? Well, Chateau is the place to call. They have the largest working collection of horse-drawn vehicles in the United States. Although they would like advance notice, they can take care of requests at any time for weddings, group rides and tours, theater connections, and overseas visitors. There is nothing quite as romantic as a ride in an authentic hansom cab—and they're so *handsome,* too.

Cars for Hire

CAREY LIMOUSINE NY
212/599-1122 (reservations)   (718) 898-1000 (office)
24 hours

Carey is considered by many to be the grandfather of car-for-hire services. They provide chauffeur-driven limousines and sedans at any time, and they will take you anywhere in almost any kind of weather. They will accept last-minute reservations on an "as available" basis.

COMPANY II LIMOUSINE SERVICE
430-6482
24 hours

Steve Betancourt provides a responsible, efficient, and confidential service at reasonable prices. His reputation for reliability is well-earned.

Chair Caning

CHAIRS CANED
371 Amsterdam Ave (2nd floor, bet 77th and 78th St)
724-4408
Wed-Sat: 11-7; Sun: 1-5

Jeffrey Weiss is an unusual, and an unusually good, craftsman. He does hand and machine caning, rush and splint seating, and wicker repair. A new addition to his business is regluing and repairing furniture.

VETERAN'S CANING SHOP
550 W 35th St   868-3244
Mon-Fri: 7:30-4:30; Sat: 10-2

Veteran's owner John Bausert has written a book about chair caning, and he claims his shop is one of the oldest in the world. Certainly, his prices and craftsmanship are among the best in town, and Bausert believes in passing along his knowledge. Customers are encouraged to repair their own chairs: the procedure is outlined in his book, and the necessary materials are sold in the shop. If you don't want to try (or have had disastrous results on your own), the shop will repair the chair. For a slight charge, they'll pick it up from your home. Since chair caning is such a specialized and limited industry, a company often has a monopoly in its neighborhood. So, it's remarkable that Bausert offers his services at such good prices. Equally remarkable are the stacks of cane—I've never seen so much. In addition to caning, Veteran's also stocks materials for chair and furniture repair; you will be encouraged to tackle these jobs, too.

Chimney Sweep

CHIMINEY CRICKET
319 W 11th St   691-0171
By appointment

Once upon a time an aspiring actress-cum-writer went shopping for an apartment. In a longshoreman's enclave too far from the subway, the hall smelled of cats, but casements overlooked a neglected garden, and an exposed brick chimney held a functional fireplace. Allayne Johnson knew she was home. Maintaining her fireplace proved difficult; a reliable chimney sweep could not be found. Johnson acquired some equipment and did the job herself. Word spread through the building and along the block. A new business was born. In exchange for a meal and maybe a theater ticket, the actress was learning a specialized (and rare) skill. It is street theater now. Some heads still turn, and she is asked to pose for photographers!

Johnson prefers her own turf (the Villages, Chelsea, SoHo) but will work almost anywhere along a viable subway route or if the client will provide transportation. Chiminey Cricket runs semiannual "black sales" in January and August, and gives group rates to neighbors. Routine service includes thorough cleaning of the firebox, smoke chamber, and flue. For a small extra charge, she will remove dead birds and other undesirables.

China and Glassware Repair

CENTER ART STUDIO
250 W 54th St (Room 901)   247-3550
Mon-Fri: by appointment

"Fine art restoration and display since 1919" is the motto here. The word "fine" should be emphasized, for owners of really good crystal, porcelain, china, or bronze art should make Center Art Studio the definitive place to go for repairs. The house specialty is restoration of antiques. They will restore or repair porcelain, terracotta, shells, and precious stones. They will also restore antique furniture and decorative objects, using original materials whenever possible. They'll even design and install display bases and cases, and will pack and crate articles for shipment. Probably the oldest and most diverse art-restoration studio in the city, Center Art can offer a multitude of special services, like designs and sketches by FAX, and multilingual personnel for overseas shoppers. The owner, Lansing Moore, has a superbly talented staff.

EARTHWORKS POTTERY/
M. SIMONDS STUDIO
1705 First Ave (bet 88th and 89th St)   534-9711
Tues-Thurs: 12-8; Fri-Sun: 12-5:30 (Earthworks)
Tues: 12-8; Thurs, Sat: 12-5:30 (M. Simonds)

Margaret Simonds ran the M. Simonds Studio for more than 15 years. It was the best place in New York for the restoration of fine-art objects. In 1979, she bought Earthworks—then located around the corner—and the merger created a comprehensive shop that caters to stoneware, pottery, and porcelain pieces from the kiln to "beyond hope" stages. The Earthworks section of the business is both a retail shop and a pottery school. The front of the shop has a fine selection of one-of-a-kind porcelain and stoneware pieces made by potters from all over the U.S. (Great for gifts!) The shop also conducts ongoing classes in pottery making, taking advantage of the on-site studio equipment. During the later part of the week (note the hours), Ms. Simonds is in residence. Her specialty is the restoration of pottery, porcelain, cloisonné, clay, and fine-art objects.

GEM MONOGRAM
628 Broadway (bet Hudson and Bleecker St)
674-8960
Mon-Fri: 9-5

Junior was playing with the prized Steuben crystal apple, thinking it was a baseball? Then it's time to call Martin Noren at Gem, who can repair chipped or damaged Steuben and Baccarat pieces. They must see the piece before they will undertake the job. Remember that they only work with fine crystal objects, like crystal chandeliers!

HESS RESTORATIONS
200 Park Ave S (at 17th St)   260-2255, 979-1143
Mon-Fri: 10:30-4; appointments necessary for later times

Hess bills itself as "repairers of the irrepareable" [*sic*], and they do a fantastic job on anything but furniture, electrical appliances, and mechanical devices. Their specialties include china, glass, handbags, ivory, jade, lamps, *objets d'art,* and virtually the entire run of items in the alphabet. The important thing, however, is that Hess can usually restore an object so that the damage is unnoticeable. (Broken crystal stemware pieces that cannot be restored are reincarnated as crystal dinner bells.) One specialty—the replacement of blue glass liners for antique silver salt dishes—is said to be unique in the city. Hess accepts parcel post-insured shipments of items to be repaired. Upon receipt, they mail an estimate for restoration. Many of Hess' best customers are museums and antique dealers.

Clock and Watch Repair

FANELLI ANTIQUE TIME
1131 Madison Ave (bet 84th and 85th St)
517-2300
Mon-Fri; 10-6; Sat: 11-5

In a beautiful new clock gallery, Cindy and Joseph Fanelli specialize in the care of high-quality "investment type" timepieces, especially carriage clocks. They have one of the nation's largest collections of rare and unusual early-American grandfather clocks and vintage wristwatches. They do both sales and restorations, will make house calls, give free estimates, and even rent out timepieces for special assignments. Granddad would be happy to see his prize in the hands of these exceptionally able folks.

FOSSNER TIMEPIECES CLOCK SHOP
1059 Second Ave (at 56th St)   249-2600
Sun-Fri: 10-6; Sat: 11-5

In Europe, fine watch repairing is a family tradition, but this craft is being slowly forgotten in our country. Fortunately, in Manhattan there is a four-generation family, the Fossners, who have passed along this talent from father to son. You can have perfect confidence in their work on any kind of watch. They will guarantee their work for one year, and in most cases, they will get your work done within a week. Besides, it's a treat to meet this outstanding Czechoslovakian family.

GRACE TIMEPIECES SERVICE
115 Greenwich Ave (at W 13th St)   929-8011
Mon-Fri: 11-7; Sat: 11-4:30; closed Mon in summer

Grace Szuwala services, restores, repairs, and sells antique timepieces. Her European training makes her particularly expert on antique watches and clocks, with a strong sensitivity for pieces that have more sentimental than real value. This amazing Grace can really do wonders with keepsakes from another time.

SUTTON CLOCK SHOP
139 E 61st St (at Lexington Ave)   758-2260
Mon-Fri: 11-5

Sutton Clock Shop takes its name from Kay Sutton, not the nearby neighborhood of Sutton Place, but the service and selection is every bit as classy as that address. While Sutton's forte is selling—and acquiring—unusual timepieces, there is at least an equal interest in the maintenance and repair of antique clocks. Some of the timepieces—even the contemporary ones—are truly outstanding, and there's a long list of satisfied customers endorsing their repair work. And now they do barometer repairing as well.

Clothing Repair

MAGIC MENDERS
118 E 59th St (bet Park and Lexington Ave, 2nd floor)
759-6453
Mon-Thurs: 9-3:30; Fri: 9-1:30

If you have an emergency with any of your clothing while you're in the vicinity of 59th Street, head over to Magic Menders. They will repair almost any type of wearing apparel, from monogrammed A's to zippers, on the spot. Of course, they prefer to be given time to work, but their reputation rests on emergency repairs. Their vast repertoire includes glove and umbrella mending, and handbag and zipper repairs. If you would like to keep Great Aunt Tilda's linens, although the monogram is all wrong, Magic Menders can fix that, too. Their mending really is invisible. They will mail your item anywhere in the country.

Craft Instruction

CRAFT STUDENTS LEAGUE
YWCA of the City of New York
610 Lexington Ave   735-9731

Because not many tools are needed to make a quilt, few stores are devoted solely to quilt making. The best instruction is to be found in such schools as the Craft Students League. There are limited classes with an average of 12 meetings. During the course, each student works on a project and, depending upon his or her proficiency, starts or completes at least one quilt. The Craft Students League also has any number of other excellent courses. All of them, while "crafty," are immensely practical as well. The bookbinding course is known for its professionalism. Send for a catalog to get a better idea of what they offer. You won't be disappointed.

Currency Conversion

FREEPORT CURRENCIES
132 W 45th St   730—8339
49 W 57th St   223-1200
554 Fifth Ave (bet 45th and 46th St)   840-2266
Daily: 9-6

If you want to make sure you have enough French francs for that weekend in Paris, this is the place to go. Usually their rates are better than most banks or hotels, and they will exchange currency for any country. Freeport will also buy and sell traveler's checks, and they sell precious metals at decent prices.

Delivery, Courier, Messenger Services

JIMINY SPLIT DELIVERY SERVICES
147 W 46th St   354-7373
Daily: 7-7

Jiminy Split can hand-deliver a package from New York to Washington, D.C., in less than five hours. That's remarkably fast; the overnight service of Federal Express can't do that, and the U.S. mail is not even in the running. (It once took three weeks for a package of mine to go from New York to Washington, D.C.—it went by way of Washington, North Carolina!) So, if you want a fast, reliable, and personal service, Jiminy Split can deliver anywhere within the continental U.S. as fast as a plane or train can deliver the messenger. (Rates include travel fare, plus delivery expense.) Within the city, rates depend upon distance traveled (the city is divided into zones) and how long delivery takes. There are several Jiminy Split branches around the city.

KANGAROO COURIER
120 E 32nd   684-2233
Mon-Fri: 8-6 (scheduled services all the time)

Messenger services range from bicycle couriers to international shipping firms. Some of them are fly-by-night operations (and I am not referring to the hours that they travel). We have personally run the gamut from rushing galleys between editors to having literally tons of books shipped cross-country. I wish I could tell you that our experience has been wonderful. Suffice it to say that no previous edition ever recommended an all-around company until we met Michael Cohen of Kangaroo Courier. Part of the problem is that no company really does it all. If you are used to sending envelopes crosstown, then you are at sea on warehouse distribution cross-country. And so are the companies you usually deal with. Kangaroo's idea is that *all* shipping is in-house, and the same company oversees the entire job. Thus, Cohen boasts that he can do everything from a rush letter (delivery completed within an hour) to a 10,000-pound shipment, and track the entire job.

NOW VOYAGER
74 Varick St (Suite 307)   431-1616
Mon-Fri: 12-5

Now Voyager runs an international courier service—and you can be a part of it. The firm has a schedule of flights to various areas, mostly Europe, South America, and the Far East, and you can go at a fraction of the regular fare if you have only carry-on luggage. Usually the flights are booked some weeks ahead, and it is a good idea to call or write as early as possible to see what might be available. Who knows, you might be able to take an exciting trip and save enough money to buy this book for all your relatives at Christmas!

Doll Repair

NEW YORK DOLL HOSPITAL
787 Lexington Ave (bet 61st and 62nd St, 2nd floor)
838-7527
Mon-Sat: 10-6

The New York Doll Hospital has been fixing, mending, and restoring dolls to health since 1900. Owner Irving Chais has been operating in the cramped two-room hospital since 1947, when he took over from his grandfather, who had begun fixing the dolls of his clients' children in his hair salon. Originally, the children wanted the dolls' hair done along with theirs. When the senior Chais obliged by keeping a supply of doll wigs, he discovered that he had a better business with the dolls than with the women. So, he abandoned the ladies and created the "hospital." Irving Chais came into the business one

Christmas season when his father was ailing and needed help. Several flipped wigs later, Chais was the latest family member in the business. He has replaced antique fingers, reconstructed China heads and German rag dolls, and authentically restored antique dolls. Additional services include appraisals, made-to-order dolls, and buying and selling antique dolls. He will even perform work on teddy bears and talking dolls with computer chips.

Dry Cleaners, Laundries

Finding a cleaning establishment that will do work on Sundays has been impossible! I have checked out dozens of places, but no one seems to want to work on a Sunday. However, if you bring your clothes in on Saturday (by early afternoon, that is), you can get them done at **111 Cleaners** (111 Third Ave, 979-6950). They are open on Sundays for receipt or pickup only. They will also do work early Monday morning and have it ready by noon. If you desire, they will even pick up and deliver orders of several items or more.

CLEANTEX
2335 Twelfth Ave (at 133rd St)   283-1200
Mon-Fri: 8-4

Cleantex specializes in cleaning draperies, balloon and Roman shades, vertical blinds, and Oriental and area rugs. They provide a free pickup and delivery service. The fact that top museums, churches, and rug dealers use their facilities underscores the fact that they offer top-grade work.

HALLAK CLEANERS
1232 Second Ave (at 65th St)   879-4694
Mon-Fri: 7-6:30; Sat: 8-3; closed Sat in July, Aug

Hallak is a family business run for four decades by Joe Hallak and his sons, John-Claude and Joseph Jr., which probably accounts for the exceptional pride they take in personal service. Much of their work comes from referrals by designers of delicate fabrics and patterns (like Georgio Armani, Valentino, and Gucci). In addition, they now have a shirt laundry and fine linen service. For those (like your author) who have trouble with salad dressing landing in the middle of a beautiful necktie, Hallak is the place to go for help. Their skilled work takes time, but they will give 24-hour emergency service.

LAUNDRY OF MISS EVANS
75 E 130th St   234-2334
Mon-Fri: 7-5; Sat: 8-4:30

As the name suggests, Miss Evans runs an establishment from a time gone by. Established in 1911, Miss Evans has hand-laundered and hand-ironed fine linens and clothing—with no markings—ever since. There are families whose heirloom linens are handed down from generation to generation, accompanied by Miss Evans' phone number. Since this plant is located in Harlem, Miss Evans picks up and delivers wherever the customers are. Prices are not cheap, but the best never is. I like the idea that *so* patrician is Miss Evans that its unmarked item is a status symbol.

LEATHERCRAFT PROCESS OF AMERICA
212 W 35th St   564-8980
Mon-Fri: 7:30-6:30

Leathercraft is all things to all suedes, sheepskins, and leathers. They will clean, redye, reline, repair, and lengthen or shorten any suede or leather garment brought in. That includes boots, gloves, clothing, and handbags, as well as odd leather items. Because leather is extremely difficult to clean, the process can be painfully expensive. However, Leathercraft has a reputation to maintain (it dates back to 1938), and their prices have remained competitive. It now shares space with Marvel Cleaners.

MIDNIGHT EXPRESS CLEANERS
921-0111
Mon-Sat: 9 a.m.-midnight

A special hint: put this number in a prominent spot near your phone. What a handy place to know about! It is eleven p.m. and you want some dry cleaning picked up? No problem. Midnight does dry cleaning, shirt laundry, luggage repair, leather and suede cleaning and repair, shoe and boot repair, and bulk laundry. Best of all (with a small minimum), they will pick up and deliver. Prompt return is assured.

MME. PAULETTE DRY CLEANERS
1255 Second Ave (bet 65th and 66th St)   838-6827
Mon-Fri: 7:30-6:30; Sat: 7:30-3 (closed Sat in summer)

This is a full-service establishment that has been in business for over a quarter of a century. They do dry cleaning (including knits, suedes, and leathers), tailoring (including reweaving and alterations), laundry, household and rug cleaning, and they provide fur and box storage. In addition, they will correct water- and fire-damaged garments, bleach-stained materials, do wet cleaning, and clean upholstery and tapestry by hand. Mme. Paulette offers pickup and delivery service throughout the city, has charge accounts, and will provide one-day service upon request. Now if they only offered service on Sundays, they would do it all!

NEW YORK'S FINEST FRENCH CLEANERS
16 Hudson St (bet Duane and Reede Sts)   791-3859
Mon-Thurs: 7:30-6:30; Fri: 7:30-7:30; Sat: 8:30-6

Three generations of the same family have operated this quality business, featuring pickup and delivery and one-day service. Tailoring and storage, as well as care for fine silks and leathers, is available.

TIECRAFTERS
116 E 27th St (at Park Ave S)   867-7676
Mon-Fri: 9-5

Old ties never die or even fade away here; instead, they're dyed, widened, straightened, and cleaned. Tiecrafters is dedicated to the philosophy that a tie can live forever, and they provide the services to make that possible. In addition to converting tie widths, they will restore soiled or spotted ties and clean and repair all kinds of neckwear. Perhaps most impressive is Andy Tarshis' willingness to discuss tie maintenance so that frequent visits to the shop won't be necessary. Tiecrafters offers several pamphlets on the subject, including one that tells how to take out spots at home. Tiecrafters accepts business via any carrier, and their charge for cleaning a tie is reasonable. They will make custom neckwear. Hint: If you roll your tie at night, wrinkles will be gone by morning.

Electricians

MICHAEL ALTMAN
681-2900
Daily: 24 hours

Usually, electrical emergencies happen at the most inconvenient times, as we all know. What do you do if the electrical socket in your living room begins to smoke an hour before guests are due for dinner? Fortunately, Michael Altman's licensed crew will respond immediately with emergency service. They are available around the clock, every day of the year. This outfit will take care of everything from small problems to big wiring jobs. They give free estimates and are very reliable, having been in business for over 50 years.

Exterminators

ACME EXTERMINATING
460 Ninth Ave (bet 35th and 36th St)   594-9230
Mon-Fri: 7-5

Are you bugged? I'm referring to the type that crawls around and causes screams when you open the kitchen closet. Well, Acme is expert at debugging a private home, office, store, museum, or hospital. Acme is state of the art in pest control.

Eyeglass Repair

DELL AND DELL
19 W 44th St (at Fifth Ave)   575-1686
Mon-Fri: 9-6; Sat: 9-1
July, Aug: Mon-Fri: 9-5:30; closed Sat

If you desperately need Dell and Dell, you probably can't read this. But no need to worry. They do on-the-spot emergency repair on glasses even if they were purchased in Peoria. There are some exceptions (if the frames were trampled by an elephant, there might be a longer wait), but this is the place to go for eyeglasses emergencies in the city. They also repair binoculars. Of course, Dell and Dell won't mind if you stop by for regular optical needs.

Fashion Schools

FASHION INSTITUTE OF TECHNOLOGY
Seventh Ave at 27th St
760-7675 (admission)   760-7654 (placement)

FIT has assumed the position as the world's premier institute serving the fashion industry. The school was founded more than 40 years ago, and includes a graduate roster that reads like "who's who" in the fashion world (Jhane Barnes, Calvin Klein, and Norma Kamali are just a few). The school offers a multitude of majors like accessories, advertising, display and exhibit, fur, toy, jewelry, interior, textile and fashion design, illustration, photography, fine arts, fashion buying and merchandising, apparel production management, pattern making, and marketing. FIT maintains a student placement service, which will match students' majors in the above fields with people looking for their talents. All students are of top caliber, as they accept only about one-quarter of the applicants. The Edward C. Blum Design Laboratory is the world's largest repository of the history of fashion, with over one million articles of clothing. It is open to the public, as are the galleries at FIT Call 760-7848 for information about current exhibits and shows.

TOBÉ-COBURN SCHOOL FOR FASHION CAREERS
686 Broadway (bet 4th and Great Jones St)   460-9600
Mon-Fri: 8:30-5:30; Sat: 10-3

Tobé Coller Davis and Julia Coburn were two of the top names in the fashion industry when they jointly founded the Tobé-Coburn school in 1937 as a training ground for careers in fashion marketing and management. Tobé was a personal friend of mine, and I had the privilege of attending many of her spectacular fashion clinics when I was in the retail business. And what a treat it was to visit with her at her brownstone apartment. She was an incredible person! Today, Patricia Niemi and her crew are keeping up the outstanding professional reputation of the great lady. Tobé-Coburn students receive an intensive two-year course in all aspects of the garment industry. Even the liberal-arts courses are oriented to industry application. Universal business-skills courses stress advertising and public-relations writing, and the history courses deal with the history of retailing and merchandising, as well as fashion trends. Over the years, the school has established a better than 95 percent placement record and a reputation as one of the best schools for training in the merchandising, marketing, and management aspects of fashion. The school has co-op programs and internships with the top names in the business, and when the students graduate, they know the city as well as they know the inside of Seventh Avenue. When these people talk fashion, they mean business!

Formal Wear Rental and Sales

A. T. HARRIS
47 E 44th St (bet Madison and Vanderbilt Ave,
    2nd floor)   682-6325
Mon, Tues, Wed, Fri: 8:30-6; Thurs: 8:30-7;
Sat: 10-4 by appointment

A. T. Harris has been in the business of outfitting gentlemen correctly since 1892. They have serviced ten U.S. presidents! This store sells and rents only current formal wear "of the better kind." You will find proper cutaways, tails, and tuxedos rather than iridescent disco wedding outfits. Shoes and accessories run in the same categories and are also readily available. The cut is decidedly English. In addition to imported shirts, Chesterfield top coats, stud and cuff-link sets, and kid and suede gloves, Harris completes the outfit by owning and renting their own Rolls Royce Silver Spur. They not only dress you in style, they make sure you get there in style. A class act!

BALDWIN FORMALS
52 W 56th St (bet Fifth and Sixth Ave)
245-8190, 246-1782
Mon, Thurs: 8:30-7; Tues, Wed, Fri: 8:30-6; Sat: 10-4

If you are suddenly called to a state dinner at the White House, one call to Baldwin will take care of all the dressing details. These folks rent and sell all types of formal attire, suits, overcoats, top hats, shoes, and everything in between. There is free pickup and delivery to many midtown addresses, and a slight charge for other addresses. Same-day service is guaranteed for orders received by early afternoon. Rapid alteration service is available.

Fur Rental

ABET RENT-A-FUR
231 W 29th St (bet Seventh and Eighth Ave, Suite 304)
268-6225
Mon-Fri: 9:30-5:30; Sat: 11-3; closed Sat in summer

Abet is one of the few places in the country that operates a fur rental business on a full-time basis. Beautiful fur coats, capes, jackets, and stoles are all available for your grand entrance on that special occasion. Many furs you see on television commercials have come from this shop, which numbers its satisfied customers in legions.

Furniture Rental

AFR (THE FURNITURE RENTAL PEOPLE)
711 Third Ave (bet 44th and 45th St)   867-2800
Mon-Sat: 9-6

AFR can provide furnishings for a single room, entire apartment, or office. They show accessories as well, and all furnishings (including electronics) are available brand-new for rent, purchase, or rent with an option to purchase. An apartment locator service and free professional decorating are available. Their stock is large, delivery and setup can often be done within 48 hours, and all styles of furniture and accessories are shown.

CHURCHILL-WINCHESTER FURNITURE RENTALS
44 E 32nd St (at Park Ave)   686-0444
Mon-Thurs: 9-7; Fri: 9-6

Say Churchill, and you think of staid old England, right? Well, *this* Churchill is starkly contemporary, as well as traditional. They can fill any size order for business or residence and can offer free interior-decorating advice and a lease-purchase plan. A customer can simply select whatever is needed from stock or borrow from the loaner program until special orders are processed. Churchill can also offer a comprehensive package, including housewares and appliances, if needed, and they specialize in executive locations (again, both corporate and personal). They will rent out anything from a single chair to entire homes and have done so for sports-team managers, executives on temporary assignment, and actors on short-term contracts.

INTERNATIONAL FURNITURE RENTALS
345 Park Ave (at 51st St)   421-0340
Mon-Fri: 9-5:30; Sat: 10-2

International claims to be the largest firm renting home and office furniture rental firm in the metropolitan area. There is a free decorating and design service, which includes on-site evaluation and layout by a design specialist. The firm offers accessories to coordinate with the furnishings, and the quality of all items is very good. Quick delivery from their own warehouse is a real plus.

Furniture Repair and Restoration

ANTIQUE FURNITURE WORKROOM
225 E 24th St (at Third Ave)   683-0551
Mon-Fri: 8-4

For years Antique Furniture Workroom was the traditional place of choice for French polishing, chair repair, and the restoration of woodwork. William Olsen added antique furniture restoration (especially American, English, Oriental, and continental originals), gold-leafing, and caning. Now Max Schneider and Son Antiques is part of the family, so even more expertise and experience has been added. If a piece of furniture in your apartment or home needs special attention, this is a very reliable place to go. Estimates are given in the home.

SACK CONSERVATION COMPANY
15 E 57th St (at Madison Ave)   753-6562
Mon-Fri: 9:30-5; Sat: 10-3; closed Sat in July, Aug (call for appointment)

This is a class act. Rumor has it that among those clients whose furniture has been deemed worthy of Sack's attention have been the White House and countless museums. If your favorite sofa is valuable enough for such exclusive attention, this is the place. The firm deals only in seventeenth- and eighteenth-century American Colonial furniture. The work is first-rate, and not inexpensive.

General Services

TOP SERVICE
845 Seventh Ave (bet 54th and 55th St)   765-3190
Mon-Fri: 8-6; Sat: 9-1

Top Service will print business cards within one day, make rubber stamps, cut keys, and do all kinds of engraving work. But that isn't all. They also are in the shoe repair business. Their specialty is working on dance shoes, and they are used by many Broadway theater groups. The folks here are the kind you're glad to have around to take care of special emergencies.

VIDEO TOWN LAUNDRETTE
217 W 80th St (bet Broadway and Amsterdam Ave)
721-1706
Daily: 24 hours

Talk about one-stop convenience; just about the only thing missing here is someone to balance your checkbook! Under one roof you have wash, dry, and fold facilities; a video rental library of over 5,000 titles; tanning facilities; FAX service; mailbox rentals; self-service copier; lottery tickets; and a postage-stamp vending machine. If you get worn out from all this activity, there is even a place to sit and relax.

Gift-Wrapping

ENFRA TRADING CO
381 Park Ave S (at 27th St)   684-3072
By appointment

This is primarily a wholesale operation, but that should not keep you from making an appointment, particularly if you are looking for a smashingly wrapped special gift. Though they are really looking for volume business here, the individual is treated graciously. You'll delight at their unusual promotional and executive gifts.

Haircuts

Children

KENNETH FOR KIDS
Macy's (at 34th St and Broadway, 4th floor)
594-1717
Sun: 10-5

Kenneth did Jackie O's hair when she was Jackie K, and for a reasonable fee (by New York standards), this salon inside Macy's will give your child's hair the Kenneth touch, too. Actually, the salon is the showpiece of the Macy's children floor, and you can bet your pogo stick it is well done.

MICHAELS' CHILDREN'S HAIRCUTTING SALON
1263 Madison Ave (at 90th St)   289-9612
Mon-Sat: 9-5; closed Sat in July, Aug

A longtime New York tradition, Michael's drawing card has always been rapport with children and the consistency of personnel and style. Nick Di Sisto, the salon's owner, is living proof of this. He worked for Michael for years, and when Michael retired, Di Sisto bought him out. Many of the hairstylists have worked under both owners. Appointments are unheard of, and lollipops, seats shaped like toy cars, and comic books are *de rigueur*. This place is totally dedicated to children, but a sprinkling of mothers get their hair cut at children's prices.

SHOOTING STAR AT F.A.O. SCHWARZ
767 Fifth Ave (at 58th St)   644-9400
Tues-Sat: 10-6; Sun: 12-5

Reflecting its location, this is a children's hair salon, not a barber-shop. Coming to F.A.O. Schwarz for something as ordinary as a barbershop? Never. This is a full-service salon that will make little boys and girls even more irresistible, with treatments, professional advice, and the latest cuts. And please, don't refer to their personnel as barbers! They suggest waiting until a child is 15 months old for his first cut (Dad will probably do it sooner.) A good cut should last six to eight weeks.

Family

ASTOR PLACE HAIR STYLISTS
2 Astor Pl (at Broadway)   475-9854
Mon-Sat: 8-8; Sun: 9-6

Astor Place doesn't need its address listed here. Just follow the mob to the spot in Manhattan where getting a haircut is an *event* not unlike being admitted to the hallowed halls of the latest ''in'' night-spot. The personnel inside what was once a modest neighborhood barbershop don't even have to actually *do* anything to generate the crowds. But they do give the trendiest, wildest, and most unusual haircuts on the scene. The real reason to stand on the sidewalk is to see and be seen. How did this all get started? Well, it seems that the Vezza brothers inherited a barbershop from their father in the East Village at a time ''when not even cops were getting haircuts.'' Enrico took note of the newly gentrified neighborhood's young trendies and their sleek haircuts and changed the name of the shop to ''Hair Styl-ists.'' Now, the shop is staffed with a resident manager, a doorman (how many barbershops need a doorman?), a loft, and an ever-increasing number of barbers. A haircut at this unique barbershop may be one of the cheapest, most fun-filled souvenirs the city has to offer.

ATLAS BARBER SCHOOL
32 Third Ave   475-1360
Mon-Fri: 9-9; Sat: 9-6

Atlas is the only barber school in the city. Haircuts here are as cheap as they come, and students, under close supervision, work on customers. Custom grooming it's not, but for the price it's excellent.

PAUL MOLE FAMILY BARBERSHOP
144 E 74th St (at Lexington Ave)   535-8461
Mon-Fri: 7:30-6:30; Sat: 7:30-5:30

Paul Mole is a find. This barbershop does a super job on kids' hair without super price tags. During holidays, Saturdays, and after school, the place is jammed, so appointments are suggested. If you want to wait even longer, pass the word along!

Men

Before getting into haircuts, first a note about shaves. Yes, gentlemen, it is still possible to get shaved at a barber shop, even if the price has gone up a bit. Most hotel barbers will perform this luxury, or you can try **Astor Place Hair Stylists** (2 Astor Place, 475-9854); **Broadway Barber Shop** (2713 Broadway, 666-3042); **Paul Mole Barbershop** (144 E 74th St, 535-8461); or **Feature Trim** (1108 Lexington Ave, at 77th St, 650-9746).

FEATURE TRIM
1108 Lexington Ave (bet 77th and 78th St)   650-9746
Tues-Fri: 10:30-7; Sat: 9-7

Salvatore Andenocci started cutting hair when he was 12 years old. For 24 years, he cut hair in a shop in the East Sixties, but some years ago, escalating rent forced him to move further uptown. His clientele followed him, and for the last decade, he has operated a seven-chair shop at the Lexington Avenue location. All those years have given Andenocci expertise aplenty. He specializes in simple haircuts that need nothing more than a combing until the next trim. And despite a clientele that includes scores of prominent businessmen, politicians, and "that sportscaster, what's his name?," Feature Trim is still reasonably priced and fairly unknown. Andenocci and his assistants offer five basic cuts. All follow the natural no-mess-no-fuss edict. Feature Trim was once named the top haircutting shop in the country by the now-defunct *New York Herald Tribune*. As the hair-care ad says, "He's not getting older—he's getting better."

JOHN ALLAN'S MEN'S CLUB
54 Stone St (at Pearl St)   422-3686
Mon-Fri: 8-7

If you have an important interview, or just feel that it's time to be pampered a bit, John Allan's is the place to visit. In comfortable, clean, and spacious surroundings you can have your hair cut, get a manicure, have your shoes polished, enjoy valet service, and even play a game of billiards. A bar and a massage service are available also. This is a classy operation, but prices are very reasonable.

PEPPE AND BILL
Plaza Hotel (Fifth Ave and 59th St)   751-8380
Mon-Sat: 9-6

Fine hair styling for men is available at Peppe and Bill, with prices that would make your hometown barber gasp. But you get the very best treatment—with skilled personnel—whether you come for a haircut, manicure, pedicure, or facial. Marie, who has been at the shop for a long time, will set up an appointment for you with Peppe, Bill, or a very talented stylist named Jacques, who happens to be her husband!

Hardware Installation

SABER'S HARDWARE ARNESTO
15 Avenue A (bet 1st and 2nd St)
473-6050, 473-6977
Mon-Fri: 9-6; Sat: 9-5

The store is a general housewares emporium with an emphasis on kitchen and bathroom fixtures. Ceramic tile, medicine cabinets, shower doors, kitchen cabinets, and hardware are house specialties. And they can install all of these items. They also have a good display of gates and locks. But where Saber's really shines is service; as their motto says: "We hang the impossible." Mirrors and shower doors are a matter of course, locksmith emergencies are answered routinely, and they even stock and hang drapery hardware. Regular customers (and it isn't hard to become one) can get Saber's to do almost any kind of handiwork. In this city—or perhaps this century—that's rare indeed. Think of Saber's, despite its location, as the city's general store and all-around handyman.

Health Clubs

With all the interest in keeping fit, health clubs have sprung up all over the place in Manhattan. Some do not last long, and it is wise to be very careful about long-term financial arrangements with any but the larger and more secure operations. Prices and facilities vary. For those who live in the city, watch newspaper and television ads for special introductory offers. For visitors, many clubs will honor reciprocal memberships, or allow one- or two-day guest memberships. A number of the newer hotels have excellent facilities, including The Peninsula, Holiday Inn Crowne Plaza, the Intercontinental, Vista International, Parker Meridien, United Nations Plaza, and Rihga Royal. There are dozens of physical-fitness trainers available; the best is Ron Filippi (753-9700, ext. 24). For all-around convenience and excellent, clean facilities with capable personnel, the New York Health and Racquet Club and the Vertical Club are the most highly recommended. Following are the better clubs, by districts:

Downtown
Executive Fitness Center, Vista International Hotel (3 World Trade Center, 22nd floor, 466-9266)

New York Health and Racquet Club (39 Whitehall St, 269-9800; 24 E 13th St, 924-4600)

Midtown
   Atrium Club (115 E 57th St, 826-9640)
   Club La Raquette, Parker Meridien Hotel (119 W 56th St, 245-1144)
   Manhattan Plaza Health Club (482 W 43rd St, 563-7001)
   New York Health and Racquet Club (132 E 45th St, 986-3100; 20 E 50th St, 593-1500; 110 W 56th St, 541-7200)
   New York Sports Club (614 Second Ave, 213-5999; 541 Lexington Ave, 838-2102; 404 Fifth Ave, 594-3120)
   Sports Training Institute (239 E 49th St, 752-7111)
   Vertical Club (335 Madison Ave, 983-5320; 139 W 32nd St, 465-1750; 350 W 50th St, 265-9400)
   YWCA (610 Lexington Ave, 735-9755) and **YMCA** (215 W 23rd St, 741-9210)

Upper East Side
   New York Health and Racquet Club (1433 York Ave, 737-6666)
   New York Sports Club (151 E 86th St, 860-8630)
   92nd Street Y Health and Fitness Center (1395 Lexington Ave, 415-5700)
   Vertical Club (330 E 61st St, 355-5100)

Upper West Side
   New York Sports Club (61 W 62nd St, 265-0995)
   Paris Health Club (752 West End Ave, 749-3500)
   West Side YMCA (5 W 63rd St, 787-4400)

Help for Hire

A.E. JOHNSON EMPLOYMENT AGENCY
   681 Lexington Ave (bet 56th and 57th St)
   644-0990
   Mon-Thurs: 8:30-4:30; Fri: 9-4
   Dating from 1890, Johnson is the oldest employment agency in the world dealing exclusively with household help. They specialize in providing affluent clients with highly qualified butlers, cooks, housekeepers, chauffeurs, valets, maids, and couples. Both temporary and permanent workers are available, many on a moment's notice.

COLUMBIA BARTENDING AGENCY
   854-4537
   Mon-Fri: 9-5
   The Columbia Bartending Agency uses students so apt at bartending that one wonders what profession they could possibly do as well after college. The service has been around a long time, and there is

none better. Columbia also supplies waiters, waitresses, and hat checkers.

DIRTBUSTERS
54 W 74th St (Apt 312-A)   721-HELP
Mon-Sun: anytime

Boy, are these handy folks! They will clean apartments, residences, and small offices for flat rates. Their staff, hours, and rates are flexible, and they are bonded. Dirtbusters can arrange upholstery and window cleaning, walk your dog, wax your floors, serve as party waiters, paint your rooms, and perform a home-maker's service for new mothers and invalids. They will also video-tape the contents of your home for insurance purposes, in case of loss or theft. A Dirtbuster gift certificate makes a great gift.

FLATIRON HOUSE AND WINDOW CLEANING
230 E 93rd St   876-8622
Mon-Fri: 8:30-4:30

Lou Marchesi, Flatiron's guiding spirit, is a stickler for "complete house cleaning," and he operates a spic-and-span operation. No request surprises him, and his staff will tackle almost any cleaning problem, including the all-time New York impossibility—windows. What is best about Flatiron is their attitude. They don't come on as if they are doing you the biggest favor in the world by handling your dirt. Marchesi offers a free advisory service that covers not only what services are needed, but the proper way to do them. Moreover, Flat-iron is capable of repairing the cleaning errors of others, be they amateur or professional, as well as handling the big cleaning jobs that should be done several times a year. All workers are bonded and insured, and Marchesi vouches for their work.

LYNN AGENCY
250 W 57th St   582-3030
Mon-Fri: 9-5

The great part of Lynn is that they are keeping up with current needs. They have developed a division called "child-care system," which offers on-site customized child-care programs for conven-tions, corporate facilities, meetings, and hotels. They are a full-service agency that can supply baby nurses, bartenders, butlers, chauffeurs, cooks, companions, couples, governesses, maids, nurs-ing aides, and housekeepers. There is also a party-planning service: the agency can supply help for any kind of function, from a small dinner party to a formal corporate affair. The owners claim that Lynn's biggest virtue is the ability to mold its services to a client's needs. They will serve outside Manhattan, their rates are reasonable, and their personnel are reliable.

Hotels

Discounts

Pay attention to rates! There are lots of special deals offered for weekends and certain times of the year. New York hotel taxes are now the highest in the nation, totaling 20 percent for rooms costing over $100. Ouch! Here is what you should know:

- Double occupancy rate: price per person, two to a room
- Double room rate: full price of room shared by two
- Rack rate: retail price of room (don't pay this rate, if you can avoid it)
- Corporate rate: price offered to corporations (must be asked for)
- Service charge: fixed percentage added to room and meal bills (not the same as taxes)
- American Plan: room rate includes breakfast, lunch, dinner
- Modified American Plan: rate includes breakfast and dinner
- European Plan: no meals included
- Park front: room facing park
- Park view: room with view of park

The following outfits can provide discounts at certain hotels (they vary by organization). In some cases, you must be a member. Give them a call:

American Association of Retired Persons (202/872-4700)
ABC Reed Travel Group (617/262-5000)
Concierge (800/346-1022)
Entertainment Publications (313/637-8400)
Hotel Reservation Systems (800/888-5898)
Hotemart (415/788-0500)
International Airline Passengers Association (800/527-5888)
International Travel Card (800/255-1487)
Privilege Card (800/359-0066)
Quest International (509/248-7512)
Travel Trust International (301/718-9500)
Uniglobe Travel International (604/662-3800)
U.S. Travel Affiliates (312/782-6870)
World International (619/558-5838)

EXPRESS HOTEL RESERVATIONS
800/356-1123
Mon-Fri: 10:30-7

This is a great number to remember! Express can save you time and money for all classes of hotel accommodations. In addition, they will request special rates for children, over weekends, and during certain seasons. They will also try for upgrades and will accept reservations, changes or cancellations right up to the last minute. Best of all, there is no service charge for their efforts. How do they do this? By being in on certain deals and working with hotels to make sure there are as few empty rooms as possible. Rates vary from approximately $80 (single) to just over $200 (double). Here are some of the New York hotels they work with:

Deluxe: Morgans, Macklowe, Royalton, Doral Tuscany, Parker Meridien, RIHGA Royal, Waldorf-Astoria.

Superior: Southgate Towers, Helmsley Windsor, Sheraton City Squire, Sheraton Centre, Mayflower, Doral Park Avenue, Warwick, Summit, New York Hilton.

Standard: Milford Plaza, New York Penta, Madison Tower, Omni Park Central.

Inexpensive digs

I am constantly asked about safe, clean, and inexpensive (less than $100) places to stay in Manhattan. These can be recommended:

Carlton Arms (160 E 25th St, bet Third and Lexington Ave, 679-0680): Funky and unique, like rooming in a museum. Half the rooms have private baths and all have sinks. Really cheap and good for dollar-strapped kids.

Excelsior (45 W 81st St, nr Columbus Ave, 362-9200): Overlooks Museum of Natural History, one block from Central Park. Beamed ceilings, large rooms, kitchenettes, room service.

Gramercy Park (2 Lexington Ave, at E 21st St, GR5-4320): 500 redone rooms and suites, many with kitchenettes, on a private park. Good restaurant and meeting rooms.

Herald Square (19 W 31st St, 279-4017): Built in 1893, near Macy's. No frills, family management.

Malibu Studios (2688 Broadway, 222-2954): Twelve blocks from Columbia University. Good for teenagers who don't mind sharing a bathroom. Really a glorified rooming house.

Olcott: (27 W 72nd St, 877-4200): A few blocks from Lincoln Center, near Central Park. Semiresidential with kitchenettes, safe but strictly utilitarian.

Roger Williams (28 E 31st, 684-7500): Budget studio-apartment hotel in the Murray Hill district. Kitchenettes, color cable TV, optional "kitchen kit" (plates, cutlery, etc.).

Stanford (43 W 32nd St, 563-1480): Handy midtown location, totally remodeled and modernized. Children under 12 stay free.

Washington Square (103 Waverly Place, 777-9515): Formerly the Earle Hotel. Restored, touristy. Good-sized bathrooms, nice lobby, good location in Greenwich Village. Ask for a front room.

Westpark (308 W 58th St, 246-6440): At Columbus Circle. Dull lobby and spartan rooms, but good value.

New hotels coming on line

Battery Park City Hotel (Battery Park City at Battery Place): Battery Park City

Journey's End Hotel (South Street Seaport): Seaport

Kalikow Hotel (Church, Dey, and Fulton St): Downtown

Ramada Renaissance Hotel (Broadway, bet 47th and 48th St): Midtown

Regent of New York (57th St, bet Madison and Park Ave): Uptown

SoHotel (382 W Broadway, bet Broome and Spring St): SoHo

South Street Seaport Hotel (Front St, bet Peck Slip and Beekman St): Seaport

Ripoffs—a few favorites

- Carefully check your in-room refrigerator
- Check room rate posted in your room against quoted price
- Keep your hotel key with you at all times
- Put your luggage tag (with name and address) on inside of bag
- Watch personnel put stamps on your letters and post cards
- Don't change foreign currency at hotels; poor exchange rates
- Ask taxi drivers the approximate fare; watch the amount of bridge and tunnel and extra baggage charges
- Cash traveler's checks at banks, where there is no service charge
- Leave your real jewelry at home; if you must bring along the family jewels, keep them in the room or a hotel safe
- Don't give out your room number to anyone you don't know

Telephone charges

Carefully examine the telephone charges at your hotel. Many outfits find this a handy way to pad the bill. A few hints:

- Don't bill calls to your room
- Ask for your own long-distance carrier
- When using a credit card, don't hang up after first call
- Beware of the phrase "standard AT&T operator-assisted rates"
- Check your bill
- Best idea: have friends and associates call you

Times Square accommodations

For years, few people wanted to stay in the Times Square area. But today things are changing rapidly! There are a number of new and remodeled hotels in this district, the best of which are listed below:

Embassy Suites (47th St and Seventh Ave, 719-1600): The flagship of the chain, atop the old Palace Theatre. The lobby is three levels above the street, the rooms are large, and electronic gadgets abound.

Holiday Inn Crowne Plaze (1605 Broadway, at 49th St, 977-4000): Big, brassy, and cold, with cramped guest rooms. It features a great health club and a David Liederman Grill.

Hotel Macklowe (145 W 44th St, 768-4400): This is a high-tech operation, both in the guest rooms (small) and meeting rooms (great). It is essentially a business hotel—very desirable for a conference. Good food!

Paramount (W 46th St bet Broadway and Eighth Ave, 764-5500): The old Century Paramount has been remodeled, with small rooms and reasonable tabs. The lobby is grander, with a good restaurant and a gourmet takeout operation by Dean and Deluca, one of New York's best caterers.

Parc Fifty One (51st St and Seventh Ave, 765-1900): Originally the Taft, then the Grand Bay, now owned by Hong Kong interests. This is a deluxe hotel, with big bathtubs and comfortable furniture. A free limo to Wall Street is offered.

ALGONQUIN
59 W 44th St (bet Fifth and Sixth Ave)   840-6800
Moderate

The Algonquin is truly a legend in the city. But years of neglect had not been helpful to this grand old lady, and things had become a bit shabby. This home of the famous Round Table, where Dorothy Parker, Harold Ross, Robert Benchley, and others sparred, has been completely refurbished and things now look great! There are only 165 rooms, so the atmosphere is intimate and friendly. The lobby and the lounge, complete with a cabaret, are good places for people watching.

CHELSEA INN
46 W 17th St (bet Fifth and Sixth Ave)   645-8989
Moderate

In the true sense of the word *inn,* the Chelsea is a small, informal European-style operation. Most rooms have kitchenettes. The two attached, refurbished townhouses offer studio rooms, guest rooms (with shared bath at a very modest price), and one- and two-bedroom suites. For those with business in the Flatiron district, this is a handy destination. Check it out with Mindy Goodfriend Chernoff; now isn't that a great name for an innkeeper?

DORAL COURT
130 E 39th St (bet Park and Lexington Ave)
685-1100, 800/624-0607
Moderate

For those with business in the garment district or visiting the United Nations, the Doral Court's location in Murray Hill is excellent. For weekend visitors, free parking is a decided advantage. 24-hour room service, dressing alcoves, and 25-inch color TVs are special amenities. A fitness center is close at hand, and an all-day dining facility—the Courtyard Cafe—is a pleasant spot for relaxation. A young and enthusiastic staff is rightfully proud of the better-than-average-sized rooms and the well-done suites, some with balconies. All suites have walk-in kitchens and stocked pantries.

DORAL PARK AVENUE
70 Park Ave (at 38th St)   687-7050; 800/847-4135
Moderate

Every room at the Doral Park Avenue is equipped with TV and radio, direct-dial telephone, refrigerator, and complimentary cable. The Saturnia Restaurant has earned an outstanding reputation for healthy meals. Nightly turndown service is provided, and exercise bicycles and VCRs are available on request.

DORAL TUSCANY
120 E 39th St   686-1600
Moderate

The Tuscany has a fine reputation for service, with the personal attention only a small hotel can offer. Large rooms, personal exer-cycles, and free overnight shoe-shine service add to the attractiveness of this well-located midtown hotel. The in-house restaurant, Time and Again, provides excellent meals. Kids under 12 stay free in their parents' room. Guests here can enjoy newly renovated rooms at a sensible price in comfortable and safe surroundings.

ESPLANADE
305 West End Ave   874-5000
Moderate

For those wishing to stay on the Upper West Side near Lincoln Center, this completely renovated hotel is ideal. Room rates for single or double occupancy are reasonable, with a small charge for each extra person. The hotel is clean, kitchens include all necessary equipment, all rooms have color cable TV and air conditioning, and on-premises dining is available, as is room service. Suites are also available at prices charged for just one room in many other hotels.

ESSEX HOUSE
160 Central Park S   247-0300
Moderate to expensive

With a great new look in a great old location, the new Essex House is open after a two-year renovation program. The lobby and public areas have been restored to their original art deco grandeur. Three restaurants (French, Japanese, and a cafe) offer outstanding dining.

The number of rooms has been cut down to allow for more space in the newly decorated units, which feature classic French and English Chippendale themes. All rooms offer marble bathrooms, two-line telephones, remote-control television, and individual climate control. A new fitness center offers a full array of services, including exercise equipment, massage, herbal wraps, and personal training.

GRAND HYATT
42nd St (at Grand Central Terminal)
883-1234, 800/233-1234
Moderate to expensive

You can't do better than the Grand Hyatt if you are staying in midtown. Close to everything, this hotel provides safe, comfortable accommodations for good value, with large rooms renting for a price comparable to much smaller accommodations elsewhere. The lobby, complete with a waterfall, is a popular meeting place. Several excellent restaurants provide informal and formal dining. The Sunday brunch is one of the best in the city, and Trumpet's, the hotel's showpiece, is a superb place to dine in truly grand style. Excellent management insures personal attention. The hotel's Regency Club rooms are top of the line, with a host of amenities like complimentary continental breakfasts, terrycloth robes and wall-mounted hair dryers. Special rooms are provided for handicapped guests.

HELMSLEY PALACE
455 Madison Ave (at 51st St)   888-7000
Expensive

You've probably heard of the Helmsley Palace Hotel, located close to Saks Fifth Avenue, one block off of Fifth Avenue itself. It's enchanting in the evening! The public rooms are exceptionally attractive, encompassing the 100-year-old Villard Mansion, one of New York's legendary landmarks. The Villard House used to be the chancery office of the archdiocese of New York. There are no convention facilities here, although there are meeting rooms available. The Helmsley Palace has several hundred apartments and suites, and even some triplex apartments. Leona isn't quite so visible these days!

LOWELL
28 E 63rd St   838-1400
Moderate to expensive

This small, classy, well-located hotel features 48 suites plus 13 deluxe rooms. There are 24-hour multilingual concierge service, at least two phones per room, VCRs and outlets for personal computers and FAX machines, marble bathrooms, complimentary shoeshine service, and all the rest that goes with a top operation. Thirty-three suites have wood-burning fireplaces, ten have private terraces, and one has a separate gym room with treadmill, stationary bicycle, weights, Nautilus system, and compact-disc stereo with built-in speaker system. (Oh yes, the latter also has *seven* telephones!)

MANHATTAN EAST SUITES HOTELS

Beekman Tower Hotel
3 Mitchell Pl (at 49th and
    First Ave)
355-7300

Shelburne Murray Hill
303 Lexington Ave
    (at 37th and 38th St)
689-5200

Eastgate Tower
222 E 39th St
687-8000

Southgate Tower
371 Seventh Ave (at 31st St)
563-1800

Lyden Gardens
215 E 64th St
355-1230

Surrey Hotel
20 E 76th St
288-3700

Lyden House
320 E 53rd St
888-6070

Dumont Plaza
150 E 34th St
481-7600

Plaza Fifty
155 E 50th St
751-5710

Moderate

These all-suite hotels are among the nicest, most reasonably priced, and conveniently located in New York. Each hotel features 24-hour attendants, and there are modern kitchens in every apartment. Suites of one, two, and three bedrooms are available at very attractive daily, weekly, or monthly rates. There are nearly 2,000 suites in all. These are particularly convenient accommodations for long-term corporate visitors and traveling families. Families can economize by putting the kids on the pull-out couches and by using the fully equipped kitchens. Women like these accommodations when they must travel and dine alone. A great buy!

THE MARK

Madison Ave (at E 77th St)   744-4300
Moderately expensive

Here's a winner! An older residency building (the Hyde Park, built in 1926) has been converted into one of the most charming hotels in New York. There are 125 guest rooms, 26 junior suites, and 34 one- and two-bedroom suites, decorated in exquisite taste. Every room has cable TV, FAX capability, and two-line phones, and most have pantries. The suites (which I strongly recommend) have separate vanities and marble baths. Some even have libraries, wet bars, and terraces with views of Central Park. The location is excellent, the personnel are extremely nice, and a very attractive dining area just off the lobby serves all meals, plus tea and brunch. If you really want to be pampered, ask for a suite with heating lamps and heated towel racks; everyone gets Frette linens, down pillows, umbrellas, and Crabtree and Evelyn soaps!

MARRIOTT MARQUIS
1535 Broadway   398-1900
Moderate to moderately expensive

The opening of this magnificent showplace in the center of Times Square in the summer of 1985 represented a major step in the rejuvenation of the area. Along with over 1,800 rooms, huge meeting and convention facilities, and the largest hotel atrium in the world, guests can enjoy a 700-seat, three-story revolving restaurant and lounge at the top of the 50-story hotel, a revolving lounge overlooking Broadway on the eighth floor, a legitimate Broadway theater on the premises, a fully equipped health club, suites with walk-in wet bars and refrigerators, oversized rooms, and a sky lounge. There are nine restaurants and lounges in all. A concierge level offers special amenities, including 24-hour room service. All rooms overlook Manhattan on the exterior and open directly to the atrium on the interior. One word describes this hotel: spectacular.

MAYFLOWER
15 Central Park W (at 61st St)   265-0060
Moderate

If you are coming to New York for cultural events at Lincoln Center or Carnegie Hall, this is an ideal place to stay. Overlooking Central Park, with most rooms and suites recently redecorated, this is a comfortable and safe hotel. There are a number of two- and three-bedroom suites, several terraced penthouses, all with refrigerators and video message features. Room service is available from seven a.m. until midnight.

MILFORD PLAZA
270 W 45th St (bet Seventh and Eighth Ave)
869-3600, 800/221-2690
Moderate

Value is the key word here. The Milford Plaza, a Best Western operation located at the edge of the theater district in midtown Manhattan, offers extraordinarily reasonable rates that are partially offset by its location. But the hotel has extremely tight security, which lessens the need to be concerned. Rooms are small yet clean, late-night dining is available, and very attractive rates are available on weekends and for groups. The Milford was recently refurbished with all new bathrooms and attractive wall coverings in guest rooms.

MORGANS
237 Madison Ave (at 37th St)   686-0300, 800/334-3408
Moderate

If a downtown location and a "boutique" atmosphere are what you're looking for, this is it. Formerly the Executive Hotel, Morgans was completely redone by a French designer, and the result is calm, comfort, and convenience. Twenty-four-hour room service is available, and room rates include breakfast. There is a stereo cassette system in all rooms.

PARC FIFTY-ONE
Equitable Center, 152 W 51st St   765-1900
Expensive

Another upscale resting place for those on an expense account. If you don't want to worry about unpacking wrinkled clothes, or packing up the dirty laundry later on, there is a personalized valet service. The lobby radiates big bucks with imported marble, Oriental carpets, and fine artwork. Beautifully appointed executive board rooms are available for meetings, and marble bathrooms and multi-line telephones are available in the guest rooms and 52 suites.

PENINSULA
700 Fifth Ave (at 55th St)   247-2220
Expensive

In Hong Kong, the name Peninsula is synonymous with quality. Now this respected hotel group has established a flagship on Fifth Avenue in New York. The recently remodeled rooms are done in art nouveau style and feature king-sized marble bathrooms. The hotel has several excellent eating places, and the lounge serves afternoon tea and goodies. But the big plus here is the tri-level, glass-enclosed fitness center, offering a superb view and swimming pool (a rarity in Manhattan). For physical fitness buffs, this is a best bet.

PIERRE
2 E 61st St (at Fifth Ave)   838-8000
Expensive

As a Four Seasons operation, you expect top quality, and that is exactly what you get. The Pierre is quiet, modest, luxurious, and expensive. There are a number of beautiful suites, excellent meeting and banquet facilities, and a three-to-one ratio of staff to guests. A number of the rooms and suites are part of a residential co-op building. Even if you don't stay here, a meal in the elegant Cafe Pierre or tea in the Rotunda is a special experience.

PLAZA
Fifth Ave and Central Park   759-3000
Expensive

In every city there is a perfect location; in New York it is the corner of Central Park and Fifth Avenue, home of the Plaza Hotel. Besides the prime setting, this grande dame of Manhattan exudes the physical charm and grace that has made it the center of activity in the city for decades. It is now a historic landmark, recently polished and shined by the Trumps to the tune of over $100 million. The guest rooms and suites (many with fireplaces), the public spaces, the restaurants, and the shops all have a new look of convenience and comfort, along with a slight tinge of nostalgia for how it used to be. The result is a gorgeous matron with a world-class facelift. Magnificent floral arrangements adorn the lobby, newly gilded ceilings shine in lobbies and rooms, fabulous chandeliers glitter in the famous Palm Court, super polite bellmen (some of whom have been there for a quarter of a century) guide you to your comfortable digs, where thirsty, king-sized towels await in marble bathrooms. Special linens with the Plaza crest enhance the beds. If you really feel like celebrating, ask for an English suite. There are horse-drawn carriages at the front door, and Eloise, the Plaza's most famous inhabitant, still stares down from her lobby painting. Young chef Kerry Simon has brought class back to the Edwardian Room, and Sunday brunch in the Palm Court is the best in New York. Top-notch managing director Dick Wilhelm has assembled a staff that brings credit to one of the must-see places in the Big Apple. A number of the rooms will be operated as condo units.

RIHGA ROYAL HOTEL
151 W 54th St (bet Sixth and Seventh Ave)
307-5000
Moderately expensive to expensive

This is the newest and tallest all-suite hotel in New York, featuring over 500 suites, 24-hour suite dining, late supper, full business center, fitness facility with sauna, and valet services. The concierge is one of New York's pleasantest and most talented. Halcyon, the hotel dining room, is a superb place for a classy meal. Foreign travelers will appreciate the fact that the staff speaks over 25 different languages. There are a number of meeting and banquet rooms, as well as six "royal" suites that are truly special (and expensive).

ROYALTON
44 W 44th St   869-4400
Moderate to moderately expensive

Run by the same people as Morgans, the Royalton is a historic hotel that's been reborn into a high-tech facility. It's sure to appeal to some modern travelers. A French designer has created stark rooms, furnished with low beds, VCRs, and finished with mahogany accents. Many of the rooms have working fireplaces, and the bathrooms are king-sized and very attractive. China Grill operates a lobby restaurant, and an attractive small bar is available near the hotel entrance. The helpful staff offers 24-hour room service and will gladly change pieces of art in each of the bedrooms.

ST. REGIS
Fifth Ave at 55th St   767-0525
Expensive

After a three-year, $100 million restoration, this historic hotel has reopened as the crown jewel of the Sheraton operation. With 307 oversized rooms and 58 suites (including a presidential suite), the hotel provides luxury accommodations with beautiful appointments. Each room has a refrigerator, classy bathroom, and all the fine extras you would expect. A private butler is assigned to each floor. Gourmet French dining is available at Lespinasse, the showpiece restaurant. Old-timers will be pleased that the St. Regis Roof, the only hotel-roof ballroom in the city, is once again in full swing. With a superb location and a grand history, the St. Regis exudes class once more.

SALISBURY
123 E 57th St   246-1300
Moderate

The Salisbury is clean and intimate, with just over 300 rooms. Most of them have been newly redecorated, and many are outfitted with butler's pantries and refrigerators. Suites are large, comfortable, and reasonably priced. This is a favorite place for lady travelers. If you want to be in the vicinity of Carnegie Hall and other midtown attractions, this hotel is for you. For those who wait until the last minute for reservations, this is a good place to call, as the Salisbury is not very well-known among out-of-towners and rooms are usually available. There is a cafe just off the lobby, and rooms are available for meetings and banquets.

SHERATON CENTRE
(to be renamed SHERATON NEW YORK in 1992)
811 Seventh Ave (at 52nd St)   581-1000
Moderate to moderately expensive

A great location, a nationwide referral service, and a wide selection of restaurants and lounges (with entertainment) add up to a very convenient and pleasant place to stay. The Sheraton Towers—the more expensive top floors—offer exclusive digs for the business or pleasure traveler. Amenities include terrycloth robes and butler service. A complete renovation of all rooms and public facilities is taking place, and by mid-1992 the hotel, to be renamed Sheraton New York, will be in place! The Centre also has a wide selection of package deals, and the price is right.

STANHOPE
995 Fifth Ave (at 81st St)   288-5800
Moderate to moderately expensive

If you are touring museums, the Stanhope is ideal. Quiet, refined, and classy describe this 141-room hotel (92 of them spacious and attractive suites). There are three excellent restaurants, an outside garden for tea and snacks, and a wonderful park view from many rooms. Manager Peter Shaindlin is always on the job, giving guests thoughtful, personal service. VCRs and FAX machines are available upon request. Rates are very attractive, considering the quality of the accommodations offered.

UNITED NATIONS PLAZA
1 United Nations Plaza (bet First and Second Ave,
   at 44th St)   355-3400
Moderate to expensive

This is a very fashionable facility in the United Nations area, a gathering spot for the international set. The hotel is very modern, but done in good taste. It has a health club and a restaurant, and it features nicely appointed rooms and international-style service. The suites are particularly attractive. The 288 rooms and suites offer spectacular views, since they begin on the 28th floor.

VISTA INTERNATIONAL
3 World Trade Center   938-9100
Moderate to expensive

If business or other needs bring you to the lower end of Manhattan, I'd suggest you try the Vista International, located right in the World Trade Center. As a matter of fact, you can go directly from the hotel into the shopping and office complex. This was the first major new hotel in Lower Manhattan in nearly 150 years, and it has a lot going for it: first-class restaurants, parking in an underground garage, and a club on the 20th and 21st floors with special accommodations, including a concierge. There's also a well-equipped fitness center and rooftop swimming pool. The fitness center includes racquetball courts, a jogging track, sauna and steam bath, plus a fully equipped exercise facility. The hotel is operated by Hilton International, which does a consistently good job. Excellent weekend rates.

WALDORF-ASTORIA

301 Park Ave (at 50th St)   355-3000
Moderately expensive

For many years the Waldorf stood as the class symbol in Manhattan. Then, sadly, over a period of years the place rested on its laurels. Now Hilton has put in more than $180 million to restore their flagship—and the work shows! The lobby, with magnificent mahogany wall panels and hand-woven carpets, is rich and impressive. In response to complaints about the size of some of the guest rooms, renovations were made, creating larger spaces by reducing the number of rooms. All-marble bathrooms and butler pantries were installed in some suites. An event at the Waldorf is sure to be something special, as their banquet service and facilities are top-cabin. Special low-price packages are usually available.

WALDORF TOWERS

100 E 50th St   355-3100
Expensive

Peter Wirth presides over a palace in the middle of Manhattan: the Waldorf Towers. Guests of the Towers have their own entrance, elevators, concierge, and all the other services you would expect from a first-rate operation. All rooms and suites, ranging from very comfortable to deluxe, are above the 28th floor, with commanding views. I can remember visiting former president Herbert Hoover in his suite here; this hotel within a hotel provides the privacy and quiet many public figures desire. All the amenities of the Waldorf-Astoria are just an elevator ride away.

HOTEL WALES

1295 Madison Ave (bet 92nd and 93rd St)
876-6000
Moderate

The Wales is a small, European "boutique" hotel that has recently been restored to its original condition. It was built in 1901 as the Chastaigneray, and it is now family-owned and -operated, unusual in this day of major chains. There is a free continental breakfast, the uptown Madison Avenue address is good for shoppers (and safe), and the Roof Garden overlooking the Central Park reservoir is attractive. Busby's (a bistro) and Sarabeth's Kitchen (an excellent restaurant) are both located on the ground floor.

WESTBURY

69th St and Madison Ave   535-2000
Moderate to expensive

Completely modernized from stem to stern, with closet safes and exceptionally tasteful décor in all rooms and suites, the Westbury is particularly suitable for the woman traveling alone or the business-man who wants quiet and comfort rather than big-city excitement. There is 24-hour room service, the outstanding Polo Restaurant on the ground floor, and refurbished bathrooms. The top-of-the-line suites are some of the nicest in the city; they are of a manageable size, done in superb taste with every comfort, yet not ostentatious.

WYNDHAM
42 W 58th St (at Fifth Ave)   753-3500
Moderate

This charming hotel is more like a large home where the owners rent out rooms. Many of the guests are folks who regularly make the Wyndham their Manhattan headquarters. The advantages are many: great location, uniquely decorated rooms and suites, complete privacy, individual attention, and no business conventions. On the other hand, the hotel is always busy, and reservations for the new-comer could be difficult. No room service is available; however, there is a small restaurant, and the suites have refrigerators. John Mados has created a winner!

Alternative Housing

. . . AAAH! BED & BREAKFAST #1
246-4000 or 800/776-4001
FAX: 212/265-4346

The principal market this outfit serves is the small business person who is more interested in the comforts of home than a fancy address. They also have a following among tourists who like to have a host clue them in about what to do and what not to do in the big city. Williams Salisbury, the manager, was a butler for many years and knows the hospitality business. A minimum stay of five nights is required for discounted rates. Hosted or unhosted apartments are available. It is desirable to contact the firm two to four weeks in advance of your stay.

ABODE BED & BREAKFAST
P.O. Box 20022
New York, NY 10028   472-2000
Mon-Fri: 9-5; Sat: 10-2

Have your heart set on staying in a delightful old brownstone apartment? Or how about a contemporary luxury apartment in the heart of Manhattan? Abode selects their hosts with great care, and all homes are personally inspected to ensure the highest standards of cleanliness, attractiveness, and hospitality. Shelli Leifer, the director, can provide clients with a maid, conference or meeting space, and whatever else is necessary for a perfect stay. Hosted accommodations with complimentary breakfast begin at $50 for singles, $70 for doubles; unhosted accommodations (minimum stay of two nights) start as low as $80 per night.

CITY LIGHTS BED AND BREAKFAST
P.O. Box 20355   Cherokee Station
New York, NY 10028   737-7049
Mon-Fri: 9-5; Sat: 9-12

City Lights lists over 400 apartments and bed-and-breakfast rooms in Manhattan and the outer boroughs. All hosts are screened, and rooms and apartments are inspected and approved by the staff. Prices depend on the length of stay, location, and elegance of the accommodation. Complimentary continental breakfasts are included with all hosted apartments. Be sure to specify the area of the city you are interested in, and chances are you will be able to save about 50 percent over commercial hotel rates. When you call, ask for Yedida Nielsen.

INTERNATIONAL HOUSE
500 Riverside Dr   316-8434
Moderate

To qualify to use these facilities, you have to pay a yearly membership fee and be a full-time graduate-level student, researcher, trainee, or intern over 21 years of age. There are all sorts of special features: a low-budget cafeteria, a clothing bank, a dark room, a TV room, a pub with dancing, public rooms, and even a gymnasium. Note the uptown address.

LEO HOUSE
332 W 23rd St
929-1010, FAX: 366-6801 (reservations)
Inexpensive

This is the answer to one of the major questions people ask about New York: Where can a visitor find a really inexpensive, safe, and clean place to stay in the city? You should have no qualms about the Leo House. This residence is a Catholic hospice; a secure, refined, quiet place still run by Sisters of St. Agnes. Reservations are required and must be made as much as a year in advance. All guests are expected to follow very reasonable house rules. A small nonrefundable deposit is required, and the maximum length of stay is two weeks. No smoking is allowed in guest and meeting rooms, and although the outside doors are locked at midnight, registered guests may still get in after that hour. Breakfast, featuring homemade bread, is available at a moderate price. A great place for the single student!

NEW YORK INTERNATIONAL AMERICAN YOUTH HOSTEL
891 Amsterdam Ave (at W 103rd St)   932-2300

Don't let the name mislead you; this facility is available to visitors of all ages. The hostel provides over 450 beds in a newly renovated, century-old landmark. They offer meeting spaces, catering, tours, self-service kitchens, and laundry facilities to individuals as well as large groups. Best of all, the price is right!

NEW WORLD BED AND BREAKFAST
150 Fifth Ave (Suite 711)
675-5600, 800/443-3800

New World specializes in serving both vacationers and business travelers. They offer accommodations in over 120 Manhattan locations, and the staff gives extra-special personalized service. Guest rooms in New York apartments begin as low as $40 a night.

92ND ST Y (DE HIRSCH RESIDENCE)
1395 Lexington Ave   415-5650
Inexpensive

This facility offers convenient, inexpensive, and secure housing for men and women between the ages of 18 and 26. There are special discounts for Y health-club memberships, and both single and double rooms are available. Lengths of stay range from several days to several months. Admission is by application, and it is nontransient.

SHORT TERM HOUSING
849 Lexington Ave (at E 64th St)   570-2288
Mon-Fri: 10-6; Sun: 1-5
Summer: Mon-Fri: 10-8; Sat, Sun: noon-5

Recently I read about Short Term Housing as an alternative to finding or buying an apartment. Since then, I've heard it mentioned dozens of times as the solution to all sorts of problems, such as marital separation, roommate problems, and extended visits of relatives or business executives. This agency serves as the go-between for those looking for an apartment and those who will not be using one for an extended length of time. Most of the clients are from North America, Europe, or the Orient, and all are individually matched to their needs. Terms are usually between one month and one year, and almost always involve sublets. One interesting wrinkle is that the fee is paid by the tenant taking occupancy, which means that Short Term works for the renter, not the owner, as most agents do. Even if that were not the case, the fact that these people offer apartments on reasonable Manhattan terms earns them an entry in my book.

URBAN VENTURES
P.O. Box 426
New York, NY 10024   594-5650
Mon-Fri: 9-5; Sat: 9-3

Mary McAulay founded this service in 1979, modeled after Britain's famous bed-and-breakfast rooms, because she felt something needed to be done about Manhattan's lack of reasonably priced lodging. After being carefully screened, 650 hosts, who live either in apartments, townhouses, brownstones, or lofts, signed up with Urban Ventures. Hosts range from older people living in big apartments to young artists; both groups need a little help with the rent, and they are friendly and interested in their guests. The spare bedrooms are found on the Upper West Side, in the Village, in midtown, on the East Side, in SoHo and TriBeCa, and even in Brooklyn. Security is good—after all, this is someone's home— and the B&B's, as they are known, are concentrated in areas heavily populated by sons and daughters trying their wings in Manhattan. Hence, these rooms are convenient for visiting parents, since their child's apartment is rarely big enough to accommodate a visitor. Some apartments are even available from two nights to two months or more without hosts. The price is right, and this is a first-rate chance to get a sense of what it's really like to live in Manhattan.

Interior Decorators

DESIGNER PREVIEWS
777-2966

Having problems finding the right decorator? Here is a great solution. Designer Previews has information on over 100 of Manhattan's most trustworthy and talented designers, and they will present information about them to you by way of slides and photographs. They will also discuss the designers' fees. Karen Fisher, the genius behind this handy service, was the decorating editor at *Cosmopolitan* and the style editor at *Esquire*. She charges $100 for her services.

NEW YORK CHAPTER OF THE AMERICAN SOCIETY OF INTERIOR DESIGNERS
685-3480
Mon-Fri: 9-3

This is not a decorating service; it's the self-monitoring professional agency to which most ethical (and qualified) interior designers belong. After an interview—during which you must specify your needs, taste, and budget—ASID will recommend up to three members who would be suitable and available for the job. They are not snobbish and treat a $200 job just as seriously as a $5,000 one.

Even if you don't go this route, be sure the decorator you *do* choose is ASID-affiliated.

PARSONS SCHOOL OF DESIGN
66 Fifth Ave (at 13th St)   741-8940
Mon-Fri: 9-5

Parsons, a division of the New School for Social Research, is one of the two top schools in the city for interior design. Folks who call will get their request posted on the school's board, and every effort is made to try and match client and prospective decorator. Individual negotiations determine price and length of the job, but it is incredibly cheaper than what a not-so-recent student charges. The disadvantage is that most of these students don't have a decorator card. (One can always be borrowed.) A good place if you just want a consultation.

Jewelry Services

B. HARRIS AND SONS
25 E 61st St (at Madison Ave)   755-6455
Mon-Sat: 10-5
Closed Sat in summer and last two weeks of Aug

William J. Harris' family started B. Harris and Sons in 1898, and since then generations of customers have relied upon the family to repair their jewelry. The competence and courtesy displayed here hail from another era, and the classic jewelry available for sale and the ancient heirlooms awaiting repair show that this is a shop of the old school. The jewelry counter is limited to antique and fine contemporary jewelry. East Side godparents have made visits there before a christening almost *de rigueur,* and the selection in baby and young children's jewelry reflects this unusual interest. Others use B. Harris as a prime source for repairs of all jewelry and timepieces. Harris is particularly proud of the restorations they do on watches and clocks, be they antique or modern.

GEM APPRAISERS LABORATORY
608 Fifth Ave   333-3122
Mon-Fri: 8:30-5; closed first two weeks of July

Leopold Woolf, who owns Gem Appraisers Laboratory, is a graduate gemologist. He is also an officer and director of the Appraisers Association of America. As such, he is entrusted with the appraisals for major insurance companies, auction houses, banks, and the New York City Department of Consumer Affairs. In an area where it can't hurt to be too careful, this is a very safe bet. In addition to doing appraisals and consultations for estate, bank, insurance, and tax purposes, Woolf also runs Gem Appraisers Laboratory Designs, which manufactures and designs jewelry. A better man would be hard to find.

GOLDFIELD'S
229 E 53rd St (bet Second and Third Ave)
753-3750
Mon-Fri: 9:30-5:45

Gino and Giuseppe personally ensure that all repairs on antique watches and clocks, jewelry, lighters, and shavers are done expertly. It isn't easy to find a place that will repair old pens, but Goldfield's specializes in this service.

RISSIN'S JEWELRY CLINIC
4 W 47th St (at Fifth Ave)   575-1098
Mon, Tues, Thurs: 9:30-5 (closed first two weeks of July)

This is indeed a clinic! The assortment of services is staggering: jewelry repair and design, antique repair, museum restorations, broken eyeglasses fixed, pearl stringing, appraisals. Joe Rissin and his wife, Toby, now run the place; Joe's father was a master engraver, so the family tradition has been passed along for decades. *Honesty* is the byword here, and customers can rest assured merchandise will be returned in excellent condition. Estimates are gladly given, and all work is guaranteed.

SALON METRO
17 E 45th St   983-3636
By appointment only

You've heard of short-term housing and clothing operations. Well, now you can add an outlet for "leasing" top-quality jewelry. Salon Metro is a new concept where you can work out a lease-option plan for spectacular pearls, diamonds, rings, necklaces, and bracelets for one-to-three year terms. They will even let you exchange your original purchase up to two months later for another item of equal value. This is not costume jewelry; this is the real thing. Hmmm, wonder if Nancy Reagan heard about this place?

ZDK COMPANY
48 W 48th St (Room 1409)   575-1262
By appointment only

Most of his work has been the creation of rare and original pieces for neighbors in the diamond district, but in his free time Zohrab David Krikorian will do the work he does wholesale for professionals for you, too. In addition to making jewelry, ZDK will mend and fix broken jewelry, as only a professional craftsman and artist can. He makes complicated repairs look easy and has yet to encounter a job he can't handle. If he can't exactly match the stones in an antique earring, he'll redo the whole piece so it looks even better than before. He loves creating the latest designs with traditional materials, and his prices are quite reasonable.

Leather Repair

ARTBAG CREATIONS
735 Madison Ave (at 64th St) 744-2720
Mon-Fri: 9-5:45; Sat: 9-4; closed Sat in summer

Artbag will make, sell, or repair any type of handbag, and they will do it well. The range goes from mounting needlepoint bags to re-lining heirloom bridal bags, as well as leather, reptile (including some of the best lizard skins in the city), and beaded evening bags. Messrs. Moore and Price are European craftsmen who modestly advertise themselves as "understanding, genteel, and good listeners. They know their business." Any of their customers could have said the same thing. Artbag is also known for its sense of style. They carry the latest and best designs, and they frequently refashion old hand-bags into chic trendsetters. It isn't every day that you come across men who know more about handbags than most women do, but these gentlemen certainly know and keep up with the latest styles.

CARNEGIE LUGGAGE
1388 Sixth Ave (bet 57th and 58th St) 586-8210
Mon-Fri: 8:30-5:45; Sat: 9-5

Carnegie is handy to most major midtown and Central Park hotels. Service can be fast, if you let them know you're in a hurry.

JOHN R. GERARDO
30 W 31st St (bet Broadway and Fifth Ave)
695-6955
Mon-Fri: 9-5; Sat: 10-2:30; closed Sat in July, Aug

Dan Gerardo manages to dispense luggage and luggage repairs at John R. Gerardo that rival Crouch and Fitzgerald's (minus the glamour). Gerardo carries all the standard brands in almost all kinds of luggage. There are sample cases, overnighters, two-suiters, and drawers with seemingly endless spare parts. There are zippers, han-dles, locks, and patches of fiber and material for emergency patch-ing. Gerardo does quick, professional repairs. They also have a pickup and delivery service for a nominal fee.

SUPERIOR REPAIR CENTER
133 Lexington Ave 889-7211
Mon-Fri: 9-6; Thurs: 9-8; Sat: 10-3; closed Sat in summer

Leather repair is the highlight of the service at Superior. Many ma-jor stores in the city use them for luggage and handbag work. They are experts in the repair or replacement of zippers on leather items. They will work on sporting equipment and fix tents and backpacks. If there is a leather problem, Superior has the answer.

Locksmiths

AAA LOCKSMITHS
44 W 46th St (at Sixth Ave)   840-3939
Mon-Fri: 8:30-5:30

You can learn a lot from trying to find a locksmith in New York. For one thing, it's the profession that probably has the most full-page ads in the Manhattan Yellow Pages. For another, this particular "AAA" is *not* the place to call about a dead battery. However, in an industry that has little company loyalty or recommendations, AAA Locksmiths has been in the business for over a half-century, and that says a lot right there.

NIGHT AND DAY LOCKSMITH
1335 Lexington Ave (at 89th St)   722-1017
Mon-Sat: 9-6:30 (24 hours for emergencies)

To be safe—just in case you're ever locked out—Night and Day is a number you should be carrying close to your heart. New Yorkers, even those who are in residence for a short time, become experts on locks and cylinders. Cocktail-party conversation is frequently peppered with references to dead bolts, Medeco, and Segal. If you haven't the vaguest idea what all the talk is about, you obviously don't live in the city, where a locksmith is about as professional an expert as there can be. He's got to be ahead of the cocktail-circuit fads, as well as the local burglar's latest expertise, and able to offer fast, on-the-spot service for a variety of devices (no apartment has *one* lock) designed to keep people out. Mena Sofat, Night and Day's owner, fulfills these rigid requirements. The company answers its phone 24 hours a day; posted hours are for the sale of locks, window gates, and keys. If you buy a lock here, you can be sure they'll be willing to help you out (or *in,* as the case may be) when the time comes.

Marble Works

NEW YORK MARBLE WORKS
1399 Park Ave (at 104th St)   534-2242
Mon-Fri: 8-4:30; closed July 1-10

Same location, same family since 1900. That's quite a record! Three generations of Louis Gleicher's family have run this business, and it's no surprise to learn that they know the marble business cold (sorry for the pun!). Gleicher will create and custom-design marble pieces and furniture for bathrooms, fireplaces, tables, and mantels. They also repair broken marble, do repolishing, plus craft consoles, pedestals, and tabletops. All of this can be done using the largest selection of floor and wall marble, granite, onyx, and slate tiles in the country. A full line of marble-care supplies is available. They will ship anywhere in the world.

PUCCIO EUROPEAN MARBLE AND ONYX
232 E 59th St (showroom on 6th floor)
661 Driggs Ave, Brooklyn (factory warehouse showroom)
688-1351

Puccio's factory and warehouse are in Brooklyn, but they qualify for a listing since they do have a showroom in Manhattan, which is open only by appointment. Paul Puccio runs both as a showcase for his sculpture and furniture designs, which range from traditional to sleekly modern. It is almost incongruous to see an angular, free-flowing sculpture made of formal marble, when Roman busts on pedestals are what comes to mind. But John Puccio boasts that his tables are found in décors that are strictly modern and very chic. "We strive for plain but luxurious," he says. He succeeds, and the results are startling as well as elegant. There are lamps, chairs, pedestals, tables, desks, sinks, and frames. They also custom-install baths, fireplaces, fountains, and staircases. A project takes from 6 to 16 weeks for delivery, since it is custom-manufactured, but a commission is not even accepted (even though there is a ready-made line) if it is not received through a decorator or designer. Puccio is just not equipped to deal with retail orders, but a visit to the factory will enable you to see the line for yourself.

Massage

JUDY MARKOVA
737-0247

The top concierges in town call Judy Markova for professional, reliable massage service. She has been a licensed operator for over 15 years, specializing in Swedish massage.

LEWIS HARRISON
40 W 72nd St   724-8782

Lewis Harrison has been an instructor at the respected Swedish Massage Institute in New York, and he is recognized as an expert in the field. He has written several books on massage and is absolutely reliable. He works on both men and women, does shiatsu and sports massage, and will take appointments at his place of business, plus home and hotel calls.

Matchmaking

FIELD'S EXCLUSIVE SERVICE
41 E 42nd St   391-2233

"New York lives by this book!" That's a pretty big challenge for one book. But I can't let anyone down, so this edition even includes a hint on matchmaking. Dan Field's company has been playing Dan Cupid for three quarters of a century. If Dan is successful for you, how about a testimonial for *Where to Find It, Buy It, Eat It in New York*—the Romance Edition, of course!

Medical Services

DOCTORS ON CALL
718-238-2100

This service answers a real need in the city. In the past, hotels always had staff doctors on call. Medical and dental associations would arrange for doctors to cover the city during off hours, and, of course, hospital emergency rooms are open 24 hours a day. But private doctors have stopped making house calls, even to regular patients. Doctors on Call was created to take care of that problem. Though most calls are to people who don't have regular city doctors —patients are usually visitors—many calls are made on residents. The fee in Manhattan is $70-95 (accurate at publication date), which covers the cost of parking and transportation, and most calls are completed within two hours of your phone call. All members of Doctors on Call are licensed, and further tests or treatments can be arranged, if necessary.

PORTNOW SURGICAL SUPPLIES
53 Delancey St (at Eldridge St)   226-1311
Sun-Fri: 9:30-6

For any kind of medical, surgical, or home nursing supplies, Portnow should be a first choice. The equipment is modern and vast in selection, and prices are discounted. In fact, for the money, there probably isn't a better source in the city for surgical supplies, convalescent aids, wheelchairs, canes, crutches, walkers, trusses, belts, supporters, and surgical stockings. Portnow's own brand of therapeutic pantyhose comes in every size. The array of blood-pressure machines, osteoscopes, blood-sugar testers, and respiratory aids would make a hypochondriac happy. The healthy come for Portnow's exercise machines and bikes, as well as the best maternity pantyhose around. Most of all, these people know their stuff, just as you'd expect from a business established in 1898. Their immediate concern is the immediate relief of pain. Portnow aims to handle any medical situation with the best, most economical treatment.

QUALITY CARE
25 W 43rd St   563-2100
Mon-Thurs: 9-6; Fri: 8-8

Quality Care is a nationwide organization dedicated to providing temporary health-care personnel on all levels. It was created to meet the changing needs of medical care: formerly, the sick were treated at home, but today they are sent to institutions, and that isn't always what patients want. So, there is a need for professionals who will work at a patient's home. Quality Care supplies registered and licensed practical nurses, home health aides, homemakers, companions (there's a term you don't see often outside nineteenth-century novels), physical occupation and speech therapists, and just about every other kind of home-care specialist imaginable. These professionals will adapt their program to special needs, such as kosher cooking and small rooming accommodations, as well as providing health screening tests and guidance to clients. They also do IV therapy. Here's hoping you won't need them, but it's nice to know that Quality Care is there and that a national organization is behind it.

UNION SQUARE DRUGS
859 Broadway (bet 17th and 18th St)   242-2725
Mon-Fri: 7:30-6; Sat: 9-3.

This store consistently offers the best prices on prescription drugs, industrial first-aid supplies, and vitamins, and is equally well-known for its reliability. The service is so conscientious that the pharmacist will call—long-distance if necessary—to verify prescriptions. (And you know how most salespeople react to the very *thought* of making a long-distance call.) Union Square will fill union prescriptions and honor other medical plans.

UPJOHN HEALTH CARE SERVICES
1 Penn Plaza (Suite 1926)   465-8400
24 hours

Upjohn is a nationwide service that provides fully screened, bonded, supervised, and trained home health aides. The type of person sent and the subsequent bill depend upon the level of care needed, but they are capable of supplying registered nurses, licensed practical nurses, home health aides, and companions. They will supply complete home-nursing service as well as hospital support.

Metal Work

AMEROM
54 W 22nd St (bet Fifth and Sixth Ave)   675-4828
Mon-Fri: 7:30-5

Florin Carmocanu is a Romanian artisan whose metal workshop mainly focused on welding and cutting metal to size. Not terribly exciting or demanding of Carmocanu's considerable talent. But then word of his handiwork got out to loft dwellers, co-op remodelers, and interior decorators, and suddenly Amerom is one of the hottest places in town. And no wonder. Carmocanu is a genius with decorative metal, structural steel, and wrought-iron furniture and gates. His spiral staircases are awesome. Amerom can even replace original artwork and wrought-iron designs of old brownstones. As for the name, which doesn't exactly come tripping off the tongue, could it be a combination of the words *American* and *Romanian*?

RETINNING AND COPPER REPAIR
525 W 26th St (at Tenth Ave)   244-4896
Mon-Fri: 9-6

Only in New York would a 75-year-old Italian retinning business be headed by a female woodworker in her thirties. Her name is Mary Ann Miles, and hers may be the only business of its kind in the city. The original business was founded on the same spot in 1916. When the second owner went bankrupt, Miles, who owned the woodworking business next door, bought it. Changing chisel for vat was not as easy as she supposed, but employees who had toiled through the two prior owners taught the current owner the business, and *voilà*, Miles became a retinning and copper expert. And an expert she is. In addition to retinning (which is basically what copper repair amounts to), Miles restores brass and copper antiques, designs and creates new copperware (almost all copper pots in use today are heirlooms), and sells restored copper pieces.

Movers

IKE BANKS
718-527-7505

Ike Banks probably breaks every rule for inclusion in this book. He's not bonded or licensed, nor is he a resident of Manhattan (he lives in Queens), but he never breaks anything, and I trust him more than anyone else listed here. He was first recommended to me by an appliance store, when a delicate and temperamental washing machine needed to be delivered. Since then, he has moved pianos, households, and dining rooms for friends. Several years ago, estimates for moving a nine-piece dining room ran from $100 to $300. Banks did it perfectly for $25. He will travel anywhere in the city, sometimes further, and will work odd hours (unless he's taking his nephew to a ballgame). He's a super guy. The only complaint I have is that he's so careful that he can be very slow. It's a good thing he doesn't charge by the hour. Ike also has a used wood furniture store.

MOISHE'S MOVING AND STORAGE
1627 Second Ave (at 84th St)   439-9191

Moishe learned the business from the bottom up, packing boxes and handling them personally to make sure the customers were satisfied. He learned well and quickly, and soon parlayed his experiences into organizing one of the largest and most successful moving and storage companies in the area. He now has dozens of bright red trucks, and several hundred bright, red-clad employees. Moishe Mana, a Tel Aviv University Law School dropout, is still only in his thirties, but he can claim he did it the hard way—from nothing to a business that now grosses millions. Document storage in modern facilities is just one feature of the storage side of his operation. Boxes and packing materials in all sizes are available for purchase.

MOVING STORE
644 Amsterdam Ave (bet 91st and 92nd St)
874-3800
Mon-Fri: 8-6; Sat: 9-3

Steve Fiore started West Side Movers in the kitchen of his studio apartment more than 20 years ago. Business was so good that he soon moved into a storefront. He was happy there until he realized the magnitude of requests he was getting from people who wanted to rent and buy dollies, and, most particularly, boxes of all sizes. A man who knows a good business opportunity when he sees one, Fiore moved into a brownstone storefront on Amsterdam Avenue to sell nothing but moving aids and paraphernalia. The main stock-in-trade is still boxes. They come in more sizes than seem possible, including three different sizes just for mirrors. He now rents and sells dollies, in addition to selling moving pads. And since all of the items are built to the specifications of professional movers, they are *very* durable.

WEST SIDE MOVERS
644 Amsterdam Ave (bet 91st and 92nd St)
874-3800
Mon-Fri: 8-6; Sat: 9-3

We came to West Side Movers via their Moving Store. But such ecumenical and diverse groups as the Union Theological Seminary and Tiffany & Company came to West Side Movers by recommendation and have added their accolades to the file. A company with a subdivision that specializes in helping people move themselves has to be top-notch. West Side Movers pays particular attention to efficiency, promptness, care, and courtesy. Customer after customer has called their staff the most courteous they've dealt with—and they don't dent the furniture, either!

Newspaper Delivery

LENOX HILL NEWSPAPER DELIVERY

502 E 74th St   879-1822

Lenox Hill Newspaper Delivery is an excellent door-to-door service. For a slight charge, they will deliver the New York papers, the *Christian Science Monitor,* the *Washington Post, Women's Wear Daily,* or the *Sunday Observer* to your door. All of these, Lenox Hill claims, can be delivered "earlier than subscriptions reach your mailbox." For many people, that's worth the service charge.

Office Services

AMAL PRINTING AND PUBLISHING

630 Fifth Ave (at 51st St, International Building,
    concourse level)   247-3270
Mon-Fri: 9-5:30 (evenings and weekends by appointment)

Run out of business cards on the day you have an appointment for a big deal? Well, don't worry, you can get them done in a day (for a bit extra) at Amal. They do all kinds of printing, from flyers to business forms to invitations, and if the order is large enough, they'll work on weekends. Overnight and while-you-wait service is available, as well as pickup and delivery. This is a good spot to remember for just about any kind of printing need.

SEEFORD ORGANIZATION

75 Varick St (bet Canal and Watts St)   431-4000
Mon-Fri: 8:30-5

Not too many outfits can say they have dealt with one customer since the day they opened . . . over 43 years ago! Seeford does quality general commercial printing, and advertising specialties of all kinds. They handle printing jobs from concept and design right through to printing, binding, and delivery. The boss, Sam Goldstein, is on the job himself, and the quality of the work and service shows that personal concern. Besides, he is one of the nicest individuals in New York to deal with!

"WE TYPE IT!"

60 W 39th St (at Sixth Ave)   354-6890
Mon-Fri: 8:30-7; Sat: 10-4

Trust the folks at "We Type It" to be in touch with the typing needs of New Yorkers. For years, they ran a center where people could rent typewriters on a daily basis. But when more and more clients began offering to pay them to do the typing for them, in came professionals who could type anything from a letter in Yiddish at three in the morning (that's their line, not mine!) to a lengthy manuscript. "We Type It" boasts the ability to do any job in record time, at record prices, in a record number of languages. When one checks out the competition, that seems to be true. "We Type It" is especially geared to the needs of travelers and businessmen who may be far from a home office and in need of a fast, efficient typist. They also offer video rentals and state-of-the-art word processing. These folks know how to strike the right keys!

WORLD-WIDE BUSINESS CENTRES
605-0200, 800/847-4276
Mon-Fri: 9-5:30; Sat, Sun: by request

Alan Bain, a transplanted English lawyer, has created a highly profitable business that caters to executives who need more than a hotel room when in New York on business. The business grew out of Bain's own frustrations in trying to put together a makeshift office, write and get out reports, answer telephones, and still attend to the matters that brought him to the city in the first place. Services by on-premises word processors and typists are available. Desk space, private offices, and conference rooms may be rented on a daily, weekly, monthly, or quarterly basis. The daily rate includes telephone answering, receptionists, and a private office. The company also operates a full-service travel agency that specializes in corporate travel and travel management service to small and medium-sized companies.

Party Services

BALOOMS
147 Sullivan St   673-4007
Mon-Fri: 10-6; Sat: 12-6; Sun: available for parties

Balooms differs from most balloon services in that customers are not only invited but requested to visit the office. That is because the Balooms office is a legitimate, albeit small, store that encourages browsing and spur-of-the-moment sales. While there are still skeptics who feel *no one* impulsively buys a balloon, Balooms' sales prove otherwise. In addition to the standard balloon bouquet, they offer party decorating and custom-designed bouquets with names, logos, and even portraits on each balloon. Balooms will deliver in Manhattan and the boroughs, but they will ship anywhere. The store also has helium rental. As befits this lighthearted business, owners Marlyne Berger and Raymond Baglietto are delightful.

EASTERN ONION/LOONEY BALLOONS
901 Sixth Ave (Room A10)   268-3900

Eastern Onion is in the New York messenger business in a new incarnation. Owner Stan Wilcox offers almost everything except the conventional telegram. Indeed, singing telegrams are as conventional as they get, but even they get pretty far-out when the singer is a professional dressed as a gorilla, Fairy Onion, or Mr. Macho. There are also belly-grams and, of course, Looney Balloons. The latter is a bouquet of 24 multicolored balloons and one mylar balloon, delivered by a suitably dressed messenger.

LINDA KAYE'S BIRTHDAYBAKERS, PARTYMAKERS
195 E 76th St (bet Lexington and Third Ave)
288-7112
Parties seven days a week

Linda Kaye got started in this business shortly after she hired a baker for her daughter's birthday party and it turned out to be a big success. Linda soon realized that there was a big market for well-organized kids' parties. Linda's successful concept is based on showcasing artist bakers who will teach partygoers how to bake a cake as part of the entertainment. Linda's staff takes care of everything; there is even a "party room" outfitted with a fireplace, kitchen, and sound system. They will do "grown-up" parties, too. There is a great catalog for birthdays from age one to one hundred plus, with specific ideas, gifts, and creative services for that special someone's birthday. A "party in a box" kit with themed paper party items is available by mail-order.

NEW YORK PARTIES
22 E 13th St   777-3565
Daily: 10-6

When you are thinking big, Jean-Michel Savoca's New York Parties is a great name to remember. These folks take charge of everything, including food, liquor, equipment rentals, tents, flowers, lighting, music, and trained personnel. When people like Frank Sinatra, Paine Webber, and Chase Manhattan use a service, you know it has to be first-rate. They can offer prime locations such as grand ballrooms or spacious yachts, if that is what you have in mind.

PROPS FOR TODAY
121 W 19th St (bet Sixth and Seventh Ave)
206-0330
Mon-Fri: 9-5

This is the handiest place in town when you are preparing for a party. Props for Today has the largest rental inventory of home decorations in New York. Whether you want everyday china and silver or unique antiques going back as far as 100 years, they have the goods in stock. There are platters and vases and tablecloths, and everything in between. There is a Christmas section, children's items, books, fireplace equipment, artwork, garden furniture, foreign items, and ordinary kitchenware. Over a million items are available—that should give you an idea of the selection. Phone orders are taken, but it is a good idea to call for an appointment and see for yourself. Ask for Dyann Klein, the proprietor.

Pen and Lighter Repair

AUTHORIZED REPAIR SERVICE
30 W 57th St   586-0947
Mon-Fri: 9-5

If a business' specialty is the repair of fountain pens and cigarette lighters in this day of disposable ball point pens and no-smoking campaigns, you might not think it would be a viable concern. But you would be wrong. Morton Winston first started the business over two decades ago, and it is still incredibly busy—perhaps because it is almost without competition. Those who use fountain pens are devoted customers. Authorized Repair sells and services nearly every brand, and the shop can refill lighters as well as all kinds of pens. (This means ball point and cartridges, as well as fountain pens.) Authorized also sells, repairs, and services electric shavers. Tourists can even pick up 220-volt appliances or adapter plugs, and the extremely polite and helpful staff is well versed in the fine points of each brand.

FOUNTAIN PEN HOSPITAL
10 Warren St (across from City Hall)   964-0580
Mon-Fri: 8-6

This establishment is one of the few places in town that repairs fountain pens. The Fountain Pen Hospital sells and repairs pens of all types—and other writing implements as well. They are probably the most experienced shop around.

Personal Services

CATHERINE VAN ORMER
238 Madison Ave   532-4446

Image-wardrobe-fashion consultant Catherine Van Ormer not only associates with diplomats, socialites, executives, and show-business personalities, but she dresses them. In fact, she was named the fashion consultant to WCBS-TV's news reporters when she owned a boutique. As more people began demanding her fashion-shopping expertise, she closed the store and went into personal shopping full time. She is quite simply the best in the business. Most of her clients have neither the time nor talent to put together a top-notch wardrobe, and they benefit from her close association with the city's top clothing designers. She scouts the lines and then shows the best to the client. Clothes can be purchased at Catherine's wholesale cost, which is roughly 50 percent less than retail, and the fashions reflect her eye for couture lines and natural fibers. Her fee is a mere pittance for those who simply must have this service. (There *are* those who simply can't keep all those cocktail parties straight.) Van Ormer offers a similar service for custom-made bridal gowns and accessories. The gowns are magnificent, and the prices do not reflect the superb quality of the work. Her one-hour consultation fee is included in the price of a wedding gown. A full range of bridal planning is also available.

EMILY CHO
14 E 90th St   289-7807
By appointment

Emily Cho is a "clothing psychologist." Have you ever met one of those before? Not too many people have. In any case, the process here begins with an in-depth interview at your home or hotel, where your wardrobe is reviewed. Emily will organize and update your wardrobe and then escort you on a shopping tour. With experience at Bloomingdale's, the Ford Model Agency, and *Seventeen* magazine, Emily is well prepared to help you with that "new look" you have always wanted. Corporate services and an intensive two-day course in personal image consulting are also available.

FASHION UPDATE
718/377-8873
Daily: 9-5

Sara Gardner is a mother of three, and naturally she wants to make sure she gets the best value out of every dollar she spends. She found she could get apparel for her family at wholesale prices from some manufacturers, so she decided to share her discovery with others. Thus she started *Fashion Update,* a quarterly publication that uncovers bargains in women's, men's, and children's designer clothing and accessories available in the garment district. She conducts special shopping expeditions to designer showrooms and maintains a fashion-update hotline (718/253-0251).

GLENN BRISTOW
218 W 10th St (at Bleecker St)
243-0571, FAX: 212/243-0675
Hours: by appointment

Financial consultant Glenn claims she can "demystify the process of managing money and paperwork." (Good luck!) Her clients include homemakers, dentists, designers, restaurant operators and horticulturists. She has had 20 years of experience in business administration, is computer literate, and comes highly recommended (although I have not personally used her services).

THE INTREPID NEW YORKER
1230 Park Ave (bet 95th and 96th St)   534-5071
Daily: 24 hours

Kathy Braddock, founder and owner of this service, is indeed "the Intrepid New Yorker." She was born, bred, and educated in the Big Apple. Like your author, she delights in trying to help folks unravel the hassles and confusion of this great city. She provides one of the most complete personal-service businesses in the area and is available at any time. Kathy can take you on private guided tours, shopping expeditions, help you find a place to live, and take care of your decorating or refurbishing needs. She also offers a membership that will give clients a number of referrals and 10 percent off regular hourly rates when her services are needed. This is handy for those who need quick and complete information or help but choose to do the work themselves. Of course, you could first look in *Where to . . .,* but calling Kathy would be the second-best alternative.

IT'S EASY
10 Rockefeller Center   586-8880
Mon-Fri: 9-5:30

Some time ago, David Alwadish found himself trying to remain cool amid an angry crowd of people at the passport office in Rockefeller Center. When someone in line told him that they would pay anything to get off that line, Alwadish took him literally, and a new business was born. Over the next decade, Alwadish did so well as a stand-in and gofer that he went national and branched out into doing research for attorneys and businesses, auto leasing, and even motor-vehicle inspection. His company will help with passports and visas. Indeed, if there is any occupation or line or work where someone else can wait in line for a client, then It's Easy will do it. Incidentally, they haven't lost the personal touch, even though the company is now owned by Alwadish's sister, Leslie Shapiro. She guarantees that no one will wait on line for reservations at It's Easy!

LA CONCIERGE
322 E 86th St (bet First and Second Ave)
737-5289
Daily: 7:30 a.m.-midnight

Handy folks to have on call! They will do cleanup work after renovation or construction, or come to a home, store, or office to put things back in shape after a party or big sale. In addition, Jessica Crosby will take care of shopping or catering needs and provide almost any kind of service personnel.

LET MILLIE DO IT!
532-8775
Daily: 10 a.m. to whenever!

Millie Emory has been in business for over a decade saving folks time, stress, and money. She especially likes to work with creative people—artists, authors, actors, conductors and those in ballet—although she will help anyone with a broad variety of tasks. She will do organizing work in home or office, make household inventories for insurance purposes, supervise remodeling jobs while you take it easy in Florida, bid at auctions so you can remain anonymous, entertain out-of-town guests, help handle financial affairs (you'll have to provide the cash), do your Christmas shopping, and even take care of all the many details when tragedy or loss of a loved one strikes your family. Millie charges by the hour and has a world of experience being an all-purpose gofer.

MANHATTAN PASSPORT
236 E 47th (bet Second and Third Ave)
832-9010
Mon-Fri: 9-5

Ina Lee Selden, a former teacher, is the brains behind Manhattan Passport—a concierge service dedicated to arranging everything for the New York visitor. They go way beyond what a travel agent will do, booking everything from breakfast in bed to a night on the town —all tailored to the individual's needs. They will arrange for guided tours or leave the client with a customized do-it-yourself itinerary. A very handy touch is their destination management service: for large or small groups, they will make sure that a group's baggage makes it safely from the airport to the hotel, and they will select places for special events. If you have ever tried to arrange group activities (especially from out-of-town), you will appreciate how helpful these folks can be.

PASSPORT PLUS
677 Fifth Ave (5th floor)
759-5540; 800/367-1818
Daily: 9:30-5:30

Larry Marsiello was another person struck by inspiration while waiting in that infamous line at the passport office at Rockefeller Center. His passport-fetching was one of the first such services, and though he has expanded nationwide, he has remained a purist concentrating on the procurement of travel documents. With the expansion, Passport Plus now offers a very personalized and complete document service. They will take care of visas, birth, death and marriage certificates, international licenses, passport photos (while you wait), and airline ticket pickups, among other things. If you've ever waited months for an errant passport or crucial certificate, you'll understand how valuable Passport Plus is. Imagine not ever having to deal with a passport office again!

SAVED BY THE BELL CORP
11 Riverside Dr   874-5457
Mon-Fri: 9-7 (or by appointment)

Susan Bell (get it?) is the genius behind this organization. Her goal is to take the worry out of planning virtually any type of job for people who are too busy or too disorganized to do it themselves. Bell says "doing the impossible is our specialty," and you can believe her. They can supervise corporate relocations and vacation trips—from making reservations right down to stocking the refrigerator or putting a great guidebook on the coffee table! They also do weddings, party planning, tag sales, shopping, delivery arrangements, and service referrals.

STRICTLY SPEAKING
445 E 80th St (at York Ave)   628-7359
Hours adjustable, depending on client

Do you get sweaty palms thinking of talking in front of people? You aren't alone! Strictly Speaking works on an individual basis (no seminars) at the convenience of the client. Services include speech writing and coaching for business executives, professional people, or anyone who wants to gain confidence talking to others. If a crisis situation arises, where you must make an unanticipated appearance, these folks will provide emergency service. Charles Nordlander is the man to call.

Photographic Services

A.A. IDENTIFICATION SERVICE
698 Third Ave (bet 43rd and 44th St)   682-5045
Mon-Fri: 8-6

A.A.'s main virtue is their ability to do passport and identification photos competently and quickly. This is no small matter, as some photo shops near passport offices can be very unreliable. A.A. has a good reputation for laminating, doing one-day business portraits, and providing one-hour photo lab services.

DAN DEMETRIAD
200 W 57th St (at Seventh Ave, Suite 200)
245-1720
Mon-Fri: 10-6:30

Dan and Iris Demetriad are European-trained artisans with offices adjacent to Carnegie Hall, but the fine tuning they do is to photographs and prints rather than to musical instruments! Because they were trained as commercial photographers, they are well skilled in their restoration work. Prices are reasonable, considering the difficulty of the work.

FRED MARCUS PHOTOGRAPHY
245 W 72nd St (bet Broadway and West End Ave)
873-5588
Mon, Wed, Fri: 9-5; Tues, Thurs: 9-8 (by appointment)

Half a century in the photography business has made this firm a favorite for weddings, parties, or any kind of business event. Children's portraits are a specialty, and Marcus offers videotaping services in a most professional manner.

GALOWITZ
511 Sixth Ave (at 13th St)   242-8115
Mon-Fri: 8:15-5:30; Sat: 10-4

In a city that has two button shops, two seashell shops, and a dozen pet groomers, you would think that there would be a number of photographic restoration establishments. No, sir. This very exacting art is a rare bird, and I am happy to recommend Galowitz as a fine practitioner whose specialty is making old photos look presentable and worth more than sentimental value. One of the specialties here is large blowups that can be used for parties or business events. Galowitz is a quality, full-service photo lab.

NEW YORK FILM WORKS
928 Broadway (at 21st St)   475-5700
Mon-Fri: 8 a.m.-9 p.m.; Sat: 9-5

Imagine a copy of a slide or print in color in six minutes! This outfit can even produce a color photograph from actual objects in six minutes. Besides this incredibly rapid service, they have a full line of photofinishing, and their prices are extremely competitive. By the way, they are the only lab in the city that processes Kodachrome.

PHOTOGRAPHICS UNLIMITED/ DIAL-A-DARKROOM
17 W 17th St (bet Fifth and Sixth Ave, 4th floor)
255-9678
Mon-Fri: 9 a.m.-11 p.m.; Sat: 10-7; Sun: noon-7

Here's another only-in-New York idea. Photographics Unlimited offers photographers of limited physical means a full range of photographic darkroom equipment and a place to work on a rental basis. The shop has everything from the simplest equipment to an 8x10 Saltzman enlarger including all manner of printing paper and film supplies, as well as a lab for on-the-spot developing of black-and-white and color. Ed Lee claims his center is a complete one for the amateur or most advanced professional photographer, and he aims to prove it. Darkrooms can be rented, and they come with advice and suggestions from the darkroom's owner. It would be hard to describe all of the resources here. Whatever could be desired in a personally owned darkroom can be rented. A technical hot line is available to answer questions.

PROFESSIONAL CAMERA REPAIR SERVICE
37 W 47th St (bet Fifth and Sixth Ave)   382-0511
Mon-Fri: 8:30-5

Rush jobs are the specialty here, so there's no need to spoil your vacation because your camera is on the blink. Professionals will work on still cameras from 35mm up. They will also do modifications and adaptations for special camera equipment.

STAT STORE
148 Fifth Ave (bet 19th and 20th St)   929-0566
Mon-Fri: 9-6:30; Sat: 10-4

In medical parlance, stat means "fast." In photo jargon, stat is short for photostat, and it has come to mean virtually any copy. The Stat Store specializes in both meanings of the word: rapid copying and photo duplication, and it offers Xerox copying, Kodaliths, color stats, cibaprints, custom transfers, photo posters, and photo murals as well as photostats. A new electronic publishing division offers high-resolution computer output and design services. They also assist clients in design, illustration, technical support, and production management of special projects.

Plant Consultation

COUNCIL ON THE ENVIRONMENT OF NEW YORK CITY
51 Chambers St (Room 228)   566-0990
Mon-Fri: 9-5

A little-known fact is that the city will loan tools free of charge to groups involved in community sponsored open-space greening projects. Loans are limited to one week, but the waiting period is not long, and for the "price," the wait is worth it. You can borrow the same tools several times a season, as long as there is no one ahead of you on the list. A group can be as few as four people. The council will also design and install paper-recycling programs for commercial businesses. They will do tree labeling for a fee, and they have a number of interesting *free* publications.

Plumbers

KAPNAG HEATING AND PLUMBING
326 E 91st St   289-8847

As an out-of-towner, I'm not often in need of a local plumber, so there's a story behind how I learned that Kapnag is a really first-rate operation. A while ago, I was visiting a friend who was having a plumbing problem. She called Kapnag, but got no response. When she called a second time, Kapnag apologized profusely and came out immediately to fix it. There was even a follow-up call to make sure the problem had been completely corrected. Ask any New Yorker, and you'll learn what a rare virtue this story illustrates. Brett Neuhauser, Kapnag's president, has got to be the reason for all this kindness. When we first published this story, Neuhauser wrote to tell us that the sudden surge in sales was due to his mother "supplying the Northeast region." May they both continue to thrive!

Postal Services

MAIL BOXES ETC USA
629-6200 (information on nearest facility)

Mail Boxes Etc has over 24 locations in New York, and they can provide convenient FAX and telex service in all time zones. They also represent all major carriers and will do professional packaging and shipping. Handy services (not all of them available at every location) include stamps and envelopes, mail forwarding, packing supplies, business cards, office stationery, notary and secretarial services, passport photos, laminating, key duplication, and computer letters. In other words, who really needs a secretary?

Reweaving

FRENCH-AMERICAN REWEAVING COMPANY
37 W 57th St (at Fifth Ave, Room 409)   753-1672
Mon-Fri: 10-6; Sat: 11-2

For more than 60 years, this company has been repairing and mending knit, lace, linen, silk, and wool fabrics with an almost invisible mending process that makes the new threads indiscernible from the originals. Even when an item is badly—and seemingly irreparably—damaged, the people at French-American claim that if they can't weave the wound, they can at least repair it so that their work is the next best thing to invisible. Needless to say, one doesn't submit a $3 tie to these costly procedures. But if an item is worth saving, it's almost a sure thing that these people can pull it off. They do a good job on suede and leather repairs, also.

Rug Cleaning

A. BESHAR AND COMPANY
611 Broadway (Cable Building)
529-7300 (gallery), 292-3301 (rug cleaning)
Mon-Fri: 9-5

Lee Howard Beshar's family has run this carpet and Oriental rug business for three generations. Consequently, there is little he doesn't know or hasn't seen in the carpet business. He can handle any kind of request competently. His expertise and experience are the basis of the Besharizing Cleaning Process, which all floor coverings submitted for correction receive. Naturally, if a rug needs only cleaning, you're ahead of the game. Beshar does not make house calls; all carpets must be cleaned at the company's warehouse. This can be expensive, so if your carpet isn't very valuable, you might be better off buying a new one. Here, too, Beshar can come to the rescue with a large range of Oriental and antique rugs. All are of good quality and value, and Beshar stands behind—and sometimes *on*—them all.

Scissors and Knife Sharpening

HENRY WESTPFAL AND COMPANY
105 W 30th St   563-5990
Mon-Fri: 9-6

A Japanese gentleman once brought in his prized Samurai sword for repair at Henry Westpfal's, so you know this place has to be expert at what it does. And they should be. They've been in business since 1874, and the same family has been in charge all that time. They do all kinds of sharpening and repair, from barber scissors and pruning shears to cuticle scissors, plus all kinds of work on light tools. And for you left-handers, they also sell those hard-to-find left-handed scissors.

Sewing Machine Repair

MILTON KESSLER
718/763-7897

More elusive than a needle in a haystack is an honest repairman, particularly one who makes house calls. Milton Kessler is one who is polite, thorough, and completely reliable. He is never home when you call, but he does get messages and can usually schedule an appointment within a week. In addition, he has a wealth of information on the care and maintenance of sewing machines, and he'll tell you how yours got into the shape that necessitated his visit. On top of his honesty, promptness, and reliability, Kessler's rates are dirt cheap. He's also one of New York's nicest people.

Shoe Repair

B. NELSON SHOE CORPORATION
1285 Sixth Ave (Paine Webber Building,
     concourse level)

Main Concourse, RCA Building
630 Fifth Ave (International Building)   869-3552
Mon-Fri: 7:30-5:15

While researching this book, I asked several luggage dealers if they knew of a good shoe repair store. I have worn out dozens of pairs of shoes while walking the city, and all of our shoe repair listings have been places that I've personally used. So, I was beginning to fear that there might be an even better spot that I had missed simply because my shoes happened to be intact when I walked by it. And I figured, who better to ask than luggage dealers? Still, I was surprised when three in a row recommended B. Nelson. I was so impressed that I dropped my planned itinerary and headed for B. Nelson. Armed only with "Rockefeller Center" as an address, I eventually found it by asking dozens of people for a good shoe repair store. I was told over and over again that B. Nelson was it. When I finally got there, Nick Valenti, the owner, was out. But there on the wall of the shop was a laudatory review of his establishment, from the fourth edition of this book! I was glad that Valenti wasn't there to see my embarrassment. It turns out that the branch stores go under the name General Shoe Repair. But under any name, at any address, this is a first choice.

JIM'S SHOE REPAIR
50 E 59th St (bet Madison and Park Ave)   355-8259
Mon-Fri: 8-5:45; Sat: 9-3:45; closed Sat in summer

This operation offers first-rate shoe repair, shoeshine, and shoe supplies. Shoe repair is a field that is rapidly losing its craftsmen, and Jim is one of the few who upholds the tradition. Jim's owner is Joseph A. Rocco, who specializes in orthopedic work and boot alteration. But people still call him Jim.

MANHATTAN SHOE REPAIR
6 E 39th St   42 E 41 St
                  683-4210
                Mon-Fri: 7:30-5:45

Manhattan Shoe Repair offers a large range of orthopedic and fashion repairs. In addition to resoling and heel repairs, Manhattan does rebinding, redyeing, and bag repair. Their motto is "Work that lasts," and 45 years in the business would seem to bear that out.

Silver Repair

BRANDT & OPIS
46 W 46 St (5th floor)   302-0294
Mon-Thurs: 8-6; Fri: 8-2

If it has anything to do with silver, Roland Markowitz can fix it. This includes silver repair, silver polishing, buying and selling estate silver, repair of silver-plated items, and fixing silver tea and coffee services. Gold plating, lamp restoration, and plating of antique bath and door hardware is a specialty. In short, Brandt & Opis are specialists in metal restoration.

THOME SILVERSMITHS
49 W 37th St (bet Fifth and Sixth Ave, Room 605)
764-5426
Mon-Fri: 8:30-5:30

Thome cleans, repairs, and replates silver, in addition to buying and selling some magnificent pieces. They have a real appreciation for the material, and it shows in everything they do. They will repair and polish brass and copper, and they also do restorations of antique silver and objects of art, silver and gold plating, pewter repair and cleaning, restoring the velvet backs of picture frames and velvet box linings, lacquering, and refining. Incidentally, *don't* attempt pewter repair yourself. Pewter is an alloy and must be handled delicately. Thome also specializes in brass. This company is one of the very few still in that business.

Stained-Glass Restoration

VIC ROTHMAN
914/965-1196

For stained-glass restoration and new fabrication, call Vic Rothman, a man with 18 years of experience. He worked on St. Paul's Chapel at Columbia University and helped restore the magnificent Lalique glass windows at the new Henri Bendel store.

Tailors

CLAUDIA BRUCE
140 E 28th St (bet Lexington and Third Ave)
685-2810
By appointment

You just can't part with that beautiful—but outdated—dress you got ten years ago on your honeymoon in Paris? You don't want to send that special gown you wore to your daughter's wedding to your dry cleaner's tailor to get a new look? Don't worry. Just call Claudia Bruce, a very talented lady who has been taking care of such problems with finesse for over a decade. Not only will Claudia take care of repairs and the rejuvenation of garments, she also will do made-to-order clothing. There are home-fitting appointments—for an extra charge, of course—and wardrobe consultations are available.

MARSAN TAILORS
897 Broadway (at 20th St, 2nd floor)   475-2727
Mon-Fri: 9:30-5:30; Sat: 9:30-5

Before Saint Laurie, one of the biggest emporiums of men's clothing in Manhattan, established its own tailor shop, all its alterations were done by Marsan. Any tailor who survives in the middle of the men's wholesale garment area must be good, and Marsan is among the best. All work is done by hand.

SEBASTIAN TAILORS
767 Lexington Ave (at 60th St, Room 404)
688-1244
Mon-Fri: 8:30-5:30; Sat 9-4:30

Tailors are a peculiar breed in New York. In a city that is the home of the garment industry, most garment repairmen build their trade as custom alteration and design specialists or dry cleaners who incidentally mend whatever bedraggled outfit has been brought in for cleaning. Sebastian Tailors is one of the few shops in the city that is exactly what it says it is—a tailor shop. The custom alterations for men and women are quick, neat, and, wonder of wonders, reasonable. Sebastian also does reweaving. Best of all, everything is accomplished without the normal ballyhoo most such New York establishments seem to regard as their due. Incidentally, Sebastian was recommended to me by another tailor. Praise from someone within the trade is the highest praise of all. And when the service includes the less common skill of ladies' tailoring, it marks a place worth trying. I use him and think he's great.

Television Rental

TELEVISION RENTAL COMPANY
13 E 31st St (2nd floor)   683-2850
Mon-Fri: 9-5

Ted Pappas runs a rental service that is fast, good, and efficient. He will rent televisions for long- or short-term periods, and will happily deliver the sets and pick them up. He also rents VCRs, camcorders, and other audiovisual aids. The prices are among the best in the city, and in a business like this, his solid reputation is a formidable recommendation in itself.

Tickets for Events

You must be prepared for hassle and confusion when you try to get tickets for events in New York. I have tried to get the latest facts, but things change very quickly. And besides, the folks in this business are among the rudest in New York. Remember that it is possible to get tickets at the last minute for most shows and performances. You just need to know how to go about doing it and must be prepared to pay a premium in some cases.

Broadway Shows: You must first decide which show (or shows) you would like to see. Naturally, getting tickets for the hits will be more difficult and costlier. To find out what is playing, consult the theater section of the *New York Times* or the theater pages of *New York Magazine* or the *New Yorker*. For information regarding theater, dance, and concert tickets, call *New York Magazine* at 880-0755 (Mon-Fri: 10:30-4:30). You may also get information from **NYC/On Stage**, a project of the Theater Development Fund. At the touch of a telephone button, at any hour of the day or night, you can get information on ticket availability, cost, seat location, how to get the tickets, similar plays in production, and information on the subject of the show and its stars (call 212/768-1818).

To secure tickets in advance, you have several choices. You may go directly to the theater's box office. If the show is a hit, be prepared to stand on line. You may order by phone; different outfits sell tickets for various shows. (The newspaper ads or the telephone information service will tell you which one sells tickets for the show you want.) **Tele-Charge**, a service of the Shubert organization, sells tickets for the Shubert shows and for several other theaters. They give good phone service and may be reached at 239-6200 (in Manhattan) or 800/233-3123 (outside the city). Remember that all phone agencies add a service charge. You may use most major credit cards, and tickets will be mailed if there is adequate time. Otherwise, they may be picked up at the box office. Be sure to carry your credit card if you are picking up tickets at the box office.

Tickets for most attractions (theater and other) are usually available from several responsible outfits, even for same-day shows. You have the advantage of large inventories; price is a disadvantage, as they charge a very hefty service fee. Two of the largest and most reliable in the business are **Continental Guest Services** (840-2800) and **Manhattan Entertainment** (582-3600 or 382-0633). Other possibilities include checking with ticket offices scattered throughout the theater area or in major hotels, or taking a chance on finding someone outside the theater of your choice who wants to get rid of their tickets (for a price, of course).

For off-price tickets for Broadway shows, the best place to go is **TKTS**. It was started as a way to fill empty seats in Broadway houses. Empty seats are lost revenue, and a half-empty house is bad for the morale of the actors, as well as that of the audience. TKTS (Broadway and 47th St, 354-5800), is open Mon-Sat: 3-8 (evening tickets); Wed, Sat: 10-2 (matinee tickets); Sun: noon to closing (matinee and evening tickets). The **Lower Manhattan Theater Center** (2 World Trade Center, mezzanine floor) is open Mon-Fri: 11-5:30; Sat: 11-1 p.m. Go early in the day for the best seats, and keep in mind that half-price tickets may not be available for the show of your choice. Note also that only tickets for that day's performances are offered.

Off Broadway and Off-Off Broadway: The best bet here is to go to the theater box office or call the theater directly. For information on some off-Broadway and off-off Broadway shows, call **Ticket Central** (daily: 1-8, 279-4200).

Music and Dance Events: Again, the newspaper and magazine listings will help you find out what is available. The **Bryant Park Music and Dance Booth** (42nd St bet Fifth and Sixth Ave) sells full-price tickets for these events, and on the day of performance only sells half-price tickets (Tues, Thurs, Fri: 12-2, 3-7; Wed, Sat: 11-2, 3-7; Sun: 12-6; 382-2323). Tickets for these events may also be purchased at the respective theater box offices.

New York Yankees, Nassau Coliseum, Radio City Music Hall, Madison Square Garden, Giant Stadium, Meadowlands, Lincoln Center: Tickets for events at any and all of these venues may, of course, be purchased directly on site. However, **Ticket Master** is a one-stop ticket center for all of them, plus certain smaller arenas and clubs and some theaters. The phone number for tickets is 307-7171, and they are very polite and helpful (for a change!). Their charge-by-phone number for Broadway theaters (**Marquis, Palace, Lunt-Fontanne, Nederlander**) and other performing arts clients is 307-4100. They will mail you tickets if there is time, or you may pick them up at the box office the day of the performance. All major credit cards are accepted. **Ticket Master** locations in Manhattan include 17 E 8th St, 955 Third Ave (at 57th St), 1302 Second Ave (at 69th St), 383 Lafayette St, 120 W 72nd St (at Columbus Ave), 32 Mott St, 40 Union Square E (at 17th St), 1595 Second Ave (at 83rd St), 1977 Broadway (at 67th St), 38 Park Row, 186 W 4th St (at Sixth Ave), and Port Authority Bus Terminal (2nd floor). Hours vary at each location. Tickets for **Radio City Music Hall** (Rockefeller Center, 247-4777) may be obtained at their box office. It is a good idea to call, write, or phone early for special attractions, especially the spectacular Easter and Christmas shows.

Television Shows: Tickets for television shows are not always easy to come by. Popular shows fill months ahead (most are taped), and taping is not always done on a regular schedule. At times, tickets are handed out to passers-by on the corner of Fifth Avenue at 50th Street. If you want to plan ahead, contact the networks as follows:

ABC (36 W 66th St, 456-7777), **CBS** (524 W 57th St, 975-2476), **NBC** (30 Rockefeller Center, Guest Relations, 664-3055). It is also possible to get tickets at the network headquarters on the day of the show. Try to be there by eight a.m. or shortly thereafter, because tickets are handed out on a first-come, first-serve basis.

Special Ideas for Less Expensive Tickets: Hit Shows (630 Ninth Ave, at 44th St, Suite 808) issues discount coupons for shows, but does *not* sell tickets. They offer a club membership; information may be obtained by calling 581-4211. The **School Theater Ticket Program** also offers coupons. They have no location or phone; word-of-mouth will lead you to distribution centers and times. Standing room for sold-out plays is often available on the day of the performance at individual box offices. The Metropolitan Opera Guild has 24 tickets available for each performance at the **Score Desk** (1865 Broadway, at 61st St, 769-7000). Standing-room tickets for the week's performances are sold at the box office beginning at ten a.m. Saturday. The **New York City Ballet**, at the New York State Theater, sells day-of performance, standing-room tickets, starting at ten a.m. (67th St and Broadway, 870-5570). A certain percentage of seats at the **New York Shakespeare Festival**'s Public Theater is sometimes sold at half price two hours before curtain (425 Lafayette St, 598-7150). The **Theater Development Fund**'s voucher plan for those who qualify (1501 Broadway, 221-0013) and the **Lincoln Center Theater** subscription program offer good values. Seats for open rehearsals of the **New York Philharmonic** are sold for peanuts on Thursday mornings. Many times, shows in preview offer tickets at reduced prices.

Star-Tix Vouchers offers sizable discounts for all kinds of shows. They are sold Monday through Friday, eight a.m. to seven p.m., and Saturday, 10:30 a.m. to four p.m., at a booth on the main concourse at Grand Central Terminal (869-7477). The **Star Theater Club**, a membership outfit, gives vouchers and passes for entertainment, dining, and parking (1457 Broadway, penthouse, 869-7477).

Here are the major Broadway theaters:

Ambassador Theatre (219 W 49th St, 239-6200)
Brooks Atkinson Theatre (256 W 47th St, 719-4099)
Ethel Barrymore Theater (243 W2 47th St, 239-200)
Vivian Beaumont Theatre (150 2 65th St, 787-6868)
Martin Beck Theatre (302 W 45th St, 246-6363)
Belasco Theater (111 W 44th St, 239-6200)
Booth Theater (222 W 45th St, 239-6200)
Broadhurst Theater (235 W 44th St, 239-6200)
Broadway Theatre (53rd St and Broadway, 239-6200)
Circle in the Square (1633 Broadway, 239-6200)
Cort Theatre (138 W 48th St, 239-6200)
Criterion Center (1530 Broadway, 764-7070)
Edison Theater (240 W 47th St, 302-2302)
Gershwin Theater (51st St, west of Broadway), 586-6510)

John Golden Theatre (252 W 45th St, 239-6200)
Helen Hayes Theatre (240 W 44th St, 944-9450)
Mark Hellinger Theatre (51st St and Broadway, 757-7064)
Imperial Theatre (249 W 45th St, 239-6200)
Walter Kerr Theatre (219 W 48th St, 582-4022)
Longacre Theatre (220 W 48th St, 239-6200)
Lunt-Fontanne Theatre (205 W 46th St, 575-9200)
Lyceum Theatre (149 W 45th St, 239-6200)
Majestic Theatre (247 W 44th St, 239-6200)
Marquis Theatre (1535 Broadway, 382-0100)
Minskoff Theatre (200 W 45th St, 869-0550)
Music Box Theatre (239 W 45th St, 239-6200)
Nederlander Theatre (208 W 41st St, 921-8000)
Eugene O'Neill Theatre (230 W 49th St, 246-0220)
Palace Theatre (1564 Broadway, 730-8200)
Plymouth Theatre (236 W 45th St, 239-6200)
Richard Rodgers Theatre (226 W 46th St, 221-1211)
Royale Theatre (242 W 45th St, 239-6200)
Shubert Theatre (225 W 44th St, 239-6200)
Neil Simon Theatre (250 W 52nd St, 757-8646)
St. James Theatre (246 W 44th St, 398-0280)
Virginia Theatre (245 W 52nd St, 977-9370)
Winter Garden Theatre (1634 Broadway, 239-6200)

Translations

BERLITZ
257 Park Ave S   777-7878

Berlitz can provide written translations in technical, advertising, legal, and commercial documents, as well as simultaneous oral translations. These people are truly masters who cannot be adequately described in writing.

Typewriter Repair

LINCOLN TYPEWRITERS AND COPY CENTER
111 W 68th St (at Broadway)
787-9397, 769-0606
Mon-Fri: 9-6; Sat: 11-4

When Abdul Majid, Lincoln's owner, branched out on his own, he took with him the skills he had learned at Francis Typewriter (a renowned repair shop in the Village). Lincoln's prices are as low as its basement-level location. They sell, rent, and repair typewriters and sell typewriter supplies. There is pickup and delivery and a tradition of service that even includes free ribbon changing. They now service word processors, calculators, and computers as well.

Uniform and Costume Rental

ALLAN UNIFORM RENTAL SERVICE
152 E 23rd St (bet Lexington and Third Ave, 5th floor)
529-4655
Mon-Fri: 9-5

Because you will probably use a costume only once, it is far less expensive to rent rather than buy. At this establishment you can rent contemporary, period, animal, Santa, or any number of other costumes. They also provide a uniform rental service.

Upholstering

RAY MURRAY INCORPORATED
121 E 24th St (bet Park and Lexington Ave, 2nd floor)
838-3752
Daily: 8:30-5

Here's the good news: Ray Murray Incorporated is a reliable, capable, talented reupholstering company. Now, the bad news: it costs just as much to reupholster your furniture as it does to replace it. Murray's specialty is creating custom-made furniture. Cheap it isn't, but the quality is superb. They can copy any design you want (including heirloom pieces or furniture from museum exhibits), but they specialize in classic, contemporary, and modern furniture. Big, overstuffed sofas are their forte. If you're redecorating and your furniture is generally in good condition, Murray can coordinate all the work, fabric, and patterns. They can make drapery and accessory pieces to match the re-covered furniture, and the total cost will be substantially less than it would be to throw everything out and start from scratch. Joe Sinis, a very talented craftsman, has taken over the Ray Murray business and carries on the tradition of excellence.

Wrapping Service

PACKAGING PLUS SERVICES
176 MacDougal St (at W 8th)   677-4788
Mon-Fri: 10-8; Sat: 10-4 (closed Sat in summer)

If you are tired of trying to get something wrapped and sent, or if you don't like standing in line at the post office, here is your salvation. Packaging Plus has all kinds of wrapping supplies, provides shipping and overnight delivery at discount, and will take care of anything from a thimble to a Taurus! In addition, they offer mailbox rental, FAXing, messenger service, and gift wrapping.

VI. Where to Buy It: New York's Best Stores

Bargains

Every month there are special bargain sales, close-outs, factory specials, and what have you. It is handy to have reference guides that tell you of these events, as many are announced just days ahead of time. Two good sources are **New York Magazine** and the **S&B Report,** published monthly by Elyse Lazar, 112 E 36th St (fourth floor), New York, NY 10016, 679-5400. A sales and bargain hot line for S&B is 1/900-820-SALE.

The Best (and Some Not So Good) Places to Shop in New York: an Exclusive List

(Please note: space limitations preclude detailed listings of some of these stores.)

Things for the Person (Men, Women, Children)

Accessories, discount: Bernard Krieger & Son (316 Grand St)
Albert Nippon apparel, discounted: Lea's (81 Rivington St)
Apparel, women's, discount: Ben Farber (462 Seventh Ave)
Aprons: Apron and Bag Supply Company (47 Second Ave)
Attitude-adjustment needed: Polo-Ralph Lauren (867 Madison Ave)
Attitude, insulting: Gucci (683 Fifth Ave)
Baby gift ensembles: Ovations (World Financial Center)
Baby gift service, mail-order: Life's Little Treasures (516/937-0511)
Bags, antique: Sylvia Pines Uniquities (1102B Lexington Ave)
Bags, leather: Ananias (A&S Plaza, 231 Thompson St, 5th floor)
Bags, overpriced: Coach Store (710 Madison Ave)
Belts, ladies': Accessorie Club (10 E 36th St)

Boots: Red Bird (464 W Broadway)

Boots, Western: Lord John Bootery (428 Third Ave)

Boots and shoes, men's handmade: E. Vogel Boots and Shoes (19 Howard St)

Bridal gowns and accessories, expensive: Vera Wang Bridal House (991 Madison Ave)

Briefcases: Jobson's (666 Lexington Ave)

Brushes: Smalley & William (806 Lexington Ave)

Buttons: Tender Buttons (143 E 62nd St)

Cartoon clothing, jewelry and accessories: Mouse 'n' Around (A&S Plaza, Sixth Ave and 33rd St)

Clothing, antique: Antique Boutique (712-714 Broadway) and Alice Underground (380 Columbus Ave)

Clothing, children's: Wicker Garden's Children (1327 Madison Ave) and Glad Rags (1007 Madison Ave)

Clothing, children's discounted: Cici Bebe (39 W 32nd St) and Jack's Bargain Store (2 W 14th St)

Clothing, children's French: Jacadi (1281 Madison Ave)

Clothing, classic men's and women's: Peter Elliot (1383 Third Ave)

Clothing, custom-made men's clothing, shirts, and ties: Ascot Chang (7 W 57th St)

Clothing, evening: Lucille Chayt (214 W 39th St)

Clothing, imported designer: India Cottage Emporium (1150 Broadway)

Clothing, infant, elegant: La Layette Et. Plus (170 E 61st St)

Clothing, Italian men's: Manitalia (24 W 55th St)

Clothing, men's, good value: Saint Laurie (897 Broadway), Gorsart (9 Murray St), and Oliver Grant (222 Columbus Ave)

Clothing, men's, department store: Saks Fifth Avenue (611 Fifth Ave)

Clothing, men's brand-name discount: L.S. Men's Clothing (19 W 44th St)

Clothing, men's custom-made: Alan Flusser (16 E 52nd St)

Clothing, men's resale: Exchange Unlimited (563 Second Ave, at 31st St)

Clothing, men's, ridiculous prices: Bijan (699 Fifth Ave)

Clothing, small-sized women's: Piaffe (841 Madison Ave)

Clothing, tall-gal: Shelly's Tall Girl Shop (13 E 41st St)

Clothing, unusual: The Gallery of Wearable Art (480 W Broadway)

Clothing, vintage: Gene London (897 Broadway)

Clothing, women's (be careful of prices): S&W (165 W 26th St)

Clothing, women's designer sportswear, discounted: PRG (307 Seventh Ave)

Clothing, women's discounted: Simply Samples (150 W 36th St, 3rd floor)

Clothing, women's good prices: Miriam Rigler (14 W 55th St)

Clothing, women's trendy: Betsey Johnson (248 Columbus Ave, 251 E 60th St)

Clothing, women's ultrasuede, discounted: Irving Katz (209 W 38th St)

Coats, lambskin: Spanish Shearling Center (345 Seventh Ave, bet 29th and 30th St)

Coats, Loden: Loden and Leather Fashions (155 W 72nd St)

Coats, suits and jackets, petite, junior and half-sizes: Rain Barrel Coat Factory (101 Orchard St)

Cosmetics, discounted: Apple Cosmetics (135 Canal St)

Cosmetics, discounted designer: Almaya Cosmetics (1214-B Broadway)

Diamonds: Rennie Ellen (15 W 47th St)

Dresses, evening and wedding, made-to-order: Jane Wilson-Marquis (124 Thompson St)

Dresses, silk/party: Sam's Knitwear (93 Orchard St)

Dresses, special occasion for teens: Sweeteen (675 Madison Ave, 2nd floor)

Earrings, custom-designed: Sheri Miller (578 Fifth Ave)

Eyewear, discounted: Superior Optical (1133 Broadway, Suite 223)

Eyewear, elegant: Morgenthal-Frederics Opticians (685 Madison Ave)

Fabrics, discounted: A&N Fabrics (268 W 39th St)

Fabrics, imported: Far Eastern Fabrics (171 Madison Ave)

Fabrics, Oriental: Oriental Dress Company (38 Mott St)

Fans, antique hand: Lune (Place des Antiquaires, 125 E 57th St)

Footwear, women's small sizes: Giordano's (1118 First Ave)

Fragrances: Scentsitivity (870½ Lexington Ave)

Fragrances, discounted brand-name: Kris Cosmetics (1170 Broadway, at 28th St)

Fur scarves and hats: Aaron Weining (348 Seventh Ave)

Furs (salespeople you can trust): G. Michael Hennessy and H.B.A. Fur (both at 333 Seventh Ave)

Gloves, discounted leather: Bernard Krieger (316 Grand St)

Hair accessories: Head Master (37 W 39th St)

Handbags: Fine and Klein (119 Orchard St)

Handbags, discounted eelskin: New Star Handbags (1010 Sixth Ave)

Hats, custom fur: Lenore Marshall (235 W 29th)

Hats, custom-made: Victoria DiNardo (68 Thompson St)

Hats, men's: Young's Hat Store (139 Nassau St)

Herbs: Meadowsweet Herbal Apothecary (77 E 4th St)

Hosiery, good values: Jacob Young and Son (329 Grand St)

Hosiery, discounted brand-name: D&A Merchandise Co (22 Orchard St)

Jeans, discounted: Classics (15 Third Ave)

Jeans, good prices: Alaska Fashions (41 Orchard St)

Jewelry: Fortunoff (681 Fifth Ave) and Hidden Treasures (Grace Garfinkel, 450 E 63rd St)

Jewelry, American Indian: Saity (Trump Tower, 725 Fifth Ave)

Jewelry, custom-made: Eurocraft Custom Jewelry (42 W 48th St)

Jewelry, gold and silver: Gold and Silver Man (2142 Broadway)

Jewelry, handmade, discounted: Bonnie and Toni (81 Orchard St)

Jewelry, special designs: Eurocraft Custom Jewelry (42 W 48th St)

Jewelry, 24-carat gold: Fu Zhou Jewelry (170-172 Canal St, Booth 15)

Jewelry, vintage costume: Norman Crider Antiques (Trump Tower, 725 Fifth Ave, Level D/5)

Kimonos: Kimono House (120 Thompson St) and East East (230 E 80th St)

Knit suits, sportswear: Sam's Knitwear (93 Orchard St)

Knitwear: Knit Couture (800B Madison Ave)

Leather goods and accessories: Fomo (61 Orchard St)

Lingerie, best values: Goldman and Cohen (55 Orchard St)

Lingerie, sexy: Samantha Jones (1074 Third Ave) and Victoria's Secret (34 E 57th St)

Lingerie, unusual: Enelra (309 E 9th St, 48½ E 7th St)

Loungewear: Enelra Uptown (309 E 9th St), Enelra Downtown (48½ E 7th St)

Massage oils: The Fragrance Shoppe (21 E 7th St)

Millinery: Victoria DiNardo (68 Thompson St)

Millinery, custom-made: Don Marshall (758-1686) and Lola (102 St. Marks Pl)

Outdoor wear: Eastern Mountain Sports (20 W 61st St)

Pearls: Sanko Cultured Pearls (45 W 47th St)

Perfume: Warwick Chemists (1348 Sixth Ave)

Perfume copies: Essential Products Company (90 Water St)

Perfumes, discounted: Round House Fashions (256 W 36th St), La Femme (110 W 40th St), and Hema Cosmetics (313 Church St)

Perfumes, discounted brand-names: (great value on Liz Taylor's "Passion"): Perfumania (1 Times Square)

Piece goods: Beckenstein (121, 125, and 130 Orchard St)

Rainwear, high fashion: Norman Lawrence (417 Fifth Ave)

Scarves: Wraps (Pier Bldg, South Street Seaport)

Shirts, custom-made: Seewaldt and Bauman (17 E 45th St)

Shirts, high-pressure salespeople: Custom Shops (many locations)

Shirts, men's, great prices: Acorn Shirts (11 E 47th)

Shirts, sport: Sosinsky's (143 Orchard St)

Shoes, athletic: The City Athlete (131, 132A, 132B, 135, and 163 Orchard St)

Shoes, big and wide: Tall Size Shoes (3 W 35th St)

Shoes, bridal: Peter Fox (105 Thompson St)

Shoes, discounted children's party: Trevi Shoes (141 Orchard St)

Shoes, discounted designer: Designer Eye Shoes (93 Nassau St)

Shoes, discounted: Aly's Hut (85 Hester St) and Stapleton Shoe Company (68 Trinity Pl)

Shoes for millionaires: Susan Bennis/Warren Edwards (22 W 57th St)

Shoes, kids' upscale: Shoofly (506 Amsterdam Ave)

Shoes, men's discounted: J. Sherman (121 Division St) and Statesman Shoes (6 E 46th St)

Shoes, women's custom-made: Mathia (20 E 69th St)

Shoes, women's, petite: In Step (1230 Second Ave)

Silk blouses and dresses (wholesale prices): Omanti Designs (530 Seventh Ave, 9th floor)

Sneakers, men and women's discounted: Shoe City (133 Nassau St)

Sportswear: C.P. Company (175 Fifth Ave)

Sportswear, discounted brand-name: Athlete's Choice (1 Times Square)

Sportswear (sizes 2-12), discounted: Joseph Vincent (575 Seventh Ave)

Sportswear, men's and women's mod: Poco Loco (106 Wooster St)

Sportswear, Swedish-designed: Marc O'Polo (44 W 69th)

Sportswear, women's, good prices: M. Friedlich (196 Orchard St) and Giselle (143 Orchard St)

Sunglasses: Shades of the Village (167 Seventh Ave S)

Sweaters, Austrian: Geiger of Austria (505 Park Ave)

Sweaters, cashmere, men's and women's: David Berk (781 Madison Ave)

Sweaters, college: Off Campus (2151 Broadway)

Sweaters, men's: Country Road Australia (335 Madison Ave)

Swimsuits: New York Body Shop (49 W 57th St, 1195 Third Ave)

Tailoring, custom: Mr. Ned (22 W 19th St)

Ties, made-to-order: De Casi (37 W 57th St)

T-shirts, discounted: Eisner Bros. (75 Orchard St)

Tuxedo shirts and accessories, discounted: Ted's (83 Orchard St) and Allen Tie & Shirt Center (146 Allen St)

Umbrellas: Uncle Sam (161 W 57th St)

Underwear, pantyhose, socks, discounted: Universal Hosiery Corp (100 Orchard St) and D & A Merchandise (22 Orchard St)

Uniforms: Dornan (653 Eleventh Ave) and Ja-Mil (92 Orchard St)

Vitamins, natural: New York Apothecary (469 Sixth Ave)

Watchbands: George Paul Jewelers (51 E 58th St)

Watches: M.A.G. Time (60 W 22nd St)

Watches, vintage: Aaron Faber (666 Fifth Ave), Time Will Tell (962 Madison Ave), and Fanelli Antique Timepieces (1131 Madison Ave)

Watches (Seiko, Casio), discounted: Foto Electric Supply Co (31 Essex St)

Wigs: Jacques Darcel International (50 W 57th St)
Zippers: A. Feibusch (33 Allen St)

Things for the Home

Air conditioners: Elgot Sales (937 Lexington Ave)
Antiques, Chinese: Jackson Chu Arts & Products (825 Broadway)
Antiques, decorative: Karen Warshaw (167 E 74th St)
Antiques, French: French Country Store (35 E 10th St)
Antiques, turn-of-the-century English: J. Zacker (97 Spring St)
Antiques, Victorian: Somethin' Else Antiques & Needle Arts (182 Ninth Ave)
Appliances, discount: Dembitzer Bros. (5 Essex St), Kaufman Electrical Appliances (365 Grand St), Sam Diamond (94 Fulton St), Price Watchers (718/470-1620 or 516/222-9100), and Bloom and Krup (206 First Ave)
Appliances, kitchen: Zabar's (2245 Broadway)
Art, Ancient, European, Oriental, and pre-Columbian: Royal-Athena Galleries (153 E 57th St)
Art, Mexican (Bustamonte): Pavo Real Gallery (Pier 17, East River, South St. Seaport)
Art, primitive: Eastern Arts (365 Bleecker St)
Art, Western nineteenth-century: J.N. Bartfield Galleries (30 W 57th St)
Art deco, French: Maison Gerard (36 E 10th St)
Artifacts: Jacques Carcanagues Gallery (114 Spring St)
Bakeware, discounted: Broadway Panhandler (520 Broadway)
Baskets, dried-flower: Galerie Felix (968 Lexington Ave)
Bathroom accessories: Elegant John (812 Lexington Ave)
Bedding, Korean embroidered: Seoul Handicraft (284 Fifth Ave)
Beds, antique: Alice's Antiques (505 Columbus Ave)
Beds, Murphy: Murphy Bed Center (110 W 17th St, 2nd floor)
Bird cages: Lexington Gardens (1008 Lexington Ave)
Brassware: Ben Karpen Brass (212 E 51st St)
Butcher-block counters, tables, chairs: Alexander Butcher Blocks & Supply (176 Bowery)
Candles: The Candle Shop (118 Christopher St)
Ceramics: Contemporary Porcelain (105 Sullivan St)
Chests, Oriental: Min Yea (79 Madison Ave)
China, Amari: Bardith (901 Madison Ave)
China and glass, discount: Lanac Sales (73 Canal St)
China, French hand-painted: Solanee (138 E 74th St)
China, odds-and-ends bargains: Fishs Eddy (551 Hudson St)
Christmas decorations, discounted (mid-Nov thru Christmas): Kurt Adler's Santa's World (1107 Broadway)
Clocks, English antique: Hymore Hodson Antiques (903 Madison Ave)

Closet fixtures: Hold Everything (1311 Second Ave)
Collectibles: Gargoyles Ltd., of Philadelphia (138 W 25th St)
Crystal: Crystal Shop (55½ Greene St)
Dinnerware, Chinese: Wing On Wo & Co. (26 Mott St)
Dinnerware, Fiesta: Mood Indigo (181 Prince St)
Dinnerware, porcelain: Bernardaud (777 Madison Ave)
Domestics, great prices: Ezra Cohen (307 Grand St)
Ecological products: Terra Verde Trading Co (72 Spring St)
Electronics, good values: The Wiz (12 W 45th St and other locations) and Vicmarr (88 Delancey St)
Engravings, Irish: Irish Books and Graphics (90 W Broadway)
Fans, ceiling: Modern Supply (19 Murray St)
Figurines, discount: East Side Gifts and Dinnerware (351 Grand St)
Floor coverings: ABC Carpets (888 Broadway)
Floral designs, Ikebana: Frank Luisi (42 E 59th)
Flowers, silk: United States Flower Co. (131 W 28th St)
Folk art: Country on Columbus (281A Columbus Ave) and Folk Art Gallery (1187 Lexington Ave)
Frames, picture: Ready Frames (14 W 45th St) and Framed on Madison (740 Madison Ave)
Frames, hand-carved picture: D. Matt (223 E 80th St)
Furnishings, traditional hand-carved: Devon Shops (111 E 27th St)
Furniture, butcher-block: J&D Brauner (316 E 59th St, 302 Bowery, 1522 Second Ave, 181 Amsterdam Ave)
Furniture, custom: Navedo Woodcraft (179 E 119th St)
Furniture, department store: Bloomingdale's (Third Ave at 59th St)
Furniture, fine mica: Room Plus (1555 Third Ave)
Furniture, French country: Pierre Deux Antiques (367 Bleecker St)
Furniture, leather: Leather Center (44 E 32nd St)
Furniture, modular: Room Plus Furniture (1555 Third Ave)
Furniture, pine: Better Times Antiques (500 Amsterdam Ave) and Evergreen Antiques (120 Spring St)
Furniture reproductions: G. Carderelli (205 W Houston St) and Foremost (8 W 30th St)
Gadgets: Brookstone (18 Fulton St)
Glass: Simon Pearce (385 Bleecker St)
Glass and tableware: Avventura (463 Amsterdam Ave)
Glassware, Steuben (used): Lillian Nassau (220 E 57th St)
Globes and maps: E. Forbes Smiley (16 E 79th St)
Home accessories: Carole Stupell (29 E 22nd St)
Housewares, unusual: D.F. Sanders and Co. (386 W Broadway, 952 Madison Ave, 57th St and Lexington Ave)
Kilims (Oriental rugs): Le Monde Des Kilims (407A Broome St)
Kitchens, custom: Regba Diran New York (1100 Second Ave)
Kitchen and bath fixtures: Windsor World (240 E 59th St)
Judaica: Hecker Corporation (164 E 68th St)

Lamp finials: Grand Brass (221 Grand St)
Lamp shades: Just Shades (21 Spring St)
Light bulbs: Just Bulbs (938 Broadway)
Light bulbs, discounted: Wiedenbach-Brown (435 Hudson St)
Lighting fixtures: New York Gas Lighting Company (145 Bowery)
Linens, antique: Jean Hoffman-Jana Starr (236 E 80th St)
Locks: Lacka Lock (253 W 46th St)
Lucite: Acrylium International (955 Third Ave)
Marble, Greek: SG Marble (900 First Ave)
Marble and stone: Petrafina (964 Third Ave)
Mattresses, good value: Town Bedding & Upholstery (205 Eighth Ave)
Medical supplies and equipment: Portnow Surgical Supplies (53 Delancey St)
Movie-star photos: Movie Star News (134 W 18th St)
Movie and TV pictures and posters, good prices: Movie Material (242 W 14th St)
Perfume bottles, vintage: Gallery #47 (1050 Second Ave)
Plants: Farm and Garden Nursery (2 Sixth Ave)
Plants, cactus: The Grass Roots Garden (131 Spring St)
Plants, orchids: Robert Lester (280 W 4th St)
Plumbing parts: George Taylor Specialties (187 Lafayette St)
Posters, best selection: Poster America (138 W 18th St)
Posters, international theater: Triton Gallery (323 W 45th St) and Jerry Ohlinger (242 W 14th St)
Poster originals from 1880-1940: Philip Williams (60 Grand St)
Potpourri: Victor Decorators (260 Madison Ave)
Prints, botanical: W. Graham Arader (29 E 72nd St)
Prints, contemporary wildlife and sporting: Sportsman's Edge (136 E 74th St)
Quilts, antique: Kelter/Malce (361 Bleecker St), Quilts of America (431 E 73rd St), and Susan Parrish (390 Bleecker St)
Rugs, old: Doris Leslie Blau (15 E 57th St)
Rugs, Oriental: Momeni International (36 E 31st St)
Screens, Shoji: Katsura Studio (389 Broome St) and Tonee Crafts (108 Wooster St)
Security devices: REM Security (11 E 20th St)
Shells: The Shell Cellar (South Street Seaport, Pier 17, East River)
Shelves: Shelf Shop II (1295 First Ave)
Silver and wedding gifts: Rogers and Rosenthal (22 W 48th St)
Silver, unusual: Jean's Silversmiths (16 W 45th St)
Silverware and holloware, good values: Eastern Silver (54 Canal St)
Soaps: The Soap Opera (30 Rockefeller Plaza)
Stationery, discounted home and office: Tunnel Stationery (301 Canal St)
Stationery, personalized: Jamie Ostrow (1142 Madison Ave)

Stone pieces: Modern Stone Age (111 Greene St)
Tableware: Fishs Eddy (889 Broadway)
Tapestries: Lovelia Enterprises (356 E 41st St) and Saint-Remy (818 Lexington Ave)
Tassels, antique silk and satin: Cobweb (116 W Houston St)
Textiles, antique: Cora Ginsburg (19 E 74th St)
Tiles (ceramic), marble and wall coverings: Quarry Tile, Marble & Granite (192 Lexington Ave)
Tools, garden: Zona (97 Greene St)
Wallpaper, discount: Pintchik (278 Third Ave)

Things for Leisure Time

Albums, out-of-print: Golden Disc (239 Bleecker St)
Art supplies: Pearl Paint Company (308 Canal St)
Athletic gear: Modell's (109 E 42nd St)
Baseball cards, best selection: Card Collectors (105 W 77th St)
Bibles (in every language): International Bible Society (172 Lexington Ave)
Bicycles: Gene's Bike Shop (242 E 79th St)
Books, art: Jaap Rietman (134 Spring St) and Hacker Art Books (45 W 57th St)
Books, astrology and artificial intelligence: New York Astrology Center (545 Eighth Ave)
Books, exam study and science fiction: Civil Service Book Shop (89 Worth St)
Books, good prices: Barnes and Noble (many locations)
Books, military: Soldier Shop (1222 Madison Ave)
Books, mystery: Foul Play Books of Mystery & Suspense (10 Eighth Ave)
Books, mystical and religious: Quest Bookshop (240 E 53rd St)
Books, rail and motor: Albion Scott (48 E 50th St)
Books, religious: Paraclete Book Center (146 E 74th)
Books, sports: James Cummings (859 Lexington Ave)
Books, theater: Theatre Arts Bookshop (405 W 42nd St)
Books, tribal art: Oan-Oceanie-Afrique Noire (9 E 38th St, 4th floor)
Books, used and review copies: Strand Book Store (828 Broadway)
Books and magazines on aviation, military, naval, and uniforms: Sky Books International (48 E 50th St)
Cameras: Grand Central Camera (420 Lexington Ave)
Cameras, professional movie: Cine 60 (630 Ninth Ave)
Comics: Village Comics (163 Bleecker St, 2nd floor)
Compact discs, rock and roll: Smash Compact Discs (33 St Marks Pl)

Computer printers, discounted: Tri State Computer (160 Broadway)

Computers: Village Computers (687 Broadway)

Crafts, contemporary: Civilisation (78 Second Ave)

Decoys: Grove Decoys (36 W 44th St)

Diving equipment: Pan Aqua Diving (166 W 75th St)

Drums: Drummer's World (133 W 45th St)

Fishing tackle: Orvis (355 Madison Ave)

Fly-fishing equipment: Hunting World (16 E 53rd St)

Games, war: Compleat Strategist (11 E 33rd St, 320 W 57th St)

Golf equipment, reasonable prices: New York Golf Center (29 W 36th St)

Guitars: The Guitar Salon (45 Grove St)

Holographs: Holographic Studio (240 E 26th St)

Horseback-riding equipment: Miller's Saddlery (117 E 24th St) and H. Kauffman and Sons Saddlery (419 Park Ave S)

Jukeboxes: Back Pages Antiques (125 Greene St)

Kaleidoscopes: After the Rain (149 Mercer St)

Kayaks: Hans Klepper (35 Union Sq W)

Kites: Big City Kite Company (1201 Lexington Ave)

Luggage: Roebling Leather Goods (207 E 43rd St)

Luggage, soft: The Bag House (58 E 8th St)

Magazines: Eastern Newsstand (Pan Am Bldg) and Magazine Store (30 Lincoln Plaza)

Magazines, back issues: A&S Book Co. (304 W 40th St)

Maps: Hammond Map Store (57 W 43rd St)

Marine supplies: Goldberg's Marine (12 W 37th St)

Movie-star photos: Movie Star News (134 W 18th)

Music (all publishers): Music Store at Carl Fischer (62 Cooper Sq)

Musical instruments: Sam Ash Music Store (160 W 48th St)

Musical items: Yamaha (142 W 57th St)

Needlecraft: The Yarn Co. (2274 Broadway)

Needlepoint: 2 Needles (1266 Madison Ave)

Newspapers, out-of-town: Hotalings News Agency (142 W 42nd St)

Papers, elegant: Il Papiro (1021 Lexington Ave and World Financial Center)

Pens, Mont Blanc, discounted: The Write Stuff (1089 Third Ave)

Photographic equipment, discounted: Tri State Photo (60 Broadway and 2 Cortlandt St)

Photo supplies: Ben Ness Camera & Studio (114 University Pl)

Pipes: Connoisseur Pipe Shop (1285 Sixth Ave)

Records: Tower Records (692 Broadway, 1961 Broadway)

Records, Broadway show: Footlight Records (113 E 12th)

Records, opera: Music Masters (25 W 43rd St)

Records, out-of-print: Dayton's (799 Broadway)

Records, used: St Marks Sounds (20 St Marks Pl)
Science fiction: Forbidden Planet (821 Broadway)
Sci-fi gifts: Star Magic (743 Broadway)
Skating equipment: SoHo Skateboards (19 E 7th St) and Blades (105 W 72nd St)
Snorkeling equipment: Scuba Network (116 E 57th St)
Soccer supplies: Soccer Sport Supply (1745 First Ave)
Soldiers, lead: Second Childhood (283 Bleecker St)
Soldiers, toy, rare: Classic Toys (69 Thompson St)
Stamps: Subway Stamp Shop (111 Nassau St)
Stereo equipment, discounted: 6th Ave Electronics City (1024 and 1030 Sixth Ave)
Tennis equipment: Jay Schweid's Grandstand (588 Columbus Ave)
Tobacco: J.R. Tobacco (11 E 45th St)
Toys, discounted: Park Row Novelty (248 Grand Ave)
Toys, handmade: Dinosaur Hill (302 E Ninth St)
Toys, museum quality (1900-1940): Bizarre Bazaar Antiques (Place des Antiquaries, 57th St and Lexington Ave)
VCRs, discount: Sound City (58 W 45th St)
Videotapes: RKO Video (1608 Broadway, 168 W 96th St, 1309 Lexington Ave, 507 Third Ave, 93 Greenwich Ave) and New Video (941 First Ave, 90 University Pl)
Videotapes, Betamax: Beta Only Store (202 W 49th St)
Videotapes, hard-to-find (buy or rent): Evergreen Video (213 W 35th St, 2nd floor)
Wine-making supplies: Milan Home Wine and Beers (57 Spring St)

Things from Far Away

Afghan imports: Nusraty Afghan Imports (215 W 10th St)
African handicrafts: Craft Caravan (63 Greene St)
Brazilian products: Coisa Nossa (46 W 46th St, 2nd floor)
British imports: 99X (84 E 10th St)
Buddhas: Leekan Designs (93 Mercer St)
Caribbean clothing: Island Trading Co (15 E 4th St)
Chinese antiques: Jackson Chu Arts & Products (825 Broadway)
Chinese goods: Chinese American Trading Company (91 Mulberry St)
Crafts, imported: Il Mercato (341 E 9th St)
English antiques, turn-of-the-century: J. Zacker (97 Spring St)
Guatemalan gift items: Artesania (274 Columbus Ave)
Hawaiian crafts: Radio Hula (169 Mercer St)
Himalayan craft items: Himalayan Crafts and Tours (1228 Lexington Ave)
Indian imports: Katinka (303 E 9th St)
Indonesian art: Eastern Arts (107 Spring St)
Irish gifts: Grafton Shoppe (22 E 54th St)

Japanese books, records, art: New York Kinokuniya Bookstore (10 W 49th St)

Japanese gift items: Five Eggs (436 W Broadway) and Katagiri (224 E 59th St)

Lambskin coats: Spanish Shearling Center (345 Seventh Ave)

Leather items, imported: Il Bisonte (72 Thompson St)

Mexican furnishings and crafts: Amigo Country (19 Greenwich Ave)

Scottish kilts and tartans: Scottish Products (133 E 55th St)

Spanish antiques: Cobweb (116 W Houston St)

Tibetan treasures: Do Kham (51 Prince St) and Tibetan Handicrafts (144 Sullivan St)

Other Things

Astrology items: New York Astrology Center (545 Eighth Ave)

Bargains (all kinds): Unredeemed Pledge Sales (64 Third Ave)

Bird and kennel merchandise: Belmont (30 Rockefeller Plaza)

Birds: Bird Jungle (401 Bleecker St)

Bottles, perfume: Gallery #47 (1050 Second Ave, bet 55th and 56th St)

Butterflies: Mariposa, the Butterfly Gallery (128 Thompson St and Pier 17, South St, Seaport)

Canvas goods: Matera Custom Canvas (5 Lispenard St)

Covert surveillance equipment: Counter Spy Shop (630 Third Ave, 5th floor)

Fire memorabilia: New York Firefighter's Friend (263 Lafayette St)

Fish, tropical: American Aquarium (810 Lexington Ave)

Flags, banners: Art Flag Co. (8 Jay St)

Flowers, silk, discounted: Holland Flowers (800 Sixth Ave)

Fun shopping: Orchard Street on Sundays

Gifts, good prices: Jompole (330 Seventh Ave)

Hologram watches, pendants, and pyramids: Baggy Pants Express (345 Sixth Ave)

Holographs: Holographic Studio (240 E 26th St)

"Ladies of the evening": Sixth Ave at 58th St (Be careful!)

Office furniture, discounted: Frank Eastern Company (599 Broadway)

Office supplies: Menash (2305 Broadway)

Pet supplies, discounted: Petland (132 Nassau St)

Pharmacy, complete (West Side): Windsor Pharmacy (1419 Sixth Ave)

Post cards: French Kisses (144 Bleecker St)

Quartz, minerals: Crystal Gardens (21 Greenwich St)

Stone items: Modern Stone Age (111 Greene St)

Thrift store: Everybody's Thrift Shop (261 Park Ave S)

Travel items: The Civilized Traveler (1072 Third Ave)

Anatomical Supplies

MAXILLA & MANDIBLE LTD.
453 Columbus Ave (bet 81st and 82nd St)   724-6173
Mon-Sat: 11-7

Henry Galiano grew up in Spanish Harlem, and on the days his parents weren't running their beauty parlor, the family often went to the Museum of Natural History. His interest in things skeletal increased when Galiano got a job at the museum as a curator's assistant. He soon started his own collection of skeletons and bones. That in turn led to his opening Maxilla & Mandible (the scientific names for the upper and lower jaw, respectively), the first and only such store in the world. That's understandable. How many people need complete skeletons (or even a single maxilla)? Apparently more than you would think. The shop started by supplying museum-quality preparations of skulls, skeletons, bones, teeth, horns, skins, butterflies, beetles, seashells, fossils, taxidermy mounts, and anatomical charts and models to artists, sculptors, painters, interior decorators, jewelry manufacturers, prop masters, medical personnel, scientists, and educators. The real business is in the basement storerooms and laboratory. It seems only natural that an anatomical supply company and bone shop should have catacombs beneath Columbus Avenue. They seem to stretch on forever, and each door yields another bony site. Unfortunately, Henry himself is a busy bag of bones and is not always available.

Animals, Fish, and Accessories

BEASTY FEAST
605 Hudson St
140 Ninth Ave (bet 18th and 19th St)
237 Bleecker St   243-3261
Mon-Fri: 12-7; Sat: 10-7

If the name intrigues you, the stock will intrigue you even more. Beasty Feast carries pet food and supplies at good discount prices, and the salespeople are thoughtful, friendly, and cooperative.

BIDE-A-WEE HOME ASSOCIATION
410 E 38th St
532-4455 (adoption shelter), 532-5884 (clinic)
Mon-Sat: 10-7; Sun: 10-6 (adoption)
Mon-Sat: 8:30-5:30; 8:30-3 (clinic)

Bide-A-Wee is the only shelter I know of in Manhattan that does not kill animals it can't place for adoption. For this alone, it deserves special mention. Dogs, cats, puppies, and kittens are available for adoption at nominal fees. Bide-A-Wee also has a veterinary clinic open to the public, and it provides a pet bereavement program.

DEDE'S DOG-O-RAMA
161 Seventh Ave So (bet Perry and Waverly)   627-3647
Daily: 8:30-6

Dede Goldsmith wants everyone to understand that this is a pet *boutique*. That means your favorite companion can find just the right turtleneck sweater, designer fabric bed, or fanciful toy to make his or her life more pleasant. Of course, they also offer more mundane things like dog grooming, leashes, collars, bowls, parkas, and (naturally) deli platters with bagels and pizza. After all, doggies are into "junk food," too!

PETLAND DISCOUNTS
132 Nassau St   964-1821
7 E 14th St   675-4102
2675 Broadway   222-8851
304 E 86th St   472-1655
Mon-Fri: 9-8; Sat: 10-6:30; Sun: 11-5

The folks at the New York Aquarium recommend this chain of stores for fish and accessories. Petland also carries birds and discount food and accessories for all pets, including dogs and cats.

Antiques

Some of New York's more interesting antique stores are described below. However, if you are an antique buff, you might want to tour various areas in Manhattan where other antique stores are located. Here are neighborhoods and stores you might include on your tour:

57th Street Area

James Robinson (15 E 57th St): Silver flatware
Doris Leslie Blau (15 E 57th St): Rugs
Israel Sack (15 E 57th St): Colonial furniture
Ralph M. Chait Galleries (12 E 56th St): Chinese art

Madison Avenue

Jenny Bailey (1326 Madison Ave, at 94th St): English
Art of the Past (1242 Madison Ave, bet 88th and 89th St): East Asian
Betty Jane Brart Antiques (1225 Madison Ave, bet 88th and 89th St): Furniture

La Mansarde (1225 Madison Ave, bet 88th and 89th St): Vases, lamps

Marco Polo (1135 Madison Ave, bet 84th and 85th St): Silver

Fanelli Antique Timepieces (1131 Madison Ave, bet 84th and 85th St): Watches

Barry Friedman (1117 Madison Ave, bet 83rd and 84th St): Art deco

China House of Arts (1100 Madison Ave, bet 82nd and 83rd St): Chinese art

Eagle Antiques (1097 Madison Ave, bet 82nd and 83rd St): English country

Guild Antiques II (1095 Madison Ave, bet 82nd and 83rd St): English country

Linda Horn (1015 Madison Ave, bet 78th and 79th St): Diverse

Navin Kumar Gallery (1001 Madison Ave, bet 77th and 78th St): Oriental art

Ursus Books and Prints (981 Madison Ave, bet 76th and 77th St): Books

Florian Papp (962 Madison Ave, bet 75th and 76th St): Furniture

Time Will Tell (962 Madison Ave, bet 75th and 76th St): Watches

DeLorenzo (958 Madison Ave, bet 75th and 76th St): Art deco

Julian Graham-White (957 Madison Ave, bet 75th and 76th St): Diverse

Stair & Company (942 Madison Ave, bet 74th and 75th St): Furniture

Cora Ginsburg (19 E 74th St): Fabrics

Galerie Metropol (927 Madison Ave, bet 73rd and 74th St): Furniture

Stubbs Books & Prints (835 Madison Ave, bet 69th and 70th St): Books

20th Century Antiques (760 Madison Ave, bet 65th and 66th St): Art nouveau

Macklowe Gallery & Modernism (667 Madison Ave, bet 60th and 61st St): Tiffany

Gorevic & Gorevic (635 Madison Ave, bet 59th and 60th St): Jewelry

ChiuZac Gallery (510 Madison Ave, bet 52nd and 53rd St): Watches

Lexington Avenue

Japan Gallery (1210 Lexington Ave, bet 82nd and 83rd St): Japanese art

Folk Art Gallery (1187 Lexington Ave, bet 80th and 81st St): American folk

Granby Books and Art (1168 Lexington Ave, bet 80th and 81st St): Books

Turner and Madden (1146 Madison Ave, bet 79th and 80th St): Chests
Sylvia Pines Uniquities (1102 Madison Ave, at 77th St): Diverse
L'Art de Viere (978 Lexington Ave, bet 71st and 72nd St): Early twentieth century
R. Brooke Ltd. (960 Lexington Ave, at 70th St): Sports
S. Wyler (941 Lexington Ave, at 69th St): Silver, china
Philippe Farley (157 E 64th St): Furniture

SoHo

Galeria Dos (84 Wooster St): Luxe deco
Alan Moss (88 Wooster St): Furniture
Michael Carey (77 Mercer St): Arts and crafts
Evergreen Antiques (120 Spring St): Furniture
Victor Antiques (65 Greene St): Furniture
Lost City Arts (275 Lafayette St): Architectural items

University Place

Philip Colleck (830 Broadway, bet 12th and 13th St): Diverse
Howard Kaplan Antiques (827 Broadway, bet 12th and 13th St): Belle époque
Kentshire Galleries (37 E 12th St): English antiques
Florence Sack (813 Broadway, bet 11th and 12th St): Furniture
Kensington Place Antiques (80 E 11th St): Furniture
Eileen Lane Antiques (52 E 11th St): Refurbished deco
Little Antique Shop (44 E 11th St): Formal antiques
Fifty/Fifty (793 Broadway, bet 10th and 11th St): Furniture
Karl Kemp & Associates (29 E 10th St): Furniture
L'Epoque (30 E 10th St): Armoires
Maison Gerard (36 E 10th St): French art deco

Bleecker Street

Susan Parrish (390 Bleecker St): Quilts
Cynthia Beneduce (388 Bleecker St): Eclectic
Whitehead & Mangan (375 Bleecker St): Prints
Pierre Deux Antiques (367 Bleecker St): French country
Kelter-Malcé (361 Bleecker St): Gothic America

ANTIQUARIUM, FINE ANCIENT ARTS GALLERY
948 Madison Ave (at 75th St)   434-9776
Tues-Fri: 10-6; Sat: 10-5; closed Sat in summer

Antiquarium is a magnificent gallery for those who appreciate museum-quality antiquities and can afford to own them. This gallery specializes in Near Eastern and classical items, with a particular emphasis on ancient glass and jewelry, marble, stone statuary and reliefs, bronzes, pottery, and coins. Virtually every ancient civilization is represented. This is definitely not the place to take your three-year-old or the Merrill Lynch bull. On the other hand, you may need Merrill Lynch's help to send a piece home!

BACK PAGES ANTIQUES
125 Greene St   460-5998
Mon-Sat: 11-6; Sun: 12-6

You provide the guests, and Alan Luchnick, the proprietor, will see to it that everyone is royally entertained. He has a fine stock of classic Wurlitzer jukeboxes, pool tables, old Coca-Cola vending machines, Edison and Victor phonographs (remember the dog?), and Regina music boxes. If nothing else, a visit here will spark a lot of pleasant memories.

CHARLOTTE MOSS
1027 Lexington Ave   772-3320
Mon-Sat: 11-5:30, closed Sat in summer

Charlotte Moss left a successful Wall Street career to open a shop that offers products and interior design services under one roof, like it is done in London. Her place is filled with attractive decorative accessories and antiques, including two furniture lines and a home fragrance line ("Virginia") developed by Moss herself.

COBWEB
116 W Houston St (bet Thompson and Sullivan St)
505-1558
Mon-Fri: 12-7; Sat: 12-5
Closed bet Christmas and New Year's Day and Sat
    during July and Aug

Cobweb (what a great name for an antique shop!) is the only store in the New York area that imports country furniture and formal antiques directly from Spain and Portugal. The stunning selection of merchandise includes armoires, brass beds, tables, chairs, benches, trunks, chests, wooden bowls, earthen olive-oil urns, and water jugs. All of these pieces are distinctive, original, and authentic. In addition, Cobweb offers customized refinishing of its own furniture. It's obvious the stock doesn't stay around long enough to house spiders, let alone cobwebs.

DARROW'S FUN ANTIQUES
309 E 61st St (bet First and Second Ave)   838-0730
Mon-Fri: 11-7; Sat: 11-4; Sun: by appointment

There are antiques, and then there are *antiques*. Darrow's specializes in whimsical antiques for all ages. So expect to find toys (the valuable and collectible, as well as the merely nostalgic), slot machines, original animation art, jukeboxes, old pay phones, Mickey Mouse watches, cast-iron banks (remember them?), and toy soldiers. Gary Darrow, the proprietor, says that at any given time there are more than 5,000 items in stock. He has customers all over the world who swear that he's the best. The store was founded by Gary's father in 1964, and they've since earned a reputation as the prime source for buying and renting props and "fun" antiques. Darrow's also sells carefully labeled reproductions that would fool most people. They don't fool Gary, though, and he won't fool you.

HYDE PARK ANTIQUES
836 Broadway (bet 12th and 13th St)   477-0033
Mon-Fri: 9-5; Sat: 10-2:30; closed Sat in summer

This gallery has the largest inventory of genuine period English furniture in the world. William and Mary, Regency, and other old English periods are represented. To accompany the furniture, there are accents, mirrors, paintings, and porcelains. If all that isn't enough, Hyde Park maintains a fine workroom for restoring the furniture.

JAMES ROBINSON
15 E 57th St   752-6166
Mon-Sat: 10-5: closed Sat in summer

Collectors and specialists in antiques (particularly silver from the seventeenth and eighteenth centuries) are familiar with James Robinson, and many of them have dealt with the store, if only by mail. James Robinson is the best at what it does, but be warned that what it does *not* do is run an establishment where tourists can pick up knickknacks. Even the Victorian period, which is best-known for its knickknack style of decorating, is represented with only the finest, most silvery, and expensive pieces. James Robinson specializes in antique silver and antique jewelry, porcelains, and glass. If something exists but is not available in the store, personnel will comb the world for it. What is no longer in existence will be perfectly reproduced in handmade silver. Nonsilver antiques in which the store specializes include seventeenth- through nineteenth-century English bone china and porcelain (many in complete services), jewelry, and glass—and none of it is inexpensive.

KURLAND-ZABAR
19 E 71st St (at Madison Ave)   517-8576
Wed-Fri: 12-6; Sat: 11-5; other times by appointment

This store is worth browsing, if nothing else. It's the only gallery specializing in British arts and crafts in this country, and what a show it is! There are outstanding pieces of British and American furniture, silver and decorative art pieces from the 1840-1940 period, including Gothic revival, the aesthetic movement, Renaissance revival, the arts and crafts movement, and modernist styles. Special services include locating particular pieces, bidding at auction in New York or London for a customer (for a fee, of course), or helping develop a collection. Pricey!

LITTLE ANTIQUE SHOP
44 E 11th St (at Broadway)   673-5173
Mon-Fri: 10-5

In a neighborhood that is borderline Village and often referred to as Strand territory, the Little Antique Shop stands out as a gem. This small store specializes in Oriental and European antiques, large and small. These are fine, delicate antiques, and the prices are equally fine. There are small accent pieces as well as large screens. All of them are quality pieces, and you'll never believe you found them on East 11th Street.

MANHATTAN ART & ANTIQUES CENTER
1050 Second Ave (bet 55th and 56th St)   355-4400
Mon-Sat: 10:30-6; Sun: 12-6

This is the oldest (1976) and largest (104 dealers) antique center in the country. Offered in this bazaar of small boutiques are eighteenth- and nineteenth-century English, French, Oriental, and continental furniture, silver, procelain, decorations, bronzes, clocks, and tapestries. The careful browser can also find some fine pieces of Tiffany glass, Japanese ivory, American quilts and folk art, and colorful lacquerware. Special services include repair of clocks, watches, silver, lacquer, and ivories; jewelry design; expert appraisals; rentals to commercial photographers; interior design consultations; rug and tapestry restorations; and packing, crating and shipping.

MAYA SCHAPER ANTIQUES
862 Lexington Ave (at 65th St, 2nd floor)   734-0176
Daily: 10:30-5:30 and by appointment

Maya Schaper has been an important player in the antique field for many years, and she enjoys a fine reputation for quality. She has moved around a number of times but has now settled into country furniture, paintings, porcelains, pottery, brass, and decorative French, English, and domestic accessories. The nice part of Maya Schaper's shop is that she personally will search out a special item you may want, saving you the time and effort.

PLACE DES ANTIQUAIRES
125 E 57th St (bet Park and Lexington Ave)   758-2900
Mon-Sat: 11-6

You'll gasp at the beauty and the variety at this antique center. Located on two levels at the base of a 32-story office tower, it houses about 50 different dealers. The galleries display different antique specialties, with an emphasis on furniture and accessories, many serving as showrooms for larger collections housed elsewhere. Some dealers are from Europe, and some have moved here from other New York locations or made this one of several showrooms in the U.S. Several outstanding dealers to visit include Edith Weber & Co., which has an outstanding collection of antique and period jewelry; Bizarre Bazaar, specializing in art deco toys of vintage caliber; Manic, featuring one of the finest icon collections in the country; Kenneth Rendell, the autograph dealer; Russissimoff, which has a beautiful collection of eighteenth- and nineteenth-century French and Russian furniture; and Ronald Hoffman, who offers a fabulous collection of American silver dating from the mid-nineteenth century. After feasting the eyes, hungry shoppers can stop by the cafe on the lower level.

PONY CIRCUS
476 Broadway (bet Broome and Grand St)   925-7589
Mon-Sat: 11:30-6:30

Wow! What a place! The antique buff will think he or she has died and gone to heaven. In this large and crowded store are hundreds of chairs, tables, cabinets, cash registers, signs, beds, bird cages, and whatever else you can think of. They are big in the rental field, with items being used for props by many shows and exhibits. Brass polishing and refinishing is also a specialty, and if they don't have what you want (which is doubtful), they will try to get it.

URBAN ARCHAEOLOGY
285 Lafayette St (bet Houston and Prince St)   431-6969
Mon-Fri: 8-6; Sat: 12-6

Nowadays people are collecting almost anything and calling it antique. Urban Archaeology offers the best trims and pieces of New York architecture from the 1880s to the 1920s. While the business specializes in house artifacts, bathroom items, lighting fixtures, and display cases, owners Leonard Schechter, Gil Shapiro, and Allen Reiven display entire "mood" settings as well. You might find furnishings from barbershops, ice cream parlors, saloons, and who knows what else!

Art Supplies

CHARRETTE
215 Lexington Ave   683-8822
Mon-Fri: 8:30-7; Sat: 10-5; Sun: 12-5; closed Sun in summer

This branch of a Massachusetts company is for serious architects, engineers, draftsmen, graphic designers, and artists. The stock includes more than 36,000 different items, which means that a practitioner in any of these fields would be hard-put *not* to find what he or she wanted. Charrette offers quality supplies and good advice; professionals will be pleased to find anything they need, while amateurs ought to study the catalog first.

EASTERN ARTISTS
5 W 22nd St (bet Fifth and Sixth Ave)   645-5555
Mon-Fri: 8:30-7; Sat: 10-6; Sun: 12-6;
     closed Sun in July, Aug

Both amateurs and professionals are served well here. Ad agencies, poster companies, and artists buy supplies from Eastern, as much for the personalized service (tailored to an artist's temperament) as for the 20 to 50 percent discount on supplies. Store manager Fred Figueroa claims there are more than 20,000 different items in stock—enough to please the fussiest artist.

LEE'S ART SHOP
220 W 57th St (nr Broadway)   247-0110
Mon-Fri: 9-7; Sat: 9:30-6

Ricky of Lee's Art Shop claims that her store is the city's most complete art supply store. Indeed, the shop is loaded with materials for both the professional and amateur artist. There is even a separate section for architectural and drafting supplies. The staff is among the city's friendliest and is extremely knowledgeable. Their help is needed to guide the uninitiated through the wealth of transfer types, lamps, silk screens, art brushes, and chart types. All are available here in various qualities. A related specialty is same-day framing; they will frame amateur or professional art for home or office the same business day. I was also impressed by the range of auxiliary services Lee's offers—mail order, catalogs, and free delivery.

NEW YORK CENTRAL
62 Third Ave (at 11th St)   473-7705
Mon-Sat: 8:30-6:15

For many years artists have looked to this firm for fine art materials, especially unique and custom-made items. There are two floors of fine art papers: one-of-a-kind decorative papers in various designs and colors, and over a hundred special Oriental papers from Bhutan, China, India, Japan, Thailand, Taiwan, and Nepal. Amateur and skilled artisans can find a full range of decorative paints and painting materials.

SAM FLAX

425 Park Ave	752-5893
747 Third Ave	630-3050
25 E 28th St	630-3040
233 Spring St	675-8571
12 W 20th St	620-3038

Mon-Fri: 9-6; Sat: 10-5 (Spring St store also open
    Sun: 12-5)

Superlatives are as common as canvas in the art supply business, and Sam Flax is yet another who claims to be the biggest and the best in the field. Since no one is going to count the paint brushes in stock, the question is moot, but Sam Flax does carry a full range of art and drafting supplies, drawing-studio furniture, and photographic products. There are also framing services at each store. The store at 12 West 20th Street is primarily devoted to furniture.

UTRECHT ART AND DRAFTING SUPPLIES

111 Fourth Ave (at 11th St)   777-5353
Mon-Sat: 9-6

We once mused about the name of this art supply outlet, and we received a letter from a reader who pointed out that Utrecht is a large city in Holland, with a long tradition of arts and crafts. Great, but we raised the question because this shop used to be called Utrecht *Linens.* In any case, Utrecht is a major manufacturer of paint and art and drafting supplies, with a large factory in Brooklyn. At this retail store, factory-fresh supplies are sold at factory discounts, and the Utrecht name stands behind every purchase. Quality is superb, as are the discounts. Utrecht also carries the lines of other manufacturers at impressive discounts.

Autographs

JAMES LOWE AUTOGRAPHS

30 E 60th St (bet Madison and Park Ave, Suite 907)
759-0775
Mon-Fri: 9-5

James Lowe is one of the most established autograph houses in the country. Catalogs, published several times a year, make a visit to the gallery unnecessary, but in-person inspections are fascinating and invariably whet the appetite of autograph collectors. There is no one specialty; the gallery seems to show whatever superior item is in stock, though there is a particular interest in historic, literary, and musical autographs, manuscripts, documents, and nineteenth-century photographs. The offerings range from autographed pictures of Buffalo Bill to three bars of an operatic score of Puccini's. It all depends on what a buyer finds intriguing. Perhaps that explains why James Lowe prefers that you drop by.

KENNETH W. RENDELL
125 E 57th St (at Lexington Ave)   935-6767
Mon-Sat: 11-6

Kenneth Rendell, from Newton, Massachusetts, has been in the business for over 30 years and offers a fine collection of pieces from famous personages in literature, arts, politics, and science. In Place des Antiquaires, Rendell shows autographed letters, manuscripts, documents, and signed books and photographs. All are authenticated, attractively presented, and priced according to the rarity of the item. Rendell evaluates collections for tax purposes and arranges the purchase or sale of items on a consulting basis.

TOLLETT AND HARMAN
175 W 76th St   877-1566
By appointment only

Autographs used to be big business in New York, perhaps because of the number of celebrities in the city. Lately, however, there are less than a handful of reliable dealers. Tollett and Harman is one of the best. They deal almost entirely by catalog and request rather than through formal retailing. They carry or will obtain original autographs, manuscripts, signed books, maps, and vintage photographs. Collectors of specific items (I collect presidents of the U.S. and of the Continental Congresses) can leave requests with them. When they come across an item, they will notify you. Each item is carefully authenticated.

Baskets

A TISKET A TASKET
475 Tenth Ave (11th floor)
967-9366, 800/955-2847, FAX: 212/967-9319
Mon-Fri: 10-6; Sat, Sun: by appointment

Sheila Nilva started A Tisket A Tasket as a sideline to her main shop, Place for Antiques. Being an energetic person, she saw to it that her new shop took off in high gear. Customers can order from a choice of over 100 baskets, and the list of recipients could fill any society page: Liza Minnelli, Ed Asner, Jimmy Buffett, Tom Cruise, Michael Feinstein, and many more. The baskets contain no perishables unless requested. They're clever, whimsical, and elegant, and they're perfect for births, birthdays, anniversaries, promotions, get-well gifts, and all holidays. There is even a $58 "New York! New York!" basket with a book (shouldn't it be this one?), a New York mug with imported coffee, a linen napkin in a Big Apple ring, and apple cookies.

Bathroom Accessories

A. F. SUPPLY CORPORATION
22 W 21st St (bet Fifth and Sixth Ave)   243-5400
Mon-Fri: 8-5 and by appointment

As far as I am concerned, the bathroom is the most important room in the house, and the folks at A. F. Supply agree. They offer a great selection of luxury bath fixtures, whirlpools, faucets, bath accessories, door and cabinet hardware, saunas, steam showers, shower doors, medicine cabinets, and spas from top domestic and European suppliers.

ELEGANT JOHN
812 Lexington Ave (bet 62nd and 63rd St)   935-5800
Mon-Wed, Fri, Sat: 10-6; Thurs: 10-7

After getting over the initial awkwardness of entering a store that displays prominently labeled "john seats" on its walls, you'll be amazed at the array of custom-made shower curtains, dressing tables, coordinated accessories, soap dishes, and, of course, seats, all sold with the aim of creating a bathroom that is every bit as comfortable and striking as the rest of the house.

SHERLE WAGNER INTERNATIONAL
60 E 57th St (at Park Ave)   758-3300
Mon-Fri: 9:30-5

If you thought the Elegant John was the definitive word in bathroom accessories, you ain't seen nothin' yet. Sherle Wagner takes a topic that even the Elegant John skirted, and places it in the most elegant location in the city, where it rubs elbows with silversmiths, art galleries, and exclusive antique shops. However, the luxurious bathroom fixtures are almost works of art and are deserving of their 57th Street location. Fixtures come in every possible material, and some are so striking that they make a glass display case seem like their natural setting. Prices are high, as might be expected. One warning! The displays are in the basement, and what seems like the world's slowest elevator will give you a good case of claustrophobia.

Books

American Indian

BOB FEIN BOOKS
150 Fifth ave (at 20th St, Room 841)   807-0489
Mon-Fri: 12-6

Bob Fein claims that his shop is the only one that's devoted to the literature of American Indians. Within this boundary, he also includes pre-Columbian art and Eskimos as subjects, and he has on hand more than 4,000 books and journals on those topics. Many of his items are out-of-print or one-of-a-kind, and Fein is considered the primary source for such material. There is also a good percentage of what Fein terms "scholarly material," along with Smithsonian publications and reports. Most of the stock is unique and rare, and if any new literature is published about Fein's specialties, there's a very good chance that he'll have it first.

Architecture

URBAN CENTER BOOKS
457 Madison Ave (at 51st St)   935-3595
Mon-Thurs: 11-7; Fri, Sat 10-6

Urban Center Books, the retail arm of the Municipal Art Society, practices what it preaches. The society was founded in 1892 to preserve the best of New York's historical architectural facades. That the society should be located in the north wing of the Villard Houses—historic homes that make up the base of the Helmsley Palace Hotel—is only fitting. And since most of the rooms in those buildings have been refurbished to resemble drawing rooms and libraries, it is equally appropriate that the society decided to retail publications on its interests in a suite that is a real library. If nothing else, a visit to Urban Center Books offers a chance to further explore the public rooms of the houses. Although only the physical amenities are left (wide doorways, parquet floors, painted ceilings), it is still a stunning look back into times gone by. The store specializes in architecture, history, and the city's physical plan. Publications on the topics of urban planning, design, and historic preservation are available.

Art

E. WEYHE
794 Lexington Ave (bet 61st and 62nd St)   838-5466
Mon-Sat: 9:30-5; closed Sat in summer

This bookstore, dedicated to the subject of art, has evolved from a small shop to a specialty store with an upstairs art gallery. Actually, it was only natural since Mr. Weyhe filled the small area with artists and art books (as well as their art) almost from its start in

1923. Over the years, Weyhe gave encouragement to scores of artists, and they reciprocated by giving him some of their paintings, tiles (note Rockwell Kent's offering on the brownstone), and sketches. Eventually, Weyhe was compelled to open the gallery to display the works of his patrons (and those he was patron to) and to prove that art literature is to be lived. Today, under the aegis of Weyhe's daughter, the store and gallery continue the work Weyhe started. The bookstore carries everything related to art, architecture, and photography. A good part of the business also involves the purchase and resale of private art-book collections.

PRINTED MATTER
77 Wooster St   925-0325
Tues-Sat: 10-6

The name Printed Matter is almost a misnomer since the store is the only one in the world devoted exclusively to artists' books (5,000 titles by over 2,500 artists). That's not books belonging to artists, or even art books, but rather a trade term for a portfolio of artwork in book form. The result is inexpensive, accessible art that can span an entire artist's career or a particular period or theme. The idea is carried further by Printed Matter's selection of periodicals and audiowork in a similar vein. Nearly all of the featured artists are contemporary, so just browsing through the store would bring you up-to-date on what is going on right now in the art world. They sell both wholesale and retail.

WITTENBORN ART BOOKS
1018 Madison Ave (bet 78th and 79th St)   288-1558
Mon-Sat: 10-5; closed Sat in summer

Possibly the ultimate art bookstore in the city, Wittenborn specializes in the arts, architecture, prints, archaeology, and fashion, and whenever fine-quality books on these topics are published, Wittenborn adds them to the stock. The staff makes a point of having it all—and having it all neatly cataloged as well. Besides contemporary tomes, Wittenborn carries out-of-print, rare, and antiquarian volumes and foreign printings. If the topic and pictures meet Wittenborn's standards, it will carry the book, no matter what language it has been published in. Artfully done!

Biography

BIOGRAPHY BOOKSHOP
400 Bleecker St (at 11th St)   807-8655
Tues-Fri: 1-9; Sat: 12-10; Sun: 12-5:30; closed one week
    in Feb, one week in Aug

Here's a New York specialty shop that deals only with books of a biographical nature. If one is researching a particular person, or if you have an interest in someone's life story, this is the place to find it. There are biographies, books of letters, autobiographies, diaries, journals, and even biographies for children.

Children's

BOOKS OF WONDER

132 Seventh Ave (at 18th St)   989-3270
Mon-Sat: 11-7; Sun: 12-6

464 Hudson St (at Barrow St)   645-8006
Mon-Sat: 11-7; Sun: 12-6

Books of Wonder established its reputation as a prime source for rare, collectible, and out-of-print children's books at its store on Hudson Street. Owners Peter Glassman and James Carey stocked the store with their own favorites and established the largest selection of Oz books for sale in the world. Books of Wonder opened a second and much larger store across the street from Barney's, which became the main store. Together they have the largest number of children's book titles in the city. Would you believe there is an Oz gift wrap and an Oz flag? At Books of Wonder they know all about it. Antique books are now available at the Seventh Avenue location.

EEYORE'S BOOKS FOR CHILDREN

2212 Broadway (at 79th St)   362-0634
Mon, Thurs: 10-8; Tues, Wed, Fri, Sat: 10-6;
   Sun: 10:30-5

25 E 83rd St (at Madison Ave)   988-3404
Mon-Sat: 10-6; Sun: 12-5

Joel Fram, Eeyore's proprietor, runs the shop as if it were a child's haven. There are books for children of every age and interest, and there is even a corner where kids can sit or browse. The majority of the books are within the price range of a good allowance, and if it's an adult who is doing the purchasing, the unobtrusive and knowledgeable staff offers guidance and suggestions. Eeyore's will order, at no additional charge, any book not in their extensive stock. The shop's highlight is its Sunday story sessions, which are attended by standing-room-only crowds. Refreshments are served after story hour. Currently, the story sessions are held for kids aged three to six at 11 a.m. on the West Side and at 12:30 on the East Side.

STORYLAND

1369 Third Ave (at 78th St)   379 Amsterdam Ave
517-6951   (at 78th St)   769-2665
Mon-Sat: 10-6; Sun: 11-6   Mon-Sat: 11-7
                              (Tues: 11-8); Sun: 11-6

Storyland is the ultimate bookstore for children. Genial owner Jeff Bergman and manager Heidi Kilgras have created an atmosphere that children will love and parents will enjoy while shopping for children's books, videos, and cassette tapes. Every Sunday (except during the summer) a writer or illustrator is on hand for story hour (1:30 p.m.). A carnival atmosphere reigns at this first-class bookstore.

Comic

ACTION COMICS

318 E 84th St (bet First and Second Ave)   249-7344
Mon-Wed: 11:30-7; Thurs-Sat: 11:30-7:30; Sun: 12-6

Comic book lovers need look no further than this remodeled establishment. You'll find new comics from all publishers, collector's comics from the 1930s through the 1980s, new and collector's baseball cards, and original comic art. The stock has been sizably expanded.

SUPERSNIPE COMIC BOOK EUPHORIUM

P.O. Box 1102, Gracie Station, New York, NY 10028
580-8843
By appointment and mail order
Call Fri, Sat: 10-4:30

The ultimate comic book emporium. Supersnipe now deals only by phone and mail order. It is well worth your time, however, because their stock is unequaled.

Food

KITCHEN ARTS & LETTERS

1435 Lexington Ave (at 94th St)   876-5550
Mon: 1-6; Tues-Fri: 10-6:30; Sat: 11-6;
    closed Aug and Sat in July

Cookbooks traditionally top the best-seller lists in bookstores, and with the renewed interest in health, fitness, and natural foods, that rule of thumb is more operative than ever. So it should come as no surprise that Nachum Waxman's Kitchen Arts & Letters should be an immediate success as a store specializing in books, literature, photography, and original art about food and its preparation. Waxman claims that his store is the only one like it in the city and one of less than ten in the country. Waxman is a former editor at Harper & Row and Crown publishing companies, where he supervised several cookbook projects. Bitten with the urge to start a specialty bookshop, he discovered almost immediately that there was a huge demand for out-of-print and original cookbooks. So while the tiny shop stocks almost 5,000 titles, as well as a gallery of photography and original art, much of the business is in finding out-of-print and "want listed" books.

Foreign

BOOK-FRIENDS CAFE
16 W 18th St   255-7407
Mon-Fri: 10-7; Sat, Sun: 12-7

Should this be in stores or cafes? Well, both really, but I decided to list it here because of the unusual combination of activities available. You can feast upon delicious chili or beef stew, pâté, salads, cheeses, scones, and wonderful desserts. You can have afternoon tea. You can meet and chat with interesting authors. You can choose from a large selection of attractive teapots. Best of all, you can browse a fine collection of new and old books centered around Paris in the 1920s.

LIBRAIRIE DE FRANCE
LIBRERIA HISPANICA
610 Fifth Ave (bet 49th and 50th St)   581-8810
Mon-Fri: 9:30-6:15; Sat: 10-6:15

115 Fifth Ave (at 19th St)   673-7400
Mon-Sat: 10-6

A short stroll through the Rockefeller Center promenade takes you by the Librairie de France and Libreria Hispanica. Inside, you will find an interesting collection of French and Spanish newspapers, magazines, tourist guides, and light reading. There are more than a million French and Spanish books and records in stock. If this isn't overwhelming enough, *all* of them are neatly cataloged and easily found. There isn't a topic on which at least several books in French or Spanish are not available, including a collection of books in Spanish about French literature and vice versa. A partial list of the available categories includes textbooks, dictionaries and encyclopedias, children's books and records, bilingual and bicultural educational records and tapes, games, posters, audiovisual aids, newspapers, magazines, French popular music on CDs and LPs, and Haitian and African literature in French. A special division stocks dictionaries and cassettes in over a hundred languages.

NEW YORK KINOKUNIYA BOOKSTORE
10 W 49th St (at Fifth Ave)   765-1461
Daily: 10-7

Kinokuniya is Japan's largest and most esteemed bookstore chain, and this is its first branch in New York. Located in Rockefeller Plaza, the store has two floors of books about Japan. The atmosphere is the closest thing New York has to Tokyo. On the first floor there are 20,000 English-language books, which leave no part of Japanese culture neglected. Art, cooking, travel, language, literature, history, business, economics, management techniques, martial arts—they're all here. The rest of the floor is rounded out with books on the same subjects in Japanese, and there are paperbacks on the second floor. Kinokuniya has the largest collection of Japanese books in the city (and possibly outside of Japan).

PARAGON BOOK GALLERY
237 W 72nd (bet Broadway and West End Ave,
   2nd floor)   496-2378
Mon-Fri: 10-6

Roberta Huber has collected more than 60,000 book titles from all over the Orient. Besides the latest art books, Huber has a fine selection of rare and old books. If you have an interest in Asian countries, you'll find nearly everything written about Asian history, culture, literature, and linguistics in stock. A very efficient mail-order service is also available.

UNIVERSITY PLACE BOOK SHOP
821 Broadway (9th floor)   254-5998
Mon-Fri: 10-5

In this out-of-the-way, dust-covered loft may be the largest collection of books on Africa and the West Indies in the world. After climbing up to its ninth-floor location, it's disconcerting to find piles and piles of books that seem to be arranged by chance. But there are some great finds here, and the salespeople are friendly and very knowledgeable. The selection includes literature in more than 35 African dialects. Compensating for the fact that many African dialects have never been written down, University stocks 200 to 300 books about them; almost any subject or group is covered. University also carries many old, rare, and out-of-print books on Africa and the West Indies. The newer books are involved with current black America. William French, owner and manager, seems to know every book in the store—an amazing feat. The books he personally values the most are the early printed books (fifteenth to seventeenth century) and the rare and out-of-print books on Africa, the West Indies, and Afro-Americans.

General

BARNES AND NOBLE
206-8800
Branches throughout city
Hours vary from store to store

Barnes and Noble is a mecca for college students, and many of the universities in the metropolitan area have branches on campus. Generations of New York students have gone through the ritual of buying books from Barnes and Noble at the start of a semester and selling them back after finals. The textbook division continues, but all other types of books are stocked as well, and all are discounted. Its particular specialty is one of the best discounts in town on any book on the *New York Times* bestseller list. As soon as a title makes the list, Barnes and Noble drastically discounts it and advertises that discount in the *Times*. There is an excellent assortment of all types of books, since Barnes and Noble has sources not available to smaller stores.

B. DALTON BOOKSELLER
247-1740 (main store)
Branches throughout city
Hours vary from store to store

The B. Dalton shop on Fifth Avenue, one of the largest bookstores in the city, is the flagship for one of the largest and best bookselling operations in the nation. Books aren't just sold here— they are theatrically produced. Dalton has access to huge lots of remainders and reprints (due to its nationwide buying power). There are sections for children, technical subjects, special interests, and the arts. Dalton doesn't excel in any one particular area, but it deserves an "A" for presentation. Their window displays are always must-sees for the latest in the publishing world.

BURLINGTON BOOK SHOP
1082 Madison Ave (bet 81st and 82nd St)   288-7420
Mon-Fri: 9:30-6; Sat: 10-6; Sun: 12-6

Burlington functions as a small-town bookstore in the big city. Their business card still lists their phone number as "Butterfield 8"! John O'Hara would love it. The store specializes in art books and literature, and offers friendly, neighborly service. How can it be otherwise when you have the name of a book in your phone number? Two specialties of this unique operation: downstairs is a fabulous collection of Burlington Antique Toys, and on the mezzanine a shop called "Compulsive Collector" features an out-of-print book department.

DOUBLEDAY BOOK SHOPS
397-0550 (main store)
Branches throughout city
Hours vary from store to store

Doubleday, the granddaddy of the Fifth Avenue bookstores, has it all. There probably isn't a topic or title in the world they don't stock; they are particularly proud of their back list. The Fifth Avenue store is the prototype of what a bookstore should be—particularly a bookstore in the city. The first floor of the 57th Street store is known for its selection of current and best-selling books and for a great travel department. If a title is newly released, Doubleday's main section has it, often before publication date. Other floors in the 57th Street store concentrate on art books, cookbooks, political issues, and back-listed publications, and that is only a partial list. But the quintessential bookstore relies heavily on its personnel, and it is in this area that Doubleday really excels. It still gives service with a capital *S*. Manager Harry Cohen and his staff are true professionals. All stores reflect their neighborhoods. The Third Avenue store is less for tourists than for homebodies, while the Citicorp branch blends perfectly with its locale. Philosophical works are basically nonexistent there, but gift books, coffee-table art books, and light fiction are runaway favorites. All Doubleday stores have a large selection of light reading: fiction, mysteries, self-improvement books, and cookbooks.

GOTHAM BOOK MART
41 W 47th St 719-4448
Mon-Fri: 9:30-6:30; Sat: 9:30-6

The Gotham is a New York institution founded by the late Frances Steloff, a legend herself. Steloff founded the store nearly 70 years ago as a very small, personal, theatrically inclined bookstore. In the early days, as today, there was a heavy emphasis on poetry and the arts because those were Steloff's passions. Steloff, who could never understand how a book could be banned (imagine what she would have said about *The Satanic Verses*), once smuggled 25 first editions of Henry Miller's *Tropic of Cancer* into the country from Paris via Mexico. She developed a deep and personal interest in authors and clients alike, and even as she grew older she would always make one daily visit downstairs to the shop around two p.m. Steloff lived to reach the century mark; her influence on this charming store will probably live on for another century. An exceptional search service is a special attraction.

McGRAW-HILL BOOKSTORE
1221 Sixth Ave (bet 48th and 49th St)   512-4100
Mon-Sat: 10-5:45

This huge shop, located downstairs in the McGraw-Hill building at Rockefeller Center, is limited in fiction and general titles, but for anything published by McGraw-Hill or written with a business, technical, or scientific bent, it is excellent. They're all sold at list price, and the wide selection of books would make any engineer happy. One-third of their books are about computers. A fine, well-run, professional store.

RIZZOLI
31 W 57th St (bet Fifth and Sixth Ave)   759-2424
Mon-Sat: 9-8; Sun: 12-8
Branches at the World Financial Center, in SoHo
(on W Broadway), and at Bloomingdale's

When you talk class in the book business, Rizzoli is right at the top of the list. They have managed to maintain the elegant atmosphere that makes a patron feel he or she is browsing a European library rather than a midtown Manhattan bookstore. The emphasis here is on art, literature, photography, music, dance (particularly ballet), and foreign language. Upstairs you will find paperbacks, Italian books, a music department, and children's books. Art objects are shown throughout the store. The SoHo store has been greatly expanded, and the Bloomingdale's department is a great place to shop for gift books. Besides that, they always feature New York's best guidebook. (I wonder what that is?)

STRAND BOOK STORE
828 Broadway (at 12th St)
473-1452, FAX: 212/473-2591
Mon-Sat: 9:30-9:30; Sun: 11-9:30

Strand at South Street Seaport
159 John St   809-0875
Daily: 10-10

For book lovers, no trip to New York is complete without a visit to this fabulous store, one of the largest bookstores in the world. For New Yorkers, this is surely the place to start looking for that volume you must have. There are eight miles of books inside and carts full of real bargains outside. The crowded quarters house secondhand, rare, and out-of-print books at reduced prices. The Strand also sells thousands of new books at a fraction of publisher's list price. Upstairs is the rare book room, where you might find a signed first edition of James Joyce's *Ulysses* for $30,000. There is a fine selection of twentieth-century first editions, limited signed editions, and art books. The store also imports English remainders, sells to libraries, and does a booming mail-order business. Be sure to meet owner Fred Bass, one of the nicest and most knowledgeable individuals in the book business. This is definitely a must-visit!

TOWER BOOKS
383 Lafayette St (at 4th St)   228-5100
Daily: 9 a.m.-midnight

The highly succssful Tower chain has now gotten into the book business in a big way. This is their first bookstore on the East Coast, and they haven't spared the horses. Under one roof you will find over 100,000 titles (including a large selection of children's books), 1,200 magazine titles, and national and international magazines. All paperbacks are discounted 10 percent; hardcovers are marked 20 percent off; best sellers are 30 percent off.

WALDENBOOKS
57 Broadway (at Exchange Pl)
279-1139, FAX: 212/809-2433
Mon-Fri: 8-6
Branches throughout city

While the other major bookstores have their flagship outlets on Fifth Avenue, Walden chose the Wall Street area for its major operation. And what an operation it is! The store literally overflows with selections in almost every category, offering one of the largest selections of business and investment books in the country (as is proper for that location). They also publish the *Walden Street Journal,* a free monthly newsletter, featuring new and noteworthy business and investment titles. But no matter what you are looking for, Waldenbooks can probably satisfy your need. The selection in this store is so vast (around 50,000 titles) that fiction browsers in one area may not realize that nearby is housed a comprehensive selection of computer and reference books, as well as travel guides and maps. In keeping with their reputation as a full-service bookstore, Walden will special order and gift wrap free of charge, send merchandise anywhere, and provide expert answers to a multitude of readers' questions. They also specialize in corporate purchasing, with bulk discounts.

SPECIAL OFFER TO MY READERS! You can purchase sets of many top-quality brand-name encyclopedias at a 35 percent discount merely by mentioning this book. Call Total Education Concepts, Inc. (718/454-1322), any time Monday through Sunday between 9:30 a.m. and 9:30 p.m.

Irish

IRISH BOOKS AND GRAPHICS

580 Broadway (bet Prince and Houston St,
    11th floor)   962-4237
Mon-Fri: 11-5; Sat: 1-4

Angela Carter has changed the name of her shop from Keschcarrigan (that was a mouthful), but she has not changed the great selection of new and used Irish books, posters, old maps, and engravings. Books are offered in both Irish Gaelic and in English.

Military

MILITARY BOOKMAN

29 E 93rd St   348-12809
Tues-Sat: 10:30-5:30

The inventory here is limited to books of a military nature. The specialty is out-of-print and rare books on military, naval, and aviation history. At any given time, there are about 10,000 such titles in stock. Topics run the gamut from Attila the Hun to atomic warfare. The Military Bookman also has a large mail-order business and maintains a subscription mail-order catalog. The proprietors are Harris and Margaretta Colt.

SOLDIER SHOP

1222 Madison Ave (bet 88th and 89th St)   535-6788
Mon-Fri: 10-6; Sat: 10-5; Sat: 10-3 in July, Aug

The military is a deadly serious business here. This is *not* for the little boy who likes to play soldier, since many of the books are extremely rare and valuable. The general specialty, however, is the military in all of its ramifications, and as a result, the Soldier Shop stocks current as well as rare military books concerning history, battles, theory, and biography. Their catalog lists 166 pages of military history books, antique soldiers, arms, and armor.

Mystery

FOUL PLAY

302 W 12th St (entrance on Eighth Ave)   675-5115
Mon-Fri: 11-9:45; Sat; 11-10:45; Sun: 11-7

1465B Second Ave (at 76th St)   517-3222
Mon-Fri: 12-10; Sat: 11-11; Sun: 11-6

If true crime fascinates you, this is your kind of place. Foul Play features a large selection in this category, as well as American and British hardbacks and paperbacks on mystery, espionage, and suspense. Note the unusually late hours, allowing you to run out and buy a good mystery to put you asleep . . . even though your dreams will probably be scary!

MURDER INK®
2486 Broadway (bet 92nd and 93rd St)   362-8905
Daily: 11-7 (Thurs: 11-10)

Murder Ink was the first mystery bookstore in the city. When Dilys Winn founded Murder Ink, she started not so much a bookstore as a way of life. Today, Jay Pearsall runs the store, which still claims to stock every murder or mystery book in print and several thousand selections no longer in print. You'll find rare books and other artifacts, but the emphasis is on good, entertaining mysteries.

MYSTERIOUS BOOK SHOP
129 W 56th St   765-0900
Mon-Sat: 11-7

Otto Penzler is a Baker Street Irregular, a Sherlock Holmes fan extraordinaire (an elementary deduction!), and the Mysterious Book Shop's owner. As a result, the shop is run as a friendly business, and spontaneous conversations among customers are the norm. On the ground floor (actually, a few steps below street level), Mysterious stocks new hardcover and paperback books that deal with any genre of mystery. ("But *not* science fiction," says the store manager. "Science fiction is not mystery.") Upstairs, via a winding circular staircase, the store branches out to the width of two buildings and is stocked floor to ceiling with out-of-print, used, and rare books. Amazingly, they seem to know exactly what is in stock, and if it is not on the shelves, they will order it. (Assume that a book not in stock *has* to be old or rare. This store has everything else.) There is as much talk as business conducted here, and you can continue the conversation at the store's next autograph party.

New York

CITYBOOKS
61 Chambers St (bet Broadway and Centre St)   669-8245
Mon-Fri: 9-5

This city government bookstore has access to more than 120 different official publications, all of which are dedicated to helping New Yorkers cope with their complex lives. *The Green Book* is the official directory of the City of New York, listing phone numbers and addresses of more than 900 government agencies and 6,000 officials. It includes state, federal, and international listings, the courts, and a section on licenses. There is also a unique collection of New York memorabilia: city-seal ties, pins, and rare New York photographs reproduced in calendars, posters, and much more.

NEW YORK BOUND BOOKSHOP
50 Rockefeller Plaza (lobby)   245-8503
Mon-Fri: 10-6; Sat: 12-4

Barbara Cohen and Judith Stonehill have assembled a printed ode to New York. The older and more esoteric a view of New York a publication has, the more these ladies covet and try to acquire it for their shop. The specialty is old, rare, out-of-print, and unusual ephemera (their word) relating to New York. History buffs will have a field day with the eyewitness accounts of early life in the Big Apple. Check out the photographs or browse through the current catalog, but definitely visit. Old New York is alive and well at New York Bound.

Occult

SAMUEL WEISER
132 E 24th St (nr Lexington Ave)   777-6363
Mon-Wed, Fri: 9-6; Thurs: 10-7; Sat: 9:30-5:30;
      Sun: 10:30-5

For stocking all kinds of publications on metaphysics, religion, and the occult, Samuel Weiser has a worldwide reputation that is well deserved. The shop is clean and modern, and its selection includes the eeriest titles found anywhere. The specialties cover almost any topic that is otherworldly: witchcraft, astrology, alchemy, magic, mysticism, ESP, flying saucers, Zen, and herb medicine. These are explored in books, magazines, periodicals, and foreign publications. (Some of the best in the field seem to be printed in foreign languages. Many are translated and sold here in both versions.) Finally, Samuel Weiser is one of the most obliging shops in town. They maintain a waiting list for out-of-print titles, and when the title arrives (by whatever mystical means), they will ship it anywhere in the world. The shop also sells topical videos, incense, and music tapes.

Out-of-Print

ACADEMY BOOK STORE
10 W 18th St (nr Fifth Ave)   242-4848
Mon-Sat: 9:30-9; Sun: 11-7

Academy has one of New York's largest selections of used, rare, and out-of-print books, records and CDs. The emphasis here is on literature, the arts, photography, architecture, philosophy, psychology, history, music, cinema, dance, and drama. In the music area, you will find a good choice of jazz recordings and a concentration on opera, contemporary classical, and early music.

CHARLOTTE F. SAFIR
1349 Lexington Ave, Apt 9B, New York, NY 10128
534-7933
Phone any time

Looking for particular book? Well, here is a lady who can save you a lot of time and effort. Charlotte Safir provides a search service for out-of-print books by mail or phone only. She has a fantastic network of contacts and can locate any kind of book, although she specializes in hard-to-find cookbooks and children's books. If you want to add to a collection or find out more about that special author you enjoy so much, this is the lady to call. Charlotte is efficient, persistent, and a pleasure to deal with.

Paperback

CLASSIC BOOK SHOP
World Trade Center (concourse level)   466-0668
Mon-Fri: 7:30-7; Sat: 10-5; Sun: 12-6

Classic Book Shop pursues the unusual, rare, and esoteric in paperbacks, and its selection is among the best. Although paperback at one time meant inexpensive, this is no longer always true. The 25-cent "pocketbook" is a thing of the past. Classic has books that cost upward of $10. Classic's forte is paperback "back stock," and it claims to have the best collection in the midtown area. Classic also carries hardcover books.

Photography

A PHOTOGRAPHER'S PLACE
133 Mercer St (at Prince St)   431-9358
Mon-Sat: 11-6; Sun: 12-5
Mail-order address: P.O. Box 274, Prince Street Station,
     New York, NY 10012

There is no doubt that photography is an art form to Harvey Zucker and the people who run A Photographer's Place. The shop is a temple to photographers, both past and present. It is *not,* however, a supply shop. Rather, it pays homage to great pictures of various eras and the people who took them. The owners claim to be "the only *all* photographic book shop in the city and perhaps the country." Their interest isn't so much in competing as in being the best they can be. It's a credo they feel is shared by every photographer, and the shop excels at offering inspiration, history, advice, and the latest in technological advances. A super catalog is free for the asking.

Rare

J.N. BARTFIELD
30 W 57th St (bet Fifth and Sixth Ave, 3rd floor)
245-8890
Mon-Fri: 10-5; Sat: 10-3

J.N. Bartfield is a legend in the field of old and rare books. His antiquarian book shop has what may be the country's largest and best collection of quality old books. The store is over 50 years old, and manager George Murray has been there for the majority of those years. There are sets of books distinguished by fine leather bindings, many of which were custom-bound for family libraries. The books themselves are often in mint condition. Today it is impossible to find editions newly bound in leather, but the antique editions are no more expensive than when they were first issued. Bartfield claims that many of these prized editions are actually less expensive than contemporary volumes of lesser quality. Bartfield's also has a strong reputation for old maps, Western art, and prints. There is an array of atlases, color-plate books, fore-edge paintings, bronzes, and watercolors.

PAGEANT PRINT AND BOOK SHOP
109 E 9th St (bet Third and Fourth Ave)   674-5296
Mon-Thurs: 10-7; Fri: 10-8; Sat: 11-7:30

This shop could be as old and rare as the stock it carries. A holdover from the days when this area was the rare- and old-book capital of the world, it displays and sometimes sells antiquarian books, maps, prints, and first editions from the fifteenth to the nineteenth centuries. I would doubt that anyone inside the shop could readily tell me what year it is today, let alone the date, but then again the shop is as timeless as its attitude. Pageant carries virtually every kind of printed matter. There are etchings and early printed items, and it would require several days just to admire the prints. But remember this is a book and print shop, and the emphasis is on the former. In the old days, this would have been one of a dozen shops. Today, it may be one of the very few places left for an authentic rare-book-buying experience.

XIMENES RARE BOOKS
19 E 69th St   744-0226
Mon-Fri: 9-5 (appointment advisable)

In a profession whose proprietorship immediately calls to mind a stooped Dickensian character peering through a pince-nez in a paneled library, Stephen Weissman of Ximenes stands alone. He has an understanding and knowledge of rare books that would seemingly come only after years of burial under dusty volumes. Furthermore, Ximenes' collection is among the more affordable (prices start at about $100), and Weissman will happily discourse on his trade, if asked. Listen carefully, because he knows his stuff. Weissman's specialties are English-language first editions printed between 1500 and 1890. In that field, he is a primary source.

Religious

CHRISTIAN PUBLICATIONS BOOK AND SUPPLY CENTER
315 W 43rd St (bet Eighth and Ninth Ave)   582-4311
Mon-Fri: 9:30-5:45; Thurs: 9:30-6:45; Sat: 9:30-4:45

This is the largest Christian bookstore in the metropolitan area. It has over 10,000 titles in stock, along with religious CDs, tapes, videos, and church and school supplies. A large number of these items are also available in Spanish, as befits the Latin neighborhood.

J. LEVINE BOOKS AND JUDAICA
5 W 30th St   695-6888
Mon-Wed: 9-6; Thurs: 9-7; Fri: 9-2; Sun: 10-5

The history of the Lower East Side is reflected in this store. Started back in 1902 on Eldridge Street, it was a fixture in the area for many years. Now things have changed, and J. Levine has moved uptown, just off Fifth Avenue. Being one of the oldest Jewish bookstores in the city, they are a leader in the Jewish-book marketplace in expanded quarters. There are also many gift items, tapes, coffee-table books, and thousands of items in Judaica, though the emphasis is still on the written word.

NEW YORK BIBLE SOCIETY
172 Lexington Ave (bet 30th and 31st St)   213-5454
Mon-Fri: 10-6

The New York Bible Society sells the world's most popular book in over 30 languages and in all kinds of editions. They can fill large church orders or special gifts. They have the greatest variety of low-cost New International Version Scriptures in the city. In addition, there are all kinds of Bibles, from pocket-sized to giant print, on audio and videotapes, and even a children's Bible storybook.

STAVSKY HEBREW BOOKSTORE
147 Essex St   674-1289
Sun-Thurs: 9-5; closed Sun in summer

This store supplies synagogues and schools with religious books and objects. While they will fill an order for ten coloring books, they are more accustomed to outfitting complete congregations, and they do it well. Their prices are fair, and service is excellent. Stavsky has the best collection of Jewish books, cassettes, CDs, Jewish videos, and everyday religious objects in the city.

Science Fiction

FORBIDDEN PLANET

821 Broadway	227 E 59th St
(at 12th St)	(nr Third Ave)
473-1576	751-4386
Mon-Wed: 10-7;	Mon-Sat: 11:30-8:30;
Thurs, Fri: 10-7:30;	Sun: 12-7
Sat: 10-7; Sun: 12-6	

When Mike Luckman started a science-fiction book-cum-toy shop in his native London, he quickly discovered that a good percentage of his customers were Americans clamoring for a similar shop at home. So Luckman obliged and first opened a satellite store at 12th Street and Broadway, directly across from the Strand. Pilgrimages have been made to the shrines of science-fiction literature and artifacts. While most of the stock is devoted to comic books and science-fiction publications, Luckman discovered in London that sci-fi devotees are not catholic in taste. First-edition collectors love Chewbacca face masks and bookends, and Darth Vadar fans browse through the vintage comic books and fantasy art. In between, there are enough toys and games to entertain the crew of *Star Trek*'s *Enterprise* during a trip to Saturn, and there is probably at least one copy of every science-fiction title ever written.

SCIENCE FICTION SHOP
163 Bleecker St   473-3010
Mon-Fri: 11:30-6:45; Sat: 11-6: Sun: 12-6

While there are other sci-fi stores, this is the only one devoted totally to science-fiction literature. There are past and current (but not future) books and magazines in the field, and that includes rare and want-listed literature. This is a special place for special people interested in a special subject.

Theater

ACTOR'S HERITAGE
262 W 44th St (bet Eighth Ave and Broadway)
944-7490
Mon-Sat: 9:30 a.m.-11:30 p.m.; Sun: 11-6:30

Actor's Heritage has an enormous stock of books, T-shirts, cards, records, scripts, and vocal selections relating to the theater. They claim to surpass every other store in the city in those areas. It certainly is worth browsing. Actor's Heritage also deserves a nod for being part of the effort to spruce up the Times Square area with interesting, legitimate businesses.

APPLAUSE THEATER & CINEMA BOOKS
212 W 71st St (at Broadway)   496-7511
Mon-Sat: 10-8: Sun; 12-6

This store offers the best selection of theater and cinema books in the world. There is great interest these days in anything having to do with theater literature, and these folks are on the cutting edge of the movement. They specialize in British plays and claim to have the play scripts for all British productions.

DRAMA BOOK SHOP
723 Seventh Ave (bet 48th and 49th St, 2nd floor)
944-0595
Mon, Tues, Thurs, Fri: 9:30-7; Wed: 9:30-8;
    Sat: 10:30-5:30; Sun: 12-5

Talk about drama! Once when we called to validate information there was a real drama going on at this bookstore: a theft was taking place! I am happy to report that there were no casualties, but the bums got away with $200 in books. Of course, things aren't always quite that exciting in this shop, which probably has the largest selection of drama books assembled outside of the Library of Performing Arts in Lincoln Center. Nearly everything in the shop relates to the written word. There are works on theater (both American and foreign), performers, scenery, props, makeup, lighting, staging, puppetry, magic, and all aspects of music and dance. One of the more scholarly undertakings is providing a catalog for each area of entertainment. The shop is best known for having the most complete selection of scores, accent tapes, libretti, arrangements, scripts, and plays in the world. While it is not always the least expensive, it is the biggest and one of the oldest (established in 1923).

RICHARD STODDARD—PERFORMING ART BOOKS
18 E 16th St (bet Fifth Ave and Union Sq, Room 305)
645-9576
Mon, Tues, Thurs-Sat: 11-6

Richard Stoddard runs a one-man operation dedicated to rare, out-of-print, and used books and to memorabilia relating to the performing arts. Despite having a Ph.D. from Yale in theater history and more than 15 years of experience as a dealer and appraiser of performing arts materials, Stoddard is determined to offer a broad range of items, not just expensive rarities. So, while there is an extensive collection of scarce books, playbills, souvenir programs, original scenic and costume designs, and back issues of performing arts magazines, Stoddard also stocks a case of paperback plays, which are within the financial reach of the most impoverished actor. There is a similar table of bargain books. Stoddard's pride, though, is his collection of scenic and costume designs. The sole agent for the estate of the late Jo Mielziner, the Broadway designer, Stoddard also has the drawings of a half-dozen other set designers. In fact, this is the only shop in the country that regularly sells such designs.

THEATREBOOKS
1600 Broadway (bet 48th and 49th St, Room 1009)
757-2834
Mon-Fri: 10:30-5; Sat: 10:30-1:30

Another example of the demand for theater literature, Theatre-books is just what its name implies. One of the only stores in the city with a selection of out-of-print and used books on the performing arts, it is also the only store with a search service for books not in stock. But the staff is proudest of being, in their own words, "the most trivia-laden staff of any theater bookstore in town." And that proves the real love of theater here. Two-fer theater tickets are available at the counter, and the staff couldn't be more helpful in discussing the current status of the Broadway theater. With their location and stock, the folks at Theatrebooks have an eye on it all.

Travel

COMPLETE TRAVELLER BOOKSTORE
199 Madison Ave (at 35th St)
685-9007; FAX: 212/982-7628
Mon-Fri: 9-7; Sat: 10-6; Sun: 12-5

An African safari? How about the Seychelles? How do I get around in China? The Complete Traveller specializes in new travel guides, books, travel literature, maps, and other travel accessories. They also have a fine collection of rare travel books. The store is very intimate, and they encourage browsing. There is an excellent catalog (only $2), which lists many travel series, travel books, maps and accessories. You can obtain it in the store or by mail.

TRAVELLER'S BOOKSTORE
22 W 52nd St (75 Rockefeller Plaza, bet Fifth and
    Sixth Ave, lobby of Time-Warner Bldg)   664-0995
Mon-Fri: 9-6; Sat: 11-5

Candace Olmsted and Jane Grossman, proprietors, practice what they sell. Theirs may be the only bookstore in the city with two distinct addresses for one location, but what could be more fitting for a bookstore for people on the move? They've developed a catalog for those who can't travel to them. As in the store, the catalog arranges books geographically, and each area is represented with a selection of maps, guides, dictionaries, fiction, and nonfiction. The ladies have a very comprehensive selection, and there is hardly a travel area they haven't covered in depth. Perhaps they've gained experience from trying to guide visitors to their single shop with double addresses!

Butterflies

MARIPOSA
South Street Seaport, Pier 17   233-3221
Daily: 10-9

Butterflies are free, but not at Mariposa, the Butterfly Gallery, where they are regarded as art. Butterflies are unique, and Mariposa (Spanish for butterfly) displays them separately, in panels, and as parts of groups. There are even butterfly farms, which breed and raise butterflies. They live their full one-month life span under ideal conditions for creating this art. I admit that sounds a little coldhearted, but Mariposa has to be seen to be appreciated. Besides, it would be impossible to appreciate so many beautiful specimens during their extremely fleeting lifetimes. A free catalog is available upon request.

Buttons

GORDON BUTTON COMPANY
222 W 38th St (near 7th Ave)   921-1684-5
Mon-Fri: 9-5

Peter Gordon's collection of old, unusual, and antique buttons is extensive. I would go to Gordon, however, for its new buttons, since the enormous stock is used by all of the neighboring garment manufacturers. Gordon's quality, selection, and variety are that good. Belt buckles, components, chains, and brass rings are also sold here at excellent discount, courtesy of the company's wholesale operation. Courtesy is the byword here. Most garment center manufacturers cannot be bothered with small retail customers, and their courtesy varies in direct proportion to the size of your order. But at Gordon, which also accepts mail orders, the size of the order seems irrelevant.

TENDER BUTTONS
143 E 62nd St   758-7004
Mon-Fri: 11-6; Sat: 11-5:30; closed Sat in July, Aug

Retail button stores can only hope to match the selection available here. Owners Diana Epstein and Millicent Safro have assembled one that is complete in variety as well as size. One antique wooden display cabinet shows off Tender Buttons' selection of natural, original buttons, many of them imported or made exclusively for them. Here are buttons of pearl, wood, horn, Navajo silver, leather, ceramics, bone, ivory, pewter, and precious stones—many of them antique. Today buttons are valuable as artwork, and a French enamel button can cost almost as much as a painting. Many unique pieces can be made by Tender Buttons into special cuff links—real conversation pieces for the lucky owner. They also have a fine collection of antique and period cuff links and men's stud sets. As a cuff-link buff, I have purchased some of my best pieces from this shop.

Candles

CANDLE SHOP
118 Christopher St (bet Bleecker and Hudson St)
989-0148
Mon-Sat: 12-8; Sun: 1-7

Thomas Alva Edison's inventions haven't made a flicker of an imprint on the folks at the Candle Shop. Ivan Smith has assembled a collection of beeswax, paraffin, and stearin candles in an assortment of sizes and colors for every possible need. In fact, it's positively illuminating to learn that candles are available in so many configurations.

Canvas

MATERA CANVAS PRODUCTS
5 Lispenard St (one block south of Canal St,
  off W Broadway)   966-9783
Mon-Fri: 10:30-5:30; closed Christmas week

John Matera is an expert with canvas. His store covers the canvas scene, from the raw product to very elaborate finished items. And since he manufactures as well as sells, he has a firm hand on the quality of everything the shop handles. There are custom-made boat covers, navy tops, automobile covers, artists' canvases, tarpaulins, and pool covers. Matera also turns out custom-made products for items that require canvas and nylon materials. (One customer used it to repair the top of a rolltop desk. It works fine!) If you need canvas, particularly large pieces, Matera should be your first choice.

China, Glassware

Superb showrooms of the best china, glass, silver, and crystal available anywhere:
Puiforcat (811 Madison Ave, at 68th St)
Daum (694 Madison Ave, at 62nd St)

Lalique (680 Madison Ave, at 61st St)
Villeroy & Boch (972 Madison Ave, at 76th St)
Although you may be able to find some items from these collections in other stores, no one has as complete a showing as these top-of-the-line houses. Madison Avenue has really become a showcase for the best in designer merchandise, both for the individual and for the home, and these relatively new stores are a part of the trend. But don't expect to find any bargains, unless you happen to drop in at sale time.

EASTSIDE GIFTS & DINNERWARE
351 Grand St (bet Essex and Ludlow St)   982-7200
Sun-Thurs: 10-6; Fri: 10-1:30

If you have been drooling over the beautiful china in the department stores but were hesitating because of the price, head down to the Lower East Side to Eastside Gifts. Here you will find Mikasa, Fitz and Floyd, Royal Doulton, Wedgwood, Haviland, Hutchenreuther, Lalique, and many others at great savings. In addition to dinnerware and crystal, they also carry a wide selection of stemware and flatware. So come here to replace those broken pieces of your best set!

LANAC SALES
73 Canal St (at Allen St)   925-6422
Mon-Thurs: 10-6; Fri: 10-2; Sun: 10-5

Across Allen Street from the old store, Lanac is still a source for chinaware, cut glass, silverware, and gifts at discount prices. Lanac has a reputation for having excellent discounts on everything in stock, and that stock includes some of the finest domestic and imported tableware and crystal in the city. *Lanac,* incidentally, is *Canal* spelled backward—just in case you get lost!

LOUIS KAPLAN RESTAURANT EQUIPMENT
250 Lafayette St (bet Prince and Spring St)   431-7300
Mon-Fri: 7-5

If you are looking for restaurant quality, heavy-duty merchandise, this is the place! You can find Lenox and Buffalo china, Libbey and imported French and German glassware, and Oneida silver, among many other well-known names. Copper, stainless steel, and heavy aluminum cookware is available at excellent prices, as are commercial-quality appliances. The real bargains are available when you buy in quantity.

ROBIN IMPORTERS
510 Madison Ave (bet 52nd and 53rd St)   752-5605
Mon-Fri: 9:30-5:30; Sat: 10-5; closed Sat in July, Aug

If you don't want to travel way downtown to take advantage of discount bargains in silverware, crystal, china, cutlery, dinner cloths, and giftware, this is a good place to shop. Prices are not as low as the Lower East Side stores, but the selection and quality are very adequate. Robin says they guarantee lowest prices for 30 days after purchase or the difference is refunded. Be sure to ask how long it will take for delivery of your purchase, as some of the suppliers in this field are notorious for lengthy waiting periods.

Christmas Decorations

CHRISTMAS EVE
1107 Broadway (bet 24th and 25th St, Room 414)
929-5500
Mon-Fri: 9-5

Some folks like to get ready for next Christmas the minute this year's event is over. If you are one of those, and you want to beat Santa to the package-wrapping fun, then this is your store. Even on the warmest day, you can cool off among a large selection of all kinds of Christmas decorations and accessories, and prices are a lot lower than they are during the holiday season, especially in the Christmas sections of the department stores. Remember this is a wholesale operation, so you will need to buy in sizable quantities. (How about setting up shop for your friends?)

Clothing and Accessories

SIZE COMPARISON CHART FOR CLOTHES

Children's clothing

				3	4	5	6	6x
American				3	4	5	6	6x
Continental				98	104	110	116	122
British				18	20	22	24	26

Children's shoes

American	8	9	10	11	12	13	1	2	3
Continental	24	25	27	28	29	30	32	33	34
British	7	8	9	10	11	12	13	1	2

Ladies' dresses, coats and skirts

American	3	5	7	9	11	12	13	14	15	16	18
Continental	36	38	38	40	40	42	42	44	44	46	48
British	8	10	11	12	13	14	15	16	17	18	20

Ladies' blouses and sweaters

American		10	12	14	16	18	20
Continental		38	40	42	44	46	48
British		32	34	36	38	40	42

Ladies' stockings

American	8	8½	9	9½	10	10½
Continental	1	2	3	4	5	6
British	8	8½	9	9½	10	10½

Ladies' shoes

American	5	6	7	8	9	10
Continental	36	37	38	39	40	41
British	3½	4½	5½	6½	7½	8½

Men's suits

American	34	36	38	40	42	44	46	48
Continental	44	46	48	50	52	54	56	58
British	34	36	38	40	42	44	46	48

Men's shirts

American	14	15	15½	16	16½	17	17½	18
Continental	37	38	39	41	42	43	44	45
British	14	15	15½	16	16½	17	17½	18

Men's shoes

American	7	8	9	10	11	12	13
Continental	39½	41	42	43	44½	46	47
British	6	7	8	9	10	11	12

Antique

ANTIQUE BOUTIQUE
712-714 Broadway (at Washington Pl)
227 E 59th St (bet Second and Third Ave)
460-8830
Mon-Fri: 10:30-9; Sat: 10:30-10; Sun: 12-8

Despite the name, clothing at Antique Boutique is more vintage than antique. Translated, this is the place to find recently recycled clothing, as opposed to a Victorian wedding gown. Prices reflect the fact that these clothes are not one-of-a-kind antiques. The selection is excellent; they carry everything from argyle socks to suede jackets and incredible sweaters in alpaca, mohair, and moth-free wools. There is rack after rack of clothing designed, as they say, to make their customers legends in any time.

HARRIET LOVE
412 W Broadway (at Spring St)   966-2280
Mon-Sat: 12-7; Sun: 12-6; closed Mon in Jan, Feb

I love that name! Harriet Love is right on the front line in the field of vintage apparel and accessories. Her shop is overflowing with beautiful alligator purses, jackets, and jewelry from Victorian days to the 1950s. Harriet also buys from vendors who interpret old pieces to create new treasures that have an old feeling. One of the nice pluses here is that Harriet takes expecially good care of gentlemen shoppers who want to purchase vintage jewelry for the lady in their life.

JEAN HOFFMAN
236 E 80th St   535-6930
Mon-Sat: 12-6 or by appointment

In a tiny space, Jean Hoffman offers one of the best selections of quality vintage items in the city. She has laces and trims, linens, jewelry, and all kinds of old clothing. For the bride-to-be who wants something really special, the stock of vintage wedding gowns is without equal in the country.

REMINISCENCE
74 Fifth Ave (near 13th St)   243-2292
Mon-Sat: 11:30-8; Sun: 1-6

It's fun to go back to the 1950s and 1960s at this "cool" emporium, which Stewart Richer created on lower Fifth Avenue. Although he is a child of this era, most of Richer's customers are between the ages of 13 and 30. The finds here are unusual and wearable, with large selections of colorful vintage clothing and attractive displays of jewelry, hats, shoes, and all kinds of accessories. Richer's goods, although vintage in style, are mostly new, and he has become a manufacturer who sells to outlets all over the world. Because of his large distribution, Richer is able to produce huge quantities and sell at low prices. Old or young, this is a store worth reminiscing about. Reminiscence Garage (175 MacDougal St, 979-9440) and Reminiscence (Ave B and 7th St, 353-0626) have better prices and more casual clothes.

SCREAMING MIMI'S
22 E 4th St (bet Lafayette and Bowery)   677-6464
Mon-Fri: 11-8; Sat: 12-8; Sun: 1-7

Owners Biff Chandler and Laura Wills, two fashion stylists, moved their landmark-upper West Side shop to new quarters in NoHo (that is, north of Houston!) Their selections feature styles from the 1950s, 1960s, and 1970s, as well as currently popular trends. A Katy K Western Boutique, a vintage housewares department, a shoe department, and the store's own line of sportswear round out a fun and exciting place to shop.

TRASH AND VAUDEVILLE
4 St. Mark's Pl (bet Second and Third Ave)
982-3590, 777-1727
Mon-Thurs: 12-8; Fri: 11:30-8; Sat: 11:30-9; Sun: 1-7:30

This place is hard to describe, since the stock changes almost constantly. What stock there is seems to have no boundaries. The store describes its stock as new and antique clothing, accessories, and original designs. Antique clothing here seems to mean 1950s to 1980s rock and roll styles, including some outrageous footwear, although there are some older—much older—things. There are some real finds here, but perhaps because this is a wholesale as well as retail business, you get the feeling that someone else has already escaped with the best values. More recently, the store has concentrated on new "new" clothing from Europe.

UNIQUE CLOTHING WAREHOUSE
726 Broadway (at 8th St)   674-1767
Mon-Thurs: 10-10; Fri, Sat: 10-12; Sun: 11-8

Harvey Russack opened his Unique Clothing Warehouse in 1973 in NoHo, and his beyond-the-fringe clothing consisted of embroidered denims, military-surplus items, and other bygone fads that are merely memories on the fashion scene. Russack started with "antique," and he has successfully worked through all of the latest trends. So the store has seen vintage menswear à la *The Sting* (Unique was one of the only sources for that style in the early days), military surplus, the Annie Hall look, surgeon's garb (remember that one?), high-tech, and clothes dyed in fluorescent hues. Shopping Unique is, well, a unique experience; the store itself is as much an experience as the clothes. One of the biggest mysteries in town is how Russack and his buyers seem to be able to predict the latest trends. There are those who have a clue. They claim Unique *makes* the trends, and that may be the answer. In any event, Unique is a bona fide success.

Bridal

I. KLEINFELD AND SON
8202 Fifth Ave	8209 Third Ave
Brooklyn, NY	Brooklyn, NY
(718) 833-1100	(718) 238-1500

Tues, Thurs: 11-9; Wed, Fri: 11-6; Sat: 10-6

The bridal business has changed a good deal. Today there are very limited collections at some specialty stores (like Bergdorf's and

Saks), but there is only one true bridal complex. I use the word *complex* because it involved two separate buildings. The half-century-old operation is called I. Kleinfeld and Son. The bridal gown collection (800 to 1,000 models in stock at all times) is located at 8202 Fifth Avenue, Brooklyn. Yes, I know, this is a book on Manhattan, but there is no store anywhere that can match Kleinfeld. The mother of the bride can find a special section called Kleinfeld's P.M., which specializes in evening wear. (Wedding guests will find this selection helpful, also). Kleinfeld carries every major name in bridal wear, including Priscilla of Boston, Carolina Herara, and Scassi. One-fifth of the collection is of international origin. A separate store for bridesmaids' gowns is located several blocks away at 8209 Third Avenue. The store prefers to operate by appointment; they can handle over 100 a day with their specialized personnel. This is *the* place to come when wedding bells will soon be ringing.

Children's—General

BEN'S FOR KIDS
1380 Third Ave (bet 78th and 79th St)
794-2330
Mon-Wed, Fri: 10-5; Thurs: 10-8; Sat: 11-5

Ben's is really a kids' department store! For youngsters up to age three you can find cribs, strollers, car seats, and playpens, as well as layettes, clothing, toys, nursing accessories, and more. This is one of New York's best juvenile outlets.

KINDERSPORT OF ASPEN
1260 Madison Ave (at 90th St)   534-5600
Mon-Fri: 10-6; Sat: 11-5

How New York! How chic! How typical! Where else but Madison Avenue would one find a shop founded in Aspen, Colorado, specializing in exclusive top lines of European clothing, sports, and ski wear for children? Did New York need such an outfitter exclusively for children? Apparently. KinderSport has made a big splash. Stylish tots aged 2 to 14 snap up KinderSport's sweaters, ski suits, and sportswear. If not all of them end up on the ski slopes for which they are intended, at least they make knockout fashion statements. And if Junior really is off for a trip to Aspen or the Alps, have no fear that KinderSport can outfit even a size two at a moment's notice. Price? The dearest. But then, what is it worth to have your two-year-old slide down the slopes in the finest togs?

M. KREINEN SALES
301 Grand St (at Allen St)   925-0239
Sun-Thurs: 9-5; Fri: 9-4

No sense in spending extra dollars to keep your kids in the most fashionable clothes. This Lower East Side establishment carries only brand-name goods, girls' sizes 7 to 14, and boys' sizes infant to 20. Discounts average about 25 percent, and you can count on the quality being as good as those at higher-priced specialty and department stores.

PETIT BATEAU BOTIQUE
930 Madison Ave (at 74th St)   288-1444
Mon-Sat: 10-6

From France comes some of the most charming outfits for kids. Petit Bateau specializes in French-designed clothing for infants, children, and teens. Most of the designs are exclusive, and the quality is absolutely top-notch.

PUSHBOTTOM FOR KIDS
252 E 62nd St (bet Second and Third Ave)
888-3336
Mon-Sat: 11-7

With a name and reputation like Pushbottom's, the goods have to be special. And indeed they are. If your kid is something special (and whose isn't?), get the young ones outfitted here. Pushbottom specializes in sweaters, but they can outfit your child from newborn to size seven. All designs are originals, so your kid can have fun telling his friends that an outfit was made just for him (or her).

RICE AND BRESKIN
323 Grand St (at Orchard St)   925-5515
Sun-Fri: 9-5

If the Lower East Side has a quality shop for children's clothing, Rice and Breskin is probably it. Wrapped in plastic, the merchandise includes good brand names at a 20 percent discount or more. They specialize in infant clothing and baby gifts. Despite its Lower East Side location, the sales help is charming, even motherly.

WICKER GARDEN
1318 Madison Ave (at 93rd St)   410-7000
Mon-Sat: 10-5:30; closed Sat in July, Aug

Want to meet a typical New Yorker? Pamela Scurry of Wicker Garden fits that category. Besides having two children and a husband who is CEO of a real-estate company, she operates a very successful business. The Wicker Garden was established as a prime source for wicker furniture and antique hand-painted adult furniture, plus accessories displayed in a Victorian garden setting. When Pam needed furniture for her children, the Wicker Garden's Baby (upstairs) was created. And when her children needed clothing to match their antique bedroom suites, the Wicker Garden's Children was set up to outfit them and other lucky kids. The infant's furnishings department has museum-quality wicker furniture and accessories, including antique quilts, linens, and lace infant furnishings along with a line of hand-painted furniture.

Children's—Used

ONCE UPON A TIME
171 E 92nd St (bet Lexington and Third Ave)
831-7619
Mon-Sat: 10-6

This children's resale shop on the Upper East Side has clothing from infants to sizes 10-14 for boys and girls. Some of the items have never been worn, and all of them are in almost new condition and attractively priced. At the end of each season, the previous season's clothing goes for a fraction of what it would sell for in department stores. In addition, the seasons are a bit more realistically timed, meaning you can buy a bathing suit in July here.

SECOND ACT CHILDREN'S WEAR
1046 Madison Ave (bet 79th and 80th St, upstairs)
988-2440
Mon: 9-2; Tues-Sat: 9-4:45 (closed Sat in summer)

The best buys here are the clothes that were bought and used for only one or two occasions, such as communion dresses, Easter outfits, and flower-girl gowns. Some of the other items don't seem worth the one-third-of-the-original-cost price tag, but everything is kept in A-1 condition. All clothing is washed and ironed or cleaned before it is put up for sale, and it is, indeed, in "like new" condition. Clothing is consigned to separate rooms according to sex, and within these rooms everything is sized in order. Sizes run from girls' infant to 14 and boys' infant to 20. In addition to clothing, there are ice skates, riding apparel, ski boots, books, and toys.

Costumes

M.I.S. RETAIL
736 Seventh Ave (at 49th St, 2nd floor)
765-8342
Mon-Fri: 10:30-6:30

Are you going to appear at your office party dressed like Groucho Marx? Is your son going to play Superman at the school benefit? M.I.S. is the specialist for both amateurs and professionals when it comes to stage makeup, wigs, beards, and all kinds of theatrical accessories.

Dance Wear

CAPEZIO'S

The various Capezio stores are the definitive outlets for dance paraphernalia, including athletic wear, aerobic shoes, and fashion shoes. The new shop (1650 Broadway, at 51st St; 245-2130) is the largest dance-theater retail store in the world. Capezio East (136 E 61st St, at Lexington Ave; 758-8833) reflects the East Side neighborhood. The most interesting shop is the one in the Village (177 MacDougal St; 477-5634), which even has a men's department. There is also a Capezio's at Steps (2121 Broadway, at 74th St); 799-7774) and a new store called Capezio at Alvin Ailey (211 W 61st St, 3rd floor; 767-0940). Hours vary, but all stores are open on Saturday. Capezio East and Capezio at Steps are both open on Sunday afternoons.

FREED OF LONDON

922 Seventh Ave (at 58th St)   489-1055, 800/835-1701
Mon-Sat: 10-6 (phone orders: 10-4)

Freed of London has landed on its toes in New York, and the venerable English establishment has brought along its tradition of supplying the best and finest in dance supplies. The style is definitely traditional, but there is virtually no piece of dance gear that Freed does not carry or cannot order. The store keeps leg warmers, leotards, ballet shoes, skirts, and tutus in stock. A list of the shop's clientele reads like a who's who of stars who've danced in London (the store carries, as a matter of course, the complete line of regulation wear for the Royal Academy of Dancing). For those who can't stop in, there's a measuring chart and mail-order catalog available. For dancers, this store is a must. If you're simply a dance fan, this is where you'd be likely to spot your favorite dancer.

Furs

BREAKAWAY

125 Orchard St (at Delancey St)   475-6660
Daily: 9-6

If price is your only objective in buying a fur or leather coat, this is a place you'll want to visit. They offer designer furs and leathers at considerable discounts, but personal advice and attention are in short supply.

FURS BY DIMITRIOS
130 W 30th St (bet Sixth and Seventh Ave)
695-8469
Mon-Fri: 9-6; Sat: 10-4; Sun: 10-4

This store is the best source for men's fur coats at wholesale prices. The racks are shaggy with furs of all descriptions and in all sizes for both genders. Prices are wholesale but go up slightly if the garment has to be specially ordered. This shouldn't be necessary, though, since the off-the-rack selection is probably the most extensive and of the best quality in the city.

G. MICHAEL HENNESSY FURS
333 Seventh Ave (bet 28th and 29th St, 5th floor)
695-7991
Mon-Fri: 9:30-5; Sat: by appointment

Furs are one item you want to be very sure of when you buy. By this, I mean you want to be sure of the people you are buying from; they must be knowledgeable and have the proper kind of stock, but more than that they must be reliable and honest. I can tell you that this firm strongly fits the mold. Michael Hennessy started as an international fur trader, ran a salon in Beverly Hills, and later became fur director of Bonwit Teller and president of Maximilian Furs. Wife Rubye, one talented and charming lady, is a former editor of *Seventeen* magazine and the *Philadelphia Inquirer*. These folks manufacture high-quality designer furs for women that are sold to stores around the world; readers of this book are fortunate because these same items are available to the public at great values. Best prices are for the in-stock furs, particularly mink, which is the house specialty. Wonderful buys are available for ladies who want a mink coat made to order. There are two new specialties: large-size furs and cashmere-with-fur coats, excellent for use from fall through spring. Hundreds of my readers have been taken care of by Rubye and Michael; every one of them has turned out to be a satisfied customer.

HARRY KIRSHNER AND SON
307 Seventh Ave (bet 27th and 28th St)   243-4847
Mon-Fri: 9-6; Sat: 10-5

Kirshner should be one of your first stops for any kind of fur product, from throw pillows to full-length mink coats. They reline, clean, alter, or store any fur at rock-bottom prices. What's even better is that they are neither pushy nor snobbish, which may make them the only place to repair Aunt Minnie's tattered but beloved lamb stole. Harry Kirshner offers tours of its factory, and if nothing available appeals to the customer, a staff member will sit down and try to draw a coat to specifications. Many times, however, the factory offers a collection of secondhand furs that the company has restored to perfect and fashionable condition. And many customers come in for a *new* fur and walk out with a slightly worn one for a fraction of what they were prepared to spend. Harry Kirshner is the only place in New York that offers such a wide choice.

H.B.A. FUR
150 W 30th St (3rd floor)   564-1080
Mon-Fri: 8:30-5; Sat (Oct-Jan): 9-1

H.B.A. was one of the first of the fur-industry garment lofts to open to the public. As a result, they are more experienced and better attuned to customer requests than some of their neighbors. The stock includes all kinds of furs, but there is a tendency to avoid trends and stick to more classic styles. As a result, this year's fads, while available, are not singled out as the *only* thing to wear. (Please note that Bob Mackie designs for H.B.A.) Rather, there's a good selection of timeless furs, which can be taken off the racks or made to order. Prices are wholesale. Harold Frishman (the *H* of the name) is a knowledgeable and absolutely honest man. Ask for him, and he'll show you one of New York's top fur collections at unbeatable prices.

RITZ THRIFT SHOP
107 W 57th St   265-4559
Mon-Sat: 9-6

Down the block and across the street from Carnegie Hall, the Ritz Thrift Shop is as much an institution as its neighbor. And its clientele is just as loyal. The Ritz Thrift Shop seems to have been in business forever, buying and selling used furs to smart shoppers. And all those years of experience have made the management as knowledgeable and fashion-conscious as the finest retail operations. The Ritz buys used furs outright. Fifty percent of the stock is bought from individual customers, and the rest comes from furriers who took them as trade-ins. Because they are not usually a consignment operation (and perhaps because they offer free repairs and storage for as long as their client owns the coat), they are very picky about what they will buy. So, if your coat is passé, damaged, or not very good to begin with, the Ritz won't be interested—unless your coat is so outdated it's "in." (Jackets from the 1940s and longhaired and silver-fox furs fall in this category. The Ritz can't get enough of them.) So, customers are offered an incredible array of modern, stylish furs at prices roughly one-third of what the fur cost originally. It's understandable why a good portion of their business is with people who trade in their furs every two years or so. The Ritz is also contemporary enough to sell 1980s men's furs.

Hosiery

FOGAL
680 Madison Ave (bet 61st and 62nd St)   759-9782

510 Madison Ave (at 53rd St)   355-3254
Mon-Sat: 10-6

Before Fogal came to New York from Switzerland, the thought of a Madison Avenue boutique devoted to hosiery was, well, foreign. But since its opening in 1982, it's hard to imagine Manhattan without it. If it's new, fashionable, and different leg wear, Fogal has it. Plain hosiery comes in over a hundred hues, at last count; the designs and patterns of the colors make the number of choices almost incalculable. You might say that Fogal's has a leg up on the competition, but there have never been any serious contenders.

JACOB YOUNG AND SON
329 Grand St (at Orchard St)   925-9232
Sun-Fri: 9-5

Jacob Young has hosiery for men and children, and pantyhose for women, at unbelievably low prices. Hanes underwear for men is also a real find. Don't look for big smiles and pleasant greetings, just grab the bargains. (P.S. They now say that they are "working on their smiles!")

LOUIS CHOCK
74 Orchard St   473-1929
Sun-Thurs: 9-5; Fri: 9-1

It's hard to find a classification for this store. It seems to stock a little of everything, but perhaps the old-fashioned term "dry goods" sums up the stock sold here. Louis Chock sells dry goods for the home, school, and the entire family. There appears to be a subspecialty in hosiery and family underwear. Children's nightwear —which is only peripherally related to the underwear category—is available in a large choice of colors and sizes, and there is something in the hosiery section for every member of the family. Furthermore, everything in the store is sold at a discount that begins at 25 percent. Another plus: there is a larger discount on items bought in quantity. Louis Chock also has a mail-order department, offering a 25 to 30 percent discount on everything in stock. A catalog can be obtained for $1.

M. STEUER HOSIERY COMPANY
31 W 32nd St (nr Fifth Ave)   563-0052
Mon-Fri: 7:45-5:20; Sat: 10-4

By walking one block from Herald Square, hosiery wearers can save a bundle. Steuer is a wholesale operation that treats each retail customer as a wholesaler, no matter how small the order. They even speak a half-dozen languages—the better to welcome visitors to New York. There is a huge selection and large inventory of name-brand hosiery, socks, pantyhose, and dance wear. Steuer has been known to fill unusual requests with aplomb.

Jeans

CANAL JEANS
504 Broadway (off Spring St)   226-1130, 226-0737
Sun-Thurs: 11-7; Fri, Sat: 10-8

From the moment you walk by the bins full of sweaters, you know Canal Jeans is not your ordinary store. And it's not. Canal Jeans buys, sells, and wholesales the latest SoHo looks and has made itself a popular place. The look is certainly casual. Even their best *new* clothing stretches the meaning of sportswear, but if it's bomber jackets, brightly colored pants, tops, and outfits you want, this is the place to shop. A large percentage of the customers are Europeans who stock up on as many pairs of jeans as they can hoard in their suitcases and backpacks. (They can sell them back home and make enough profit to pay for their trip.) Other clothing items include punk outfits, bins of junk clothes (don't bother— they're just that), and closeouts.

CLASSICS
15 Third Ave (bet 7th St and St. Marks Pl)
475-7170
Mon-Sat: 12:30-8:30; Sun: 1-7

If you can find this place, you are in for some real bargains in 501 and 505 Levis, flight jackets, casual shirts, chinos, and grubby wear. The service is minimal, the ambiance hardly Fifth Avenue, but the savings make up for it.

Leather

BARBARA SHAUM
69 E 4th St   254-4250
Wed-Fri: 1-8; Sat: 1-6

Barbara Shaum does magical things with leather. The main stock is custom-made sandals, although there are some ready-made pairs available for emergencies. In addition, there are bags, sterling silver buckles, belts (with handmade brass, nickel-silver, inlaid wood, and copper buckles), attaché cases, and briefcases. Everything is designed in the shop, and Barbara Shaum meticulously crafts each item, using only the finest materials. She's a wonder.

NORTH BEACH LEATHER
772 Madison Ave (at 66th St)　　772-0707
Mon-Fri: 10-7; Sat: 10-6; Sun: 1-6

If leather wear connotes home on the range or some motorcycle bar on the Village waterfront, then you are obviously unaware that leather is the flip side of fur and can be just as elegant. North Beach Leather's locations are proof enough of that (with stores in Houston, Los Angeles, and San Francisco, to name but a few), and the fashions are further evidence. Madison Avenue isn't the place to look for an outfit to wear when cleaning the barn, and North Beach couldn't oblige, even if it wanted to. But if you need a leather ensemble for an outing in the Mercedes, then North Beach is the place to look. There is, of course, an emphasis on jackets, coats, and outerwear, but there are also suits and even skirts and dresses for women. Their leather jackets for men are just the thing to round out an outfit. But they aren't cheap.

SAN MICHEL LEATHER
379 Fifth Ave (bet 35th and 36th St)　　481-4110
Call for store hours

Right in the heart of Manhattan, just one block from the Empire State Building, San Michel features the finest leather and suede apparel for both men and women. Designer names are available on some of the merchandise. The store claims that every piece of merchandise is sold at a price that is from 40 to 60 percent lower than elsewhere; you might check around before you buy to make sure this is true for the item you select.

Men's and Women's—General

BARNEY'S
111 Seventh Ave (at 17th St)　　929-9000
Mon-Thurs: 10-9; Fri: 10-8; Sat: 10-7; Sun: 12-6

World Financial Center (200 Liberty St)　　945-1600
Mon, Tues, Wed, Fri: 10-7; Thurs: 10-9; Sat: 10-6;
Sun: 12-6

For years the best place in New York to shop for men's and boy's clothing and furnishings, Barney's has now grown into a two-unit operation that features women's merchandise as well. Additional property next door to the original location now houses a stunning women's store, with floor after floor of stylish goods. In addition, a number of boutique sections of accessories, home furnishings, gifts, and the like have been created to make the store a very upscale specialty operation. But it is still in the men's area where the store shines. Nowhere will you find the selection and depth of merchandise that Barney's offers in such a wide range of styles and prices. Practically every major menswear designer is represented here. Shopping in the main store is not easy, however. First, one has to look in section after section to see all the clothing in a particular style or size, and the store's owners are obsessed with the possibility of pilferage. Then, their paper-flow system is annoyingly slow and complex, and the average salesperson here reminds one of some of those found in used-car lots. The new store at the World Financial Center carries only the men's classifications. Prices are hefty, but sales events at Barney's can provide some excellent bargains. By the way, Barney's has always had some of the best tailors in town.

CASHMERE-CASHMERE
840 Madison Ave (bet 69th and 70th St)   988-5252

595 Madison Ave   935-2522
Mon-Fri: 10-6; Sat: 12-6

Silk, thanks in part to the growth of Silk Surplus, is no longer a luxury fabric in this city. Not so cashmere! At this shop, every possible type of clothing from all over the world is available. The weights vary, so that it is possible to wear cashmere year round. The styles vary as well to reflect different lifestyles. There's clothing for men and women, as well as cashmere accessories for the home. A visit here makes cashmere a necessity in one's life!

CHARIVARI
(locations and phones noted within review)
All stores open daily, late Thurs nights, and Sun

The Upper West Side was a fashion desert until Selma Weiser arrived on the scene with her first Charivari. With a smart merchant's sense of location and fashion, Selma and her family have guided the growth of this organization into a six-store chain. Mother Selma still has a major hand in most of the operation, while daughter Barbara and son Jon do most of the buying. The men's store (2339 Broadway, at 85th St; 873-7242) is where the more conservative businessman can find office clothes. Charivari for women (2315 Broadway, bet 83rd and 84th St; 873-1424) has the same image for women. The sports store (201 W 79th St, at Amsterdam; 799-8650) is brimming with fun play clothes at reasonable prices. The Workshop (441 Columbus Ave, at 81st; 496-8700) features avant-garde Japanese-designed merchandise for both men and women. Charivari 72 (257 Columbus Ave, at 72nd St; 787-7272) and Charivari 57 (18 W 57th St; 333-4040) feature high-fashion designer clothing for men and women. The 72nd Street store is more intimate; the 57th Street store is cold and uninviting. Running an operation as spread out as this one is difficult at best. The Weisers, who possess a unique flair for the dramatic in merchandise presentation, might well concentrate on passing on that same expertise to their struggling salespeople.

COCKPIT
595 Broadway (bet Houston and Prince St)
925-5455
Mon-Sat: 12:30-7; Sun: 12:30-6

This is a fascinating store for anyone interested in flying. A fabulous collection of flight jackets (the best in the city), Flying Tiger shirts, China-Burma baggies, athletic jerseys, T-shirts, coveralls, trench coats, flight boots, sweaters, insignias, books, watches, bags, flight suits, and dozens of gift items are displayed to create an attractive, aviational atmosphere. Royal Air Force jackets, European jeans, sweaters, boots, and insignias, are also available. One of the more interesting specialty items is a collection of pilot's manuals from World War II. I was fascinated by the Army Air Force pilot's cloth charts, printed by the Army Map Service in May 1945 for the Allied invasion of the Japanese mainland. They are great gifts for the World War II military buff.

DAFFY'S
111 Fifth Ave (at 18th St)   529-4477
Mon-Sat: 10-9; Sun: 11-6

335 Madison Ave (at 44th St)   557-4422
Mon-Fri: 10-9; Sat: 10-6; Sun: 11-5

Daffy's describes itself as a bargain clothing outlet for millionaires. Well, I guess a lot of folks got to be millionaires by saving money, so perhaps they have something going for them. But millionaire or not, you can find great bargains here in better clothing for men, women, and children. Fine leather items are a specialty. This is not your usual "off-price" store; they have done things with a bit of flair.

DOWN HOME AMERICA
1367 Third Ave (at 78th St)   861-4200
Mon-Fri: 11-8; Sat: 11-7;
Sun: 1-5 (March-June, Sept-Dec)

Hurrah for the red, white, and blue. It sure is refreshing to see a store that is proud to boast that all of their items are made in this country! Featured are men's and women's unisex sportswear, shirts, sweaters, pants, shorts, and T-shirts in dozens of different colors at sensible prices. The selection includes more good Yankee merchandise like umbrellas, blankets, picnic baskets, yo-yos, barbecue sauces, and relishes. You almost expect George M. Cohan to appear from behind the counter!

EMPORIO ARMANI
110 Fifth Ave (at 16th St)   727-3240
Mon-Sat: 11-7

In the lower canyons of Fifth Avenue, where lofts feature off-priced men's clothing, you can now walk into one of the classiest designer showrooms in the city. Emporio Armani clothes for both men and women are shown with style and taste, befitting the hefty price tags. There is sportswear and dress-up wear, accessories and jeans, all with the distinct Armani look. It well could be that this boutique will be the forerunner of a move from pricey Madison Avenue for some of the better-known names in the ready-to-wear business. Don't miss this one, especially if you're "just looking"!

HOUSE OF LODEN
155 W 72nd St (bet Broadway and Columbus Ave,
    5th floor)   362-7443
Mon-Fri: 11-6 (may be closed in summer)

If you can figure out when they are open and snag an "appointment," you will be treated to a room full of the finest Austrian Lodenwool coats, car coats, wools, and capes for men and women. This outlet will custom-order exact sizes, fabrics, and designs. Better still, there is an incredible in-stock selection in sizes and designs. In a city where the top department and specialty stores have a very limited selection of the Loden coat, this is amazing.

MATSUDA

461 Park Ave
  (at 57th St)
935-6969
Mon-Fri: 11-7
Sat: 11-6

156 Fifth Ave
645-5151
Mon-Fri: 11-7
Sat: 11-6
Sun: 12-5

Mitsuhiro Matsuda is one of Japan's most successful fashion designers. For both men and women he designs lines of business wear, casual and sportswear, and active sportswear. There is also a line of apparel and accessory basics, including bedding, bath items, nightwear, hats, glasses, jewelry, ties, gloves, belts, socks, and shoes. Madonna and Cher are customers here, so you know the place is at the forefront of fashion.

OTTO PERL
HOUSE OF MAURIZIO
18 E 53rd St (5th floor)   759-3230
By appointment only

Otto and Susanne Perl cater to women who like the functional, fashionable tailored look that suits create. Although they can copy almost any kind of garment, the Perls are known for their coats, two-, three-, or four-piece suits, and mix-and-match combinations. Usually, this look is favored by busy executives, artists, or journalists who have to look very well-dressed but don't have hours to spend dressing. Perl creates blazers (or suits) in a range of 2,000 different fabrics, but those in silk, linen, cotton, or a solid virgin wool are sensational. In addition to the women's garments, the Perls can design and create coats and suits for men in the same broad range of fabrics. They promise fast service, expert tailoring, and moderate prices on everything they do, but no alterations.

POLO-RALPH LAUREN
867 Madison Ave (at 72nd St)   606-2100
Mon-Sat: 10-6; Thurs: 10-8

I am a Ralph Lauren fan. He has probably done as much as anyone in this period to bring a classic look to American fashion and furnishings. His showpiece store in Manhattan is fabulous, housed in the magnificent remodeled Rhinelander mansion. There are four floors of merchandise for men, women, and the home, beautifully displayed and expertly accessorized. You will see a much larger selection here than in any of the specialty Polo boutiques in the stores. There are several things to be aware of, however. One is an attitude problem of the help: I'm sure that Ralph himself would not put up with the above-it-all way some of his people greet customers who don't look like they have big bucks to spend. Then again, although the clothes and furnishings are stylish and classy, one can find items of equal or better quality elsewhere at considerably lower price tags. But then, shopping elsewhere is not nearly as stylish as carrying your item out in one of those popular green bags. And that little horse says something about you!

Men's Formal Wear

JACK AND COMPANY FORMAL WEAR
128 E 86th St   722-4609, 722-4455
Mon-Fri: 10-7; Sat: 10-4; Sat in July, Aug: 10-2

Jack and Company rent and sell men's ready-to-wear formal wear. They carry an excellent selection of sizes (nearly all) and names (After Six, Lord West, and Palm Beach), and they have a good reputation for service since 1925. In sales or rentals, Jack's can supply head-to-toe formal wear. The people here are excellent at matching outfits to customers, as well as knowing exactly what is socially required for any occasion. Same-day service is available, and you can rent with an option to buy!

ZELLER TUXEDOS

201 E 56th St (at Third Ave)   355-0707
Mon-Fri: 9-7:45; Sat: 10-4:45

1010 Third Ave (at 60th St)   688-0100
Mon-Fri: 9-7:45; Sat: 10-4:45; Sun: Noon-4:45

Zeller Tuxedos is tops in sales and rentals of tuxedos, formal shirts, capes, overcoats with fur collars, and all the accessories necessary for that big night on the town. Merchandise from Canali, Belvest, Bill Kaiserman, Bally, Valentino, and Burberry is featured. They'll even fit you with appropriate shoes. Zeller provides made-to-order service for those who require special attention.

Men's—General

CAMOUFLAGE

141 Eighth Ave (at 17th St)   741-9118
Mon-Fri: 12-7; Sat: 11-6; Sun: 1-5 (Sun hours in
     April, May, Nov, Dec only)

Camouflage has never been just another store, and more often than not, it has managed to shine out of all proportion to its small size. If you've got patriotic tastes, this may be the store for you. It is one of the few shops that eschews foreign designers, selling only American clothing. New resources are Jeffrey Banks, Pendleton, Ruff Hewn, New Republic, Heartland, and Calvin Klein, plus private label trousers, shirts, ties and accessories. Prices range from very reasonable (their chinos may be one of the best buys in the city) to good, considering those pricey designer names. But one of a Camouflage's best virtues is the ability to dress its customer with a dignified but special appearance. There's nothing at Camouflage that would blend into the wallpaper.

EISENBERG AND EISENBERG

85 Fifth Ave (6th floor)   627-1290
Mon-Wed, Fri: 9-6; Thurs: 9-7; Sat: 9-5:30; Sun: 10-4

The Eisenberg and Eisenberg style is a classic one that dates from 1898, the year they opened. Although Eisenberg and Eisenberg has a loft in the menswear garment district, it consistently offers top quality and good prices on suits, tuxedos, coats, and sportswear. E & E also stocks outerwear, slacks, name-brand raincoats, cashmere sports jackets, and 100 percent silk jackets. All are sold at considerable discounts, and alterations are available. London Fog coats are featured here, and no label is better known for wet-weather needs.

GILCREST CLOTHES COMPANY
900 Broadway (at 20th St)   254-8933
Mon-Fri: 8-5; Sat: 8:30-5; Sun: 9:30-4

No fancy fixtures in this upstairs loft, just very good buys on many top names in quality men's clothing. If you are looking for suits by Ralph Lauren, Alexander Julian, Lanvin, Perry Ellis, or Adolfo, and if the prices uptown make you go back to wearing that same old suit in your closet, then take an hour off to see the Gilcrest operation. The folks here are helpful and knowledgeable, and they are not pushy. While you are looking, ask to see their own line of suits—excellent tailoring at sensible prices. There is no charge for alterations.

GORSART
9 Murray St   962-0024
Mon-Fri: 9-6; Sat: 9-5:30

Gentlemen! If you are the natural-shoulder type, read on. And if you find the style and quality of Brooks Brothers or Paul Stuart appealing but the prices appalling, head downtown to this little known jewel. In 1921, two brothers started catering to the financial community with a new twist at that time: quality merchandise at a discount. Moe Davidson and Neil Roberts purchased the store from the founders in 1975 and carry on the same tradition in a loft that offers classy suits made by H. Freeman and Arthur Freedberg (among others) at prices that will make you smile. These are not seconds or mark-downs. In addition to suits, there is a nice selection of sportswear and furnishings, all discounted. The reason for the great prices? Simple: low overhead. You can pick up a tux for about half the uptown price, and you don't pay for tailoring on anything, unless of course it's a complete restructuring. They have 35 tailors in-house on the job all the time. This is a special store, fellows, and you will enjoy shopping here. No high-pressure selling, no gimmicks, just value and service.

IRVING BARON CLOTHES
343 Grand St (at Orchard St)   475-1718
Mon-Thurs: 9:30-6; Wed: 9:30-7:30; Sat, Sun: 9-5:30;
summer: Sun-Fri: 9:30-6

Once inside, a customer at Irving Baron might think he's in a posh Fifth Avenue store. Such brand names as Groshire, Marzotto, Corneliani, Yves St. Laurent, Halston, Le Baron, Louis Roth, London Fog, Mondo, Torras, Countess Mara, Damon, and Calvin Klein are part of the stock, which, the staff says, can dress a man from top to bottom. (Shoes are an exception.) It is only when the bill is presented that the customer realizes that this is, indeed, a Lower East Side store, for the discount starts at 25 percent. Suits, sport jackets, pants, overcoats, raincoats, outerwear, shirts, sweaters, and ties are carried to suit men sized from 36 short to 50 long. The salespeople are excellent.

J. PRESS
7 E 44th St (bet Fifth and Madison Ave)   687-7642
Mon-Sat: 9-6

As one of New York's classic, conservative men's stores, J. Press prides itself on its sense of timelessness. Its salespeople, customers, and attitude have changed little from the time of J. Press to that of Richard Press today. Styles are impeccable and distinguished, if not distinguishable. Blazers are blue, and shirts are button-down and straight. Even in the days when button-down collars were out, Press was such a bastion of support for them that it went so far as to make them available in colors other than blue.

LESH CLOTHING
115 Fifth Ave (at 19th St, 6th floor)   255-6893
Mon-Fri: 9-6; Sat: 9-4; Sun: 10-3

Irving Lesh claims that his family business was one of the first, if not *the* first, wholesale men's clothing lofts. He has a certain pride in the bare-piped surroundings, and the quality of the suits, sports jackets, slacks, and outerwear seems designed to prove that here the dollar goes for the merchandise rather than the décor. Lesh manufactures its own suits, and when the overhead (i.e., rent) gets to be too much, they move to another (read: cheaper) loft. Consequently, it always pays to call before paying Lesh a visit. Speaking of overhead, that's where you'll find the merchandise. It literally hangs from the rafters and the pipe racks. The selection and quality of suits, tuxedos, and sports coats is great. Lesh has been manufacturing them since 1935, and they adhere to the fine nuances of tailoring.

LOUIS BARALL AND SON
58 Lispenard St (bet Canal St and Broadway)
226-6195
Mon-Fri: 9:30-6; Sat: 9:30-5; closed Sat in July, Aug

Although it has been in existence for 75 years and Louis Barall has been succeeded by Irving Barall, this store is one of the best-kept secrets in town. The only possible reason is that the savvy Wall Street types who shop here have no desire to share the market with anyone else. Styles are conservative and traditional at best. But that doesn't mean old-fashioned or even out of season; it simply bypasses the ultratrendy. If your style runs to the tried and true, try Barall. Prices *begin* at one-third off list price and go down from there. Garments—all with recognizable names—come in first-quality or clearly marked irregulars, with the latter going for about 50 percent off list price and more.

L. S. MEN'S CLOTHING
19 W 44th St (Room 403)   575-0933
Mon-Thurs: 9-7; Fri: 9-4 (Sun: 10-4 at 19 W 44th St)

L. S. bills itself as the "Executive Discount Shop," but I would go further and call them a must for the fashion-minded businessman. For one thing, their midtown location precludes a trip downtown to the Fifth Avenue-in-the-teens area that is the usual spot for finding men's discount clothing. Better still, as owner Israel Zuber puts it, "There are many stores selling $200 suits discounted, but we are one of the few that discount the $400 to $600 suits *and* are located in mid-Manhattan." The main attraction, though, is the tremendous selection of styles in stock. Style is primarily executive class, and within that category a man could almost outfit himself entirely at L. S. The natural and soft-shoulder designer suits are available in all sizes. This is one of the top spots for top names. I would make it number one on the midtown shopping itinerary.

MANO A MANO
580 Broadway (bet Houston and Prince St)
219-9602
Mon-Thurs: 12-7:45; Fri: 12-8:45; Sat: 11-7:45;
   Sun: 12-6:45

There are monkeys in cages, very hip salespeople, and a general carnival atmosphere here, but don't let all of that keep you from investigating the huge selection of stylish sportswear, leather items, suits, and accessories for men. If you have seen it in one of the men's fashion magazines, you no doubt will find it here at less than uptown prices. Although there is a selection of women's items available, this is definitely the store for the modern man.

NAPOLEON
Trump Tower (Fifth Ave at 57th St)   759-1110
Mon-Sat: 10-6

Trump Plaza
1048 Third Ave (at 62nd St)   308-3000
Mon-Sat: 10-7

Plaza Hotel Lobby
768 Fifth Ave   759-8000
Mon-Sat: 10-6:30

This is one of the number-one men's boutiques in the city—or anywhere, for that matter. The customer is emperor here, and what an empire he has! Napoleon stocks only the finest in haberdashery. The style is set by modern Italian designers; there's an extensive line by Brioni, Mila Schon, Stefano Ricci, and Ermenegildo Zegna. Its superb quality and style are matched only by an incredibly personalized service that makes each person who enters the shop feel that he or she is someone special. Prices are in the if-you-have-to-ask-you-can't-afford-it class, but the merchandise and ambiance make it all worthwhile. Napoleon really does carry clothes fit for a king and his consort.

PAN AM SPORTSWEAR AND MENSWEAR
50 Orchard St (bet Grand and Hester St)   925-7032
Sun-Wed: 9-6; Thurs: 9-8; Fri: 9:30-3 (winter);
    9-5 (summer)

With more stores like this, the Lower East Side could become synonymous with class as well as bargains. From the shiny glass windows (as opposed to the clutter of hangers that usually denotes an entrance) to the extremely fine stock, Pan Am is distinctive enough to be on Madison Avenue, except for its prices. They are nothing short of super! Perry Ellis, Mani by Georgio Armani, Polo by Ralph Lauren, and Andrew Fezza are but a few of the names that adorn the racks in all their glory, but sans the excessive price tag (at least a third off the uptown price). What's more, styles are *au courant;* they often preview here first, and they're in classic good taste. There are no screaming purple parachute suits and no 1940s (or even last year's) lapels. Finally, the sales help is a major exception to the Lower East Side norm. They are prompt and courteous, although they may be a little too quick to pounce on any customer who walks through the door. But at these prices, that's a minor annoyance. Besides, who ever heard of complaining of too much service on the Lower East Side?

PARKWAY
30 Vesey St   962-7500
Mon-Fri: 8:30-7; Sat: 10-5

12 Gold St   809-6636
Mon-Fri: 10-6

Parkway carries most major brands for men, including Manhattan, Botany, Chaps, Perry Ellis, Bill Blass, and London Fog. Prices are excellent, reflecting an average discount of 30 percent. The stores are noted for their selection of outerwear, sportswear, dress shirts, and ties as well.

PAUL STUART
Madison Ave at 45th St   682-0320
Mon-Wed, Fri: 8-6; Thurs: 8-7; Sat; 9-6

If you are the kind of shopper who doesn't really know what you want, if you have trouble putting things together to make a "look," or if you worry about quality, this is the store for you. In both men's and women's apparel and accessories, you would be hard pressed to find a better selection of fine merchandise. But there is little excitement here, either in the presentation or in the merchandise. The men's suits and sports jackets are first-class, as is the collection of handmade English shoes.

ROTHMAN'S
200 Park Ave S (at Union Sq)   777-7400
Mon-Wed, Fri: 10-7; Thurs: 10-8; Sat: 9-6; Sun: 12-5;
   closed Sun in summer

Forget your mental picture of the old Harry Rothman store. Harry's grandson, Ken Gidden, runs this classy new men's store, which offers a huge selection of quality clothes at discount prices (up to 40 percent) in a contemporary and comfortable atmosphere. He carries top-of-the-industry names, like Hickey-Freeman, Norman Hilton, Perry Ellis, Ralph Lauren (Polo), and Alexander Julian, all at off prices. Gentlemen, be sure to check out the Alexander Julian clothes in particular; no one has more interesting fabric and color combinations. They have also added Italian clothing like Canali and Lubiam. Sizes at Rothman range from 36 to 56 in regular, short, long, extra long, extra short, portly short, and portly. Raincoats, slacks, sports jackets, and accessories are stocked in-depth at the same attractive prices. It's great to see the third generation just as eager and as capable as Grandpa himself!

SAINT LAURIE
897 Broadway (at 20th St)   473-0100
Mon-Wed, Fri, Sat: 9:30-6; Thurs: 9:30-7:30; Sun: 12-5

If you want selection, quality, and value, this is the place to go first. Saint Laurie is a manufacturer that does not sell its retail line anywhere else in the city; it distributes entirely outside Manhattan. Consequently, the customer can take advantage of the missing middle man. So here you have thousands of garments in sizes 35 to 48, regular, short, long, and extra long. All are arranged for easy looking and selection. The professional salespeople are informed but not pushy. Saint Laurie also manufactures women's classic business suits made of 100 percent worsted wool. They are outstanding. Custom shirts made in-house are first class. The relatively new building has a "living museum," demonstrating Saint Laurie's production of its clothing as well as a tour of the workrooms and an exhibit showing various suit styles over the years. Custom-made clothing at truly reasonable prices is a new service offered. In addition, a mail-order swatch brochure program is available for the out-of-town shopper. If you are looking for extremely high-fashion goods, this is not the place. If you want the best in comfortable, practical, and stylish clothing at a very attractive tab, march on down to 20th and Broadway.

SOSINSKY'S
143 Orchard St (bet Delancey and Rivington St)
254-2307
Mon-Thurs: 10-5; Fri: 10-3; Sun: 9-5

Three generations of the Sosinsky family have been in business at this same location for over 75 years. This says something for the bargains offered here on men's dress and sport shirts, sweaters, and robes by such famous names as Arrow and Alexander Julian. Unlike many of their neighbors, these folks are polite and helpful and will provide first or irregular (always marked) merchandise at one-quarter to one-half off normal uptown prices. The Julian sport shirt selection is especially impressive, both in variety and value.

Men's Hats

VAN DYCK HATTERS
94 Greenwich Ave   929-5696
Mon-Fri: 7:30-6; Sat: 9-4

The quintessential hatter, Van Dyck is the first choice for anything that has to do with men's hats in New York. Since 1940, Van Dyck has been known for the quality of its own brand, which it manufactures and sells. Prices and quality can't be beat, but should you not trust its brand (New Yorkers do), Van Dyck also discounts Stetson and Borsalino hats at a minimum of 25 percent. No matter what the brand, Van Dyck can also clean, block, restyle, reband, or renovate any hat brought in.

Men's Large Sizes

IMPERIAL WEAR
48 W 48th St   719-2590
Mon-Wed, Fri, Sat: 9-6; Thurs: 9-8

Among New York's specialty shops, several are devoted exclusively to clothing in extra-large and extra-tall sizes. The salespeople at this one are well trained in the problems that large men usually encounter, and quality is not sacrificed in garments that require more material. It is this, perhaps, that has guaranteed Imperial its clientele *and* kept them returning. Many stores cater to big men, but having a captive audience causes some stores to relax their standards. The many regular customers who return to Imperial again and again prove that this is not the case here. The new line of designer fashions for big men is also a major attraction.

Men's Shirts

PENN GARDEN GRAND SHIRT CORPORATION

58 Orchard St (at Grand St)   431-8464
Sun-Wed, Fri: 9-6; Thurs: 9-8

G&G INTERNATIONAL

62 Orchard St (bet Grand and Hester St)
431-4530
Sun-Wed: 9-6; Thurs: 9-8; Fri: 9-6 (summer),
    9-4 (winter)

And you thought the Lower East Side pickle business was in-bred! It's got nothing on the local men's haberdashery dynasties, and these stores are probably the most typical of the breed. Each considers itself a distinct entity, to the point that the people at Penn Garden will not tell you to go next door to G&G if you can't find what you want with them. (Tell you? Ha! They won't even give out the other's phone numbers!) Taken separately, however, each store is a gem, and the sales help can sometimes be charming.

SHIRT STORE

51 E 44th St (bet Vanderbilt and Madison Ave)
557-8040
Mon-Fri: 8-6:30; Sat: 10-5

The attraction here is that you buy directly from the manufacturer, with no middle man to increase the price. The Shirt Store offers 100 percent cotton shirts for men, from the smallest (14x32) to the largest (18½x37). Although the ready-made stock is great, they will also do custom work and even come to your office with swatches. Imagine excusing yourself from the rest of the office crew to have your shirt maker do some measuring! How's that for status? Even better than those cuff initials! Additional special services include home-order visits, alterations, and monogramming.

VICTORY SHIRT COMPANY

96 Orchard St (bet Delancey and Broome St)
677-2020   1/800/841-3424
Sun-Thurs: 9-5; Fri: 9-4

Victory manufactures and retails their own 100 percent cotton ready-to-wear and made-to-measure shirts. They have the facilities to taper, shorten, alter or monogram any shirt to individual specifications. Sizes run from 14x32 to 18½x36. Periodic sales make their already reasonable prices even more attractive.

Men's Underwear

UNDER WARES
1098 Third Ave (bet 64th and 65th St)   535-6006,
800-237-8641
Mon-Fri: 10-7; Sat: 10-6; Sun: 12-5

It used to be that the average fellow not only couldn't tell you what kind of underwear he wore, he probably didn't even buy it himself. All that changed with the ads featuring Jim Palmer and other celebrity jocks. These days a man's underwear can make a fashion statement. Ron Lee was on top of the new trend and opened a fashionable shop that sells fashionable underwear in over 100 styles of briefs and boxer shorts—the largest selection of men's undergarments in the whole world. There are also T-shirts, hosiery, swimwear, and gift items. If you are shy about browsing through all the sexy styles, you can call for one of their free catalogs.

Men's Western Wear

BILLY MARTIN'S
812 Madison Ave (at 68th St)   861-3100
Mon-Fri: 10-7; Sat: 10:30-6; Sun: 12-5

If Western wear is on your shopping list, head right to Billy Martin's, where you will find a great showing of deerskin jackets, shirts, riding pants, skirts, Western hats, and parkas. They also have one of the best collections of boots in the city for both men and women. Great accessory items like bandannas, jewelry, buckles, and belt straps complete the outfit. The items here are well-tooled and designed, and are priced accordingly.

Outerwear

COUNTRY ROAD AUSTRALIA
335 Madison Ave (bet 43rd and 44th St)   949-7380
Mon-Fri: 10-7 (Thurs: 10-8); Sat: 10-6

199 Water St (entrance on Front St)   248-0810
Mon-Sat: 10-7; Sun: 11-6

When it comes to styling clothing, particularly sportswear, the Australians are right at the top. This is only natural, as they are a nation of outdoor enthusiasts. At Country Road you will find great men's and women's casual attire, including separates, suits, slacks, and shoes. The sweaters are especially attractive and wearable. The best part of shopping in these stores is that the famous Aussie friendliness has been transported to Madison Avenue and the South Street Seaport!

C.P. COMPANY
175 Fifth Ave (Flatiron Bldg, bet 22nd and 23rd St)
260-1990
Mon-Sat: 10-7 (Thurs: 10-8); Sun: 12-5

In a spectacular location in the historic Flatiron Building, Massimo Osti, a noted Italian designer, has put together one of the classiest collections of unisex sportswear in the city. The space presently occupied by his C.P. Company was originally a cigar store. The whole area is now making a comeback, and this store is sure to add to the interest. There are shirts and jackets that spell style and comfort, but with true lasting appeal. You can find jackets with built-in goggles in the hood and special built-in watch windows on the sleeve. An "ice jacket" that changes colors when exposed to the cold is both unusual and extremely stylish. This is one store that shouldn't be missed by anyone interested in the fashion picture; it is just another indication that the Italians are Number One when it comes to design. Besides the quality of the merchandise (price tags are hefty), the ambiance is first-class and the personnel exceptionally friendly and helpful.

Rainwear

NORMAN J. LAWRENCE
417 Fifth Ave (at 38th St, Suite 1116)   889-3119
Mon, Wed, Fri: 10-3

I have known Norman for more years than either of us would like to admit. Every year he would come to the family department store to show his line of coats, always very special, always high style and high quality. The tradition has endured, and now he has probably the finest selection of daytime and after-five raincoats in the country. He designs the coats himself, and if you're not able to fit into any of the stock items, he will make one for you in any of the water-repellent materials available: cashmere, velvet, silk faille, or ultrasuede. All of the coats may be buttoned-in or buttoned-out fur-lined, with your own fur or in one of the real furs Norman features. Men can also find some spectacular silk raincoats here. Norman is an engaging guy, a wonderful salesman, and a superior storyteller. His prices are superior, too!

Shoes—Children's

RICHIE'S DISCOUNT CHILDREN'S SHOES
183 Avenue B (bet 11th and 12th St)   228-5442
Mon, Tues, Thurs-Sat: 10-5; Sun: 10-3

Richie's offers an experience your children's feet will never duplicate. Inside, the décor is probably as old as the surrounding environment outside, but the stock includes the very latest shoes at a fraction of the prices found anywhere else. Brands include Stride Rite, Buster Brown, Blue Star, Jumping Jacks, and Keds sneakers, and the clincher is that the fit will be extraordinary. Considerable time is spent with each customer, and for each time a pair of shoes has been sold here, a pair has also *not* been sold. Reasons for the latter include the customer's being told that the child's old ones are still good. (Has that ever happened elsewhere?) Salesmen have even admitted that the quality desired just wasn't in stock or that Richie's would not sell a lesser quality to a customer. So, the drawback? The neighborhood. Gentrification hasn't quite reached this block of the East Village.

SHOOFLY
506 Amsterdam Ave (bet 84th and 85th St)
580-4390
Mon-Sat: 11-7; Sun: 12-6

This store is included for two special groups! Shoofly (isn't that a great name?) carries attractive and reasonably priced shoes mainly for the younger set, infants to 14-year-olds. But there are lots of women with tiny feet who have a difficult time finding an adequate selection of footwear. As a matter of fact, this is one of the most common questions I am asked on the call-in radio talk shows. Look no further, my petite friends. Shoofly takes care of your needs with styles and sizes that will be a surprise and a delight.

Shoes—Family

BUFFALO CHIPS BOOTERY SOHO
116A Greene St (bet Spring and Prince St)   274-0651
Mon-Wed, Fri-Sat: 11-7; Thurs: 11-9; Sun: 11-6

The best of the West comes East! You'll be all set for a dude ranch visit or plain old Western comfort and ambiance with the wall art, Indian and contemporary Western jewelry, leather items, artifacts, pottery, rugs, and blankets from this attractive outlet. Best of all are the unique Western boots, all designed by the store's own personnel. If you have ever fantisized about having a pair made especially for you, they can produce custom-made boots in about 12 weeks!

THE CITY ATHLETE
131, 132A, 132B, 135, and 163 Orchard St (five stores)
475-4875
Daily: 9-6

What used to be separate stores has now been combined into five outlets with the same name, offering good prices on brand-name sneakers, casual and rugged footwear, and children's shoes. Brands featured include Bally, Zodiac, Timberland, Adidas, Nike, Puma,

Reebok, and New Balance, among many others. These stores are usually so crowded that you'll probably need a new pair of shoes after all the bargain-hunting customers step on your toes. Family management ensures a hands-on operation.

KENNETH COLE
353 Columbus Ave (bet 76th and 77th St)
873-2061
Mon-Sat: 11-8; Sun: 12-7

This is not a run-of-the-mill shoe store. For one thing, the walls are adorned with clever, irreverent posters poking fun at well-known personalities like Imelda Marcos and Michael Dukakis. But the real treats are the fashionable and trendy shoes for men and women at sensible prices. Cole is a master of public relations, and he has developed a deserved reputation for a quality product. I suggest you browse at the high-style shops like Susan Bennis-Warren Edwards, where prices are absurd, and then come here to buy.

LEACH-KALE
1261 Broadway (at 31st St, Suite 815-816)
683-0571
Mon-Fri: 9-5

While some custom shoe craftsmen are determined to prove that their product can (and should be) owned by every man, Andre S. Feuerman of the Leach-Kale Company is not among them. Perhaps he has been burned too many times by the bargain hunter who thought that the gap between a high-class shoe salon's product and Leach-Kale's couldn't be as great as it is, or by customers who, prepared to shell out money, think at that price the shoe should cure all their orthopedic problems for life. Feuerman is careful to point out that this is not the case. The business has customers who have been loyal patrons for 25 to 30 years (Joan Crawford was one), and these are the people Feuerman would rather court. They have neither unrealistic expectations nor impossible dreams, but appreciate the quality item that Leach-Kale produces. Leach-Kale specializes in orthopedic work, which is probably why many of their customers come here and pay the price without batting an eye. They have no choice. Shoes start at about $700 for the first pair, but some first orders, and all subsequent orders, can be substantially less.

LESLIE'S BOOTERY
319 Grand St (bet Orchard and Allen St)   431-9196
Sun-Wed, Fri: 9:30-6; Thurs: 9:30-7

For over 20 years, this business has been selling top name ladies' and men's shoes at discount prices. Normal prices reflect a 20 percent discount. At sales times in January and July, the prices are even better on Bally, Cole-Haan, Timberland, Reebok, Bass, Rockport, Bostonian, Clark's of England, and other nationally advertised brands.

LORD JOHN BOOTERY
428 Third Ave (bet 29th and 30th St)   532-2579
Mon-Fri: 10-7; Sat: 10-6; closed Sat in July, Aug

Now here's a real "shoe dog" store. John Kyriannis and two generations of his family have been happily working together for four decades, and this happiness spills over to their customers. They carry Dan Post and Justin Western boots, in all kinds of leathers for men and women, and discounted by 20 to 30 percent, as well as discounted Timberland and Dexter boots and shoes. There are also imported brands like Evan Picone, Nickels, Joan and David, and many more. It's refreshing to be helped by people who really know the business.

MANUFACTURERS SHOE OUTLET
537 Broadway (bet Spring and Prince St)
966-4070
Mon-Fri: 8-6; Sat: 9-5; Sun: 10-6

The hours and phone number are nebulous, and the attitude is "go help yourself, don't bother me." But if a lack of amenities doesn't bother you, then run, don't walk, to this dirty store in SoHo. It carries a wide variety of shoes, slippers, and hosiery, and the sizes range from infants' to large men's. And if that isn't inducement enough, there are such top brand names as Nunn Bush and Freeman sold at a discount. Finally, note the hours. If your son breaks a buckle at nine a.m. or the heel falls off a shoe an hour before *the* business meeting, this is the place to go for a quick replacement at discount prices. They claim to keep these hours because "everyone else here does." Now you know another difference between SoHo and the Village!

T.O. DEY
9 E 38th St   683-6300
Mon-Fri: 9-5; Sat: 9-1

It is immensely satisfying when words in this book stimulate the firms that have been included to do a better job. For years I have included T.O. Dey, because they are a good, fancy, jack-of-all-trades operation. Though thier specialty is custom-made shoes, they will also undertake any kind of repair on any kind of shoe. They will create both men's and women's shoes, based on a plaster mold taken of the customer's feet; their styles are only limited by the customer's imagination. They also make arch supports and will cover shoes to match your garment. They sell sports shoes for football, basketball, hockey, boxing, and running. So when I mentioned in the last edition that I had heard complaints about their service, the telephone wires burned. I am happy to say that recent reports have been that the usual superior service has returned; thank you, T.O. Dey, for reading not only what is *on* the line but *between* the lines.

VOGEL BOOTS AND SHOES

19 Howard St (one block north of Canal St,
    bet Broadway and Lafayette St)   925-2460
Mon-Fri: 8-4:30; Sat: 8-2
Closed Sat in summer and first two weeks of July

The Vogels—John, Hank, and Dean (who are the third and fourth generations to join this 110-year-old-business)—happily fit and supply made-to-measure boots and shoes for any adult who can find the store. Howard is one of those streets that even native New Yorkers don't know exists. The many who *have* found it beat a path to the door for top-quality shoes and boots, personal advice, excellent fittings, and prices which, while not inexpensive, are reasonable for the service involved. The fit is not to be taken lightly, for made-to-measure shoes do *not* always fit properly. At Vogel, they do. Once you have a shoe pattern on record at Vogel, they will make up new shoes without a personal visit and ship anywhere. For top craftsmanship, this spot is top-drawer. There are more than 600 Vogel dealers throughout the world, but this is the grandfather store, and the people here are super.

Shoes—Men's

ADLER SHOE SHOPS

141 W 42nd St (bet Sixth Ave and Broadway)
382-0844
Mon-Sat: 9-7

Adler's is a chain of men's shoe stores in New York, featuring Weyenberg, Stacy Adams, and Nunn-Bush brands. At this store, all of the rejects, overruns, unsalables (for whatever reason), and odd lots are sold at big reductions. Incidentally, after having checked out over 100 shoe stores, I still remember the staff here as having been exceptionally friendly.

CHURCH ENGLISH SHOES

428 Madison Ave (at 49th St)   755-4313
Mon-Fri: 9-6; Sat: 9-5:30

Anglophiles have a ball here, not only because of the *veddy* English atmosphere, but for the pure artistry and Englishness of the shoes. Church has been selling English shoes for men since 1873 and has long been known for classic styles, superior workmanship, and fine leathers. The styles basically remain unchanged year after year, although one or two new designs are occasionally added as a concession to fashion. All are custom-fitted by shoe salesmen. If a style or size does not feel right, Church's will make up a customized special order for approximately $150 more than the regular price. The salesmen are very professional. Foot problems? This is the place for competent advice.

J. SHERMAN SHOES
121 Division St (bet Orchard and Ludlow St)
233-7898
Mon-Thurs: 9:30-5:30; Fri: 9:30-3:30; Sun: 9-5:30

Upholding the Lower East Side tradition, J. Sherman has excellent prices on its merchandise. But its shoes are nothing less than top-of-the-line quality. So here's the place to pick up Bally, Bruno Magli, French Shriner, Polo, Rockport, Clarks, Dexter, Bass, Zodiac, Timberland, Frye, and other brand-name shoes for 20 to 60 percent off list price. J. Sherman boasts that they have the best buys on brand-name shoes in the city. They may be right.

MCCREEDY AND SCHREIBER
213 E 59th St (bet Second and Third Ave)
759-9241
Mon, Thurs: 9-9; Tue, Wed, Fri, Sat: 9-7;
   Sun: 12-6

37 W 46th St (bet Fifth and Sixth Ave)
719-1552
Daily: 9-7

How about a department store for shoes and boots? Well, here is one that features Lucchese, Tony Lama, Frye, Justin, Larry Mahan, and Timberland boots, as well as (among others) Bass, Cole-Haan, and Clark's English and Italian shoes. There are boots in large sizes (like 14 and 15), prices are competitive, and made-to-order footwear is available.

STAPLETON SHOE COMPANY
68 Trinity Pl (at Rector St)   964-6329
Mon-Thurs: 8-6; Fri: 8-5

Their motto is "better shoes for less," but that doesn't begin to cover the superlatives that Stapleton deserves. Gather around, gentlemen, because here is the place to get Bally, Alden, Allen-Edmonds, Johnston Murphy and a slew of other top shoe names at a discount. Stapleton is located on the same block as the Amex

(American Stock Exchange). With the money saved here, there should be enough left over to take a flyer in the stock market. There probably isn't a better source for quality shoes anywhere. And that's a free tip on the market!

TO BOOT
256 Columbus Ave (at 72nd St)   724-8249
Mon-Fri: 12-8; Sat: 11-7; Sun: 1-6

Bergdorf-Goodman Men
Fifth Ave at 57th St (3rd floor)   339-3335
Mon-Wed, Fri, Sat: 10-6; Thurs: 10-8

To Boot features high-quality men's footwear for the sophisticated urban man. They carry casual, dressy, and business shoes in fine leathers, suedes, and exotics, with designer collections by Armani, Ralph Lauren, and Cesare Paciotti. Western boots are also featured here. There are two collections: To Boot New York, their signature line, and To Boot II, with "gentler" prices. To Boot Woman is available only at the Columbus Avenue store. If you just want a "little something" to wear around the house, take a peak at the John Lobb collection at Bergdorf's; this custom shoe and boot-maker from London makes things for Prince Charles (and you, if you so desire) starting at about $2,000!

Shoes—Women's

ANBAR SHOES
93 Reade St (bet Church St and W Broadway)
227-0253
Mon-Fri: 8-5:30; Sat: 11-5; closed Sat in July, Aug

You can't judge a shoe store by its décor! As long as you walk out wearing the best shoes for your money, who cares what the store's windows look like? Certainly not the people at Anbar, who just may offer the best shoes in town for the best prices. Names like Charles Jourdan, Julianelli, Lamarea, Garolini, Mr. Seymour, and Andrew Geller are always discounted, often as much as 50 percent. Overlook the grubby setting. Anbar is a gold mine!

GIORDANO'S SHOES
1118 First Ave (at 61st St)   688-7195
Mon-Fri: 11-7; Sat: 11-6

Susan Giordano has a very special clientele. In fact, if you're a woman whose shoe size is larger than 6½, you can't imagine how important this store is. And if you're a woman with a shoe size in the 3½ to 6 medium or 5½ to 6½ AA range, learning about Giordano's will make the purchase of this book more than worthwhile.

Giordano stocks a fine selection in a range of tiny sizes of women's shoes. While there are women with smaller sizes still, Giordano's range is nonexistent in regular shoe stores. (Occasionally 5Bs, a sample size, can be found in closeout shops.) Most women in this category shop in the children's shoe departments or have shoes custom-made, either of which can cramp your style. For these women, Giordano's is a godsend.

IN STEP
1230 Second Ave (bet 64th and 65th St)   734-7484
Mon-Fri: 11-7; Sat: 11-6

Petite ladies take note! "In Step" carries fashion footwear catering to sizes 3½ to 6½ medium and 5½ to 6½ narrow. Dale Feinblatt, the owner, comes from a family with small feet, so she well knows the frustrations of trying to find fashionable footwear in small sizes. Her store not only carries stylish name brands (like Stuart Weitzman, Bally, and Amalfi, among others), but also has work shoes, evening shoes, and boots, plus coordinated handbags and gloves. Pumps may be special-ordered in a variety of colors, and mail orders are encouraged.

LACE UP SHOE SHOP
110 Orchard St (at Delancey St)
475-8040 or 800/488-LACE
Sun-Fri: 9-5:30

The unusual part of this operation is that it is a full-service shoe store in an area where such a thing isn't supposed to exist! The folks at Lace Up actually help put on your shoes, will special order a particular style, if it is available, and will discount your purchase. They carry a large selection of top-name, current-season merchandise for both men and women. You will find Mephisto, Arche, Cori, Bruno Magli, Evan Picone, and many other designer names. If your young one gets bored while you are trying on some super styles, "Shoo-Guy" will entertain them. No, he is not a shoe-dog! He is their mascot, a yellow nape parrot!

PETER FOX SHOES
105 Thompson St (bet Prince and Spring St)
431-6359

378 Amsterdam Ave (at 78th St)   874-6399

Mon-Sat: 12-8; Sun: 12-7

Peter Fox was the downtown trailblazer for women's shoes. Everything sold in the shop is exclusive, limited-edition designer footwear. Perhaps because of the store's original location, Fox's designs seem more adventurous than its uptown competitors, but then, no one ever accused Maud Frizon or Susan Bennis/Warren Edwards of being staid. However, the look seems younger and more casual here than it does with other designers. For those looking for shoes to be seen in, Michael (uptown) and Jacques (downtown) are the people to see. Bridal shoes are available next door to the Thompson Street store (431-7426).

SOLE OF ITALY
119 Orchard St (at Delancey St)   674-2662
Sun-Fri: 9:30-6

Sole of Italy is the soul mate to Fine and Klein, and it is fittingly located above the latter store. Fine and Klein carries classy handbags and attaché cases, and Sole of Italy offers the perfect complement in footwear. The selection is limited to those labels sold in the finest boutiques; the collection of so many brands and sizes in one spot is awesome. The Fine and Klein (or Lower East Side) discount policy also applies here, which makes Sole of Italy a contender as the sole source for fashionable footwear. Some name dropping is in order: Beverly Feldman, Sudini, Mosaic, Adige, Pierre Balmain, Jacques Cohen, Collette, Courreges, Caiman Mode, Xavier Danand, Delman, Charles Jourdan, Ted Lapidus, Bally, Walter Steiger, Madame Gres, Vitto Latvada, Menin, and J. B. Martin are just some of the labels Sole of Italy carries. There are few places to find them all under one roof and virtually none that discounts.

TALL SIZE SHOES
3 W 35th St (at Fifth Ave)   736-2060
Mon-Wed, Fri, Sat: 9:30-6; Thurs: 9:30-7

The tall gals do not have an easy time finding a good selection of shoes. But walk easily, ladies. Tall Size Shoes has come to your rescue, with super service, polite sales help, and an outstanding selection. They only sell women's shoes in sizes 10 to 15, from narrow to wide widths, and feature their own brand, as well as shoes from designers like Bandolino, Jazz, Liz Claiborne, Amalfi, Evan Picone, and Zodiac. They will take phone orders and ship anywhere in the country.

Sportswear

FINALS
487 Broadway (at Broome St)
431-1414, 800/431-9111
Mon-Sat: 10-6; Sun: 12-6

This is the case of a catalog having a store rather than the other way around. For years, Finals has published a catalog offering competition swim and running wear to schools, clubs, and YMCAs across the country. In that time, they have garnered 75 percent of the market, in part because no one could match their "factory direct" prices and in part because a majority of the customers were located far from other sources for that equipment. The business operated out of New York, and it finally decided to open an outlet store in SoHo. Prices are the same as those in the catalog, but they are so sensational that visitors should not feel that the only savings is the cost of postage and handling. An added fillip is the chance to comb through whatever outdated, discarded, or non-catalog merchandise might be around. But it's really not necessary when you can get the finest apparel at true factory prices!

GERRY COSBY AND COMPANY
Madison Square Garden
3 Pennsylvania Plaza (at 32nd St and Seventh Ave)
563-6464
Mon-Fri: 9:30-6:30; Sat: 9:30-6; Sun: 12-5

There's a lot to like about this company. For one thing, they know how to spell my first name correctly! Although it will be difficult for an out-of-towner to find them, they are a briskly professional business that is located at the most appropriate spot for its wares. And those wares are sportswear—as in what people active in sports *wear,* not as in people wearing two-piece sweater outfits. In particular, Gerry Cosby designs and markets protective equipment and covers. The covers cover both bodies and equipment, and the protective equipment and bags are designed exclusively for professional use but are available to the general public as well. Much of it is designed for football. Gerry Cosby's designs are coveted and frequently copied, but why not get the original? They accept mail and phone orders for all of their equipment, including personalized (with either team or name) jerseys and jackets. And even if your name isn't Gerry, the staff seems competent enough to spell any name right.

HOWRON SPORTSWEAR
295 Grand St (bet Eldridge and Allen St)   226-4307
Sun-Fri: 9-5

Howron was transformed from a typical Lower East Side shop into a fashionable boutique without sacrificing Lower East Side prices. They carry an excellent selection of men's sportswear, including top names like Damon, Lee's, and Blacker. If you are looking for a Spanish-leather coat, this is the place. For that cool summer sport shirt, no one has a better selection.

WOMEN'S WORKOUT GEAR
121 Seventh Ave (at 17th St)   627-1117
Mon-Fri: 11-7; Sat: 11-6; Sun: 1:30-5:30

Here is a store that specializes in clothes for today's health-conscious woman. Paula Shirk, an avid runner herself, has put together a great collection of women's aerobic and running wear; walking, running, and aerobic shoes; bathing suits and goggles; sports bras; and weights and exercise mats. Paula and her crew give professional advice to their customers, along with brand-name merchandise from Baryshnikov, Dance Basics, City Lights, Brooks, New Balance, Avia, Speedo, and Triangle. Almost everything is specially designed for women, and careful shoppers can find outstanding bargains on off-season merchandise.

Surplus

59th STREET ARMY AND NAVY
221 E 59th St (bet Second and Third Ave)
755-1855
Mon, Thurs: 10-7:45; Tues, Wed, Fri: 10-6:45;
    Sat: 10-6; Sun: 1-5:45

328 Bleecker St (at Christopher St)   242-6665
Mon-Thurs: 10-7:45; Fri, Sat: 10-8:45; Sun: 1-6:45

110 Eighth Ave (bet 15th and 16th St)   645-7420
Mon-Fri: 9-6:45; Sat: 10-6:45; Sun: 1-5:45

SECOND AVENUE ARMY NAVY
1598 Second Ave (corner E 83rd St)
Mon-Sat: 10-7:45 Sun: 12-6

I have long sung the praises of so-called army-navy stores, although the genuine outlets for surplus military supplies have been gone for years. These shops are the best sources for camping supplies as well as durable and practical clothes and equipment. Instead of navy dress pants and sailor uniforms, this chain of stores specializes in rugged outdoor wear, including the largest inventory of 501 Levi's on the East Coast. There are sweat outfits, sneakers (the top brands at excellent prices), Timberland, Nike, and Rockport shoes, Schott leather jackets, Ocean Pacific, Gotcha, and Quicksilver.

KAUFMAN SURPLUS
319 W 42nd St (bet Eighth and Ninth Ave)
757-5670
Mon-Wed, Fri, Sat: 11-6; Thurs: 11-7

One of the last surviving surplus stores in the city, Kaufman's has long been a favorite among New Yorkers and visitors alike for its extensive selection of genuine military surplus from around the world. Kaufman's is not your average army-navy store! Over the last half century, Kaufman's has outfitted dozens of Broadway and TV shows and has supplied a number of major motion pictures with military garb. The store is a treasure trove of military collectibles, hats, helmets, dummy grenades, uniforms, and insignias. Over a thousand military pins, patches, and medals from armies the world over are on display. Kaufman's is the building painted red, white, and blue, with two U.S. Army cannons outside. You can't miss it!

Sweaters

BEST OF SCOTLAND
581 Fifth Ave (bet 47th and 48th St, penthouse)
644-0403
Mon-Fri: by appointment; Sat: 10-6

If you've been to London recently, you must have noticed that the price of cashmere sweaters has skyrocketed. Some of the British companies, like N. Peal, have opened up branches in Manhattan, offering beautiful sweaters at beautiful prices. But if you walk about ten blocks from Peal (at 118 E 57th St) to Best of Scotland, you'll find attractive, well-made Bryant cashmere sweaters for men and women being sold at half the price. Best shopping is in the fall, when the showroom is open all the time; in the spring, it is advisable to call for an appointment. This is a real find!

GRANNY-MADE
381 Amsterdam Ave (bet 78th and 79th St)
496-1222
Mon-Fri: 11;7:30; Sat: 10-6; Sun: 12-5

Michael Rosenberg did what many others have often wanted to do. He turned his grandmother's handiwork into a business. Michael's grandmother, Bert Levy, who is in her nineties, handknitted sweater designs that are now made on knitting machines (hand-loomed). Like all good grandmothers, Granny-made looks after the little ones. The store carries an extensive collection of newborn, infant, toddler, and children's sweaters up to size 14. In addition to the sweater collection, skirts, pants, mittens, scarves, hats, cotton sweaters, classic cable knits, and 100 percent alpaca sweaters are all first-quality and attractively designed. I sure wish I had been fortunate enough to have a grandmother like Michael's. When you shop here, you can still say, "Granny made this for me!"

Thrift Shops

ARTHRITIS FOUNDATION THRIFT SHOP
121 E 77th St (bet Lexington and Park Ave)
772-8816
Mon-Sat: 10:30-4:45

This very friendly store carries donated clothing, furniture, bric-a-brac, and oddities that will appeal to bargain hunters. Their donors include people whose family members have suffered from arthritis.

ENCORE
1132 Madison Ave (bet 84th and 85th St, upstairs)
879-2850
Mon-Wed, Fri, Sat: 10:30-6; Thurs: 10:30-7;
    Sun: 12:30-6; closed Sun from July to mid-Aug

There are thrift shops, and then there are thrift shops. Encore is so chic and select that it prefers to be billed as a "resale shop of gently worn clothing," and when one sees the merchandise and the caliber of the clientele, Encore can be forgiven its conceit. For one thing, Encore is a consignment boutique, not a charity thrift shop. Its donors receive a portion of the sales price, and according to owner Carole Selig (who bought the store upon the death of Florence Barry, who founded the business more than three decades ago), many of the donors are socialites and other luminaries who can't afford to be seen in the same outfit twice. So Selig can afford to be picky, and so can you. The fashions are up-to-date, and if Jackie O doesn't mind dropping off her better items here, why should a customer mind grabbing these top fashions at 50 to 70 percent off original retail prices? At any time, there are over 6,000 items in stock, and all of it sells. Prices range from reasonable to astronomical, but just think how much more they sold for originally! Encore may be the only way to go if you're going to appear on the pages of *W* four times in a week and want to look fresh each time. If the sheer savings don't appeal to you, then maybe you should be an Encore donor.

EVERYBODY'S THRIFT SHOP
261 Park Ave S   355-9263
Mon-Fri: 10-5; Sat: 10-4; closed Sat in summer

This shop was founded in 1921 to support the "Bundles for Britain" program, one of the recovery efforts after World War I. Today it serves as the umbrella organization for six charities and has an impressive list of supporters. Knowing who they are and when they donate (the list includes many manufacturers and retail stores) is the reason a queue forms outside the store on some mornings.

Everybody's features designer clothing, bric-a-brac, jewelry, furniture, and donations from large corporations.

I, MICHAEL, RESALES
1041 Madison Ave (bet 79th and 80th St)   737-7273
Mon-Sat: 9:30-6; Thurs: 9:30-8;
    summer: Mon-Fri: 9:30-6

It's not too common to find bargain prices on designer clothes on trendy, expensive Madison Avenue. I, Michael, is an exception. You can find an excellent selection of quality merchandise in sizes 4-12 at very substantial discounts in this consignment shop.

MEMORIAL SLOAN-KETTERING CANCER CENTER THRIFT SHOP
1440 Third Ave (at 82nd St)   535-1250
Mon-Sat: 10-4:45

Because of its location on the affluent Upper East Side, Memorial benefits from its big-name donors. Try this shop for accessories, and don't miss its designer room, which is better stocked than the ones in some retail stores.

REPEAT PERFORMANCE
220 E 23rd St (bet Second and Third Ave)
684-5344
Mon-Fri: 10-5:45; Thurs: 10-6:45; Sat: 10-5

Repeat Performance is run for the benefit of the New York City Opera, a cause near and dear to the hearts of wealthy donors and major department and specialty stores. So, while there are the usual thrift-shop furniture, jewelry, bric-a-brac, and occasional paintings, the strong suit here is brand-new, designer-name, often store-labeled clothing at ridiculously inexpensive prices.

T-Shirts

EISNER BROS.
76 Orchard St (bet Grand and Delancey St)
431-8800, 800/426-7700 (telephone orders)
Mon-Thurs: 9-6:30; Fri: 9-3; Sun: 9-5

Except for its tiny, cramped quarters and its adherence to the local practice of hanging merchandise from every available space on walls and ceilings, Eisner Bros. does not fit the usual Lower East Side shopkeeper's mold. Whereas its neighbors sell everything from handbags to shoes to designer clothes, Eisner Bros. specializes in T-shirts. They claim to have the biggest assortment of colors and sizes in the world, and about half of their business is custom orders. So although every neighborhood seems to have at least one T-shirt store, this is the granddaddy of them all. Eisner Bros. also carries jogging suits, sport shirts (that's *sports* as in baseball, football, soccer, etc., *not* dress shirts with an open collar), nightshirts, and baseball jackets and caps (official licensed team-baseball caps and hot, neon ones). Sweat shirts have become popular, and this is the place to get them. There's a tremendous selection, and the magnificent discount doesn't hurt, either. Eisner Bros. is constantly upgrading its line. A free catalog is available upon request.

Umbrellas

UNCLE SAM
161 W 57th St (bet Sixth and Seventh Ave)
247-7163, 582-1976
Mon-Fri: 9:30-6; Sat: 10-5

This is a New York specialty store at its very best. Uncle Sam sells, canes, services, recovers, and customizes umbrellas. There are umbrellas for children, golfers, fashion models, travelers, chauffeurs, doormen—and for the beach. All are hand-carved, hand-sewn, and hand-assembled. Uncle Sam also sells umbrella accessories, and they remake old umbrellas and canes.

Uniforms

DORNAN
653 Eleventh Ave (bet 47th and 48th St)
247-0937 (outside New York State: 800/223-0363)
Mon-Wed, Fri: 8:30-4; Thurs: 8:30-6

Dornan is the largest supplier of chauffeur uniforms in the country, and they carry many other lines of work uniforms as well. This includes outfits for butlers, maids, beauticians, hospital workers, doormen, bellboys, bartenders, chefs, stewards and stewardesses, pilots, firemen, police, doctors, nurses, and . . . well, you get the picture. They have been in the business for nearly 70 years, so they know what they are doing. They are capable of setting up a uniform program and customizing and distributing the outfits anywhere.

JA-MIL UNIFORMS
92 Orchard St (at Delancey St)   677-8190
Mon-Thurs, Sun: 10-5; Fri: 10-3

This is *the* bargain spot for those who wear uniforms and do not want to spend a fortune on work clothes. There are outfits for doctors, nurses, and technicians, as well as good values on white nursing duty shoes.

Women's Accessories

ACCESSORIE CLUB
10 E 36th St   213-3336
Mon-Fri: 9-6

If you are one of those gals whose waist size changes each season, you should head down to the Accessorie Club, where they feature the largest selection of ladies' belts in the city. You can choose from many different styles and colors, all at very reasonable prices. In addition, there are scarves, hats, and hair accessories. With a moderate-size purchase, they will make you a member of the club, which entitles you to a special discount on all merchandise.

BERNARD KRIEGER & SON
316 Grand St   CA6-1929
Mon-Thurs, Sun: 8-4:30; Fri: 8-3; Sun hours may
    vary in summer

The assortment of items here is limited, but they do have one of the best selections anywhere of millinery, handkerchiefs, scarves, accessories, and gloves. If this is the Christmas you're giving your grandfather that most exciting of all gifts (a dozen hankies), this is the place to go, because everything is discounted. It also looks as though they have more berets than any store in Paris, and the price tags are certainly a lot more reasonable.

FINE AND KLEIN
119 Orchard St (at Delancey St)   674-6720
Sun-Fri: 9-5:30

No, the finest handbag store for value and selection is not located in Rome or Paris or London. It is not even located on Fifth Avenue in New York. It is on the Lower East Side, and the name is Fine and Klein. What a selection! There is a bag for every purpose, for any time of day, and in any fabric. If top labels are what you're looking for, they sell them for a fraction of the price you would pay at Bergdorf's. Besides, shopping at Fine and Klein is fun. The crowds, especially on Sundays and holidays, are so great that the number of persons allowed to enter is controlled! One Saudi princess bought $9,600 worth of bags here. My good friends Julius Fine and Murray Klein are the epitome of old-time merchants. Tell them I sent you, and you will be delighted with the service.

HYUK BAGS
39 W 29th St   685-5226, 685-5399
Mon-Fri: 7:30-6; Sat: 7:30-1

Hyuk K. Kim runs an importing company exclusively dedicated to handbags. Importing and wholesaling companies are common in this area. What is uncommon is the courtesy and selection the company gives individual retail customers. Kim has a knack for making everyone feel like a valued customer, and she does not take offense when a finicky lady picks through the entire stock in search of the right handbag—and it shouldn't be too hard to find, within certain guidelines. *Imported* here usually refers to origins from points west rather than east. So rather than an "LV," expect to see "Made in Hong Kong." Hyuk seems to import every type of handbag— leather, vinyl, canvas, and nylon. Most of this is your average, serviceable stuff. But there are a few stars in the line, and prices border on magnificent. Spoken English is at a premium here.

J. S. SUAREZ
26 W 54th St (bet Fifth and Sixth Ave)   315-5614
Mon-Fri: 9:30-6; Sat: 10-5:30

J. S. Suarez has been in business for over 42 years, and in that time, he has made his reputation by selling name-brand bags at a 30 to 50 percent discount, and copies of name-brand bags (and *big* names at that) at even better prices. For years, Suarez was the source for unlabeled Gucci bags that were identical to the real thing (naturally, since they came from the same factory) for less than half the price. And, unlike Gucci, Suarez doesn't have some of the most obnoxious clerks this side of Italy. In fact, Suarez and his people are downright pleasant. He discounts name brands as well as "fake" (read "unlabeled") Bottega Veneta, Celine of Paris, Chanel, Fendi, and Hermes items. There is also a great selection of exotic skins. Suarez takes it as a matter of course that you are *supposed* to deliver top quality, great service, good selection, and excellent prices to all customers. Gucci could learn a few things from J.S. Suarez.

MICHAEL KLEIN'S FOMO
61 Orchard St   925-6363
Mon-Fri, Sun: 9:15-5:30

The name Klein is world-famous on Orchard Street because of Fine and Klein. A second-generation Klein wanted to continue the family tradition of being in the handbag business, but he wanted to flap his own wings. Thus Michael Klein's FOMO. And what does FOMO stand for? *Finally on my own!* Michael offers an outstanding collection of briefcases and bags, including such top names as Courreges of Paris, Carlos Falchi, and Cosci of Italy. Prices reflect a 25 to 50 percent discount, and the imported merchandise includes belts and wallets, as well as handbags.

ST. REGIS DESIGNS
58 E 7th St (bet First and Second Ave)   533-7313
Mon-Sat: 10-7:30; Sun: 12-6:30

From this unlikely spot in the East Village, Andrew Pelensky, who used to work for a top handbag designer, turns out hand-made, original custom-designed handbags and belts from the finest leathers, including snake and alligator skins. The workmanship is both unique and magnificent, and items can be custom-ordered. For the quality, prices are outright cheap. George Pelensky is listed as being in charge of "sales." I hope this doesn't mean they are going into mass production. Right now, it's the personal touch, like a final fitting before a belt leaves the premises, that makes St. Regis so special.

Women's Evening Wear

KHANITHA
1034A Lexington Ave (at 74th St)   570-0015
Mon-Sat: 10-7

There are few human beings more graceful than the hostesses on Thai Airways. They are always clad in magnificent Thai silk clothes, beautifully made in spectacular colors. Now one can find this same quality in evening wear at Khanitha, the only one of its kind in this country, although they have five sister operations in Thailand. The designer is Thai, as is the charming store manager, Annette Akaranithikul.

ONE NIGHT STAND
905 Madison Ave (bet 72nd and 73rd St)
772-7720
Mon-Fri: 10-6 by appointment; Sat: 10-3 by
   appointment; closed Sat in July, Aug

Now here's a great idea. You are invited to a gala, and you "don't have a thing to wear." Don't buy. Rent. One Night Stand has over 700 pieces of ladies' evening wear for rent in sizes 2 to 16. Jewelry, evening bags, and cloaks are also available for hire. You can even select your outfit and pick it up the same day. Sure beats shelling out big bucks for a dress you may not need for another two years, if ever.

TAMARA BOUTIQUE
134 E 70th St (bet Park and Lexington Ave)
628-0902
Mon-Sat: 9:30-5:30 (closed Sat in summer)

If you are looking for a place to find dinner, cocktail, evening or other special-occasion apparel that you will not see in every other store in town, then Tamara is worth a try. Individual attention in the choice of garment and in alterations is a tradition here. Naturally, you pay for the personal interest and the exclusive designs, but if it is a once-in-a-lifetime event, why not go for the best?

Women's—General

For one of those New York-only experiences, drop by the starkly unusual *Romeo Gigli* boutique at 21 E 69th St (744-9121). It is so chic there is no name on the door. Inside you will find clothing by one of Italy's most exciting designers, with prices beginning at $35 (for men's socks) and going as high as $15,000 for some of the women's clothes. The atmosphere is rather decadent, but then they *want* people to talk about it, and that is just what we are doing here!

ATELIER/45
347 Madison Ave　　687-6877
Mon-Fri: 10-7:30; Sat: 11-6

ATELIER/55
101 W 55th St (at Sixth Ave)　　245-3650
Mon-Wed, Fri: 10-7; Sat: 11-6; Thurs: 10-7:30

ATELIER/86
144 E 86th St　　427-2211
Mon-Fri: 10:30-8; Sat: 10:30-7; Sun: 12-6:30

When a store down the street from ABC and Burlington calls itself a "small family kind of place," it may be a little hard to believe. But Atelier, a store with great fashions from American designers, does just that. Indeed, Atelier even claims that the 86th Street store attracts browsers and tourist clientele, while the 55th Street shop has loyal and devoted customers who, with all of the midtown Manhattan stores to choose from, pick their wardrobes from Atelier, season after season. The reason is simple. Atelier's prices on quality garments are excellent.

BEN FARBER
462 Seventh Ave (at 35th St, 3rd floor)
736-0557, 800-223-6101
Mon-Fri: 9-5; Thurs: 9-8; Sat: 9-4; Sun: 10-4

I'll put my reputation on the line for this one: it's the best women's fashion discount house in New York. Thousands of satisfied customers must agree, because Ben Farber (located just catty-corner from Macy's) has expanded into a bright, attractive new space that gives them nearly three times the area they previously had. This pipe-rack, two-level, fully stocked house offers the finest labels in the fashion industry at savings you'll find hard to beat. Ben Farber carries coats, suits, dresses, outerwear, sportswear, and rainwear in all sizes, even for the hard-to-fit half-size lady. All the merchandise is fresh and seasonal, and there are no irregulars passed off as first quality. Ben's son, Don Farber, and his always-on-the-job sidekick, Joe Halperin, go out of their way to satisfy the individual customer. When you go in, be sure to mention this book, and you'll get an even more attentive service. And for gentlemen who get bored waiting for the ladies to make up their minds, there are chairs in a comfortable waiting area.

BETSEY JOHNSON
248 Columbus Ave (bet 71st and 72nd St)
362-3364

130 Thompson St (bet Prince and Houston St)
420-0169

251 E 60th St (at Second Ave)   319-7699

Mon-Sat: 12-7; Thurs: 12-8; Sun: 1-7

In the 1960s and 1970s, Betsey Johnson was *the* fashion designer. Her designs appeared everywhere, as did Betsey and her personal life. As an outlet for those designs not sold to exclusive boutiques, Betsey helped found Betsey Bunky Nini, but her own pursuits led to more designing and ultimately a store in SoHo. The SoHo store proved so successful that Betsey moved first to larger quarters and then up and across town, as well as into such department stores as Bloomingdale's. While her style has always managed to be avant-garde, it has never been way-out. Johnson believes in making her own statement, and each store seems unique despite the fact that over 500 outlets carry her line. Prices, particularly at the SoHo store (which started as an outlet), are bearable and wearable. Incidentally, it's hard to overlook the shop—it's pink, with pink neon accents and what she simply refers to as "great windows."

FORMAN'S
82 Orchard St (bet Grand and Broome St)
FORMAN'S PETITE
94 Orchard St
FORMAN'S PLUS SIZES
78 Orchard St

228-2500
Sun-Wed: 9-6; Thurs: 9-8; Fri: 9-3

Forman's bills itself as "the fashion oasis of the Lower East Side." While you can determine for yourself if that overstates the case a bit, it is true that they have enjoyed a good reputation for years and years. By Lower East Side standards, the store is enormous. It is laid out in such a way that a teenage daughter, mother, and grandmother can all head for sections designed for their needs and not meet for hours. Even then, it might be at one of the dozen (do you believe it?) dressing rooms or the cash register. Denim reigns here, but so does casual sportswear, separates, and trendy outerwear. The main floor dazzles the customer with designer sportswear (Calvin Klein must have a direct line here) and such better-made separates as Jones of New York and Adrienne Victtatini. The basement—excuse me, the lower level!—is dedicated to young, suburban-type separates and sportswear. Forman's made its reputation outfitting these images. Prices are the obligatory Lower East Side discount. Read that to mean *very* good.

GALERIES LAFAYETTE
Trump Tower
E 57th St (bet Fifth and Madison Ave)

This first American branch of the famous French store carries only women's clothing and accessories, placed in a number of boutiques in a space that once housed Bonwit Teller. There are no *haute couture* clothes; the store carries "better," "bridge," and "designer" fashions. "Bridge" means clothes priced in between "better" and "designer." Only French designers are featured.

GALLERY OF WEARABLE ART
480 Broadway (bet W Houston and Prince St)
425-5379
Mon: 10-6; Tues-Sun: 11-7

The best phrase to describe this innovative business is "anti-trendy." The Gallery carries what is probably the largest collection of unusual clothing, jewelry, and accessories from all over the world that one can find in New York. It is primarily a cottage industry, with a specialty in creating and designing special-occasion and bridal wear, plus all the accessories that go with the main item. If you are looking for unusual evening gowns, cocktail suits, bridal alternatives for nonclassic weddings, attractive jewelry, lace collage ensembles, and antique collaged suede suits, make this your destination. One thing is for sure: you won't see similar apparel on a friend or relative!

HONEYBEE
7 E 53rd St (bet Fifth and Madison Ave)   688-3660
Mon-Fri: 10-6:30; Sat: 10-5:30

7 Hanover Sq (at Water St)   269-8110
Mon-Fri: 8-6

HoneyBee is a different shop to different people. To many of the city's fashion models, it is a small, intimate shop with a good collection of desirable clothing easily accessible on a quick visit. To out-of-towners, particularly those from Missouri, this is the flagship of a catalog and local branch store, with modern but not far-out sportswear. To the rising class of executive women, it is a shop where you may call to have a few things set aside for a trip to Pittsburgh and know that they will be both appropriate and ready whenever you get there. Primarily, though, HoneyBee relies on its ability to be "totally service oriented." Salespeople carry books that record likes, needs, and previous purchases of customers. Shopping via the catalog is encouraged, and long waits for either service or checkout are taboo. With all this service, prices could be unreasonable. They aren't. In fact, prices in the catalog designed to appeal to Middle America do not differ at all from what is offered in the heart of Manhattan. And styles that appear across the country are au courant enough for fashion models.

LAURA ASHLEY

21 E 57th St (bet Fifth and Madison Ave)   752-7300
Mon-Fri: 10-7; Sat: 10-6

398 Columbus Ave (at 79th St)   496-5110
Mon-Wed, Fri, Sat: 11-7; Thurs: 11-8; Sun: 12-6

4 Fulton St (at South Street Seaport)   809-3555
Mon-Sat: 10-8:45; Sun: 11-7

714 Madison Ave   735-5000
Mon-Fri: 10-7; Sat: 10-6

For Laura Ashley, time and space have stopped in an Edwardian English countryside. Twenty-odd years ago, in response to the growing blue-jean trend and because she was always enamored of the romantic turn-of-the-century dress styles, Ashley and her husband, Bernard, turned out their first dress on their kitchen table. In the years since, the style and fabric have come to be known as Laura Ashley classic, distinguishable in over 130 exclusive shops. And Ashley's death didn't change a thing. There are now three Laura Ashley stores that specialize in clothing in Manhattan. A fourth store on Madison Avenue carries only home furnishings. The dresses are always in a small print fabric, which seems to emerge from the mills looking well worn. (Laura Ashley Ltd. designs and produces its own fabric.) The fabric is then used in a few classic, simple designs that vary only slightly from year to year. It always follows a romantic Victorian-Edwardian theme. In summer, the fabrics are 100 percent cotton; in winter, a light woolen tweed. Except for the seasonal fabric switch, the clothing is timeless, in terms of style and wearability. In recent years, Laura Ashley has expanded to include fabrics for home furnishings as well. There are wallpapers, curtains, and even loose fabric available, as well as Laura Ashley dresses for infants and children.

LEA'S DESIGNER FASHION
81 Rivington St and 98 Orchard St (nr Allen and
Delancey Sts)   677-2043
Sun-Thurs: 10-5:30; Fri: 10-3

You don't have to pay full price for your Albert Nipon (or other famous designer) dresses and suits if you head to this popular Lower East Side outlet. Lea discounts her merchandise up to 30 percent and sells previous season's styles for as little as $50. Don't expect much in the way of amenities, but you'll save enough here to afford a special dinner to show off your new outfit!

LUCILLE'S
33 W 55th St (Hotel Shoreham, Suite 2B)
245-7066
Mon-Sat: 11-5:30; closed July 1-Aug 15

Women who wear sizes 6 to 20 can save substantial sums on designer fashions at Lucille's, a shop that specializes in classic designer clothing at good discount prices. The best part of all—as if that were not enough—is Lucille herself, who presides over her beautifully organized emporium with incredible taste and style. Exactly where Lucille gets her merchandise is uncertain, but somehow she gets fantastic designer clothing in striking colors, patterns, and ensembles. And the labels are intact, unlike nearly every other designer outlet I can think of. Lucille also has an instinct for the needs of her customers. Most are middle-age, very well-dressed, and classically fashionable rather than fad-conscious. So Lucille's styles show a prejudice for the larger sizes. They start at 6, and the higher you go (including a very unusual designer 20), the more varied the selection is. Lucille's concern is shown in her selection of summer outfits with coordinating sweaters (to wear when there's air conditioning), jerseys that pack easily, and three-piece ensembles in striking patterns that can be interchanged for various occasions. Finally, don't miss Lucille's formal wear; her dressy outfits are really special. And did I mention that all of these fashions are sold at a 20 to 40 percent discount?

M. FRIEDLICH
196 Orchard St (bet Stanton and Houston St)
254-8899
Daily: 9:30-5:30

Another typical Lower East Side boutique, Friedlich has the usual fabulous finds in both quality and price as well as the usual abrasive service people. Starting with the good points, Friedlich stocks women's fine imported sportswear in sizes 3 to 14, a range that includes misses and juniors sizes and is somewhat limited on the larger sizes. M. Friedlich seems to favor imports from France and Italy—perhaps because they are the best—but there is a healthy assortment of better-quality American sportswear as well. Another plus is Friedlich's selection of coats and outerwear, which consists of great designer coats and better-brand offerings from both Europe and America. The only problem with a visit here is what one would facetiously call ambiance. Perhaps the sales help are always too swamped with customers, or maybe handling all those good-looking fashions while wearing a smock gets to them. In any event, *surly* is a polite way to describe their behavior. Never ask a question, unless being yelled at in the midst of a horde of tightly packed people turns you on. And that is the final point. The fantastic buys at Friedlich's are not a secret, so the store is always crowded. Would anyone whose pet peeve is standing in line and begging people to take his money come here? You betcha! It's that good!

MIRIAM RIGLER
14 W 55th   581-5519
Mon-Sat: 10-6 (Thurs: 10-7)

Miriam Rigler is the quintessential ladies' dress shop. They seem to have it all—personal attention, expert alterations, wardrobe coordination, custom designing, and a large selection in everything from sportswear to knits to evening gowns, in sizes from 4 to 20. Despite the location, all items are discounted, including specially ordered outfits that are not in stock. This store meets all of my criteria for being one of the very best.

S&W
Coats:
287 Seventh Ave (at 26th St)

Bags, Shoes, Accessories:
165 W 26th St

Dresses, Sportswear:
165 W 26th St
   (at Seventh Ave)

924-6656
Mon-Wed: 10-6:30; Thurs: 10-8; Fri: 10-4; Sun: 10-6

Each location of S&W features a specialty, as indicated above. While it is unclear exactly what the source of supply is, it is a well-known fact that S&W is one of the best places in the city for ladies' designer clothing. Clothing orders include elegant—the suedes and leathers in the coats and suits are magnificent—and top-of-the-line garments only. Unlike so many of the other discount boutiques, S&W maintains a consistent level of quality. It is *not* the place to uncover the buy of the year. Prices, incidentally, are not incidental. The discount is a minimum of 40 percent, but 40 percent off a $300 suede suit still takes a lot out of a working girl's budget. Two serious drawbacks: prices are not marked for the customer to read, and rudeness seems to be a way of life at S&W.

SHULIE'S
175 Orchard St (bet Stanton and Houston St)
473-2480
Sun-Fri: 9:30-5:30

You probably wouldn't think that Orchard Street is the place to come for designer clothes, but think again. Look around uptown in some of the fancier shops for top-label clothing and accessories, then phone or come down to Shulie's. The merchandise will be the same, but the shopping bag, the ambiance, and most important, the price, will be very different. Special orders are taken here, and service is above the norm for this area.

SPITZER'S CORNER STORE
101 Rivington St   156 Orchard St
477-4088   473-1515
Mon-Fri: 9:30-5:30; Sun: 8:30-6

Spitzer on Rivington is a Lower East Side landmark. There is just one good reason for shopping at these stores: excellent selection at the best prices. You have to put up with less than helpful salespeople, unmarked merchandise, and, at the Rivington store, three rooms jammed with goods. Be especially careful in any store that does not mark its merchandise; make sure you're getting the best price possible. A bit of "bargaining" may be necessary. Now that you know the up side and down side of shopping here, you'll be able to get some great bargains and memorable shopping experiences. Good luck.

THREE WISHES
355 W Broadway   226-7570
Sun-Fri: 12-7; Sat: 11-7

Not too many stores in SoHo are true discount operations all year round, but Three Wishes is just that. They feature knit suits, dresses, sweaters, separates, silk dresses, blouses, and evening wear at sizable savings. This is not a sample or overstock type store; their merchandise is first-quality and fashion-current.

Women's Knitwear

SCALERA KNITS
796 Madison Ave (at 67th St)   988-3344
Mon-Sat: 10-6

In this store devoted entirely to knitwear, women can pick up outfits in silk, wool, cashmere, cotton, or blends of those materials in sizes from 8 to 20. If that isn't impressive enough, Scalera is the only direct importer of Italian silk knits in the country.

Women's Large Sizes

ASHANTI

872 Lexington Ave (bet 65th and 66th St)
535-0740
Mon-Wed, Fri, Sat: 10-6; Thurs: 10-8

Its name is a throwback to the days when ethnic boutiques were popular in Manhattan, but Ashanti's current image couldn't be more in vogue. Today, Ashanti carries better dresses, clothing, and accessories solely for the "larger woman." What they can't buy, they have made to order. In fact, says Bill Michael, 75 percent of his merchandise is of Ashanti's own design and manufacturing. And, adds Sandra Michael, the craftsmen who work exclusively for Ashanti are often supplied with patterns as well as designs, since the field is so new. There is more to large sizes than letting out seams or sewing up caftans in polka-dot polyester. Now, for the first time, there are boutiques that operate on the belief that big ladies deserve a positive, stylish fashion image. Ashanti will do alterations and ship anywhere. It may be the only place that carries classic, quality clothing up to size 28. There is even a bargain basement.

FORGOTTEN WOMAN

888 Lexington Ave   60 W 49th St
(at 66th St)   247-8888
535-8848

Mon-Wed, Fri, Sat: 10-6; Thurs: 10-7:30

Nancye Radmin, a former partner in the Farmer's Daughter Boutique, was so appalled by the dearth of size 20 clothes that she opened her own boutique. The Forgotten Woman thus became the first store in New York devoted exclusively to the larger-size woman and, in the process, became a trailblazer for Seventh Avenue manufacturers as well. The selection was so small in the beginning that Nancye designed much of her own merchandise. (She still creates about 25 percent of what is sold.) Eventually, manufacturers followed her lead, and the Forgotten Woman now stocks everything from Diane von Furstenberg's wrap dress to bathing suits with coordinated skirts for cocktail wear. Better still, as a "forgotten women" herself, Nancye knows what looks good and what styles have become almost a uniform for large women. Nicest of all, sizes at the Forgotten Woman range from 14-24. Even if she is really a 44, the Forgotten Woman is one place where the well-endowed woman can feel wanted—and definitely *not* forgotten.

LANE BRYANT
452 Fifth Ave (at 39th St)   764-3550
Tues, Wed, Fri, Sat: 10-6; Mon, Thurs: 10-8; Sun: 12-5

In days of yore, Lane Bryant was the store of choice for women who were either overweight or pregnant. But the store was heavy-handed as well, and over the years it failed to pick up on the popularity of outlets for both of those markets. The Limited purchased Lane Bryant and almost immediately applied its much vaunted marketing techniques to the faded lady. The results have been startling. This store is now the prototype of a chain of Lane Bryants stretching across the country. The image is still large, but it is now high-fashion as well. Clothing is displayed much like it is at the Limited, with highlighted top fashions and mini-departments for different lifestyles.

Women's—Maternity

THE EXECUTIVE MOTHER
757 Third Ave (bet 47th and 48th St)
753-4993
Mon-Wed, Fri: 10-7; Thurs: 10-8; Sat: 11-6; Sun: 12-5

The busy business woman who is going to have a new addition at home will find this store a real help. Business suits, conservative dresses, sportswear, lingerie, nightwear, infant apparel, and toys are all available in one convenient location. This is definitely an up-scale operation. They will assemble clothing for you, deliver it anywhere in the country, and also provide alteration services. Christine LaBastille, herself a successful investment analyst, knows what the busy mother-to-be needs, and she has put together a first-class operation.

FORMAL EXPECTATIONS
341 W 24th St (at Ninth Ave)   675-4859
By appointment only

This is the only formal maternity-wear rental company in the area. They offer top-of-the-line formal wear at a fraction of the retail price, with individualized attention. They will even send a videotape to out-of-town customers to give them an idea of what is available.

LADY MADONNA
793 Madison Ave (at 67th St)   988-7173
Mon-Wed, Fri, Sat: 10-6; Thurs: 10-7; Sun: 12-5

I'd like to reaffirm that I personally visited nearly every one of the stores listed in this book—even the maternity shops. I wasn't exactly a regular customer, but my visits were pleasant and informative and not half as embarrassing as one might think. Okay, back to business. Lady Madonna started with the premise that most pregnant women are adults who would like to dress as adults rather than as Raggedy Ann or Pollyanna. The idea took off beyond anyone's imagination. It was helped along by the rising number of women who combined careers with families and who, therefore, needed good clothing that was stylish even in the advanced stages of pregnancy. Old-fashioned ideas fell by the wayside. One such idea was that a pregnant woman should be hidden, either by staying home or by being swathed in voluminous clothing. Another was that maternity clothes should be inexpensive, since no one wants to pay a lot of money for an outfit worn a maximum of five months. Lady Madonna banished these concepts once and for all with fashionable, functional maternity clothing.

Women's Millinery

DON MARSHALL
(call for address)   758-1686
Mon-Sat: 10:30-5; closed Sat from April to Sept

Even in fashion-conscious New York, personal milliners are a rare breed. In fact, Don Marshall, who's been in business over 40 years, says his is a dying art, and he can see the writing on the wall. "It's too bad," he says. "This is a beautiful profession. Years from now, people will look at these hats and be amazed at the care that was taken to make each piece." And he's right, although it shouldn't take years for Marshall's work to be appreciated; Princess Di has already given hats a new lease on life. All of Marshall's hats and clothing (often in matching ensembles) are custom-made. Your purchase could well be an instant heirloom, while its quality and style will always keep it fashionable. Marshall, who could be a crabby old craftsman or even a fashion snob, is neither. He is one of the friendliest guys you'll ever meet.

HATS IN THE BELFRY
Pier 17 Pavilion, South Street Seaport (1st floor)
406-2574
Mon-Thurs: 10-9; Fri, Sat: 10-10; Sun: 11-8

The Pier 17 Pavilion, an addition to the South Street Seaport, is a popular gathering place for the young financial-district crowd as well as tourists. Many of the shops have sister stores in Rousse-inspired redevelopment projects in other cities, and Hats in the Belfry is among them. So if you're from Washington, Baltimore, Philadelphia, Annapolis, St. Louis, or New Orleans, you may already be familiar with the shop, which has a stock as cute as its name and a reputation that's unusual for such a location. Novelty hats for children and adults (the Statue of Liberty was big in 1986; animals are more popular now) and theatrical-style hats are lined up alongside ladies' designer hats and some of the sharpest men's hats found anywhere. They're also one of the few places that will still steam, brush, or stretch hats. What about that! First-rate service and selection, and all at the charming Seaport.

MANNY'S MILLINERY SUPPLY COMPANY
63 W 38th St   840-2235
Mon-Fri: 9-5:30; Sat: 9-3:30

Manny's is another New York institution. It carries millinery supplies, and that's an understatement. There are drawers, row after row, built up against the walls, and each is dedicated to a particular aspect of head adornment. The section for ladies' hatbands alone takes up almost 100 boxes and runs the gamut from thin pearl lines to wide leather belts, Western style. They have rhinestone banding and an enormous selection of artificial flowers and feathers. The center of the store is lined with tables that display accumulated odds and ends, as well as several bins of larger items that don't fit in the wall drawers. Hat forms can be found here on hat-tree stands in the front. The front, incidentally, displays sample hats in no particular order. Manny's will help fix up any hat and play with interchangeable decorations for it. Manny's also sells completed hats, closeouts, and samples, and will even re-create an old hat.

PAUL'S VEIL AND NET
66 W 38th St (bet Fifth and Sixth Ave)   391-3822
Mon-Fri: 8:30-4:30; Sat: 8-2:30

It is inconceivable that the mob scene here is being repeated up and down the block, and that even *that* is a mere fraction of the bridal business nationwide. Despite the competition of its neighbors (or perhaps because of it), Paul's would be a first-choice recommendation for any bride-to-be who wants to put together her own bridal headpiece. Although they deal in illusion (lace, that is), they are one of the few stores on the block that does not maintain the illusion that they are a wholesale-only outfit, doing the lowly retail customer a big favor by unbarring the doors to her. The staff at Paul's seems genuinely glad to see you—glad to share your joy and overjoyed to help you create a truly unique bridal veil or crown. The store stocks all the equipment needed for the rest of the bridal party, as well as unusual accessories, bridal supplies, and a great collection of imported headpieces created from flowers. The lucky bride will find the savings—and the outfit—extraordinary.

Women's Small Sizes

PETITE PLEASURES
1192 Madison Ave (at 87th St)   369-3437
Mon-Fri: 10:30-6:30; Sat: 10:30-6; Sun: 12-5 (Sept-Dec, March-May)

Just because you are small doesn't mean that you have to accept less than stylish clothes. No more do you have to shop in the young people's departments. Petite Pleasures caters exclusively to the high-fashion woman who happens to be under 5'4". They carry dresses, suits, coats, blouses, sweaters, and pants in petite sizes 2-8 from such well-known designers as St. Gillian, Carole Little, Andrienne Vittadini, and Lloyd Williams. There is also an outstanding private-label collection.

PIAFFE
1412 Broadway (Room 702)   921-7183, 869-3320
Mon-Fri: 9-5, by appointment

This is a personalized shopping service for the petite woman 5'4" and under, size 2-12. They will search out fashionable and unique merchandise for the "little lady."

Women's Tall Sizes

SHELLY'S TALL GIRLS SHOPS
13 E 41st St (nr Fifth Ave)   697-8433
Mon-Wed, Fri, Sat: 9:30-6; Thurs: 9:30-7

Tall ladies don't have much of a choice when shopping for clothing, even in New York. So, it's a bonus when a store specializing in fashions for tall women offers current name-brand fashions at reasonable prices. And Shelly's does. Shelly stands for Sheldon, not Rochelle, and that's the name for the designer line of tall fashions carried exclusively in the shop. Actually, that line is the only such line carried anywhere in the country. And while those fashions are particularly exciting for women who have heretofore been letting hems down no matter what the fashion experts decree, there's more. The store offers a complete wardrobe in sizes 8 to 22; there are sweaters, dresses, tops, skirts, pants, and even coats. That's *complete*. Filling all those requirements is a tall order. Since they are virtually unique, Shelly's also maintains an extensive mail-order business. They will ship anywhere in the country.

Women's Undergarments

A. W. KAUFMAN
73 Orchard St (bet Broome and Grand St)
226-1629, 226-1788
Sun-Thurs: 10:30-5; Fri: 10-2

With three generations in the business, Kaufman handles only the finest in ladies' lingerie and lounge wear, at prices that are substantially less than what uptown stores charge. In fact, Kaufman's discounts are so good that top-quality merchandise here is competitively priced with lesser quality available elsewhere. Kaufman's line includes good, quality practical wear, such as lounge wear, hostess gowns, pajamas, slips, bikini briefs, terry robes, quilted velour robes, and flannel gowns, plus some items, such as the pure silk underwear and hand-embroidered accessories, that are both luxurious and downright frivolous. However, frivolity here is not as expensive as elsewhere, and if you're going to indulge yourself, it's nice to know you can do it at a bargain price. And quality is so good at Kaufman's that everything could last forever.

BRIEF ESSENTIALS
1407 Broadway (bet 38th and 39th St)   921-8344
Mon-Fri: 8:30-5:30

You should shop here, if for no other reason than to be able to brag that you got your sensational lingerie at 1407 Broadway—that veritable bastion of inaccessibility in the wholesale Garment Center. No matter that the store is off the lobby and is a legitimate store (or even that 1407 is known for junior sportswear, and the only thing junior about Brief Essentials' stock is the sizes); if you can buy anything in this building, you've arrived! Not incidentally, the selection is great, if only slightly risqué. "Sensuous lingerie for the sensual woman" is their boast, and you'd better believe that a women's lingerie store doing business in a building full of men who wholesale women's fashions has got to offer the best items in terms of quality, fashion, and price. The ladies' lingerie business has really taken off in the New York area. Brief Essentials is just one of the many lingerie specialty stores with cute names that have sprung up all over. No longer are undergarments limited to bras and girdles purchased in a department store. These intimate boutiques consider such items as camisoles, corsets, and nightwear essential. And all of it is made up in such luxury fibers as silk, satin, and the more plebian, yet highly popular, 100 percent cotton.

D&A MERCHANDISE COMPANY
22 Orchard St (bet Canal and Hester St)   925-4766
Sun-Thurs: 9-5; Fri: 9-3

Elliott Kivell claims that a good reason to shop at D&A is "my sweet adorable smile," but even he concedes that his mother is probably the only person who would make that the first reason to come here. Most people come because it is a one-stop place to get underwear for the entire family at a minimum 25 percent discount, while ladies are impressed by the large selection of bras, gowns, lingerie, and underwear. (There is also a bit of sportswear.) But really smart shoppers come to D&A for the labels they carry. Dior robes, designer tennis wear, nightwear, and top-of-the-line lingerie at these discount prices would convince anyone to shop here, whether Elliott smiles or not.

GOLDMAN AND COHEN
55 Orchard St   966-0737
Sun-Fri: 9-5:30

Goldman and Cohen specializes in name-brand underwear and lingerie for women at a great discount—up to 70 percent! The lines include almost anything that falls within those two categories. This is one of the best.

IMKAR COMPANY
(M. KARFIOL AND SON)
294 Grand St (bet Allen and Eldridge St)   925-2459
Sun-Thurs: 10-5; Fri: 9:30-2; Sun (summer): 10-3

Imkar carries pajamas, underwear, and shifts for both men and women at about one-third off retail prices. A full line of Carter's infants' and children's wear is also available at good prices. The store has a fine line of women's lingerie, including dusters, gowns, and layettes. Featured names include Model's Coat, Barbizon, Vanity Fair, Arrow shirts, Jockey, Lollipop, and Munsingwear.

MENDEL WEISS
91 Orchard St (at Broome St)   925-6815
Sun-Thurs: 9:30-5:30; Fri: 9:30-4

Mendel Weiss is one of the stalwarts in the Lower East Side tradition of selling ladies' undergarments and lounge wear at sizable discounts. Depending on the dates of the merchandise, prices can range from wholesale at 10 percent above cost to other items marked down as much as 75 percent. Weiss includes T-shirts and bathing suits in his collection. Trained specialists are available to aid mastectomy fittings. This is not a glamorous shopping environment, but lingerie styles don't change much from season to season and you can save money here.

SAMANTHA JONES
1074 Third Ave (bet 63rd and 64th St)   308-6680
Mon-Sat: 11-7; Sun: 1-5

Samantha Jones, the owner and operator of her own namesake boutique, specializes in contemporary and glamorous lingerie. Her collection consists of art deco styling in robes, gowns, teddies, and camisoles, and an interesting collection of undergarments, silk scarfs and wraps, and Samantha Jones fragrances. When you're in trouble at home, fellas, this is the place to come for something special for a special lady.

SCHACHNER FASHIONS
95 Delancey St (bet Orchard and Ludlow St)
677-0700
Sun-Fri: 9-5:30

For over 35 years Schachner has been a Lower East Side institution, selling brand-name robes, sleepwear, underwear, and lounge wear at discount prices. They are still doing what they do best!

VICTORIA'S SECRET
34 E 57th St (bet Park and Madison Ave)
758-5592
Mon-Wed, Fri: 10-7; Thurs: 10-8; Sat: 10-6; Sun: 12-5

This has to be one of the sexiest stores in the world. I mean in ambiance, dear reader. The beautiful lingerie and bedroom garb, bridal peignoirs, exclusive silks, and accessories are displayed against the most alluring backdrops. Combine all of this with absolutely charming personnel and, gentlemen, this is *the* place to buy the most personal gifts for your lady.

Coins, Stamps

HARMER ROOKE NUMISMATISTS
3 E 57th St (6th floor)   751-1900
Mon-Fri: 9:30-5; Sat: 10-2:30

Harmer Rooke is a virtual cornucopia of coins, antique items, and fine collectibles, all stocked to abundance and available in hundreds of different styles and price ranges. Howard Rose, one of the managers, says: "In antiquities alone, we have thousands of items on display, priced from a few dollars to $10,000. We feature Greek, Roman, Judaic, pre-Columbian, Egyptian, and Middle Eastern coins, jewelry, and artifacts." There are also collections of American antiques, paper money, and tribal arts among others. Each collection can stand among its peers throughout the country. Taken together, under one roof, it's positively staggering. The personnel behind the counters are knowledgeable and helpful, even if you don't make a purchase.

STACKS RARE COINS
123 W 57th St (nr Sixth Ave)   582-2580
Mon-Fri: 10-5

Stacks, established in 1858, is the country's oldest and largest rare coin dealer. With a specialty in rare coins, medals, and paper money of interest to collectors, Stacks has a solid reputation for individual service, integrity, and knowledge of the field. In addition to specific sales of rare coins and the walk-in business, Stacks runs ten public auctions a year. Both neophyte and experienced numismatists will do well at Stacks.

SUBWAY STAMP SHOP
111 Nassau St (bet Ann and Beekman St)
227-8637, 800/221-9960
Mon-Fri: 9:30-5:30

Subway has operated a stamp shop for over half a century, offering discounts to collectors and bearing one of the most intriguing store names in the city. In that time, they have become the largest mail-order stamp and coin supply company in the world. A look at their 50-page catalog ($1 postage) will explain why they are so successful. The prices are right for all their merchandise, including reference books, stamps and stamp products, and a new-issue service.

Computers

SOFTWARE, ETC.
101 Fifth Ave (bet 17th and 18th St)   727-3280
Mon-Fri: 9:30-8; Sat: 9:30-6:30; Sun: 11-6

1120 Ave of the Americas (corner 44th St)   921-7855
Mon-Fri: 9:30-7; Sat: 10-6; Sun: 11-5

162 E 53rd St   753-7780
Mon-Fri: 9-6:30; Sat: 12-5

666 Fifth Ave (at 52nd St)   315-4744
Mon-Fri: 8:30-7; Sat: 9:30-6:30; Sun: 11:30-5

396 Ave of the Americas (at 8th St)   529-6985
Mon-Sat: 10 a.m.-midnight; Sun: 12-7:30

2300 Broadway (bet 83rd and 84th St)   362-3460
Mon-Thurs: 10-8; Fri, Sat: 10-10; Sun: 12-8

Software, Etc. is the largest resource for computer accessories, books, and software in the area, with highly competitive prices.

Their staff, in the main, are very knowledgeable, and their return policy is generous. Customers may make use of computer demonstration equipment, and they will special order any book or piece of software.

VILLAGE COMPUTERS
687 Broadway (bet 3rd and 4th St)   254-9191
Mon-Fri: 10-7; Sat: 11-6

Finding a place to buy computer supplies is no problem. There are dozens in nearly every neighborhood. But the trick is finding an establishment that will help the amateur properly use the items. Here is where Village Computers shines. This is one of the oldest computer stores in the city, and their people are patient and gentle in leading us nonprofessionals through the wonders of the computer age. The selection is complete (don't be put off by the small store; they have a huge warehouse), and prices are competitive.

Cosmetics, Drugs

BOYD CHEMISTS
655 Madison Ave (at 60th St)   838-6558, 838-5524
Mon-Fri: 8:30-7; Sat: 9:30-6; closed Sat in July, Aug

Boyd is a drugstore in a city full of drugstores, so it has to have something special to be worthy of mention. Naturally, it does. In addition to a complete drug and prescription service, Boyd carries a complete line of cosmetics, soaps, jewelry, and brushes. The latter range from the common to the esoteric: i.e., nail brushes and mustache combs in a variety of sizes and shapes. I started my retailing career in the drug department of the family store, and I do not hesitate to say that Boyd has one of the largest and most complete selections I have ever seen of drugs, cosmetics, and sundries. But shopping in this store is not always a pleasant experience, because of an attitude problem. A new boutique department has handbags, gloves, jackets, and hair accessories.

COSMETIC WORLD AND GIFT CENTER
431 Fifth Ave (bet 38th and 39th St, 2nd floor)
213-4047
Mon-Sat: 10-6:30

Right in the heart of the city you can find cosmetics, crystal pieces, figures, handbags, jewelry, ties, and men's and women's fragrances at discounts that range from 15 to 50 percent. You will not find every major brand in stock at all times, but there are excellent buys on such well-known (read: expensive) names as Chanel, Opium, Estee Lauder, Calvin Klein, Krizia, and Albert Nipon. Cosmetic World has a multilingual staff, a corporate gift program, and telephone and mail-order facilities.

ESSENTIAL PRODUCTS
90 Water St (bet Wall St and Hanover Sq)
344-4288
Mon-Fri: 9-6

Essential Products has been manufacturing flavors and fragrances for nearly 100 years. They know that an enormous percentage of the price of colognes and perfumes pays for advertising and packaging. So they set out to see how closely they could duplicate expensive scents at cheaper prices. They describe their fragrances as "elegant interpretations" of designer names sold at a small fraction of the original's price. Essential features 68 sensual perfumes and men's colognes, and offers a money-back guarantee. If you send them a self-addressed stamped envelope, they will send you five scented cards and all ordering information.

KAUFMAN PHARMACY
557 Lexington Ave (at 50th St)   755-2266
Daily: 24 hours

I hope Kaufman's is one phone number in New York you will never need, but it's wonderful to know it's there. In addition to the usual drugstore operation—soda fountain, sundries, cigarettes, electrical goods, and traveling needs—Kaufman's has a prescription department that's always open. Should the nightmare of being ill in a New York City hotel room actually happen to you, it's nice to know a pharmacy is open and ready to deliver your prescription by cab. Bless them! Incidentally, should you need a doctor to write that prescription, check this book's special telephone numbers.

KIEHL'S
109 Third Ave (bet 13th and 14th St)   677-3171
Mon-Fri: 10-6; Sat: 10-4:30

Kiehl's has been a New York institution since 1851. It is a fourth-generation, family-owned company unlike any you have ever visited. Their special treatments and preparations are made by hand and distributed internationally. Natural ingredients are used in the full lines of cleansers, scrubs, toners, moisturizers, eye-area preparations, men's creams, masques, body moisturizers, bath and shower products, sports items, ladies' leg-grooming formulations, and hair shampoos, conditioners, and treatments. Customers can also enjoy an unusual collection of memorabilia related to aviation, an interest of the Aaron Morse family, who runs this famous shop.

SOAP OPERA
30 Rockefeller Plaza   245-5090
Mon-Fri: 10-6

The Soap Opera calls itself a "bath boutique," but its specialty is soaps and soap products rather than bathroom furnishings. There is a full range of over 400 natural and herbal soaps, as well as soap powders, bath oils, and bath additives. Some, in fact, are packaged so that they make great gifts. The scents are long-lasting without being sickly sweet, and add a pleasing aroma to any room. There is a good selection of oatmeal soaps, which are supposed to be excellent for the complexion. The store carries a line of decorative bathroom sinks and accessories, and such gift items as potpourri and lace- and flower-adorned baskets.

Crafts

ALLCRAFT TOOL AND SUPPLY COMPANY
45 W 46th St (3rd floor)   840-1860
Mon-Fri: 9-4:45

If there is a definitive jewelry-making supply store, Allcraft is it. Its reputation is so old and solid that even the name of its manager, Catherine Grant, is legendary. Allcraft's catalog is so all-inclusive that it's impossible to describe. (To obtain one, write 666 Pacific Street, Brooklyn, NY 11217.) There is a complete line of tools and supplies for jewelry making, silversmithing, metal smithing, enameling on metal, lost wax casting, and much more. Out-of-towners usually deal with the mail-order catalog, but New Yorkers don't miss the opportunity to visit this gleaming cornucopia.

ANN JACOB AMERICA
756 Madison Ave (bet 65th and 66th St)   988-5143
Mon-Sat: 10-6

Ann Jacob has finally fulfilled her dream of having a gallery on Madison Avenue in New York. Originally from Manhattan, Jacob started her collection in Atlanta and has come back to offer the Big Apple unique American folk-art pieces, contemporary crafts, and American antique and primitive furniture. Many of the items have a Southern drawl, and all have charm and class.

CERAMIC SUPPLY OF N.Y. & N.J.
534 LaGuardia Pl (bet Bleecker and 3rd St)
475-7236
Mon-Fri: 9-6; Sat: 10-5

Ceramic Supply runs the whole wheel of pottery. They have a school, they sell supplies and equipment, and they hand-make pottery, all from the same location. These people eat and breathe pottery, and their enthusiasm shows in all of their projects. There are even special programs for the handicapped. If classes aren't convenient, Ceramic Supply has books and materials available for the self-starter. In short, one can do everything at this location, from buying an ashtray to casting a mold.

CLAYWORKS
332 E 9th St (bet First and Second Ave)
677-8311
Mon-Thurs: 4-7; Fri: 4:30-8:30; Sat: 12:30-8:30;
    Sun: 2:30-8:30 (best to call ahead)

All of Clayworks' pottery is lead-free and dishwasher- and microwave-safe. It is also handmade on the wheel. You can watch the talented artist, Helaine Sorgen, at work and ask questions about what is going on. Small classes in wheel throwing are given for adults. Everything here is individually produced, from teapots to casseroles, honey pots, mugs, and sake sets. Decorative pieces include vases, platters, and bowls. You won't see them duplicated anywhere else!

COMMON GROUND
19 Greenwich Ave   989-4178
Mon, Tues, Thurs, Fri: 11:30-7:30; Wed: 11-6:30;
    Sat: 11-7; Sun: 1-7

Please note that the address is Greenwich *Avenue,* not Greenwich *Street.* Greenwich Avenue is a crosstown street in the Village, and Greenwich Street runs north-south from the Village down into TriBeCa. Coming from Oregon, where a multitude of artifacts and crafts are made and sold by native Indians, I am familiar enough with this kind of merchandise to know that Common Ground has an excellent selection of American Indian jewelry, furniture, rugs, baskets, and the like. The folks in the shop are very proud of their stock, and they will take time to explain the origin of each item.

ELDER CRAFTSMEN
846 Lexington Ave (bet 64th and 65th St)
535-8030
Mon: 11-5:30; Tues-Sat: 10-5:30; closed Sat in July, Aug

The Elder Craftsmen is a shop that epitomizes all that is great about New York. It is strictly a nonprofit organization. Everything sold here is certifiably handmade by a senior citizen who's at least 55 years old. Often in desperate need of both money and something to do, these talented people are able to satisfy both needs, keeping half of the purchase price for everything they make (the remaining money goes to operating expenses for the shop). Most of the work is of a higher quality than that of comparable machine-made items.

ERICA WILSON
717 Madison Ave (at 63rd St, 2nd floor)
832-7290
Mon-Wed, Fri, Sat: 10-6; Thurs: 10-7

Erica Wilson is a lady of many talents. This British émigré not only writes books and newspaper columns about needlework, but also finds time to do TV shows and run a store that supplies almost anything a needlework enthusiast might require. There is a huge stock of knitting yarns, ranging from alpaca to cashmere, and the city's finest selection of hand-painted needlepoint patterns from London and elsewhere. You can select hand-knitted sweaters or beautiful accessories from Erica's stock. Her chintz bags are very special. Blocking, padding, mounting, finishing—and classes in these skills—are available at prices that are, well, not inexpensive.

IL MERCATO
341 E 9th St (bet First and Second Ave)   260-6329
Mon-Fri: 12:30-8:30; Sat: 12:30-9; Sun: 1-7:30

"Il Mercato" means "the Market," and that is exactly what you will find here. The prices are right at this international crafts bazaar, where you can scoop up dolls from Peru, bags from Guatemala, rugs from Afghanistan, as well as a host of other bargains from all over the world. This house will also rent items that you might want to use for a party, television show, or other special event.

LOVELIA ENTERPRISES
356 E 41st St (in Tudor City)
490-0930, FAX: 212/697-8550
Mon-Fri: 9:30-5 (by appointment only)

Lovelia F. Albright and her establishment are one of New York's great finds. From a shop in Tudor City, overlooking the United Nations, she dispenses the finest European Gobelin and Aubusson machine-woven tapestries at a price that is often one-third that of any other place. The tapestries are exquisite. Some of the designs depict the ubiquitous unicorns cavorting in a medieval scene; others are more modern. They come in all sizes. The latest additions include tapestries for upholstery, wool-pile miniature rugs for use as mats under *objets d'art,* and an extensive line of tapestry-woven borders. They're designed by Albright and made exclusively for her in Austria. There is also a very impressive catalog for mail orders.

PERFORMERS OUTLET
222 E 85th St   249-8435
Tues-Thurs: 12-7; Fri: 3-7:30; Sat: 11-5:30

Performers Outlet was started as a cooperative venture to market the non-show-business talents of show-business people who have lots of time and very little money on their hands. The concept worked so well that several would-be performers gave up the lively arts to develop full-time crafts careers. Today, very little of the crafts are of amateur quality, and the standards are so high that very few performers are even represented. Most of the items are made by professional craftsmen from this country and France, and the evolution has been such that the gallery now goes by the name of Francophilia Americana Gallery, as well as Performers Outlet. There is a search service, and craftsmen can be commissioned for specific projects. There is also color coordinating of glass, pottery, rag rugs, picture frames, candles, flowers, and other decorating accessories. The atmosphere is still homey.

RADIO HULA
169 Mercer St (bet Houston and Prince St)   226-4467
Tues-Sat: 12-7

This is the only retail gallery on the East Coast dedicated to the native culture of Hawaii and the South Pacific. They carry traditional and contemporary Hawaiian arts and crafts, including wood carving, weaving, clothing, gourmet foods, jewelry, books, and other unusual items.

SCULPTURE HOUSE
30 E 30th St (nr Madison Ave)   679-7474
Mon-Fri: 10-4

In 1918, Bruner F. Barrie's family established a small sculpture and pottery workshop in Manhattan. The business grew and grew, and today, after a move further downtown, it offers everything necessary for the serious sculptor. Note the word *serious,* because Sculpture House, while pleasant and informative, hasn't the time or space to initiate neophyte sculptors. It's assumed that the customer knows exactly what he wants. Sculpture House offers 16 different types of clay bodies, tools for ceramics and pottery, and more than 1,000 wood-carving tools that the Barrie business manufactures itself. While sculpture normally implies ceramics and clay, Claire Brush says that 40 percent of the business is related to wood-carving. Sculpture House offers a wide variety of services as well. There are no formal classes, but every conceivable related book can be found here.

A SHOW OF HANDS
531 Amsterdam Ave (at 86th St)   787-1174
Mon-Sat: 11-7; Sun: 11-6

Remember the CCC? (Civilian Conservation Corps, for those who don't.) Well, this is another kind of a CCC that could be of real interest to you. In this case the three C's stand for Contemporary Crafts Cooperative, an organization that represents crafts people from all over the country who are considered tops in their respective fields. Over 100 artists show an outstanding collection of functional and decorative pottery, magnificent scarves, unusual jewelry, quilts, and home accessories, including furniture. Prices are reasonable for the quality of merchandise offered. Who knows? You may find a treasure signed by an artisan who one day will be on the collectors-item list!

SUNRAY YARN
347 Grand St (bet Essex and Ludlow St)   475-0062
Sun-Fri: 9:30-5; closed one week in July and Dec

Sunray is another of the Lower East Side needlework shops with all of the stock and discounts characteristic of the area. In addition to the best prices on DMC and precut rug yarns, Sunray also has yarns for knitting (hand and machine), needlepoint kits and components, stitchery, latch-hook and punch rugs, and crocheting. They also do a brisk business in custom pillow design and needlework framing. Instructors write out knitting and crocheting pattern instructions for customers and help them with any difficulties.

WOMEN'S EXCHANGE
1095 Third Ave (at 64th St)   753-2330
Mon-Sat: 10-6

The Women's Exchange was started over 100 years ago to provide a marketplace for the crafts of women widowed by the Civil War. Over the years it evolved into a source of income for retired governesses, housekeepers, and down-at-the-heels gentlewomen. In recent years it has regrouped and moved, but the tradition as a showcase for women's crafts continues. They are particularly known for their hand-smocking on children's clothing. Every item is one-of-a-kind. There are dolls, shawls, mittens, fabrics, pillows, and model furniture for sale. While prices are not cheap, they are certainly competitive. The women receive 75 percent of the sale, so you are helping to support them while dressing your children.

YARN CENTER
1011 Sixth Ave   719-5648
Mon-Wed, Fri: 10-6; Thurs: 10-7; Sat: 10-5

The New York Yarn Center has become a discount establishment that concentrates heavily on needlecraft items and accessories. They have one of the largest selections of DMC yarns in the area —over 3,000 different colors and textures. You'll find Persian and tapestry yarns; cross-stitch books; kits for cross-stitch, embroidery, and crewel; and a tremendous assortment of wools for knitting and crocheting.

Dance Items

BALLET SHOP
1887 Broadway (bet 62nd and 63rd St)   581-7990
Mon-Sat: 11-8

This shop is a mecca for ballet fans. While the name presupposes that one would be inundated with tutus and leotards, the store has only a few decorating the walls. The entire display area of the store is devoted to books, records, and other memorabilia. Available are new books, gift and novelty items, rare and out-of-print books, limited editions, albums, programs, posters, art, collector's items, ballet and opera videotapes, and autographs of stars. I list it all only to show that truly there are no ballet supplies. But now you know where to get a Nureyev T-shirt in your choice of several poses.

Department and Specialty Stores, Malls and Factory Outlet Stores

The word that best describes the department- and specialty-store scene in Manhattan in recent years is *turmoil*. Never before has there been so much change in ownership and management in a short space of time. The economic problems of some of the organizations have resulted in store closings. In other cases, changes have taken place in the merchandising direction of the store.

We have seen the closing of Bonwit Teller and B. Altman, two long-time major players on New York's retail scene. The space formerly occupied by Bonwit at Trump Tower features Galeries Lafayette, the famous French department store. There is some speculation that Bonwit Teller may reappear on the scene in another location.

Bloomingdale's and Macy's have each had their financial difficulties, but their Manhattan flagship stores remain the city's dominant quality retailers. A major (and successful) addition to the midtown retail scene has been A&S, an operation that is a step down price-wise from Macy's and Bloomingdale's. Henri Bendel has moved around the corner into beautiful new digs facing Fifth Avenue. Bergdorf Goodman has expanded across Fifth Avenue with a sparking new (and expensive!) men's store, while Barney's is planning an additional store on the Upper East Side. Saks Fifth Avenue's Middle Eastern ownership has put substantial money into a major expansion, with added space on every floor, a remodeled street floor, and relocated departments. Alexander's, a lower-priced store, is not a major player. Lord & Taylor, long a quality operation, is now operating successfully under new ownership.

There are four major malls in the Manhattan area, although they differ from the usual conception of a suburban shopping mall because of property costs and size limitations. Trump Tower (Fifth Ave near 56th St) is a vertical mall, with upscale stores, many of which are showcases for leading overseas retailers. Don't expect to find bargains, but the ambiance is top-notch. A spectacular waterfall and atrium dominate the scene. Outstanding stores include Blantree (European and Oriental art), La Petite Etoile (high-fashion clothes for infants and children), Abercrombie and Fitch (clothing, gifts), David Saity (sterling silver jewelry), and Saity Jewelry.

The new A&S department store is a major tenant in A&S Plaza (Sixth Ave and 33rd St), formerly the home of Gimbel's. In a busy, glitzy Herald Square setting only a stone's throw from Macy's, this new development has brought renewed vigor to the area. A food fair and a large number of specialty stores make for interesting shopping. Worth visiting are Accento (hand-made sweaters), Forest Club (outdoor clothing), Anania's (leather bags), Jungle Fever (just as it sounds), and Mouse 'n Around, Too (Mickey headquarters).

Next door is a less successful mall. In what was once Saks 34th Street and later Korvettes, Herald Center has never really gotten off the ground (although the building is eight stories tall). A poorly designed facility and shaky retail operations have led to a declining volume of business. The only shot in the arm—a major one, at that —has been the opening of a large branch of the nation's top toy retailer, Toys 'R' Us, in the street and basement levels.

Further downtown, another new, quality mall is located in the World Financial Center (Battery Park City). The centerpiece is the magnificent Winter Garden, an open space used for concerts, benefits, and just plain resting. The waterfront setting is very special. Surrounding the Winter Garden in both directions and on several levels is a collection of better stores, some of which are struggling because of light traffic. There are several eating facilities of varying quality and price range (see Restaurant section). Some of the more interesting stores worth visiting are Barney's (clothing), Outfitters (outer apparel), Sports International (clothing), Ovations (gift baskets) and Il Papiro (fine stationery).

Across town is the South Street Seaport, a picturesque and historic area that has tended to attract more visitors than city residents. As a result, year-round traffic has fallen and a number of businesses have closed or changed hands. Pier 17, however, remains a vital mall, with a food fair and interesting places for shopping or browsing. This area is not the best for eating establishments, however. In the summertime, outdoor entertainment is offered, and the waterside activities are worthwhile. Some of the better shops in the area include a branch of the Strand (books), Hats in the Belfry (millinery), Brookstone (housewares), Mariposa (butterflies), and Country Road Australia (clothing).

Factory Outlet Shopping has become a way of life for bargain-happy New Yorkers. Although this book is Manhattan-oriented (with a very few special exceptions), I feel that it is important to list the better factory outlet malls in surrounding states. Thus, for the first time, a special section follows with the best of this exciting (and money-saving) shopping pastime.

Factory Outlet Stores

LIBERTY VILLAGE
1 Church St, Flemington, NJ 08822
201/782-8550
Daily: 10-5:30

Approximately 65 stores including Anne Klein, Anne Klein Petites, Bass Shoes, Calvin Klein, Capezio Factory Direct Shoes, Carole Little, Carter's Little Gallery, Coat World, Corning/Revere, Eire (Waterford, Aynsley), Harve Bernard, Joan & David Shoes, Jones New York, Lady Leslie Fashions, L'eggs/Hanes/Bali, Manhattan, Perry Ellis Direct, Ribbon Outlet, Van Heusen, Villeroy & Boch, and others.

THE FACTORY OUTLETS AT NORWALK
East Ave, Norwalk, CT 06855
203/838-1349
Mon, Tues, Wed, Sat: 10-6; Thurs, Fri: 10-9; Sun: 12-5
For map and guide: 11 Rowan St, Norwalk, CT 06855

Twenty-six stores, including Bag and Baggage, By the Yard, Bed, Bath & Beyond, Company Store, Crazy Horse/Russ Togs, Adolfo 11, Dress Barn, Dunham Boots/Quoddy Shoes, Fashion Shoe Outlet, Gentlemen's Wearhouse, Harve Bernard, Head Over Heels, Intimate Eve, Just Coats & Swimwear, Old Mill, Royal Doulton, Shoe Manufacturers Outlet, Top of the Line Cosmetics, Van Heusen, and more.

READING OUTLET CENTER
801 North 9th St, Reading, PA 19604
215/373-5495
Mon-Wed: 9:30-6; Thurs-Sat: 9:30-8; Sun: 12-5

Seventy-five stores, including Allen Edmonds, Bag and Baggage Outlet, Bass Shoes, Bostonian, Carole Hochman/Lily of France, Carter's Childrenswear, Corning/Revere, Crazy Horse, Children's

Bootery/Jumping Jacks, Delta Hosiery, Dooney & Bourke Handbags, Eric Allen, Evan Picone, Farah, Fashion Shoe Outlet, Fenn Wright & Manson, Flemington Fashions, Gant Company Store, Gilligan and O'Malley, Hart Schafner & Marx, Harve Bernard, Izod-Lacoste, J. Crew, Ship 'n Shore/Monet, Jaeger Outlet, J.G. Hook, Kitchen Collection/Wearever, L'eggs/Hanes/Bali, Leslie Fay, Liz Claiborne, London Fog, Maidenform, Nautica, Norton McNaughton, Polo/Ralph Lauren, Rawlings Sporting Goods, Timberland, Van Heusen, Windsor Shirt, and more.

HARMON COVE OUTLET CENTER
20 Enterprise Ave, Secaucus, NJ 07096
Mon, Tues, Wed, Sat: 10-6; Thurs, Fri: 10-9;
    Sun: noon-5
Fifty stores, including American Tourister, Bally Outlet Store, Barbizon Lingerie, Bass Shoes, Capezio Factory Direct, Gitano, Hosiery Mill Outlet, Izod-Lacoste, Ship 'n Shore/Monet, Jonathan Logan, N.T. Tahari, Sportswear Systems, Urban Clothing, Van Heusen, and more.

OUTLETS AT THE COVE
45 Meadowlands Parkway, Secaucus, NJ 07096
Mon, Tues, Wed, Sat: 10-6; Thurs, Fri: 10-9;
    Sun: noon-5
Ten stores, including Bass Shoes, Bugle Boy, Calvin Klein, Fenn Wright & Manson, Harve Bernard, Jones New York, Leather Loft, Luggage World, and Van Heusen. (Note: For a map and guidebook to Harmon Cove Outlet Center and Outlets at the Cove, call or write: Hartz Mountain Industries, 400 Plaza Drive, Secaucus, NJ 07096; 201/348-1200, ext. 425.)

CALVIN KLEIN WAREHOUSE STORE
50 Enterprise Ave N, Secaucus, NJ 07096
201/330-0373
Mon-Sat: 9:30-5:30; Thurs: 9:30-8:30; Sun: 12-5

LIZ CLAIBORNE
4 Emerson Lane, Secaucus, NJ 07094
201/319-8411
Mon-Sat: 10-6; Thurs and Fri: 10-9; Sun: 12-6

UNITED STATUS APPAREL
25 Enterprise Ave N, Secaucus, NJ 07094
201/867-4455
Mon-Wed: 10-6; Thurs, Fri: 10-9; Sat: 10-7; Sun: 11-6

WOODBURY COMMON
FACTORY OUTLETS
Route 32, Tower Building, Central Valley, NY 10917
914/928-7467
Mon-Sat: 10-6; Sun: 11-6 (Thurs, Fri: 10-9, May-Dec)

Over 95 stores, including Adidas, Adolfo Sport, Adrienne Vittadini, American Tourister, Anne Klein, Anne Klein Petites, Calvin Klein, Carlos Falchi, Carole Little, Carter's Childrenswear, Charles Jourdan Factory Outlet, Corning/Revere, Dansk Factory Outlet, Delta Hosiery, Ellen Tracy, Fenn Wright & Manson, Gitano, Gucci, Hanes Activewear, Harve Bernard, Izod-Lacoste/Ship 'n Shore/Monet, Joan & David Outlet, Jones New York, Lady Leslie Fashions, L'eggs/Hanes/Bali, Leslie Fay Factory Outlet, Liz Claiborne, Sergio Valente, Sultra/Camp Beverly Hills, Tahari, Van Heusen, and more.

BERGDORF GOODMAN
754 Fifth Ave (at 58th St)   753-7300
Mon-Wed, Fri, Sat: 10-6; Thurs: 10-8

Sitting in a prime location on Fifth Avenue, just off a corner of Central Park, Bergdorf is the epitome of class. The operation has broadened its appeal in recent years, reaching out to young and affluent customers scared away by the cold atmosphere of previous years. Many sections of the store have been redone into smaller boutiques. Lines have been expanded, and an efficient transportation system has been completed. Dollar sales per square foot are among the highest in the nation. Bergdorf emphasizes top fashion names in all departments; many of the styles shown are found exclusively in this store. Their windows usually show a fine selection of this apparel. The top floor presents an exciting array of home-accessory merchandise, carefully selected and beautifully displayed. Several trendy eating places allow shoppers to spend more time in the store. Personnel here are great if they know you; if not, don't appear in your grubbies. A new men's store (see adjacent write-up) has opened across the street. It is, however, more like a museum than a store (ridiculous prices, top-quality goods, difficult shopping, "don't touch me" feel).

BERGDORF GOODMAN MEN
745 Fifth Ave (at 58th St)   753-7300
Mon-Wed, Fri, Sat: 10-6; Thurs: 10-8

What used to be the home of the fabled toys of F.A.O. Schwarz is now a showroom for fabled items of menswear from all over the world. This separate new men's store is a first for Bergdorf Goodman, and is a strong statement for the upper end of the gentlemen's market. The attempt is only partially successful. The range of stock and the showing of top designer names are awesome (as are many of the prices). But the service borders on being ultra-pretentious, and the physical layout is confusing and inconvenient at best. Still, if you are looking for that price-does-not-matter gift for the man in your life, or if you are a gentleman intent on wearing the best of the best, you will surely find this a happy hunting ground.

BLOOMINGDALE'S
1000 Third Ave   355-5900
Mon, Thurs: 10-9; Tues, Wed, Fri, Sat: 10-6;
     Sun: 12-6

"Like no other store in the world." These are the words used by management to describe this store, which has been a New York institution occupying the same spot since 1879. Although there have been some rather serious financial problems at the corporate level, Bloomingdale's continues to be the standard by which other retailers judge their own operations. Having a sense of style and being just a bit ahead of everyone else are two reasons for their success. When something new appears on the market, either in clothing or home furnishings, chances are you will find it first at Bloomingdale's. Their fashion departments carry just about every famous name in the business. The newly expanded men's sections are a vast improvement, with a fine selection of imported clothing. In home furnishings, no one is better. Their furniture department and home-accessories areas are without equal. Dining in "Le Train Bleu" (the restaurant) is almost like being in the old Twentieth-Century Limited! Gourmets will go wild in the food area and a tempting bakery section with in-house products. Special promotions featuring countries from around the world (and various regions of America) draw huge crowds. Bloomingdale's appeals to middle- and upper-income shoppers, but everyone will find something to intrigue them, even if it is only a Bloomie's nightshirt for pleasant shopping dreams.

HENRI BENDEL
712 Fifth Ave (bet 55th and 56th St)   247-1100
Mon-Sat: 10-6:30 (Thurs: 10-8); Sun: 12-6

Having spent a major portion of my adult life in the retail business, I know stores pretty well. There are not many fine stores in this country or abroad that I have not visited in recent years. I can say, without equivocation, that the new Henri Bendel store on Fifth Avenue is one of the classiest around. Founded in 1896 as a millinery store, Bendel's was a fixture on West 57th Street for years. In a boutique setting, the store catered to high-fashion women's apparel for the upwardly mobile New Yorker. The new store, in the former Coty Building, keeps the same boutique atmosphere but expands it into a series of shops that just speak fashion, quality, and excitement. You will want to buy something in every section you visit; it is that colorful and attractive! Wood is used prominently throughout the store, and the magnificent original windows by René Lalique have been incorporated into the store design in a most appealing manner. The store re-creates the ambiance of Paris in the 1920s. Don't miss the Parfumerie, the "Kidz" section, the Salon de Thé (sandwiches, salads, pastries, and more by Les Delices Guy Pascal), and the Tabletoppings by McIntosh. A concierge service is provided, and the store includes the only American branch of the Institut Jeanne Gatineau, a French spa. No salespeople (just "stylists") can take you from boutique to boutique by oval staircases—there are, happily, no escalators in the building! Top billing is given to young, up-and-coming designers, and today's shopper will find a spectacular setting for her wardrobe selections.

LORD & TAYLOR
424 Fifth Ave (at 39th St)   391-3344
Mon, Thurs: 10-8:30; Tues, Wed, Fri, Sat: 10-6:45;
      Sun: 12-6

"Red, white, and blue" might be an appropriate way to describe this long-time player on the New York merchandising scene. For many years, this was *the* store for the working girl, an image that the legendary Dorothy Shaver cultivated when she headed Lord and Taylor. Today the store is owned by the May Company, successful merchants who have carved out a middle territory—price and fashion-wise—for their stores. So far, the strategy has been to strive for high volume with popularly priced goods that are actively promoted. If there is an underlying image, it is an emphasis on American designers. The store showcases good lines from local sources, both in their ads and window displays. No longer is there a significant home furnishings showing, and the men's areas have never been strong. But for the average woman who is looking for good value for her clothing (and who does not want to put up with discount-store shopping), Lord & Taylor is an ideal alternative. What the store lacks in physical attractiveness (the first floor is one of the dullest in the city), it makes up in aggressive merchandising.

MACY'S
151 W 34th St (at Herald Sq)   695-4400
Mon, Thurs, Fri: 9:45-8:30; Tues, Wed: 9:45-6:45;
      Sat: 10-6:45; Sun: 10-6

The heart of New York might just be the giant Macy's store at Herald Square, "the world's largest department store." At one time, this was certainly the heart of the retail world, as Macy's and Gimbel's fought it out across the street (with Saks 34th Street in between). In the battle, Macy's emphasized quantity rather than quality, and the store began to slip. Enter Ed Finkelstein, one of retailing's stars. He brought his successful Macy's California formula to Manhattan, spruced up the store (beautiful new main floor, redone departments throughout), brought back top names and top-quality goods, and set out to reclaim the Macy's heritage. Now the retail battle pits Macy's and Bloomie's. A new element has been added, however, with the arrival of A&S as a neighbor, which has brought back traffic to the area. Macy's excels in home furnishings and offers good values on children's merchandise, a great "Cellar" for fine foodstuffs and accessory items, and a dazzling main floor cosmetic section. Numerous eating nooks are available, as is most every customer service known in the industry. At Easter time, the store is a magnificent garden scene, with live plants, flowers, and fountains. Macy's sale events offer special value and large selections. Shopping here is an experience; if you are addicted to the pastime, you'll love this place.

SAKS FIFTH AVENUE
611 Fifth Ave (at 50th St)　　753-4000
Mon-Wed, Fri, Sat: 10-6:30; Thurs: 10-8; Sun: 12-5

Now there is even more of Saks to drool over! A new 36-floor office and retail tower has been built adjoining the original store, and 15,000 square feet of merchandising space has been added behind the escalators on each of the store's nine floors. The main floor has been completely and attractively redone. A new designer's shop for women has opened on level three, and an expanded section for men's European clothing has been added on level six. Cafe S.F.A., on the eighth floor, provides a rest stop for your feet and pocketbook. With a Bahrain-based holding company as a parent, financing here is not a problem. The store remains a quality institution of the highest order, where men and women (and kids) can be outfitted with the top names in the business. The career woman, the well-heeled young matron, and the society dowager will all find a huge selection of sportswear, dresses, formals, coats, suits, furs, and accessories with moderate to very expensive tabs. The men's clothing section is one of the best in the city. Ask for Dennis Weiner in this department; he is one of the last of the breed of really concerned salesmen! (Hint: Smart shoppers save their dollars until Saks has a sale.)

Display Accessories

NIEDERMAIER DISPLAY
435 Hudson St　　675-1106
Mon-Fri: 9-5

The main business here is conducted in trade shows. Niedermaier designs and creates all kinds of displays, and they are considered

tops in the business. They usually discourage retail customers looking for just "the right thing" for some special need at home or the
office, but if you talk nicely (and mention this book) they probably
will take care of you. Think of the fun you can have with all kinds
of model pieces of human anatomy at that next birthday party!

Domestics

AD HOC SOFTWARES
410 W Broadway (at Spring St)
925-2652, FAX 212/941-6910
Mon-Sat: 11:30-7; Sun: 11:30-6

What does the name of this store mean? Just what it says: soft
textures for modern living. There is furniture, clothes for kids and
adults, luggage, table top items (china, glassware), sheets and
towels, blankets, and table linens. You will also find pile and sisal
rugs, American folk-art antiques, and steel occasional tables.
You'll have a soft spot in your heart after you visit this unusual
establishment!

D. PORTHAULT
18 E 69th St   688-1660
Mon-Fri: 10-6; Sat: 10-5

Porthault, the French queen of linens, needs no introduction.
Custom-made linens are available in a range of 600 designs (or
more, if you count custom designs), scores of colors, and weaves
of super luxurious density. Wherever the name Porthault appears
(some fancy hotels), you know they run a top-notch operation.
The folks here are definitely top-notch. Their printed sheets seem
to last forever; they're passed along from one generation to another. Porthault can handle custom work of an intricate nature
for odd-sized beds, baths, and showers. Specialties include signature prints; printed terry towels; decorative accessories like trays,
wastebaskets, tissue-box covers, drawer liners, and room sprays;
and a large selection of other unusual gift items.

EZRA COHEN
307 Grand St (at Allen St)   925-7800
Sun-Fri: 9-5

Ezra Cohen is the first of the Lower East Side linen and dry-
goods stores you encounter when coming from Allen Street. While
the entire street—on both sides—is lined with them, Ezra Cohen is
the only one you really need to know. Its floors are stocked with the
finest linens, bedspreads, quilts, and draperies at prices that, at the
very least, match the department stores' sale prices. Quality is always top-notch, and at a time when bed linens have styles and fashions like clothing, Ezra Cohen not only carries what's current, but

what will become current. The first floor is dedicated primarily to linens, and most customers never go any farther, since the vast selection can make up complete trousseaus. The second floor is dedicated to bed coverings, and note the use of the word. It used to display bedspreads by Nettlecreek and custom-made designs, but as the "unmade" bed motif has spread, it has adapted as well. Today, it has coverlet, comforter, and sheet ensembles and such hard-to-find items as sheets for water beds and throws and comforters for platform beds. Ezra Cohen features Croscill products in the bedspread department. There is also a great selection of pillows. There are custom-made comforters, dust ruffles, pillow shams, and custom-sized sheets and blanket covers, as well as vertical blinds and all types of custom draperies. Lighter drapery is on the first floor, along with the Fieldcrest and Martex towel lines. Ezra Cohen has been a family business for as many generations as it has floors. The current generation—Bob, Jerry, and Marvin Cohen—are great people, who are as well versed as their ancestors in selling the best for the least.

J. SCHACHTER'S
85 Ludlow St (near Delancey St)
533-1150, 800/INTO BED
Mon-Thurs: 9-5; Fri: 9-2; Sun: 9-4

J. Schachter's is the foremost purveyor of quilts in the New York area and perhaps the entire continent. If your grandparents had a quilt, at one time in its life it probably had some connection with Schachter's. It was either purchased, restuffed, mended, or sewn anew there, but, at some point, almost all quilts but those found in museums have been to Schachter's. In the days before the home-crafts and comforter craze in home decorating, Schachter's managed to do a good business. Today, when everyone owns not only quilted coverlets but down-filled jackets and hoods, Schachter's business is booming. This is the oldest quilting firm in New York, and Schachter's knows everything there is to know about quilts and their making. They also do work in polyester, lamb's wool, and cotton. The talented staff can make a quilt in any size and in 20 different quilting patterns from any fabric given to them. Schachter's has a complete line of linens as well. Custom pillows can be made while you wait. When both lines are combined, entire bedrooms or bathrooms, from rugs to ceiling and wall coverings, can be completely coordinated.

PILLOW SALON
313 E 61st St   755-6154
Mon-Fri: 11-6

Pillows are king here. Pillow Salon's complete line changes constantly but always involves unique designs. There are decorative pillows, custom-made pillows, and antique textile pillows, all of which are available to the trade and general public.

PRATESI LINENS
829 Madison Ave (at 69th St)   288-2315
Mon-Sat: 10-6

Pratesi says it carries the best linens the world has to offer, and they're probably right. Families hand them down for generations. In fact, the new customers probably don't have affluent ancestors and wish to avail themselves of the two new collections that come out in the spring and fall. The only other reason to buy new Pratesi linens (since they don't wear out) is for redecorating needs. The Pratesi staff is unexcelled in coordinating linens to décor or creating a custom look. Nearly all of the linens are of natural fiber cloth (the upstairs maid can always do the ironing!), although there are some easy-care versions of late. The three-story store boasts a winter garden, which sets the mood for the luxurious linens. Towels are made in Italy exclusively for Pratesi and are of a quality and thickness that has to be felt to be believed. Bath robes are magnificent—in natural fibers, plush, and quietly understated. So are the price tags. The baby boutique has been expanded, and a new Pratesi men's collection is outstanding.

SOHO MILL OUTLET
490 Broadway (bet Spring and Broome St)   226-8040
Mon-Thurs: 11-6; Fri: 11-7; Sat: 11-6; Sun: 11-5

This is hardly an area where you would expect to find a linen factory outlet store. But indeed here are Cannon, Fieldcrest, and other quality comforters, sheets, blankets, towels, pillows, mattress pads, tablecloths, and dust ruffles at good prices. Both first-quality merchandise and seconds are carried, and the savings are substantial. While browsing, you can also pick up some good hosiery bargains.

TIGER'S EYE
157 W 72nd St (bet Broadway and Columbus Ave)
496-8488
Mon-Wed, Fri: 10-7; Sat: 10-6; Thurs: 10-8; Sun: 12-6

Tiger's Eye offers the Upper West Side one of the largest selections of bath towels, shower curtains, bathroom rugs and accessories, shower heads, robes, toilet seats, sheets, and bedding in the city. This is truly a bedroom and bathroom specialty store. Pillows, rugs, and window treatments can be custom-ordered to match other accessories in your home. This is a "must visit" if you are planning to remodel or have just moved into new digs.

Electronics, Appliances, FAX Machines

Don't say I didn't warn you! When visiting the numerous electronics, camera, and stationery supply stores along Fifth Avenue and in the 50s along Sixth Avenue, don't be misled by the discounts quoted off the marked retail figure. In many cases, those prices are grossly inflated. It is a very wise idea to shop around at reputable stores before deciding on your purchase.

BERNIE'S DISCOUNT CENTER
821 Sixth Ave (bet 28th and 29th St)
564-8582, 564-8758
Mon-Fri: 9-5:30; Sat: 11-3:30; closed in July, Aug

Bernie is nowhere to be seen, but the *discount* in the store's name is certainly apt. If you want to get first-class treatment, ask for George Vargas. Bernie's was the first appliance dealer in the country to discount the 1,000 RCA Selectavision video recorder *before* the machine officially came out and at a time when it was the most popular item in town. Bernie's stocks electrical appliances, TVs, videogames, phone machines, refrigerators, washers, dryers, radios, tape recorders, and air conditioners from the finest names in the business (e.g., Mitsubishi, Sony, Panasonic, and Norelco). The discount is better at some of the other stores mentioned here, but Bernie's is more conveniently located. Bernie's also services wat it sells.

DEMBITZER BROS.
5 Essex St (at Canal St)   254-1310
Mon-Thurs: 10-5; Fri: 10-2; Sun: 10-5

Dembitzer was one of the first discount appliance stores on the Lower East Side, and it was so successful that it spawned many imitators. This is good for the consumer. With a host of imitators nearby, Dembitzer is constantly alert to keep the business it has garnered so far. They specialize in appliances that work in 220-volt, 50-cycle applications for overseas use. Dembitzer's motto is, "If it plugs in, we have it," but even that doesn't do justice to the stock. Left out of that description are pens, luggage, soda makers, cameras, film, *ad infinitum*. Dembitzer also breaks the Lower East Side rudeness code. Between them, the brothers speak 8 or 11 languages (depending on whom you ask). While they clearly don't have time to traffic with people who are "just looking" or comparing prices, they can be charming to real customers in any of those languages.

GREATER NEW YORK TRADING
81 Canal St (bet Eldridge and Allen St)
226-2808, 226-2809, 226-8850
Mon-Thurs: 10-6; Fri: 10-3; Sun: 9:30-6

Perhaps influenced by its proximity to the Jewelry Exchange on the Lower East Side, the Greater New York Trading Corporation dabbles in fine housewares while selling appliances. In addition to the toasters, VCRs, TVs, stereos, and refrigerators that almost everyone else carries, Greater New York stocks many types of china, silverware (even discontinued silver patterns), and gifts. All are sold at good discounts. Despite the location and the fact that it carries brands and products not readily available elsewhere, prices are said to be wholesale. Even more than the prices, I liked the personnel's boast, "Every one of our staff smiles and is helpful." It matters to them, and that certainly matters to me. In this messy store, one can unearth great buys on brand-name crystal, china, and flatware unavailable elsewhere on the Lower East Side. They even quote prices over the phone!

HARVEY ELECTRONICS
2 W 45th St (nr Fifth Ave)   575-0527
Mon-Fri: 9:30-6; Sat: 10-6

Not everyone understands all the fine points of the new technology flooding the markets these days. For those who need advice and individual attention, Harvey's is the place to shop for state-of-the-art consumer electronics. They offer top-of-the-line audio and video components and fully integrated audio and video systems. Harvey has developed an in-home design and installation division for both new and existing residences.

J&R MUSIC WORLD
15, 23, 27 Park Row (one block south of City Hall)
732-8600
Mon-Sat: 9-6:30; Sun: 10-5

These folks bill themselves as New York's most complete home entertainment department store, and I believe them. You can find cameras, radios, televisions, speaker systems, VCRs, cassette and CD players, personal electronics, records, tapes, compact discs, computer systems, telephone answering machines, telephones, typewriters, microwave ovens, and even bread makers. The place is well organized but gets rather hectic at times. The prices are very competitive, and they guarantee all merchandise.

PHONE BOUTIQUE
828 Lexington Ave (at 63rd St)   319-9650
Mon-Sat: 10-6:30

In my opinion, the breakup of Ma Bell was one of the saddest episodes in American corporate history. The confusion with the phone system since then has overwhelmed nearly everyone. Fortunately, there is a place in Manhattan where, under one roof, you can buy or rent new and antique-style phones, have them repaired, see all kinds of answering machines, FAX machines, and telephone-related accessories, and even have your phone painted.

SHARPER IMAGE
4 W 57th St (at Fifth Ave)   265-2550

900 Madison Ave   794-4974

Mon-Wed, Fri: 10-7; Thurs: 10-8; Sat: 10-6; Sun: 12-5

If you are a gadget freak like me, you'll go wild at the Sharper Image. This is truly a grown-up's toy store! The very latest in electronic gadgets, household helpers, sports items, games, and novelties makes browsing in this fascinating emporium a unique experience. Vinnie Trinkwald, the able manager at 57th Street, and his well-trained crew seem to delight in demonstrating things you'll think you just can't live without. There's also a branch on Pier 17 at the South Street Seaport.

SPECTRA RESEARCH GROUP
762 Madison Ave (bet 65th and 66th St)   744-2255
Mon-Sat: 9-6

Spectra offers electronic solutions to contemporary problems. If that problem includes being overheard on the telephone, not being able to find and work a pocket-sized computer, or having difficulty spelling *deceive* (is it *ei* or *ie*?), then Spectra can be of great help. While the unreliable Fifth Avenue electronics stores major in customer deception and price ripoff, these people have a one-price policy and offer only state-of-the-art items.

VICMARR STEREO AND TV
88 Delancey St   505-0380
Sun-Fri: 9-6

In the middle of famed Delancey Street on the Lower East Side, Mal Cohen presides over a treasure house of electronics, including microwave ovens, stereo and hi-fi equipment, telephones, and camcorders, as well as such items as organs, sunglasses, fans, and answering machines. Unlike many electronics outfits, this place has all items on display, well organized and marked, with none of the high-pressure selling you often encounter. Best of all, the prices are right, and you can be assured of not getting secondhand merchandise. Vicmarr is one of the largest JVC outlets in the area. You can save yourself some time by calling for prices.

WAVES
32 E 13th St (bet University Pl and Fifth Ave)
989-9284, FAX 201/861-9659
Tues-Fri: 12-6; Sat: 12-5

The past lives on at Waves, and Bruce and Charlotte Mager try to make it last forever with their collection of vintage record players, radios, receivers, and televisions. They have scorned the electronic age in favor of the age of radio; their shop is a virtual shrine to the 1930s and before. Here you'll find the earliest radios (still operative) and their artifacts. There are even radio promotion pieces, such as a radio-shaped cigarette lighter and recording discs (as in crank-handled phonographs, not video recorders). Gramophones and anything dealing with the radio age are available, and Waves is capable of repairing privately owned instruments. Waves also rents phonographs, telephones, neon clocks, and photographica [*sic*] for media shoots. They also make appraisals and will help with any questions on repair, sale, or rental.

Fabrics, Trimmings

A.A. FEATHER COMPANY (GETTINGER FEATHER CORPORATION)
16 W 36th St (bet Fifth and Sixth Ave, 8th floor)
695-9470
Mon-Thurs: 9-5; Fri: 9-3

Suppose you've made a quilt and want to stuff it with feathers? What if your latest outfit just has to have an ostrich plume, feather fan, or feather boa? Well, in New York, you're in luck with A.A. Feather, a.k.a. Gettinger Feather Corporation. The Gettingers have been in the business since 1915 and have passed the trade down from grandfather to father to Dan Gettinger, who is the first Gettinger grandson. There aren't many such family businesses around now, and there are even fewer sources for really fine quality feathers. This is a find!

A. FEIBUSCH—ZIPPERS & THREADS
33 Allen St   226-3964
Mon-Fri: 9-5; Sun: 9-4; closed Sun in summer

Would you believe a large store dedicated entirely to zippers? Well, in New York, nothing is impossible. One of the many amusing aspects of my visit here was hearing the boast, "We have one of the biggest selections of zippers in the USA." *One* of the biggest selections? It's as if they really think there are zipper stores throughout the country! Anyway, Feibusch has zippers in every size, style, and color, and if it's not in stock, they will make it to order. There isn't much demand for that service, however, since there are 200 colors in stock, in an almost infinite selection of sizes and styles. Should you need the matching thread to sew in a zipper, Feibusch carries that as well. A selection of threads rivaling the number of zippers is available in all varieties. Eddie Feibusch assured me that no purchase is too small or too large. When I saw one woman purchase tiny zippers for doll clothes, I wasn't sure if he meant physical or financial size! In both senses, he was right. And he gives each customer prompt, personal service.

ART MAX FABRICS
250 W 40th St   398-0755, 398-0754, 398-0756
Mon-Fri: 8:30-6; Sat: 9-5

The fabric wholesale district is conveniently adjacent to the garment district, and the usual retail-shopper traditions of that area apply here. Some stores welcome the retail customer, some don't, and some fluctuate with the market. Art Max is dedicated to the retail customer. Its three floors are filled to overflowing with outstanding fabrics for clothing. They now carry full lines of fabric for everyday wear: linens, wools, cotton prints, and solids and silks. The really striking brocades, metallics, and laces require an experienced touch. It would be a shame for a novice to ruin such beautiful fabrics. The real specialty here, however, is bridal fabrics. When the fabrics mentioned above are made into gowns, the wedding party could rival a *Vogue* layout. There are even a dozen different types of nets for bridal veils and infinite combinations of heavier materials. Try to look at the fabrics in the basement, not so much for the fabrics as for the basement. It looks like the catacombs!

BECKENSTEIN MEN'S FABRICS
121 Orchard St   677-6663

BECKENSTEIN LADIES' FABRICS
125 Orchard St   475-4305

BECKENSTEIN HOME FABRICS
130 Orchard St   475-4887

Sun-Fri: 9-5:30

And now it is three! Samuel Beckenstein began business as a pushcart peddler in 1918; when he prospered, he opened a store selling wools for men's garments. This was the start of an empire that is synonymous with quality and selection in the fabric business. As is so often the case in a family business, the time comes when succeeding generations want to be on their own. The third generation of this famous name recently divided the operation into three separate and distinct stores, some still run by members of the family. In one of the three operations you will be able to find any kind of fabric you want at great prices. No one does it better than Beckenstein, with added features like a find selection of trimmings and accessories (ladies' store) and a home decorating department (home fabric store).

CINDERELLA FLOWER AND FEATHER COMPANY

60 W 38th St   840-0644
Mon-Fri: 8-5:15; Sat: 9-4:15

A few years back, in the midst of a particularly cold and dreary winter, Seventh Avenue fashions began to blossom with artificial flowers in every possible spot as the "in" look for spring. The department stores quickly got the message, and in just a few weeks, people were removing their fur-lined gloves to hand $10 over the counter for a single flower for their lapel. Many of these transactions were made along 34th Street or Fifth Avenue, and only a few wise New Yorkers walked an extra two blocks to the "trimmings district," where they could buy an identical flower for 35 cents. There were even buyers of the $10 variety who *knew* of the district and assumed that they couldn't get in. Cinderella Flower and Feather Company is for them. Jonathan Wolff, Cinderella's president, brags that they have the country's largest selection of feather trimmings, decorations, craft supplies, and conversation pieces, as well as silk and other artificial flowers. "And," he adds, "since we're the importer, our prices are unbeatable."

FABRIC WAREHOUSE

406 Broadway (bet Canal and Walker St)   431-9510
Mon-Wed, Fri: 9-6; Thurs: 9-7:30; Sat, Sun: 10-5

Fabric Warehouse has three very full floors of every imaginable kind of fabric and trimming. Since all of it is sold at discount prices, it's one of the best places to buy fabrics. Some of the attractions include an extensive wool collection and such dressy fabrics as chiffon, crepe, silks, and satin. There's enough to equip a wedding *and* all the guests. But most amazing are the bargain spots, where remnant and odd pieces go for so little it's laughable. Since the Fabric Warehouse isn't exactly in the heart of the city, they sell patterns, notions, and trimmings at the same low prices, with the same excellent selection, so that customers don't have to make several stops.

FAR EASTERN FABRICS

171 Madison Ave (at 33rd St)   683-2623
Mon-Fri: 9-5

Far Eastern Fabrics is a small company that imports and retails some of the world's lushest fabrics from some of the world's most exotic places. From India, there are cotton prints, madras cottons, brocades, and silks. There are even silk saris and stoles. From China, there are more brocades and silks, plus damasks and woven and Jacquard tussah silk. Indonesia is represented by batiks, weavings, and cotton sarongs. Japanese silk pongee is among the cheapest silks Far Eastern offers, while Thailand is represented with a selection of cotton prints and silk scarves and stoles. And to show that Far Eastern is really global in its intent to pick the finest and the best, there are striking wax and java print cottons from the Netherlands. Prices for these often unique fabrics are excellent, and discounts are offered for trade orders.

GAMPEL SUPPLY
39 W 37th St (bet Fifth and Sixth Ave)   398-9222
Mon-Fri: 8:30-4

This is the kind of business New York does best—esoteric. The sole stock in trade here is beads, and they know more about them than you will ever need to know. Just make a request, and you'll find that they have it—cheap. While single beads go for a dollar each at a department store one block away, Gampel sells them by bulk for a fraction of that price. Though they prefer to deal in bulk and at wholesale, individual customers are treated as courteously as institutions, and the wholesale prices remain the same for all. As for the stock, well, a visit to Gampel is an education. Pearlized beads alone come in over 20 different guises, and they are used for everything from bathroom curtains to earrings and flowers. Since many of its customers are craftspeople, Gampel diverges slightly from its specialty to sell a few craft supplies—for bead-related crafts only. They stock needles, cartwheels, cord (in enough colors to match each bead), threads, poly bags, glues, jewelry tools, and jewelry findings.

HANDLOOM BATIK
214 Mulberry St (at Spring St)   925-9542
Wed-Sat: 12-7; Sun: 1-6; Mon, Tues by appointment

Note the hours here since the limited time can be a problem for anyone who wants to see one of the best collections of batiks outside a crafts museum. Carol Berlin runs Handloom Batik with near reverence for her merchandise. All of the fabrics are handmade, and she is quick to show how each can be set off to its best advantage. Imported hand-woven and hand-batiked fabrics (primarily from India and Indonesia) are sold by the yard as fabric, or made up as clothing, napkins, tablecloths, or handiwork. Handloom Batik will also use its own fabrics for custom-made shirts and other garments. In addition, a gift selection features handicrafts of wood, stone, brass, and paper from the aforementioned countries. Pillows, bed covers, curtains, and napkins can be custom-made from the store's cotton ikat and cotton batik. Incidentally, Carol Berlin says her collection is the largest in the country.

HARRY ZARIN FABRIC WAREHOUSE
72 Allen St (at Grand St)   925-6112
Sun-Fri: 9-5:30

This is a square city block containing all kinds of decorative upholstery and drapery fabrics, as well as window treatments, vertical blinds, mini blinds, draperies, and cornices. As featured in the *New York Times,* Harry Zarin Fabric Warehouse is *the* source for fine upholstery and drapery fabrics, and prices are well discounted. A complementary supply business at 105 Eldridge Street features rods, trimmings, and other necessary accessories.

HYMAN HENDLER AND SONS
67 W 38th St (bet Fifth and Sixth Ave)   840-8393
Mon-Fri: 9-5:30

Although Hyman Hendler has passed away, the store that proudly bears his name is in the capable hands of his sons and niece. In the middle of what may be the trimmings center of the world, Hyman Hendler is one of the oldest businesses (established in 1900) and probably the crown head of the ribbon field. This organization manufactures, wholesales, imports, and acts as a jobber for every kind of ribbon imaginable. It's really hard to believe as many variations exist as are jammed into this store.

INTERCOASTAL TEXTILE CORPORATION
480 Broadway (at Broome St)   925-9235
Mon-Thurs: 9-6; Fri: 9-5; closed first two weeks in July;
    Sun: 10-4 (Oct to Dec)

Intercoastal is an eight-story shop that carries decorator fabrics at wholesale prices. You must buy ample amounts of a particular item and know what you want when you come. The employees are accustomed to dealing with large department stores and decorators. Bloomcraft, Scalamandre, and Schumacker are some of the name brands that can be found here.

LEATHER FACTS
262 W 38th St (bet Seventh and Eighth Ave)
382-2788
Mon-Fri: 9:30-6; Sat: 11:30-3:30 (closed Sat in summer)

Francois George dispenses all manner of leather, suede, and exotic skins. He concentrates upon custom-made, actual skin clothing.

PARON FABRICS
60 W 57th St (bet Fifth and Sixth Ave)   247-6541
Mon-Sat: 9-6; Sun: 11-3
    (closed Sun in Dec-Feb, July, Aug)

Amazingly, you can find an excellent selection of designer fabrics uptown at discount prices! Paron carries the vary latest, and many of their goods are available only in their store. At their outlets (Paron II, 56 W 57th St, second floor; Paron West, 239 W 39th St) you can find a large selection of quality goods priced at 50 percent off. This is a family operation, so personal attention is assured. Hard-to-find Vogue and Burda patterns are also available.

PIERRE DEUX—FRENCH COUNTRY
870 Madison Ave (at 71st St)   570-9343
Mon-Sat: 10-6

Pierre Deux, the French Country home furnishings company, specializes in authentic, hand crafted products from the provinces of France. Everything from eighteenth-century antique and reproduction furniture to fabrics, brightly colored pillows, faience, table linens, glassware, and bed linens can be found here. A personalized bridal registry and custom orders are also available.

SHERU ENTERPRISES
49 W 38th St (nr Fifth Ave)   730-0766
Mon-Fri: 9-6; Sat: 9:30-5

Sheru is almost impossible to describe. If you're into hobbies, crafts, or do-it-yourself decorating, Sheru has what you need. If you are an incurable bargain hunter, Sheru will satisfy your wildest dreams. And if you are none of these things, Sheru will guide, teach, and instruct you. Officially, Sheru is a wholesaler of beads and trimmings. Its stockpile includes bases for clips, shoe clips, ear posts, trimmings, artificial flowers, cords, ribbons, notions, buttons, and stringing supplies. You will need help from the friendly personnel, because these treasures are thrown about. Without a guide, many may well be overlooked. Antiquated and unwanted things are stored in the basement in probably the most haphazard order in the entire city. Amazingly, Mr. I. Sherwin seems to know what's down there.

SILK SURPLUS
235 E 58th St (bet Second and Third Ave)   753-6511

1147 Madison Ave (at 85th St)   794-9373

Mon-Sat: 10-5:30

Silk Surplus is the exclusive outlet for Scalamandre closeouts of fine fabrics, trimmings, and wallpaper, as well as its own line of imported and domestic fabrics and trimmings. At each store, Scalamandre is sold for a minimum of one-third less than retail prices, and there is a choice selection of other equally luxurious fabrics at similar savings. There are periodic sales, even on fabrics already discounted. Lest it appear that Silk Surplus is a run-of-the-mill fabric store, we hasten to add that everything is elegantly run. Each store has a personal manager, and each manager strives to maintain an establishment more like an exclusive boutique than a fabric store. It is felt that the fabrics merit this kind of attention, and they do. Silk Surplus has the qualities I most like to see in a shop: quality, service, *and* a good discount price.

TINSEL TRADING
47 W 38th St   730-1030
Mon-Fri: 10-5; Sat: call for hours

Time at Tinsel Trading stopped around 1933, and anyone who spends any time here could come to believe that (a) all the traffic outside is caused by Model T cars, and (b) a couple of hundred yards of various trims are absolutely mandatory. A comment from the personnel at Tinsel Trading: "We're the only firm in the United States specializing in antique gold and silver metallics, and we have everything from a gold thread to lamé fabric." Tinsel Trading offers an array of tinsel threads, braids, fringes, cords, tassels, gimps, medallions, edging, banding, gauze lamés, bullions, tinsel fabrics, ribbons, soutache, trims, and galloons. All of these trimmings are genuine antiques, but many customers buy them for the accents they lend to modern clothing. The collection of military gold braids, sword knots, and epaulets is unexcelled anywhere in the city.

Fans

MODERN SUPPLY COMPANY
19 Murray St (bet Broadway and Church St)
267-0100
Mon-Fri: 10-5; Sat: 12-5

The name was not an anachronism when Modern Supply conducted business for 42 years at a site now usurped by the World Trade Center. Today, however, it's hard to reconcile *modern* with a store that sells fans and only fans. But Leo Herschman is not about to change his habits of over 50 years, so he still maintains the business name and a firm conviction that fans are the best way to keep things cool and comfortable. From *un*-air-conditioned offices on the third floor, Herschman dispenses all kinds of fans. The floors are overcrowded with fans, and they hang from the ceiling in abundant formations that resemble a jungle out of *Casablanca*. Incidentally, did you know that Casablanca is a brand name of fan? Herschman says that if you want the movie version, don't order a Casablanca fan, because it is nothing like the one in the classic Bogart movie. Instead, ask for "the kind in the movie."

Fireplace Accessories

EDWIN JACKSON

307 E 60th St (Alessandro Building)   759-8210
Mon-Fri: 10-1, 2-5

New Yorkers have a thing for fireplaces, and Edwin Jackson caters to that infatuation. Just as New York fireplaces run the gamut from brownstone antique to ultramodern blackstone, Edwin Jackson's fireplaces and accessories range from antique pieces to a shiny, new set of tools that look like plexiglass and silver. (They're really chrome. Do you know what would happen to silver in front of a fireplace?) The expanded two-store shop also stocks salvaged marble and sandstone mantelpieces, antique andirons, and an incredible display of screens and tool kits. In the Victorian era, paper fans and screens were popular for blocking fireplaces when not in use. Jackson's collection of surviving pieces is great for modern decorating. Edwin Jackson will also custom-order mantels, mantelpieces, and accessories. This is primarily a fireplace *accessory* source, however; neither advice nor information is given on how to put a fireplace in working order. Edwin Jackson has been in business over 100 years, and he assumes every New Yorker who has a fireplace knows how to use it.

WILLIAM H. JACKSON

3 E 47th St (at Fifth Ave)   753-9400
Mon-Fri: 9-4:30

"WBFP" in the real-estate ads stands for "wood-burning fireplace," and they are the rage in New York. William H. Jackson is reaping the harvest of this resurgence in fireplace usage. In business since 1827, the company is familiar with all the various types of fireplaces in the city. In fact, many of the fireplaces were originally installed by the company. William H. Jackson has hundreds of mantels on display in its showroom. The variety ranges from antique and antique reproductions (in wood or marble combinations) to stark modern. There are also andirons, fire sets, screens, and excellent advice on enjoying your own fireplace. Jackson does some repair work (removing and installing mantels is a specialty), but it is better known for fireplace paraphernalia. A handy item: a "Damper is open"/"Damper is closed" reversible hanging sign.

Flags

ACE BANNER AND FLAG COMPANY

107 W 27th St   620-9111
Mon-Fri: 9-5

Rally round the flag, boys, and if you need a flag, Ace is the place to go. Established in 1916, Ace prides itself on having the flag of every country in the world readily available; other flags can be ordered. They range from lapel pins to George Washington Bridge banner size. (For those who don't know, the largest flag flown in the world is the Stars and Stripes, which hangs from the New Jersey side of the bridge every holiday.) For those who are not flag-waving types, Ace also sells custom banners, buttons, pins, patches, balloons, and pennants. If you're running for office (school or national), all of the campaign paraphernalia can be ordered with a promise of quick delivery. Carl Calo, Ace's owner, does not exist on flags and campaigns alone, however. A large part of his business consists of outfitting grand openings and personalizing equipment, such as boat flags. If your boat already has a flag and you're not planning to run for office (as a lot of my friends do), you can always try the T-shirts here. There's a full line, and all are custom-printed.

Floor Coverings

ABC CARPET COMPANY
881 Broadway (at 19th St)

ABC INTERNATIONAL DESIGN RUGS
888 Broadway (at 19th St)

473-3000
Mon, Thurs: 10-8; Tues, Wed, Fri: 10-7; Sat: 10-6;
Sun: 11-6

ABC has been in business for over 100 years, supplying carpet for such famous places as Madison Square Garden and William Paley's private suite. Starting as a pushcart business, it expanded into a wholesale source for decorators. Then it became a retail store. Now it's a major home-furnishings center. Along the way, it earned a reputation as the best carpet place in town when price is a consideration. ABC claims to have the largest readily available floor-covering inventory in the world. Oriental rugs are available, as well as a major antique furniture department and a bed-and-bath shop.

COUNTRY FLOORS
15 E 16th St   627-8300
Mon-Wed, Fri: 9-6; Thurs: 9-8; Sat: 9-5; closed Sat
in summer

Country Floors is one of New York's biggest success stories, probably because they are offering a magnificent product. Begun in 1964 in the tiny, cramped basement under the owner's photography studio, Country Floors has grown to include huge stores in New York, Philadelphia, Miami, Los Angeles, Sydney and Melbourne, Australia, as well as spacious New York headquarters and 35 affiliated representative stores nationwide. Customers from across the country have learned that Country Floors carries the finest in floor and wall tile. Their sources include a wide variety of styles and artisans from all over the world. All are unique, and a visit—or at least a look at their catalog—is really necessary to appreciate the fineness and intricacy of each design. Some of the more complex patterns are hard to imagine as a whole when one concentrates on individual tiles. The common denominator is that even the simplest solid-color tiles are beautiful.

DESIGNED WOOD FLOORING CENTER
281 Lafayette St (bet Prince and Houston St)
925-6633, FAX: 212/941-8005
Mon-Fri: 9-5; Sat by appointment

A couple of decades ago, the epitome of good decorating was wall-to-wall carpeting. Even 10 years ago, industrial carpeting covered floors, walls, and even seating in the most modern homes. But nowadays, bare floors are in, and people who can provide those floors and care for them are as successful as can be. So it's no wonder that Designed Wood Flooring Center is in demand. Conventional homes are installing, finishing, or refinishing wood floors, while DWF's neighbors in former lofts have to deal with industrial flooring totally unacceptable for residential use. With the latter customer, the store can lay subfloor preparations as well as some magnificent wooden floors. These people are experts, and the floors come in almost as many varieties and patterns as that old-time wall-to-wall carpeting. And don't worry about their expertise. Despite the fact that they will accept the smallest private job, they are the choice of several major museums and department stores, as well as major showrooms and building lobbies. From now on, I won't walk over a wood floor without noticing it.

ELIZABETH EAKINS
21 E 65th St   628-1950
Mon-Fri: 10-5:30

Collectors choose Elizabeth Eakins' shop as a first-class source for hand-woven rugs. Here they custom-design and make their hand-woven rugs in standard and hand-dyed colors. To complete the look, they offer coordinated upholstery fabric and throws. Custom-designed hand-hooked wool rugs are also available.

IDEAL TILE
405 E 51st St   759-2339, FAX: 212/826-0391

Broadway and 70th St   799-3600

Mon-Fri: 9-5:30; Sat: 10-5

Ideal Tile imports ceramics, porcelain, marble, granite, and terra cotta from Italy, Spain, Portugal, and Brazil. They have absolutely magnificent hand-painted Italian ceramic pottery as well! This outfit guarantees installation of any of their tiles by skilled craftsmen. They also offer marble and granite fabrication for fireplaces, countertops, saddles, window sills, and tables.

LE MONDE DES KILIMS
470A Broome St (entrance on Greene St)   431-9064
Tues-Sun: 11-7

Kilims are flat-woven Oriental rugs that come mainly from Turkey, Caucasus, Russia, Iran, and Afghanistan. Le Monde, the only store in New York dealing in kilims, is a part of a Belgian company that has its own studio and workshops in Brussels and Istanbul. Because they import directly, they have beautiful merchandise available at reasonable prices. The selection is fantastic, with over 600 antique and decorative kilims on display in their gallery.

MOMENI INTERNATIONAL
36 E 31st St (2nd floor)   532-9577
Mon-Fri: 9-5

The people here will tell you that they are wholesale only, and they will do everything short of saying "don't come," but try it anyway. Those who do will be rewarded by what may be the single best source for Oriental rugs in the city, because Momeni is a direct importer. Since they don't suffer individual retail customers officially, their prices reflect wholesale rather than retail business. That doesn't make them cheap (good Oriental rugs never are), but it does assure the very best quality and the best price. So, don't let the wholesale-only policy scare you. They're really pussycats. (But don't tell them I said so!)

PASARGAD CARPETS
95 Madison Ave (bet 28th and 29th St)   684-4477
Mon-Sat: 9-6; Sun: 11-5

Pasargad is a fifth-generation family business, established in 1904. They know what they are talking about when it comes to antique, semi-antique, and new Persian and Oriental rugs. They have one of the largest collections in the country, and they provide decorating advice, repair and cleaning, and a pickup and delivery service. Pasargad will also buy quality antique rugs.

PILLOWRY
19 E 69th St (at Madison Ave, 3rd floor)
628-3844
Mon-Fri: 11:30-5:30; Sat: by chance or appointment;
   closed Aug

Sandwiched between two generations of New York guidebook writers (her mother wrote one for the 1964 World's Fair, and her son, Peter, wrote *A Kid's New York*), Marjorie Lawrence specializes in Oriental rugs and kilims at her latest shop. How she came to sell kilims while her relatives sold books is another story, but Lawrence has been doing so since 1971, and she is the best in the business. The name of the shop comes from the pillows that are made of tapestries, old rugs, and old textiles on the premises. Customers can select fabric from the kilims, knotted rugs, and Oriental carpets lying around the shop, or they can have them made to order. Her fabrics are old, authentic, and come from all parts of the world, and the Pillowry does expert rug restoration, as well as pillow creations from old textiles, needlepoints, and rugs. You might say Lawrence has the subject covered. Thank goodness she didn't join the family in the guidebook business. She'd be tough competition!

RUG WAREHOUSE
220 W 80th St (nr Broadway)   787-6665
Mon-Sat: 10-6; Thurs: 10-8; Sun: 11-5

One of the largest collections of antique and semi-antique Oriental rugs in the city is available at the Rug Warehouse. The current owners come from a family tradition of five decades in the rug business. A huge inventory of over 5,000 antique and contemporary rugs includes creations from 13 countries. Recent modernization has provided an attractive setting for the rugs that are offered (in many cases at good discount prices). The word *warehouse* is, in fact, hardly applicable to the new digs!

SAFAVIEH CARPETS
153 Madison Ave (at 32nd St)   683-8399
Mon-Fri: 9-6; Sat: 10-6; Sun: 12-5

Time was when it was possible to visit the teeming markets of Tehran and find some real bargains in rugs. No more. But one is still able to see a vast selection of these beautiful works of art, even if the setting is a little less glamorous. Safavieh has one of the finest collections of Iranian, Indian, Pakastani, and Chinese rugs in this country. They're displayed in a showroom spacious enough for you to see the prize pieces spread out so that you can visualize how they would look in your own home or place of business. These rugs are truly heirlooms, and you will want to spend time with the folks here while they tell you of the differences in their exotic products. Prices, although certainly not inexpensive, are competitive for the superior quality represented. It doesn't hurt to do a little haggling, even if it isn't in that foreign bazaar.

Flowers, Plants, Planters

CLAYCRAFT
101 W 28th St   242-2903
Mon-Fri: 7-4:30; Sat: 10-5

Pottery World claims to have the largest selection of planters, fiberglass display pieces, garden ornaments, and pottery for plants in the city. With a location in the wholesale flower market, they operate on a wholesale-retail basis as well. (This is supposed to mean wholesale prices for retail customers.) Owner Robert Lapidus claims that his years in the business have made him an expert in supplying the best planter and vase for any plant. With such a selection and location, he really does have an excellent vantage point. If Pottery World does not have *the* piece you're looking for, Lapidus will search for and usually locate any type of planter. Any plant that needs a new home can find one here.

FARM AND GARDEN NURSERY
2 Sixth Ave (bet White and Walker St)   431-3577
Daily: 9-6; Jan, Feb: Tues-Sat: 10-5

Don't miss this—it's one of New York's most unusual enterprises. First, a little background. The towering buildings in this neighborhood are the two spires of the World Trade Center. However, a decade or so ago, the surrounding area was made up of 50-year-old buildings housing government offices, while the site of the future WTC housed tiny and dirty electronics, job-lot, and gardening shops. When construction began on the World Trade Center, all of the small businesses were dislocated. Some retired. Many vanished. A few historic buildings were relocated to the new Independence Plaza several blocks away, and an even smaller handful re-established their businesses in proximity to the old neighborhood. Those that relocated have done remarkably well. Of the garden centers, Farm and Garden Nursery was the only one to remain in the area. Thus, it is part of a long and honored tradition, and it has done its best to maintain it. Farm and Garden operates like a suburban nursery, dispensing grass seed, fruit trees, vegetables, and sprays, and yet its nursery is, in its own terms, an "outdoor lot," while its customers' lawns are usually six-foot terraces. Oblivious of this fact, the nursery blissfully sells all manner of garden plants, indoor tropical plants, and trees under the assumption that they will grow anywhere. Usually, they do. In addition, one holdover from the old days is the prices. They are cheaper than uptown.

FRANK LUISI'S IKEBANA ROSE
42 E 59th St (bet Madison and Park Ave)   888-1224
Mon-Sat: 10:30-6

Frank is the master of ikebana, which is the art of Japanese floral design; he and his wife do special things with silk and fresh flowers. He has taken ikebana one further step by creating floral sculptures, using wood and copper as well as flowers. They specialize in custom work and have done work for a number of famous businesses and individuals, such as David Rockefeller.

GRASS ROOTS GARDEN
131 Spring St (bet Wooster and Greene St)   226-2662
Tues-Sat: 9-6; Sun: 12-6

Larry Nathanson's grass-roots movement began years ago when he turned his hobby into a full-time vocation. The possessor of a genuine green thumb, Nathanson couldn't understand why city pavement had to be an inhibiting factor for would-be urban farmers. So, he blithely set up his Grass Roots Garden, paying no mind to the boutique atmosphere or cutesy merchandising that marked the shops of his peers. Every square inch in Nathanson's shop is crammed with a sprouting green plant. The cityscape is still irrelevant to him. The business is evenly divided between indoor and outdoor plants, and no one here blinks an eye at the sale of a six-foot orange tree or a quarter-inch tall cactus. Somewhere in this city, it will make someone happy. And if having to prune and water plants infringes on your happiness, Grass Roots can handle that, too. In addition to soil, plants, lighting units, insecticides, fertilizers, gardening tools and equipment, and a consulting business, Grass Roots makes house calls "all over town" and runs a plant maintenance service. They also have a large selection of terra cotta clay pots.

NEW YORK BOTANICAL GARDEN'S
SHOP IN THE GARDEN
IBM Plaza Garden
590 Madison Ave (bet 56th and 57th St)   980-8544
Mon-Sat: 10-6

Right in the center of the city you can find one of the most colorful and interesting garden shops around. In the plaza of the grandiose IBM castle, this small shop is overflowing with plants and flowers, seeds, garden books, tools, and all the other things that green thumbers (and the rest of us) need in dealing with nature! The Botanical Garden also operates a plant information service where folks can get telephone or walk-in advice five days a week for gardening, plant and other horticultural questions (212/220-8700). If you have the time, a visit to the Garden is well worth the trip. If you are driving from Manhattan, take the Triboro Bridge and Bruckner Expressway east to Bronx River Parkway north. Then take the exit marked "Botanical Garden" to Southern (Kazimiroff) Blvd. You can also go by train (Conrail's Harlem line) from Grand Central to the Botanical Garden Station.

PRESTON BAILEY
88 Lexington Ave (16C)   683-0036
By appointment

Bailey has established himself as one of the most sought-after freelance florists in the city. He is known for his creative talents and his abundant floral arrangements for such top clients as *Architectural Digest, House and Garden,* the *New York Times Magazine,* and Oscar de la Renta. Best be on an expense account when you call on this master. But you'll get top quality, and no green leaves for fillers!

PUBLIC FLOWER MARKET
479 Second Ave (at 27th St)   684-2850
Daily: 9-6

The Public Flower Market is not *the* flower market, but it is open to the public. It specializes in supplying flowers to retail florists, as well as creating lavish floral decorations for its own retail sale. Most of the latter are destined for weddings or funerals, which, while occupying opposite ends of the emotional spectrum, are pretty much the same thing to florists. Ordering in advance assures top quality, and Public Flowers guarantees wholesale prices to retail customers.

RENNY
159 E 64th St   288-7000
Mon-Sat: 9-6

Renny's headquarters is a brownstone with an enclosed courtyard, complete with an antique fountain filled with a spectacular array of orchids and other exotic plants. Although primarily a florist, Renny Reynolds really specializes in party pieces. Renny also runs a plant maintenance and landscaping service, and he carries materials for centerpieces, bouquets, sprigs, and plain flower decorations.

RIALTO FLORISTS
707 Lexington Ave (bet 57th and 58th St)
688-3234
Daily: 24 hours

A good place to know, Rialto is one of the few florists in New York that is always open and will make deliveries until midnight. Great for patching up late-night quarrels.

ROBERT LESTER ASSOCIATES
280 W 4th St   675-3029, 215/258-6075 (weekends)
Tues-Thurs: 8-9 a.m. by appointment only; closed Aug

Robert Lester sells bamboo plants from the greenhouse on the roof of his townhouse. He has at least 150 different plants available at any time. The catch is that you have to phone for an appointment (hours are limited) and see for yourself. Lester will overwhelm you with information about plants that range in size from 8 inches to 25 feet in height.

SIMPSON & COMPANY
1318 Second Ave (bet 69th and 70th St)   772-6670
Daily: 8-8

You only have to step into the fragrant and crowded Simpson store to realize that these folks have the quality and selection necessary for any floral need. The place is overflowing with unusual flowers, plants, and arrangements for use at home, at parties, or at weddings. Unlike many Upper East Side operations, this one has reasonable prices and sales help you can talk to without being hassled. It is easy to understand why they are so busy, but they still take a personal interest in even the smallest order. I would especially recommend Simpson if you have your mind set on some very uncommon flower or plant. They're also open every day until eight p.m., even on Sundays.

SURA KAYLA
484 Broome St   941-8757
Daily: 11-6

The minute you walk into this colorful establishment you will see things that would look just right in every room of your apartment or home. Dried and fresh flower arrangements are beautifully executed, and their topiary tree selection is as good as any in the city.

Furniture, Mattresses

AMERICANA WEST
120 Wooster St   966-WEST
Daily: 12-6

Paralleling the current interest in foods from the Southwest, Americana West shows New York's best selection of furniture and accessories from that part of the country. Color and style are the name of the game here; the merchandise will light up any dreary corner. Nearly everything is made in Santa Fe, New Mexico. There are tables, chairs, beds, cabinets—just about everything a cowboy or -girl likes to use when away from the saddle!

ARISE FUTON MATTRESS COMPANY

Numerous locations throughout city
Mon-Sat: 11-7; Sun: 1-5

Futons are thick sleeping mats popular in Japan. They look like upholstered cushions with cotton batting and unbleached muslin casings. Arise claims to have introduced them in 1970, and their success has been such that in a few years, no one will need a further introduction to them. There are four different styles currently available, ranging from the standard futon to the "Living Health Imperial" models. So, while the classic futon has all-cotton batting, Arise's other models incorporate cores of various fibers for greater resiliency. In addition, the adaptation to New York has been made with the introduction of folding futon beds and even convertible sofas. These don't pull out; they simply drape the furniture. Frames are also available. All products are American-made.

AU CHAT BOTTE DECORATION

903 Madison Ave (bet 72nd and 73rd St)
772-7402, FAX 772-3381
Mon-Sat: 10-6

Au Chat Botte is known for the finest imported clothing for babies and children. Now, the perfectly dressed child can hang his overalls or her dresses on the perfectly executed bedpost in a room that's color coordinated and designed by Au Chat Botte Decoration. This store is a source for bassinets, toy chests, tea tables, high chairs, and various other baby furnishings. Bibs, changing pads, bassinet linings, towels, linens, quilts, and even doll accessories can be ordered and color-coordinated. When Au Chat Botte is finished with a baby and its room, it is apparent that they have dealt with an heir apparent—and his or her parents.

BAR MART—B. KASNER & SON

123 Bowery (at Grand St)   226-7148
Mon-Fri: 8:30-5; Sat: 10-3:30

If you are looking for a home bar, tables and chairs, and bar or counter stools, no place has a better selection than Bar Mart. Custom-made bars for home or commercial use are a specialty. You can even pick up accessory items like ice buckets and glassware at sensible prices.

BUNBURY ANTIQUES

489 Broome St   925-3000, 800/622-7377
Fri-Sun: 11-5

In a 12,000-square-foot warehouse gallery, these folks show the largest selection of popularly priced European art deco furniture in the city. They specialize in armoires, dining room and bedroom sets, and cocktail bars from the 1925-1938 period. Bars were first used in homes then, and some of the models are outstanding conversation pieces. English and Scotch country pine furniture and Victorian and art nouveau pieces are also specialties. Refinishing and rental services are available.

CHARLES P. ROGERS BRASS BED COMPANY
899 First Ave (bet 50th and 51st St)   594-8777
Mon-Fri: 11-7; Sat: 10-6; Sun: 12-5

Anyone who has been in the bed business for a century and a half should know almost everything about good looks and comfort when it comes to the sleeping department. Rogers shows over 50 models in four-posters, contemporary, canopied, and hand-painted-finish styles. There are replicas of original designs, and all sizes are available in stock or on order. These folks sell factory direct, so prices are competitive.

DEUTSCH
31 E 32nd St   683-8746
Mon-Fri: 9-5; Sat: 10-4; closed Sat in summer

Wicker and rattan became popular in the mid-1970s, but Deutsch had been in the business for 20 years by that time. They originally sold mainly to interior designers, furniture stores, and large businesses, but now the public can benefit from this high-quality merchandise. All of it is imported, and there are no cheap weaves here. Roger Deutsch is rightfully proud of his position in the field, and you should seek him out for advice when you shop.

FOREMOST FURNITURE SHOWROOMS
8 W 30th St (at Fifth Ave, 10th floor)
242-3354, 889-6347
Mon-Wed, Fri, Sat: 9-4; Thurs: 9-7; Sun: 11-4

Decorators recommend Foremost to friends who want to avoid decorator commissions, because it's a good place to get quality furniture at a 20 to 50 percent discount. Foremost has four floors full of furniture, laid out by floor and room plans, and the personnel are friendly, knowledgeable, and helpful, making this an excellent source. Comparison and window shopping are particularly difficult here, and though the values are indeed very good, it isn't obvious unless you've shopped around. So, make this one of your last stops.

FRANK EASTERN COMPANY
599 Broadway (at Houston St)   219-0007
Mon-Fri: 9-5; Sat: 10-2; closed Sat in summer

First things first. No, I'm not related to this particular Frank, and I'm resisting the use of all the puns on the name that I've accumulated over the years! For business supplies and furniture, however, Frank Eastern Company should be a first choice. They are capable of completely furnishing a business office or corporate headquarters with tables, desks, chairs, files, bookcases, partitions, and a full line of computer work stations for home or office. Frank Eastern Company specializes in advanced ergonomic seating chairs that prevent backache and premature fatigue. The company president has personally conducted 20 years of extensive research in this field and has actually tested over 1,700 different chairs (from all over the world) in an ongoing attempt to find the ultimate chair for the person who works at a desk or a computer. And all of it is sold at a discount. Custom jobs are a specialty. Smart people, these Franks!

GRANGE
831 Madison Ave (at 69th St)   737-8080
Mon-Sat: 10-6 (Thurs: 10-7)

Superb French furniture and accessories dominate the two small selling floors of this very attractive Madison Avenue boutique. The goods are all French-inspired, and the furniture in particular is clean-lined, functional, and in great taste. What the Italians have contributed to the classy look in ready-to-wear, the French have achieved in home collections. However, this is not a place for bargain hunters.

JENSEN-LEWIS
89 Seventh Ave (at 15th St)   929-4880
Mon-Wed, Fri, Sat: 10-7; Thurs: 10-8; Sun: 12-5

Jensen-Lewis had its origins in the late nineteenth-century sail-making business of Charles Jensen and the canvas-awning business of Edward Lewis. In 1932, the two businesses united to become the premier canvas-awning dealer in the country. In 1964, the business expanded to include the making and retailing of canvas furniture. In very short order, the canvas furniture took off, and the business now concentrates on canvas products and accessory pieces. Nowadays at Jensen-Lewis, there are bunk beds and bedroom sets, wardrobes in two heights and four sizes, home and office furniture, dining-room tables, lamps, and kitchen accessories. There's loads more, too, and we haven't even touched on basic items such as canvas chairs, bags, pillows, and futons. Not all of this is in canvas, but it does all fit the "Jensen-Lewis look." You'll recognize it when you see it. It's relaxed, practical, and very comfortable.

KENTSHIRE GALLERIES
37 E 12th St (bet University Pl and Broadway)
673-6644
Mon-Fri: 9-5; Sat: 10-2 (Oct-Apr)

Kentshire presents eight floors of English furniture and accessories, circa 1690-1870, with particular emphasis on the Georgian and Regency periods. This gallery has an excellent international reputation, and the displays are a delight to see, even if the price tags are a bit high. There is also a collection of eighteenth- and nineteenth-century English jewelry.

KLEINSLEEP/CLEARANCE
176 Sixth Ave (bet Spring and Prince St)   226-0900
Mon-Sat: 10-7; Sun: 11-6

Kleinsleep is a chain of stores in the New York area specializing in bedding needs. At each store, the byword is *discount,* and at this downtown location, everything is reduced even further. This is the final resting place of Klein's floor samples, closeouts, weird no-sells, mismatches, and just plain mistakes. Since almost all of these pieces are going to be covered with linens, almost none of the mistakes matter in the least, and a trip down here is a must for anyone in need of a bed. They boast that all sizes and types of sleeping furniture are available, including brass headboards. In particular, they claim to have New York City's largest showing of inner-spring and platform box springs. At the very least, this is a company that is experienced and knows what it's doing. The customer gets advice, expertise, and exceptional bargains. Shipping is additional, but considering the neighborhood, it is usually well worth it. It is against the New York City health code to sell a used bed. Therefore, the leftovers sold here are just that; they're not used.

NORTH CAROLINA FURNITURE SHOWROOM
12 W 21st St (at Fifth Ave, 2nd floor)   260-5850
Mon-Wed, Fri, Sat: 10-6; Thurs: 10-8; Sun: 12-5

Finding quality furniture at a decent price is not too easy these days. North Carolina Furniture Showroom is a unique establishment. Previously known as Apartment Living, they specialize in furnishings for apartments. It is the kind of merchandise New Yorkers need and love: lots of drawers, shelves, and storage space in functional form for those who have to live in somewhat cramped space where there are never enough closets. Now new lines have been added. They offer over 400 famous name brands in furniture and bedding, all at very substantial discounts. They will order items not shown on the sales floor. It pays to take a look at their living rooms, bedrooms, dining rooms, dinettes, den furniture, wall units, sofa beds, and recliners before making a final selection.

OAK-SMITH & JONES
1321 Second Ave (bet 69th and 70th St)   535-1451
Daily: 10-8

Stuart Sackin runs a shop dedicated to fine, old-fashioned furniture. Besides an outstanding collection of antique pine items, brass and iron beds, and leaded-glass lamps, Sackin has added a major upholstery line and unique iron, stone, and mahogany merchandise. He also offers a decorating service.

OOPS (ORIGINALS ON PERMANENT SALE)
528 LaGuardia Pl (bet Bleecker and 3rd St)   982-0586
Mon, Tues, Wed, Fri, Sat: 11-7; Thurs: 11-9;
    Sun: 12-6 (May-Sept)

OOPS is no accident for the clever furniture shopper. It deals with a class of furniture normally available only to designers and architects but sold to the public due to some mishap that occurred on its way to wholesalers. It may be damaged, but it is just as likely to be a cancellation, overstock, discontinued stock, or a showroom sample. So the chances of getting a bedroom suite or living-room conversation pit with matching end tables are small, but OOPS is a top-notch source for distinctive individual pieces and vastly reduced prices. Since they deal in designer pieces (they claim the majority of their furniture can be seen in the Museum of Modern Art's permanent collection), it is possible to collect specific names or styles, if not specific suites. The stock is not limited to current manufacturers; in fact, a store specialty is finding originals or creating approved reproductions of recent trends, such as Eero Saarinen's art deco. They are also quite frank about an item's origin and how it wound up at OOPS.

OSBORNE & OSBORNE
508 Canal St   431-7075
Daily: by appointment

Since 1975 Kipp and Margot Osborne have been building custom-made hardwood furniture for private and corporate clients. Each of their pieces is signed, dated and numbered, marking both the continuing evolution of their work and the unique nature of each piece. They are shown in a 1827 landmark row house in Tri-BeCa. Traditional, time-proven cabinetmaking techniques and joinery provide the quality basis for Osborne furniture. Using these methods in conjunction with a careful process of wood selection and a sensibility that book-matches and balances wood grain, the Osbornes have created a body of work that to date numbers more than 1,200 pieces.

T&K FRENCH ANTIQUES
120 Wooster St   219-2472
Mon-Fri: 11-6; Sat: 12-6

If you have the craving to accent your home with interesting French antiques, then T & K should be one of your first stops. They import directly from France and display an unusually interesting collection of antiques, including turn-of-the-century coffee dispensers, oak ice-cream boxes, chicken coops, baskets, doctor's cabinets, and a fine collection of iron items. For unusual chairs and bird cages, look no further. I even saw a magnificent antique walnut doctor's table.

WICKERY
342 Third Ave (at 25th St)   889-3669
Mon-Fri: 10:30-6:30; Sat: 10:30-6

The Wickery handles wicker, rattan furniture, and accessories in tortoise shell, rolled bamboo, burned bamboo, and rattan core. Items range from basket to hamper size, and discounted prices range from pennies to hundreds of dollars.

WIM AND KAREN'S SCANDINAVIAN FURNITURE
319 E 53rd St   758-4207
Mon-Wed, Fri: 10-6; Thurs: 10-7:30; Sat: 10-5

Wim Sanson's collection of Scandinavian furniture is light, airy, and functional. Unlike most Scandinavian and modern imports, they look and feel solid, which make them a good investment. Wim and Karen import oak, cherry, ash, teak, and rosewood furniture for every room in the house. All of it is made in factories abroad. If you think that all Scandinavian furniture is blond Danish modern, Wim and Karen deserve your visit. Most noteworthy is the encouragement they have given native Scandinavian designers. Many of the styles sold here are unique and suited for life on both sides of the Atlantic. It is possible that the mobile New York lifestyle finds its most sympathetic counterpart in Scandinavia. The convenient wall units in particular seem to bear this out, but there are also bedroom suites and super leather furniture for living-room seating.

Games—Adult

COMPLEAT STRATEGIST
11 E 33rd St (at Fifth Ave)   685-3880
Mon-Wed, Fri, Sat: 10:30-6; Thurs: 10:30-9

320 W 57th St (bet Eighth and Ninth Ave)
582-1272
Mon-Sat: 11-8; Sun: 12-5

630 Fifth Ave (Rockefeller Center)   265-7449
Mon-Fri: 10:30-5:30

The Compleat Strategist was established as a fortress for military games and equipment. As the only such sanctuary in the city (possibly the country), it was an overwhelming success and was soon overrun with military strategists. As time went on, they branched out into science fiction, fantasy, murder mystery games, and adventure games and books. And when this, too, seemed to capture the imagination of the public, the Compleat Strategist opened two more outposts. So today people who are refighting the Civil War can browse alongside Dragon Masters at three locations in the city. The stock is more than ample for any military or Dungeons and Dragons addict, and the personnel are knowledgeable and friendly. For the less feisty, they have chess and backgammon sets, and even Monopoly. These are adult games with no sneering or innuendo—unless you're playing the villain.

DOUBLING CUBE
80 E 2nd St   420-8557
Mon-Fri: 11-6:30

Only in New York! This outfit is the only business in the country that supplies backgammon sets, monogrammed poker chips (ten kinds), chess equipment, and all kinds of gaming devices for home use. No need to go to Atlantic City; just head to the Doubling Cube and pick up your blackjack, craps, and roulette layouts; handmade chess, backgammon, and Chemin de Fer boards; wheels, dice, and other game parts. They will even tell you where you can play all these games right here in Manhattan.

GAME SHOW
474 Sixth Ave (bet 11th and 12th St)
633-6328, FAX: 212/633-6208
Mon-Sat: 12-7 (Thurs: 12-8); Sun: 12-5

If you can't find the kid's or adult's game you have heard about at the Game Show, it probably doesn't exist. This store is crammed with the best of the lot, and the folks here love to talk to customers about their stock. I wonder if they were able to finance their inventory with some winnings from Monopoly?

MARION & COMPANY
315 W 39th St (16th floor)   868-9155, 594-1848
Mon-Fri: 8-5:15

When you think of casino and game equipment, think Marion!
This outfit has been in business for nearly a century, and it is still
presided over by family member Ed Weinstein. Marion distributes
backgammon and domino items, KEM cards, and casino equipment for home or professional use. They also make personalized
poker chips and offer a wide range of gaming tables and roulette
wheels. It is both a wholesale and retail operation.

VILLAGE CHESS SHOP
230 Thompson St (bet Bleecker and 3rd St)   475-9580
Daily: noon-midnight

People who enjoy chess can play a game at the Village Chess
Shop for about $1.50 an hour. And those who are searching for
really unique chess pieces would be wise to patronize this shop.
Chess sets are available in pewter, brass, ebony, onyx, and more.
Many boards can be flipped over for backgammon, and, in fact,
Village Chess—its name notwithstanding—has outstanding sets for
that game as well. In short, the Village should be a first stop for
moving chess pieces, whether they are being moved from one
square to another or from their store to your home.

Gifts, Accessories

ADELE LEWIS
227 W 29th St   594-5075
Mon-Fri: 8-5

This operation may be called a pottery specialty shop. Everything
is neat, clean, and well organized, and each item appears to be
something special. In addition to baskets and pots, they have a fine
collection of one-of-a-kind decorative pieces for the home. Prices
are high, but the service and selection more than make up for it. You
can find one-of-a-kind wicker log holders, Mexican jugs in descend-
ing order, and decorative accessories. There are also display pieces
for stores; imported baskets from China, Spain, the Philippines, and
Indonesia; and stone and pottery pieces from Mexico. And this is
just a start. Partly because of its location and name, this is one of
the city's biggest secrets.

AMETHYST
32 E 7th St   979-9458
Tues-Fri, Sun: 12-7; Sat: 12-9

Be forewarned that East 7th Street is not a through street as you
would expect. Cooper Square is a good place from which to find this

hidden street. Guy de Ville and Mario Cavallini have assembled a marvelous collection of lavender and purple antique and designer jewelry pieces, collectibles, and kimonos. Only in the Big Apple could you find a store specializing in goods of just one color.

BERTABRASIL BUTIK
151 W 46th St (bet Sixth and Seventh Ave,
    7th floor)   354-9616
Mon-Fri: 9-5:30; Sat: 9-2

This is a loft discount boutique featuring a number of well-known names in watches, sunglasses, electronics, cosmetics, and some clothing items. Don't expect to find depth in any classifications, but you can find some good bargains if you don't mind disinterested salespeople and zero ambiance. The folks here have promised me (after seeing previous write-ups) that they are trying to improve their service! (Let me know.) This is a good place to get a birthday gift for Aunt Gertrude, who sends you three handkerchiefs each year for Christmas!

BRASS LOFT
499 Broadway (bet Broome and Spring St)   226-5467
Daily: 11-6:30

Michele Rosenthal and Ruth and Gayle Hoffman run the Brass Loft. After a visit here, any other metal pales in comparison, and that isn't just due to the brightness of polished brass. Nearly everything in the shop is made of brass or copper, and many of the configurations are most unusual, if not unique. Brass fireplace equipment, screens, sconces, candlesticks, hurricane lamps, chandeliers, and planters (large and small) are just a few of the Hoffmans' items. In addition, the Brass Loft will repair and polish almost any brass and copper item, and they even electrify vases for lamps. Completed, many of them are unusually striking. Bar rails, handrails, and carpet rods are custom-made for homes and restaurants. This factory outlet is the best source in the city for brass gifts at any price, and the 25 percent discount doesn't hurt.

CAROLE STUPELL
29 E 22nd St   260-3100
Mon-Sat: 10-6

Imagine the fun of being able to set a table with the most beautiful accessories available anywhere! The first place anyone able to do this should visit is Carole Stupell. In my opinion, this is the finest home-accessory store in the country. The taste and thought that has gone into the selection of the merchandise is simply unmatched. Keith Stupell, second generation chip-off-the-old-block, has assembled a fabulous array of china, glassware, silver, and gift treasures, and displays them in spectacular settings. In addition, the store offers a large range of special china and glassware replacement patterns which date back over 30 years. The prices are not in the bargain range, but the quality is unequalled. Film companies often use Stupell merchandise to decorate their productions.

CAT STORE
562 Amsterdam Ave (at 87th St)   595-8728
Mon-Sat: 11-6; Sun: 12-5 or by appointment

Meow. I have to admit I'm not a cat lover, but this place is a find for those who are. The largest selection of cat-related merchandise in the city is available here, including cat-motif jewelry, accessories, and houseware. They point out that the items relate to both domestic and wild cats; read that to mean there are some unusually "catty" things for sale in this emporium!

CERAMICA GIFT GALLERY
1009 Sixth Ave (bet 37th and 38th St)
354-9216, 800/666-9956, FAX: 201/568-1046
Mon-Fri: 9:30-6; Sun: 12-5

We've been looking a long time for a place that has good bridal-registry giftware at discount prices. It's one of the most frequent requests from readers. Well, finally, we've found just the place, and the convenient midtown location is an extra bonus. At Ceramica Gift Gallery, you'll find most, if not all, major brands of china, crystal, tableware, and collectibles, including Waterford, Royal Doulton, Gorham, Minton, Wedgwood, and Lenox. In addition, they ship anywhere in the cuontry and will accept mail and phone orders. Discounts can go as high as 50 percent, and they will quote prices over the phone.

CONTEMPORARY PORCELAIN
105 Sullivan St (bet Spring and Prince St)
219-2172
Tues-Sun: 12-7

This is the only gallery in Manhattan exclusively showing ceramics from the United States and Europe. The pieces focus on functional and decorative design, and the majority are one-of-a-kind. Tea sets, plates, mugs, vases, and bowls are among the many attractive treasures. Don't bring Junior along to play.

CRYPTOGRAPHICS
40 E 32nd St   685-3377
Mon-Fri: 8:30-5

Whether it's a bowling trophy or the Man of the Year award, Cryptographics can design a piece that will be exactly right. Their basic line is anything that has to do with awards, and that includes plaques, nameplates, badges, signs, executive gifts, trophies, premiums, laminations, and signs. Any of these can be personalized quickly on the premises, but given ample time, Cryptographics can design outstanding pieces. The personalized gift items make really unique presents.

CURACAO
20 W 57th St (4th floor)   581-6970
Mon-Sat: 9-5:45; Sun: 9-2

This is a special find only for those with non-U.S. passports. There is a great selection of pens, electronics, perfumes, gifts, and some clothing at considerable savings. For visitors from overseas, Curacao is a bonanza. For New York residents, go along with someone who has a foreign passport and share in the savings.

FLIGHTS OF FANCY
450 E 78th St (bet First and York Ave)   772-1302
Mon-Fri: 12-7 (Wed until 8)

Flights of Fancy's shop exudes charm, with its 1850 clapboard facade, soft music gently beckoning passers-by, and the Americana "treasures" Don Detrick has arranged in a Victorian parlor setting. Many of the gifts are handmade and exclusive to the shop, and the window display, which changes weekly, often showcases only one item in a line. That item is often so unusual and special that orders pour in from customers around the country. Prices range from $2 to $2,000, so there is something for every kind of gift giving. July is the month to save 15 percent on holiday items. Some suggestions? It's hard to be specific since the stock is always changing. But there is a handmade American theme that runs through the selection, and the best sellers include Pet Portrait Dolls, jewelry, and home-accessory designs. (The Pet Portrait Dolls incorporate a photo of any pet on a doll resembling it, which is then dressed in historical or literary costume.) There are other dolls, toys, soft sculptures, beautiful handcrafted eggs, and miniatures available on the premises or by customer order, plus the largest selection of one-of-a-kind gifts in the city.

JENNY B. GOODE
1194 Lexington Ave (bet 81st and 82nd St)
794-2492
Mon-Fri: 10-6:30; Sat: 10-6

Jenny B. Goode appears on everybody's list as *the* place for special household gifts. It is a super source for really unusual gift items; in fact, it's the type of place where you're tempted to buy something for yourself! Jenny keeps the store stocked with contemporary and antique jewelry and pottery, tapestry pillows, lace shams, majolica pottery, all kinds of scarves, silver and silver-plated items, plush toys for the kids, handmade tapestry-and-lace photo albums, and imported frames. There's something for everyone. Jenny B. Goode could charm Old Scrooge himself!

JOMPOLE COMPANY
330 Seventh Ave (at 29th St, 3rd floor)   594-0440
Mon-Wed, Fri: 10-5; Thurs: 10-7; Sat: 10-3;
    closed Sat in summer

When the local bank offers an electric blanket to anyone depositing $500, or the boss gives every employee a clock radio for Christmas, or the academy gives every graduate a silver pin, odds are that it was bought here. Jompole is a dynamite company. They offer great service at super prices, and Irving Jompole and Shirley Smith are two of the friendliest, funniest people around. They bill themselves as suppliers of business gifts, sales incentives, premiums, and awards, and they claim to have supplied everything from lollipops and imprinted toothpicks to diamonds, color televisions, and Cadillacs. Their stock in trade is crystal, sterling silver, china, and top-name watches. There is no name they don't carry or can't get, and it is sold at a substantial discount (30 to 50 percent). "Very nice," you say, "but I'm not a bank, employer, or school." No problem, Jompole provides service to individuals at the same discount price. Jompole warns that everything is not always in stock (this is mostly a brokerage operation), but anything can be ordered. Customers are invited to call or come in to peruse the catalogs and place orders. Shipping is reasonable (sometimes free), and the prices may be the lowest in town.

LEONARD'S OF NEW YORK
New York Hilton (downstairs)
1335 Sixth Ave (at 54th St)   582-4184
Daily: 7:30 a.m.-11:15 p.m.

It's not often that you find a really good specialty shop in a hotel, but the New York Hilton has an exception. Leonard's of New York is one of the most complete gift, novelty, and food shops in the midtown area. Quality items for special occasions, snacks for the hotel room, and unusual souvenirs of the Big Apple are attractively displayed *and* attractively priced. Unlike most hotel gift shops, this one does not inflate the price tag for the captive hotel customer.

L S COLLECTION
765 Madison Ave (at 66th St)   472-3355
Mon-Sat: 10-6

Even if you have no intention of buying a thing, you'll get a thrill out of seeing this superb collection. Seldom have I seen home and office accessory items done in such superb taste. Each piece is almost museum quality. You'll find dishes, vases, glassware, tea and coffee sets, nifty-gifties, desk pieces, and leather goods that would be just the thing for your "dream pad." Prices are not low, but for the quality represented, they are not out of line.

MABEL'S
849 Madison Ave (bet 70th and 71st St)   734-3263
Mon-Sat: 10-6

Mabel, owner Peaches Gilbert's black-and-white cat and business trademark, has gone to cat heaven, but her namesake store continues to delight hordes of Madison Avenue shoppers. The store is jam-packed with handmade accessories for decorating body and home, and virtually everything is made around an animal or fantasy theme. They have elegant to whimsical hand-painted furniture, hooked rugs, old-fashioned lamps, and chic wearables, and all are inspired by animals! Mabel must be looking down on this scene with "cataleptic" glee!

NATURE COMPANY
Seaport Marketplace
   8 Fulton St   422-8510
Mon-Sat: 10-7; Sun: 11-6 (Jan 2-March 31)
Mon-Sat: 10-9; Sun: 11-8 (rest of year)

One of the most fascinating of the newer trends in merchandising is the appeal to the naturalist, and no one does it better than the Nature Company. The store is a treasure chest for the browser or the buyer; you don't have to be a nature lover to appreciate the unusual selection. There are beautiful marble desktop boxes, attractive jewelry, nature posters, books for the outdoors lover, inflatable toys, telescopes and watches, bird feeders and birdbaths, and all sorts of items that a stargazer would find irresistible. My favorite is a set of sound recordings on tape or CD that reproduce the music of the environment. Imagine being lulled to sleep by the rippling charm of a mountain stream!

NEW GLASS GALLERY
345 W Broadway (bet Broome and Grand St)
431-0050
Tues-Fri: 12-7; Sat, Sun: 12-6

This gallery is a sight for the eyes! Beautiful contemporary hand-blown colored glass from small studios all over the world is on display and for sale. The crafts here are in tune with modern design, and this is one of the largest collections of glass works in the country.

ONLY HEARTS
386 Columbus Ave (at 79th St)   724-5608
Mon-Sat: 11-8; Sun: 12-7

This is one of the most fun shops in New York. Helena Stuart offers the romantic in the family a fascinating array of intimate apparel and lingerie, heart-shaped or printed jewelry, balloons, boudoir pillows, soaps, tissues, and even plungers decorated with heart-shaped tops.

QÜARK
537 Third Ave (at 36th St)   889-1808
Mon, Thurs: 10-9; Tues, Wed, Fri, Sat: 10-8;
    Sun: 12-6:30

There is just one word to describe this store: *fantasy*. Whether it is spy equipment, telescopes, remote-controlled boats and airplanes, or unusual electronics, you'll find it here. A great place to shop for the person who has everything.

SEASHELL BOUTIQUE
208A Columbus Ave (bet 69th and 70th St)
877-4354
Daily: 12-9

Seashell Boutique shares its very precious space with designer jewelry (semiprecious stones, porcelain, and sterling), small gifts, and other items in addition to shell objects. What they all have in common is their natural origins and their size.

TROPICA ISLAND TRADERS
170 Fifth Ave (at 22nd St)   627-0808
Mon-Fri: 8:30-7; Sat: 10-6; Sun: 12-5

All that is missing here are the hula dancers in their native outfits! If your travel wishes take in Hawaii, but the budget won't allow it, then head to the Flatiron district and feast your eyes and tummy on attractive and tasty island specialties. There are fun gifts, tropical clothing and accessories, handmade jewelry, carvings, baskets, and a delicious variety of Hawaiian food items, including those great Maui potato chips. There is always some flavorful coffee brewing, and you can get goodies to go along with your drink.

WOLFMAN-GOLD & GOOD COMPANY
116 Greene St (bet Prince and Spring St)   431-1888
Mon-Sat: 11-6; Sun: 12-5

This SoHo shop is described as a "marriage of contemporary and antique table settings," and that probably says it best. There are linens available by special order that would look classy in a Park Avenue penthouse, and a series of white-on-white tableware that would blend with the starkest loft in SoHo. Some of the tableware is imported from France, Italy, and England; some is domestic. But all of it is elegant. The store also stocks baskets, cutlery, glasses, linens, doilies, home accessories, furniture, and one of the best collections of cloth napkins in the city. The linens can be specially ordered, and Holophane light fixtures can be similarly ordered for the ultimate table setting. This is a first-choice source for an exquisite house gift.

Greeting Cards

GREETINGS
45 Christopher St (bet Sixth and Seventh Ave)
242-0424
Daily: 11-11

This store claims to have the largest collection of contemporary greeting cards and gifts in the country, and one would be hard-pressed to prove them wrong. The sheer number of cards is mind-boggling, and the types and titles cover topics Hallmark never thought of. "Congratulations on your divorce" is one wry example. Don't overlook the stationery department; it's really unique and well stocked with a collection of New York City memorabilia. It makes the "I Love New York" campaign look malnourished. For any type of stationery, Greetings deserves a hearty "hello."

UNTITLED
159 Prince St (at W Broadway)   982-2088
Mon-Sat: 10-9; Sun: 12-8

The Metropolitan Museum and the Louvre each have approximately 1,500 art cards. Untitled, whose reputation is not nearly as well known, has 4,000-plus cards in stock at any given moment. Those cards include modern-art post cards, greeting cards, and note cards, many of which are unused or old cards. The post cards are filed as either pre- or post-1945, and they're further ordered within those classifications by artist's name. There are also post cards of famous photos and depictions of every possible type of art known. Some of these items are good for gags, and some are suitable for framing.

Hearing Aids

EMPIRE STATE HEARING AID BUREAU
25 W 43rd St   921-1666
Mon-Wed, Fri: 9-5:30; Thurs: 9-6; Sat: 9-1;
    closed Sat in summer

If President Reagan left no other legacy, he did set a shining example of not being ashamed to wear a hearing aid. The new aids are so small that most people are not even aware of their use. Empire State has been in the business for over 30 years and carries the top names in the field: Seimens, Starkey, Bosch, and Danabox. They have mature and skilled personnel who will do the proper testing and fitting in a quiet, unhurried atmosphere.

Hobbies

AMERICA'S HOBBY CENTER
146 W 22nd St   675-8922, FAX: 212/633-2754
Mon-Wed, Fri: 8:45-5:30; Thurs: 8:45-6:30; Sat: 8:30-3:30

Hobbies and models are a serious business here, but there's a lighthearted touch to remind everyone that hobbies are *fun*. It is evident everywhere in the shop, but nowhere more so than when Marshall Winston introduces himself as the "known authority on vehicular hobbies." Winston's vehicular hobbies include model airplanes, boats, ships, trains, cars, radio-controlled materials, model books, helicopters, tools, and "everything for model builders." They also sell wholesale to dealers and by mail order to retail customers, as well as doing export business. In fact, they fill more orders by mail than at the store. Ask for the catalog for a good indication of what they have regarding your specific interests.

JAN'S HOBBY SHOP
1557 York Ave (bet 82nd and 83rd St)   861-5075
Mon-Sat: 10-7; Sun: 12-5 (closed Sun in July, Aug)

When Fred Hutchins was young (he's now in his 30s), he was obsessed with building models and dioramas, particularly on historical themes. Eventually, it became economically viable for his parents to buy his favorite source of supply. Now, he runs the shop. So, while the front of the store is still a run-of-the-mill hobby shop, the star of the show is clearly the grown-up Fred and his childhood hobby. You can bet that Fred will keep Jan's stocked with everything a serious model builder could possibly want. Jan's has a superb stock of plastic scale models, model war games, paints, books, brushes (and other paraphernalia), toys, trains, planes, ships, and tank models. But in the meantime, Fred has gone professional. He creates models and dioramas to order for television, advertising, and private customers. In addition to his craft skills, he is also noted for his accurate historical detail. And there is yet a third business: showcase building. Because any hobbyist likes to show his wares, Fred builds custom-made wood and plexiglass showcases for that purpose. Incredibly, he even offers two-day service. He also has remote-controlled cars, ships, and tanks. The shop has become a full-service center for electrically remote-controlled cars. Did I mention that Jan's is one of my favorite examples of New York retailing?

Housewares, Hardware

AMERICAN STEEL WINDOW SERVICE
108 W 17th St (bet Sixth and Seventh Ave)
242-8131
Mon-Fri: 7:30-4:30

Peter Weinberger has one of the most esoteric businesses in the city, a business that his family has been in for over 75 years. What he does (just down the block from Barney's men's store) is sell window hardware. If you need a lock, latch, handle, or bracket, American undoubtedly has it. The "store" itself is a tiny office, but the warehouse is right next door. It resembles nothing so much as someone's garage crammed full of window hardware. How he stays in business is beyond comprehension.

BARSON HARDWARE
35 W 44th St (bet Fifth and Sixth Ave)   944-8181
Mon-Fri: 8:30-6; Sat: 10-5

A hardware store in the middle of Manhattan that is well-organized and competitively priced? Impossible? No, sir. Founder Barney Rubin's daughter, Anita, and David Schneiderman operate a store that has everything from first-aid kits to drill bits, 29 sizes of scissors, hair curlers, and fire extinguishers. They specialize in travel needs, unique kitchen and houseware items, tools, and plumbing needs. The best part is that the personnel know their stock and can come up with the item to fix that "whatjamagig" in the bathroom. And if you have a language problem, the staff is fluent in six languages, including Hebrew, Yiddish, Chinese, and Russian.

BLACK AND DECKER
50 W 23rd St (bet Fifth and Sixth Ave)   929-6450
Mon-Fri: 8:30-5:30; Sat: 9-4

Black and Decker is a name well-known for power tools. At this location, the company sells, services, and reconditions Black and Decker tools and small appliances. If you already own such power tools, this is the place to bring them when they don't work, since the company knows its products better than anyone else. If you wish to purchase tools, this is also a good source. New tools are sold at a discount, while reconditioned items go for even better prices. And everything is sold with a two-year guarantee. This is a real find. Imagine buying a power saw on your trip to ultra-urban New York!

BRIDGE KITCHENWARE
214 E 52nd St   688-4220
Mon-Fri: 9-5:30; Sat: 10-4:30

Bridge Kitchenware is a unique-to-New York store that supplies almost every restaurant and institution within 500 miles. Bridge carries bar equipment, cutlery, pastry equipment, molds, glassware, copperware, cast-iron ware, woodenware, flatware, stoneware, and kitchen gadgets. All goods are professional quality and excellent for the home gourmet. Be sure to see the line of imported copperware from France, as well as the professional knives and baking pans. After trying them, people use no other. The peppermill collection, while not abundant in choice, has several top-quality items designed for function. Bridge takes its name from owner Fred Bridge, not from the nearby 59th Street Bridge. Ask for their new catalog.

BROADWAY PANHANDLER
520 Broadway (bet Spring and Broome St)
966-3434
Mon-Fri: 10:30-6; Sat: 11-5:30; closed Sat, Sun in summer

Over 8,000 different items of cutlery bakeware and cookware are available at this SoHo store. Broadway Panhandler made its reputation supplying restaurants and hotels, and it sells everything at low prices.

CK&L SURPLUS
307 Canal St (at Broadway)   966-1745
Mon-Fri: 9-6; Sun: 10-5:30

In New York, a shopping trip for hardware wouldn't mean a thing without a trip to Canal Street. And on Canal Street, CK&L is the oldest and best. Years ago, these very same Canal Street stores dealt in industrial and war surplus. With the passing demand for military supplies and an influx of electronics, the Canal Street surplus stores turned to areas best described as "hardware whatever." All of the stores do business the same way. Sawed-off cardboard boxes, containing an assortment of homogeneous but totally implausible merchandise, are "displayed" in front. The junk in the front is there to draw customers inside, where the *real* merchandise is sold. There are power tools, simple tools, plumbing and electrical goods, accessories, and supplies. Prices, even for the complete line of hardware, are much lower than retail ones uptown. When you see the place, you'll understand why the overhead is so low.

CLOSET KING
113 W 10th St (bet Sixth and Greenwich Ave)
741-0027
Mon-Sat: 10-6

Spend any time in New York, and you'll know that rarer than a parking space is a place to park yourself and your belongings. Living quarters in the city have always been notoriously tight, but with the current economy, people are staying put, and small apartments are being measured for every inch of usable space. Frequently, closets—if they exist at all—are the first things to go. They are reincarnated as nurseries, bars, bathrooms, eating areas, and even at-home offices. So, it was inevitable that there would be experts who would specialize in organizing closet space, and Don Constable and his Closet King staff do just that. The overall aim is to provide a maximum amount of storage space customized to the customer's needs. Since the store exists to sell components, they encourage "do-it-yourselfers." A customized system can be planned out and purchased here, then self-installed at a fraction of the cost a professional closet organizer would charge. Yes, such people exist. And they're not mothers!

CONRAN'S
2-8 Astor Pl (at Broadway)   505-1515
Mon-Sat: 10-9; Sun: 12-7

160 E 53rd St (at Third Ave, Citicorp Center)
371-2225, 800/431-2718
Mon-Sat: 10-9; Sun: 11-7

Terence Conran's enterprise is not new to the home-furnishings and housewares business. His Habitat stores exist across Europe, and the same operating style has been brought to the New York stores. The look is young. The furniture is sleek, modern, clean of encumbering frills and decorative accents, comparatively inexpensive, and, most important, portable. A good percentage of Conran's line can be carried out of the store at the time of purchase, and that is one of its canons. Some of the furniture items are blatant copies of more expensive lines. Conran's also has linens, lighting, bath accessories, and toys.

D. F. SANDERS

386 W Broadway (bet Spring and Broome St)
925-9040
Mon-Sat: 10:30-7; Sun: 12-6

952 Madison Ave (at 75th St)   879-6161
Mon-Sat: 10-6; Sun: 12-5

In addition to the usual (which in any other city would seem highly unusual) assortment of kitchenware, Sanders specializes in commercial and industrial products for home use. Sanders delights in offering the best industrial products for individuals. The formula has paid off; the store has expanded into several locations. Industrial shelving, butcher-block tables (meant for a butcher, not a suburban buffet), and shelving are solid, substantial pieces and worthy additions to any home. The store's emphasis is on the best the industrial world has to offer a homemaker, period. And many members of the comfortable yuppie generation love it.

GARRETT WADE

161 Sixth Ave (at Spring St)   807-1155
Mon-Fri: 9-5:30; Sat: 10-3

The Garrett Wade customer is a person who uses and appreciates fine woodworking tools, for the store prides itself on offering only the best-made tools from all over the world. The main business is the mail-order selling of the finest tools available. The catalog is all-encompassing. It lists every imaginable woodworking aid and makes a point of explaining each piece's function and advantage over its peers. It reads like a "how to" guide. While some of the pieces are incomprehensible to a layman, Garrett Wade never accepts that supposition. They assume that anyone could put together a rocker or, at the very least, appreciate the function of their lightweight spokeshave. And after a visit here, you may become a believer, too.

GEORGE TAYLOR SPECIALTIES CO.

187 Lafayette St (bet Broome and Grand St,
    4th floor)   226-5368, FAX: 212/274-9487
Mon-Thurs: 7:30-6; Fri: 7:30-4

Taylor stocks plumbing replacement parts to fit all faucets, and custom faucets can be fabricated for your special order. There are also reproduction faucets and custom designs of fittings for unique installations. Antique towel bars, bath accessories, and pedestal sinks are a specialty. The business was founded in 1869 and is a family-run operation. Ask for Chris, his daughter Valerie, and son John.

GRACIOUS HOME
1220 and 1217 Third Ave (bet 70th and 71st St)
517-6300
Mon-Sat: 9-7; Sun: 10:30-5:30

This is the local hardware store, New York style. It's run more like a personal boutique and offers both services and products geared for New York life. So they sell appliances, wall coverings, security systems, sinks, sporting goods, china, casual furniture, shelving, television sets, umbrellas, pots and pans, heaters, and moldings, along with a hundred other items. Their services include cooking demonstrations, rental of tools, a repair and service department, installations, and delivery worldwide. The latter is free in Manhattan. They will try to order any item for you.

LEESAM KITCHEN AND BATH CENTER
124 Seventh Ave (at 17th St)   243-6482
Daily: 9:30-6 (Thurs: 9:30-8); Sat: 12-5

For over a half century these folks have been fixing up kitchens and bathrooms. Whether it is medicine cabinets, kitchen cabinets, faucets, shower enclosures, or counters, you will see top brands from both domestic and foreign suppliers. No excuse now for that leaking shower door or the kitchen cabinet that has outgrown its capacity!

LUDLOW HARDWARE AND VARIETY
246 Broome St (at Ludlow St)   673-1642
Mon-Fri, Sun: 9:30-5; closed Fri in July, Aug

This is one of the last "mom and pop" hardware stores in the city, and the ambiance and prices reflect its advantages. Ludlow just about has the lowest price tags around on hardware, housewares, paint, and tools. They also make keys and can speak Russian, Polish, Yiddish, and even a good bit of English.

M. WOLCHONOK & SON
155 E 52nd St (bet Third and Lexington Ave)
755-2168, 755-0895
Mon-Fri: 8:45-5:45; Sat: 9-4:30; closed Sat in July, Aug

Wolchonok has been a family wholesale-retail business in the midtown area for over six decades. In those years, the neighborhood has influenced their business and vice versa. So while they might have been a general hardware store elsewhere, in Manhattan Wolchonok is a prime source for furniture hardware, particularly legs and replacement pieces. Their business card says, "legs, legs,

legs.'' (I wonder if they get calls from people expecting the Rock-ettes.) If a given limb, as the Victorians would call it, is not in stock, Wolchonok can make it to order. They do the same with towel bars, cafe curtain rods, brass switch plates, and decorator hardware. Speaking of the Victorians, the line of porcelain plumbing fixtures is authentically reproduced, while the other end of the bathroom spectrum features futuristic metal and Lucite fixtures. And while legs are the business specialty, they can stand on an equally extensive line of casters, sockets, and glides.

NEW CATHAY HARDWARE CORPORATION
49 Mott St (at Canal St)   962-6648
Daily: 10-8

In the heart of Chinatown, this gem of a shop has been dispensing Chinese cooking items, utensils, hardware, small appliances, and restaurant equipment since 1928. There's no more authentic place to get your wok, chopsticks, steamer, or egg-roll roller, and prices and quality are geared for the professional. This is also a great place to find an unusual housewarming or shower gift.

P.E. GUERIN
23 Jane St (bet Greenwich St and Eighth Ave)
243-5270
Daily: 9-4:30 by appointment only; closed first two
     weeks of July

Andrew F. Ward, P.E. Guerin's current president, is the fourth generation of the oldest decorative hardware firm in the country and the only foundry in the city. What's more, they've been on Jane Street for the more than 125 years of the firm's existence. In that time, though, the firm has grown into a worldwide operation. The main foundry is now in Valencia, Spain (although work is still done at the Village location), and there are branches and showrooms across the country and in Puerto Rico. The Jane Street location is still headquarters for manufacturing and importing decorative hardware and bath accessories. Much of it is done in brass or bronze, and Ward boasts that the foundry can make virtually anything in those materials, including copies and reproductions. The Gueridon table has garnered design and production awards and has a worldwide reputation. Their fixtures enjoy a similar reputation, yet no job is too small for this firm. It operates like the hometown industry it thinks it is. So they offer free estimates (for blueprints, etc.) and help with such hardware problems as locks that don't seem feasible. Their work is impressive.

PRO KITCHEN WARE
4 Bleecker St (bet Bowery and Elizabeth St)
529-7711
Mon-Fri: 10-5

If you are a serious cook, then this is the place to shop. That goes for both home and restaurant chefs! Under one roof, you will find commercial kitchen supplies like glassware, china, pots, pans, bakeware, and just about every imaginable houseware utensil or gadget. Ask for Eva Taub; she is second generation in the business.

SIMON'S HARDWARE
421 Third Ave (bet 29th and 30th St)   532-9220
Mon-Fri: 8-5:30; Sat: 10-4:30

This is really a hardware supermarket. Customers take numbers just as they would at a bakery counter. No one minds waiting, because Simon offers one of the city's finest selection of quality hardware items, including custom-made decorative fixtures. The personnel are extremely patient, even if you just need something to fix the handle on the chest of drawers grandmother left you.

VAN WYCK DRAPERY HARDWARE SUPPLY
39 Eldridge St (near Canal St)   925-1300
Mon-Thurs: 8-5; Fri: 8-4; Sun: 9-4;
    closed Sun in summer

New York has four pages of listings in the Yellow Pages devoted solely to *retail* hardware stores, so to be singled out, a particular store has to be special. Van Wyck merits this distinction by virtue of its specialty in drapery hardware. Harold Lamm stocks all manner of drapery hardware, as well as supplies, urethane foam, and drapery trimmings. This is a particular boon to do-it-yourself drapery makers, since they can buy the materials in the neighboring fabric shops, pick up the hardware here, and set it all up with one shopping trip. Should the draperies be ready-made (and these, too, can be purchased at a discount from stores close by on Grand Street), the same holds true. Even if your draperies were purchased elsewhere, the discount at Van Wyck makes a trip to the Lower East Side for hardware worthwhile.

W. G. LEMMON
755 Madison Ave (bet 65th and 66th St)   734-4400
Mon-Fri: 9-6; Sat: 9-5:30

W. G. Lemmon is a neighborhood housewares and hardware store that is totally aware of its location. Considering that the neighborhood is the Upper East Side in general and Madison Avenue in particular, it has to be just a bit special, and it is. While they stock run-of-the-mill hardware and housewares, W. G. Lemmon manages to make this home-supply store look like a veritable boutique and gift center.

WILLIAMS-SONOMA
20 E 60th St (bet Madison and Park Ave)
980-5155
Mon-Fri: 10-7; Sat: 10-6; Sun: 12-5

From humble beginnings in the wine country of Sonoma, California, this store has expanded over the nation and is now referred to as the "Tiffany of cookware stores." The serious lady or gentleman of the kitchen will find a vast display of quality cookware, bakeware, cutlery, kitchen linens, specialty foods, cookbooks, small electricals, kitchen furniture, glassware, and tableware. The store also offers a gift and bridal registry service, cooking demonstrations, free recipes, gift baskets, and assistance for corporations or individuals with their shopping needs. Ask for their very attractive catalog, whch includes a number of excellent recipes.

Icons

GALERIE MANIC
125 E 57th St   755-0640
Mon-Sat: 11-6

Authentic icons of good quality are becoming increasingly difficult to find, and those available have risen considerably in price. It used to be that a visitor to Beirut could obtain some fine Russian pieces, but no more. Manic, in the antiques center, has a fine selection of fifteenth-to-nineteenth-century icons from its sister store in Paris.

Imports

Afghan

NUSRATY AFGHAN IMPORTS
215 W 10th St (at Bleecker St)   691-1012
Daily: 1-9

Abdul Nusraty has transformed a corner of the Village into a corner of Afghanistan that is fascinating and free of politics. There are magnificently embroidered native dresses and shirts displayed alongside semiprecious stones mounted in jewelry or shown individually. Another part of the store features carpets and rugs, while yet another displays antique silver and jewelry. Nusraty has an unerring eye; all of this is of the very best quality, and often it is unique as well. The business also operates on both a wholesale and retail level. Nusraty is probably the best source for Afghan goods on this continent.

Arctic

ALASKA SHOP/
GALLERY OF ESKIMO ART
31 E 74th St (nr Madison Ave)   879-1782
Tues-Sat: 11-6

This store/gallery is New York's most complete source for Eskimo art. Rare antiquities and artifacts of centuries-old Arctic cultures are displayed next to sculptures of Indians of the Northwest. Periodic shows highlight different aspects of Northern culture. A number of contemporary Eskimo artists whose works have been shown here have gained international acclaim.

Chinese

CHINESE PORCELAIN COMPANY
822 Madison Ave (bet 68th and 69th St)   628-4101
Mon-Fri: 10-5:30; Sat: 11-4; closed Sat in summer

Khalil Rizk and his partners began this company in 1985 as a source for Chinese decorative arts, with a particular emphasis on porcelain and furniture. Soon they had outgrown their quarters. Having to climb half a flight of stairs sets the mood for one to become enthralled with the porcelain, period hardwood and lacquer furniture, cloisonné, woodcarvings, prints, and watercolors that make up the colorful stock. And that half-flight climb helps keep the overhead down!

WING-ON TRADING
145 Essex St   477-1450
Daily: 10-6

No need to go to Hong Kong to get your set of Chinese porcelain or earthenware. Wing-On, even though it is located on the disorganized Lower East Side, has a clean and complete stock of household goods, Chinese and Oriental groceries, vases and the like. One of their specialties is Chinese tea, and they have just about any kind at prices considerably lower than your local grocery store.

General

BACK FROM GUATEMALA
306 E 6th St   260-7010
Mon-Sat: 12-11; Sun: 2-10

CHRYSALIS
340 E 6th St (bet First and Second Ave)   533-8252
Tues-Sun: 2:30-10:30

Even if these weren't two of the most intriguing import stores, I'd patronize them just for their names. Joe Grunberg and Susan Kaufman are the owners and buyers, and their devotion to Guatemalan artifacts is obvious. Their merchandise includes ethnic clothing, wall hangings, and jewelry from Central and South America and from Asia as well. There are both exotic and classic styles of ethnic clothing. (Ms. Kaufman is a specialist in antique Tibetan jewelry.) Back from Guatemala also has the city's best collection of cloisonné earrings from mainland China. And there's more: preshrunk cotton clothing, masks, handmade sweaters, and artifacts from many different countries. Back From Guatemala has contacts with 35 countries and hundreds of world travelers, so it offers the best. Grunberg and Kaufman are among the most charming of New York's store owners. Their other store, Chrysalis, offers beautiful crystals, contemporary and ethnic jewelry, puppets, stationery, handmade chiffon scarves, body scents, and accessories.

JACQUES CARCANAGUES
114 Spring St (bet Greene and Mercer St)
925-8110, FAX 212/274-8780
Tues-Sun: 11:30-7

After a stint in the diplomatic service, Frenchman Jacques Carcanagues decided to assemble and sell the best of the world's artifacts that he had run across in his travels. So while the store has no particular ethnic or historical persuasion, it is, in his own words, "a complete ethnic department store, not a museum." Afghan textiles and Japanese tansus (dressers) are everywhere, as is more jewelry and lacquerware than can be counted. What it all has in common is that it is (despite protestations to the contrary) all of museum quality. It is also very appealing to SoHo shoppers, who may choose among Indian sculptures of many periods, or kilims and rugs from places like Turkey, Afghanistan, and Tibet. The overall effect is like nothing so much as an Eastern marketplace; all that is lacking are the water pipes and music.

KATINKA
303 E 9th St (at Second Ave)   677-7897
Daily: 2-6 (call as hours may vary)

This is an import paradise, with jewelry, natural-fiber clothing, shoes, scarves, belts, hats, musical instruments, incense, and various artifacts from India, Thailand, Pakistan, Afghanistan, and South America. The most popular items are colorful shoes from India and embroidered silk skirts that look like they just came out of the Taj Mahal. The place is small, but so are the prices. Jane Williams and Billy Lyles will make you feel like you have just embarked on a worldwide shopping expedition!

PUTUMAYO
857 Lexington Ave (bet 64th and 65th St)   734-3111
Mon-Sat: 11-7; Sun: 12-5

341 Columbus Ave (at 76th St)   595-3441
Mon-Sat: 11-7; Sun: 12-6

147 Spring St   966-4458
Mon-Sat: 11-7; Sun: 12-6

The merchandise is mostly designed by Putumayo and mostly imported from Bali, Java, India, Sri Lanka, Portugal, Guatemala, China, and Uruguay. The emphasis is on fashion from around the world, and there is an extensive collection of folk art. In the fall, Putumayo displays a variety of hand-knit virgin-wool sweaters and jackets made from primitive fabrics. For summer, there are cotton sun dresses, skirts, and loose-fitting pants—all of them cool, comfortable, and practical.

Himalayan

HIMALAYAN CRAFTS AND TOURS
1228 Lexington Ave (at 23rd St)   744-8892
Mon-Sat: 11-7

There's more to the Himalayas than Mt. Everest and the Abominable Snowman. Shozo and Yoko Miyahara preside over an emporium of imports from Nepal, Tibet, and northern India—in short, any country that even remotely can claim contact with the Himalayan Mountains. Despite the image of exotic tundra this description evokes, many of the items are easily adaptable for city life. The hand-detailed boots are desired as much for their warmth as for their show-stopping fashion quality. The Tibetan rugs are also conversation pieces. And, of course, the shop houses much more—batik paintings, art, statues, antiques, carpet bags from Afghanistan, African beads, and incredibly attractive sweaters.

True to its name, the shop also arranges tours of the Himalayas; there is probably no one more knowledgeable on the subject outside the mountains. But the real attractions here are the boots and sweaters. If you run into the Abominable Snowman on your trip, at least you'll be properly dressed.

Indian

HANDBLOCK
487 Columbus Ave (bet 83rd and 84th St)   799-4342
860 Lexington Ave (bet 64th and 65th St)   590-1816

Mon-Wed, Sat: 10-7; Thurs, Fri: 10-8; Sun: 11-7

Handblocking, an ancient art of India, gives this store both its name and wares. The four partners divide their time between overseeing production in India and merchandising at this store and other ones in Canada. There are linens, place mats, napkins, tablecloths, bedcovers, and dish towels, all created in India of cotton tinted in brilliant colors and handblocked in designs that range from traditional to contemporary. One can also find rugs, dishes, jewelry, and pottery. The merchandise is distinctive and fashionable.

HIND INDIA COTTAGE EMPORIUM
1150 Broadway (at 27th St)   685-6943, 685-2460
Mon-Fri: 9:30-6:30; Sat: 11-5

Hind India Cottage Emporium features clothing, jewelry, handicrafts, and gifts imported directly from India. Moti R. Chani has a sharp eye for the finest details, and the saris and other Indian clothing he sells reflect that. The clothing is prized by both Indian nationals and neighborhood residents for its sheer beauty. The garments, made completely of cotton and featuring many unique madras patterns, come in sizes small, medium, and large. Pay particular attention to the leather bags and jewelry.

Irish

THE GRAFTON SHOPPE
22 E 54th St (bet Madison and Fifth Ave)
826-6511, FAX: 212/644-0976
Mon-Sat: 11-9

A delightful touch of Ireland in the middle of all the hustle and bustle. You can stop in the afternoon for a cup of tea with Bernadette Ryan and her daughters, Mary Jo and Aileen. On the way out pick up some beautiful Irish imports, including sweaters, capes, blouses, hats, scarves, jewelry, and even Irish food, crystal, and china.

MATTIE HASKINS SHAMROCK IMPORTS
A&S Plaza, 901 Sixth Ave (at 32nd St, 6th floor)
564-7474
Mon, Thurs, Fri: 10-8:30; Tues, Wed, Sat: 10-6:45;
    Sun: 11-6

Several editions back, I commented about the housekeeping at the former home of this charming shop. To say the least, they were not happy. Now Cathy, Tom, and Kathleen have moved to sparkling new quarters, and their delightful bit of Old Ireland would pass any inspection. You can find anything and everything Irish, from tapes to candy, newspapers, tweed caps—and wonderful accents.

Italian

CAROSELLO MUSICALE COMPANY
119 Mulberry St (nr Canal St)   925-7253
Mon: 10 a.m.-11 p.m.; Tues: 10-10; Wed-Sun: 11-11

Every section of New York with a concentrated ethnic population has a group of stores that serve the specific needs of that nationality. Usually, the group will include a bakery and coffee shop, a bookstore, and an import shop featuring various items of the homeland. There is often one shop devoted to a distinctive characteristic of that nationality as well. What, therefore, could be more natural than a shop in Little Italy dedicated to recordings and music? Carosello is primarily a music shop specializing in Italian recordings and operas. But Carosello is also a bookstore, import store, and gift shop. So you can find perfumes, Italian newspapers, magazines, and gifts, as well as Caruso recordings. The atmosphere is informal—but proud—and frequently the customers can be heard humming an aria while checking record labels. Even if you don't buy anything here, check out the espresso and breads at any of the neighboring cafes.

Japanese

O-ZORA
238 E 6th St (at Second Ave)   228-1325
Mon-Sat: 11-7

O-Zora, which in Japanese means "limitless," features virtually anything Japanese, with an emphasis on tools. Japanese tools, which range from antique to power saws and drills, are prized for their design and quality, and they are often exclusive to this shop. Artisans seek out this place, and amateurs are carefully instructed in the use of the tools.

THINGS JAPANESE
1109 Lexington Ave (bet 77th and 78th St, 2nd floor)
249-3591
Tues-Sat: 11-5

Things Japanese believes that the things Japanese most in demand are prints. So while there are all sorts of Japanese artworks and crafts, the prints highlight the selection. They know the field well and believe that the market for prints, while almost exhausted on the high-priced, established end, is only just beginning for newer and unknown artists. The store will help would-be collectors establish a grouping or assist decorators in finding the right pieces to round out the décor. And to round out the print image, there are also original eighteenth- to twentieth-century Japanese woodblock prints. Okay, you say, that's *still* prints, so be assured that there are porcelains, baskets, chests, lacquers, and books as well. Prices range from ten to several thousand dollars, and everything is accompanied by a certificate of authenticity. Things Japanese claims that you need to appreciate both the subject matter and the artistry in the works it sells, and that's not a difficult task at all.

Korean

SEOUL HANDICRAFT TRADING
284 Fifth Ave (at 30th St)   564-5740
Mon-Sat: 9-6; closed first week in July

If you want to really dress up your bedroom or dining room, the Korean hand-embroidered bedding, linens, tablecloths, and comforters from this house are unique and beautiful. Besides, the price is right!

Middle Eastern

PERSIAN SHOP
534 Madison Ave (bet 54th and 55th St)   355-4643
Mon-Sat: 10-7

Persia, of course, no longer exists; today, that area is more or less Iran. But the Middle Eastern mystique is strong enough at this shop to encompass the ancient kingdom. Merchandise includes a representative sample of past and present Oriental jewelry in silver and gold available in a large selection of rings, earrings, bracelets, necklaces, belts, and heirloom pieces set with precious and semiprecious stones. The magnificent brocades—the kind that used to hang behind a sheik in his palace—are obtainable by the yard or are styled in neckties and cummerbund sets for men. The Persian Shop has caftans, Bedouin dresses, gifts, *objets d'art,* water pipes, and authentic Turkish coffee grinders. Men check out the sensational ties while women are awed by the colorful scarves.

Russian

VICTOR KAMKIN
149 Fifth Ave (at 21st St)   673-0776
Mon-Fri: 9:30-5:30; Sat: 10-5

With the lessening of tension between the superpowers, more interest is being shown in all things Russian. Fluency in the Russian language is increasingly prized in business and government, and Victor Kamkin can be of great help in this area. His store features books in Russian, translations from Russian, guidebooks, art albums and reproductions, textbooks, and dictionaries. There is also an excellent stock of Russian music items (records and CDs), souvenirs (like lacquer boxes and dolls), and videocassettes. An added feature is a subscription service for Soviet magazines and newspapers.

Ukrainian

SURMA "THE UKRAINIAN SHOP"
11 E 7th St (nr Third Ave)   477-0729
Mon-Sat: 11-6

Since 1918, Surma has conducted business as the "general store of the Slavic community in New York City." My only quarrel with the description is that it should be limited to the city, since it seems capable of serving the entire hemisphere. More than a store, Surma is a bastion of Ukrainianism, and once inside, it is difficult to believe you're in New York. Another quote sums it up: "Visit Surma and spend time in the Old Country." Fortunately, language is not much of a problem. The clothing here is ethnic opulence. There are dresses, vests, shirts, hand-tooled and soft-soled leather dancing shoes, hundreds of blouses, dresses, vests, and accessories. All are hand-embroidered with authentic detailing. For the home, there are accent pieces (including an entire section devoted to Ukrainian Easter-egg decorating), imported brocaded linens, and Surma's own Ukrainian-style honey (very different and very good). Above all, Surma is known for its records, stationery, and books; not surprisingly, the business is also known as the Surma Book and Music Company. Particularly note the collection of paintings and the stationery, which features modern-day depictions of ancient Ukrainian glass painting. Surma has even published *A Guide to the Ukraine,* a listing of Ukrainian-related spots in New York.

Jewelry

Pearls are very "in." Make sure you fully understand what you are buying. Practically all pearls on the market these days are cultured pearls, in which a mother-of-pearl bead is implanted in an oyster to start the pearl-coating process.

Akoya pearls: From Japan. The best ones are round, very white, with high luster and a slight rose tint.

South Sea pearls: Very large, from the South Pacific.

Black pearls: Grown in black-lipped oysters in Tahiti.

Baroque pearls: Less expensive, unusual shapes.

Mabé pearls: Grown as a blister on the inside of an oyster shell, these can be brittle and break easily. Prices have become inflated.

Dome pearl: Grown in Tennessee, these are more durable.

Freshwater pearls: Inexpensive and attractive, grown by a type of mollusk that produces many pearls simultaneously.

A correct description follows each misnomer. When it comes to buying any of the rocks listed below, be careful.

JAPANESE AMETHYST synthetic amethyst
ALASKAN BLACK DIAMOND hematite
HERKIMER DIAMOND colorless quartz
MATURA DIAMOND colorless zircon
MOGOK DIAMOND colorless topaz
RANGOON DIAMOND colorless zircon
CHATHAM EMERALD synthetic
GILSON EMERALD synthetic
ORIENTAL EMERALD green sapphire
GOLDSTONE glass with copper crystals
AUSTRALIAN JADE chrysoprase quartz
INDIAN JADE aventurine quartz
KOREAN JADE serpentine
MANCHURIAN JADE soapstone
MEXICAN JADE dyed-green calcite
SOOCHOW JADE serpentine, soapstone
GERMAN LAPIS dyed-blue jasper
SWISS LAPIS dyed-blue jasper
ATLAS PEARL imitation
RED SEA PEARL coral
ADELAIDE RUBY garnet
AUSTRALIAN RUBY garnet
BALAS RUBY spinel
BOHEMIAN RUBY garnet
BRAZILIAN RUBY tourmaline

CAPE RUBY garnet
LUX SAPPHIRE iolite
WATER SAPPHIRE iolite
MADEIRA TOPAZ quartz
PALMEIRA TOPAZ quartz
RIO TOPAZ quartz
SMOKY TOPAZ smoky quartz

BILL SCHIFRIN
National Jewelers Exchange
4 W 47th St (Booth 86)   221-1873, 944-1713
Mon-Fri: 10-5

From a booth in the National Jewelers Exchange—better known for its diamond engagement rings than its plain wedding bands—Bill Schifrin presides over a collection of 1,873 unusual wedding bands. Prices range from a few dollars to several thousand, depending upon the complexity of the work and the stones used. If you have the time, Bill Schifrin will tell you a story about each ring: where it came from, how he got it, or about someone who bought a similar one recently. He's been doing this for over 40 years, and after all this time, you'd think he'd be cynical. He's not; he's "just cautious," and his stories and prices draw customers from all over the world. The selection isn't bad, either.

FORTUNOFF
681 Fifth Ave (at 54th St)   758-6660
Mon-Wed, Fri, Sat: 10-6; Thurs: 10-8

This is one of the best stores in Manhattan devoted to quality merchandise. Prices on all items are very competitive, and the store has a reputation for meeting or beating any legitimately quoted price in town. Although there are extensive and well-stocked houseware and gift departments, it is in the jewelry area that the store really shines. There is a jeweler in residence at all times. Fortunoff shows one of the largest and finest collections of 14-, 18-, and 24-karat gold jewelry in the city, as well as a fine selection of precious and semiprecious stones and name-brand watches from the top watchmakers around the world.

GALERIA CANO
Trump Tower
725 Fifth Ave (at 57th St, Level C-4)   751-0946
Mon-Sat: 10-6

Galeria Cano is a third-generation jewelry and accessory business with items made from 24K gold-plated brass. If you want to attract some attention at the next big party, put on one of their dramatic, handcrafted reproductions of original pre-Columbian artifacts from the family collection. If you mention this book, they will smile upon you with some special prices for 18K jewelry!

JAN SKALA
1 W 47th St   246-2814
Mon-Sat: 9:30-5

Jan Skala is located in the diamond district, that mysterious one-block area of Manhattan that purportedly handles every diamond imported into this country. The retail customer's place here is nebulous at best. Jan Skala, a reliable, non-"tourist trap" diamond dealer, is not averse to retail customers. Jan Skala is ostensibly wholesale only, but its ground-floor storefront is the first spot off Fifth Avenue to welcome retail customers. In addition to diamonds, there is a large selection of pocket watches, antique watches, and jewelry. The latter includes a good selection of Russian enamels, Fabergé eggs, and the like. Quite a sight to see, even if you don't buy.

MAX NASS
118 E 28th St (bet Park Ave S and Lexington Ave)
679-8154
Mon-Fri: 9:30-6; Sat: 9:30-4

The Shah family members are jewelry artisans; Arati is the designer, and Parimal ("Perry") is the company president. Together, they make and sell handmade jewelry, and they also service, repair, and restore antique jewelry. At Max Nass, they deal in virtually any type of jewelry—antique (or merely old), silver, gold, and semiprecious. Two special sales every year bring their low prices down even lower. One lasts for the last three weeks in January (33 percent discount); the other runs for two weeks in July (25 percent discount). In between, Arati will design pieces on whim or commission. The necklaces are particularly impressive; his work is often one-of-a-kind. The store also restrings and redesigns necklaces. I can only assume Max Nass is the name of a previous owner. He sure isn't Parimal S. Shah.

MURREY'S
1403 Third Ave (bet 79th and 80th St)
879-3690, FAX: 212/879-7957
Daily: 9:30-6:30

Murrey's, family jewelers since 1936, sells find jewelry and giftware. In the service area, they do machine engraving, stringing, watch repair, and they have a talented goldsmith for custom-designed pieces.

MYRON TOBACK

25 W 47th St (bet Fifth and Sixth Ave)   398-8300
Mon-Fri: 8:30-4; closed first two weeks in July and
    Dec 25-Jan 1

You must meet Myron Toback. Ostensibly, he is a refiner of precious metals with a specialty in findings, plate, and wire. Not very exciting or helpful to the average customer, you might think. But you'd be wrong. Note the address. Toback is not only in the heart of the diamond district, he is a bona fide landlord of a new arcade that is crammed full of wholesale artisans of the jewelry trade. Taking their cue from Toback, they are open and friendly to individual retail customers. So note Toback as a source of gold, gold-filled, and silver chains sold by the foot at a wholesale price. And don't overlook the gold and silver earrings, beads, and other jewelry items at prices laughably less than those at establishments around the corner on Fifth Avenue. Even though most of the customers are professional jewelers or wholesale organizations, Toback is still simply charming to do-it-yourselfers, schools, and hobbyists. Toback delights in showing people how to bypass jewelry middlemen in putting together their own custom-made items.

OCINO

66 John St (bet Nassau and William St)   269-3636
Mon-Fri: 8:30-6

Ocino is a fantastic find right in the middle of the financial district. At Ocino, there are diamonds, custom-made jewelry (both to individual customer's specifications and corporate advertising or logo inscriptions), handmade jewelry, resetting and redesigning, top brand-name watches, and gold chains sold by weight for those who want to make their own jewelry. For the latter, Ocino claims the lowest prices in the city. Ocino calls itself the "quality store downtown" and offers tableware by Lenox, Royal Copenhagen, Waterford, Kosja Boda—you get the idea. Despite having a virtual monopoly on those brands in the area, everything is sold at enough of a discount to be among the best priced anywhere in the city.

PEDRO BOREGAARD

48 W 48th St (Suite 904)   819-1060
Mon-Fri: 10-5:30 by appointment

Pedro Boregaard's credentials as a master jeweler are impressive, to say the least. He apprenticed under masters in Germany and England, then came to this country in 1974 to work at Tiffany's. He ended up co-supervising a large crew there, and he also did some designing for top names in the field. Few have the native talent Boregaard possesses, and his unusual pieces are sure to attract attention for any occasion. Magnificent necklaces, earrings, and bracelets are all one-of-a-kind.

RENNIE ELLEN
15 W 47th St (Room 401)   869-5525
Mon-Fri: 10-4:30 by appointment only

A trip to New York without meeting Rennie Ellen is a trip without experiencing what New York shopping is all about. For openers, she is a wholesaler offering the discounts that the city's wholesale businesses are famous for. Second, she deals in diamonds—the real thing—which are certainly knockout souvenirs to bring back from the city. Third, not only was she the first woman diamond dealer in the male-dominated diamond district, but feminism has made her a world-renowned consumer advocate. Rennie Ellen personally spent so much time and effort to keep the diamond district straight and honest that she earned the title "Mayor of 47th Street." Finally, only a fool would negotiate a purchase in any wholesale area without knowing the merchant. This is particularly true when one is dealing with diamonds, since thousands of dollars depend upon quirks visible only to a jeweler's eye. In such a field, Rennie Ellen's reputation is impeccable. Her store deals exclusively in diamond jewelry. There are pendants, wedding bands, engagement rings, and diamonds that, Rennie says, fit all sizes, shapes, and budgets. All sales are strictly confidential and are made under Rennie Ellen's personal supervision.

ROBERT LEE MORRIS
409 W Broadway (bet Spring and Prince St)   431-9405
Sun-Fri: 11-6; Sat: 12-7

AT&T Building
550 Madison Ave (at 56th St)   593-3388
Mon-Fri: 11-6

ARTWEAR
456 W Broadway   673-2000
Sun-Fri: 11-6; Sat: 12-7

Robert Lee Morris often sets the pace in the jewelry world. Betweern periodic exhibitions of the latest in contemporary jewelry, Artwear sells the works of 29 different artists. If you want to be noticed, merchandise from any of these three shops will make wonderful conversation pieces. The real emphasis here is on *art*.

SAITY JEWELRY
Trump Tower
725 Fifth Ave (at 57th St, Level 5)   308-6570
Mon-Sat: 10-6

Saity is a gallery of one-of-a-kind treasures, featuring the world's largest collection of authentic Native American jewelry. Over

8,000 original masterpieces, handcrafted by artisans of the Zuni, Navajo, Hopi, and Santa Domingo tribes, are shown here. The collection spans 40 years, featuring sterling silver, turquoise, coral, jet, and mother-of-pearl gemstones. Next door at David Saity, you can see an array of handcrafted sterling silver designs from China, Tibet, Nepal, and Africa.

SAVAGE UNIQUE JEWELRY

59 W 8th St	267 Columbus Ave
(near Sixth Ave)	(at 72nd St)
473-8171	724-4662
Mon-Sat: 11-7; Sun: 1-5	Mon-Sat: 12-9:30; Sun: 1-6

Outrageous is the word here! Very unusual and unique watches, flamboyant accessories, and spectacular earrings will dazzle your eye. This is not a place for the conservative matron, but the fashion-conscious will be able to rub shoulders with many soap-opera actors and rock stars. Be sure to check out the large assortment of gold rings. As a special service, they will make appointments after hours for out-of-city visitors.

UNDERGROUND JEWELER

147 E 86th St	175 E 86th St (at Third Ave)
348-7866	369-0920
Mon-Fri: 10-8; Sat: 10-7	Mon-Sat: 10-8; Sun 12-6

Subway arcades are neglected areas of commerce in New York (unlike in Vienna, for example), and with good reason. There is very little sold deep underground that could withstand scrutiny in the light of day. Furthermore, most shops whose sales depend upon bright, open displays that attract casual passers-by do not believe a potential clientele exists in a subway. There are two exceptions. The nut concessions are pretty universal and depend almost entirely upon impulse buying. The Underground Jeweler is the other exception, and it's worth the trip to see why. They carry jewelry from 60 countries. Most is of a whimsical nature and not made of valuable metals or precious stones, but all of it is very attractive and definitely not of the costume-jewelry class. One of Underground's specialties is gold with real stones. The stones are mostly semi-precious, and gold settings are used primarily because they won't make your finger turn green. The African wood carvings—rings, gifts, and statues—are sensational, and some of the genuine folk jewelry is great. Imagine row upon row of hand-worked silver pendants of international origins. This is not the place to go for an engagement ring, but it's perfect for many other types of jewelry. They also do ear piercing.

Ladders

PUTNAM ROLLING LADDER COMPANY
32 Howard St (bet Lafayette St and Broadway)
226-5147
Mon-Fri: 8-4:30

This is a great esoteric shop on an esoteric street. What, you might ask, would anyone in New York do with those magnificent rolling ladders used in traditional formal libraries? And could there possibly be enough business to keep a place like this running all those years? The answer is that Putnam has been in existence since 1905. Clever New Yorkers turn to Putnam for designing access to their lofts (especially sleeping lofts). Here's a partial list of ladders, which come in many different hardwoods: rolling ladders, rolling work platforms, telephone ladders, portable automatic ladders, scaffold ladders, pulpit ladders, folding library ladders, library stools, aerial platforms, library carts with steps, steel warehouse ladders, safety ladders, electric stepladders for industrial use, and mechanics' stepladders. Then there are Alpine, Crosby, Peerless, Durable, twin, and dual-purpose stepladders; extension ladders; window cleaners' ladders; sectional ladders; shelf ladders; extension trestle ladders; custom ladders; and many more. Putnam is a step up.

Leather Goods, Luggage

ANANIAS
231 Thompson St (bet Bleecker and W 3rd St)
533-5135
Mon-Thurs: 2-10; Fri-Sat: 1-midnight; Sun: 1-10

Herald Center, 34th and Broadway (4th Floor) 695-2052
Daily: 10-7

This interesting store probably has the city's largest selection of natural leather items handmade from cowhide. There are knapsacks, travel and school bags, purses, sandals, belts, wallets, and accessories. Everything is made by their own people on the island of Crete, although the owners are German and Chinese! I can vouch for the durability of cowhide; I have a suitcase that has literally traveled millions of miles around the world in the past 40 years, and it is still providing great service!

BETTINGER'S LUGGAGE SHOP
80 Rivington St   674-9411, 475-1690
Sun-Fri: 9-6

This tiny shop can be located by keeping an eye peeled for a mound of luggage heaped all over the sidewalk in front of the store.

Inside, it is even more crowded, but, amazingly, the people who run Bettinger's can put their hands on almost any type of luggage in only a few minutes. Their merchandise includes Samsonite, American Tourister, Ventura, and Mark and Andiano luggage, camp trunks, briefcases, and leather envelopes in both first quality and irregulars. The prices are among the best in New York, being at least 30 percent lower than you'd pay uptown.

JOBSON'S LUGGAGE
666 Lexington Ave (bet 55th and 56th St)
355-6846, 800-221-5238
Mon-Sat: 9-6

Apparently, the key to a successful luggage store in New York is to offer a vast selection at discount prices. With the exception of a store such as T. Anthony, which depends on quality and service to offset its high prices, most of the stores we've checked out offer good variety and a range of discounts. Naturally, the stores we've listed are the best of the genre. At Jobson's, they claim to have the largest selection of brand-name luggage, attaché cases, and small leather goods in the metropolitan area. (It *is* enormous.) They also claim that their large volume in sales enables them to sell at guaranteed low prices that are close to wholesale. Believe it or not, that is not enough to gain recognition in this book. There must be a dozen other stores with similar claims, but Jobson's sales staff and personal attention set it apart. The staff guides each customer, pointing out the advantages and disadvantages of each model. You need such guidance, and getting the best prices is a bonus. They also offer free monogramming and free delivery in Manhattan.

T. ANTHONY
480 Park Ave (at 58th St)   750-9797, 800/722-2406
Mon-Fri: 9:30-6; Sat: 10-6

T. Anthony handles luxurious luggage of distinction. Anything purchased here will stand out in a crowd as being of really fine quality, and that is a distinction that T. Anthony customers expect and receive. Every person who comes into the store receives courteous attention. Luggage comes in sizes from small overnight bags to massive pieces that just fall short of being steamer trunks. Gifts have a similar range. All are based on the leather-luggage theme, but the wallets, key cases, and billfolds are distinctive gifts, individually or in matched sets. Don't come looking for discount prices here, but the quality and service are well-established New York traditions. Exclusive T. Anthony products are also available through the store's catalog.

Lighting Fixtures and Accessories

JUST BULBS®
938 Broadway (at E 22nd St)   228-7820
Mon-Fri: 9-6

From a practical point of view, this is probably the only shop in the world that can supply certain types of bulbs. In addition to the obvious ones, Just Bulbs has a collection for use in old fixtures. The staff boasts that the store houses almost 25,000 different types of bulbs. It's hard to imagine half that many exist. The shop looks like an oversize stage dressing-room mirror, and everywhere you look there are bulbs connected to switches that customers are invited to flick on and off.

JUST SHADES
21 Spring St   966-2757
Thurs-Tues: 9:30-4

This store specializes in shades. They are experts on the proper shade for the proper lamp, and they share their expertise with retail customers. Their experience encompasses the entire subject, and they carry only the finest shades. They have lampshades of silk, string, parchment, and just about any other material imaginable. Interestingly, they say their biggest peeve is customers who "neglect" (a polite way of putting it) to take the protective cellophane off their shades, because the shade actually collects ruinous dust.

LIGHTING PLUS
676 Broadway (bet 2nd and 3rd St)   979-2000
Mon-Sat: 10-7; Sun: 11-7

Few things are more annoying than not having that special electrical gadget you need to use or fix a lamp, computer, hair dryer, or whatever. Running around from one store to another trying to find an elusive item is even more frustrating. Take heart. Go straight to Lighting Plus. In a thankfully well-organized store, you can find just about anything that has any connection with electricity. And the personnel are eager to help amateur shoppers.

LOUIS MATTIA
980 Second Ave (bet 51st and 52nd St)   753-2176
Mon-Fri: 9-6

Few stores repair or stock parts for lamps. Louis Mattia does. In his crowded shop, he has enough spare parts to fix almost any lamp. Consequently, he is patronized by a wide variety of customers: socialites who need a priceless heirloom repaired; decorators such as Denning-Fourcade; and other merchants who need quick repairs on slightly damaged merchandise for their customers. All of them receive prompt and courteous attention from one of the most knowledgeable staffs in New York.

NEW YORK GAS LIGHTING COMPANY
145 Bowery (bet Grand and Broome St)   226-2840
Mon-Fri: 9-5; Sat, Sun: 10:30-5

The definitive source for traditional and elegant quality lighting, New York Gas Lighting Company is mentioned repeatedly by decorators. Consumers will find a wide array of merchandise for all lighting applications at good prices. Be sure to go through all the rooms. There's lots to see!

ROSETTA ELECTRIC CO
21 W 46th St (bet Fifth and Sixth Ave)   719-4381
Mon-Fri: 9-6; Sat: 9-5

Right in the middle of Manhattan under one roof you can buy top-name lighting fixtures like Lightolier, Stiffel, and Kovacs and also find a great selection of electrical supplies. Rosetta started on Fulton Street in 1936, and it has been a reliable electrical-goods store for over half a century. Special orders are taken, delivery service is available, and best of all, prices are in the discount category.

SHADES BY PERRY
247 E 77th St (bet Second and Third Ave)   472-1140
Mon-Sat: 8-5

When it comes to ordering a custom-made shade or some other special lighting accessory, this is the place to go. The designs here are unique and attractive, and all work is very professionally done.

TUDOR ELECTRICAL SUPPLY
222-26 E 46th St (bet Second and Third Ave)   867-7550
Mon-Thurs: 9-5; Fri: 9-4:30

Although you may feel like you need an engineering degree to enter Tudor Electrical, the staff is geared to explaining everything in stock to even the proverbial novice who doesn't know how to replace a light bulb. Light bulbs are the store's forte. No one has ever counted the varieties available, but they are cataloged by wattage, color, and use by a staff who can almost immediately pull out the best bulb for your needs. If Tudor stocks it, you can believe there's a reason for it. Quartz, tungsten, and halogen bulbs don't distort light, while incandescent and fluorescent lamps offer the best of both kinds of lighting for desk work. Energy-efficient bulbs come with vital instructions, which is a boon to people who don't know wattage from lumens output. And better still, while discounting at least 20 percent off list price, Tudor Electrical Supply will guide a customer to the best bargains.

UPLIFT
506 Hudson St   929-3632
Daily: 1-8

The big question is what the name Uplift has to do with a store that mainly sells art deco and Victorian lighting fixtures. In any event, Uplift has one of the largest collections of original American art deco chandeliers in the country. They also have some less expensive reproductions and a full line of fantasy figures, like wizards and dragons made of pewter. They will rebuild old torchier lamps so that they are like new, but taller. Uplift also has accessories for lighting fixtures: lamps, wiring, bases, glass bowls, and shades, including glass ones for lamps suspended from the ceiling and replacement slip shades for slip-in deco fixtures.

Magic

FLOSSO AND HORNMANN MAGIC
45 W 34th St (Room 607)   279-6079
Mon-Fri: 10:30-5:30; Sat: 10:30-4

Harry Houdini got his tricks and kicks here, which is not surprising, since he was but one of a score of professional magicians who have owned this shop since its creation in 1856. Flosso and Hornmann is proof that magic is timeless, not only because its clientele spans all ages, but because the store seems unchanged since Houdini's time. In part, that's due to the dim light and dust, but mostly it's because the stock is so complete. It's hard to think of a trick that's *not* stocked here. The staff, if asked, will show you what's new. You have to visit the store to understand how amazing that is. In addition to magic acts, the shop carries books, manuals, historical treatises, and photographs, and they'll even create stage sets. For their final act, ladies and gentlemen, they'll produce a professional magic catalog in which many of the tricks are explained in detail. Don't tell a living soul!

LOUIS TANNEN
6 W 32nd St (4th floor)   239-8383
Mon-Wed, Fri: 9-5:30; Thurs: 9-7; Sat: 9-3

Levitate upstairs to this jam-packed magic store, and Tony Spina (or any of the other helpful personnel) will cheerfully demonstrate the latest in magic. Unlike many such shops, this one welcomes amateurs, and there is a large stock of simple, inexpensive acts. In case they *do* leave the customer baffled, the staff will patiently explain them. The annual *Catalogs of Magic* contain the store's inventory—over 8,000 individual items and 350 books about magic. But unlike the store, the catalogs seem to be for people who know what they are doing.

Maps

HAGSTROM MAP AND TRAVEL CENTER
57 W 43rd St (at Sixth Ave)   398-1222
Mon-Fri: 9-5:30

The Hammond Map store was one of the finest in the business for three-quarters of a century. Now as Hagstrom, under the supervision of Mr. Warner, the map specialist, it is a big name in maps in its own right. As the only complete maps and charts dealer in the city, they highlight the maps of other manufacturers and five branches of the U.S. government, as well as their own. There are also nautical, hiking, global, and travel guides. They publish a free periodic newsletter, and they ship maps virtually all over the map!

Memorabilia

ANNA SOSENKO
25 Central Park W (bet 62nd and 63rd St)   247-4816
Mon-Sat: by appointment

After a quarter of a century in business, she has moved the operation to her home. Anna Sosenko sells and maintains a magnificent collection of autographs and personal memorabilia. Most of the collection is show-business oriented, and the better items are framed. Anna Sosenko loves what she is doing, and it shows. Her advice is to stick to a particular specialty; she has merchandise to start you in your collecting career with hundreds of samples, and most are reasonably priced.

LOST CITY ARTS
275 Lafayette St (bet Prince and Houston St)   941-8025
Mon-Fri: 10-6; Sat, Sun: 12-6

Are you looking for a special old Coca-Cola advertising piece or a souvenir from a New York World's Fair? Lost City specializes in such items, with an emphasis on architectural antiques, old advertising fixtures, and a great collection of old New York souvenirs.

MEMORY SHOP
109 E 12th St (off Fourth Ave)   473-2404
Daily: 11-6

This dirty basement is virtually a Hollywood archive. The Memory Shop claims to have 1 million posters, 500,000 press books, and over 8 million photographs in stock. If it exists, it's buried here somewhere. Customers don't browse; they know exactly what they want, hand in the order, and the counter clerk gets it. This is probably because *only* the clerk could find it. If you have a fetish for *Gone with the Wind* or some other old movie, this is the place for you. The Memory Shop is especially eager to fill requests from libraries and film students.

MOTION PICTURE ARTS GALLERY

133 E 58th St (10th floor)   223-1009
Tues-Fri: 11-5:30; Sat: 12-5; closed Sat from
Memorial Day to Labor Day and all of Aug

Ira Resnick runs the world's only gallery that treats movie posters as works of art. His Motion Picture Art Gallery is just that: a gallery that displays the original posters and lobby cards from motion pictures as artwork and sells them. His customers include film buffs and vintage poster collectors and investors. (A *Casablanca* poster could be had for a couple of dollars in the early Sixties. Today, the same poster fetches upwards of $4,500.) There are over 15,000 items in stock here.

MOUSE 'N AROUND

901 Sixth Ave, 7th floor, A&S Plaza
(bet 32nd and 33rd St)   947-3954
Mon, Thurs, Fri: 9:45-8:30; Tues, Wed, Sat: 9:45-6:45;
Sun: 1-6

Mouse 'n Around has moved to the sparkling new A&S Plaza, and Mickey seems happy in his new digs. In addition to all the Disney character merchandise, you will find Snoopy, Betty Boop, Looney Tunes, Flintstones, and Tiny Tunes. The largest selection of cartoon watches in the city can be found here. The big stock is in clothing; there are sizes for all members of the family. Now wouldn't Uncle Harry love that reversible sweat shirt with Mickey's likeness on it?

MOVIE STAR NEWS

134 W 18th St (bet Sixth and Seventh Ave)   620-8160
Mon-Sat: 10-6

In what is becoming the movie memorabilia center of the city, Movie Star News claims to have the world's largest collection of movie photos. If you thought the heyday of movie stars was long gone, don't tell the folks here, because stars past and present still shine brightly in this shop. Movie Star News offers posters, press books, and other cinema publicity materials as well. The selection is arranged like a library, and the Kramers, who run Movie Star News, do a lot of research for magazines, newspapers, and the media. This is the closest thing to Hollywood on the East Coast.

MYTHOLOGY UNLIMITED

370 Columbus Ave (bet 77th and 78th St)   874-0774
Mon-Sat: 11-11; Sun: 11-6

You have to see Mythology Unlimited to understand it. You'll find anything from an autograph party for the author of a book on diners to an exhibit of contemporary art and objects that can be politely described as unusual. There's the regular stock of tons of archaic post cards, pins, posters, tin toys, assorted rubber stamps, screen prints, masks, toys, knickknacks, jewelry, salt and pepper shakers, antique toys, Mexican masks, and Burmese puppets. This eclectic shop is a celebration of whimsy and pop art, right across the street from the Museum of Natural History.

ONE SHUBERT ALLEY
1 Shubert Alley (bet Broadway and Eighth Ave)
944-4133, 800/223-1320 (mail order only)
Mon-Sat: 9 a.m.-11:30 p.m.; Sun: 12-7:30

Shubert Alley is a narrow alleyway in the Broadway theater district that is often used as a shortcut between theaters. One Shubert Alley is the only retail establishment on the alley, and it's a fascinating place to browse. You will find T-shirts, posters, recordings, buttons, and other paraphernalia from current shows both on and off Broadway. There is a mail-order catalog and a special number for telephone orders.

PERFORMING ARTS SHOP
Metropolitan Opera House at Lincoln Center
(downstairs)   580-4356
Mon-Sat: 10-9; Sun: 12-6

This little-known shop on the lower level of the Metropolitan Opera House is an aria unto itself. Everything on sale has a tie to the performing arts, no matter how tenuous. All of it is high quality, and all is done in good taste. So there are top-notch gifts—all with a performing-arts motif—an enviable collection of printed matter that is so encompassing that there are rumors of an underground link to the Library of the Performing Arts one building over, and much more. CDs and tapes are balanced by beach towels and Beethoven T-shirts. And if you want to check out that underground rumor, the Performing Arts Shop also arranges tours of Lincoln Center. (They should start with better directions to their own shop!)

SILVER SCREEN
35 E 28th St (bet Park and Madison Ave)   679-8130
Mon-Fri: 12-7

If the 1950s were the silver years for you, this is your shop. Ken, Carol, and Irma sell posters, autographs, movie magazines, and other theatrical memorabilia. In addition, they rent out old photographs in either black-and-white or color. The place is jammed with memories of old movie and stage personalities and events, and they evoke tears and thrills of glamorous yesteryears. Clients must write or phone their wants. *No browsing!*

Mirrors

SUNDIAL-SCHWARTZ
1388 First Ave (at 74th St)   734-0838, 873-8154
Mon-Fri: 8-4:30; Sat: 10-4

The people at Sundial claim they supply "decorative treatments of distinction," and anyone who has ever seen a cramped New York apartment suddenly expand with the use of a few strategic mirrors will understand how they can make that claim. Sundial deals with professional decorators as well as do-it-yourselfers, and both reap the benefit of the staff's years of experience. There are mirrors for home, office, and showroom. In addition, Sundial will remodel, resilver, and move mirrors. Sundial also custom-designs window treatments, doors, blinds, shades, storm windows, room dividers, and more. The primary service here, however, is the decorating advice.

Museum and Library Shops

One of the greatest advantages of living in a city with so many museums and libraries is that almost all of them have gift shops. Museum and library gift shops in New York are very specific. They're short on Empire State Building salt-and-pepper shakers and long on really unique, classy items. The MOMA store inspires a cult following of its own. The Museum Watch and the Museum Kettle are just two designs made and marketed purely for display at the MOMA shop. It's like an award in design. In addition, the wares at most of these shops directly relate to the organization's forte, as well as current and past popular exhibits. These are wonderful places for gifts or household decorating.

AMERICAN CRAFT MUSEUM
40 W 53rd St   956-6047
Tues: 10-8; Wed-Sun: 10-5

The American Craft Museum, which is across from MOMA, has a gift shop that highlights American crafts, featuring selections from recent shows. Most of the exhibitors are contemporary, so original works are also sold.

AMERICAN MUSEUM OF
NATURAL HISTORY
Central Park West and 79th St   769-5100
Sun, Mon, Tues, Thurs: 10-5:45; Wed, Fri, Sat: 10-9

Located inside the museum are several gifts shops. One on the lower level is a "junior" shop for kids. Despite the dinosaur models, bins of rubber animals, and a superb balcony of books and prints on the upper level of the rotunda, this is not an appealing place. There may be treasures here, but I can't find them.

ASIA SOCIETY BOOKSTORE AND GIFT SHOP
72 Park Ave (at 70th St)   288-6400
Tues-Sat: 11-6-Sun: noon-5

The Asia Society highlights John D. Rockefeller's collection of Asian art. Although there are changing exhibits, little is added, so it's not terribly innovative. But exactly the opposite is true in the corner gift shop downstairs. Although it is tucked away, it's really a gallery all by itself. Here, one will find Asian prints, posters, artwork books, jewelry, and toys. The items are clever and quite striking. If you're looking for something with a Far Eastern motif, this is the place to come!

THE CATHEDRAL SHOP/CATHEDRAL OF ST. JOHN THE DIVINE
1047 Amsterdam Ave (bet 112th St and Amsterdam Ave)
222-7200
Daily: 9-5

The world's largest cathedral, St. John's, has been undergoing construction for over a hundred years, and the task will continue well into the next century. Work stopped for many years. When they began anew, instead of importing artisans, they trained local craftsmen in the ancient arts of stonecutting and glassmaking. The gift shop has samples of their work, such as hand-cut stone and stained-glass pieces, as well as books on the cathedral arts and architecture. There's also jewelry, Biblical books and herbs, religious articles, and giftware. Tickets for concerts at the cathedral are also sold at the gift shop.

COOPER-HEWITT
2 E 91st St   860-6878
Tues: 10-9; Wed-Sat: 10-5; Sun: noon-5

Since this museum is dedicated to interior display and household design, the gift shop should be the best source in town for wallpaper, prints, and tea sets. (These are all things they've had exhibits on.) It is not, though. The shop is cramped beside the main staircase, and very little of a permanent nature is sold therein. Most of the items are supposed to relate to the current exhibit, but when we tried to find a copy of something we really liked, it wasn't available.

JEWISH MUSEUM
The New York Historical Society (until late 1992)
Central Park W at 77th St   860-1895
Mon, Wed, Thurs: noon-5; Tues: noon-8; Fri: 11-3;
    Sun: 11-6

The Jewish Museum gift shop prides itself on its selection of
Judaica. They are particularly well stocked with Jewish ceremonial
items, including what is possibly the city's largest collection of
menorahs and kiddush cups. But don't overlook items for the Sab-
bath and everyday giftware with a Jewish theme. Prices range from
inexpensive to more costly one-of-a-kind or limited-edition levels.
They also stock T-shirts, sterling silver jewelry, and posters and
books relating to past and current exhibits and the practice of
Judaism.

METROPOLITAN MUSEUM OF ART
Fifth Ave at 82nd St
(There are also branches at the Cloisters, the 42nd Street
    Library, 15 W 59th St [opposite Rockefeller Center],
    and Macy's.)   535-7710
Tues: 9:30-8:45; Wed-Sun: 9:30-5:15

Virtually everything in the Met's gift shops is a copy, reproductions, or sister piece to something in the permanent collection. For
years the Met rented out paintings on a monthly basis, but prints
relating to past and current exhibits are so magnificent and so
reasonable that much decorating is done with them. (You've seen
them on the walls of homes in decorating magazines.) The Met
mounts several shows a year, and the gift shops reflect the art and
artists from those showcases. It's no wonder that the Met gift shop
has spawned branches and imitators around town. It is surely one
of the best.

MUSEUM OF AMERICAN FOLK ART
2 Lincoln Sq (Columbus Ave bet 65th and 66th St)
496-2966
Mon, Tues, Sat: 11-6; Wed, Thurs, Fri: 11-7:30; Sun: 12-6

62 W 50th St (at Sixth Ave)   247-5611
Mon-Sat: 10:30-5:30

Since the motif of this museum is contemporary American folk
art, I'm not quite sure who makes the distinction as to what goes on
display and what gets sold in the "country store" gift shop. But
country is what you're getting, and since most of the craftsmen are
very much alive, you can purchase an original work of art by someone who has a piece on display in the museum. Not everything is
museum-priced. In fact, very little is. There are accent pieces—
breadboxes, knickknacks, butter churns, and weathervanes—as

well as quilts, wooden toys, and hand-carved furniture. Prices vary accordingly, but most of these pieces are *not* reproductions. It's all modern work in the style of early folk crafts.

MUSEUM OF THE CITY OF NEW YORK
Fifth Ave at 103rd St   534-1672
Tues-Sat: 10-5; Sun: 1-5

Most everything in this museum's gift shop is New York related. History buffs will be in seventh heaven. There are books and many cute, old-fashioned toy reproductions. They might consider trying to reflect more of the museum's collection in the gift shop. Still, New Yorkphiles could live here!

MUSEUM OF MODERN ART/ MOMA DESIGN STORE
44 W 53rd St   767-1050

MOMA Bookstore   708-9700
11 W 53rd St
Mon-Wed, Fri: 11-6; Thurs: 11-9

Grand Central Terminal   599-3260
Mon, Tues, Fri: 9-7; Wed, Thurs: 8-7

This is where it all started. MOMA, in addition to displaying modern art, also displays home furnishings, including watches, books, prints, children's activities, contemporary cookware, and innovative designs. Museum goers weren't satisfied with viewing these items. They wanted to *own* them, and MOMA soon amassed a collection of the very best, most functional and artistic items, from kettles to sofas. All of it was offered for sale in its gift shop. Educators prized the children's items as well. Many of the toys and games were unique to MOMA (and were quite afield from modern art). Eventually the toys, games, books, and prints were fighting for space with the home furnishings. An annex down the street was installed, but it was too distant from the museum and inadequate from the start. The MOMA Design Store is brand-new, located in custom-designed quarters across the street from the museum. The basement gift shop is now the bookshop, and it is still a first choice for wrapping paper, books, prints, games, and toys.

NEW YORK HISTORICAL SOCIETY
170 Central Park W (at 77th St)   873-3400
Tues-Sun: 10-5

This overlooked museum has an equally overlooked gift shop, which is a shame. The stock reflects the Historical Society's interest in New York and broader American history. The museum takes wing with the collection of Audubon prints (the Historical Society owns 433 of the 435 originals in Audubon's *Birds of America* series), house reproductions (actual homes in miniature), and home furnishings, such as baskets, tiles, and tableware. The majority are authentic reproductions. Don't overlook the toys, dolls, and games, derived from the Colonial era in American history.

NEW YORK PUBLIC LIBRARY SHOP
Fifth Ave at 42nd St (Room 116)   930-0678
Mon-Wed: 11-6; Thurs-Sat: 10-6

Everything for sale here is literary in nature. The majority has a connection to the library stacks, rather than a particular show the library might be presenting at any given time. The literary motif is reflected in the wrapping paper, note paper, fictional characters on wall hangings and mementos, and a really great selection of "Ex Libris" bookplates. At Christmas time this is a one-stop gift-finding paradise. But it's low to the point of nonexistence on books; it could do a best-seller business with prints from the library's own collection. My favorite "in" joke is the bookends of Patience and Fortitude. Those were the names given by Mayor LaGuardia to the two lions that guard the main entrance. It's also a perfect piece of trivia to determine if someone is a *real* New Yorker.

THE PIERPONT MORGAN LIBRARY
29 E 36th St   685-0610
Tues-Sat: 10:30-4:45; Sun: 1-4:45

Step back into the era when J. P. Morgan was alive and this could be a gentlemen's club. The stock, salespeople, and general atmosphere all reflect the esoteric tastes of J. P. Morgan (although there is very little of his interest in Egyptology), from his own private blend of tea to the leather-bound books that may or may not be reproductions. Still, there's something here for every modern man (or child). Beatrix Potter lives in post cards, posters, and Peter Rabbit paraphernalia. (You can even find dishes.) The store reminds you of an English library; they do everything possible to reinforce that image. Books are reverently displayed on tables and walls, and the accessories are all literary-minded. There is note paper, bookmarks, bookplates, and book preservatives, all adding to the atmosphere. In short, a first-rate place for well-stated gifts.

SOUTH STREET SEAPORT
MUSEUM SHOPS
14 Fulton St, Cannon's Walk, 209 Water St   669-9400
Mon-Sat: 10-9; Sun: 11-7

The addresses above are specifically sanctioned by the Seaport Museum for the sale of Seaport mementos. However, since the entire Seaport is a working period piece, that doesn't rule out all the shops—particularly those along Front and Water Streets that offer authentic seaport wares. Check them out. Those listed above, however, are special. The Museum Shop (14 Fulton St) carries T-shirts, pens, little games, and sweat shirts. The Book & Chart Shop (209 Water St) is one of the oldest in the restored Seaport. It carries authentic and reproduced charts, books, ship models, scrimshaw, and maps, as well as a fair amount of printing. Along Cannon's Walk are several functioning period stores. The Curiosity Shop is what the Museum Shop would have looked like a hundred years ago. Note the old post cards, posters and sea-related products.

THE WHITNEY MUSEUM'S STORE NEXT DOOR

943 Madison Ave (bet 74th and 75th St)   606-0200
Tues: 10-8; Wed-Sat: 10-6; Sun: noon-6

It took the Whitney a long time to open its gift shop, but the wait was worth it. The autonomous Store Next Door resembles an artist's high-tech loft, and everything displayed under the sleek black ceiling is American-made and *very* sharp. The jewelry is that of Lisa Fidler, Lisa Jenks, Thomas Mann, and Steve Vaubel, among others. There are quilts by Pea Ridge Purdies, wooden toys, and Dan Mack's miniature Windsor chairs. Even the obligatory T-shirts and tote bags are unique. While much of this is standard, the Store Next Door always gears its merchandise to the museum's exhibitions. Would that they all did so!

Music, Musical Instruments

BLEECKER BOB'S GOLDEN OLDIES RECORD SHOP

118 W 3rd St (bet MacDougal St and Sixth Ave)
475-9677
Sun-Thurs: 12-1 a.m.; Fri, Sat: 12-3 a.m.

Let us sing the praises of Bleecker Bob's, who is nothing if not perverse. (Name another store open till three a.m. on Christmas Day!) For one thing, although there is a real Bob (Plotnik, the owner), the store isn't on Bleecker Street. For another, Bleecker Bob is an institution to generations of New Yorkers who have sifted through the selection of virtually every rock record ever recorded. Yet what did the *New York Times* finally cite Bleecker Bob's for? "The archetypal punk-plus record store." Come on, folks! With a stock that includes all those old records (including rare jazz), autograph parties for rock stars, and a boast that they can fill any wish list from their stock, Bleecker Bob's is obviously much more than a punk-rock store. It is also *the* gathering place in the wee hours of the morning in the Village (where that *ain't* the wee hours of the morning). But above all, it's one great source for out-of-print, obscure, and imported discs.

DAYTON'S RECORD ARCHIVES
799 Broadway/80 E 11th St (same location; 2nd floor)
254-5084
Mon-Fri: 11-6:30; Sat: 11-6

Dayton's is to records what the Strand Book Store (their neighbor) is to books. They both have the same sources—reviewers' copies and promotional materials—and they both pass on the savings to retail customers. Dayton's specializes in long-playing phonograph records, particularly those that are out-of-print.

DETRICH PIANOS
211 W 58th St (nr Broadway)   246-1766
Mon-Fri: 10-6; Sat: 10-4

Kalman Detrich fled Hungary for the United States many years ago, bringing his love and knowledge of pianos with him. His shop, within earshot of Carnegie Hall, ministers to any of the myriad needs the piano player might have. Detrich will tune, repair, polish, rent, buy, sell, and even buy back a piano with all the finesse of his Old World training. But his specialty is antique pianos. He lovingly restores them, and the few that he can't restore, he polishes to a gloss and sells as furniture rather than as musical pieces. The small shop is jammed with the cream of whatever is being revitalized at the moment, and passers-by cannot help but understand Detrich's pride when viewing the finished results.

DRUMMERS WORLD
147 W 46th St   840-3057
Mon-Fri: 10-6; Sat: 10-4

Rat-tat-tat! This is a great place, unless the patron is your teenager or an upstairs neighbor. In any case, Barry Greenspon and his staff take great pride in guiding students as well as professionals through one of the most well-rounded percussion stores in the country. Inside this drummer's paradise you'll find everything from commonplace equipment to one-of-a-kind antiques and imports. All of the instruments are high-quality symphonic percussion items, and customers receive the same attention whether they are members of an orchestra or kitchen-spoon rappers. For the latter, the store offers instructors, instruction, and how-to books. And there are esoteric and even ethnic instruments for virtuosos who want to experiment. Drummers World has a catalog and will ship anywhere in the country.

FOOTLIGHT RECORDS
113 E 12th St (bet Third and Fourth Ave)   533-1572
Mon-Fri: 11-7; Sat: 10-6; Sun: 12-5

Footlight Records has a passion for rare and odd records, but there's an emphasis on show tunes and jazz rather than a general hodgepodge of discounted current recordings. This is not to say that Ed McGrath and Gene Dingenary's prices aren't good. In fact, for many of the albums, their prices are the best around, but that is really the point—these records just *aren't* around elsewhere. If an original cast album was made of a Broadway show, Footlight has it. Often, its customers are the artists themselves, who are without copies of their own performances! What is more impressive is the organization that enables the store's personnel to know almost at a glance what is and is not available. Not an easy task when the stock is constantly being sold and much of it is out-of-print or hard-to-find recordings. There are show tunes, whole collections of 1940s, 1950s, and 1960s artists, and probably every big-band record ever made. Their compact disc selection is also impressive.

FORD PIANO SUPPLY COMPANY
4898 Broadway (bet 204th and 207th)   569-9200
Mon-Fri: 8:30-5:30

John Ford's father was in the piano-repair business. When John took over, he began collecting odds and ends whenever he found them, and he soon had more piano parts than pianos in his shop. Along with the best collection of supplies for piano repairs, Ford garnered a reputation as *the* place to go for piano tuners. So, Ford all but abandoned buying and selling instruments and concentrated on rebuilding pianos (often from scratch) and supplying piano parts. The Ford family can refinish, tune, rebuild, or adjust any kind of acoustic piano. They will custom-make covers and benches, as well as pedals, and there is an array of piano-tuning tools, lamps, chairs, and coasters. The Fords will happily conduct tours of their piano-rebuilding factory, which is a sight to see. But for the most part, Ford's customers never come to the shop. When you're the only store in town supplying everything for pianos, most customers order by mail or telephone. The Fords also rent and tune pianos. Truly a family business, they are awaiting the day when little John Ford III is old enough to join the family ranks.

GRYPHON RECORD SHOP
251 W 72nd St (2nd floor)   874-1588
Mon-Sat: 11-7; Sun: 12-6

Gryphon is one of a handful of stores specializing in rare and out-of-print LPs. They're world-famous for their collection. Raymond Donnell knows his business; he's able to help customers search out the most elusive LP, be it classical, jazz, Broadway, pop, or the spoken arts. But the emphasis is on classical recordings.

THE GUITAR SALON
45 Grove St (Sheridan Sq, Seventh Ave and Bleecker St)
675-3236
By appointment; closed July

Beverly Maher's salon is a unique one-person operation located in a historic brownstone in Greenwich Village. Here you will find fine handmade classical and flamenco guitars for serious students, priced from $1,800. The shops buys and sells fine instruments, giving outstanding personal service from a talented guitarist. The salon specializes in nineteenth- and twentieth-century vintage instruments. Appraisals are available, and lessons are given on all styles of guitars. Maher even appraised Segovia's guitars, which he donated in 1987 to the Metropolitan Museum.

HMV U.S.A.
1280 Lexington Ave (at 86th St)   348-0800
Mon-Thur: 10-10; Fri, Sat: 10-midnight; Sun: 11-7

This is truly a musical supermarket! There are separate departments for rock and pop, classical, dance, jazz, and video. Listening booths are available, and a discount club is offered to regular patrons. This outfit is 90 years old, with outlets all over the world. They know their business. If you are looking for CDs, cassettes, records, VHS tapes, laser discs, or accessories, HMV is a good place to visit.

JAZZ RECORD CENTER
135 W 29th St (12th floor) 594-9880
Tues-Sat: 10-6; June 1-Labor Day: open Mon-Fri,
    closed Sat

This is the only jazz specialty store in the city. The house specialty is out-of-print jazz records, but there are also CDs, videos, books, posters, photos, and periodicals on the topic. The Center buys and sells collections, runs a search service, fills mail orders, offers appraisals, and holds an annual jazz rarities auction. All of this is run by an amazing man, Frederick Cohen. Here's a world-famous specialist on jazz history running his shop from the 12th floor of an old office building. Business is so good that he moved to larger quarters several years ago, and now all records are arranged in browser bins. Cohen is a charming guy who really knows his business.

JOSEPH PATELSON MUSIC HOUSE
160 W 56th St   582-5840
Mon-Sat: 9-6; closed Sat in summer

Located behind Carnegie Hall, Joseph Patelson is a shop known to every student of music in the area. From little first-graders in need of theory books to artists from Carnegie Hall in need of an extra copy of sheet music, everyone stops here first because of the fabulous selection, as well as the excellent prices. The stock includes music scores, sheet music, music books, and orchestral and opera scores. All are neatly cataloged and displayed in open cabinets, and one can pore through the section of interest—be it piano music, chamber music, orchestral scores, opera scores, old popular songs, concerts, ethnic scores, or instrumental solos. Sheet music, incidentally, is filed the way records are elsewhere. You flip through the files to find what you want, then bring it up to the counter to be checked out. There are some musical accessories, like metronomes and pitch pipes, as well. Patelson's is an unofficial meeting house for the city's young artists. Word goes out that "we're looking for a violinist," and meetings are often arranged in the store.

LAST WOUND-UP
889 Broadway (at 19th St)   529-4197
Mon-Thurs: 10-6; Fri, Sat: 10-8; Sun: 11-6

This super store is dedicated to any kind of object that can be wound up, with a roughly equal division between music boxes and windup toys. Owner Nathan Cohen harbors a slight prejudice for the former. He makes many of the boxes in stock, and his avocation is helping customers make their own music boxes out of almost any suitable container. The Last Wound-Up also sells the components to do this. The completed boxes range from valuable antiques to modern models.

LYRIC HIGH FIDELITY
1221 Lexington Ave (bet 82nd and 83rd St)
535-5710, 439-1900
Mon-Sat: 10-6

2005 Broadway (bet 68th and 69th St)   769-4600
Mon-Wed, Fri, Sat: 10-6; Thurs: 10-8

Lyric is the place for sound fanatics who know what they're doing. As Lyric's Michael Kays says, they're not for beginners. But anyone who has the knowledge and necessary cash can indulge his wildest audio fantasies here. Cash is as important as knowing the merchandise; you can part with between $1,000 and $60,000 in a morning's worth of shopping here. Lyric has been in business for over 30 years, selling equipment to people who want the best. Kay sniffs at names like Sony, which the average person considers top-of-the-line. Lyric carries only the best lines of each component, and the names of its suppliers are unknown to all but the most discriminating audiophile. If that's you, this is your store.

MANNY'S
156 W 48th St (bet Sixth and Seventh Ave)   819-0576
Mon-Sat: 10-6

Manny's is a huge discount department store for musical instruments. "Everything for the musician" is their motto, and it is borne out by a collection of musical equipment so esoteric that different salesmen are experts in different departments. There is an emphasis on modern music, as evidenced by the hundreds of autographed pictures of contemporary musicians and singers on the walls, and the huge collection of electronic instruments. Even the photos tend to be of the musicians who rely on electronic components rather than classical music. This does not, however, preclude classical instruments, and there is a good collection of them as well. The best part is that all of the musical instruments, accessories, electronic equipment, and supplies are sold at very good discount prices. They have full audio facilities. If you're into electronic music, Manny's should be your first choice.

MUSIC STORE AT CARL FISCHER
62 Cooper Sq (at 7th St and Fourth Ave)   677-0821
Mon-Sat: 10-5:45

Outside the Carnegie Hall area, the Music Store at Carl Fischer offers the best selection of sheet music from all publishers and categories, including pop, jazz, folk, rock, and classical. Everything is reasonably priced, with real bargains to be found in the older music. The store also has extended research facilities and background information for piano, vocal, instrumental, band, orchestral, and choral music. And that pretty much covers it all.

NOSTALGIA . . . AND ALL THAT JAZZ
217 Thompson St (bet Bleecker and 3rd St)   420-1940
Mon-Thurs: 1-8; Fri: 1-9; Sat: 1-10; Sun: 1-7:30

Guess what they sell here! The answer is—envelope please—nostalgia records, especially jazz LPs. Most of the recordings are of early radio programs, jazz programs, and soundtracks of old shows. There are a few vocal LPs, too. All are very reasonably priced. The shop has set up a sideline in photography, and Kim Deuel and Mort Alavi do a healthy business in the production, cataloging, and reproduction of photos. Nostalgia will reproduce any photograph, in any size or quantity, up to 30″ × 40″. They also have a good collection of posters, movie and jazz stills, and large (16″ × 20″) show-business photos, in black-and-white *and* color. Prices are excellent.

RITA FORD
19 E 65th St (at Madison Ave) 535-6717
Mon-Sat: 9-5

Rita Ford collects antique music boxes, and in the process she has become an expert in all aspects of the business. Her stock consists of valuable old music boxes, not-so-valuable old pieces, and pieces in various states of disrepair. (Rita Ford also does repairs.) The main stock in trade is expertise; Rita Ford knows all there is to know about the music-box business. She is an acknowledged expert on various music-box scores, workings, and outer casings. Some of her pieces are rare, one-of-a-kind antiques and are priced accordingly. Somewhat more reasonable are the contemporary pieces based upon original antiques.

TOWER RECORDS
See below for addresses and phone numbers
Daily: 9 a.m.-midnight

Tower Records provides a selection of music that can satisfy any New Yorker, young or old. Their stores are busy, crowded, noisy, and fun. There is almost as much amusement watching the parade of shoppers as there is enjoying the music. The stores at 692 Broadway (at East 4th Street; 505-1500) and 1961 Broadway (at 66th Street; 799-2500) carry records, tapes, and CDs; the annex at 4th St and Broadway (505-1500) features classical, Western, and used records. Tower Video Stores (discs and equipment) are located at 1977 Broadway (at 67th Street; 496-2500); 215 East 86th Street (between Second and Third Ave; 369-2500), and Fourth Ave and Lafayette St (505-1166).

VENUS RECORDS
13 St. Mark's Place (bet Second and Third Ave)
598-4459
Mon-Thurs: 12-8; Fri: 12-12; Sat: 11 a.m.-midnight;
    Sun: 12-6

For the rock and roll enthusiast, Venus offers one of New York's finest selections of 1950s and 1960s reissues and original editions, hard-core, punk, and new and used rock records not usually found in the Top Twenty. They also carry imported and independent releases, many out-of-print items, and a large selection of 45s. They are the only store in Manhattan with used cassettes. You can bring in used LPs, CDs, and cassettes at any time to sell for cash or trade. A wholesale service is available, and they will place special orders for individual customers.

VINYL MANIA RECORDS
Carmine St (three stores)   924-7223
Mon-Fri: 11-9; Sat, Sun: 11- 7

There is no other record store quite like this one. If you can't find it at one of their three outlets, it probably doesn't exist. The specialties are as follows: 60 Carmine (12″ dance, R&B, funk, rap, hip-hop, and house); 41 Carmine (12″ dance, rock, industrial, oldies, 45s, and CD singles); 43 Carmine (CDs, LPs, cassettes, R&B, dance, jazz, and rock.) You can see why they call these places "adventures in recorded music"!

Newspapers, Magazines

A&S BOOK COMPANY
304 W 40th St (bet Eighth and Ninth Ave)
695-4897, 714-2712
Mon-Fri: 10:30-6:30; Sat: 11-5

For some reason, the sleazy Times Square area has always had backdated-periodical shops, even before the ubiquitous porno dives. A&S, one of the best, is a source of back issues of nearly every possible periodical. The more respectable the magazine, the better the possibility of finding it. Prices for what was originally very cheap but is now hard to find are reasonable, though they often surprise people who once threw out the very issue they now seek. A&S specializes in cinema, sports, and fashion magazines. You can avoid the neighborhood altogether and shop by mail or phone.

HOTALINGS NEWS AGENCY
142 W 42nd St   840-1868
Mon-Fri: 7:30 a.m.-9 p.m.; Sat, Sun: 7:30 a.m.-8 p.m.

As every homesick out-of-towner should know, hometown newspapers can be picked up at Hotalings for the regular price, plus the cost of transportation. Domestic and foreign newspapers are sold on the day of issue (or soon thereafter), and many non-natives keep in daily contact with their homes through these papers. However, as many a Hollywood movie will attest, Hotalings also carries back issues (thereby enabling the hero to learn that his adversary has ceased to exist months ago, so he can return home). Back issues are erratic at best, and the days of sending the secretary out for the papers from Peoria for the past six months probably never existed, but there is still a pretty ample selection here.

Occult

MAGICKAL CHILDE
35 W 19th St (at Fifth Ave)   242-7182
Mon-Sat: 11-8; Sun: 12-6

I asked the proprietor, Herman Slater, how one could describe this incredible place to readers of a book on New York. He answered that his shop was an "occult emporium," and I guess that is the best formal description. You have to see this place to believe it; there is nothing else quite like it in New York. There are shelves and bins of quartz crystals, gemstones, books, ritual accessories, videos, herbs and oils, powders and incense, curios and tarot cards, jewelry, and just about anything else that fits the occult image. The aisles are filled with readers and lookers, and they are just about as fascinating as the merchandise. Oh, yes, there are skulls, too.

Optical

GRUEN OPTIKA CORPORATION
1225 Lexington Ave (bet 82nd and 83rd St)   628-2493
599 Lexington Ave (bet 52nd and 53rd St)   688-3580
1076 Third Ave (bet 63rd and 64th St)   751-6177

GRUEN OPTIKA WEST
2382 Broadway (at 88th St)   724-0850

Mon-Fri: 9:30-6:30; Sat: 9:30-4:30; open Sun on
    West Side: 12-5

Gruen boasts the same faces and personal quality care year after year. The firm enjoys a reputation for excellent service, be it emergency fittings or one-day turnaround, and there's a super selection of specialty eyewear. Their sunglasses, theater glasses, sport spectacles, and party eyewear are particularly noteworthy. The atmosphere is summed up by the continuous music and availability of Dom Perignon and caviar. It's plain to see that these people care.

MORGENTHAL-FREDERICS OPTICIANS
685 Madison Ave (bet 61st and 62nd St)   838-3090
Mon-Fri: 9-6; Sat: 10:30-4:30 (closed Sat, July and Aug)

If you are looking for state-of-the-art creative and elegant eyewear, this is the place. Owner Richard Morgenthal, a very knowledgeable and helpful gentleman, is on the job himself. He features his own designs, manufactured in Europe and created in-house. As an added service, they will make appointments with some of New York's best-known ophthalmologists. The fact that they have been in business in the city for eight decades says something about the caliber of their products and service.

PILDES
111 Nassau St   227-9893, 800/427-4564
Mon-Fri: 8-6; Sat: 8:30-3:30

1010 Third Ave (at 60th St)   421-1322
Mon-Wed, Fri: 9-7; Thurs: 9-7:30; Sat: 10-6; Sun: 12-5
(closed Sun in summer)

Pildes is the only "while-you-wait" eyeglass chain in New York, and it has an impeccable reputation. Nothing fancy here, just frames, styles, and service, and all are first-class.

Photographic Equipment and Supplies

ALKIT CAMERA SHOP
866 Third Ave (bet 52nd and 53rd St)   832-2101
222 Park Ave S (at 18th St)   674-1555

Mon-Fri: 8:30-6:30; Sat: 9-5

If you're professional enough to want to go where the photographers of the Elite and Ford modeling agencies go, Alkit is the shop for you. But come here even if you haven't the faintest idea which end of a camera to look into. Most establishments that deal with the real pros have little time for rank amateurs. Not so here. Nothing gives Edward Buchbinder, the store's owner, more pleasure than introducing the world of photography to a neophyte. And few stores are better equipped to do so. Alkit maintains a full line of cameras, film, and equipment, as well as stereos, TVs, VCRs, and electronics, and they have a one-hour professional processing lab on premises. The shop repairs and rents photographic equipment, and it also maintains a professional catalog of preferences for and gripes about particular models. The attitude is always briskly professional. Buchbinder hastens to point out that the stereo and TV line is not an extraneous frill: many of his best customers find it essential to work with one or both playing in the background.

BIG APPLE CAMERA AND SOUND
178 Church St   791-5869
Mon-Sat: 9-6; Sun: 11-5

Big Apple specializes in selling the best cameras, Walkmans, telephones, home stereo equipment, and the handiest beepers at the best prices. They are not averse to phone or mail inquiries; they will even quote prices over the phone. Equipment stocked by Big Apple represents all of the major names, and the staff will instruct customers on the merits of each of them. And now for the best part: tell the folks you read about them in Gerry's *Where to . . .* and you'll get a special discount!

CARLYLE CAMERA CORP.
971 Madison Ave (at 76th St)   535-2800
Mon-Fri: 9-6; Sat: 10-5

With camera stores going in and out of business with regularity (particularly on Fifth Avenue), it is comforting to find an establishment that has been in the business since 1956. Carlyle has a large selection of cameras, films, albums, portable stereos, and frames. The personnel know what they are talking about and can be of great professional help to we amateurs who just want to "aim the camera and shoot."

47th STREET PHOTO
67 W 47th St   398-1410

115 W 45th St (bet Sixth Ave and Broadway)
398-1410

116 Nassau St   608-8080

38 E 19th St   398-1410

Mon-Thurs: 9-6; Fri: 9-1:45; Sun: 10-4

Before shopping here, be sure to check the Sunday *New York Times* ads. You will find some great prices on cameras and photographic equipment, FAX machines, computers, phones, video items, CD and cassette players, and sunglasses. Don't try to call the stores, as the phones are always busy. Note that they are not open on Saturdays.

NEWMAN PHOTOGRAPHICS
400 Lafayette St (at 4th St)   505-1840
Mon-Fri: 9-5:30 (evenings and weekends by appointment)

Whether you are a professional or an amateur, Newman can take care of your photographic needs. They do excellent work producing Cibachrome prints, all of them exhibition quality. The nice part is that they are patient and understanding with those of us who need counseling and advice. They are not professional retouchers, but they can spot and make minor changes. Lamination and print-mounting service is available on premises.

WILLOUGHBY'S CAMERA STORE
110 W 32nd St (bet Sixth and Seventh Ave)   564-1600
Mon-Wed, Fri: 9-7; Thurs: 9-8; Sat: 9-7; Sun: 10-6

This is the largest camera shop in the world, boasting a huge stock, extensive clientele, and a good reputation. Willoughby's can handle almost any kind of camera order. For those in doubt, there is always the mail-order division. Write and ask for something really esoteric; Willoughby's can probably fill it without a problem. In addition to selling all kinds of cameras, Willoughby's also services them, supplies photographic equipment, and recycles used cameras. This is truly a photographic emporium *plus*. A large new computer division has been added, in addition to electronics and copiers.

Pictures, Posters, Prints

ARGOSY BOOK STORE
116 E 59th St   753-4455
Mon-Fri: 9-6; Sat: 10-5; closed Sat in summer

Ostensibly, the main stock in trade here is books (the older and rarer, the better), but knowledgeable browsers usually pass the books by in favor of the antique maps and prints. There is an excellent collection of Early American paintings and prints (Currier and Ives, among others) and a combination of maps and prints that makes a marvelous background. In fact, if a bookstore could be classified as a decorating accessory store, Argosy would qualify. The books are valued as much for their appearance and bindings as for their age and rarity, and maps and prints are similarly rated. Argosy handles first editions and Americana garnered from estate sales, and they will buy books from private sources. The specialties are antique prints, maps, autographs, and, surprisingly, medical books. The personnel seem very impressed with their own knowledge and position, so some customers feel intimidated here. Too bad. Otherwise, it's a great place to browse and shop.

JERRY OHLINGER'S MOVIE
MATERIAL STORE
242 W 14th St   989-0869
Daily: 1-7:45 p.m.

Do you need a *Bonnie and Clyde* poster for the den? Or the *Empire Strikes Back* for the boss's office? Jerry Ohlinger has a huge selection of movie and television posters and photographs, and he will gladly provide a catalog to help with the selection.

OLD PRINT SHOP
150 Lexington Ave (bet 29th and 30th St)
686-2111, 683-3950
Mon-Sat: 9-4:30; closed Sat in summer

Strolling down Lexington Avenue and glancing at the Old Print Shop, one might think that time was suspended in the nineteenth century. Established in 1898, the shop exudes an old-fashioned charm that makes it appear timeless, and its stock only reinforces that impression. Kenneth M. Newman specializes in Americana. That includes original prints, paintings, town views, Currier and Ives prints, and original maps that reflect America as it used to be. Most of the nostalgic bicentennial pictures that adorned calendars and stationery were copies of prints found here. Historians, amateur and professional, have a field day in this shop, often purchasing things that simply strike their fancy and have nothing to do with their original request. Kenneth Newman also does custom framing—"Correct period framing," he hastens to add—and prints in his frames are striking. Everything bought and sold here is original. (Newman also purchases estates and single items.) A great place.

POSTER AMERICA
138 W 18th St (bet Sixth and Seventh Ave)   206-0499
Tues-Fri: 11-7; Sat, Sun: 12-5

You've never seen a poster gallery more interesting than this one! Jack Banning's store features original posters circa 1870 to 1950, nearly all of which are lithographs. But ah, the setting! For ten years, he ran Poster America, the oldest gallery in the country devoted to vintage poster art. When that gallery on Ninth Avenue proved too small, he found and renovated a former stable and carriage house that used to serve the department stores on Ladies Mile in the 1880s. These new quarters sport a magnificent mahogany-and-glass storefront, a huge, well-appointed gallery, and elegant living quarters for Banning. Poster America is known for the brilliant graphics and sheer magnitude of its pieces. It is also the exclusive agent for California designer David Lance Goines.

TRITON GALLERY
   323 W 45th St (bet Eighth and Ninth Ave)   765-2472
   Mon-Sat: 10-6

Theater posters are the show here, and Triton presents them like no one else. The complete list of current Broadway posters is but a small part of what's available, and it's balanced by an almost equally complete range of older show posters from here and abroad. Show cards are a standard 14″ × 22″ size and seem to be the most readily available items. Posters range in size from 23″ × 46″ to 42″ × 84″ and are priced according to rarity, age, and demand. None of these criteria, incidentally, has much to do with the actual success of the show. Often, hundreds of posters were printed for shows that lasted less than a week and no one has a use for. At the same time, a hit like *Annie* has produced more posters than anyone could use, so its show cards cost no more than some of the totally obscure ones. The collection is not limited to Broadway or even American plays, and some of the more interesting pieces are of plays from other times. Triton also does custom-framing, and much of the business is done via mail and phone orders. Ask for Triton's catalog.

Plastics

PLASTIC PLACE
   309 Canal St (bet Mercer St and Broadway)   226-2010
   Mon-Fri: 8:30-5; Sat: 8:30-3:30

This large loft is dedicated to plastics, both the Lucite and soft plastic variety. Primarily wholesalers, they will cut anything from cubes to wall coverings free of charge. Their line includes waterproofing material, Lucite cubes, and sheets of plastic. They are particularly accommodating to do-it-yourself customers.

PLEXI-CRAFT QUALITY PRODUCTS
   514 W 24th St.   924-3244
   Mon-Fri: 9:30-5; Sat: 11-4

Plexi-Craft offers anything made of Lucite® and Plexiglas® at wholesale prices. If you can't find what you want among the pedestals, tables, chairs, shelves, and cubes, they will make it for you. The personnel are extremely helpful in pointing out the various styles in cocktail tables, shelves, magazine racks, and chairs.

Religious Arts

GRAND STERLING SILVER COMPANY
345 Grand St (bet Essex and Ludlow St)   674-6450
Sun-Thurs: 10:30-5:30

Ring the bell, and you will be admitted to a stunning collection of silver religious art. You'll also find almost anything from silver toothpick holders to baroque candelabras over six feet tall. Grand Sterling will also repair and resilver any silver item, be it religious or secular. They are manufacturers and importers of fine sterling holloware, and silver is revered with a dedication unmatched elsewhere.

HOLY LAND ART COMPANY
160 Chambers St (bet W Broadway and Greenwich St)
962-2130
Mon-Thurs: 9-4:30; Fri: 9-4; Sat: 9-2 (bet Thanksgiving
   and Christmas)

Across the street from Cheese of All Nations, there's another world at Holy Land Art Company. The store offers all kinds of religious articles to churches and the public. On hand is everything from Bibles to altars, although the latter, along with custom-made statues of wood, bronze, and marble, are usually special-ordered by churches rather than individuals. In December, Holy Land is anything but pastoral, as customers snap up crèches, nativity scenes, and chalices. There's a tremendous selection, and the prices are reasonable. The company says that its work for churches is evenly divided between new buildings and refurbishing or reconstruction.

Rubber Goods

CANAL RUBBER SUPPLY COMPANY
329 Canal St (at Greene St)   226-7339
Mon-Fri: 9-5; Sat: 9-4:30

"If it's made of rubber, we have it" is this company's motto, and that sums up the supply at this wholesale-retail operation. There are foam mattresses, bolsters, cushions, pads, pillow foam, pads cut to size, hydraulic hoses, rubber tubing, ventilation, vacuum hoses, and sheet rubber products of various kinds. And there is much, much more. They are right. If it's made of rubber, Canal Rubber Supply has it.

Screens

TONEE CORPORATION
108 Wooster St   966-4213
Mon-Fri: 9-5; Sat: 10-4

The lovely screens that slide back and forth between rooms and between house and garden in Oriental settings are usually Shoji screens, and the genuine article is seldom available outside of Asia. Some years ago, however, the natural connection between light, free-standing space dividers and studios, lofts, and even offices dawned on some Japanese merchants, and this outpost of Japanese construction came to SoHo, an area where it was especially needed. Though this is one of the few Shoji outlets anywhere—and may be the only one manned by authentic native craftsmen—Tonee is not limited solely to Shoji screens. For example, the Fusuma screen is also available. The screens are defined by use, size, style, and material. An expert such as Tonee is the perfect person to guide a customer through the maze of screens, tatami mats, and general construction that the company offers.

Security Devices

CCS COUNTER SPY SHOPPE
675 Third Ave (at 42nd St)   557-3040
Mon-Fri: 9-5:30 by appointment

Fascinated by James Bond and all of his gadgets? You'll marvel at this shop, which supplies security items for business and private use. There are covert video systems, night-vision equipment, de-bugging devices, FAX scramblers, voice-stress analyzers, and bulletproof cars. They even have bulletproof T-shirts! These people are the best in the business, and they advertise themselves as the only anti-terrorist boutique in Manhattan. Appointments are a must, and confidential demonstrations and security consultations can be arranged.

EMPIRE SAFE COMPANY
433 Canal St (at Varick St)   226-2255
Mon-Fri: 9-5; Sat: 10-3; closed Sat in July, Aug

Things have been safe around here since 1904! The same family has been in the business for three generations, and now they have the largest showroom of safes in the country. You can find vaults and safes for homes, offices, and restaurants. A great exhibit of an-tique and art deco safes is well worth seeing. Empire also services all makes of safes.

Signs

CRYPTOGRAPHICS
40 E 32nd St   685-3377
Mon-Fri: 9-5

This is a handy service place to know about. They offer a complete service for signs, awards, advertising specialties, executive gifts, bulletin boards, and directories. Customized merchandise for businesses, organizations, and individuals is done quickly and accurately with engraving and silk-screening facilities on the premises.

LET THERE BE NEON CITY
38 White St   226-4883
Mon-Fri: 8:30-6; Sat by appointment

Though the image of neon is modern, it harks back to Georges Claudes' capturing of it (from oxygen) in 1915. And while "the flashing neon sign" is perhaps the ultimate urban cliché, Rudi Stern has turned the neon light into a modern art form. So, Let There Be Neon operates as a gallery. At any given moment, there is an assemblage of sizes, shapes, functions, and designs to entice the browser. Though they all have a common neon base (with a transformer in the base), that is all they have in common. Almost all of Let There Be Neon's sales are custom-made, commissioned pieces. Stern claims that even a rough sketch is enough for them to create a figurative (literal or abstract) sculpture within days. Each project is proof that neon is a versatile art form. There's a glow about the place!

Silver

EASTERN SILVER COMPANY
54 Canal St (2nd floor)   226-5708
Sun-Thurs: 9:30-5; Fri: 9:30-1 (showroom closed Fri)

Ascend to the second floor, ring the bell, and you enter a wonderland of silver, from floor to ceiling. Not all of it is clean or polished, but it has the potential of becoming as beautiful as only silver can be. The stock includes virtually any product made of silver or pewter, and the amazing thing is that Robert Gelbstein seems to be able to put his hand on any desired item almost immediately. Eastern has a large collection of Jewish ceremonial silver and secular silver items, such as candlesticks and wine decanters. However, most of the collection would be perfect gracing any home. Prices are extremely reasonable, and the quality is A-1. This place is a real find.

JEAN'S SILVERSMITHS
16 W 45th St (at Fifth Ave)   575-0723
Mon-Thurs: 9:15-4:45; Fri: 9:15-3:45

Having a problem replacing a fork that accidentally went into the garbage disposal? No worry. Proceed directly to Jean's, where you will find over 1,000 discontinued, obsolete, and current flatware patterns. They specialize in antique and secondhand silver, gold, and diamond jewelry and watches.

ROGERS AND ROSENTHAL
22 W 48th St (Room 1102)   827-0115
Mon-Fri: 10-3

Rogers and Rosenthal are two big names in the elegant place-setting business, and while this store claims that it is just a coincidence and that *their* Rogers and Rosenthal are merely the founders' names, the shop's title is an excellent sign of what is inside. Rogers and Rosenthal has to be one of the very best places in the city, if not *the* best, for silver, china, and crystal. A visit to verify this statement isn't necessary, since nearly all their business is done by mail. ("Very slow delivery," they warn!) This shop features every major brand name, and a 25 percent discount on every piece by mail is an added bonus. They will send price lists upon request, and what isn't in stock will be ordered. They are very accommodating.

TIFFANY AND COMPANY
727 Fifth Ave (at 57th St)   755-8000
Mon-Sat: 10-5:30

What can you say about a store that's such an institution it has appeared in plays, movies, books, and even slogans? Almost nothing, except that the store really isn't *that* formidable or forbidding, and it can even be an exciting place to shop. For the curious, let's begin by stating that, yes, there really is a Tiffany Diamond, and it can be readily viewed on the first floor. That floor also houses the watches and jewelry departments, and while browsing is welcome, salespeople are quick to approach lingering customers. The second floor houses clocks, silver jewelry, sterling silver, flatware, bar accessories, centerpieces, leather accessories, stationery, scarves, and knickknack gifts. The third floor highlights china and crystal. The real surprise—and a fact not known to many New Yorkers—is that Tiffany has an excellent selection of reasonably priced items. Many come emblazoned with the Tiffany name, wrapped in the famed Tiffany blue box, and at prices less than those of some neighborhood variety stores.

Sporting Goods

Art

CROSSROADS OF SPORT
36 W 44th St (bet Fifth and Sixth Ave)   764-8877
Mon-Fri: 10-5

Crossroads here seems to refer to intersecting country lanes, and the store's personnel are quick to tell you that sports to them is decidedly not team sports. In addition to an admirable collection of books, artwork, prints, and paintings relating to the store's definition of sports, there is also a variety of tankards, serving pieces, and tableware decorated with sporting motifs. Many of the books are collector's items, as is the artwork (note particularly the eighteenth-century prints). Crossroads is a primary source for appraisals and purchase of sporting art, and they are accomplished enough to trace and find any item they don't have in stock. If there's a bit of country gentleman in you, stop by. It's the closest thing to a hunt club you'll find in the city.

Bicycles and Accessories

BICYCLE RENAISSANCE
491 Amsterdam Ave (at 84th St)   724-2350
Mon-Sat: 10-7; Sun: 10-5; summer: 10-7 daily

Biking here is a way of life, just as health foods are to most of the staff. Services include the custom building of bikes. Their mechanics aim for same-day service on all makes and models. As for brands—well, they are all here, with an accent on racing and mountain bikes. In stock are specialized Trek, Giant, and Cannondale, and custom frames for Stronglight, Campagnolo, Ideale, and many others. I appreciate the fact that this was the only bike shop that did not pretend to have discount rates. And, in fact, its prices were exactly on par with the so-called discount stores.

GENE'S DISCOUNTED BICYCLES
242 E 79th St (at Second Ave)   288-0739
Mon-Fri: 9:30-8; Sat, Sun: 9-7

This is *the* bike shop in New York. Gene's features children's bikes, racing bikes, tour bikes, fat-tire bikes, and BMX bikes—all made by leading manufacturers from around the world. Names like specialized Raleigh and Peugeot are represented in quantity, and all kinds of accessories are available. Gene will repair or rent any kind of bike, and now he offers a big selection of exercise equipment, including aerobic bikes, treadmills, and home gyms. He also guarantees that he'll meet or beat any competitor's price. The service is good, the personnel knowledgeable, and the selection tremendous.

STUYVESANT BIKE SHOP
349 W 14th St   254-5200
Mon-Fri: 9:30-6:30; Sat: 10-6; Sun: 12-5

When a customer comes into his shop, Salvatore Corso and his crew take time to find out what he or she really wants. Stuyvesant features a large selection of mountain bikes, models for off-road cycling, and all the new city bikes that are so hot and trendy. They cater not only to professionals, but to family riders as well. A great deal of their business is in road cycling and sport touring. A large clothing and shoe department has been added, with merchandise from Italy as well as top American manufacturers. Corso will store bikes over the winter months, and he will take care of most repairs within 24 hours from his large stock of spare parts.

Billiard Equipment

BLATT BILLIARD
809 Broadway (bet 11th and 12th St)   674-8855
Mon-Fri: 9-6; Sat: 10-4; closed Sat in summer

Blatt is outfitted from top to bottom with everything for billiards. You also get friendly pointers from a staff that seems, at first glance, to be all business.

Darts

DARTS UNLIMITED
30 E 20th St (bet Park Ave S and Broadway)   533-8684
Tues-Fri: 12-5:30; Sat: 11-4

Most towns have sporting goods shops, but few have even a department (or display) for darts. In New York, things are different. There's Darts Unlimited, an emporium dedicated solely to darts and darting equipment. The collection of darts, dartboards, accessories, and English darting equipment (England's pubs are where it all started, you know) makes you wonder why they are not more prominent in other sports stores. Indeed, it seems that darts is a neglected game in America. Which is a shame, since it's good not only for exercise but for channeling aggression!

Diving

RICHARDS
233 W 42nd St (bet Seventh and Eighth Ave)   947-5018
Mon-Sat: 9-7:30

Aside from being near the Port Authority bus terminal, there's nothing positive that can be said about the neighborhood, but much can be said about Richards' stock. The store calls itself an aqua-lung and skin-diving center, but there's also all kinds of sporting goods, clothing, and cameras. The clothes are of the army/navy surplus variety. And in keeping with the low rent (and lowlife) of the area, everything in the store is discounted. They claim to be the largest diving shop in the country.

Exercise Equipment

THE GYM SOURCE
45 E 51st St (bet Park and Madison Ave)   688-4222
Mon-Fri: 9-6; Sat: 10-5 (closed Sat in July and Aug)

This is the largest exercise equipment dealer in the Northeast. They carry treadmills, bikes, rowers, and more. They will rent equipment or provide a visitor with an item to be used in a hotel room while in Manhattan. President Bush has used their products. Maybe his example will help you get into that suit that seems to have shrunk around the waistline.

Fishing Equipment

CAPITOL FISHING TACKLE COMPANY
218 W 23rd St (Chelsea Hotel, nr Seventh Ave) 929-6132
Mon-Fri: 8-5:30; Sat: 9-4

Historical records show that over 100 years ago, the 42nd Street Library and the adjacent Bryant Park were once a cemetery and later a reservoir—an indication of just how distinct and countrified was their location in relationship to the rest of the city. In 1897, when Capitol Fishing Tackle Company was established, its present location would have justified a store dedicated to fishing. Today, in the hustle and bustle of Chelsea, the store is totally incongruous and yet it is typical of New York. Where else would one find a fishing store so totally landlocked that a subway roars beneath it, yet one that offers bargains unmatched at seaport stores? Capitol features a complete range of fishing tackle with such brand names as Penn, Shimano, Tycoon Finnor, Garcia, and Daiwa at the lowest possible prices. There is a constantly changing selection of specials and closeouts that can only be described as fantastic. All of it is achieved by Capitol's buying up surplus inventories, bankrupt dealers, and liquidations. Almost nothing in the store was purchased at full wholesale, and those savings are passed on to the customer.

Game Equipment

V. LORIA AND SONS
178 Bowery (bet Kenmare and Spring St)   925-0300
Mon-Fri: 11-6; Sat: 11-4; closed Sat in summer

This family business, established in 1912, is a mecca for indoor sports enthusiasts. One can find a complete line of equipment. There are bowling and billiard items, pool tables and such supplies as cues and chalk, plaques, and awards—not to mention ping-pong equipment and poker tables. When the family champion is triumphant, the winner's trophy can be ordered from Loria as well. It is impossible *not* to try out some of the equipment right on the premises, and Vernon and Roger Loria don't seem to mind.

General

EASTERN MOUNTAIN SPORTS (EMS)
20 W 61st St (bet Broadway and Columbus Ave)
397-4860

611 Broadway (at Houston St)   505-9860

Mon-Fri: 10-8; Sat: 10-6; Sun: 12-6

Eastern Mountain Sports started in Wellesley, Massachusetts, at the height of the backpacking craze. Despite its geographic origins, there's a natural connection with New York, which is cold (weatherwise, of course), and the residents are fanatics for anything that is compact and functional. What could be more functional than thermal clothing that fits in a pocket? So, EMS' camping grounds in New York were an immediate success. In fact, it was so successful that it spawned a branch in SoHo, as well as in several suburban malls, and became the flagship store for a European conglomerate. It's the place to go for authentic outdoor clothing and gear (service, too), although prices can be bettered elsewhere. Still, for one-stop shopping, it's an excellent source and the merchandise is of better quality and price than that of the department stores. Incidentally,

EMS covers virtually *all* outdoor sports. That includes mountain climbing, backpacking, skiing, hiking, tenting, kayaking, and camping. And there's much more.

G&S SPORTING GOODS
43 Essex St (at Delancey St)   777-7590
Mon-Fri, Sun: 9:30-6

If you have a sports buff in the family and are looking for a place to buy him (or her) a birthday or Christmas gift, I'd recommend G&S. They have a large selection of sneakers, balls, gloves, toys and games, sports clothing, and accessory items any jock would like to receive. That isn't all the good news; the prices reflect a 20 to 25 percent discount. Brand names include Adidas, Puma, Converse, Nike, Reebok, Spaulding, New Balance, Wilson, Prince, Head, Avia, LA Gear, Champion, and Keds.

HERMAN'S
110 Nassau St   233-0733
Mon-Fri: 9-6; Sat: 9-5

135 W 42nd St   730-7400
Mon-Fri: 9:30-7; Sat: 9:30-6

39 W 34th St   279-8900
Mon-Fri: 9:30-7; Sat:
   9:30-6:30; Sun: 12-5

845 Third Ave (at 51st St)
688-4603
Mon-Fri: 9:30-7; Sat: 9:30-6

1185 Avenue of the Americas   944-6689
Mon-Fri: 10-7; Sat: 10-6

With only a moderate selection of women's and children's gear, Herman's is almost no *her* and almost all *man*. Long before the running and physical-fitness craze, this chain of sporting goods shops was set up to equip men for the enjoyment of sports, and the more macho, outdoorsy, or competitive the sport, the better. There are woodsmen's vests, plaid flannel shirts, and camping equipment, but there is more emphasis on clothing than equipment. As for price—in general, you can do better. But there is a sale every week on something, and those prices can be good. Add the convenience of a vast selection of equipment for all types of sports, and you know why the Herman's chain is growing.

PARAGON SPORTING GOODS
871 Broadway (at 18th St)   255-8036
Mon-Fri: 10-8; Sat: 10-7; Sun: 12-6

This is truly a sporting-goods department store, with over 80,000 square feet of specialty shops devoted to all kinds of sports equipment and apparel. There are separate departments for skis, team equipment, athletic footwear, skateboards, ice skates, racquet sports, aerobics, swimming, golf, hiking, camping, diving, biking, sailing, and whatever else you want to do in the great outdoors. There are also gift items, and the stock is arranged for easy shopping. It is a pleasure to shop in this vast wonderland of fun.

SPIEGEL'S
105 Nassau St (at Ann St)   227-8400
Mon-Fri: 9-6; Sat: 10-5; closed Sat in summer

You wouldn't expect to find a good, competent place to buy sporting goods in this neighborhood, but Spiegel's is here, and they would be top-notch in any location. The most advantageous point (aside from the lack of competition) is their discount prices, which are as good as those anywhere in the city. In addition, the selection is ample, the sales help excellent, and the supply amazing for a store of its size. Call first, and they will tell you if they have what you are looking for. They run advertisements in the *Times* for special items, and then their prices can't be beat.

Guns

JOHN JOVINO GUN SHOP
5 Centre Market Pl (at Grand St)   925-4881
Mon-Fri: 9-6; Sat: 8-1

These folks have been in business since 1911, and they are recognized as leaders in the field. They carry all major brands of handguns, rifles, shotguns, and accessories, including ammunition, holsters, bulletproof vests, knives and scopes. Major brands represented include Smith & Wesson, Colt, Ruger, Beretta, Browning, Remington, Walther, Glock, Winchester, and Sig Sauer. Jovino is an authorized warranty repair station for all the gun manufacturers, and they have two licensed gunsmiths on the premises.

Horseback-Riding Equipment

H. KAUFFMAN AND SONS
419 Park Ave S   684-6060
Mon-Sat: 9:30-6:30; Sun: 11-5

If you're into horses and horseback riding, Kauffman's is the place to seek out. Kauffman's handles the field so well that no one even stops to think that one of the world's finest equestrian supply shops is located in the midst of one of the world's largest cities (not to mention miles from the borough's only bridal paths). It is taken for granted that for the very best in riding equipment, Kauffman's is the place to go. This specialty store has literally everything for horse and rider. They even manage to sell a good amount of hay! In addition to saddles, bridles, and riding equipment, there is a good line of gifts for horse lovers. Ladies' side saddles, Kauffman told me, are about the only thing he doesn't stock. A catalog is published for $3. Being a horse fancier, I found this place a fascinating spot, and it is very well stocked.

MILLER'S
117 E 24th St   673-1400
Mon-Sat: 10-6 (Thurs: 10-7); Sun: 11-4

The Miller symbol (two boots) is displayed in hundreds of shops across North America that carry all or part of the exclusive Miller line. That line is so distinctive it covers a rider and his horse from head to hoof. Sizes suit men, women, children, stallions, mares, and colts. The haberdashery offers proper riding gear and saddles. (The Hermes saddles are registry numbered and go for $2,800 and up!) There are boots, helmets, riding shirts, plaques, and riding potpourri. That makes Miller's a good bet for those who have never ridden, as well as for the U.S. equestrian team. For horse lovers, this is a super place to find gifts for both horses and owners. The Sultan of Brunei was so impressed here he bought 40 T-shirts, six pairs of breeches, and two pairs of cowboy boots.

Marine

GOLDBERGS' MARINE
12 W 37th St (at Fifth Ave)   594-6065
Mon-Wed, Fri: 9:30-5:45; Thurs: 9:30-7:45;
   Sat: 9:30-3:45

Goldbergs' sells marine supplies as if it were situated in the middle of a New England seaport rather than in the heart of Manhattan. The staff looks like a ship's crew on leave in the Big Apple, and they are as knowledgeable as if that were the case. They carry marine electronics, sailboat fittings, big-game fishing tackle, lifesaving gear, ropes, anchors, compasses, clothing, clocks, barometers, and books. Many of those items—the ropes and compasses, for example—are of professional quality, and Goldbergs' is an excellent source for purchasing such items for dry-land purposes. Foul-weather suits are a star attraction, but there is also a line of clothes suitable for yacht owners. Landlubbers are treated kindly, since Goldbergs' realizes that some of the gear is purchased for other purposes. (The fishing line is used in many crafts; artists buy it by the yard.) They are even kinder to genuine marine people and weekend sailors.

HANS KLEPPER CORPORATION
35 Union Sq W (nr Broadway and 17th St)   243-3428
Mon-Fri: 9:30-5:30; Sat (April-Aug): 10-4

Hurry down to Union Square to get your own portable boat. That means folding kayaks, rigid kayaks, and even sailboats. In fact, Hans Klepper considers itself New York's portable boat center, and as compact as its products may be, this is not a small business. Klepper has expedition equipment, boating accessories, and more information than even the most avid enthusiast could absorb. Most remarkable, however, is that nearly all of the equipment is easily transported.

Outdoor Equipment

HUDSONS NEW YORK
97 Third Ave (bet 12th and 13th St)   473-7320
Mon-Thurs: 10-8; Fri, Sat: 10-7; Sun: 12-6

This family-owned emporium has been in the same location for more than 70 years. They offer a huge selection of classic American clothing and accessories for town and country living. The lower level features camping and outdoor gear. Someone described the store as "a sort of new-age rough-wear emporium." A store catalog features 100 pages describing what is available by mail order.

TENT AND TRAILS
21 Park Pl (bet Broadway and Church St)
227-1760 FAX: 212/267-0488
Mon-Wed, Fri, Sat: 9:30-6; Thurs: 9:30-7; Sun: 12-6

Whether it is for a weekend camper or an expedition to Mt. Everest, Tent and Trails is ready for the outfitting! In the canyons near City Hall (they are not nearly as beautiful as the canyon destinations of this outfit's customers), you will find a store exclusively devoted to camping, with help that is both experienced and knowledgeable. There are boots from Hi Tech, Nike and North Face, and camping gear from Lowe, Madden, Camp Trails, Moonstone, Jansport, Gregory Packs, Eureka Tent, Coleman, Moss Tent, and others. You'll find backpacks, sleeping bags, tents, down clothing, and much more. Tent and Trails rents camping equipment on a first-come, first-served basis.

Running

ATHLETIC STYLE
118 E 59th St (bet Park and Lexington Ave)   838-2564
Mon-Thurs: 10-6:30; Fri, Sat: 10-6

This was originally a running-shoe shop, because the owners were and are avid joggers. But the store has prospered and grown, and it is now one of the top outlets for sports clothing in terms of quality and attitude. One of the reasons is that owners Vic and Dave are always on the job. There is an expanded variety in footwear, including Reebok, Tiger, Nike, Topsider, and Avia. In clothing, you can find Russell Athletic, Speedo, and Hind. Adults and children will find a well-selected stock of clothing and accessories and an atmosphere conducive to fun shopping.

SUPER RUNNERS SHOP

1337 Lexington Ave   360 Amsterdam Ave
  (at 89th St)   369-6010   (at 77th St)   787-7665

1170 Third Ave (at 68th St)   416 Third Ave (at 29th St)
249-2133   213-4560

Mon-Wed, Fri: 10-7; Thurs: 10-9; Sat: 10-6; Sun: 1-5
  (Lexington store: 12-5)

Gary and Jane Muhrcke are runners, as is every member of their staff. And when they are *not* running, they are advising other runners at Super Runners Shop. The original store was located in Huntington, Long Island. Gary or Jane would grab a handful of shoes whenever they ventured into Manhattan and peddle them on the street to whoever ran by. Their reputation grew so fast that the handful became a van full, the street a permanent spot, and then a legitimate store, and ultimately branches of that store. Although their prices have risen with the move, they are still probably the most knowledgeable and reasonable athletic shoe store around. Unlike many such stores, they do not stock one brand exclusively. The staff of Super Runners Shop really believes that each person has to be fitted individually, both in terms of sizing and need. What's more, if a mistake in sizing is made, they will cheerfully correct it (although they claim such mistakes are few and far between). Super Runners Shop stocks men's and women's sizes (a few children's, too) and a full range of paraphernalia for devotees. In fact, they consider themselves a running-equipment source.

Skating

BLADES WEST

105 W 72nd St (at Columbus Ave)   787-3911
Summer: Mon-Fri: 12-9; Sat: 10-9; Sun: 10-6
Winter: Mon, Tues, Wed, Fri: 12-7:30; Thurs: 12-9;
  Sat: 10-7:30; Sun: 10-6

Everything for the skater can be found here! In-line skates (Rollerblades), ice skates, skateboards, and snowboards are available for rent and sale. You can even look the part by taking advantage of their skating apparel! Party rentals are a specialty.

PECK AND GOODIE
919 Eighth Ave (bet 54th and 55th St)   246-6123
Mon-Wed: 10-6; Thurs, Fri: 10-8; Sat: 10-6; Sun: 12-6

Skating is a popular means of summer transportation in Manhattan, so there are plenty of skate shops. But Peck and Goodie seems to have been in business forever, offering equipment and apparel to skaters who need the best with minimum fuss. Now, they are doing the same for the scores of people who have suddenly rediscovered skating. The store offers a complete stock of roller and ice skates, Rollerblades, skateboards, and accessories. Boots, blades, brackets, and braces are available, along with expert advice. And with faddish skates costing a hundred dollars a pair or more, it's wise to go to an expert.

Skiing

SCANDINAVIAN SKI SHOP
40 W 57th St (bet Fifth and Sixth Ave)   757-8524
Mon-Wed, Fri, Sat: 9-6; Thurs: 9-7

Despite its name, this shop is really an all-around sporting goods store with an emphasis on skiing and other winter sports. They have a full range of goods, from skis and skiwear to a complete department that offers repairs and ski advice, as well as outfitting. The shop has also developed a good reputation for serving other, decidedly non-Scandinavian sports as well. It is capable of outfitting its customers in tennis and hiking gear, as well as in skis, and its selection of competition swimwear rivals the namesake specialty. The store also carries exercise equipment.

Soccer

SOCCER SPORT SUPPLY COMPANY
1745 First Ave (bet 90th and 91st St)
427-6050, 800-223-1010
Mon-Fri: 10-6; Sat: 10-3

Max and Hermann Doss, the proprietors of this half century-old soccer and rugby supply company, operate as if they were located in merry old England instead of New York. And, indeed, they are international; half the business is involved in importing and exporting equipment around the world. Soccer Sport garners the finest rugby and soccer equipment available and ships it to its customers. Visitors to the store have the advantage of choosing from the entire selection, as well as having guidance from a staff that knows the field perfectly.

Tennis

MASON'S TENNIS MART
911 Seventh Ave (bet 57th and 58th St)   757-5374
Mon-Sat: 9-7; Sun: 10-4

This is a loyal family shop. It was supplying tennis paraphernalia long before the tennis craze hit, and it will probably continue to do so long after it has peaked. They outfit for tennis, stock for it, play it, etc. In fact, as owner Mark Mason puts it: "We have everything but the courts, and if real estate wasn't so high, we'd have that, too." They carry the clothing lines of these tennis designers: Ellesse, Fila, Maser, Nike, and Tacchini, a selection Mason claims is unrivaled anywhere. And once you're looking good on the court, Mason can supply rackets, ball machines, bags, and any other tennis paraphernalia you could possibly think of. They even offer a same-day stringing service for the unfortunates who didn't bring three or four rackets to the U.S. Open. Watch for their sales events!

Stationery

JAMIE OSTROW
1142 Madison Ave (bet 84th and 85th St)   734-8890
Mon-Fri: 11-7; Sat: 11-6

For contemporary personalized stationery and invitations, you can't do better than Jamie Ostrow. They design and manufacture their own items to the specifications of the individual customer. A good selection of boxed Christmas and holiday cards is shown, and personalized Christmas cards are a specialty.

JAM PAPER/HUDSON ENVELOPE
111 Third Ave (at 14th St)
473-6666, FAX: 212/473-7300
Mon-Fri: 8:30-7; Sat: 10-6

621 Sixth Ave (at 19th St)   255-4593
Mon-Fri: 8:30-6; Sat: 10-6

770 Second Ave (at 41st St)   986-6000
Mon-Fri: 9-6

These folks have become the largest single paper and envelope store in the city and, they say, perhaps the world! Stationery can be purchased from as little as 100 sheets of paper and 25 envelopes on up. Their inventory of paper stocks is about half recycled merchandise. Over 150 different kinds of papers, with matching card stock and envelopes, are available. They also have a vast selection of presentation folders. Closeouts and discounted items provide excellent bargains at all times.

KATE'S PAPERIE
8 W 13th St (at Fifth Ave)   633-0570
Mon-Fri: 10-7; Sat: 10-6

Here you will find one of the largest selections of decorative and exotic papers in the country. Kate has papers of all kinds and descriptions, including papyrus, hand-marbled French paper, Japanese lace papers, handmade paste papers, and just about anything else you can think of in the paper classification. But that isn't all at this unique store. There are leatherbound albums and journals, classic and exotic stationery, and paper-related items like jewelry, crafts, boxes, and desk accessories. They will do custom printing and engraving, and personal or business embossing.

RITE STATIONERY
113 Ludlow St (at Delancey St)   477-0280, 477-1724
Sun-Fri: 9-5

Considering the company this shop is keeping, there should be a fence, hedge, or at the very least a warning separating Rite Stationery from its fellow stores in this category. While all these stores deal in paper and the accessories necessary for correspondence, a visit here is more inclined to make you put pen to paper for an angry letter of complaint than to invite friends for cocktails at eight. This is just about as far from Tiffany's and Fifth Avenue as you can get. This Lower East Side store's claim to fame is its proximity not to the Plaza Hotel, but to the Ludlow Street entrance to the Municipal Garage. So why, you ask, do we mention it? Because of its great prices and because it takes all kinds to create mail. And besides, there are many times when you really don't need formal engraved calling cards. They specialize in school supplies.

Tobacco and Accessories

BARCLAY-REX
7 Maiden Lane	70 E 42nd St (bet Madison
(nr Broadway)	and Park Ave)
962-3355	692-9680
Mon-Fri: 8-6	Mon-Fri: 8-6:30; Sat: 10-5:30

This is a tobacco connoisseur's shop, and a specialty tobacco shop at that. The specialty is pipes (cigars are an anathema and cigarettes more so), and third-generation owner Vincent Nastri knows the field inside out. His shop is prepared to create a pipe from scratch, fill it with any imaginable type of tobacco (including a good house brand), repair it if it should break, and offer all sorts of advice on proper pipe care and the blending of pipe tobacco. Nastri has a good reputation for prompt quality repairs and reasonable prices. If you have no sentimental attachment to the pipe, it might pay to buy a new irregular pipe that can be had for a surprisingly low price. As with most specialties, there are esoteric models available at astronomical prices. If you have upwards of $1,000 to send up in smoke, Nastri can come up with something really extraordinary.

CONNOISSEUR PIPE SHOP
1285 Ave of Americas (concourse level)   247-6054
Mon-Fri: 8-6

Edward Burak is essentially an artist. A pipe artist, that is. At his shop he has assembled a collection of hand-carved beauties that range in price from $27 to over $3,500. His store features natural unvarnished pipes, custom-made pipes, custom-blended tobacco, and expert repair of all kinds of pipes. Burak will also do appraisals for insurance purposes. Although you have to be careful these days *where* you smoke a pipe, if it comes from Connoisseur you'll probably get admiring glances from anyone who really knows quality.

INTERNATIONAL SMOKE SHOP
153 E 53rd St (Citicorp Center)   755-8339
Mon-Sat: 7-7

The Citicorp Center is one of the city's best tourist haunts, in part because its trilevel lobby is full of restaurants and other interesting shops that keep "tourist hours." Despite this (and despite an intense campaign to make the shopping area a mecca for browsing), the area can seem cold and impersonal. So even if it had no other virtues, Citicorp's International Smoke Shop would be noteworthy as a friendly oasis in a frigid zone. True to its name, the store stocks all kinds of tobacco and tobacco paraphernalia. But it also carries books, magazines (including foreign publications), gifts, Lotto tickets, New York souvenirs, and imported chocolate.

J. R. TOBACCO
11 E 45th St (at Madison Ave)   983-4160
Mon-Fri: 7:45-5:45; Sat: 9-3:45

219 Broadway (at Vesey St)   233-6620
Mon-Fri: 7:45-5

1410 Broadway (bet 38th and 39th St)   921-9360
Mon-Fri: 7:45-6

For years, Lew Rothman has claimed that he offers the world's largest selection of cigars at the world's lowest prices. Now that cigar smoking isn't quite as popular as it used to be, he has diversified into the fragrance business, offering discount prices on most major fragrance lines. The cigars come in over 3,000 different brands, and the fragrances in over 50 top names. Prices are 20 to 50 percent off regular retail.

PIPEWORKS & WILKE
16 W 55th St   956-4820
Mon-Fri: 9-5:45; Sat: 9:30-5

Elliott Nachwalter started creating briar pipes in Stowe, Vermont, more than a decade ago. He then moved to New York and established Pipeworks as the outlet for his exclusive handmade, custom-designed pipes. Nachwalter can create a pipe from a customer's design, as well as his own. Only Grecian Plateux briar is used for each pipe, and each goes through a 130-step process between design and the finished product. Once a pipe is in hand, customers can return to Pipeworks for custom tobacco blends, antique pipes, and repairs. Chances are that it won't be a Pipeworks pipe that needs repair. Each is guaranteed for five years for most parts, and Nachwalter says they are created to last a lifetime. There is also a great assortment of antique pipes.

Toys, Trains

BIG CITY KITE COMPANY
1201 Lexington Ave (at 82nd St)   472-2623
Mon-Wed, Fri, Sat: 10-6; Thurs: 10-7;
   Sun (seasonally): 12-6

Of course you would expect New York to have a store dedicated totally to kites, and of course it is a great one. David Klein sells kites for people's houses: mobiles and wall hangings. He sells custom-made specialty kites and brilliantly colored fighter kites made of tissue paper. He also has a kite-repair service. Prices begin at about $2 and go as high as $300. The lack of fanatacism and the presence of genuine devotion is most evident in the community programs that Big City sponsors. There are kite festivals, kite exhibitions, even "kite-ins." They have now added a full line of dartboards, darts, and dart accessories for recreational and competitive throwers.

B. SHACKMAN AND COMPANY
85 Fifth Ave (at 16th St)   989-5162
Mon-Fri: 9-5; Sat: 10-4

In the midst of the wholesale toy district, B. Shackman has been playing house since 1898. But their play is a very serious business devoted to the manufacturing, importing, and sale of toys, novelties, and miniatures. Though a large portion of their business is still on the wholesale level, it is obviously run by people who enjoy what they are doing. They are willing to take time to share their vocation with amateurs and single retail customers. This is one of the few such firms in the area to do so. Shackman carries a full line of aforementioned specialties. However, the items of interest to retail customers are their miniatures and a striking collection of Victoriana. Again, this is not at all in keeping with its neighbors, but Shackman excels in Victorian post cards, Christmas tree decorations, old-fashioned greeting cards, and children's books. There are also Steiff toys, lead hand-painted soldiers, antique dolls, contemporary stuffed toys, and paper dolls.

BURLINGTON ANTIQUE TOYS
1082 Madison Ave (at 82nd St)   861-9708
Tues-Sat: 12-6 and by appointment; closed Sat in summer
Anyone who has been to the Forbes Gallery knows that toy soldiers are not just for children. Anyone who has been to Burlington Antique Toys has undoubtedly discovered that this is definitely not kid's stuff. The toy soldiers are antiques, as is virtually everything else in the store. That roll call includes toy cars, airplanes, boats, and other tin toys. There is a new "used car" lot specializing in out-of-production, die-cast car models. Best of all, Burlington proves that not only fabulously rich men can play with toy soldiers or float their own armadas. This is a place for everyone. And the folks here couldn't be nicer.

CLASSIC TOYS
69 Thompson St (bet Spring and Broome St)   941-9129
Wed-Sun: noon-6:30
You can tell in a minute when the owner of a business is in love with his operation. This is surely true at Classic Toys, where pieces that have passed through the hands of several generations of kids are still in fine shape and are awaiting new owners. Traditional toys, die-cast vehicles, stuffed toys, playroom toys, Christmas figures and more, both old and new, are available in this SoHo operation. The folks here try to stock playthings based on real situations, rather than fantasies. Come to think about it, isn't that a much healthier approach for our kids?

DOLLHOUSE ANTICS
1343 Madison Ave (at 94th St)   876-2288
Mon-Fri: 11-5:30; Sat: 11-5
The expanded Dollhouse Antics is straight out of childhood dreams. Their official claim is that they are a shop dedicated to miniatures, but the shop is run more like a playroom, and either of the two owners always seems to be ready to join in the games. But

dollhouse-making is serious business here. Ever hear of custom-made dollhouses? Or mouse houses? The most popular orders are for replicas of ancestral homes, and you can bet your made-to-order miniature needlepoint rug that these dollhouses aren't made for eager little children. Dollhouses come in kit form, but when money is no object (or if the fun of assembling it yourself wanes), the store will put it together for you. But be wary: like real houses, these models need to be furnished. If you can afford the scaled-down Oriental rugs, custom upholstery, special wallpaper, lumber, electrical supplies, and made-to-order furniture, you'll eventually want to redecorate the whole house.

ENCHANTED FOREST
85 Mercer St (bet Spring and Broome St)   925-6677
Mon-Sat: 11-7; Sun: 11-6

The Enchanted Forest is one of the very few shops that physically and philosophically matches its name. The husband-and-wife team of owners, David Wallace and Peggy Sloane, hired theatrical set designer Matthew Jacobs to create an enchanted-forest backdrop for a collection of toys, whimsies, and artwork. The announced intention of the shop was that it would be a "gallery of beasts, books, and handmade toys celebrating the spirit of the animals, the old stories, and the child within" with an emphasis on *gallery*. One can enter a crystal cave that transforms into an old wooden wardrobe, through which one passes into a small Victorian room. Other featured items include a fine selection of fairy tales, mythologies, children's stories, and various eclectic gems. This is truly an enchanted place.

F.A.O. SCHWARZ
767 Fifth Ave (bet 58th and 59th St)   644-9400
Mon-Wed, Fri, Sat: 10-6; Thurs: 10-8; Sun: 12-6

Long-time readers of this book will remember that I was not very gentle with F.A.O. Schwarz in previous editions. I was unhappy with the service and lack of sales supervision. Well, this prestigious, world-famous toy store has since moved to new and larger quarters in the General Motors building, across the street from the old store. The result is a distinct improvement in appearance and service. Schwarz is the "cutting edge" of the toy business, and toy manufacturers are just as eager to get their new items in this store as ready-to-wear manufacturers are to see their goods at Bloomingdale's. The new store has two floors, arranged into small shops that specialize in stuffed animals, bears, games, electronics, dolls, and all the other gadgets you'd expect to find in a first-rate toy emporium. Thank goodness there seems to be a new regime of sales help; they attentively follow you around the store as you pick out gifts for the kids (and for yourself). If you're in a hurry but want to get Susie and Sam a little something, you can stop at a special counter right at the door and pick up an already wrapped present. Now if they would just get some supermarket carts to help you shop, I might take back all those nasty things I once said. Anyway, I have to confess that I have always been a rather loyal Schwarz customer. After all, their catalog was one of the first things I was able to read. Hmmm, that goes back a few years!

MANHATTAN DOLL HOUSE
176 Ninth Ave (at 21st St)   989-5220
Mon-Fri: 11-6; Sat: 10-5

Time marches on, and sadly some of New York's most talented folks are no longer with us. Jenny Grunewald, who handled the doll hospital part of this operation, has passed away, so now her son-in-law Edwin Jacobowitz operates the Manhattan Doll House. It boasts the city's largest collection of dolls (including Madame Alexander), doll houses, and doll paraphernalia. Jenny's husband, Herman, still comes in the shop from time to time, so you could have the pleasure of visiting with him. He can create a castlelike home for the new princess you might purchase for your grandchild!

MINT & BOXED
1124 Madison Ave (at 84th St)   794-4000
Mon-Sat: 10-6

There is a bit of nostalgia in most of us when it comes to memories of childhood toys. Mint & Boxed has a superior collection of vintage trucks, trains, tin toys, and the like that will recall exciting moments from Christmas mornings past. But that is where the fun ends. Shopping here is like touring the U.S. Mint, only without the courteous people who man that public operation. The noses here are so high, and the snobbish "by appointment only" atmosphere so unfriendly, I have a feeling those great toys are not going to find many happy homes. Prices? Don't ask!

RED CABOOSE
16 W 45th St (bet Fifth and Sixth Ave, 4th floor)
575-0155
Mon-Fri: 10-7; Sat: 10-5:30

At the Red Caboose, owner-operator Allan T. Spitz will tell you that 99 percent of his customers are not wide-eyed children but sharp-eyed adults who are dead serious about model railroads. Since these are the people Spitz serves, it is difficult for a Christmas-morning engineer to adequately describe his stock, but I'll try. The Red Caboose claims to have 100,000 items in stock. That includes a line of 300 hand-finished, imported brass locomotives *alone*. That doesn't begin to cover the tracks or track gauges available. (Spitz claims that the five basic sizes—1:22, 1:48, 1:87,

1:161, and 1:220, in a ratio of scale to life size—will allow a model railroader to build layouts sized to fit into a desk drawer or a basement.) The store also carries the city's largest model-ship selection, and HO and N gauge equipment. If there is a model-train district, it is located on the upper floors of the buildings on this block. For that reason, Spitz offers a 20 percent discount on purchases over $10 (on most lines).

TOY BALLOON
204 E 38th St   682-3803
Mon-Fri: 9-5:30

I wandered in here by accident, but you'll want to wander in on purpose. This is a serious adult business. Balloons are dealt with in exactly the same manner that any business would deal with its product, but how *can* one be serious when the product is balloons? The Toy Balloon tries. Balloons are sold individually or in multitudes of up to 50,000. Types are so varied that there are graduations in diameter, thickness, style, and type (including Mylar balloons). Sizes range from peewees to blimps, while shapes include dolls, rabbit heads, hearts, dachshunds (a personal favorite; they're often used to advertise hot dogs), and extra-elongated shapes. Most of the business is done for advertising campaigns, and the Toy Balloon will make up and sell personalized logos, styles, or two-colored messages. This specialty store also sells complete kits and everything the balloons require.

TOYS 'R' US
1293 Broadway (Herald Center, at 33rd St)   594-8697
Mon, Fri: 9-9; Tues, Wed, Sat: 9-8;
Thurs: 9 a.m.-9:30 p.m.; Sun: 10-6

This is the "big one" in the toy business! With over a million toys in stock, and a location right in the heart of the city, this place is a zoo—as you might expect! If you're looking for ambiance and an easy-to-shop-in store, this is surely not it, as the aisles are crowded and there is not the excitement of an F.A.O. Schwarz. However, if selection and price are your main interests, you can't do better. The adjoining Kids 'R' Us does the same for clothing.

TRAIN SHOP
23 W 45th St (basement)   730-0409
Mon-Fri: 10-6; Sat: 10-5

The second major resident of model-train row, this shop differs from its fellow traveler only by its basement location and its insistence that it has *no* specialty. It merely stocks everything. The Train Shop's manager (engineer?) is Paul Schulhaus, who is about as knowledgeable as they come. He sums up the stock by saying,

"Look around. If you need help, just give us a holler." Now isn't that just the way they'd do it at the local station? To name *some* specifics, the shop claims to have at least 30,000 different model pieces in stock. What is not in stock can be ordered, but they do not maintain their own catalog. (They accept phone and mail orders.) *Walther's Catalog* includes the Train Shop and lists the unique items they have. (One favorite is a train engine, complete with its own realistic sound system.) But the stock can in no way be described. It is simply incredible and an awful lot of fun! Prices are competitive with the store's neighbors, and where else would you find two such shops within hollering distance of each other?

Travel Goods

THE CIVILIZED TRAVELLER
1072 Third Ave (bet 63rd and 64th St)   758-8305
Mon-Sat: 10-7; Sun: 12-6

If you are like me and are on the go a great deal of the time, this is an important store to visit. Under one roof one can choose from a selection of unique and hard-to-find travel items like personal grooming pieces, pocket tailors, shoe kits, water purifiers, packable rainwear and slippers, travel-size games, special travel alarm clocks, world time calculators, automatic language translators (some even talk), doorknob burglar alarms, highway tool kits, atlases and guides, workout kits, and even portable showers. There is a special section for meeting the travel needs of kids and pets, and you may even be able to pick up a copy of New York's number one guidebook. A "Civilized Traveller Club" provides interesting information for members and sponsors a number of special activities relating to travel.

Typewriters

CENTRAL TYPEWRITER AND
APPLIANCE COMPANY
42 E 33rd St   686-0930
Mon-Fri: 9-7; Sat, Sun: 10-5

In this age of word processors and computers, some people still use the trusty old typewriter. Central is the name for those folks to remember. They wholesale, retail, repair, rent, and sell all kinds of typewriters and business machines. Now they have added computers, cellular phones, car stereos, home audio, televisions, and video equipment to their stock. Central has been known for years for their excellent selection, fine service record, and best of all, reasonable prices.

TYTELL TYPEWRITER COMPANY
116 Fulton St (bet William and Nassau St, 2nd floor)
233-5333
Daily: 10:30-4 by appointment

Detective story readers know that a typewriter's keys are as individual as fingerprints, and in New York Martin and Pearl Tytell have made a name for themselves by identifying typefaces. Today, the so-called "questioned document" service has become a major operation that requires the full-time expertise of Pearl and the Tytell's son, Peter. Martin devotes his time to running the typewriter sales and repair business, with rentals on the side. They have also become a rehabilitation center for old and antique typewriters. With a 62-year-old collection of typewriters and typewriter parts, they can restore virtually any machine. Tytell's is also the United Nations, the Smithsonian, and the Elaine's of the typewriter business. They have in stock type changes required for 145 languages, as well as IBM Selectric elements for all the languages IBM had calls for during the years they were manufacturing the Selectric typewriter. If you're in a hurry, he's farsighted enough to have made up foreign-language typewriters for emergencies. In addition to typewriters for every language, he can make up keys of corporate logos, six-pitch double-case type (good for teleprompter reading), phonetic alphabets, stencil cutting, and jumbo type. There are over 2 million pieces of type in stock, as well as typewriters so old they're rented by movie studios for props. Tytell's list of clients reads like a who's who of typewriter users.

Variety, Novelty

ABRACADABRA
10 Christopher St   627-5745
Mon-Sat: 12-8; Sun: 12-6 (special seasonal holiday
      hours)

Does that stuffy boss of yours need a whoopie cushion placed on his chair? Do you need a Lincoln beard for the church play? How about an exploding toilet or a set of Frankenstein hands? This place has it all; it bills itself as the great American masquerade, gag, gift, and gadget shop. They carry a full line of magic items, costumes for rent or purchase, theatrical makeup, and all the things to make your entrance memorable. There are even "menus" listing all of their items in specific categories, like horror, gags and jokes, magic, and costumes.

BARGAIN SPOT
64 Third Ave (at 11th St)   674-1188
Mon-Sat: 8:30-5

In one of Cynthia Freeman's books, the heroine makes her money by starting out in a pawnshop. The Bargain Spot also started in a pawnshop, but in this case, it's the consumer who makes the money. Established in 1909, the Bargain Spot is also known worldwide as the Unredeemed Pledge Sales Company, and that name says it all. If something has been pledged and left, the Bargain Spot will purchase and resell it. But the heyday of pawnshops in New York is long gone, so no one could rely on that angle alone for business. Today, the company uses its base of pawnshop spoils to buy, rent, sell, and exchange a tremendous variety of items. The clientele is hard to believe (my office didn't believe it included me!), but all of them are obviously smart shoppers who know great bargains when they see them. At this aptly named shop, it's possible to buy everything from diamonds to typewriters to antiques. If you call first, they will happily tell you what is in stock. Cynthia Freeman's protagonist isn't the only one to know a fortune can be made in pawnshop redemptions.

COME AGAIN
353 E 53rd St (at First Ave)   308-9394
Mon-Fri: 11-8:30; Sat: 11-6:30

Come Again? Yes, you have it right. This book contains something for everyone's taste! Come Again is a one-stop shopping center for all your sexual needs. There are vibrators, bondage equipment, exotic lingerie for men and women, adult books, oils and lotions, gift baskets, party gifts and favors. Now they boast the first of its kind: an X-rated shop-at-home adult toy and lingerie video catalog. They claim it "combines an hour's hot entertainment with the convenience of shopping at home." If the entertainment gets too hot, you can always turn it off and return to reading this book. Bet it doesn't have quite the same sizzle!

EVE'S GARDEN
119 W 57th St (4th floor)
757-8651, FAX: 212/977-4306
Mon-Sat: 12-6:30

One of the real pleasures of the "New York Is Book Country" fairs each September on Fifth Avenue is the opportunity to meet and exchange views with readers and business folk who are, or who would like to be, featured in this book. During one of these fairs, Dell Williams, who runs Eve's Garden, suggested I visit her unusual emporium. The descriptive line in her literature is "We grow pleasurable things for women." Well, you get the picture. It may not be a must-see place on your shopping list, but after all, this is a book designed for every type of reader, and some will find a unique selection of merchandise at this liberated garden. Dell claims her items are featured with "sex-positive experiences in mind."

HOME TO HARLEM
1 W 125th St (bet Fifth Ave and Malcolm X Blvd
  [Lenox Ave])   831-7367
Tues-Sat: 10-7; Sun: 1-5

Kevin McGruder has parlayed his hobby (the study of Harlem history) into a unique business. In his shop you will find souvenirs and educational items celebrating Harlem's history (post cards, pictures, books, etc.). In addition, McGruder offers lectures and readings on topics related to Harlem history, and he will conduct walking tours for groups from 4 to 30 in size if arrangements are made at least two weeks in advance.

JOB LOT TRADING COMPANY— THE PUSHCART
140 Church St   962-4142   80 Nassau St   619-6868
Mon-Sat: 8-6   Mon-Fri: 7:45-6:15

After only a day in New York, even the most casual visitor becomes aware of black-and-white paper bags (depicting jam-packed pushcarts) being carried around by all sorts of New Yorkers. Close examination would reveal that these bags all emanate from Job Lot Trading. Job Lot and the Pushcart were originally two separate stores that were dislocated by the World Trade Center. Of those original residents, only a few survived, and none survived as spectacularly as these two stores, which merged (on different floors of the same store), took over a building, and week after week offered some of the best bargains in the city. Job Lot carries an odd number of consignments that are unsalable through normal retail channels for one reason or another. Absolutely everything is sold below wholesale. The stock changes constantly, so some people make weekly shopping trips. There is no telling what will turn up.

JUNGLE FEVER
A&S Plaza
901 Sixth Ave (bet 32nd and 33rd St, 7th floor) 947-3956
Mon, Thurs, Fri: 9:45-8:30; Tues, Wed, Sat: 9:45-6:45;
  Sun: 11-6

The only thing missing here is Tarzan himself! This store features merchandise from and about the jungles of the world. Leopards, toucans, elephants, and lions leap out from T-shirts, and stuffed

monkeys and gorillas hang overhead from bamboo rods. Tropical
jewelry, straw bags, and hats are packed next to Rainforest crunch
and animal mugs and posters. Many items sport a World Wildlife
Fund sticker, which means that organization receives a portion of
the proceeds from the manufacturer.

ODD JOB TRADING
7 E 40th St (bet Fifth and Madison Ave)   686-6825

66 W 48th St (bet Fifth and Sixth Ave)   575-0477

149 W 32nd St (bet Sixth and Seventh Ave)
   564-7370

10 Cortland St   571-0959

Mon-Fri: 8-5:50; Sun: 10-5

Another of the jobbers in the wake of Job Lot, Odd Job has been
around for a while and seems to consistently come up with good
buys on quality merchandise. What differentiates Odd Job from
the other half-dozen stores of its type is that its quality merchandise
is more *au courant*. You never know what is going to turn up here;
it can be anything from book racks to perfume, but it's always interesting. It's also the perfect place for gifts for the folks back
home, where they'll never know how little they cost unless you tell.
Odd Job is perhaps the most aggressive of the closeout stores. They
are expanding rapidly and now have the reputation of being the
best of its kind.

ROMANO
628 W 45th St (entrance on 12th Ave)   581-4248
Mon-Fri: 8-5; Sat: 8-4

Nomenclature is a problem here. Romano goes under at least two
other names: Paris-Rome and Rome Outlet. Not terribly well-
known to New Yorkers, it is as patronized by visitors (especially
foreign visitors) as the airports. Perhaps the various names came
about from the confusion of customers seeking it out in dozens of
languages. What do they know that natives don't? Simply that this
part of town—best known for redeeming impounded cars and
boarding the Circle Line tour boat—operates like a miniature Hong
Kong. The only ships to speak of are the aforementioned Circle
Line and cruise ships, but the neighborhood seems to think that
crewmen and ship stevedores are docking every day with money to
spend for gifts back home. So, the stock is a hodgepodge of American—distinctly American—culture. Luggage, watches, Ray-Ban
sunglasses, bath towels, pens, cordless phones, electronic games,
designer scarves and umbrellas, tennis rackets, china, and small

electric appliances are all in stock at excellent discount prices. There has to be a good reason for landlubbers to come all the way over here. Nothing is sold at list price, and many of the items (watches in particular) are sold at the best prices in town.

SOHO EMPORIUM
375 W Broadway (bet Spring and Broome St)   966-7895
Mon-Fri: 12-8; Sat, Sun: 11-8

Shopping here is a fun experience that can also be a serious venture. The SoHo Emporium is a consortium of individual shops selling an eclectic mixture of clothing, accessories, antique and contemporary jewelry, new and old artifacts, and gifts. A visit here will indeed brighten your spirits and give proof that innovation is still an important part of the American dream.

STAR MAGIC
743 Broadway (bet 8th St and Astor Pl)
228-7770

275 Amsterdam Ave (at 73rd St)
769-2020

1256 Lexington Ave (bet 84th and 85th St)
988-0300

Mon-Sat: 10-10; Sun: 11-8

Step through Star Magic's door, and you step through a time warp into the future. For Star Magic—from its midnight-black ceiling with suspended galactic spheres to its spacecraft-like walls—is designed to make a visitor forget contemporary New York and enter into a timeless universe. The setting is inducement enough to pay a visit. Star Magic's theme is "Yesterday's magic is today's science," and that perhaps is the only way to describe the eclectic selection that owners Shlomo Ayal and Justin Moreau call space-age gifts. There are toys (in this case, literally for children of all ages) with a scientific bent and scientific items strictly for fun. There are books specifically chosen for their ability to make a reader "ponder the cosmos." Star Magic offers minerals and prisms, scientific instruments to explore the universe, high-tech toys, and new-age music that is positively futuristic. Over and out.

THINK BIG
390 W Broadway (bet Spring and Broome St)   925-7300

313 Columbus Ave   769-0909
Daily: 11-6

If you are one of those *big* thinkers, then this is the ideal place for you to shop. In this unique store, you'll find larger-than-life architect's lamps, toothbrushes (57″), erasers, desk calendars, paper clips, crayons, toy chests, baseball bats (66″), soccer balls, and even a 7″ (in diameter) aspirin. If they don't have your own big idea in stock, tell them your desire and they might have it made especially for you and other customers.

Videotapes

PALMER VIDEO STORE
470 Hudson St   463-9377
Daily: 10 a.m.-midnight

The nice thing about this store is that you are able to see all the titles easily; they are displayed in a neat and orderly way. This store carries popular titles, as well as unusual ones. There is a membership plan, a discount for frequent users, reservation privileges, many titles for sale, and no deposit required for members.

VIDEO ACCESS
2617 Broadway (at 99th St)   316-6666

2821 Broadway (at 109th St)   749-3900

Open seven days a week, hours vary by store
(open late weekends)

Video Access offers over 8,000 of the latest movies for sale or rent, and you can visit them every day of the year. They will transfer foreign tape formats to the standard used in this country. They rent and repair camcorders, VCRs, and TVs, and sell a full range of accessories and prerecorded movies at reasonable prices.

Visually Impaired Helps

LIGHTHOUSE SHOPPING
& INFORMATION CENTER
111 E 59th St (bet Park and Lexington Ave)
355-2200 (ext. 1801)
Mon-Fri: 9:30-5

This is a wonderful place for the visually impaired! In this store, blind folks can browse, touch and feel merchandise before they buy. Over 200 articles are carried, including reading and writing supplies, talking articles (talking clocks are a great item), and cassette players and recorders. An especially nice gift is the Old or New Testament on tape in a self-locking, dustproof cover, narrated by J. Bridges Dugan.

Wall Coverings

PEARL PAINT COMPANY
308 Canal St (at Broadway) 431-7932
Mon-Sat: 9-5:30; Thurs: 9-7; Sun: 11-4:45

With ten floors and more than a hundred clerks on duty at all times, Pearl claims to be the world's largest art and graphics discount center. Who can disagree? Besides these ten floors of fine-arts discounts, Pearl has another building at 42 Lispenard Street (226-3717), which is an art-furniture showroom. Pearl's new first-floor entrance opens onto a jam-packed store divided into specialty sections of all kinds. Pearl is the kind of place where house painters shop next to batik craftsmen, and moldings and castings are sold beside materials for etchings and silk screenings. Pearl's personnel are also very friendly, which is quite rare for a professional supply house.

PINTCHIK
278 Third Ave (at 22nd St) 982-6600, 777-3030
Mon-Fri: 8:30-7; Sat: 9-6; Sun: 11-5

Discount wallpaper shops are few and far between in Manhattan, despite its reputation as the discount center of the world. But Pintchik is one such source. They discount paint and wall coverings, as well as the supplies that go with them. Two of the better wall coverings they carry are Laura Ashley and Marimeko patterns—by coincidence, two manufacturers with large stores in Manhattan. Nonetheless, Pintchik can always beat even the manufacturer's prices, except during the rare clearance sales at the previously named stores. An advantage (besides price) is that unlike the fabric stores (and basically that is Laura Ashley's and Marimeko's trading card), Pintchik's staff is well-versed in the city's painting and wall-covering needs. They are very good at coming up with solutions to problem walls (and there probably isn't an apartment in the city without a problem wall), as well as making accommodations to city living. Needless to say, white backgrounds don't go over very well with city soot.

SHELIA'S WALLSTYLES
DECORATING CENTER
274 Grand St (bet Eldridge and Forsyth St) 966-1663
Sun-Thurs: 9:30-5; Fri: 9:30-2

Grand Street is a strange place for a wallpaper store, since those locals who are into wall decorating almost universally use the paint-pattern-on-paint school of design. But Shelia opened her shop about a decade ago, and it proved so successful that she now has imitators. And why not? She took her cue from the retail motif of the Lower East Side, selling everything at a good discount. And then she located her store on a block that is quickly becoming a mecca for fashion and budget-conscious home decorators. The result is the very best in wall coverings, fabrics, drapes, bedspreads, vertical and horizontal blinds, shades, and coordinated accessories. Those who want a tissue box to match the boudoir can find it at Shelia's—and at a discount, to boot.

Watches

Don't be taken by the watch peddlers who tackle you along Fifth Avenue, near Bloomies, and on side streets in midtown. Most of the pieces they are selling are fake, and you have no recourse if there are problems. For reliable watches (and service), here are the best:

Aaron Faber Gallery (vintage) 666 Fifth Ave, at 53rd St)
Aaron M. Jewelers (526 Seventh Ave, at 38th St)
Cartier (653 Fifth Ave, at 52nd St)
Fortunoff (681 Fifth Ave, at 54th St)
Jerry Grant's (276 Columbus Ave, at 73rd St)
Stanley & Son (1006 Ave of the Americas, at 37th St)
Tourneau (500 Madison Ave, at 52nd St; and 635 Madison Ave, at 59th St)

WHAT ARE THE DIMENSIONS OF MANHATTAN ISLAND?

Manhattan is 13.4 miles long, 2.3 miles across at its widest point, and 22.5 square miles in area.

VII. Where to "Extras"

Auctions

There are basically two kinds of auction action in New York. The first is the very proper and formal auction house. Most of these are quite well known and make the papers when they record sensational sales. The second kind is the surplus auction, be it governmental or private. Of late we're experiencing a third kind: real-estate auctions. While New York City has auctioned off surplus land (usually sliver-sized odd lots) for years, private developers are now unloading condos, co-ops, and foreclosures the same way. A word of warning: Auctions are attended by professional buyers. You won't beat them. The best you can expect to do is to top their wholesale price, which will still be less than retail. Check the *New York Times* antique pages on Fridays and Saturdays for announcements of upcoming auctions.

CHRISTIE'S
502 Park Ave (at 59th St)   546-1000

Today there may be only a few big auction houses in New York, but ten years ago there were none. Much like their prices, the city's auction scene has its highs and lows. Look for antiques, art, books, coins and numismatics, clocks and timepieces, furniture, photographs, and porcelain art and sculpture here. The American touch (from a British house) is seen in the almost weekly auctions of Americana. Christie's also offers an "Auctiontalk" series (same phone number) on shopping at auctions. They are informative, entertaining, and free!

CHRISTIE'S EAST
219 E 67th St   606-0400

Christie's East is the junior branch of Christie's. It sells anything of value that "would not pass the clientele at the big Christie's," says the lady at the reception desk. We're still talking about big names and bigger bucks, but the prices, styles, and collections are somewhat more whimsical. Look for pop art and collections of toys, stamps, paintings, and folk art.

SOTHEBY PARKE BERNET
1334 York Ave (at 72nd St)   606-7000

As the other major hitter on the scene, Sotheby holds the really grand sales and males headlines with record-setting bids and no-sales. If you have time for only one auction, come here and watch a master deal with the old masters. If it is very, very valuable, then Sotheby handles it. The Sotheby Arcade, in the same building, holds a couple of auctions a week (depending upon the market) for more affordable antiques and artwork. Sotheby is open as a gallery even when there is no immediate auction. It's an experience you shouldn't miss.

WILLIAM DOYLE GALLERIES
175 E 87th St (bet Lexington and Third Ave)
427-2730

This is the local talent on the auction scene. It is American-owned and -oriented, and the sales reflect that fact. The merchandise is often from estate collections of books, jewelry, artwork (including sculpture), and furniture.

As the seat of regional government and a major port, New York City is the site of many auctions designed to clear warehouses. Lots range from 400 Korean human-hair wigs (from a customs auction) to Wallace sterling silver for 12 (the post office). Despite the wide variety and types of merchandise, the rules are remarkably similar at all of them. First, there is usually no on-site viewing and only a few days or a week of prior notice. Very often the merchandise and auction are miles and even states apart. Again, professionals abound at these. If you can't match their bankrolls, at least there is consolation when you shop the jobbers and discount stores and see the same merchandise. You'll know where it came from and "how he does it."

Nearly every such action requires that you put down a deposit (in cash or certified check) to bid with a paddle or number. The account must be settled quickly when you make a successful bid or else it goes back on the block. Professionals establish a reserve beforehand. You probably can't do that, but your advantage is that they will usually ignore small or esoteric lots. And even if you get nothing, it is a lot of fun!

NEW YORK CITY DEPARTMENT OF GENERAL SERVICES
669-8546

They will answer the phone "surplus," but what is in surplus here is not brains, intelligence, or information. Some of the people who work at this office don't even know who they work for or where they are! (I was told to call 411 for this information.) They oversee the general auctioning off of vehicles and furniture excessed by the city about once every two weeks at the Brooklyn Navy Yard. Commercial real estate (obtained through foreclosures for taxes) is auctioned off about every two months at 1 Police Plaza. Most of the lots are vacant, commercially zoned lots located throughout the city.

NEW YORK CITY PARKING VIOLATIONS BUREAU
791-1450

One of the hazards, sports, and dangers of life in the city is having a car towed for a parking infraction. Well over 10,000 cars get towed every year. Those who do not redeem their cars lose them forever in a short period of time. A surprising number of "good" cars are put up for auction. (To redeem a towed car, you must settle outstanding fines at once.) If you're in a tow-away zone and don't care, odds are it's not your first offense. Sometimes it's cheaper to buy a new car. All cars are sold "as is" at weekday auctions at one of three sites—Pier 50 (20th St), Pier 26 (6th St), and the 203rd Street yard. Exactly what is up for auction on a given day is printed in the *New York Times* classified pages. Viewing begins only an hour before the eleven a.m. auction, which precludes detailed inspection under the hoods. Sometimes there *is* nothing under the hood! And sometimes you can chance upon a real steal—legally, of course.

NEW YORK CITY POLICE DEPARTMENT AUCTION
Property Clerk Division
1 Police Plaza (bet Chambers and Centre St)
406-1369 (recording), 374-5905

The city should take a leaf from the auction notebook of the police department. These people know how to run things in an orderly way and give out helpful information. Several times a year the police department holds auctions that are, depending upon your point of view, exhilarating or depressing. The merchandise that's auctioned off is all recovered contraband that couldn't be returned to its rightful owners. Giving New York's finest credit, assume that half of all stolen goods is returned. What one inspects at the auction viewing (usually held the day before the auction) is a fraction of what is stolen annually. The selection will boggle the mind. Wheelchairs, car seats, radios, toilet seats, bicycles, and furniture are represented in the hundreds. There are enough vehicles to have a separate auction devoted solely to that category. Auctions are usually held on Tuesday at 1 Police Plaza. Viewing is usually in Queens; it is an absolute requirement for bidding during the auction. The department also publishes notices the weekend before the auction in the *New York Daily News* and the *New York Times* and has the most informative tape I've heard.

POST OFFICE AUCTION
General Post Office
380 W 33rd St   330-2931

If you have time for only one auction, this is it! The Post Office auction is huge and a lot of fun. Auctions are usually held once a month, with viewings scheduled from 8-10:30 a.m. the day of the auction. Pickup is the day after sale. Don't attend the auction if you haven't been to the viewing, as everything is sold in lots that are poorly identified in the catalog. "Lot 75—books" could be 43 volumes of *Snow White* in Korean or a complete set of encyclopedias. (Actually, there is a separate auction for printed matter.) You may write ahead, but nowadays they will only furnish information about upcoming auctions. Phoning is better.

Churches and Synagogues of Note

Abyssinian Baptist Church (132 W 138th St, nr Lenox Ave) The oldest black church in the city and the largest place of worship for blacks in the country.

Central Synagogue (E 55th St and Lexington Ave) The city's oldest Jewish (Reform) synagogue still in use.

Grace Church (E 10th St and Broadway) A Renwick masterpiece, especially worth seeing for its Gothic revival architecture.

Holy Trinity Greek Orthodox Cathedral (319 E 74th St, bet First and Second Ave) You might think you're in ancient Greece when you visit this architectural masterpiece.

Marble Collegiate Church (W 29th St and Fifth Ave) Dr. Norman Vincent Peale made this one famous.

New York Islamic Center Mosque (E 96th St and Third Ave) A new and lavish addition to the city's religious landscape.

Riverside Church (W 122nd St and Riverside Dr) John D. Rockefeller was responsible for this huge, 22-story edifice, which is a must for all to visit.

St. Bartholemew's Church (E 50th St and Park Ave) This midtown Episcopal Church, has been in the midst of a controversy over the use of its air space, a valuable commodity in New York real estate.

St. John the Divine Cathedral (W 112th St and Amsterdam Ave) One of the largest cathedrals in the world.

St. Nicholas Russian Orthodox Cathedral (15 E 97th St, bet Fifth and Madison Ave) Here you can see what Russian churches used to be like.

St. Patrick's Cathedral (E 50th St and Fifth Ave) Probably the best-known church in the city, another work of architect James Renwick.

St. Peter's Lutheran (E 54th St and Lexington Ave) Cozily housed inside the towering Citicorp Center, it is a modern beauty.

Temple Emanu-El (E 65th St and Fifth Ave) A large, magnificent Jewish house of worship.

Trinity Church (Broadway and Wall St) A treasure trove for history buffs; the churchyard is not to be missed.

Cooling Off

Even in the midst of bustling Manhattan you can enjoy the tranquility of running water, both inside and out. Here are a few soothing sites:

Bankers Trust Plaza (Liberty and Greenwich St)
Crystal Pavilion (E 50th St, nr Third Ave)
Exxon Garden (1251 Sixth Ave, nr 49th St)
Grand Hyatt Hotel (42nd St, at Grand Central Station)
Greenacre Park (217 E 51st St, nr Second Ave)
McGraw Hill Plaza (1221 Sixth Ave, nr 48th St)
Olympic Tower (645 Fifth Ave, bet 51st and 52nd St)
Paley Park (E 53rd St, nr Fifth Ave)
Park Avenue Plaza (Park Ave, bet 52nd and 53rd St)
Tishman Building (666 Fifth Ave, nr 52nd St)
Trump Tower (725 Fifth Ave, nr 56th St)
Wall Street Plaza (88 Pine St)

Flea Markets

Annex Antiques Fair & Flea Market: Sixth Ave, from 24th and 26th St (243-5343). Sat, Sun: 9-5 (Mar-Dec). Probably the oldest and best.

Antique Flea & Farmer's Market: P.S. 183, E 67th St, bet First and York Ave (737-8888). Sat: 6-6.

Canal West Flea Market: 370 Canal St (718/693-8142). Sat, Sun: 7-6. Cheaper merchandise, lower prices.

Greenwich Village Flea Market: P.S. 41, Greenwich Ave at Charles St (752-8475). Sat: noon-7.

I.S. 44 Flea Market: Columbus Ave, bet 76th and 77th St (316-1088). Sun: 10-5:30.

Tower Market: Broadway, bet W 4th and Great Jones St (718/273-8702). Hours vary. Higher quality, funky, and crafty.

Walter's World Famous Union Square Shoppes: 873 Broadway, at 18th St (255-0175). Tues-Sat: 10-6. A number of independent dealers.

Yorkville Flea Market: 351 E 74th St (535-5235). Sat: 9-4 (closed in summer).

Some basic ground rules: Remember to take cash (credit cards sometimes don't work). Don't be hesitant about haggling. Be fair and decent with the merchants and that courtesy will be returned. Finally, plan to be around at the end of the day, when the dealer is packing up; he or she might well have lowered prices.

Japanese Visitor Hints

Accommodations at Hotel Kitano (66 Park Ave).

Books at N.Y. Kinokuniya (10 W 49th St).

Business meetings at the Nippon Club (115 E 57th St).

Designer clothes at Hanae Mori (27 E 79th St), Kenzo (824 Madison Ave), and Matsuda (156 Fifth Ave, at 20th St).

Gift items at Things Japanese (1109 Lexington Ave), Maki Fifth Avenue (575 Fifth Ave, at 47th St, 2nd floor), and Takashimaya (509 Fifth Ave, at 42nd St).

Hand tools at O-Zora (238 E 6th St).

Japanese screens, ceramics and sculptures at Naga Antiques (145 E 61st St).

Japanese-style breakfast at the following hotels: Edwardian Room, Plaza Hotel (Central Park South and Fifth Ave), Grand Hyatt (42nd St and Grand Central Station), Hotel Pierre (2 E 61st St) and Drake Hotel (440 Park Ave).

Kobe beef at Old Homestead (56 Ninth Ave).

Specialty Foods at Katagiri (224 E 59th St).

Sushi at Hatsuhana (237 Park Ave and 17 E 48th St).

Table pot cooking at Shinwa (Olympic Tower, E 51st St).

Tasty Japanese cuisine at Nippon (155 E 52nd St).

Tempura at Kitcho (22 W 46th St).

Miscellaneous Activities

Billiards

Billard Club: 220 W 19th St (206-7665)
Cafe Society: 10 E 21st St (529-8600)
Chelsea Billards: 54 W 21st St (989-0096)
Julian's Billiard Academy: 138 E 14th St (475-9338)
Tekk: 75 Christopher St (463-9282)

Miniature Car Racing

MANHATTAN RACEWAY
893 Broadway (bet 19th and 20th St)
1/800-852-RACE
Mon-Sat: noon-2 a.m.; Sun: 12-12

Here is special excitement for the miniature race-car enthusiast! Manhattan offers 32 lanes of racing on lazy L, American king, hill-climb, figure-eight, and drag-strip tracks. Youngsters and adults may rent cars and controllers or buy them at the counter. Folks here will repair and upgrade cars and allow the use of demo cars for test drive and rental. Portable tracks are offered for home use, refreshments are available on the premises, and birthday and private parties are encouraged. Fun is the name of the race here!

Miniature Golf

PUTTER'S PARADISE MINIATURE GOLF
48 W 21st St (bet Fifth and Sixth Ave)   727-7888
Wed, Thurs: 2-midnight; Fri: 5 p.m.-1 a.m.; Sat: noon-
    1 a.m.; Sun: noon-10 p.m.

This is a great place to come to amuse the kids, have a private party, or just do something out of the ordinary. Putter's Paradise is the only miniature golf course in Manhattan. It is an 18-hole layout, done in a tropical theme. Alligators, gorillas, and rotating bananas all present obstacles to the golfer's game.

Tennis Instruction

EVE ELLIS SCHOOL OF TENNIS/
EVE ELLIS CENTRAL PARK SPORTS
Central Park Tennis House
93rd/96th St and Central Park W (park entrance)
289-3133
April-Dec 1: 7 a.m.-dark

This is New York's only school of tennis, and it is handily located at the 30 tennis courts in Central Park. Tennis buffs can find tennis instruction, tournament information, 24-hour stringing, group lessons, plus a nice assortment of tennis apparel and shoes. Eve Ellis is a well-known tennis writer and personality, and she is accessible to those who attend the school.

Museums (see also "Museum and Library Shops" under "Where to Buy It")

ABIGAIL ADAMS SMITH MUSEUM
421 E 61st St   838-6878
Mon-Fri: 10-12 (group reservations only), 12-4 (all
    visitors); Sun: 1-5 (Sept-May); Tues: 5:30-8 p.m.
    (June, July); closed Aug

Constructed in 1799, the Abigail Adams Smith Museum is a historic building that originally served as a carriage house for a 23-acre East River estate planned by Colonel William Stephens Smith and his wife, Abigail Adams Smith, daughter of President John Adams. In 1826, the carriage house was converted into the Mount Vernon Hotel, a popular day resort. Today, this New York City landmark features Federal and Empire decorative arts in Greek revival interiors. As the only historic house museum in midtown Manhattan, the AASM offers guided tours of its nine-period room exhibitions and eighteenth-century garden, lectures, neighborhood walking tours, concerts, craft workshops, Christmas candlelight tours, and children's events. Call for current programs.

AMERICAN BIBLE SOCIETY
1865 Broadway (at 61st St)   408-1200
Mon-Fri: 9-5

This free gallery houses every kind of Bible from rare historic editions to at least one copy in every language known to man. In addition, they have a collection of current and interpretive Bibles and an ongoing exhibit on the Dead Sea Scrolls. Free guided tours are available on request.

AMERICAN CRAFT MUSEUM
40 W 53rd St   956-6047
Tues: 10-8; Wed-Sun: 10-5

Sponsored by the American Craft Council, this museum is just settling into its new, custom-made quarters opposite the Museum of Modern Art in a condominium building owned by CBS. A spiral staircase sports a free-floating canoe (I suppose they have a broad definition of *craft*), and many of the showcases and exhibits are objets d'art themselves. Several shows are mounted at the same time to display various aspects of American crafts. The time frame, perhaps in homage to its neighbor, is always modern, and the museum is more of a showcase than an archive. Even the "historical" aspect of the permanent collection brushes off the origins of contemporary crafts and starts its chronicle with crafts created after World War II.

AMERICAN MUSEUM OF NATURAL HISTORY
Central Park W at 79th St   769-5100
Sun-Thurs: 10-5:45; Fri, Sat: 10-8:45 (free Sat: 5-9)

This is the granddaddy of all the city's museums. A remnant from Theodore Roosevelt's era (in case you couldn't guess), it has something for everyone. To see everything from dinosaurs and an enormous suspended whale (the new favorite leviathan after the fall of the dinosaurs) to gems and minerals can take several days. The special shows and collections inspire visitors to return again and again. The Naturemax Theater's four-story-high screen is the largest in the city.

ASIA SOCIETY GALLERY
725 Park Ave (at 70th St)   288-6400
Tues-Sat: 11-6; Sun: noon-5

The foundation of the Asia Society's collection is John D. Rockefeller's Asian art collection. There are many changing exhibits on all aspects of Asian art, as well as cultural programs. Guided tours are given at 12:30 Tuesday through Saturday. And don't miss the gift shop!

AUNT LEN'S DOLL AND TOY MUSEUM
6 Hamilton Terrace (at W 141st St)   926-4172
Daily: by appointment

This one is a charmer. Aunt Len is Mrs. Leon Holder Hoyte, an octogenarian and former schoolteacher who shares her doll collection with the public. *Shares* isn't exactly the right word—Aunt Len makes a visitor to her townhouse on Hamilton Terrace feel like a member of the family when she shows off her collection of more than 5,000 dolls, from the Queen Anne era to the present. And her Harlem house is as charming as the dolls. There is a $2 admission fee, and Aunt Len doesn't receive visitors without an appointment.

BLACK FASHION MUSEUM
155 W 126th St   666-1320
Daily: noon-8 by appointment

Located in a renovated brownstone, this museum was founded in 1979 by Lois Alexander, who wrote her master's thesis on fashions designed by Afro-Americans. The museum's display guides visitors through 3,000 garments from the 1800s to the 1980s. A stitch-by-stitch duplicate of the gown worn by Mary Todd Lincoln at her husband's inaugural ball is here. The collection includes an authentic slave dress from Staunton, Virginia; the yellow dress Rosa Parks was making for her mother when she was arrested for refusing to give up her bus seat; and the costumes created for *Grind, The Wiz,* and other productions.

CARNEGIE HALL MUSEUM
154 W 57th St 903-9629
Tues-Sat: 11-4 (and at concert time)

This new addition to the famous showplace features a documentary history of Carnegie Hall and the studios that are a part of the landmark building. Approximately half of the space houses temporary exhibits related to music, musicians, and events that have taken place in this important house.

CENTER FOR AFRICAN ART
54 E 68th St (bet Park and Madison Ave) 861-1200
Tues-Fri: 10-5; Sat: 11-5; Sun: 12-5

Housed in adjoining townhouses, the Center for African Art covers traditional and contemporary art from Africa with two changing exhibits. The exhibits are augmented by films, slide shows, lectures, and artifacts.

CHILDREN'S MUSEUM OF MANHATTAN
212 W 83rd St 721-1234
Tues-Fri: 2-5; Sat, Sun: 10-5

This place has undergone several changes in name, location, administration, and emphasis. It is left with a somewhat befuddled image that has not been enhanced by major breakdowns and malfunctions. When founded in a storefront by Bette Korman, the basic idea was that there should be an interactive museum on the city's environment for city kids. From the beginning the emphasis was on programs and classes supplemental to school activities. The age level to which they are geared was never high, but now a bright seven-year-old would be bored. The reviews have been mixed. The Brainatarium, a multimedia walk through the brain, has never made waves. The hands-on media center and TV studio get higher marks, but they are very often preempted by school groups and preregistered classes. There are also art, music, dance, and theater classes and programs.

CHINA HOUSE GALLERY
125 E 65th St 744-8181
Mon-Sat: 10-5

China House Gallery is a museum operated by the China Institute, a nonpolitical, nonpartisan bicultural organization founded in

1926 by a group of American and Chinese educators. The gallery presents innovative exhibitions of Chinese art and artifacts, as well as educational exhibitions on the subject of China and its culture. China Institute also houses a school of Chinese studies, featuring painting, cooking, language, and calligraphy classes and workshops.

CITY GALLERY
2 Columbus Circle   974-1150

This white elephant of a building was originally the Huntington Hartford Museum. When it fell upon hard times, it was taken over by the city for the Department of Cultural Affairs and the Visitors and Convention Bureau. The space also serves as an exhibit area for the two groups. You might see the unveiling of a new map or a showcase for a new exhibit either group may be mounting. The gallery changes whenever there is something to show. Admission is free.

THE CLOISTERS MUSEUM
Fort Tryon Park   923-3700
Tues-Sun: 9:30-5:15 (March-Oct); 9:30-4:45 (Nov-Feb)

Situated on the northernmost tip of Manhattan Island, the Cloisters was brought over brick by brick from Europe and reconstructed from several monasteries on land donated by the Rockefellers. They also donated land to create the Palisades Interstate Park on the other side of the Hudson, so that the view from the Cloisters would always be pristine. This branch of the Metropolitan is devoted to medieval art and architecture, and the very building helps create the mood. Tuesday through Thursday there are group tours at three p.m., and throughout the year there are various festivals in period mode.

COOPER-HEWITT MUSEUM
Fifth Ave at 91st St   860-6868
Tues: 10-9; Wed, Sat: 10-5; Sun: noon-5

Quite recently, museum visitors have been given an opportunity to see the absolute best at Cooper-Hewitt, the Smithsonian Institution's National Museum of Design. Although the museum was founded 100 years ago as the Cooper Union Museum downtown, it only found its present identity with a move into Andrew Carnegie's Fifth Avenue mansion in 1975. Throughout its history, the museum has never had the space to show off even a minute part of its collection. Dianne H. Pilgrim, the museum's current director, saw the numbers on the bottom line and the handwriting on the wall. Her solution was to mount an exhibit based entirely upon the museum's permanent collection. The emphasis will be on contemporary design and social diversity; it won't all look like "the Astors take tea." Every department in the museum has had a hand in the exhibit, contributing items that have never been shown before. It almost makes one grateful for the budget crunch!

EL MUSEUM DEL BARRIO
1230 Fifth Ave   831-7272
Wed-Sun: 11-5

El Barrio is the local name for Spanish Harlem, the area above the Upper East Side and below Harlem (although I haven't heard the name used in a very long time). This is the only museum in the country that highlights the culture and art of Latin America. There are special programs, concerts, films, and classes, and the accent is Puerto Rican.

FORBES MAGAZINE GALLERIES
62 Fifth Ave   206-5548
Tues, Wed, Fri, Sat: 10-4

Malcolm Forbes was an eclectic collector of treasures and people. His funeral was attended by everyone from Elizabeth Taylor to Hell's Angels, and it stands to reason that his private collection would mirror the man. Housed on the first floor of the Forbes Building in a space he had custom-built in 1985, the Forbes Magazine Galleries were an outgrowth of his desire to share his prized possessions with the world. The star of the galleries is the world's largest collection of Fabergé Imperial Eggs. Each egg is valued at over $1 million. You might think the rest of the collection would pale by comparison, but it doesn't. Forbes was a man who could afford to fulfill his whims and share them with others. There are 500 toy boats (some are so incredible in detail they look seaworthy), 12,000 lead soldiers, and a roomful of 200 inscribed trophies commemorating the sublime and the ridiculous. Changing exhibits of paintings, photographs, American historical documents, and related memorabilia fill two additional galleries.

FRICK COLLECTION
1 E 70th St   288-0700
Tues-Sat: 10-6; Sun: 1-6

The Frick Collection is housed in the former home of Henry Clay Frick, whose interest was in art of the fourteenth century through the nineteenth century. Though absolutely unreceptive to children, the Frick offers help to any serious student of painting, sculpture, European antique furniture, enamel images, and European and Asian procelain. This is a quiet, romantic, serious place off the tourist trail. They also sponsor free concerts and lectures.

HAYDEN PLANETARIUM
81st St at Central Park W   769-5920
Skyshows: Mon-Fri: 1:30, 3:30; Sat: 11, 1, 2:15, 3:30,
    4:45; Sun: 1, 2:25, 3:30, 4:45 (Oct-June).
    Mon-Fri: 1:30, 2:30, 3:30; Sat, Sun: 1, 2, 3, 4
    (July-Sept)

An adjunct to the American Museum of Natural History, Hayden Planetarium is quasi-independent. The sky show, included in the cost of a ticket, is a classic that everyone should see at least once. The weekend double bills sell out quickly. Then there are two floors of space exhibits to explore. You can learn your weight on the Moon, and various planets, view lunar rocks, and so forth.

HISPANIC SOCIETY OF AMERICA
Broadway at 155th St   926-2234
Tues-Sat: 10-4:30; Sun: 1-4

There are four museums on a square that are collectively known as the Washington Heights Museum Group on Audubon Terrace. Of them, the Hispanic Society of America is clearly the star. (The Museum of the American Indian has been in the process of moving out for years.) It has a very impressive collection of decorative and fine arts of the Iberian Peninsula, from ancient to modern times. Goya, El Greco, Velazquez, Sorrolla, and Ribera are just a few of the painters represented.

INTERNATIONAL CENTER OF PHOTOGRAPHY
Fifth Ave at 94th St   860-1777
Tues: noon-8; Wed-Fri: noon-5; Sat, Sun: 11-6
    Free on Tuesday evening

1133 Sixth Ave at 43rd St   768-4682
Tues, Wed, Fri-Sun: 11-6

This is the city's only museum totally devoted to photography and every aspect of it. Founder Cornell Capa (brother of photographer Robert Capa) had as his aim that photographs should be treated as serious art in the same manner as paintings. Since photography is not as old a medium, he was able to incorporate it all under one townhouse roof, but this is definitely a museum. Items on display date from historical to current, with over 10,000 pictures to draw on. For a taste of the permanent collection, catch one of the rotating shows.

INTREPID SEA-AIR SPACE MUSEUM
Pier 86 (W 46th St at Hudson River)   245-0072
Wed-Sun: 10-5

The *Intrepid* is a circa World War II aircraft carrier that was mothballed into an ode to sea, air, and space travel. It isn't really all that military, although there are many displays on naval exploits. The flight deck is full of all types of aircraft. The *Intrepid* stays current, with contributions from the Persian Gulf War already in place and pictures of various craft in operation. Your ticket also grants admission to a submarine and another ship moored at the dock.

JEWISH MUSEUM
1109 Fifth Ave (at 92nd St)   399-3430
Sun, Tues-Thurs: 10-5; Fri: 10-3

Until the end of 1992, the Jewish Museum is being housed in the quarters of the New York Historical Society (170 Central Park West, at 77th Street) while their own home, the former Warburg Mansion, undergoes extensive renovations that will greatly expand its exhibition space. It's an interesting New York relationship: an institution showcasing 5,000 years of Jewish history being hosted by a bastion of Colonial life. Only in New York! The collection of the museum has great strengths in contemporary and ancient Jewish art and artists. Marc Chagall and George Segal are represented, as are clay oil lamps from ancient Israel. It is the only museum in the area with a permanent exhibition on Israeli archaeology. While in its temporary home, the museum continues to mount timely shows and ongoing exhibits. The new construction should greatly increase its ability to showcase a very impressive collection.

LOWER EAST SIDE TENEMENT MUSEUM
97 Orchard (bet Delancey and Broome St)   431-0233
Tues-Fri: 11-4 (gallery hours)

After you've toured historical mansions, it's a change of pace to see how the common folk lived. This is the first urban living history museum in the country, and it does for the city's immigrant experience what the Williamsburg and Richmondtown restorations do for Colonial times. Of course, comparing a tenement to Williamsburg is not really apt, but the museum does a great job of charting new territory. They are preserving the history of waves of immigrants that came to the Lower East Side through living history models set inside a genuine tenement building. There are ongoing exhibitions that change constantly. While the gallery hours are limited, the real role of the museum lies in its walking tours of the Lower East Side. They are held every weekend and Wednesday afternoon and are led by period-costumed guides who really make it seem as if you are walking the streets of the tenement era. Most weeks there are at least two tours a day around lunchtime. And it doesn't hurt to have a guide to the Lower East Side on a Sunday!

METROPOLITAN MUSEUM
Fifth Ave at 82nd St   879-5500, 535-7710 (recording)
Tues-Thurs, Sun: 9:30-5:15; Fri, Sat: 9:33-8:45

No visit to New York is complete without spending at least part of a day at the Met. The collections are fabulous and extensive, including ancient Egyptian, Greek, Roman, ancient Near East, medieval, Renaissance, Asian, Oceanic, pre-Columbian, and contemporary American Art. The American Wing houses the finest collection of American paintings, sculpture, and decorative arts in the country. The Lila Acheson Wallace Wing houses contemporary art. The Astor Court replicates a famous Chinese scholar's garden. The Lehman Wing exhibits furniture and paintings as they were in the Lehman house. Many other period rooms are breathtaking, submerging visitors in another lifestyle and time. Upstairs, there are countless masterpieces—so many that even the greatest philistine will likely have seen at least a dozen of them as reproductions at some time in his life. New Yorkers congregate on the front steps, the choicest meeting and lounging spot in the city. The parking lot underneath the museum is the most reasonable in the area. A marvelous program of art appreciation and hands-on art is held after school and Saturdays (879-5510, ext. 3310). The waiting list is long, because it is very popular.

MUSEUM OF AMERICAN FOLK ART
2 Lincoln Sq (Columbus Ave, bet 65th and 66th St)
595-9533, 977-7298
Daily: 9-9

This unusual museum is devoted to folk art made between 1776 and 1914. You'll be fascinated by all the old pieces and impressed by the works on display, as well as the reproductions in the two gift shops. The story of this museum is a bit of folk history itself. For years, it was quartered in rented space near MOMA. When it lost that space, it was literally homeless, until the folks at 2 Lincoln Square ran afoul of public accommodations zoning regulations. The compromise was that the museum found a home at a nominal rental (a dollar a year), and its new home reserved the right to remain overbuilt. So the new setting (circa 1989) is untramodern, in sharp contrast to the country-homespun crafts. It's free!

MUSEUM OF THE AMERICAN INDIAN
Broadway at 155th St   283-2420
Tues-Sat: 10-5; Sun: 1-5

George Heye started building a world-renowned collection with the purchase of a deerskin shirt in 1896. His fascination with the native customs of the Navajo Indians led to what is now a world-famous institution. The museum presently holds a million artifacts, some 86,000 pictures and negatives, and a 40,000-volume library. In 1989, President Bush signed legislation establishing the National Museum of the American Indian as a new museum of the Smithsonian. The centerpiece will be located on the mall in Washington on a site adjacent to the National Air and Space Museum. A second exhibition site will be located in the Old U.S. Custom House in lower Manhattan.

MUSEUM OF THE AMERICAN PIANO
211 W 58th St (Broadway)   246-4646
Tues-Fri: 12-4

Adjacent to Detrich Pianos, this museum is an outgrowth of Kalman Detrich's love of esoteric and antique pianos. When his own showroom grew overrun with oddities, he was forced to split the new collection from the old, and the Museum of the American Piano was born. Visitors with a specific interest in period instruments are invited to play pianos built as early as the turn of the nineteenth century. There is a collection of about thirty restored American pianos, dating from the late 1700s to the 1940s. In addition, there is a "rogue's gallery," featuring such oddities as the remains of a concrete grand piano and a portable piano intended for use on long trips by train or ship.

MUSEUM OF THE CITY OF NEW YORK
Fifth Ave at 103rd St   534-1034
Tues-Sat: 10-5; Sun: 1-5
Guided tour reservations: 534-1672, ext. 206 (Tues-Fri)

This is an incredible place, dedicated to the world's most incredible city. The aim is to trace the history of the city from its origins as a Dutch pioneer settlement to the world's biggest metropolis. They accomplish this via a sensational permanent collection of artifacts, innovative and timely shows and programs, and a fabulous Sunday walking tour schedule in the spring and fall. This museum believes in getting outside to demonstrate how thoroughly they know the streets of New York. The permanent collection includes Dutch, marine, fire, doll-house, silver, furniture, print, map, and painting galleries; period alcoves; the John D. Rockefeller, Sr., rooms; and exhibitions on costumes, theater, photography, and toys. One perpetual favorite is the Volunteer Fire Gallery. Don't miss the multimedia film *The Big Apple*. This was one of the first museums to host birthday parties for children in the museum, and every Saturday there's a "please touch" demonstration in a re-created seventeenth-century Dutch New York bedroom that's been reserved just for touching.

MUSEUM OF HOLOGRAPHY
11 Mercer St (bet Grand and Canal St)
925-0581, 925-0526 (recording)
Mon-Sun: 11-6

This museum has the world's largest collection of holograms. When it started, it was necessary to provide very basic information on holography, but over the years holograms and three-dimensional images created with laser light have become an accepted part of modern life. Both the gallery and gift shop offer unique shows.

THE MUSEUM OF MODERN ART
11 W 53rd St   708-9480, 708-9490 (film listings)
Fri-Tues: 11-6; Thurs: 11-9
Pay what you wish Thurs evening

MOMA is popular even among non-museum lovers for its gift shops, concert series, film festivals, and tranquil meeting spots, such as the sculpture garden. MOMA's attitude is modern and up-to-the-minute in both themes and acquisitions. A recent renovation has doubled the exhibition space, but even that is not enough. The galleries hold priceless paintings, design objects and furniture, architectural models, sculpture, and the famed Film Institute downstairs. There are always several rotating shows highlighted at the museum. When Margaret Thatcher left office, the museum did a retrospective of British photography through her years as Prime Minister. Each spring the Film Institute screens the films nominated for the Academy Award in the short, documentary, and foreign-language categories. MOMA visitors probably see more nominated films than Academy members, and without question they are some of the best-educated patrons of modern art in the world.

THE MUSEUM OF TELEVISION AND RADIO
25 W 52nd St   752-7684
Wed-Sat: noon-5; Tues: noon-8

A dream of William Paley (an executive legend at CBS), the Museum of Television and Radio (formerly the Museum of Broadcasting) was really the first institution in the country to preserve television archives as historical artifacts. The early idea was to operate the place more as a library than a museum, and the general form has followed through. Tickets are purchased on the first floor. You then go to the archives' computerized file for access to the 20,000 tapes of radio and television broadcasts in the museum's collection. Scattered on different floors in a brand-new custom-designed building are 96 video terminals and 25 radio booths. You are free to watch for up to two hours. If video consoles are not available, there are two screening and listening rooms (one seats

200, the other 90) and two 45-seat rooms. All broadcast retrospectives with various themes. Kids love it here (the morning hours are reserved for school groups and students), but adults do, too!

NATIONAL ACADEMY OF DESIGN
1083 Fifth Ave (89th St)   369-4880
Tues: noon-8; Wed-Sun: noon-5

This museum's setting is part of the exhibit, since it's housed in the handsome *beaux-arts* mansion that was the former home of Archer M. Huntington and his wife, sculptor Anna Hyatt. The museum sponsors an annual exhibition, a permanent collection on American Art (on the fourth floor), and rotating exhibitions of American and European art.

NEW MUSEUM OF CONTEMPORARY ART
583 Broadway (bet Houston and Prince)   219-1222
Wed, Thurs, Sun: 12-6; Fri, Sat: 12-8

The Museum of Modern Art is pure establishment, compared to this storefront show at the historic Astor building in SoHo. Exhibits change on a regular basis, and they walk a fine line between what is "museum quality" and what is being exhibited in the neighborhood galleries. At least the exhibits set the parameters of what passes for art on the current scene. It's a good place to come for a quick study on the contemporary art scene.

NEW YORK CITY FIRE MUSEUM
278 Spring St (bet Hudson and Varick St)   691-1303
Tues-Sat: 10-4

The Fire Department Museum is funded by a private, not-for-profit agency. Remember that. It means that when all the other city museums (like the Police Academy) are subject to the whims of budgetary constraints, this one sails on. They have their eye on the public, and they mount a very impressive exhibit. The collection includes hand- and horse-drawn fire trucks dating as far back as 1735. A permanent exhibit highlights the role of water in the social fabric of New York City life. A temporary exhibit may deal with the role of women in firefighting in the city. Kids will love to see some of the old fire trucks, and parents will be intrigued to learn more about the practical side of fighting fires.

NEW YORK HISTORICAL SOCIETY
170 Central Park W (at 77th St)   873-3400
Tues-Sun: 10-5
Pay what you wish Tues

This is the oldest museum in New York (founded in 1804), so its very existence is a part of the city's history. It also *made* history when it offered temporary housing to the Jewish Museum while the latter's own home was being reconstructed. In the interim, the two museums are sharing the 32 gallery spaces of the Historical Society, which are used to show off collections of American historical artifacts, art, and antiques. But the Historical Society is more than a museum. It houses a reference library that holds over 4,000,000 manuscripts, historical photos, music sheets, rare books, and so many prints of historical worth that they are exhibited as a separate collection. The museum features 433 of Audubon's 435 original *Birds of America* watercolors; Colonial silver; early American toys, arts and crafts; collections in Tiffany glass and lamps; advertising art; and New York silver. There are free tours daily, plus programs and movies for the whole family and children's story hours.

NEW YORK PUBLIC LIBRARY
Mid-Manhattan branch
Fifth Ave at 42nd St   930-0800
Mon-Sat: 10-6

The 42nd Street Library, as it is known locally, is the intellectual center of the city. The library was created in 1895 when the Astor and Lenox libraries merged with the Tilden Trust. Prior to that time, there were private clublike libraries, vestiges of what still exist in the city. (The Mercantile at 17 E 47th St, 755-6710, is one. Until very recently, there was no charge to members for library usage.) The new library was built on the Fifth Avenue side of Bryant Park, which had previously been a reservoir and potter's field. At the time it was built, it was the exact population center of the city, which shows how much New York has grown in 100 years. The combined collections today boast more than 30 million cataloged items. In addition to special areas that delineate the original collections in the *beaux-arts* building, there are 21 specialty rooms for such subjects as maps; American history; art; periodicals; Bibles; rare books in American and English literature; and Jewish, black, Oriental, Slavic, and local history and genealogy. The main reading room is a work of art in itself, and anyone can fill out a call slip that will gain access to the stacks. The information desks at the library handle 5 million questions a year—so many that in 1989 it published *The New York Public Library Desk Reference*! There are 82 branch libraries in the system, and several of them specialize as well. For example, the Donnell Library Center (20 W 53rd St, 621-0618) specializes in education, while the branch in Lincoln Center (111 Amsterdam Ave, 870-1630) is the premier library for the performing arts.

NEW YORK TRANSIT MUSEUM
Boerum Place and Schermerhorn St, Brooklyn
718/330-3060
Tues-Sat: 10-4

Housed in the old, circa-1936 Court Street shuttle station in Brooklyn, the New York Transit Museum is the only transportation museum so situated. To get there, take the A or F train to Jay Street, the M or R to Court Street, or the 2, 3, 4, or 5 to Borough Hall, and then follow the signs. The museum aims to teach visitors the history of public transportation in the city. To do this, they demonstrate actual subway cars of various vintages going back to 1903, a working signal tower, and many antique artifacts such as seats, tokens, turnsites, maps, advertisements, and the "Miss Subways" campaign posters. (Ellen Sturn of Ellen's Cafe was a "Miss Subway," and is now the leader of the alumni club.) There's also a scale model of the entire subway system. Groups are offered full-fledged programs and guided tours Tuesday through Friday, while individuals can take a self-guided tour. Unfortunately, the museum is presently in serious financial trouble.

PIERPONT MORGAN LIBRARY
29 E 36th St   685-0610
Tues-Sat: 10:30-5; Sun: 10-5

Pierpont Morgan started collecting literature when he was just a boy. His collection of books, etchings, manuscripts, and sketches became one of the most extensive in the city. Ultimately, it outgrew the West Room of his Renaissance-style palazzo and overtook the whole house. Today there are changing exhibits based upon the house collections of autographs, letters, music manuscripts, original texts and first editions, medieval manuscripts, master drawings, and rare books. In addition, the permanent exhibits include the West Room, which was J.P. Morgan's private study; a Gutenberg Bible; medieval gold and decorative art; and art and sculpture.

SCHOMBURG CENTER FOR RESEARCH IN BLACK CULTURE
515 Lenox Ave (at 135th St)   862-4000
Mon, Wed: noon-8; Tues, Thurs, Fri: 10-6

This is one of the research branches of the New York Public Library, but it also stands by itself as the premier place for research and artifacts on black culture. In addition to an extensive collection of literature, photography, and archives on the black experience, there are many displays of African art, changing exhibits, and lectures on black culture.

SOLMON R. GUGGENHEIM
1071 Fifth Ave (at 89th St)   360-3500
Wed-Sun: 11-4:45; Tues: 11-7:45
Free on Tues evening

The Guggenheim, a Frank Lloyd Wright building, is as sleekly modern as its collection of paintings. It was designed around a continuous ramp that looks like an inverted snail, according to some critics. Because of its radical design, fine collection of modern paintings, and rotating exhibits, the recently restored Guggenheim is a must on every museum goer's list. A satellite in SoHo is being planned.

SOUTH STREET SEAPORT
East River at Fulton Street

There are dozens of different aspects to the South Street Seaport, which is a restoration of the Port of New York and the prototype for many reclamation projects all over the country. So successful has the Seaport been, there is even talk of a similar project in Brooklyn, directly across the East River (which is not a river but an estuary). Wall Streeters use the Seaport as an informal base for lunch and after-work meetings. Tourists take in the Seaport Museum (669-9400 or 669-9424 [recording]), the multimedia movie *The Seaport Experience* (210 Front St, 608-7888), and the ships. There are always at least three tall ships in residence. And while there are three museum shops per se, the whole place brings back the magical feel of New York's thriving seaport of 150 years ago!

STATUE OF LIBERTY MUSEUM
Liberty Island   363-3200
Daily: 9-4

Located at the base of the Statue of Liberty, the museum is really only accessible on the way out. It purports to tell the story of immigration to the United States from the founding of New Amsterdam to the present time, as well as the story of the construction of the statue itself. Unfortunately, it doesn't do a very good job of either task. Most of the thunder for the immigration story has been taken by nearby Ellis Island. The exhibits here were never historically accurate. People used to eagerly await the exhibit on their ethnic group, until they came upon it. Then there were howls of laughter or outrage. Better things can be said for the construction of the statue.

STEINWAY HALL
109 W 57th (nr Sixth Ave)   246-1100
Mon-Wed, Fri: 9-6; Thurs: 9-9; Sat: 9-5; Sun: 12-5

Steinway Hall is a monumental sales gallery and a fitting showcase for the famed Steinway & Sons piano. It is a museum housing memorabilia of Steinway accomplishments, past and present. Steinway pianos are displayed in the main showroom, a classical rotunda with a domed, painted ceiling worthy of a Renaissance palace. (Steinway Hall has been used as the backdrop for several movies.) Other equally impressive salons situated on the two floors off the grand foyer house the most comprehensive collection of Steinway pianos in the world. Films that take you step-by-step through the manufacture of a Steinway piano are featured.

STUDIO MUSEUM IN HARLEM
144 W 125th St   864-4500
Wed-Fri: 10-5; Sat, Sun: 1-6

This pioneering institute is in newly renovated quarters to better display black art in different mediums. The permanent collection is very contemporary and yet has enough of a base to mount several shows a year on a changing schedule. Note the sculpture and folk art. There are special exhibits, workshops, concerts, and movies.

THEODORE ROOSEVELT BIRTHPLACE
28 E 20th St (bet Broadway and Park Ave)   260-1616
Wed-Sun: 9-5

Theodore Roosevelt was a born-and-bred New Yorker, although the site more commonly associated with him is his family's Long Island homestead, Sagamore Hill, in Oyster Bay. This building, on the site of the brownstone that was demolished in 1916, was reconstructed in 1923 to simulate his boyhood home. It is run as a national memorial. Approximately 40 percent of the furniture is original to the house and another 20 percent was gathered from family members. The adjoining lot originally held the companion brownstone purchased by T.R.'s grandfather for his son Robert at the same time he purchased #28 for Theodore Sr. During the 1923 reconstruction, it was purchased and turned into museum galleries and other facilities. Today, it is operated by the National Park Service, which makes this a national park on East 20th Street!

TRINITY MUSEUM
Trinity Church
Broadway at Wall Street   602-0847
Mon-Fri: 9-11:45, 1-3:45; Sat: 10-3:45; Sun: 1-3:45

At one point, Trinity Church was the most powerful church in the city. It is rumored to still own (or to have owned) some of the choicest real estate in town. The original building was built in 1697, and the present building dates back to 1846. Columbia University was founded at this site, and George Washington worshiped here.

(His pew is preserved in St. Paul's Chapel.) There are guided tours weekdays at two p.m. They include the churchyard where Robert Fulton and Alexander Hamilton, among others, are buried.

UKRAINIAN MUSEUM
203 Second Ave (at 12th St)   288-0110
Wed-Sun: 1-5

Located in the heart of the Ukrainian community in New York, this museum has a fine collection of Ukrainian folk art in both permanent and rotating exhibitions. There are exhibits on Ukrainian life both abroad and in this country, and fabulous crafts, including over 900 of the famous Easter eggs. Courses are taught in baking and culinary art, jewelry making, fabric design, and decorating. Yes, they even attempt to teach the art of "pyansky" (making Easter eggs).

WHITNEY MUSEUM OF AMERICAN ART
945 Madison Ave (at 75th St)   570-3676
Tues: 1-8; Wed-Sat: 11-5; Sun: noon-6

Federal Reserve Plaza
33 Maiden Ln   943-5655

Equitable Center
787 Seventh Ave   554-1113
Tues, Wed-Fri: 11-5; Thurs: 11-7:30; Sat: noon-5

Philip Morris
120 Park Ave (at 42nd St)   878-2550
Mon-Sat: 11-6; Thurs: 11-7:30
Courtyard open 7:30-9:30 p.m.

A young man was out on a blind date. He called the girl and suggested they "meet at the Whitney. You do know where that is?" he asked. "Of course," she responded. "I work right there." So he went uptown and waited, while she stepped outside her office and waited downtown. Take this as a warning. The Whitney, the repository of the foremost collection of twentieth-century art, believes in taking art to the people. Currently there are three branches that are every bit as worthwhile as the main branch, and people genuinely believe that "their" branch is the real thing. The epitome of a contemporary urban art museum, the Whitney was founded by Gertrude Vanderbilt Whitney to house her collection of contemporary American art and sculpture. (Whitney was a sculptor herself.) The collection eventually grew to include over 6,000 pieces, and the museum's management decided to make it more accessible to the people of the city by establishing branches in public spaces in office buildings.

YESHIVA UNIVERSITY MUSEUM
2520 Amsterdam Ave (bet 184th and 185th St)
960-5390
Tues-Thurs: 10:30-5; Sun: noon-6; closed Aug

Located on the main campus of Yeshiva University, this museum houses outstanding exhibits of contemporary art, decorative arts and crafts, and Jewish culture and history. There are programs and workshops for children and adults, as well as tours.

New York on the Water

Central Park: Dine at the Boathouse, then take your date for a rowboat spin. Located on the lake, off East Drive at 72nd Street. Prices are reasonable, and boats are available seven days a week in nice weather. (517-3623)

Circle Line: A number of boat tours, leaving at different times during the day, give you a great view of Manhattan Island. The circuitous tour lasts three hours, and it starts at Pier 83 at West 42nd Street. (563-3200)

Honey Fitz: Make believe you are the president, and go deluxe on this ex-presidential yacht. Private cruises are available. (233-4800)

Pan Am Ferry Boat to LaGuardia Airport: High-speed ferryboats whisk you from Wall Street to the plane in 45 minutes, at a cost of around $25.

Petrel: Cruises of varying lengths are available on this 70-foot yawl, which operates from Battery Park. The *Petrel* is in service seven days a week, and the 90-minute "executive lunch hour" trips are very popular. (825-1976)

Pioneer: You can take your choice of cruises in the summer months on this 106-year-old sailboat. Call ahead to book one that will fit your schedule. (669-9400)

Seaport Line: The *DeWitt Clinton* and the *Andrew Fletcher* sail from Pier 16 (South Street Seaport) with a variety of excursions. There are luncheon sailings and 90-minute sightseeing trips. Young folks will enjoy the evening music cruises. (385-0791)

Spirit of New York: A red, white, and blue experience for patriots and romantics. The address is Pier 19, East River, near Wall Street. Meals are available, and it is a good idea to call for reservations for moonlight fun on weekends. (480-2970)

Staten Island Ferry: The *Hong Kong Star Ferry* and the *Staten Island Ferry* are the last two great bargains on the water. The *Staten Island Ferry* costs 50¢ per round trip, and the view of Manhattan is sensational.

World Yacht Cruises: Feel like the VIP you are while the crew does all the work of preparing noon buffets, dinner and dancing, or Sunday brunch. The food is really excellent. Prices are in keeping with the luxury class. The address is Pier 62 (at W 23rd St and Twelfth Ave). It is a good idea to call ahead to make sure what you want is available. (929-7090)

Parks and Recreation

Through New York City's Department of Parks and Recreation, you can find facilities for almost any interest you might have. In Manhattan there are 2,598 acres of parkland—equal to 17 percent of the borough!

Badminton: Call 718/699-4231 for information.

Baseball: For permits to use diamonds, call 408-0209.

Basketball Courts: Central Park, the Great Lawn near 85th St, midpark; Riverside Park, W 101st to W 111th St.

Bicycling: Central Park drives are closed to motor vehicles on holidays, on summer weekdays (10-3, 7-10), and on weekends (from seven p.m. Friday to six p.m. Monday). Bicycle rentals at Loeb Boathouse (861-4137).

Bird Watching: Central Park, the Ramble (73rd to 79th St) and the Hallet Nature Sanctuary (nr E 59th St and Fifth Ave); Fort Tryon Park, Heather Garden, north of Fort Washington Ave; Riverside bird sanctuary, W 114th to W 120th St.

Boating Area: Central Park, Loeb Boathouse, the Lake, off East Dr at 74th St (April-Oct); 517-2233.

Boccie Courts: 34 courts at the Cuvillier, East River, Harlem River Dr, Highbridge, Thomas Jefferson, Roosevelt, and Walker parks; playgrounds at 96th St and First Ave, and East River Dr and 42nd St; Thompson St playground; and Randall's Island and Wards Island.

Bowling Lawn: Central Park, near Sheeps Meadow, 67th St near West Dr (May-Nov). For permits, call 360-8133.

Bridle Paths and Stables: Central Park, Claremont Riding Academy (724-5100).

Carriage Rentals: Central Park S, $17 for first half hour, $5 each additional quarter hour (246-0520).

Carrousels: Central Park, 65th St, midpark (879-0244).

Chess and Checkers: Central Park, Chess and Checkers House, 64th St, midpark (indoor play, weekends only, 11:30 a.m.-4:30 p.m.; outdoor play, weekdays, terrace of Chess and Checkers House), pieces available at the Dairy, 64th St; Washington Square Park, southwest corner; Manhattan Chess Club, 154 W 57th St, 10th floor (admission charge).

Croquet Lawns: Central Park, near Sheeps Meadow, 67th St near West Dr (May-Nov). For permits, call 360-8133.

Day Camps: Central Park, N Meadow Center, off 97th St transverse, midpark; Columbia Playground, 143 Baxter St; Morningside Park, 410 Morningside Ave; Jackie Robinson Play Center, W 146th St and Bradhurst Ave; Payson Playground, Dyckman St and Payson Ave.

Fishing: Riverside Park, Hudson River, along the Esplanade, W 72nd to W 84th St, and W 91st to W 100th St.

Folk Dancing: Central Park, east shore of Turtle Pond, 81st St, midpark, Sun: 2-6 p.m.

Golf Courses: none in Manhattan.

Handball Courts: Central Park, North Meadow Center, off 97th St transverse, midpark; Riverside Park, W 72nd St and Hudson River, W 101st to W 111th St, and W 147th to W 152nd St.

Ice Skating: Sky Rink, 450 W 33rd St, 16th floor (697-6555); Wollman Rink, Central Park, East Dr and 63rd St (517-4800); Lasker Rink, Central Park, near 110th St and Lenox Ave (397-3106); Rivergate Ice Rink, E 34th St and First Ave; Rockefeller Center (757-5730).

Kite Flying: Central Park, Sheeps Meadow.

Marinas: Riverside Park, 79th St Boat Basin, Hudson River (362-0909).

Model Boat Ponds: Central Park, Conservatory Water, 74th St and Fifth Ave.

Picnic Areas: Central Park, Sheeps Meadow, East Meadow, pool shores; Riverside Park, W 93rd to W 98th St, W 147th to W 152nd St.

Recreation Centers: Carmine (Clarkson St and Seventh Ave, 397-3107); Mount Morris/Marcus Garvey (Mount Morris Park W and 122nd St, 397-3118); Alfred E. Smith (80 Catherine St, 397-3108); E 54th St (348 E 54th St, 397-3155); W 59th St (533 W 59th St, 397-3166); Hansborough (35 W 135th St, 397-3136).

Rodeo: Randall's Island, Black World Championship Rodeo (675-0085).

Roller Skating: Central Park rental, Mineral Springs Pavilion, Sheeps Meadow, enter at W 69th St.

Running Tracks: Central Park Reservoir; Downing Stadium (Olympic), Randall's Island; Riverside Park at 74th St; Hansborough Recreation Center (indoor); Carmine Street Recreation Center (indoor); E 54th St Recreation Center (indoor); Thomas Jefferson Park.

Soccer Field: Central Park, Great Lawn, 81st to 85th St, midpark; North Meadow, 97th to 103rd St, midpark.

Swimming Pools (indoor): E 54th St (397-3154); Hansborough (35 W 134th St, 397-3134); W 59th St (533 W 59th St, 397-3159); Carmine Street (Seventh Ave and Clarkson St, 397-3107).

Swimming Pools (outdoor): E 23rd St (Asser Levy Pl, nr FDR Dr, 397-3123); Hamilton Fish (128 Pitt St, 397-3171); Carmine Street (Clarkson St and Seventh Ave, 397-3107); John Jay (east of York

Ave on 77th St, 397-3177); Thomas Jefferson (111th St and First
Ave, 397-3112); Lasker (110th St and Lenox Ave, 397-3106);
Highbridge (Amsterdam Ave and W 173rd St, 397-3173); Marcus
Garvey (124th St and Fifth Ave, 397-3124); Jackie Robinson
(Bradhurst Ave and W 146th St, 397-3146); Sheltering Arms
(Amsterdam Ave and W 129th St, 397-3128); Szold Place (E 10th
St, bet Ave C and D, 397-3110); Wagner Houses (E 124th St, bet
First and Second Ave, 397-3125).

Tennis Courts: Central Park, East River Park, Inwood Hill Park,
Frederick Johnson Playground, Randall's Island, Riverside
Park, and Fort Washington Park. There are 92 courts in all.

Zoos: Central Park Zoo (439-6500); Children's Zoo, Central Park
(408-0271).

CENTRAL PARK
59th St to 110th St (bet Fifth Ave and Central Park W)

There is enough to see and do in Central Park to occupy several
days. The most romantic way to see the park is by horse and carriage. They are very strictly regulated. A 30-minute ride has a standard rate posted right on the side of the carriage. No matter what
the driver tells you, that's all you have to pay, unless you strike a
deal for a longer ride.

Central Park consists of 840 acres smack-dab in the center of the
city. Landscaped pathways, two rowing lakes, numerous meadows,
two ice-skating rinks, and grounds dedicated to recreation—this
magnificent park is Fredrick Law Olmsted's legacy to the city. And
what a legacy it is! There's Belvedere Castle (722-0210), near the
West 79th Street entrance, which often serves as the backdrop for
plays in the open-air Delacorte Theater. Originally, the castle
served as a weather center. Nowadays it is a learning center for science and nature programs. Call for a list of programs and hours.

Central Park is best known for its playgrounds. All are modern,
child-safe, and outfitted with some of the most imaginative equipment in the country. Two of the best are on the East Side: the Sand
Playground at 85th Street, across from the Metropolitan Museum,
and the Estee Lauder Adventure Playground, next to the zoo entrance at 71st Street. On the West Side there's more celebrity status,
but the playgrounds themselves aren't as special.

The newly renovated Central Park Zoo (64th St, 439-6500) is run
by the New York Zoological Society, the same folks who run the
Bronx Zoo. There are three biomes (climate zones), which feature
arctic pools, tropical rain forests, and man-made "natural" habi-
tats. Visitors nostalgic for the Victorian cages and inhabitants of
the old zoo are likely to be disappointed. Penguins, red pandas, sea
lions, harbor seals, otters, and snow monkeys are on view, but the

larger animals (elephants, zebras, rhinoceroses, etc.) can now be seen only at the Bronx Zoo. The Children's Zoo (408-0271) remains unchanged. It's a marvelous place, featuring better fairy-tale attractions and animals than many tourist parks. Don't miss the huge Delacorte Clock at the entrance to the Children's Zoo. There is a modest admission charge for both zoos.

The merry-go-round nearby is another recent restoration. Located in almost the exact center of the park (62nd St entrance), it is almost as wonderful to look at as it is to ride.

The Dairy (nr 64th St, west of the zoo, 397-3156), another restored building, really was a dairy where children could stop for a glass of milk. (There are differing opinions as to whether cows were ever actually in residence.) Today it is the park information office and a center for free family activities throughout the year. It also has a semipermanent display of pictures and artifacts relating to the park. It is so picturesque that one of the most popular "family activities" at the Dairy is getting married.

Next to the beautifully restored Bethesda Fountain are two boating lakes (Loeb Boathouse, E 72nd St, 517-2233) and a pond devoted to toy sailboats.

In the summer the park resounds with activity. Softball games are played throughout the park. There are leagues for Broadway plays, TV soap operas, magazine staffs, Wall Street tycoons, and all kinds of companies and organizations. Joseph Papp's New York Shakespeare Festival presents full, star-studded productions of Shakespeare's plays at the Delacorte Theater throughout the summer, and the admission is free.

When the temperature drops, it is ice-skating season. The rehabilitation of the Wollman Memorial Skating Rink (off E 64th St, 517-4800) was a *cause célèbre* for years, until Donald Trump glided to the rescue and rebuilt it in six months. Trump runs the rink, and it is beautifully maintained. The Louise Lasker Skating Rink (996-1184), also run by Trump, at the very northern end of the park (107th St and Central Park N), is an unknown gem patronized mostly by the locals and hockey professionals. In the summer, it is a pool.

The next big project in Central Park is the creation of an 11-acre lake complete with a small island in what was once Hatlem Meer, about 150 feet from the Lasker rink. It will be a bit of unspoiled nature at the north end of the park.

Party Places

Abigail Adams Smith Museum (421 E 61st St, 838-6878) Old carriage house.
American Zephyr (124 E 27th St, 764-6266) Private railroad cars.

Asia Society (725 Park Ave, at 75th St, 288-6400) Stunning facilities for members or nonprofit groups.

Bridgewaters/Museum Club (19 Fulton St, 608-8823) River views.

Burden Mansion (1 E 91st St, 722-4745) Former Vanderbilt mansion.

Circle Line Sightseeing Yachts (Pier 83, at 42nd St, 563-3200) Fun on the water.

Cooper-Hewitt Museum (2 E 91st St, 860-6898) Former Carnegie mansion.

Delegate's Dining Room, United Nations (UN Building, Room 414, 963-7098) East River view.

Delia's (197 E 3rd St, 254-9184) Queen Anne and country-chic décor.

Empire State Building Observatories (350 Fifth Ave, 86th floor, 736-3100) Manhattan at your feet.

Federal Hall National Memorial (26 Wall St, 264-8711) Washington's inaugural setting.

Four Seasons (99 E 52nd St, 754-9494) Class.

Fraunces Tavern (54 Pearl St, 425-1778) For history buffs.

Grande Promenade (Lincoln Center Visitor's Services, 140 W 65th St, 877-1800) For really big shindigs.

Hard Rock Cafe (221 W 57th St, 459-9320) Kids will love it.

Intrepid Sea-Air-Space Museum (Pier 86, W 46th St at 12th Ave, 245-0072) Ship setting, hangar and flight decks.

Loeb's Boat House (Central Park, 72nd St and Fifth Ave, 988-0575) Park setting, inside and outside.

Manhattan Mansions (627-8838) A fine private home.

Museum of the City of New York (Fifth Ave at 103rd St, 534-1672) Fascinating museum.

Museum of Modern Art (11 W 53rd St, 708-9480) Prestige setting for receptions.

New Yorker (929-7090) Grand-scale cruises.

Palladium (126 E 14th St, 473-7171). Big-time nightclub.

Passenger Ship Terminal (711 12th Ave, at 52nd St, 246-5450) Enormous space.

Patrick O'Neal's Penthouse Loft (236 W 26th St, 399-2355) Loft with floor-to-ceiling windows.

A Perfect Space (260 W Broadway, 941-0262) Dramatic 100 year-old building.

Pierpont Morgan Library (29 E 36th St, 685-0008) Fascinating palazzo.

Plaza Hotel (Central Park S and Fifth Ave, 759-3000) Heart of Manhattan.

Prince Street Club (117 Prince St, 353-0707) Classy digs.

Radio City Music Hall (1260 Sixth Ave, 247-4777) World famous.

Rainbow Room (30 Rockefeller Center, 632-5000) Elegant, dramatic.

Russian Tea Room (150 W 57th St, 265-0947) East European chic.
SOB's - Mango Tree Cafe (204 Varick St, 243-4940) Native Brazilian color.
Space II XI (211 W Broadway, 966-1183) TriBeCa charm.
Tiffany Hall (2 E 37th St, 685-8019) Landmark setting.
The Tower (45 W 185th St, 620-0505) Uptown beauty.
Tower Suite (Time-Life Building, 1271 Sixth Ave, 48th floor, 586-2100) For big groups.
Tribeca Film Center (375 Greenwich St, 941-4000) Multimedia center.
21 Club (21 W 52nd St, 582-7200) Great address.
Whitney Museum of American Art (945 Madison Ave, 570-3676) Summer spot.
Windows on the World (1 World Trade Center, 107th floor, 938-0030) Fabulous views.
Winter Garden (World Financial Center, 945-7200) Simply spectacular.

Sights

THE AT&T INFOQUEST CENTER
550 Madison Ave (at 56th St)   605-5555
Tues: 10-9; Wed-Sat: 10-6

This multifloor, multimedia, hands-on ode to science and technology (with an emphasis on communications) is free and just may be the best show in town. (New York kids carry around their Infoquest ID cards like adults carry a credit card.) From the spectacular entry through the atrium of the Johnson designed AT&T Building to the glass elevator and on into the hall, where you are given an ID card, there are explorations, exhibits, and games to interest the whole family. They cover such fields as voice recognition, energy, color coding and matching, satellites, holograms, microchips, and recording studios. The most popular exhibits involve creating your own music video, navigating a communications network through a series of crises, and painting computer pictures with your fingers. You could easily spend a day here. The price is right!

BATTERY PARK
Southern tip of Manhattan

This is basically the southernmost point of Manhattan Island, excluding the islands in the harbor, so it was the site of the city's earliest fortifications. Castle Clinton (344-7220) was an 1812 fort that later served as Castle Garden and later still was the home of the New York Aquarium. (The latter is now in Coney Island, Brooklyn.) Today you can catch ferries to Ellis Island, Staten Island, and the Statue of Liberty here or just stroll the promenade and park. I qualified my opening sentence with *basically,* because much of this end of Manhattan is built upon landfill. The most recent extension is Battery Park City, which, as its name implies, is almost a city unto itself and was built on the land displaced by the building of the World Trade Center. The World Financial Center has activities and shopping for the whole family, and the Winter Garden takes its name from the original, which stood in Battery Park 150 years ago.

CARNEGIE HALL
57th St and Seventh Ave
247-7800 (box office), 903-9600 (information)

The oldest New York joke is "How do you get to Carnegie Hall?" (Answer: "Practice, practice, practice.") In the old days there was Carnegie Hall, City Center, and the Met. Lincoln Center was built to supplant all three, and it has succeeded in becoming the musical and cultural mecca of the city. City Center was overpowered by CitiSpire which bought its air rights, illegally built 11 feet too tall, and whistles to the utter despair of its neighbors. The Met merely moved into Lincoln Center, and everyone sounded the death knell for Carnegie Hall. Well, everyone was wrong. It has always been preferred for its acoustics by many performers, and it has a classy history that will never be matched by Lincoln Center. The hall is the historical and ongoing home of concerts, performances, and recitals for a variety of groups. For its 100th birthday, Carnegie Hall was renovated and now looks better than ever. Fifty-seventh Street is the home of the city's great piano and music showrooms, as well as sheet music, records, and instruments. As always, the Russian Tea Room is "slightly to the left" of Carnegie Hall. (*Tootsie* was filmed here.) There are guided tours on Tuesdays and Thursdays at 11:30 a.m. and two and three p.m. (247-7800) The tour goes backstage and through the archives. They are not free, but the Visitors and Convention Bureau has discount coupons.

CATHEDRAL CHURCH OF
ST. JOHN THE DIVINE
1047 Amsterdam Ave (at 112th St)   316-7540
Daily: 7-5
Tours: Tues-Sat at 11; Sun at 12:45

The largest gothic church in the world, St. John's is still not completed and won't be anytime soon. In the meantime, local craftsmen are being trained in the ancient arts of stained-glass making, stonecutting, and Biblical architecture and horticulture. The 13 acres of grounds in Harlem include a Biblical garden and extraordinary architecture in virtually every corner. Admission is free, although there is a suggested donation. The sense of community spirit is so overwhelming you'll want to contribute.

CHINATOWN
West of Chatham Square

Chinatown is over a hundred years old and is bursting at the seams of the narrow, winding streets just east of the municipal buildings. (City Hall turns its back on Chinatown.) Check out the restaurants, food stores, and fascinating poultry shops. This is Chinatown, New York-style: crowded and teeming, where even the phone booths look like pagodas.

CHRYSLER BUILDING
405 Lexington Ave (at 42nd St)

The illuminated building in the night skyline that is *not* the Empire State Building is the Chrysler Building. Erected in 1929 as the showcase and showroom for the Chrysler Corporation, this classic art deco building was the world's tallest until the Empire State Building came along. Chrysler moved out a long time ago, and the magnificent elevator banks in the lobby—festooned with art deco car grills and automobile friezes—went the way of its trademark gargoyles. Recently, the new owners restored the lobby, including those magnificent elevators, to their former glory. The walls are done in African marble, and the building's version of the Sistine Chapel is a ceiling with a mural depicting the transportation industry and the workers who created the building.

CITICORP CENTER
53rd St and Lexington Ave
559-2330, 935-2200 (program information)

Citicorp was one of the first of the new breed of skyscrapers (it is the world's eighth tallest building) that was built with various zoning concessions. One was that the building would offer a "public accommodation" space. With its three-floor skylit atrium known as "the Marketplace," Citicorp succeeded in creating one of the best and most gracious spaces in town. Almost every day there is free entertainment, and around holidays there are puppet shows, choral societies, and jazz concerts serenading brown baggers at meal time. Another concession was the rebuilding of St. Peter's Church in a corner of the Center, in exchange for the original St. Peter's land. Here, too, everyone benefited. St. Peter's got a sparkling new building and a vigorous infusion of capital and parishioners. The community got a religious institution that offers its own space in concert with Citicorp's efforts. St. Paul's sponsors a midtown, midday jazz festival and dozens of other programs. Incidentally, the Citicorp Center's distinctive slanted roof was designed for solar energy, but it isn't used. Rumor has it that snow slid off the roof at an acute angle, causing problems below.

COMMODITIES EXCHANGE CENTER
Visitor's Gallery
4 World Trade Center   938-2025
Mon-Fri: 9:30-3

It's not as well known, exciting, or large as the Stock Exchange, but the Commodities Exchange Center (COMEX) has two things going for it over the "Big Board." It's open and what's there works, and it's in the World Trade Center. It's also free. If you're interested, go now. Every couple of years, COMEX makes noises about moving to New Jersey.

ELLIS ISLAND
Ferry departs from Battery Park   363-3200
Mon-Fri: 9-5; Weekends: 9-6

Ellis Island is currently the hottest ticket in town, but the bloom is already off the rose. For one thing, people objected violently to the very high ferry fare, especially when it was discovered that the island can literally be walked to from New Jersey over a construction bridge that was left in place. The long lines didn't help, either. Then Lee Iacocca's "Wall of Glory," for which donors paid $100 to inscribe their immigrant ancestor's names, began to run, ruin, and fade after less than a year. Despite all this, the lines continue. They want to see the restoration of the buildings that served as the entrance point for 80 percent of the immigrants who entered the country. Most of the island is not yet restored (and may never be), but the Great Hall, with arches and staircases leading to the Registry Room, lend enough atmosphere that more is not necessary. Those entering Ellis Island had to climb the stairs so that inspectors could detect any infirmity. Also on exhibit are the button hooks used to peel back eyelids to check for eye disease. The overall effect gives the lie to Emma Lazarus' words—"Give me your tired, your poor. . . ."—inscribed on the base of the nearby Statue of Liberty.

EMPIRE STATE BUILDING
Fifth Ave at 34th St   736-3100
Daily: 9:30-midnight (in good weather)

Built on the site of the original Waldorf-Astoria Hotel (which, in turn, was built on the site of the two Astor homes), this 102-story building has come to represent New York. Some New Yorkers still swear it is the tallest building in the world, even though they have probably never been to the top of the observation deck. (Real New Yorkers don't go to tourist sights unless they are escorting tourists.) There are 73 elevators. Next to the observatory ticket office is the Guinness World Record Exhibit Hall (947-2335). Some Empire State trivia: The point on the top of the building was created as an anchor for dirigibles. Leona Helmsley's contribution to the skyline is that the lights on the top (visible for 50 miles) glow different colors for different occasions. A plane crashed into the building in the 1940s. Fourteen people died during its construction. Enough!

GENERAL GRANT NATIONAL MEMORIAL
Riverside Drive at 122nd St   666-1640
Wed-Sat: 9-5

So who is buried in Grant's Tomb? The correct answer is not only General Grant but Mrs. Grant, who lies here as well. Admission is free. This is *not* the Soldiers and Sailors Monument, further down Riverside Drive, and if you wonder what the general and the missus are doing here anyway, you've got a good question. The exhibit inside explains part of the story. Suffice it to say that even his burial was controversial.

GRAND CENTRAL STATION
42nd St and Park Ave   935-3960
Tours: Wed at 12:30

One of the grandest buildings in the world, Grand Central Station's *beaux-arts* structure is unfortunately in serious danger of becoming a white elephant. Many years ago, the Pan Am Building was erected over the station, and that was followed by an effort to tear down the station altogether. Such celebrities as Jackie Onassis led the fight to save Grand Central, lest it go the way of Pennsylvania Station. (The latter was torn down to make way for the latest incarnation of Madison Square Garden, which is nowhere near Madison Square. Penn Station now exists solely in subterranean tracks beneath the replacement building, which is itself being replaced.) But Penn Station got the last laugh. The last long-distance train pulled out of Grand Central in 1991. This national landmark building and its cavernous main concourse are now used by commuters catching local trains. As for the long-haul trains, they all terminate in Pennsylvania Station. The Municipal Art Society sponsors free tours, which meet on the main concourse at Chemical Bank. (In spring and summer, the society sponsors all kinds of walking tours around the city for a nominal fee. They are among the best in town.)

IBM GARDEN PLAZA
590 Madison Ave (at 56th St)

IBM has always been a class act. The bamboo court of their public space features some of the largest living bamboo plants in captivity. The New York Botanical Gardens runs a kiosk and gift shop here almost as a testament to the skill of the plaza's gardeners. It's a fantastic place to bring a brown-bagged lunch.

JACOB JAVITS CONVENTION CENTER
From 35th to 39th Streets (bet Eleventh and
Twelfth Ave)   216-2000

It's hard to come up with superlatives that will express the massiveness of this building. Until it was built, New York never had a viable convention center. The I.M. Pei latticework glass and metal structure has been likened to an erector set. It encompasses 22 acres, five blocks, 900,000 feet of exposition area, and almost 2 million square feet of total space. The center's showcase is a 15-story atrium, and the building's walls reflect the New York skyline. One major problem: Aside from some hastily rerouted buses, there is no convenient public transportation or parking. Parking in private lots or hailing a taxi while your arms are loaded with mementos can be costly or bothersome.

LINCOLN CENTER FOR THE PERFORMING ARTS
Broadway, bet 63rd and 66th St   877-1800

Remember *West Side Story?* Specifically, do you remember that it was set in a slum? Well, that slum was replaced by Lincoln Center. So even if Lincoln Center had not furnished a home for the New York Philharmonic (whose conductor, the late Leonard Bernstein, wrote *West Side Story),* the Metropolitan Opera, the New York City Opera, the New York City Ballet, or the Julliard School, it would deserve a round of applause for turning a blight on the scene into a cultural wonderland. But there's more. New York never had a cultural center before. Aside from changing the face of the entire neighborhood, Lincoln Center made the city music-conscious and socially aware. There are programs out of the center (and Julliard) to bring music to the local schools and populace. There are tickets available for open rehearsals of the Philharmonic. And in the summer, the Met and Philharmonic give free concerts in parks around the city. The complex houses several different buildings and companies around a plaza. Damrosch Park and the Guggenheim Bandshell (in the Amsterdam Ave and W 62nd St corner of the plaza) is home to the Big Apple Circus (268-2500) every winter from October to January. Avery Fisher Hall is the home of the Philharmonic. This celebrated orchestra is the oldest in the country and has maintained a tradition of excellence. The hall itself is not fantastic. (Very little of Lincoln Center's architecture is.) It had to be completely reconstructed a short time after its opening. Alice Tully Hall in the Julliard School building is home to the center's Chamber Music Society, which has performances every weekend through the fall, winter, and spring. Center Court is the Metropolitan Opera, with its Chagall panels. When the Met isn't in residence, the American Ballet Theater (Mikhail Baryshnikov's company) is. The New York State Theater is the home of the New York City Ballet and the New York City Opera. The Vivian Beaumont and Mitzi E. Newhouse Theater is the most striking building at the Center. Designed by Eero Saarinen, it skirts a fine line between repertory theater and innovative productions while trying not to duplicate Broadway. And finally, the Performing Arts Library and Museum in the far corner has an extensive collection devoted to its namesake. It also houses the Bruno Walter Auditorium and Hecksher Oval, which hosts many free performances and concerts.

If all this is more than a little overwhelming, there is a one-hour Lincoln Center tour daily from ten a.m. to five p.m. (877-1800, ext. 512). It leaves from the concourse level downstairs at both the New York State Theater and Avery Fisher Hall. It is not cheap. To cut the cost, check out open rehearsals, standing room, volunteering, and the TKTS Bryant Park Music and Dance Ticket Booth (382-2323), which offers same-day tickets at greatly reduced rates. (Unlike the other TKTS booths, a phone call will elicit information about availability and likelihood.)

MADISON SQUARE GARDEN
4 Penn Plaza (33rd and Eighth Ave)   563-8300

Madison Square is downtown, around 23rd Street and Madison Ave in the heart of insurance-company headquarters. Now in its third incarnation, Madison Square Garden was originally in Madison Square and served largely as a boxing ring. The second Madison Square Garden was displaced by expansion of the Port Authority, and this building in turn displaced the magnificent Pennsylvania Station. When that happened, there was a very belated outcry, and the historic nature of the station accentuated the loss. The city's grief was vented at this third Madison Square Garden, which was deemed inadequate almost before it was completed. In every edition of this book, we have cautioned that by the next edition it may be leveled while yet another Madison Square Garden arises miles from Madison Square. Aside from being tired of making the same prognostication edition after edition, we have another reason for refraining this go-round: that is, economic conditions being what they are, no one is currently beefing about MSG. (And speaking of beef, the Wendy's across the street at 34th Street has the highest volume of business in the *nation*.) In any event, the Garden is home to the Knicks, the Rangers, the circus, trade shows, and countless rock concerts and exhibitions. The Garden is an amazing place. There's even a 48-lane bowling alley in addition to the 4,500-seat Felt Forum and the 20,500-seat Garden.

NEW YORK PASSENGER SHIP TERMINAL
From 48th and 55th St, at Twelfth Ave and
Hudson River   765-7437

If you're in town for a convention or to depart on a cruise, note the address. Odds are this is your destination. The Passenger Ship Terminal serves double duty as both an exhibit hall and a debarkation point. Tours of the cruise ships that dock here are available; call the above number for information. There's parking for 1,000 cars, but it isn't cheap. There's a cheaper lot on 42nd Street off Twelfth Avenue.

RADIO CITY MUSIC HALL
Sixth Ave at 50th St   247-4777
Tours: 632-4041

The home of the world-famous Rockettes, Radio City Music Hall has become a landmark attraction. Every trip to New York should include Radio City. Nowadays, movie premières have been replaced with concerts and special shows. Don't forget to check out the art deco bathrooms. The rest of this fabulous theater, including the labyrinthine backstage, can be seen via a daily tour (246-4600). The spectacular Christmas show is a must-see New York experience.

ROCKEFELLER CENTER
From Fifth to Sixth Ave, bet 47th and 52nd St
489-2947

Planned and erected in the Depression, Rockefeller Center stood as an ode to capitalism and private enterprise meant to be as American as apple pie. Perhaps that explains the hue and cry when the entire complex was bought by the Japanese. The original complex included 14 buildings (including Radio City) constructed as a city-within-a-city around Rockefeller Plaza. Workers erected the first Rockefeller Center Christmas tree atop the unfinished building during the first Depression Christmas, and the tradition has continued to the present day. High points of the center include the skating rink (which becomes an outdoor cafe in summer) under the statue of Prometheus. You've seen it (and Rockefeller Center) on NBC television. Channel Gardens, leading to the rink from Fifth Avenue, has a constantly changing seasonal floral display while the many restaurants vary from soda shop to the restored and renovated Rainbow Room. There are several layers to a 24-acre underground concourse, which can be explored with help from a free map available in the lobby of the General Electric Building.

STATUE OF LIBERTY NATIONAL MONUMENT

Liberty Island Ferry information:
269-5755, 201/435-9479
Statue information: 363-3200

The Lady was spiffed up for her centennial, and she is now said to be the top tourist attraction in the country (even ahead of Disney World!). While New York and New Jersey have been disputing each other's claims for jurisdiction over Liberty Island, for years the National Park Service has operated the monument with access from both states. The New Jersey ferry, which leaves from Liberty State Park, is quicker, cleaner, and has shorter lines. The latter is no small consideration when you are visiting the country's number one tourist attraction! Remember when you land that everyone on the island got there the same way you did. There are usually two lines; one each for the two viewing areas. The one for the top of the pedestal is quicker, and the pedestal is wide enough so that there's no rush to move for the next crowd. The trek to the top of the crown is entirely indoors, and the end is an indoor view of the harbor through the crown. After that, you descend the same very narrow spiral staircase you climbed. Not for the faint of heart! The platform at the top of the torch has been closed for years.

TIMES SQUARE

42nd St and Broadway

The famous square takes its name from the tower at the intersection of the lower part of a double *X* formed by the merging and crossing of Broadway and Seventh Avenue. It was originally the home of the *New York Times,* which is still just down the block on West 43rd Street. The around-the-building electronic news tape still remains, as does the tradition of dropping a ball (or apple) from the tower on New Year's Eve. On the side streets in the mid-40s and along Broadway are the legitimate Broadway theaters. The Times Square Redevelopment Project has been trying to get off the boards for years. Maybe in our lifetime!

UNITED NATIONS

First Ave from 43rd to 49th St
Tour information: 963-7713

The United Nations offers a chance to visit international territory in New York. The land, donated by the Rockefellers, is an international zone, and the UN boasts its own postage system, security force, dining facilities, and gift shop, none of which are subject to New York taxes and regulations. (The Delegates Dining Room [963-7625], which is open to the public weekdays for lunch and is available for banquets, is one of the best and cheapest meals in town, with fabulous views. See the Restaurants section.) Free tickets to open meetings of the Security Council, General Assembly, and various committees are available on a first-come, first-serve basis in the lobby of the General Assembly building. You can call 963-7113 to learn what's in progress, or check the second page of the *New York Times*. Guided tours (in English) leave from the lobby of the General Assembly building every 30 minutes daily, and on demand in other languages (963-7539). There are 159 members of the United Nations, and tours have been conducted in 20 languages. Be warned that security measures forbid strollers and baby carriages on UN grounds, and touring with children is uncomfortable at best. Children under five are not admitted on tours.

WORLD FINANCIAL CENTER
From Vesey to Liberty St at the Hudson River
945-0505
Mon-Sat: 10-7; Sun: noon-5

Four granite and reflective glass buildings, designed by Cesar Pelli, comprise the World Financial Center. Each has a series of stores and shops, as well as offices, and all are centered around the Winter Garden court. The glass-and-steel atrium is 120 feet high. It includes live palm trees and a sweeping grand staircase of marble. The structures were built on landfill over the Hudson River and are accessible via two covered walkways from the World Trade Center. Throughout the center there are free shows and entertainment to both attract shoppers and to add to the atmosphere of the area.

WORLD TRADE CENTER
West, Vesey, Church, and Liberty St   466-4170

The twin towers enjoyed their claim to fame as the world's tallest buildings for about a year, and they are still the tallest buildings in New York. They offer breathtaking views of the city, the harbor, and New Jersey. (It's not true that you can see as far as Pennsylvania.) The observation deck on the 107th floor of 2 World Trade Center (466-7397) is the world's largest exposed deck. For safety's sake, it is glass-enclosed. There's an even higher observation deck on the rooftop promenade on the 110th floor. The entire complex is bigger than some cities. It includes seven buildings, a hotel (Vista International), a TKTS office (which should be a first choice—it is *never* crowded), and hundreds of floors of offices.

Special Days
1992
New Year's Day .... Wednesday—January 1
Martin Luther King's Birthday .... Monday—January 20

Lincoln's Birthday	Wednesday—February 12
St. Valentine's Day	Friday—February 14
Washington's Birthday	Monday—February 17
St. Patrick's Day	Tuesday—March 17
Good Friday	Friday—April 17
Passover (1st Day)	Saturday—April 18
Easter	Sunday—April 19
Mother's Day	Sunday—May 10
Memorial Day	Monday—May 25
Father's Day	Sunday—June 21
Independence Day	Saturday—July 4
Labor Day	Monday—September 7
Rosh Hashana	Monday—September 28
Yom Kippur	Wednesday—October 7
Columbus Day	Monday—October 12
Halloween	Saturday—October 31
Election Day	Tuesday—November 3
Veteran's Day	Wednesday—November 11
Thanksgiving Day	Thursday—November 26
Hanukkah	Sunday—December 20
Christmas	Friday—December 25

1993

New Year's Day	Friday—January 1
Martin Luther King's Birthday	Monday—January 18
Lincoln's Birthday	Friday—February 12
St. Valentine's Day	Sunday—February 14
Washington's Birthday	Monday—February 15
St. Patrick's Day	Wednesday—March 17
Passover (1st Day)	Tuesday—April 6
Good Friday	Friday—April 9
Easter	Sunday—April 11
Mother's Day	Sunday—May 9
Memorial Day	Monday—May 31
Father's Day	Sunday—June 20
Independence Day	Sunday—July 4
Labor Day	Monday—September 6
Rosh Hashana	Thursday—September 16
Yom Kippur	Saturday—September 25
Columbus Day	Monday—October 11
Halloween	Sunday—October 31
Election Day	Tuesday—November 2
Veteran's Day	Thursday—November 11
Thanksgiving Day	Thursday—November 25
Hanukkah	Thurday—December 9
Christmas	Saturday—December 25

Special Telephone Numbers

Emergency Services

AAA Highway Conditions 757-2000
AAA Road Service 757-3356
Alcoholics Anonymous 683-3900
Ambulance 911
Arson Hotline 718/403-1300
Babysitters Guild 682-0227
Better Business Bureau 533-6200
Child Abuse 800/342-3720
Child Care (part-time) 757-7900
Crime Victims Hotline 577-7777
Day Care Council of New York 398-0380
Day Care (NYC Health Dept) 334-7814
Doctor Line Referral (free) 876-5432
Emergency Dental Service ....679-3966 or 677-2510
Emergency Medical Service 718/326-0600
FBI 335-2700
Fire 911
Gas, Electric, and Steam Emergency (Con Edison) 683-8830
Immunizations 349-2664
Legal Aid 577-3300
New York Women Against Rape 777-4000
Parents League of New York 737-7385
Passport Office 541-7700
Poisoning ....340-4494 or 764-7667
Police 911
Police Precinct Locations 374-4303
Rape Hotline 267-7273
Sanitation, Garbage, and Snow Removal 334-8590
Sewers 966-7500
Suicide Prevention 532-2400
Telephone Repair Service 611
Tips Concerning Violent Crimes 577-TIPS
Victim Services Agency 577-7777
Water 285-9503

Complaints

Consumer (stores, services, etc.) 577-0111
Corruption 825-5900
Housing 960-4800
Mail Fraud 330-3844
Noise 966-7500
Pets 285-9503
Rats 285-9503
Sidewalks 323-8501
Smells 966-7500

Taxes 718/935-6000
Trash 334-8590

Entertainment
Folk music 666-9605
Madison Square Garden (sports events) 563-8300
New York Convention and Visitors Bureau 397-8222
New York Public Library 340-0849
Sportsphone 540-1313

Information
Airports 800/AIR-RIDE
Bureau of Labor Consumer Price Index 337-2405
City Phone (general) 567-9930
Customs Services 466-5550
Federal Information Center 264-4464
Health Department 285-9503
Hospitals 566-8650
Marriage License Information 269-2900
Plant Hotline 220-8681
Postal 967-8585
Public Library 340-0849
Sky Reporter 769-5917
Social Security 800/234-5772
Stock Market 976-4141
Tel-Med (health topics) 439-3200
Time of Day 976-1616
Vaccinations (travel) 349-2664
Veteran's Benefits 620-6901
Weather 540-4000
Weather Trak (access code needed) 540-3000
Welfare 553-5997
Zip Code Hotline 967-8585

Transportation

Trains
Amtrak 800/872-7245
Long Island Railroad 718/454-5477
Lost Property (bus, subway) 718/625-6200
Metro North 532-4900
Metroliner 582-6387
New Jersey Transit 201/460-8444
PATH Train 732-8920
PATH Train (Newark Airport) .466-7649
Staten Island Rapid Transit 718/447-8601
Subway Information 718/330-1234

Buses

Carey Transportation (airports) 718/632-0500
George Washington Bus Terminal 564-1114
Greyhound Bus 971-6363
NYC Bus Information 718/330-1234
Port Authority Bus Terminal 564-8484

Taxis

NYC Taxi and Limo Commission
  (lost property, complaints) 869-4513

Air Travel

Manhattan Air Lines Terminal
  (tickets, information) 986-0888
JFK Airport 718/656-4520
LaGuardia Airport 718/476-5000
Newark Airport 201/961-2015

One final number: If you don't trust your alarm clock, try 540-WAKE. Dial-a-Wakeup will get you out of the sack for $2!

Tipping Etiquette

Babysitter	0-15%
Barber/Beautician	15%
Bartender	10%**
Bellboy/Skycap	50¢ per bag ($1.00 min.)
Buffet waitress	10%**
Busboy	No Tipping*
Chambermaid	50¢-75¢ per night
Cloakroom	50¢ per coat
Cocktail waitress	10%**
Delivery boy	25¢-$1.00
Doorman	50¢ per assistance
Lunch counter	10%** (15¢ minimum)
Maitre'd	No tipping*
Masseur/Masseuse	20%
Parking attendant	50¢-$1.00
Rest room	15¢-25¢ (if assisted)
Shoeshine	50¢
Taxi	15% (25¢ minimum)
Waiter/Waitress	15-20%
Wine steward	10%**

 *unless special service provided
**up to 15% for extra service

INDEX

Burke and Burke, 79, 229
Burlington Antique Toys, 563
Burlington Book Shop, 368

C

C.A.S.H./Student Employment
  Office, 267
C K & L Surplus, 498
C. P. Company, 1, 13, 342, 410
Cabana Carioca, 62
Cabana Carioca II, 42, 96
Cadillac Bar, 83
Cafe, 42, 96
Cafe at Between the Bread, 52
Cafe de Bruxelles, 56, 59, 60
Cafe de la Gare, 55, 56
Cafe des Artistes, 43, 55, 56, 62,
  71, 73, 76, 78, 96
Cafe des Sports, 43, 65, 76, 97
Cafe Europa & La Brioche, 43,
  50, 82, 97
Cafe Galette, 53
Cafe Greco, 60, 67
Cafe Lalo, 62, 64, 208
Cafe L'Etoile, 80
Cafe Masada, 54, 70
Cafe Mortimer, 54
Cafe New York at the Hilton, 68
Cafe Orlin, 63
Cafe Pierre, 61, 69, 78
Cafe SFA, 80, 81
Cafe Society, 581
Cafe Suisse, 68
Cafe Trevi, 78
Cafe Un Deux Trois, 43, 98
Cafe Vienna/Bergdorf-Goodman,
  80
Caffé Bianco, 51
Caffe Bondi, 13, 64
Caffe Dante, 43, 52, 53, 63, 74,
  98
Caffe Fontana at Sheraton (New
  York) Centre Hotel, 69
Caffe Reggio, 63, 225
Caffe Roma, 224
Caffe Vivaldi, 51, 62, 63, 78
Cakes by Cliff, 209
Calligraphy Studios, 271

Cameos, 43, 60, 71, 98
Camouflage, 401
Canal Bar, 72
Canal Jeans, 395
Canal Rubber Supply Company,
  545
Canal West Flea Market, 580
Canard and Company, 230
Candle Shop, The, 343, 382
Canton, 43, 99
Capezio's, 391
Capitol Fishing Tackle Company,
  551
Carcanagues, Jacques, and
  Gallery, 343, 506
Card Collectors, 346
Carderelli, G, 344
Carey Limousine NY, 272
Carey, Michael, 353
Carlton Arms, 293
Carlyle Camera Corp, 541
Carlyle Hotel, 61, 68
Carmine's, 43, 62, 99
Carnegie Deli & Restaurant, 3,
  43, 52, 53, 55, 61, 64, 65, 70,
  79, 82, 100
Carnegie Hall, 18, 606
Carnegie Hall Museum, 585
Carnegie Luggage, 312
Carnevale, P., and Son, 57
Carolina, 60, 76
Carosello Musicale Company, 509
Carrot Top Pastries, 51
Cartier, 575
Cashmere-Cashmere, 397
Cat Store, 490
Catalano's Fresh Fish, 258
Caviarteria, 230
CBS, 335
CCS Counter Spy Shoppe, 546
Cellar in the Sky, 82
Center Art Studio, 274
Center for African Art, 585
Central Fish Company, 53, 259
Central Park, 1, 2, 3, 12, 28, 30,
  32, 599, 600, 601, 602
Central Park Zoo, 602
Central Synagogue, 579
Central Typewriter and Appliance
  Company, 567

F

O

U

V

NOTES

NOTES

NOTES

NOTES

NOTES

NOTES